Decision Making from a Cognitive Perspective

Decision Making from a Cognitive Perspective

Edited by **Jerome Busemeyer*** and **Douglas L. Medin**
Reid Hastie†

Department of Psychology
*Department of Psychology
Northwestern University
Purdue University
Evanston, Illinois
West Lafayette, Indiana

†Department of Psychology
University of Colorado
Boulder, Colorado

THE PSYCHOLOGY OF
LEARNING AND MOTIVATION, VOLUME 32
Advances in Research and Theory

ACADEMIC PRESS #195

San Diego   New York   Boston   London
Sydney   Tokyo   Toronto

Academic Press, Inc.
A Division of Harcourt Brace & Company
525 B Street, Suite 1900, San Diego, California 92101-4495

United Kingdom Edition published by
Academic Press Limited
24-28 Oval Road, London NW1 7DX

International Standard Serial Number: 0079-7421

International Standard Book Number: 0-12-543332-8

PRINTED IN THE UNITED STATES OF AMERICA
95 96 97 98 99 00 BC 9 8 7 6 5 4 3 2 1

CONTENTS

COGNITIVE APPROACHES TO JUDGMENT AND DECISION MAKING

Reid Hastie and Nancy Pennington

AND LET US NOT FORGET MEMORY: THE ROLE OF MEMORY PROCESSES AND TECHNIQUES IN THE STUDY OF JUDGMENT AND CHOICE

Elke U. Weber, William M. Goldstein, and Sema Barlas

v

CONTENT AND DISCONTENT: INDICATIONS AND IMPLICATIONS OF DOMAIN SPECIFICITY IN PREFERENTIAL DECISION MAKING

William M. Goldstein and Elke U.Weber

AN INFORMATION PROCESSING PERSPECTIVE ON CHOICE

John W. Payne, James R. Bettman, Eric J. Johnson, and Mary Frances Luce

ALGEBRA AND PROCESS IN THE MODELING OF RISKY CHOICE

Lola L. Lopes

UTILITY INVARIANCE DESPITE LABILE PREFERENCES

Barbara A. Mellers, Elke U. Weber, Lisa D. Ordóñez, and Alan D. J. Cooke

Contents

COMPATIBILITY IN COGNITION AND DECISION

Eldar Shafir

PROCESSING LINGUISTIC PROBABILITIES: GENERAL PRINCIPLES AND EMPIRICAL EVIDENCE

David V. Budescu and Thomas S. Wallsten

COMPOSITIONAL ANOMALIES IN THE SEMANTICS OF EVIDENCE

John M. Miyamoto, Richard Gonzalez, and Shihfen Tu

VARIETIES OF CONFIRMATION BIAS

Joshua Klayman

CONTRIBUTORS

Numbers in parentheses indicate the pages on which the authors' contributions begin.

Sema Barlas, Department of Medical Education, University of Illinois at Chicago, Chicago, Illinois 60612 (33)

James R. Bettman, Fuqua School of Business, Duke University, Durham, North Carolina 27708 (137)

David V. Budescu, Department of Psychology, University of Illinois, Champaign, Illinois 61820 (275)

Alan D. J. Cooke, Department of Psychology, University of California, Berkeley, Berkeley, California 94720 (221)

William M. Goldstein, Department of Psychology, University of Chicago, Chicago, Illinois 60637 (33, 83)

Richard Gonzalez, Department of Psychology, University of Washington, Seattle, Washington 98195 (319)

Reid Hastie, Psychology Department, Center for Research on Judgment and Policy, University of Colorado, Boulder, Colorado 80309 (1)

Eric J. Johnson, Wharton School, University of Pennsylvania, Philadelphia, Pennsylvania 19104 (137)

Joshua Klayman, Center for Decision Research, Graduate School of Business, University of Chicago, Chicago, Illinois 60637 (385)

Lola L. Lopes, College of Business, University of Iowa, Iowa City, Iowa 52242 (177)

Mary Frances Luce, Wharton School, University of Pennsylvania, Philadelphia, Pennsylvania 19104 (137)

Barbara A. Mellers, Department of Psychology, University of California, Berkeley, Berkeley, California 94720 (221)

John M. Miyamoto, Department of Psychology, University of Washington, Seattle, Washington 98195 (319)

Lisa D. Ordóñez,[1] Department of Psychology, University of California, Berkeley, Berkeley, California 94720 (221)

John W. Payne, Fuqua School of Business, Duke University, Durham, North Carolina 27708 (137)

Nancy Pennington, Psychology Department, University of Colorado, Boulder, Colorado 80309 (1)

Eldar Shafir, Department of Psychology, Princeton University, Princeton, New Jersey 08544 (247)

Shihfen Tu, Department of Psychology, University of Miami, Coral Gables, Florida 33124 (319)

Thomas S. Wallsten, Department of Psychology, University of North Carolina, Chapel Hill, North Carolina 27599 (275)

Elke U. Weber,[2] Graduate School of Business, University of Chicago, Chicago, Illinois 60637 (33, 83, 221)

[1] Present Address: Management and Policy Department, University of Arizona, Tucson, Arizona 85721.
[2] Present Address: Department of Psychology, Ohio State University, Columbus, Ohio 43210.

PREFACE

Decision processes are the gatekeepers mediating between thought and action. Every response to any conceivable cognitive task—signal detection, memory recognition, conceptual categorization, problem solving—must be approved by a decision process. Furthermore, every choice in any imaginable decision task—medical diagnosis, consumer choice, investment planning—entails cognitive processes such as memory, inference, and problem solving. These processes are so highly interconnected that it is impossible to examine one without evoking another. Accordingly, research on decision and cognitive processes should be tightly interwoven. However, as Wallsten (1980) pointed out over fifteen years ago, a *schism* exists between the decision and cognitive sciences. To a large extent, this schism still exists today, and the reasons for its persistence warrant a close examination.

Decision science is an interdisciplinary field comprising researchers from business, consumer research, economics, management science, marketing research, operations research, and psychology. For some, the goal is to develop a rational or normative theory of decision making that identifies the optimal way to make decisions (e.g., Savage, 1954). For others, the goal is to develop a behavioral or psychological theory of decision making that empirically describes how we make judgments (e.g., Kahneman, Slovic, & Tversky, 1982). Finally, the goal for some is to develop a prescriptive or supportive approach that tries to aid or help make better decisions (e.g., Keeney & Raiffa, 1976), and this is done by bringing the way we *do* make decisions closer in line with the way we *should* make decisions.

Cognitive science is also an interdisciplinary field comprising researchers from anthropology, computer science, electrical engineering, library science, linguistics, philosophy, and psychology. For some, the goal is to develop theories of computability or competency that identify the requirements for an ideal intelligence system (e.g., Chomsky, 1965). For others, the goal is to develop a general theory of human cognition that explains how we actually perceive, think, and move (e.g., Anderson, 1983). Finally, the goal for some is to build artificial intelligence or expert systems that perform as well as or sometimes even better than humans on complex cognitive tasks (e.g., Newell, 1991). This is done by combining ideal theories of computability with theories of human cognition.

Certainly there is sufficient overlap across these two sets of goals to produce some intersection of ideas. Cognitive scientists have borrowed optimal principles from decision theory to form the foundation of their cognitive theories (e.g., Anderson, 1990). Decision theorists have borrowed methodology from cognitive science to investigate decision behavior (e.g., Payne, Bettman, & Johnson, 1993). Sometimes a common formal model has been applied to perception, memory, and decision making research (Link, 1992; Ratcliff, 1978; Busemeyer & Townsend, 1993). Striking parallels between phenomena from decision and cognitive research have also been noted (Medin, Goldstone, & Markman, 1995).

The few cases of intersection mentioned above are overwhelmed by numerous other examples where research in one field proceeds without taking notice of findings from the other field. Cognitive theorists are quite willing to adopt optimal principles of Bayesian inference, bypassing findings by decision researchers that humans systematically violate the axioms of these optimal theories. Decision theorists are quite willing to adopt strictly serial processing architectures for information processing, bypassing findings by cognitive researchers that humans do a great deal of parallel processing of information. Sophisticated models of decision making in memory or perception have been proposed that lack references to the decision making literature. Information processing models of decision making have been proposed without references to the current cognitive literature. In sum, there is still a large gap between the vast majority of work in decision making and cognition that needs to be understood.

The answer might be found by analyzing theories from decision and cognitive science in terms of Marr's (1982) levels of explanation. According to Marr, intelligent systems can be explained in terms of three different levels: (a) the computational level, which describes the objectives of the system; (b) the algorithmic level, which symbolically describes how the system achieves these goals; and (c) the implementation level, which describes the mechanisms that physically carry out the process. For example, human performance in pattern recognition tasks may be explained at the first level by assuming that the human's objective is to maximize the probability of a correct category response (e.g., the optimal observer in Green & Swets, 1966), but details regarding how the subject learns to achieve this goal are left unspecified. Alternatively, performance in this task may be explained at the second level by assuming that humans learn to categorize according to a connectionistic model (Rumelhart & McClelland, 1986). Finally, performance in this task may be explained at the third level by describing the detailed neurophysiological mechanisms involved in learning (Gluck and Rumelhart, 1990). Some theories may fall between levels, such as neural network models that attempt to be consistent with known neurophysiological facts (e.g., Grossberg, 1988).

A quick survey of the major theories in decision making reveals that decision theorists prefer the computational level of explanation. For example, popular rank dependent utility theories provide a general formula describing an individual's preference over actions. But they provide no explanation for the processes used to calculate this formula.

A quick survey of the major theories in cognition reveals that cognitive scientists prefer the algorithmic level of explanation. For example, popular production rule based artificial intelligence theories provide a highly detailed description of different processes underlying cognition. But they fail to identify the overall global objectives of the system.

Thus cognitive scientists generally find that decision theories fail to provide sufficient depth of explanation, and decision scientists generally find that cognitive theories are too complex. So this leads us to the question of what we can hope to gain by bringing these two fields closer together. How can cognitive scientists benefit from incorporating decision theory, and how can decision scientists benefit from incorporating cognitive theory?

Cognitive science can benefit by organizing an arbitrary collection of algorithmic level processes into a unified theory glued together by a small set of objectives. The computational objectives would also place constraints on the construction of process models. For example, different process models of perception and memory would be required to satisfy a common computational goal, and additionally, their joint operation would need to optimize this same objective. Processes that failed to achieve the organizing objective could be eliminated from consideration. Note, however, that it would be critical to adopt objectives consistent with decision research.

Decision science can benefit by expanding the theory's domain to new independent variables and extending the theory's range to new dependent variables. For example, consider once again rank dependent utility theories (see Luce, 1988, for a general review). These theories are restricted to two basic independent variables: (a) the probability distribution over outcomes, and (b) the values of outcomes. A cognitive process interpretation would increase the capability to explain the effects of variation in stimulus display, presentation order of information, time pressure, and effects of memory on decision making. Furthermore, a process level description could expand the explanatory power to new dependent variables such as decision time, confidence, and other measures of the decision process, which currently cannot be explained. Once again, it would be critical to construct a process model consistent with cognitive research.

One danger in the construction of process models is the tendency to create issues that are not scientifically meaningful. To illustrate this problem, consider the following issue: Are decisions made by production rules or neural networks? This is probably a question that has no meaningful answer. Production rules and neural networks are best considered as theoretical approaches or formal languages for constructing theories. It is quite likely that a production rule model can be mimicked by an appropriately constructed neural network model. For example, Usher and Zakay (1993) describe a neural network that can mimic many of the popular production rule models used in multiattribute decision research. At best, one can compare and test a specific production rule model with a specific neural network model. Often it is appealing to bring up broad and general issues, but frequently such global questions have no empirically testable answer.

The purpose of the present book is to provide readers with a survey of new decision research that is closely integrated with research from cognitive psychology. The chapters will be of interest to both decision and cognitive scientists. Chapters 1 and 2 examine the role of memory in decision making, including discussions of the implications of parallel distributed processing models for decision making. Chapters 3 through 7 investigate the effects of stimulus context and problem content on the construction of decision strategies, including discussions of the connections between algebraic and process models of decision making. Chapters 8 through 10 analyze the relations between natural language and probabilistic inference, including discussions of fuzzy set and semantic theories of evidence. The ensemble contains exciting new empirical findings as well as revolutionary new ideas for bringing together cognitive and decision sciences.

Jerome R. Busemeyer
Purdue University

REFERENCES

Anderson, J. R. (1983). *The architecture of cognition.* Cambridge, MA: Harvard Univ. Press.
Anderson, J. R. (1990). *The adaptive character of thought.* Hillsdale, NJ: Erlbaum.
Busemeyer, J. R., & Townsend, J. T. (1993). Decision field theory: A dynamic–cognitive approach to decision making in an uncertain environment. *Psychological Review, 100,* 432–459.
Chomsky, N. (1965). *Aspects of a theory of syntax.* Cambridge, MA: MIT Press.
Gluck, M. A., & Rumelhart, D. E. (Eds.) (1992). *Neuroscience and connectionistic theory.* Hillsdale, NJ: Erlbaum.

Green, D. M., & Swets, J. A. (1966). *Signal detection theory and psychophysics.* New York: Wiley.

Grossberg, S. (Ed.) (1988). *Neural networks and natural intelligence.* Cambridge, MA: MIT Press.

Kahneman, D., Slovic, P., & Tversky, A. (Eds.), (1982). *Judgment under uncertainty: Heuristics and biases.* London: Cambridge Univ. Press.

Keeney, R., & Raiffa, H. (1976). *Decisions with multiple objectives.* New York: Wiley.

Link, S. W. (1992). *Wave theory of difference and similarity.* Hillsdale, NJ: Erlbaum.

Luce, R. D. (1988). Rank dependent, subjective expected-utility representations. *Journal of Risk and Uncertainty, 1,* 305–332.

Marr D. (1982). *Vision.* San Francisco: W. H. Freeman.

Medin, D. L., Goldstone, R. L., & Markman, A. B. (1995). Comparison and choice: Relations between similarity processes and decision processes. *Psychonomic Bulletin and Review, 2,* 1–19.

Newell, A. (1991). *Unified theories of cognition.* Cambridge, MA: Cambridge Univ. Press.

Payne, J. W., Bettman, J. R., & Johnson, E. J. (1993). *The adaptive decision maker.* Cambridge, MA: Cambridge Univ. Press.

Ratcliff, R. (1978). A theory of memory retrieval. *Psychological Review, 85,* 59–108.

Rumelhart, D. E., & McClelland, J. L. (Eds.), (1986). *Parallel distributed processing; Explorations in the microstructure of cognition (Vol. 1, Foundations).* Cambridge, MA: MIT Press.

Savage, L. J. (1954). *The foundations of statistics.* New York: Wiley.

Usher, M., & Zakay, D. (1993). A neural network model for attribute-based decision processes. *Cognitive Science, 17,* 349–396.

Wallsten, T. S. (Ed.) (1980). *Cognitive processes in choice and decision behavior.* Hillsdale, NJ: Erlbaum.

COGNITIVE APPROACHES TO JUDGMENT AND DECISION MAKING

Reid Hastie and Nancy Pennington

I. Introduction

There is a fair amount of consensus on the scope of the field of judgment and decision making. The gist of the proposed conceptual definitions is that decision making involves the deliberate choice of a course of action with the intention to produce a maximally desirable outcome. There are many subtle variations on this basic definition: Some theorists do not think that the condition of deliberateness is necessary, others do not include reference to "maximally desirable." There are also some common elaborations; for example, many theorists want to emphasize the distinctive focus on the integration of value (or preference or desire) with belief (or judgment or perception). However, all the popular definitions converge on a common set of components: a choice set of options or courses of action, a background of controllable and uncontrollable events that determine the outcome of the action–event combination that occurs, and subjective satisfaction that is a consequence of the objective outcome.

Mathematicians, philosophers, and other thoughtful people have also converged on an ideal calculus for the basic decision process and on the details of its implementation in probability theory and a rational computation of maximum utility. (Of course there are variant approaches, but the amount of convergence on a unitary, most popular model is remarkable.) The result is a useful shared vocabulary to describe decision making tasks

1

and to identify the most important elements of these situations, and an agreement on how to calculate optimal outcomes.

A definitional method that is common in the judgment and decision making area is to describe a representative sample of decision situations. Even when, as is the case today in judgment and decision making, there is a successful conceptual definition, examples play a key role in clarifying the scope and application of a concept. A list of decision tasks like the following could be compiled by perusing the chapters in this volume: choosing or rating monetary gambles or multioutcome lotteries, deciding who to hire or who to marry, choosing which apartment to rent or which product or vacation package to purchase, deciding which job to accept, and rendering a verdict in a criminal trial. A list of examples like this can help specify the appropriate conceptual level and provide a guide to instantiations of general concepts (e.g., "choice options") in the larger conceptual framework. Also, of course, generalization from concrete examples can serve as the basis for judgments about the inclusion of new instances in the category of decision tasks.

It is important to distinguish between the *decision task,* described as a system of events and relationships in the "objective" external world (the experimenter works hard to control or to describe this system), and the system of *cognitive processes and mental representations* that occur in the "psychological" world inside the decision maker's head. One seductive characteristic of theories (like modern utility theories) is that they do such a good job of describing both tasks and plausible computational processes that the task analysis and the psychological analysis get mixed together. When the duplication of the theoretical frameworks is deliberate, as it is in the hands of many sophisticated theorists, problems do not arise. However every so often, conceptual confusion will occur because of the failure to separate carefully the task from the cognitive parts of the overall theoretical account of behavior.

A common theoretical tactic is to define a typology of tasks and a typology of cognitive strategies, then to combine the two typologies into a predictive claim about the relationships between strategies induced by tasks (Hammond [1988, 1990] provides an elegant example of this theoretical strategy). There are several useful decision task typologies available today. First, there are typologies that are derived from the components of the utility theory framework. For example, we might distinguish between individual decisions under certainty (choice), individual decisions under uncertainty (a further distinction between ignorance, uncertainty [ambiguous probabilities], and risk [known probabilities] is sometimes made), group decision making (with common motives), and decisions in mixed-motive conflict games (cf. Luce & Raiffa, 1957). Second, there are typologies (usually dichotomies) that are based on the task requirements imposed on subjects in experimental situations: singular stimulus judgments versus multiple stimulus comparative choices, static one-shot decisions versus dynamic sequential decisions, decisions among positively valenced gains versus among negatively valenced losses versus among mixed gain and loss options, and so on. Third, there are typologies that are motivated by more psychological considerations. For example, Hammond proposes that tasks can be assigned to locations along a hypothetical continuum defined by the cognitive processes induced by performance, ranging from intuitive cognition-inducing tasks (e.g., many continuous, perceptual, and redundant cues are simultaneously available to the decision maker) to analytical cognition-inducing tasks (e.g., few discrete, low redundant cues are available in a sequence).

Keeping in mind that the model of the decision task and the model of the decision maker's thought processes should be kept distinct, although the relationship between the two is a crucial component of any good theory, we now turn to cognitive approaches to psychological theory.

II. Cognitive Symbolic Information Processing Approach to Judgment and Decision Making Phenomena

The field of epistemology is concerned with questions about the nature of knowledge and how people obtain it. The fundamental question addressed by epistemological theories is how do we make contact with the outside world? One popular solution to this question, called cognitivism, is to posit a mind, internal to the self, and to reframe the question in terms of the transfer of information from the outside environment into representations inside the mind that reflect the objects and relations that exist in the outside world. In the current cognitive psychological jargon, the fundamental assumption of cognitive psychology is that a person creates mental models of situations in the environment that are most relevant to current or anticipated actions. Many theorists would claim that most of our mental life is devoted to the task of creating and updating mental situation models that allow us to navigate through our daily lives. Furthermore, because these mental situation models are the causal mediators of stimulus–response (environment–behavior) relationships, we must study these mental models to predict and explain behavior.

There are many arguments for the cognitive approach, from attempts to prove that cognitive theories are more general and more parsimonious, to claims that even behaviorist theories are implicitly mentalistic in spite of their authors' intentions to stay with pure public behavior. In our view, none of these reasons to "go cognitive" is absolutely compelling; we can only rely on our own experience in trying to account for empirical findings and on the many successful examples of theoretical accounts for behavior in perception, memory, reasoning, problem solving, and judgment tasks. Furthermore, there is something inherently satisfying (critics would say seductive) about a theoretical account that explains the contents of conscious thoughts as well as successfully predicting behavior.

Once the decision has been made to theorize at a cognitive level, there is a host of additional considerations that must be addressed. In spite of its intuitive appeal, it is difficult to be clear about what constitutes a cognitive theoretical account: Where is this ineffable cognitive level of reality? There seems to be considerable agreement that cognitive analysis occurs at one level of a system of theoretical levels that comprises levels above the cognitive level (e.g., a level at which theories concerned with optimally rational solutions to behavioral–environmental problems are framed) and levels below the cognitive level (e.g., a level at which cognitive processes are implemented in the neural medium of the brain; J. R. Anderson, 1987; Marr, 1982; Newell, 1990; Pylyshyn, 1984). However, proposals to identify the cognitive level (sometimes called algorithmic or symbolic) tend to be tentative lists of characteristic features rather than crisp operational definitions tied to distinct theoretical systems with long histories (e.g., the distinctions between biochemical and anatomical models in the neurosciences). The clues for identifying the cognitive level usually include two primary features: (1) "conscious availability" or verbal reportability, and (2) "penetrability" or flexibility associated with changes in a person's conscious goals or intentions.

Another complexity for the theorist once the cognitive road has been chosen concerns the particular brand of cognitive theory to adopt. Fortunately, there are several useful guides to alternate approaches within the information processing cognitive theory domain. Massaro and Cowan (1993) and Palmer and Kimchi (1986) provide helpful overviews and defenses of the information processing approach.

First, there are theoretical systems that include computer programming languages within which models to perform specific intellectual tasks can be written (e.g., J. R. Anderson's ACT*, 1983, and ACT-R, 1993; Newell's Soar, 1990; Rip's PSYCOP, 1994). It is important to realize that these systems are much more than just computer programming tools; each is justified with a comprehensive review of empirical findings and theoretical precedents, and each includes a conceptual specification of the principles that underlie implementation of the programming language. Of the current systems, Newell's Soar, which emphasizes *learning* procedural knowledge more than its competitors, is the least strongly characterized as a descriptive psychological theory. J. R. Anderson's ACT* and ACT-R systems have been the most widely applied to produce descriptive models and are surely the king of the hill in psychology today. Rip's PSYCOP has been applied primarily to model human deductive and plausible reasoning, although the system has been persuasively described as the heart of a general cognitive architecture that is especially relevant to judgment and decision making phenomena.

A second option is to theorize in a Cognitive Algebra tradition in which mental processes are modeled as equations that are instantiated within a general processing system (N. H. Anderson, 1981, 1991; Stevenson, Busemeyer, & Naylor, 1991). There has been some ambiguity about the status of algebraic equations as models of cognitive processes. This ambiguity was expressed in the principle of paramorphic representation introduced in a landmark paper by Hoffman (1960). Hoffman reported the results of several studies to "capture clinical judgment policies" by fitting linear regression models to predict judgments on the basis of five to ten cues presented in sets of more than 50 to-be-judged cases. He observed that subjects' self-reports were often discrepant with linear weighting and adding statistical models. However, rather than simply accepting the statistical analysis as the behaviorally validated description of the judgment process (such models often account for more than 80% of the variance in individual judgments), Hoffman concluded that although the observable judgments were well fit by algebraic equations, they might actually be produced by fundamentally different mental operations.

Hoffman's cautious conclusion has been reinforced by subsequent findings concerning the "omnivorousness" of linear models and the imprudence of accepting large stimulus–response correlations as the sole evidence for conclusions about underlying processes (N. H. Anderson & Shanteau, 1977; Dawes & Corregan, 1974). However, cognitive algebrists still claim that equations are good models of mental processes and they have advanced to new levels of methodological sophistication in verifying hypotheses about the form of the descriptively valid model (N. H. Anderson, 1982).

A third option is to invent a limited purpose, sometimes partly formalized cognitive framework (e.g., Payne, Bettman, & Johnson's "adaptive decision maker" framework, 1993; Pennington & Hastie's explanation-based decision making framework, 1993; Lopes' 1990 SP/A; Beach's Image Theory, 1990; Gigerenzer's Probabilistic Mental Models, 1991; Tversky & Kahneman's cognitive heuristics, 1974). What makes these varied approaches "cognitive" is that each one attempts to address the following issues.

1. Mental computational algorithms are specified as the central components of models to explain behavior in judgment and decision tasks. A collection of elementary information processes is assumed (although often

they are not explicitly listed) and more complex processing strategies are proposed that are sufficient to "compute" responses that mimic human behavior. Payne, Bettman, and Johnson's (1993) mental "toolbox" of contingent choice strategies provides the clearest example of this approach to modeling mental processes. For example, we can outline a production system that will compute the expected values for a pair of choice alternatives (e.g., apartments to rent) and then make a choice of the alternative with the highest expected value. The "pseudocode" description is composed of elementary operations (e.g., MOVE TO, CALCULATE PRODUCT) and assumes that there are "addressable" storage locations in working memory (WM) and long-term memory (LTM):

MOVE TO (Attribute$_1$ of Apartment$_1$)
READ VALUE OF (Attribute$_1$ of Apartment$_1$)
RETRIEVE FROM LTM (Weight (Attribute$_1$))
CALCULATE PRODUCT (wgt$_1$ × val$_{1,1}$)
STORE PRODUCT (wgt$_1$ × val$_{1,1}$) IN WM sumproducts$_1$
MOVE TO (Attribute$_2$ of Apartment$_1$)
READ VALUE OF (Attribute$_2$ of Apartment$_1$)
RETRIEVE FROM LTM (Weight (Attribute$_2$))
CALCULATE PRODUCT (wgt$_2$ × val$_{2,1}$)
ADD ((PRODUCT(wgt$_2$ × val$_{2,1}$) + sumproducts$_1$) = sumproducts$_1$)
STORE sumproducts$_1$ IN WM

. . . continue until all information about Apartment$_1$ has been processed, then:

MOVE TO (Attribute$_1$ of Apartment$_2$)
READ VALUE OF (Attribute$_1$ of Apartment$_2$)
RETRIEVE FROM LTM (Weight (Attribute$_1$))
CALCULATE PRODUCT (wgt$_1$ × val$_{1,2}$)
STORE PRODUCT (wgt$_1$ × val$_{1,2}$) IN WM sumproducts$_2$

. . . continue until evaluation of both apartments is complete, then:

COMPARE sumproducts$_1$, sumproducts$_2$
CHOOSE apartment with the larger sumproducts.

2. Mental representations of task-relevant information play a major role in the theoretical explanation. In some cases (e.g., Pennington & Hastie,

1986) considerable effort is expended to make detailed claims about mediating representations and to test these claims empirically. Again, the venerable message of the cognitive approach is that people create models of the outside world inside their heads and that these cognitive representations mediate most complex deliberate behaviors.

3. The focus of the information processing analysis is on goal-driven behavior, rather than on behavior that is controlled by the immediate stimulus environment. The control processes that organize behavior are usually conceptualized in terms of hierarchical goal structures (e.g., J. R. Anderson, 1983; Newell & Simon, 1972) with superordinate (e.g., choose an apartment) and subordinate goals (e.g., judge how noisy Apartment j will be in the evening). They are designed to ensure that cognitive processes are executed relatively efficiently, to avoid between-goal and between-process conflicts, and to coordinate mutually supportive goals (Sacerdoti, 1977; Wilensky, 1983).

4. A closely related principle of "adaptive strategic variety" is assumed to describe human behavior. People are expected to create or select one of several optional processing strategies contingent on environmental conditions such as the consequences of the decision and the form in which decision-relevant stimuli occur in the environment (e.g., J. R. Anderson, 1990b; Payne, Bettman, & Johnson, 1993). This is a very old theme in the judgment literature, which has long acknowledged that a person making a judgment can "substitute" one intercorrelated cue for another, yielding observable behaviors that cannot be used to identify the controlling cue in any specific judgment (see Brunswik, 1956, on "vicarious functioning"). The advent of more complex mental models has broadened the notion of adaptive strategic variety to include changes in the entire judgment process, as well as changes in reliance on one cue or another within a fixed strategy (Mellers, Ordóñez, & Birnbaum, 1992, provide one recent example among many).

The cognitive approach is accompanied by several persistent methodological problems. One set of problems is associated with the emphasis on the centrality of information representations in cognitive explanations of behavior: If there are problems with specifying the cognitive "level" of theorizing, how can convincing arguments be made about the particulars of mental representations?

In our view, the key to solving the problem of nailing down the representation is to start with a precise hypothesis about the form and format of the mental representation. Recent developments in computer science have been the critical ingredient in this solution; theoreticians are now able to spell out representations and to study the properties of information structures in several computer programming language media (Winograd, 1975; Rumelhart & Norman, 1988). The problem of creating a precise hypothesis about representations can often be solved by relying on subjects' verbal reports of their task-relevant memories, by the analysis of think-aloud reports during the comprehension process, and by measures of the structure of complex recall output sequences. Turning this kind of rich verbal material into precise hypotheses still requires considerable ingenuity and hard work from the researcher, and computer language representational media are often indispensable here. However, the result is not "circular," although additional independent empirical tests are required before such a hypothesis is convincingly validated.

Once a precise hypothesis is in hand, there are many effective means for evaluating claims about representation. The strongest arguments for a representational hypothesis always involve multiple operationalized tests, which, if the hypothesis is true, converge in providing support for the claim. For example, Suh and Trabasso (1993; Graesser, Singer, & Trabasso, 1994) recommend a three-pronged attack, combining think-aloud verbal reports, reading time measures, and post-comprehension recognition memory-priming tasks to evaluate hypotheses about inferences and representations during text comprehension (for related methodological advice, see also Balota, d'Arcais & Rayner, 1990; Kieras & Just, 1984; and McKoon & Ratcliff, 1992).

One of the interesting empirical facts that has emerged from a few decades of research on mental representations is that people seem to be concrete thinkers. We seem strongly to prefer task-specific, concrete representations and, outside of deliberately trained expertise, it is rare to find reliance on abstract task representations. This principle implies there will be a remarkable amount of task specificity in cognitive skills, that transfer of learned solutions on the basis of abstract relationships will be rare, and that problems that only admit abstract solutions will be difficult to solve. This general conclusion is supported by a preponderance of findings in almost all domains of cognitive skills, including decision making and judgment (see chapter by Goldstein & Weber, this volume).

The recognition that there is considerable strategic variety has promoted the task × strategy predictive approach to theory development that we mentioned earlier. However, strategic variety, not only across tasks and across subjects but also across trials within a fixed task for a single subject, also poses substantial methodological challenges. The traditional solution has been to average over measurements collected from many subjects. This strategy has much to recommend it, particularly when it is preceded by a careful examination of distributions and followed by theoretical statements that acknowledge or model the distribution of responses, not just central tendencies (N. H. Anderson, 1982; Ratcliff, 1993). However, there are a number of perils in averaging data and conclusions based on only averaged data are always ambiguous concerning individual cognitive strategies (e.g., Siegler, 1987). The basic prescription to cure the methods problems raised by strategic variety is to spell out detailed hypotheses about plausible alternative strategies and then to collect lots of data, preferably on (somewhat) independent, potentially converging operations (Garner, Hake, & Eriksen, 1956). Many ambiguities about individual cognitive strategies are convincingly resolved when truly "dense behavioral data" are collected. So, for example, if a subject's reasoning is studied via on-line think-aloud reports, continuous response time analyses (with responses separated into task completion components), error patterns, and retrospective reports of strategies (Ericsson & Simon, 1993), there is usually little uncertainty about the subject's algorithmic cognitive strategy.

A second related methodological tactic has been to select tasks and subjects for which the strategies would be especially visible (consciously reportable) and stable (over time, if not across subjects). This tactic has led to the proliferation of studies of "zero background knowledge tasks" like the Tower of Hanoi and River Crossing brain teasers or tasks with an isolated well-defined background knowledge base like cryptarithmetic and chess. It has also led to the focus on very large skill differences (novice [less than 1 year of experience] vs. expert [more than 10 years of experience] comparisons) when designing studies to identify differences in strategies. In general, these tactics have supported big advances in the understanding of slow, serial information processing strategies. Success has been considerably more limited in studies of relatively rapid, probably parallel judgment cognition. We will return to the question of good research strategies for the cognitive assault on judgment and decision making behavior after we review some substantive contributions.

III. A Selective History of the Major Precursors to Current Cognitive Approaches

One historical thread that has taken a cognitive turn entered psychology when Ward Edwards (1954) introduced psychologists to the work of early subjective probability theorists and decision theorists (e.g., von Neumann & Morgenstern, 1947; Ramsey, 1931; Savage, 1954). Edwards initiated a program of research to explore the extent to which human judgments and decisions matched those from optimal rational models, and he concluded that human thought, although fundamentally probabilistic, did not exactly follow the laws of mathematical probability theory (1962). This tactic, comparing human behavior to the prescriptions of optimal rational models, is still the favorite comparative method in judgment and decision research.

Edwards (1968) concluded that people are approximately Bayesian (an essay by his students was titled, "Man as an Intuitive Statistician," Peterson & Beach, 1967), in that they derive the implications from individual items of evidence but they misaggregate these implications. Edwards' laboratory was apparently a model of tolerance for alternative hypotheses (indeed, the classic 1968 paper was written by Edwards as a congenial debate among colleagues) and cognitive strategies were entertained as interpretations of many of the experimental results (e.g., Beach, Wise, & Barclay [1970] and Marks & Clarkson [1972], proposed that anchoring and insufficient adjustment could account for the central finding of conservatism in belief updating).

In the early 1970s, Amos Tversky (an Edwards student) and Daniel Kahneman outlined a collection of cognitive judgment heuristics to account for most of the major results from Edwards' research program and their own original empirical findings (Tversky & Kahneman, 1974). Tversky and Kahneman proposed that people make judgments under uncertainty via basic cognitive strategies previously studied in research on recall and recognition memory (availability), similarity judgments (representativeness), and logical reasoning (simulation), plus a procedural interpretation of the ever-popular weighted averaging combination rule (anchor-and-adjust). Although there had been earlier proposals of cognitive procedural heuristics for some judgment behaviors, there had been nothing as comprehensive as Tversky and Kahneman's proposal of a mental toolbox of cognitive heuristics sufficient to explain a very broad sample of empirical findings. In addition, Tversky and Kahneman reported numerous infectious new judgment phenomena to illustrate their heuristics; and many of the new phenomena provided devastating challenges to traditional Bayesian interpretations.

There have been many critical responses to the tidal wave of research on heuristics and biases in judgment under uncertainty. However, for most researchers in psychology and in nearby fields of behavioral science, Tversky and Kahneman's work was the most exciting and inspiring empirical research ever conducted on human judgment. Among other virtues, it firmly established the cognitive approach as an appropriate theoretical and methodological level for the explanation of judgment and decision phenomena.

A second, historically continuous thread in the history of cognitive approaches to judgment and decision making phenomena was introduced in Herbert Simon's (1955, 1959, 1979; see also March, 1978) proposal to account for choice and decision making phenomena in terms of an adaptive, but boundedly rational system behaving in a complex, uncertain environment. One motivating idea in Simon's proposal was the convergence among cognitive psychologists on the concept of a limited capacity short-term memory (e.g., Broadbent, 1958; Miller, 1956). Simon proposed several cognitive strategies to describe behaviors exhibited by managers, consumers, and other economically significant actors. The most famous example is the "conjunctive satisficing" strategy that explains the behavior of consumers seeking "good enough" options in an uncertain environment in which search is costly. Under such conditions, people appear to stop with the first option that is "satisfactory" on one or more important attributes, rather than continuing the search until they are convinced that they have found the maximally satisfying option.

The major proponent of Simon's boundedly rational choice strategies has been John Payne. He is the quintessential example of the cognitive information processing approach as we have characterized it. Over the years, he developed Simon's general information processing system into a mental toolbox of cognitive choice strategies. Furthermore, he has attempted to specify the major determinants of the adaptively contingent selection of one strategy or another from the "toolbox." Also, more than any other researcher in the field of judgment and decision making, Payne has applied the Ericsson, Simon, and Newell methodological techniques, inventing a widely used method to study "externalized" information search and using think-aloud protocols to identify individual subjects' choice strategies.

A third historical thread (more properly a collection of threads in the historical fabric) is the cognitive algebraic approach usually associated with the monumental contributions of Norman Anderson (1981, 1991) and Kenneth Hammond (Brehmer & Joyce, 1988; Hammond, 1966). These theorists asserted that algebraic processes, conveniently expressed in equation form, provide valid representations of most fundamental cognitive processes. In particular, integration of information from diverse sources that appears to be the fundamental step in most judgment and decision tasks can be represented by algebraic operations such as those involved in calculating a weighted average or a difference.

One of the great advantages of this approach is that once algebra has been selected to represent mental processes, then a host of statistical methods (i.e., those associated with the analysis of variance and other regression models) is immediately available to suggest and construct experimental designs and procedures. Both Anderson and Hammond are acknowledged master artists in the methodological realm and the straightforward connection between algebraic theories and research methods is of inestimable value to these approaches, especially in contrast to the clumsier and often criticized methods associated with the cognitive heuristics and contingent choice strategy approaches.

The parallels and divergences among the three general cognitive approaches are important and instructive. First, all three make the assumption of strategic variety as a central principle. In the cognitive heuristics approach, the image of a procedural memory store containing at least four multipurpose computational schemes (availability, representativeness, anchor-and-adjust, and simulation heuristics) is assumed. In the cognitive algebra approach, several alternative algebra combination rules (averaging, adding, subtracting, etc.) are candidate process models when each new judgment or decision task is studied. Finally, in the adaptive contingent choice strategy approach, at least seven basic strategies (weighted additive rule, equal weight rule, satisficing strategy, lexicographic strategy, elimination by aspects strategy, majority of confirming instances rule, frequency of good and bad features rule) and several hybrid strategies are proposed.

The wisdom expressed in the Rational Expectations Principle of utility theory is represented by the prominent role assigned to weighting and adding judgment rules (anchor-and-adjust, weighted averaging, and weighted additive rule) in each system. Obviously, the three approaches differ in format and detail of the specifications of the cognitive strategies they propose. Tversky and Kahneman have stayed with verbal statements of their heuristic mechanisms; Anderson, Hammond, and the other algebrists have relied on equations to represent their hypotheses about cognitive processes; and Payne and his colleagues have presented detailed computational subroutines (in a generic pseudocode similar to a computer programming language).

The three approaches have different concepts about the role of prediction and the identification of strategies. The cognitive heuristics approach is most casual on this issue, and it has frequently been criticized for not making a priori predictions about which strategy will be adopted in new tasks and for lacking strong methods for strategy identification during or after a subject has performed a judgment task. This approach has relied heavily on empirically observed "signature biases" to indicate, post hoc, which heuristic has been adopted by a subject.

The cognitive algebra approach also makes limited a priori predictions, mostly based on simple empirical generalizations (if weighted averaging was the most common strategy in Task A, and Task B is similar to Task A, then predict weighted averaging in Task B). But the inductive approach to strategy identification is supported by powerful, well-defined measurement methods imported from least-squares statistical modeling (N. H. Anderson, 1982; Stewart, 1988). These methods allow a skillful investigator to make very strong claims after the fact, on the basis of empirical results, concerning subjects' judgment strategies.

The adaptive contingent choice strategies approach is the most ambitious, with its development of information search and think-aloud report analyses to identify individual strategies on single choice tasks. Furthermore, Payne, Bettman, and Johnson (1993) have recently proposed an adaptive principle as the basis for making a priori predictions about strategy adoption by decision makers attempting to trade off cognitive effort against the costs and benefits of error and accuracy to make maximally satisfying choices.

The three approaches take very different tacks in addressing the role of memory in judgment and choice processes. All three rely on the concept of a limited capacity working memory to motivate predictions about adaptive strategy selection and about judgment errors and biases that are likely to be associated with the execution of a selected strategy. However, none of them has addressed the implications of modern cognitive theories of complex memory-encoding processes, representational structures, or retrieval processes to a substantial degree.

The cognitive heuristics approach has proposed one heuristic, availability, essentially covering the effects of any factor that is known to affect memory for evidence: "People assess the frequency of a class or the probability of an event by the ease with which instances or occurrences can be brought to mind" (Tversky & Kahneman, 1974, p. 1127). The other heuristics also involve memory processes; for example, discussions of the representativeness heuristic usually assume that the person making judgments can retrieve representations of relevant categories (e.g., bank teller, feminist), in the form of lists of prototypical features, from long-term memory. However, the cognitive heuristics approach has made few detailed proposals about memory representations and their role in judgment, even in explorations of availability phenomena.

The adaptive contingent choice strategies approach has also had little to say about memory representations for choice-relevant information. Perhaps the use of perceptually available information displays in most experiments has led these theoreticians to underemphasize the role of long-term memory, although the limits on short-term working memory are of central importance in explanations for errors and for people's use of nonoptimal, but practical, choice strategies under low incentive and high time pressure conditions. Still, direct claims and measures of memory load and memory representation have not been part of the approach.

The cognitive algebra approach, as formulated by Norman Anderson, has had the most to say about memory representations. Anderson and Hubert (1963) found that when subjects made judgments of likeability based on a sequence of eight trait adjectives, recall memory serial position curves diverged from judgment weight serial position curves, summarizing the impact of each item of information on the final likeability rating. This led to the "two-memory hypothesis," that is, the raw concrete trait adjectives were stored in memory independent of the abstract impression that had been extracted from them. Additional research (notably N. H. Anderson & Farkus, 1973) led to a more comprehensive functional memory framework (N. H. Anderson, 1991a), elaborating the basic insight that judgments and other abstractions from evidence need to be treated as independent memories. The functional memory perspective is an important precept about memory and judgment; however, to date, only the simplest judgment tasks have been considered, and it is not yet clear what cognitive algebrists have to say about more complex memory representations.

The underdeveloped state of knowledge about evidence–judgment memory relationships is the stimulus for a research program that we review in the remainder of this chapter. We summarize our research on the effects of *memory on judgment* and the effects of *judgment on memory*. The former is represented by the seminal discovery of the independence of memory and judgment effects in trait adjective-based impression formation experiments (N. H. Anderson & Hubert, 1963; Dreben, Fiske, & Hastie, 1979) and demonstrations of memory availability effects on frequency and risk judgments (Hastie & Park, 1986; Tversky & Kahneman, 1973; Slovic, Fischhoff, & Lichtenstein, 1979). The latter is represented by research on social judgments that has focused on the relative memorability of evidence for and against a judgment after the judgment has been made (Hastie & Kumar, 1979; Hamilton, Katz, & Leirer, 1980; Ostrom, Lingle, Pryor, & Geva, 1980).

IV. Illustrations from Our Own Research

A. THE ROLE OF MEMORY REPRESENTATIONS IN JUDGMENT

The orientation of our research on memory–judgment relationships depends on the manner in which we conceptualize memory. We have adopted the basic framework that is presented in most current cognitive psychology textbooks and monographs (e.g., J. R. Anderson, 1990a; Baddeley, 1990; Bourne, Dominowski, Loftus, & Healy, 1986; Rumelhart & Norman, 1988). Briefly, we assume: (1) Memories are symbolic "things" that are stored in geometrically described structures that are located somewhere in the head (this assumption is not concerned with the physical substrate of the remembered ideas, we do not claim there is a simple correspondence between the cognitive symbolic representation and the neural representation); (2) we have limited capacities to keep memories "active" and immediately available to influence thought processes (i.e., we have limited working memory capacities); (3) forgetting occurs when we are unable to "find" memories in the long-term memory store because we lack effective retrieval routes or cues; (4) long-term memory contains a mixture of specific, concrete, episodic memories, abstract conceptual memories, "what" memories about events and facts, and "how" memories about procedures that do things; and (5) what is remembered, which inferences are drawn and stored in memory, and our ability to retrieve particular memories is highly dependent on our current goals and mental models of the situation about which we are thinking.

One simple implication of the cognitive information processing assumptions we have outlined is that the form of the memory representation of the situation about which judgments or decisions are to be made will have effects on judgments and on confidence in judgments. Thus, we expect that if evidence relevant to a decision is learned in a manner that produces an orderly, highly interconnected memory representation, the judgment or outcome favored by that evidence will dominate responses. Furthermore, we have hypothesized that if decision-relevant information is structured in an orderly manner, judgments will be made with higher confidence than when the information is scrambled and disorderly.

We will briefly summarize two experiments that support these hypotheses. The first experiment took a very direct route to assess the prediction that "orderly" memory structures will lead to more extreme and more confident memory-based judgments than will "disorderly" memory structures. Subjects were told that they were participating in an experiment to study human memory and that the experimenters were interested in how memory drills would affect long-term memory (no mention of a judgment task was made). Then, the subjects performed a memory drill task designed to allow the experimenters to manipulate the structure of interitem links in the subjects' memories for sentences describing the actions performed by characters described as other college students. For example, a subject might be trained on 16 "facts" describing the behavior of a hypothetical student named Jack. Jack performed four actions that implied he was intelligent (e.g., "Won the university chess tournament 2 years in a row."), reckless (e.g., "On a dare, jumped from the balcony of a third floor apartment into a swimming pool"), sociable (e.g., "Organized a square dance club that met every week for dances and other social activities"), and dishonest (e.g., "Pretended he worked at the theater to cut in front of people waiting in line at a concert to buy a ticket").

One-third of the subjects learned the facts in a memory drill task in which they attempted to recall the 15 remaining facts when they were presented with one (randomly selected) cue fact. The remaining two-thirds of the subjects learned the facts in four clusters: for one-third of the subjects, these clusters were orderly, the facts were grouped by organizing personality traits so that the four intelligent facts were clustered together, the four reckless facts were clustered together, and so on; for the last one-third of the subjects, the four-fact clusters were disorderly, each to-be-learned cluster contained one fact from each personality trait grouping (e.g., the preceding four illustrative facts might be learned together as one disorderly cluster).

After studying the facts and learning them to a criterion of 2 perfect cued recall trials, subjects were surprised by a request from the experimenter to make three types of judgments about Jack based on the facts. First, subjects were asked to rate Jack's personality on 7 personality trait scales (e.g., "Make a slash mark through the scale below to indicate how *athletic* you think Jack is compared to other University of Colorado undergraduates"), then they rated his suitability for 11 jobs (e.g., "How suitable do you think Jack would be for a job as a door-to-door salesman?"), and finally they made judgments about his future behavior in 13 hypothetical situations (e.g., "Jack has a choice between going to hear a world-renowned chamber music concert or to a hockey game—good friends have invited him to both events on the same evening and the expensive tickets are a gift to him in either case—which do you think he would choose?"). Each of these judgments was accompanied by a confidence rating on a 6-point scale: "For each rating, we also want to ask you to rate your confidence in the accuracy of your judgment by circling a number on . . . a 6-point scale labeled 'very uncertain' to 'very confident.'"

The focus of the analysis was on the effects of memory structure on the subjects' confidence in their judgments. Our prediction was that confidence ratings would be lowest when subjects learned the judgment-relevant facts in a disorderly memory structure, with facts with mixed implications for Jack's personality grouped together. This basic result was obtained; average confidence was consistently and significantly lowest for personality, job suitability, and future behavior judgments in the disorderly memory structure condition (average confidence rating of 2.70 on the 0–5 scale). The confidence ratings were indistinguished in the global cluster (all 16 facts learned together) and in the orderly cluster (facts implying a single trait grouped together) conditions (average confidence ratings of 3.47 and 3.34, respectively).

We should emphasize that this is an initial finding that is confirmatory of our view that variations in memory structure will have an effect on memory-based judgments. Our interpretation is that it is the orderliness of the memory structures that leads subjects to feel that they know Jack's character well. We assume that subjects have imposed orderly memory structures on the to-be-learned facts in the global 16-fact drill condition (the subject imposes this structure by habit when creating a "subjective organization" of the list during learning) and in the orderly four-fact, four-cluster condition (in which the experimenter has grouped the facts in a subjectively orderly trait-defined structure), and, of course, these are the conditions in which we observe high confidence. However, there are alternative interpretations of this effect with reference to availability effects. Suppose that confidence depends on the subject's ability to retrieve quickly judgment-relevant information from memory and that the orderly structures support the retrieval of relevant facts more effectively than the disorderly structures, then, we would predict the same pattern of ratings we obtained (Tversky & Kahneman, 1973; see also Jacoby, Kelley, & Dywan, 1989, for additional examples of "authority" given to a belief from its accessibility in memory).

We can partly address the alternative interpretation in terms of availability by looking at the correlations between fact recall and judgment confidence across experimental conditions and within experimental conditions (across subjects). The examination of these correlations provides weak disconfirmation of the availability interpretation. At the mean level, the big differences in recall occur when we shift from the global cluster (16 items learned together, average recall 15.5 items out of 16) to the four-cluster conditions (13.13 items recalled on average in the orderly condition, 12.84 items recalled in the disorderly condition), but the big differences in confidence occur when we shift to the disorderly (four cluster) condition from the orderly conditions. At the individual subject level (within cluster drill conditions), the correlations between overall recall (of all 16 facts) and the subjects' average confidence ratings are modest (the median correlation is +.14). More research is required to tease apart the support for these alternate interpretations; but whatever the conclusion of further research, the basic finding that memory structure has an influence on confidence in memory-based judgments has been established.

A second study on the relationship between memory structures and judgments comes from our program of research on legal decision making. The juror in a typical criminal trial has the difficult task of making sense of a large collection of conflicting evidence presented at trial, learning some novel decision options (verdicts) and decision procedures (application of a presumption of innocence and a standard of proof), and putting the two new sets of knowledge together to render a verdict. Prior research has established that in most criminal trials, jurors spend their time during the individual decision process attempting to construct a unitary narrative summary of the evidence, which is then used to render a verdict. We varied the ease with which one narrative story structure or another could be constructed by manipulating the order in which evidence was presented in a mock juror judgment task. Our primary goal was to test the claim that the structure of stories constructed during evidence evaluation causes decisions. A secondary goal was to determine whether story coherence and uniqueness influenced confidence in the correctness of verdicts.

The logic of the experiment was summarized in our hypothesis that (manipulated) ease of story construction would influence verdict decisions; easy-to-construct stories would result in more decisions in favor of the corresponding verdicts. Stories were considered easy to construct when the evidence was ordered in a temporal and causal sequence that matched the occurrence of the original events in the crime situation (story order), with the temporally and causally prior events (e.g., an instigating quarrel between two men) presented in the earliest testimony heard by the juror and the final consequential events (e.g., evidence from the autopsy) heard last. Stories were considered difficult to construct when the presentation order did not match the temporal sequence of the original events (e.g., the autopsy presented first). We based the non-story order on the sequence of evidence as conveyed by witnesses in the original courtroom trials used as stimulus materials in the study (witness order).

Mock-jurors listened to a tape recording of a 100-sentence summary of the trial evidence (approximately 50 prosecution statements and 50 defense statements), followed by a judge's charge to choose between a murder verdict and a not guilty verdict. The 50 prosecution statements, constituting the first-degree murder story identified in our initial interview study (Pennington & Hastie, 1986), were presented either in a story order or a witness order. Similarly, the defense statements, the not guilty story, were presented in one of the two orders creating a four-cell factorial design. In all four order conditions, the prosecution evidence preceded the defense evidence, as per standard legal procedure. After listening to the tape recorded trial materials, the subjects completed a questionnaire indicating their verdict, their confidence in the verdict, and their perceptions of the strengths of the prosecution and defense cases.

As predicted, subjects were likeliest to convict the defendant when the prosecution evidence was presented in story order and the defense evidence was presented in witness order (78% chose guilty), and they were least likely to convict when the prosecution evidence was in witness order and defense was in story order (31% chose guilty). Conviction rates were intermediate in conditions in which both sides of the case were in story order (59% convictions) or both were in witness order (63% convictions). Furthermore, the perceived strength of one side of the case depended on both the order of evidence for that side *and for the other side* of the case. This finding supports our claim that the *uniqueness* of the best-fitting story is one important source of confidence in the decision.

Again, there remain open questions about interpretations of these results. We favor an interpretation in terms of "orderliness" of the memory structures for evidence supporting one verdict or the other; making the construction of a story easy (via our manipulation of evidence presentation order) produces a more orderly, more complete memory structure and this in turn leads to verdicts commensurate with the most orderly structure.

The message from these studies is that people making trivial or important everyday judgments often invest a substantial amount of their thinking in the construction of a mental representation of the object, person, or situation about which they are making a judgment. The person making the judgment attempts to construct a complete, internally consistent model that explains or covers as much of the judgment-relevant evidence as possible. This model is central to the judgment process, when the process is "explanation-based," and it plays a causal role in determining the ultimate decision and the degree of confidence that is associated with the decision.

B.   THE EFFECTS OF JUDGMENTS ON MEMORY STRUCTURE

Our first set of empirical studies focused on the effects of memory structure on judgments, but we can turn the coin over and look at the effects of a judgment on subsequent memory for judgment-relevant evidence. Here, there seem to be two apparently contradictory findings. Hastie, Srull, and many others have reported an incongruity-enhanced recall effect such that after making a social judgment (e.g., personality ratings, likeability ratings), the judge can best recall the subset of information that most strongly disconfirms the implications of the larger evidence set for the ultimate judgment (e.g., Hastie & Kumar, 1979; Rojahn & Pettigrew, 1992; Srull, 1981; Stangor & McMillan, 1992). At the same time, the intuitively appealing result that evidence that most strongly confirms the ultimate judgment will be best remembered has also been obtained (Dellarosa & Bourne, 1984).

In a typical study finding incongruity-enhanced recall, a subject is asked to study a list of (10 to 20) facts describing the behavior of a hypothetical college student and then is asked to make judgments about the student's personality (e.g., Hastie & Kumar, 1979). This would be called an on-line judgment task, as the subjects were attempting to form impressions and preparing to render judgments as they studied the judgment-relevant facts (Hastie & Park, 1986; Hastie & Pennington, 1989). A key feature of many of these experiments is that the subject is shown a set of traits before studying the list of facts (usually descriptions of behaviors performed by the fictional student), and these traits were selected to induce an initial impression of the student's personality. For example, the subject might learn that friends of the fictional student described him as "dull, stupid, slow-witted," thus leading the subject to expect to hear about a relatively unintelligent person. The list of facts providing additional information about the fictional student contained three kinds of descriptions: behaviors congruent with the initial traits (e.g., "Failed his written driver's examination three times"), behaviors incongruent with the initial traits (e.g., "Won the university-wide chess tournament"), and behaviors irrelevant to the personality judgment task (e.g., "Ordered a cheeseburger with french fries for lunch"). Subjects would make personality impression ratings of one or more fictional characters and then, without prior warning, be asked to recall all of the behaviors they could remember from the experimental lists.

Early experiments on this paradigm found that the incongruent items were best recalled, the congruent items were second, and the irrelevant items were least well remembered (Hastie & Kumar, 1979). Subsequent research established the reliability of this finding and showed that the recall advantage for incongruent items depended on the numbers of these items in the list, although incongruents were still better recalled when equal set sizes of the various items were presented (Hastie & Kumar, 1979; Srull, 1981). For example, Hastie and Kumar found that the recall advantage (in terms of the probability of recalling an item) for a single incongruent item was .79, versus .60 for congruent items, and that the advantage dropped to .67 versus .61 when there were equal numbers of the two items in a 14-item list. Recall probabilities for judgment-irrelevant items were substantially lower (e.g., approximately .45 in a 14-item list) than for either of the sets of judgment-relevant items.

Meanwhile, other researchers reasoned that when a schematic organizing principle could be imposed on a set of facts (e.g., a trait, race, or gender stereotype), the principle would serve as a retrieval plan and guide recall to yield superior memory for schema-relevant facts (e.g., Taylor & Crocker, 1981). Dellarosa and Bourne (1984) report a set of experiments that support this hypothesis that an on-line judgment will serve as the basis for retrieval and produce better memory for facts consistent with a decision than for facts in opposition to it. In one of their experiments, subjects studied 12 items of information, one-half favoring a positive outcome and one-half favoring a negative outcome, about a legal, medical, or business situation. Subjects then made decisions about the outcomes of the cases (e.g., Is the defendant guilty or innocent? Should the patient be hospitalized or not? Will the price of the stock go up or down?) or did not make decisions. Recall, after a 48-hour delay, was biased to the advantage of decision-consistent facts for subjects who made a decision (.50 probability of recall of decision-consistent facts vs. .35 recall of decision-inconsistent facts), but there was no apparent differential memory for pro or con facts for subjects who did not make a decision.

Dellarosa and Bourne interpreted their result by hypothesizing that when a decision was made, it was entered into the long-term memory representation of the 12 evidence items and associatively linked to confirmatory evidence. When recall was requested by the experimenter, the decision itself served as a primary entry point for the search and retrieval of the evidence items.

Hastie (1981) attempted to reconcile these two hypotheses, that is, following a judgment process, both incongruent and congruent evidence would show better memory in comparison to judgment-irrelevant information and in comparison to memory in a nonjudgment task. His proposal was that the process of making an on-line judgment would invoke considerable inferential activity and that these inferences would produce associative links between relevant facts; these links would later serve to facilitate memory retrieval either in terms of search through a network of associative paths for unrecalled items or in terms of spreading activation of items from connected items (e.g., J. R. Anderson & Bower, 1973; Rumelhart & Norman, 1988).

Using the concept of interconnectedness of memory traces as an explanatory construct, Hastie proposed that a U-shaped function would best summarize the relationship between a measure of the probability of an event given an expectation and the probability of recalling that event. Assuming that a candidate judgment, impression, or schema would produce expectations about the nature of "new" information, the hypothesis was that both unexpected (incongruent) information and expected (congruent) information would be well remembered. Judgment-irrelevant, undiagnostic information (with intermediate conditional probabilities on the probability of the event given the expectation dimension) would be least well remembered.

Hastie (1984) elaborated this hypothesis by proposing that in social judgment studies (e.g., the Hastie & Kumar and Srull person memory studies), incongruent information would produce the most inferential activity, as subjects attempt to explain or make sense of apparently contradictory, incorrigible facts about a to-be-evaluated person. This inferential activity would produce a relatively elaborate collection of associative links between incongruent events and other facts already learned about the object of judgment. Essentially, the subject would be searching through known facts to construct an explanation (cf. Pennington & Hastie, 1993) of the new unexpected fact. Expectancy-congruent information would also evoke inferential activity and receive associative links as the subject used this information to make spontaneous on-line judgments, to construct explanations of anomalous information, and to create a "theory" of the person described by the facts (cf. Murphy & Medin, 1985; Schank, Collins, & Hunter, 1986; Thagard, 1989). The irrelevant information would be treated as uninformative, and would be unlikely to evoke inferential activity and, thus, would not be associatively linked to other information.

The message from the literature on judgment effects on memory is not so clear. It does seem that judgment-relevant material is much better remembered than irrelevant material, and that memory for the same material is poorer and does not discriminate between relevant and irrelevant when encountered outside of a judgment of decision task. However, the relative memorability of information as a function of its implications for the outcome of a judgment or decision does not support a simple summary conclusion.

C. DEMONSTRATIONS OF STRATEGIC VARIETY

Two lines of research in our laboratories illustrate the theme of strategic variety. The first set of experiments (Hastie & Park, 1986) manipulated the timing of subjects' judgments and the source of the information they considered when making the judgments. These experiments compared on-line judgment strategies, in which subjects made judgments while information was available through perceptual processes, with memory-based strategies, in which subjects made judgments on the basis of information retrieved from long-term memory some time after it had been perceived and encoded in memory. The second set of experiments examined different types of on-line judgment strategies that are induced by variations in task and response demands manipulated by the experimenter. For example, the difference between judgments expressed only once (after all relevant evidence is presented) versus judgments expressed repeatedly item-by-item as evidence was presented.

Hastie and Park (1986) report the results from several experiments designed to vary subjects' judgment strategies in social judgment tasks. One method used to manipulate subjects' strategies relied on presenting subjects with an anticipated or a surprising judgment task after information relevant to the judgments had been presented. One-half of the subjects were told they would be asked to play the role of a personnel officer making occupation suitability judgments about applicants for jobs in a large company. They were given detailed instructions about the attributes of a good candidate for the job they were evaluating. For example, they might be told that good candidates for a job as a computer programmer would be precise, quantitative thinkers who were also relatively unsociable. With this judgment task in mind, the subjects listened to a tape-recorded conversation in which one man made a series of statements implying that he had five favorable attributes (e.g., "I did quite well on the graduate school quantitative aptitude test") and five unfavorable attributes (e.g., "I can't stay still indoors, I really get restless working inside") in reference to the profile of a good computer programmer.

The other half of the subjects in this experiment were told nothing about the job suitability judgment task before they heard the taped conversation. Rather, they were told that they were subjects in a social psychology experiment and that they should listen to the conversation, after which they would be asked "some questions." After listening to the tape-recorded conversation, these subjects were instructed to play the role of a personnel officer and to make the same job-suitability judgments as the other subjects. Thus, both groups of subjects heard identical evidence and were given an identical judgment task, however for one-half of the subjects, the task was presumably anticipated and on-line judgment strategies were followed, whereas for the other subjects, the task was unanticipated and memory-based judgment strategies were followed.

As predicted, subjects performing under instructions that led them to anticipate the job-suitability judgment task and to follow on-line strategies made judgments that were independent of their memory (tested after the judgments were made) for the contents of the conversation. For these subjects, the correlation between their recall of pro-computer programmer and anti-computer programmer remarks was nonsignificant (median correlation of +.09). In contrast, in the surprise judgment condition, designed to induce a memory-based strategy, the correlations were substantial (median correlation of +.46).

Hastie and Park (1986) also used a method that relied on interference with on-line judgments (rather than surprise) to produce another comparison between on-line versus memory-based judgments. In these experiments, one-half of the subjects were simply told that they would be making judgments about a person's personality and then they listened to a tape recording describing the person's behaviors. As they listened to the tape they made ratings of the likeability of the person described by each of the 50 behaviors. At the end of the tape, after a short distracting task, these subjects made personality trait ratings of the person described on the tape. The other half of the subjects were told that they were participating in a psycholinguistics experiment, and they listened to the same tape recording and made judgments on the grammaticality of each of the 50 sentences describing the person's behaviors. This grammaticality-rating task was chosen to interfere with subjects' natural tendency to make spontaneous judgments of the person's personality. After the tape and the grammaticality ratings, these subjects were treated in the same manner as the first group of subjects, and all subjects attempted to recall as many of the 50 behaviors as they could remember.

Again, as in the first experiment, the hypothesis was that in the straightforward likeability judgment condition an on-line judgment strategy would be induced, whereas in the interfering grammaticality judgment condition a memory-based strategy would be induced. As in the first experiment, insignificant and small correlations were observed between subjects' judgments and memory for the relevant evidence in the on-line condition (median correlation of +.15), whereas significant and large correlations were obtained in the memory-based condition (median correlation of +.67).

Relying on the results of previous legal decision making research, Pennington & Hastie (1992, Experiments 2 and 3) manipulated the decision strategy followed by subjects making judgments of guilt or innocence in a felony case. They assumed that under normal, global judgment task conditions in which subjects were only required to render one ultimate judgment, an explanation-based strategy would be followed. Subjects would spend considerable time reasoning about the evidence to construct a story that they believed would best explain the evidence deemed to be true from the trial. A second set of task conditions, based on a requirement that the subject make repeated judgments after each block of evidence was presented, was designed to induce an item-by-item, anchor-and-adjustment judgment strategy (Hogarth & Einhorn, 1992; Lopes, 1982; Tversky & Kahneman, 1974).

Three versions of an embezzlement case originally used in research by Schum & Martin (1982) were created: a basic version of the case with evenly balanced pro-conviction and pro-acquittal evidence, a convict version of the case in which additional information was added supporting inferences that would lead to a conclusion the defendant was guilty, and an acquit version of the case in which evidence was added supporting the defendant's innocence. Two rating tasks were created, one in which the subject made only one global rating of probability of guilt after reading all of the evidence and the other in which several ratings were required after blocks of the evidence were read with a final rating after all of the evidence was presented.

Comparisons of the final ratings from the two conditions showed that the single global rating task yielded more extreme ratings (either in the guilty or innocent direction depending on the version of the case being judged) than the item-by-item rating condition. This result was as predicted on the assumption that the global rating condition induced an explanation-based reasoning strategy that would facilitate the inferences implicit in the convict version and acquit version evidence additions and on the assumption that the anchor-and-adjustment process would lead to "conservative" and insufficient adjustment from the initial anchor (as has been reported by other researchers, e.g., Tversky & Kahneman, 1974). In addition, efforts to fit an anchor-and-adjust differential weighting algebraic model were relatively successful for ratings from the item-by-item judgment task, but not for ratings from the global judgment task.

One message from these studies is simply that the same sets of evidence can be connected to judgment responses via several alternate reasoning strategies. This is, of course, an old message in cognitive psychology and in the field of decision making (e.g., Payne, Bettman, & Johnson, 1993; Tversky & Kahneman, 1974). We believe that the distinction between on-line versus memory-based judgment or decision strategies (some have called it stimulus-based vs. memory-based; cf. Lynch & Srull, 1982) is fundamental and warrants the increasing attention it is receiving by empirical researchers. At a minimum, our studies demonstrate the value of the judgment–memory correlation as a "signature" of subjects' reliance on a memory-based strategy.

We also think that explanation-based decision strategies are very common and that the distinction between these strategies and others is especially important. The Pennington and Hastie (1992) studies show that subtle predictions about the outcomes of judgments made via alternative strategies can be framed and that there are real differences between the judgments reached via one strategy and another.

V. Conclusions

The cognitive approach to judgment and decision making behavior is gradually developing and expanding in scope and in number of adherents. We have presented a collection of experimental methods and results from one laboratory studying several different judgment tasks to illustrate some major trends that are central in the cognitive approach: evidence representation in the form of a model or explanation of the decision situation, enhanced memory for decision-relevant information after a decision has been made, and adaptive flexibility in individual decision strategies in response to variations in task conditions (with fixed evidence bases and outcomes).

One obstacle for the development of cognitive theories of judgment and decision making behavior is that there are considerable differences among the theories that (appropriately) are called cognitive. Of course, this situation is probably good for the eventual development of cognitive theories, but it is troublesome for individual researchers, especially those who are currently attempting to spread the faith to new task domains. As attested to by our own example, we do not believe that researchers should wait for convergence on one general cognitive theory before addressing cognitive themes in their research. Rather, general issues, such as those concerning mental representation and strategic variety, are appropriate subjects of research today. When the time comes to state theoretical interpretations, it seems that any of the major options (computer simulation, algebraic modeling, or middle range, partly formalized theories) offer good solutions.

In the field of judgment and decision making, it is essential to think about the relationships between alternate theoretical developments and formulations based on traditional Expected Utility Theory (von Neumann & Morgenstern, 1947). The cognitive psychological approach begins with observations of human behavior and works toward a descriptive theory of behavior. This bottom-up development of a judgment and decision making theory is facilitated by the accumulating store of successful examples of cognitive accounts for complex behaviors in other intellectual tasks. In contrast, the development of Expected Utility Theory has been essentially top-down, beginning with a succinct set of assumptions about rationality and optimal adaptation and concluding with deductions about appropriate behavior in judgment and decision making tasks.

There is, in principle, no reason why the two theoretical enterprises might not converge; indeed, cognitive psychologists often refer to models of optimal behavior to guide the development of descriptive models (e.g., Green & Swets, 1966; J. R. Anderson, 1990b). However, when clear comparisons to normative standards are possible in controlled experiments, the Expected Utility Theory formulations repeatedly fail to describe human decision behavior (N. H. Anderson, 1991b; Camerer, 1992; Lopes, 1987; Luce, 1992; Tversky & Kahneman, 1974). Thus, the cognitive theories developing bottom up from the empirical base do not converge with the top-down applications of Expected Utility Theory.

For better or for worse, we do not see that cognitive theoretical developments will have much impact on Expected Utility formulations in the near future. The enterprise of developing normative models to prescribe optimal performance is of obvious value outside of its implications for descriptive psychological theory. Furthermore, the belief that human behavior is rationally adaptive is enormously appealing and also appears to support the assumption that normative theories are descriptive. What seems to be happening is that an intermediate form of theory is appearing. These non-expected utility theories start with the basic Expected Utility Theory formulation and then depart of modifying or supplementing its basic assumptions to create systems that have more accurate behavioral implications (many of these non-expected utility theories have been proposed by economists, e.g., Machina, 1989, but several formulations have been authored by psychologists: Kahneman & Tversky, 1979; Luce, 1988; Lopes, 1990; Tversky & Kahneman, 1992). Our expectation is that the crucible of empirical evaluation will force all of the approaches to converge on a common theoretical framework; and we believe that cognitive precepts, like the ones we have reviewed in this chapter, will be the core of the next generation of theories of judgment and decision making.

ACKNOWLEDGMENTS

The authors thank Mary Luhring for her assistance with the preparation of the manuscript, and Jerry Busemeyer and Doug Medin for helpful comments. The authors were supported in part by National Science Foundation Grants SES-9122154 and SES-9113479.

REFERENCES

Anderson, J. R. (1983). *The architecture of cognition.* Cambridge, MA: Harvard University Press.

Anderson, J. R. (1987). Methodologies for the study of human knowledge. *Behavioral and Brain Sciences, 10,* 467–505.

Anderson, J. R. (1990a). *Cognitive psychology and its implications* (3rd ed.). New York: Freeman.

Anderson, J. R. (1990b). *The adaptive character of thought.* Hillsdale, NJ: Erlbaum.

Anderson, J. R., & Bower, G. H. (1973). *Human associative memory.* Washington, DC: V. H. Winston.

Anderson, N. H. (1981). *Foundations of Information Integration Theory.* New York: Academic Press.

Anderson, N. H. (1982). *Methods of Information Integration Theory.* New York: Academic Press.

Anderson, N. H. (1991a). Functional memory in person cognition. In N. H. Anderson (Ed.), *Contributions to Information Integration Theory: Vol. 1. Cognition* (pp. 1–55). Hillsdale, NJ: Erlbaum.

Anderson, N. H. (1991b). A cognitive theory of judgment and decision. In N. H. Anderson (Ed.), *Contributions to Information Integration Theory: Vol. 1. Cognition* (pp. 105–142). Hillsdale, NJ: Erlbaum.

Anderson, N. H., & Farkas, A. J. (1973). New light on order effects in attitude change. *Journal of Personality and Social Psychology 28,* 88–93.

Anderson, N. H., & Hubert, S. (1963). Effects of concomitant verbal recall on order effects in personality impression formation. *Journal of Verbal Learning and Verbal Behavior, 2,* 379–391.

Anderson, N. H., & Shanteau, J. (1977). Weak inference with linear models. *Psychological Bulletin, 84,* 1155–1170.

Baddeley, A. (1990). *Human memory: Theory and practice.* Boston: Allyn and Bacon.

Balota, D. A., d'Arcais, G. B. F., & Rayner, K. (Eds.). (1990). *Comprehension processes in reading.* Hillsdale, NJ: Erlbaum.

Beach, L. R. (1990). *Image Theory: Decision making in personal and organizational contexts.* Chichester, England: Wiley.

Beach, L. R., Wise, J. A., & Barclay, S. (1970). Sample proportion and subjective probability revisions. *Organizational Behavior and Human Performance, 5,* 183–190.

Bourne, L. E., Dominowski, R. L., Loftus, E. F., & Healy, A. F. (1986). *Cognitive processes* (2nd ed.). Englewood Cliffs, NJ: Prentice-Hall.

Brehmer, B., & Joyce, C. B. R. (Eds.). (1988). *Human judgment: The SJT view.* Amsterdam: North-Holland.

Broadbent, D. E. (1958). *Perception and communication.* London: Pergamon Press.

Brunswik, E. (1956). *Perception and the representative design of psychological experiments.* Berkeley, CA: University of California Press.

Camerer, C. F. (1992). Recent tests of generalizations of expected utility theory. In W. Edwards (Ed.), *Utility theories: Measurements and applications* (pp. 207–251). Boston: Kluwer.

Dawes, R. M., & Corrigan, B. (1974). Linear models in decision making. *Psychological Bulletin, 81,* 95–106.

Dellarosa, D., & Bourne, L. E., Jr. (1984). Decisions and memory: Differential retrievability of consistent and contradictory evidence. *Journal of Verbal Learning and Verbal Behavior, 23,* 669–682.

Dreben, E. K., Fiske, S. T., & Hastie, R. (1979). The independence of evaluative and item information: Impression and recall order effects in behavior-based impression formation. *Journal of Personality and Social Psychology, 37,* 1758–1768.

Edwards, W. (1954). The theory of decision making. *Psychological Bulletin, 51,* 380–417.

Edwards, W. (1962). Subjective probabilities inferred from decisions. *Psychological Review, 69,* 109–135.

Edwards, W. (1968). Conservatism in human information processing. In B. Kleinmuntz (Ed.), *Formal representation of human judgment* (pp. 17–52). New York: Wiley.

Ericsson, K. A., & Simon, H. A. (1993). *Protocol analysis: Verbal reports as data* (2nd ed.). Cambridge, MA: MIT Press.

Garner, W. R., Hake, H. W., & Eriksen, C. W. (1956). Operationalism and the concept of perception. *Psychological Review, 63,* 149–159.

Gigerenzer, G., Hoffrage, U., & Kleinbölting, H. (1991). Probabilistic mental models: A Brunswikian theory of confidence. *Psychological Review, 98,* 506–528.

Graesser, A. C., Singer, M., & Trabasso, T. (1994). Constructing inferences during narrative text comprehension. *Psychological Review, 101,* 371–395.

Green, D., & Swets, J. A. (1966). *Signal detection theory and psychophysics.* New York: Wiley.

Hamilton, D. L., Katz, L. B., & Leirer, V. O. (1980). Cognitive representation of personality impressions: Organizational processes in first impression formation. *Journal of Personality and Social Psychology, 39,* 1050–1063.

Hammond, K. R. (Ed.). (1966). *The psychology of Egon Brunswik.* New York: Holt, Rinehart, and Winston.

Hammond, K. R. (1988). Judgment and decision making in dynamic tasks. *Information and Decision Technologies, 14,* 3–14.

Hammond, K. R. (1990). Intuitive and analytical cognition: Information models. In A. Sage (Ed.), *Concise encyclopedia of information processing in systems and organizations* (pp. 306–312). Oxford: Pergamon.

Hastie, R. (1981). Schematic principles in human memory. In E. T. Higgins, C. P. Herman, & M. P. Zanna (Eds.), *Social cognition: The Ontario Symposium* (Vol. 1, pp. 39–88). Hillsdale, NJ: Erlbaum.

Hastie, R. (1984). Causes and effects of causal attribution. *Journal of Personality and Social Psychology, 46,* 44–56.

Hastie, R., & Kumar, A. P. (1979). Person memory: Personality traits as organizing principles in memory for behaviors. *Journal of Personality and Social Psychology, 37,* 25–38.

Hastie, R., & Park, B. (1986). The relationship between memory and judgment depends on whether the judgment is memory-based or on-line. *Psychological Review, 93,* 258–268.

Hastie, R., & Pennington, N. (1989). Notes on the distinction between on-line versus memory-based judgments. In J. N. Bassili (Ed.), *On-line cognition in person perception* (pp. 1–18). Hillsdale, NJ: Erlbaum.

Hoffman, P. J. (1960). The paramorphic representation of clinical judgment. *Psychological Bulletin, 57,* 116–131.

Hogarth, R. M., & Einhorn, H. J. (1992). Order effects in belief updating: The belief adjustment model. *Cognitive Psychology, 24,* 1–55.

Jacoby, L. L., Kelley, C. M., & Dywan, J. (1989). Memory attributions. In H. L. Roediger III, F. I. M. Craik (Eds.), *Varieties of memory and consciousness: Essays in honor of Endel Tulving* (pp. 391–422). Hillsdale, NJ: Erlbaum.

Kahneman, D., & Tversky, A. (1979). Prospect theory: An analysis of decisions under risk. *Econometrica, 47,* 263–291.

Kieras, D. E., & Just, M. A. (Eds.). (1984). *New methods in reading comprehension research.* Hillsdale, NJ: Erlbaum.

Lopes, L. L. (1982). *Toward a procedural theory of judgment* (Tech. Rep. No. 17, pp. 1–49). Madison, WI: Wisconsin Human Information Processing Program.

Lopes, L. L. (1987). Procedural debiasing. *Acta Psychologica, 64,* 167–185.

Lopes, L. L. (1990). Remodeling risk aversion: A comparison of Bernoullian and rank dependent value approaches. In G. M. von Furstenberg (Ed.), *Acting under uncertainty: Multidisciplinary conceptions* (pp. 267–299). Boston: Kluwer.

Luce, R. D. (1988). Rank-dependent subjective expected utility representations. *Journal of Risk and Uncertainty, 1,* 305–332.

Luce, R. D. (1992). Where does subjective expected utility fail descriptively? *Journal of Risk and Uncertainty, 5,* 5–27.

Luce, R. D., & Raiffa, H. (1957). *Games and decisions: Introduction and critical survey.* New York: Wiley.

Lynch, J. G., & Srull, T. K. (1982). Memory and attentional factors in consumer choice: Concepts and research methods. *Journal of Consumer Research, 9,* 18–37.

Machina, M. J. (1989). Dynamic consistency and non-expected utility models of choice under uncertainty. *Journal of Economic Literature, 27,* 1622–1668.

March, J. G. (1978). Bounded rationality, ambiguity, and the engineering of choice. *Bell Journal of Economics, 9,* 587–608.

Marks, D. F., & Clarkson, J. K. (1972). An explanation of conservatism in the bookbag and pokerchips situation. *Acta Psychologica, 36,,* 145–160.

Marr, D. (1982). *Vision.* San Francisco: W. H. Freeman.

Massaro, D. W., & Cowan, N. (1993). Information processing models: Microscopes of the mind. *Annual Review of Psychology, 44,* 383–425.

McKoon, G. A., & Ratcliff, R. (1992). Inferences during reading. *Psychological Review, 99,* 440–466.

Mellers, B. A., Ordóñez, L. D., & Birnbaum, M. H. (1992). A change-of-process theory for contextual effects and preference reversals in risky decision making. *Organizational Behavior and Human Decision Processes, 52,* 331–369.

Miller, G. A. (1956). The magical number seven, plus or minus two: Some limits on our capacity for processing information. *Psychological Review, 63,* 81–97.

Murphy, G. L., & Medin, D. L. (1985). The role of theories in conceptual coherence. *Psychological Review, 92,* 289–316.

Newell, A. (1990). *Unified theories of cognition.* Cambridge, MA: Harvard University Press.

Newell, A., & Simon, H. A. (1972). *Human problem solving.* Englewood Cliffs, NJ: Prentice-Hall.

Ostrom, T. M., Lingle, J. H., Pryor, J. B., & Geva, N. (1980). Cognitive organization of person impressions. In R. Hastie, T. M. Ostrom, E. B. Ebbesen, R. S. Wyer, Jr., D. L. Hamilton, & D. E. Carlston (Eds.), *Person memory: The cognitive basis of social perception* (pp. 55–88). Hillsdale, NJ: Erlbaum.

Palmer, S. E., & Kimchi, R. (1986). The information processing approach to cognition. In T. J. Knapp & L. C. Robertson (Eds.), *Approaches to cognition: Contrasts and controversies* (pp. 37–77). Hillsdale, NJ: Erlbaum.

Payne, J. W., Bettman, J. R., & Johnson, E. J. (1993). *The adaptive decision maker.* New York: Cambridge University Press.

Pennington, N., & Hastie, R. (1986). Evidence evaluation in complex decision making. *Journal of Personality and Social Psychology, 51,* 242–258.

Pennington, N., & Hastie, R. (1992). Explaining the evidence: Tests of the Story Model for juror decision making. *Journal of Personality and Social Psychology, 62,* 189–206.

Pennington, N., & Hastie, R. (1993). A theory of explanation-based decision making. In G. A. Klein, J. Orasanu, R. Calderwood, & C. E. Zsambok (Eds.), *Decision making in action: Models and methods* (pp. 188–204). Norwood, NJ: Ablex.

Peterson, C. R., & Beach, L. R. (1967). Man as an intuitive statistician. *Psychological Bulletin, 68,* 29–46.

Pylyshyn, Z. W. (1984). *Computation and cognition.* Cambridge, MA: MIT Press.

Ramsey, F. P. (1931). Truth and probability. In R. B. Braithwaite (Ed.), *The foundations of mathematics and other logical essays* (pp. 156–198). London: Routledge & Kegan Paul.

Ratcliff, R. (1993). Methods for dealing with reaction time outliers. *Psychological Bulletin, 114,* 510–532.

Rips, L. J. (1994). *The psychology of proof: Deductive reasoning in human thinking.* Cambridge, MA: MIT Press.

Rojahn, K., & Pettigrew, T. F. (1992). Memory for schema-relevant information: A meta-analytic resolution. *British Journal of Social Psychology, 31,* 81–109.

Rumelhart, D. E., & Norman, D. A. (1988). Representation in memory. In R. C. Atkinson, R. J. Herrnstein, G. Lindzey, & R. D. Luce (Eds.), *Stevens' Handbook of Experimental Psychology* (Vol. 2, pp. 511–587). New York: Wiley.

Sacerdoti, E. D. (1977). *A structure for plans and behavior.* New York: North-Holland.

Savage, L. J. (1954). *The foundations of statistics.* New York: Wiley.

Schank, R. C., Collins, G. C., & Hunter, L. E. (1986). Transcending inductive category formation in learning. *Behavioral and Brain Sciences, 9,* 639–686.

Schum, D. A., & Martin, A. W. (1982). Formal and empirical research on cascaded inference in jurisprudence. *Law and Society Review, 17,* 105–151.

Siegler, R. S. (1987). The perils of averaging data over strategies: An example from children's addition. *Journal of Experimental Psychology: General, 116,* 250–264.

Simon, H. A. (1955). A behavioral model of rational choice. *Quarterly Journal of Economics, 69,* 99–118.

Simon, H. A. (1959). Theories of decision making in economics and behavioral science. *American Economic Review, 49,* 253–280.

Simon, H. A. (1979). Rational decision making in business organizations. *American Economic Review, 69,* 493–513.

Slovic, P., Fischhoff, B., & Lichtenstein, S. (1979). Rating the risks. *Environment, 21*(3), 14–20.

Srull, T. K. (1981). Person memory: Some tests of associative storage and retrieval models. *Journal of Experimental Psychology: Human Learning and Memory, 7,* 440–462.

Stangor, C., & McMillan, D. (1992). Memory for expectancy-congruent and expectancy-incongruent information: A review of social and social developmental literatures. *Psychological Bulletin, 111,* 42–61.

Stevenson, M. K., Busemeyer, J. R., & Naylor, J. C. (1991). Judgment and decision-making theory. In M. D. Dunnette & L. M. Hough (Eds.), *Handbook of industrial and organizational psychology* (Vol. 1, 2nd ed., pp. 283–374). Palo Alto, CA: Consulting Psychologists Press.

Stewart, T. R. (1988). Judgment analysis: Procedures. In B. Brehmer & C. R. B. Joyce (Eds.), *Human judgment: The SJT view* (pp. 41–74). Amsterdam: North-Holland.

Suh, S. Y., & Trabasso, T. (1993). Global inferences in on-line processing of texts: Converging evidence from discourse analysis, talk-aloud protocols, and recognition priming. *Journal of Memory and Language, 32,* 279–300.

Taylor, S. E., & Crocker, J. (1981). Schematic bases of social information processing. In E. T. Higgins, C. P. Herman, & M. P. Zanna (Eds.), *Social cognition: The Ontario Symposium* (Vol. 1, pp. 89–134). Hillsdale, NJ: Erlbaum.

Thagard, P. (1989). Explanatory coherence. *Behavioral and Brain Sciences, 12,* 435–502.

Tversky, A., & Kahneman, D. (1973). Availability: A heuristic for judging frequency and probability. *Cognitive Psychology, 5,* 207–232.

Tversky, A., & Kahneman, D. (1974). Judgment under uncertainty: Heuristics and biases. *Science, 185,* 1124–1131.

Tversky, A., & Kahneman, D. (1992). Advances in prospect theory: Cumulative representation of uncertainty. *Journal of Risk and Uncertainty, 5,* 297–323.

von Neumann, J., & Morgenstern, O. (1947). Theory of games and economic behavior (2nd ed.). Princeton, NJ: Princeton University Press.

Wilensky, R. (1983). *Planning and understanding: A computational approach to human reasoning.* Reading, MA: Addison-Wesley.

Winograd, T. (1975). Computer memories: A metaphor for memory organization. In C. Cofer (Ed.), *The structure of human memory* (pp. 133–161). San Francisco: W. H. Freeman.

AND LET US NOT FORGET MEMORY: THE ROLE OF MEMORY PROCESSES AND TECHNIQUES IN THE STUDY OF JUDGMENT AND CHOICE

Elke U. Weber, William M. Goldstein, and Sema Barlas

I. Introduction

Can you remember the last time that memory was *not* involved, in some form or other, in a decision or judgment you had to make? When asked to predict the July temperature in your city on the occasion of an impending in-laws' visit, you probably recalled July temperatures over the last few years. When thinking about a new car, you probably retrieved car models you had recently seen and admired on the highway. When deliberating about the job offer from the East Coast, you might have remembered the good times you had in that city during college and weighed those memories against the traffic congestion and high housing prices you recalled from your recent visit there. Considering the prevalent use of memory at many decision stages—including the generation of feasible alternatives, the determination of the utility of different outcomes, and the prediction of the likelihood of outcomes—it may come as a surprise to nonspecialists in the area of human judgment and decision making (J/DM) that, with some notable exceptions, most models of decision or judgment performance do not explicitly combine considerations of memory processes and of the representation of information in memory with other stages of the decision process.

THE PSYCHOLOGY OF LEARNING
AND MOTIVATION, VOL. 32

33

This is not to say that memory considerations are new to J/DM researchers. However, the integration of memory concepts into theoretical and empirical work has been uneven and nonsystematic. Thus, memory processes have been adduced as explanations for particular phenomena, as in Tversky and Kahneman's (1973) theory that people judge the relative frequency of events by their availability, that is, by the frequency and ease with which instances can be retrieved. Hindsight bias is usually explained as a reconstructive memory problem, that is, as an inability to reconstruct one's prior state of knowledge after additional information has been added (Fischhoff, 1975; Hawkins & Hastie, 1990). Memory-related mechanisms such as the biased encoding and biased retrieval of information are also used to explain why people fail to learn the relationship between variables from experience (Brehmer, 1980), why their predictions are typically overconfident (Einhorn & Hogarth, 1978; Lichtenstein, Fischhoff, & Phillips, 1982), or why the utilization of base rate information appears to be sensitive to elicitation procedure and the knowledge base of respondents (Gigerenzer, Hell, & Blank, 1988; Weber, Böckenholt, Hilton, & Wallace, 1993).

Moreover, beyond the explanation of particular phenomena, memory considerations have had a broad, if indirect and diffuse, effect on general theory in J/DM research. Recognition that human working memory is of limited capacity (e.g., Miller, 1956) has had lasting impact on J/DM models through the work of Simon (1955, 1956), whose theories redefined the image of the typical decision maker from that of a "rational calculator" to that of a creature of finite resources forced to find practicable strategies for processing information in a "satisficing," and not necessarily optimal, fashion. This image of the decision maker as a limited capacity information processor contributed to the subsequent identification of different decision heuristics (Kahneman, Slovic, & Tversky, 1982) and decision strategies (Payne, 1982).

This indirect effect of memory considerations probably presents its greatest impact to date because of the central role that has been accorded in J/DM research to the concept of *decision strategy*. Numerous task and context effects have been attributed to the use of different decision strategies, that is, to the operation of different rules and procedures for the weighting and combination of information. For example, decisions have been shown to be sensitive to a variety of task and context characteristics, including "irrelevant" filler alternatives (Goldstein & Mitzel, 1992), time pressure (Ben Zur & Bresnitz, 1981; Böckenholt & Kroeger, 1993; Busemeyer, 1985), and the response mode subjects use to report their decisions (Goldstein & Einhorn, 1987; Huber, 1980; Lichtenstein & Slovic, 1971; Mellers, Ordóñez, & Birnbaum, 1992; Tversky, Sattath, & Slovic, 1988). To contain the proliferation of decision strategies postulated to account for these effects, unifying metatheories have been suggested to explain how adaptive and goal-directed organisms select strategies to tailor their decisions to the information, constraints, and tasks at hand (Hogarth & Einhorn, 1992; Payne, 1982). One widely held metatheory states that decision strategies are selected on the basis of an error–effort trade-off analysis (Payne, Bettman, & Johnson, 1988, 1990, 1993; Smith, Mitchell, & Beach, 1982). Metatheories about contingent strategy selection also exist in the domains of problem solving (Friedrich, 1993) and hypothesis testing (Klayman & Ha, 1987). In summary, memory *limitations* have impressed J/DM researchers more than other findings about memory, and J/DM researchers have mostly made use of memory limitations to motivate a concern for issues of strategy selection.

The idea that people select their decision strategies on the basis of an error–effort (or, more generally, cost–benefit) trade-off analysis represents one of the two main metatheoretical frameworks that have been proposed to account for the sensitivity of decision behavior to manipulations of the task and context (Payne, Bettman, & Johnson, 1992). The other approach is a perceptual framework, which attributes behavioral variability not to shifts in strategy, but to changes in the way that relevant information is framed (e.g., Tversky & Kahneman, 1981, 1986).

Strategy selection and information framing are important explanatory constructs within J/DM research and will continue to explain a broad range of phenomena. However, there is an increasing concern within the J/DM community that the theoretical and empirical focus of the field may be too narrow (Beach, 1993; Frisch & Clemen, 1994; Holbrook, 1987; Lopes, 1994). Much of this concern raises questions about the relative merits of psychological versus economic approaches, discussing, for example, whether descriptive or prescriptive models should serve as a theoretical starting point in the explanation of choice behavior. In this chapter, we argue that there is a need to enlarge the current set of explanatory constructs and experimental tools even *within* the confines of descriptive, psychological models of decision making, and we argue further that insights from the field of memory can help to supplement and enrich the explanatory constructs that are the focus of the strategy selection and perceptual frameworks.

First, we will argue that recent models of memory representation and memory processes have the potential to enlarge the set of explanatory constructs that J/DM researchers bring to bear on issues of strategy and strategy selection. Specifically, we describe some recent assumptions about the *format* in which information is represented, stored, and retrieved from memory, which offer new perspectives on whether the integration of information necessarily requires the deliberate use of an effortful decision strategy. We show in Experiment 1 that judgments thought to require the use of effortful information integration strategies (under traditional assumptions about memory) may, in fact, arise more effortlessly, as the automatic by-product of the way information is stored and retrieved. Not only does this show that the "work" of a decision strategy (i.e., information integration) might be accomplished nonstrategically, that is, without the use of processes deliberately invoked for this purpose, but this result also suggests that definitions and measures of cognitive "effort" should be reconsidered. We also review the gains in the predictability of judgment and decision making performance that arise from making several functional distinctions about the *content* of memory (i.e., semantic vs. episodic memory; declarative vs. procedural memory).

Second, we will consider the implications of memory research for the perceptual framework, which emphasizes the influence of information en-coding. Research on information encoding within J/DM has been surpris-ingly circumscribed. Although Kahneman and Tversky's (1979) prospect theory included an editing phase that encompassed a variety of coding operations, J/DM research within the perceptual framework, with some notable exceptions (e.g., Brainerd & Reyna, 1992; Reyna & Brainerd, 1991), has concentrated mostly on just three: (1) the framing of outcomes as gains versus losses relative to a reference point (Kahneman & Tversky, 1979), (2) the aggregation versus segregation of events and options (Thaler, 1985), and (3) the restructuring of alternatives to reveal or create a dominance relation (Montgomery, 1983). Without denying the importance of these three coding operations, we consider the implications of memory research for relevant issues that may have been overlooked by this focus. Memory researchers are certainly not the only psychologists to have considered matters concerning the encoding and representation of information. How-ever, because memory researchers traditionally divide their field into issues of encoding, storage, and retrieval of information, they have given more thought than most to matters of encoding. Specifically, we discuss the influence of prior experience (as opposed to concurrent task conditions) on the encoding of information. Then, in Experiment 2, we present an example in which short-term memory limitations lead to preference rever-sals, not as the result of changes in decision strategy, but as the result of simplification in the encoding of presented information. We conclude with a discussion of the way presented information may be elaborated in light of prior knowledge.

Finally, we will argue by review and by example that apparently unobserv-able mental events can be studied by means of experimental procedures that examine the memorial aftereffects of information encoding and prior processing. That is to say, memory can be used the way physicists use cloud chambers: to study otherwise unobservable events via the residue they leave behind. The use of memory techniques as experimental tools may thus allow researchers to distinguish between J/DM models that make similar outcome predictions but differ in their assumptions about underlying processes.

II. Memory Structure and Processes in J/DM Models

A. BEYOND STRATEGY: AN EXPANDED SET OF
    EXPLANATORY CONSTRUCTS

1. Microlevel Assumptions about Memory

Most decision models, either explicitly or implicitly, assume a structure of knowledge representation that dates back to the 1960s and 1970s, that is, to a Newell and Simon (1972) cognitive architecture with localized representation of information and serial storage and retrieval processes. Alternative cognitive architectures with distributed representation of information and parallel storage and retrieval processes have since found widespread use in research on learning and memory, but their implications for models of judgment and decision making have not yet been fully investigated. We suggest that J/DM researchers consider new assumptions about cognitive architecture that include the possibility of distributed representation and parallel processing (Humphreys, Bain, & Pike, 1989; Metcalfe, 1990; Murdock, 1993; Rumelhart & McClelland, 1986; Townsend, 1990). We show that these distinctions are important, because different assumptions about the properties of memory representation and processes allow for different mechanisms by which information can be stored and combined and thus make different predictions about the cognitive "effort" required to implement particular processing strategies.

a. Distributed versus Localized Representation of Information. Cognitive architectures modeled on the architecture of a serial computer (e.g., Newell & Simon, 1972) have assumed that an item of information is represented in a localized way such that it can be stored in and subsequently retrieved from a single memory location. However, different cognitive architectures have since been suggested, including architectures modeled on a hologram in which an item of information is represented in a distributed way. *Distributed representation* gets its name from the fact that an item of information is distributed over numerous memory locations. A given item should thus be thought of as a vector of features, where a "feature" in a distributed-memory model is an abstract, usually numerical, variable that need not correspond to any physical or psychological feature, and the representation of a typical item is a vector of several hundred such "features." An advantage of such a distributed representation is that distinct vectors representing several different pieces of item information can all be placed and stored into a common memory vector; that is, different vectors can be superimposed without losing their individual identities. As a result, an overall impression can thus be created by the superposition of individual item vectors. A visual example of such a composite memory is a "photograph" in the front pages of a conference volume edited by Hockley and Lewandowsky (1991) that provides an impression of the prototypical attendee through the superposition of the negatives of the portraits of all conference participants.

The combination of different pieces of information into a composite impression of a judgment or choice alternative, which lies at the heart of many decision strategies, is similar to the formation of a prototype as a composite of multiple exemplars. In many current memory models applied to categorization, and in contrast to analogous decision models, prototypes emerge without deliberate, strategic, or effortful computation as the consequence of a single memory store into which the (distributed) representations of all exemplars are superimposed and merged (J. A. Anderson, Silverstein, Ritz, & Jones, 1977; Chandler, 1991; Metcalfe, 1990). The integration of exemplar information into prototypes or composite impressions may also occur at the time of information retrieval rather than storage (but still without deliberate computation), an assumption made by a different set of models (e.g., Kruschke, 1992). Superposition of memory traces (e.g., different exemplars of a category) allows for the emergence of an average impression or prototype in the form of a composite memory vector. Thus, assumptions about memory representation and processes different from the localized representation and serial processing of a Newell and Simon (1972) cognitive architecture have some desirable by-products. One emergent property of the superposition of distributed representations of information into a common memory vector is that prototype formation and composite–impression formation are "automatic."

A well-developed theory of distributed memory representation and processes that is capable of reconstructing both individual item information and overall impressions from such composite memory vectors is Murdock's (1982, 1983, 1989, 1993) theory of distributed associative memory (TO-DAM). Weber, Goldstein, and Busemeyer (1991) used TODAM to model observed dissociations between people's evaluative judgments of alternatives and their memory for the alternatives' characteristics and found that some of TODAM's assumptions (e.g., the assumption of memory decay) predicted observed phenomena such as serial position effects in the judgment task different from those in the memory task. However, other memory theories exist that also assume distributed representation of information but postulate different storage and retrieval processes, for example, Metcalfe's composite holographic associative recall model (CHARM; Metcalfe Eich, 1982; Metcalfe, 1990) and the matrix model of Humphreys et al. (1989).

   b. *Automatic versus Controlled Processing.* Decision strategies describing the nature of information use and combination are often depicted as something requiring mental effort. However, Schneider and Shiffrin (1977) showed in visual search experiments that the effortfulness of the task depends on the learning history of the person performing the task, and that effortful processing can sometimes (with sufficient practice in consistent environments) become automatic. Automatic processing is fast, autonomous (i.e., grabs attention in an obligatory way), unavailable to conscious awareness, and relatively effortless (Logan, 1988). Strategic processing, in contrast, is both under conscious control and effortful.

   There is a growing literature that documents unconscious influences of memory on performance for a variety of tasks (for reviews see Bargh, 1989; Bornstein, 1989; Jacoby, Lindsay, & Toth, 1992; and Roediger, 1990). Implicit memory, that is, effects of prior experience on task performance in the absence of any intent or instructions for memory and without any conscious awareness, seems to be accessed automatically and effortlessly by a different set of processes than explicit, consciously controlled use of memory. Young and DeHaan (1990) found dissociations between performance on direct versus implicit memory in amnesics, consistent with different routes of access to stored knowledge that make it possible to interfere with consciously controlled access without affecting unconscious automatic access. Jacoby, Toth, and Yonelinas (1993) had people study a list of words, then later presented them with the first three letters of each word as a cue for one of two tasks. In the exclusion condition, people were instructed to complete the word stem with a word that was *not* on the studied list. The proportion of such words that were produced anyway (i.e., contrary to instructions) permitted Jacoby et al. to estimate the joint probability that a word would fail to be recalled consciously (and thereby rejected as a permissible response) and yet would be produced by unconscious, uncontrollable memory processes. In the inclusion condition, people were instructed to complete the word stem with a word that *did* appear on the studied list. Performance in this condition reflects conscious recall as well as unconscious memory processes. Thus, the *difference* in performance between the two conditions yields a measure of conscious recall. This measure, in turn, can be used to obtain an estimate of the contribution of *un*conscious processes to performance in the exclusion condition. By using this method of obtaining separate estimates of the conscious and unconscious components of memory, Jacoby et al. demonstrated that a manipulation of attention during study of the initial word list (i.e., attention divided between visual list learning and auditory monitoring of digits) impaired the conscious component of memory while leaving the unconscious component unchanged. Thus, there are memory processes that in addition to being unconscious and obligatory seem not to be affected by attention and effort during study.

Payne et al. (1988, 1990, 1993) characterized decision strategies as sequential series of effortful production rules. In the next section, we apply the work on distributed memory and automatic processing to a judgment task. We offer an information integration process (i.e., superposition) in which a distributed memory representation does the work of an information integration strategy, but does so in an apparently automatic, effortless manner. The following results of Experiment 1 suggest that current assumptions about the effortfulness of information integration may need to be qualified.

2. Experiment 1: "Effort-free" Impression Formation

Hastie and Park (1986) suggested that overall impressions of people or objects can be formed by two types of processes. The first type is *on-line* processing of information; that is, new information is integrated into an overall judgment as the information is seen, while the overall judgment is constantly being updated. The second type is *memory-based* processing; that is, in the absence of an up-front warning that information needs to be integrated, people have to recall the relevant information from memory when asked at a later point to form an overall impression and thus base their impression on what they recall. In the study described in this section (and in greater detail in Weber, Goldstein, Barlas, & Busemeyer, 1994), we hypothesize the operation of a third mechanism for impression formation, a different type of memory-based processing, namely the retrieval of a composite impression that is formed effortlessly in memory by the spontaneous superposition of informational items during memory storage. We will refer to this mechanism as *composite-memory recall.*

The study was designed to demonstrate that impression formation can be achieved relatively effortlessly and without prior warning or conscious strategy by this third mechanism as the by-product of a "distributed" memory representation which makes it possible to place different pieces of information or different impressions into a common storage vector that represents the category to be judged. The critical evidence is the response time (RT) needed to integrate several impressions into a single overall judgment. As further explained, if an overall impression is produced by composite-memory recall, then the RT to make the judgment will not depend on set size, that is, on the number of items that need to be integrated. This set-size logic was first introduced by Lingle and Ostrom (1979) to discriminate between retrieval versus nonretrieval judgment strategies.

   a. Dependent Measure. The use of RT as a dependent measure is widespread in many areas of cognitive psychology. Payne et al. (1988) used choice RT as a proxy for the effort involved in making a decision. In the effort–accuracy framework of their metatheory for strategy selection, they model the cognitive effort of a decision strategy as the weighted sum of the effort associated with the elementary information processing steps (eips) necessary to execute the strategy in a given situation. Weights represent the hypothesized effort of different eips (e.g., reading an attribute value in short-term memory or adding the values of two attributes in short-term memory), and total effort is assumed to be proportionate to RT. Payne et al.'s (1988) implicit assumption of a cognitive architecture with localized representations of items and serial processes leads to the prediction that the effort (and thus RT) for the formation of an overall impression should increase with the number of items of information that need to be recalled and integrated; that is, RT should increase with set size.

   When arriving at an overall impression through the process of recalling a composite memory into which individual items have been stored, set size should have no effect. The overall impression (be it a composite vector of superimposed item feature vectors or a composite matrix of superimposed negatives, as in the example of the group–prototype photo mentioned earlier) requires only a "readout" from the common vector or matrix into which the individual items have been superimposed, an operation that is not a function of a number of items that went into the vector or matrix. A photograph that is the composite of 25 researchers is just as easily processed as a photograph that is the composite of only 5 researchers. In each case, we see a single composite portrait; in the case of the Hockley and Lewandowsky (1991) conference honoring Bennet Murdock, the image was of the prototypical memory researcher, a spectacled and balding middle-aged man with just the hint of a moustache. Set-size effects occur at storage, where it takes longer to place more items into the composite store, but not at retrieval.

   We hypothesized that set-size-free composite-memory-based impression formation would occur when task and instructions made it possible for people to superimpose relevant item information into a single vector. According to our model, the composite storage vector represents the category that is to be evaluated, and the superposition of item vectors into the category-representation vector yields a prototypical impression or overall judgment as a "free" by-product of the storage operation (namely, superposition). We hypothesized that such composite memory storage would happen spontaneously, that is, without conscious attention or effortful strategy initiated by task instructions as long as people were aware that all item information describes the same category, and that people need not be prewarned about having to make the final overall category evaluation to store information in this way.

b.   *Design and Instructions.*   This microcomputer-administered experiment was advertised as a consumer-research study. Respondents ($N = 350$) were informed that their task was to help the designer of a TV game show to assess whether a recently developed show (the Green Show) was better in terms of its prizes than the previously cancelled Blue Show: "This study investigates how young people like yourself evaluate consumer goods that they might win as prizes in a TV game show." Respondents were divided into nine groups that differed factorially in the instructions they received about the evaluation of the list of prizes they were shown (three Tasks) and in the number of prizes to be won in the show and thus the number to be evaluated (three levels of Size that ranged from 4 to 20 prizes). Participants saw one prize at a time and were asked to evaluate either how safe it would be to take the prize home assuming that they had a toddler at home (Task 1) or how attractive the prize was to them (Tasks 2 and 3). Respondents in Task 3 (but not in Tasks 1 or 2) were also *forewarned* that they would be asked later to rate the overall attractiveness of the Green Show. To encourage them to integrate the information about the attractiveness of individual prizes into an overall attractiveness impression for the show (i.e., to do on-line processing), respondents in Task 3 were asked to indicate how much they liked the show so far after every two prizes. After evaluating all prizes, participants in all three Task groups were asked to evaluate the overall attractiveness of the Green Show. For respondents in Tasks 1 and 2, this request came as a surprise. The magnitude of people's evaluations (of individual prizes and of the show's overall attractiveness), as well as their RT for these judgments, were recorded. Respondents had an incentive to make the final overall attractiveness evaluation as fast as possible while still being confident of its consistency with their previous evaluations: A $50 prize was awarded to the person with the fastest response that was consistent with his or her individual item evaluations, for which "consistency" was deliberately left undefined.

c.   *Results.*   We predicted and obtained a Task–Size interaction for the RT required to make the final overall attractiveness judgment ($F(4, 340) = 5.89$, $p < .0001$). The mean RT (in 1/100 sec) of people's final judgments of the overall attractiveness of the Green Show are shown in Fig. 1. Because

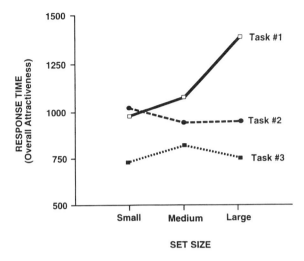

Fig. 1.   Mean response time for final judgment of overall attractiveness of game show as a function of the number of prizes evaluated (i.e., set size). Respondents in Task 3 were forewarned about the final overall attractiveness judgment. Respondents in Task 2 were not forewarned, but judged the attractiveness of the individual prizes. Respondents in Task 1 were also not forewarned, but judged the safety of the prizes.

respondents in Task 3 updated their overall game show impression *on-line,* as the prizes were seen and evaluated, no set-size effect was predicted for the final judgment RT in this group, and none was observed. Because respondents in Task 1 did not know that they would have to evaluate the show's overall attractiveness and did not even evaluate the attractiveness of individual prizes (but instead the prizes' "safety"), *memory-based processing* in the Hastie and Park (1986) sense was necessary to make the overall show attractiveness judgment: Subjects had to recall the different prizes, evaluate their attractiveness, and integrate those into an overall game show impression at the time that they were asked for that final judgment, resulting in the prediction of a strong set-size effect for their RT, which was clearly observed. Finally and most crucially, we hypothesized that respondents in Task 2 would spontaneously store their evaluations of the attractiveness of the different prizes to be won on the Green Show into a common memory storage vector. By categorizing all prizes as belonging to the same show (the Green Show) and by showing them on the computer screen in green color to facilitate such common-category encoding, we hypothesized that people would "set up" such a common-memory storage vector for their individual prize-attractiveness judgments without any instructions to do so. If so, then the surprise question about the game show's overall attractiveness should be answerable by a single operation that retrieved the value of the composite vector, that is, by *composite-memory recall,* with the result of no set-size effect in RT. In the absence of such composite storage, set-size effects in Task 2 should be similar to those of Task 1. Figure 1 clearly shows the absence of any set-size effect for Task 2, whose nonsignificant slope makes it more similar to Task 3 than to Task 1. The difference in intercept between Tasks 2 and 3 can be attributed to different memory retrieval operations: The prewarned respondents in Task 3 needed to recall only their last explicitly stated overall game show impression that they had generated on-line. For respondents in Task 2, on the other hand, the request for an overall impression of the game show's attractiveness came as a surprise. To give this judgment, they could recall all prizes and integrate their attractiveness at the time of the request, like the people in Task 1. However, the absence of any set-size effect argues against this mechanism. Instead, the results for Task 2 are consistent with the assumption that respondents in this group retrieved the composite-memory vector for the show's attractiveness that was created when the show's individual prizes were judged for attractiveness. This retrieval operation took longer than the simple recall of a previous overall judgment (an average of 9.7 sec for Task 2 rather than 7.7 sec for Task 3), probably because a composite-memory trace is noisier than a simple item trace and thus may take longer to disambiguate. This difference in retrieval time provides evidence against the alternative explanation that Task 2 respondents may have generated overall show attractiveness on-line, just as Task 3 respondents did, even though they were not prewarned to do so. The results of Experiment 1 demonstrate that information can become integrated under some circumstances relatively effortlessly. The assumption of a distributed memory structure that allows for composite storage is one way in which such effortless information integration can occur, as a by-product of the storage operation.

Complementing and supporting our demonstration of relatively effort-free information integration, courtesy of a distributed memory store in Experiment 1, is a recent study by Kashima and Kerekes (1994), who provide a model of impression formation that capitalizes on distributed representations of both item information and rating scale anchors. In contrast to the semantic network representations commonly assumed in person memory research (e.g., Hastie, 1988) in which a concept or proposition is localized in a single node or unit, person information in their model is represented by a pattern of activation over a set of units. Memory storage takes the form of a matrix into which associated item vectors are placed, with storage and retrieval operations similar to the models of J. A. Anderson

(1972) and Humphreys et al. (1989). The model further assumes that the anchors of the judgment scale on which the person impression is reported have a distributed representation that is compatible with the distributed representation of person information, such that new information is integrated by vector operations that compare it to the upper and lower anchors of the judgment scale. Kashima and Kerekes (1994) show that N. H. Anderson's weighted averaging model of impression formation (e.g., 1981), which has been shown to fit empirical data but has been criticized as a judgment strategy for being cognitively too effortful (e.g., Fiske & Neuberg, 1990), actually falls out as the natural consequence of their hypothesized encoding, storage, and retrieval processes. Their data suggest that it may be misleading to speak of the use of the weighted averaging rule as a conscious strategy, and that averaging behavior may not be cognitively effortful.

Bruce, Hockley, and Craik (1991) provide evidence consistent with composite-memory storage and recall under appropriate conditions in a different domain, namely, category frequency estimation. Although some studies have found a positive correlation between the recall of exemplars cued by the category name and frequency estimation (e.g., Tversky & Kahneman, 1973, whose availability theory is based on this positive correlation), other studies have failed to find one (e.g., Barsalou & Ross, 1986). Bruce et al. (1991) produced both the presence and the absence of a significant correlation between availability measured by cued recall and frequency estimation of category size under different conditions. When they encouraged exemplar encoding of the type previously described in Experiment 1 as enabling overall category impressions by composite-memory recall (e.g., by having people name the category name of exemplars during list presentation, possibly allowing them to "set up" a composite memory vector for each category into which exemplars can be placed), the correlation was not significant. After such encoding, judgments about the frequency of exemplars in each category presumably could be made on the basis of composite-memory strength of the category storage vector, rather than by inference from the recall of exemplars. When such encoding was not encouraged by experimental instructions, there was a positive correlation between the number of exemplars recalled per category and category frequency judgments.

3. Macrolevel Assumptions about Memory

We now turn our attention away from issues concerning the format of stored information (i.e., distributed vs. localized representation) to consider some distinctions related to the source and content of information in memory (i.e., semantic vs. episodic vs. procedural memory). In contrast to the preceding section, in this section, we do not find that memory considerations reveal alternatives to the concept of strategy so much as they present ways to broaden the notion of strategy, and embed it in a richer context with both theoretical and methodological implications.

   a.   Semantic versus Episodic Memory.   For more than 20 years, memory researchers have maintained a distinction between (1) episodic memory for information about specific experiences, outcomes, or events, and (2) semantic memory of abstract knowledge, for example, rules abstracted from a series of prior experiences or prototypes abstracted from a series of exemplars (Tulving, 1972). This distinction offers an interesting parallel to different philosophies of instruction. Both theory-based learning and learning by apprenticeship or case study can lead to the establishment of "rules." The first approach does so directly, whereas the second approach requires induction from episodic knowledge on the part of the learner.

   A great deal of controversy in social cognition and categorization research has centered on the twin issues of memory representation of categories (exemplar storage in episodic memory vs. prototype formation and storage in semantic memory) and memory processes (induction of prototypes from specific exemplars at storage vs. at retrieval) (Smith, 1990; see also Nisbett, 1993). Early models assumed that knowledge about categories was abstract, and was represented in semantic memory as prototypes (Posner & Keele, 1968) or as networks of associations or rules (Elstein & Bordage, 1979). Later models favored the representation of specific, concrete knowledge about category exemplars in episodic memory (Brooks, 1978; Medin & Schaffer, 1978). Barsalou (1990) argued that it may be difficult to differentiate between these different types of memory representations on the basis of behavioral data, because any difference in representation can usually be compensated for by appropriate retrieval processes. However, in some special cases differences may be detectable (Nosofsky, 1992). Recent evidence has favored hybrid models of memory representation that include memory for particular exemplars, that is, an episodic memory component, as well as generalized semantic knowledge. Evidence for such hybrid models has been found in medical diagnosis (Brooks, Norman, & Allen, 1991; Weber et al., 1993) and in people's judgments of the frequency of past events (Means & Loftus, 1991). Whittlesea, Brooks, and Westcott (1994) demonstrated that people acquire both types of knowledge during categorization learning, but that the subsequent utilization of general semantic knowledge versus particular episodic knowledge depends on subtle characteristics of the judgment task and information display.

   The implication of this controversy for decision researchers is that behavior that appears to involve the manipulation of abstract information may, in fact, reflect the (possibly unconscious) comparison of the current situation to concrete episodes encountered in the past. Decision researchers have tended to conceive of decision strategies as sets of abstract rules and procedures for evaluating the attributes of choice alternatives (e.g., elimination-by-aspects, additive rules, lexicographic rules, etc.). Undoubtedly, people often do implement abstract rules (Nisbett, 1993), and semantic knowledge clearly plays a role in "analytic" rule-based decisions, as well as in people's post hoc justifications of their decisions. However, decision researchers have tended to overlook the fact that episodic knowledge about prior decisions and their outcomes may also play a role, for example, in "intuitive" decisions that are made on the basis of similarity to previous experiences (see Goldstein & Weber, 1995). There has been more attention to these issues in the area of artificial intelligence, for example, the work on case-based reasoning (e.g., Kolodner, Simpson, & Sycara-Cyranski, 1985). These considerations suggest that decision researchers may have been unduly restrictive in conceiving of strategies as the application of semantic knowledge only.

As an illustration of the utility of distinguishing between the use of semantic and episodic knowledge in decision making, consider the issue of whether people utilize base rate information when making predictive judgments about the likelihood of future events. When base rate utilization is defined as the knowledge and application of Bayes' theorem to numerical base rate information (i.e., as an application of semantic knowledge), people without formal instruction in statistics fail at the task (Eddy, 1982; Wallsten, 1981). If, on the other hand, utilization of base rate information is operationalized as an episodic knowledge task, both undergraduates (Medin & Edelson, 1988) and physicians (Weber et al., 1993) can quite accurately incorporate the frequencies of different *experienced* events into their predictions and diagnoses. Episodic knowledge allows for the operation of similarity-based diagnostic strategies which reflect differences in the base rates of different diagnoses without any deliberate calculations or conscious awareness (see Weber et al., 1993). Semantic knowledge about differences in base rates, on the other hand, requires deliberate, conscious strategies (i.e., equivalents of Bayes' theorem) to utilize such knowledge.

b. Declarative versus Procedural Memory. J. R. Anderson (1976) contrasts procedural knowledge with the declarative knowledge of episodic and semantic memory in his taxonomy of functional memory systems, and neuropsychological evidence favors the existence of different memory systems. For example, some amnesics have been shown to have practically normal learning curves for new procedural skills (e.g., the Tower-of-Hanoi problem), without any episodic memory of ever having performed the task before (Cohen, 1984). As another example, patients with prosopagnosia show galvanic skin responses to familiar faces without the subjective experience of recognizing those faces (Young & De Haan, 1990).

As mentioned earlier, a number of metatheories have tried to explain how adaptive and goal-directed organisms select strategies to tailor their decisions (Hogarth & Einhorn, 1992; Payne, 1982; Payne et al., 1988, 1990, 1993; Smith et al., 1982), problem solutions (Friedrich, 1993), or hypotheses (Klayman & Ha, 1987) to the information, constraints, and task at hand. Implicit in these metatheories about strategy selection is the presupposition that people have a representation of different processing strategies that allows them to "compute" the relative pros and cons of each strategy for a particular task environment accurately on-line. Given the prominent role attributed to knowledge about procedures in strategy selection, there is a crucial need to better understand the representation, storage, and retrieval of procedures, as well as the knowledge people have *about* procedures.

J. R. Anderson (1987) likens the acquisition of (cognitive) skills (i.e., the establishment of procedural knowledge) to the "compilation" of general problem-solving methods that are applied to declarative knowledge about the content domain. The initially conscious, effortful, and verbalizable application of general rules to a specific problem produces a set of domain-specific production rules which, by repeated use, becomes "compiled" or automatized. Logan's (1988) instance theory of automatization similarly assumes that practice in consistent environments leads to the automatized retrieval of stored instances of previous exposures to the task, that is, a compilation of episodic memory retrieval into procedural memory. Compilation of skills into procedural knowledge explains why expert performance tends to be faster (Chase & Simon, 1973; Joseph & Patel, 1990), but at the cost of being less verbalizable and open to introspection (Adelson, 1984). Anderson's (1987) theory of the development of procedural memory through automatization thus has a variety of interesting and untested implications for the quality of novice versus expert metadecisions about strategy selection that may fruitfully be explored. Moreover, the fact that people may be able to perform certain tasks without being aware of all procedural steps also raises questions about the completeness of information obtained by methodologies like verbal protocols and the accuracy of self-assessment of cognitive effort in well-practiced judgment or decision situations. Finally, the fact that automatized procedures are less open to introspection implies that the selection of a procedure or strategy may often rely on metacognitive knowledge *about* the procedure, rather than information derived directly by introspection of the procedure itself. This suggests that metatheories about strategy selection should be elaborated with research on people's metastrategic knowledge about strategies, in addition to research on the performance characteristics of the strategies in operation.

B.   BEYOND FRAMING: AN EXPANDED SET OF ENCODING AND
     REPRESENTATION ISSUES

Having considered the implications of memory research for one branch of metatheory in decision research, that is, the adaptive selection of a decision strategy, we now turn to the other main branch of metatheory, the perceptual framework. As mentioned earlier, J/DM research within the perceptual framework has concentrated mostly on (1) the framing of outcomes as gains versus losses relative to a reference point (Kahneman & Tversky, 1979), (2) the aggregation versus segregation of events and options (Thaler, 1985), and (3) the restructuring of alternatives to reveal or create a dominance relation (Montgomery, 1983). In this section, we first consider the effect of prior events and experiences on encoding; second, the simplification of information as a coding operation; and third, the elaboration of presented information on the basis of prior knowledge.

1. Differences in Perception Resulting from Prior Experience

Encoding has been defined as follows: "between the external world and a human's memorial representation of that external world there operate certain processes that translate external information into internal information. These processes may in part be selective, or elaborative, or transformational; some may be optional while others are obligatory" (Melton & Martin, 1972, p. xii). Given the basic ambiguity of information, encoding processes have elements of selection and interpretation (e.g., Fiske & Taylor, 1991) which frequently involve a loss of information (e.g., Brainerd & Reyna, 1992). Much of psychology, from early psychophysics to current social cognition, concerns itself with the question of how physical stimuli map into subjective experience (e.g., how choice outcomes map into utility). Subjective experience is important because it forms the basis for judgments, actions, and choices. The same "objectively" described outcomes of choice alternatives, if experienced differently, may and perhaps should lead to different decisions (Frisch, 1993). Differences in the encoding of outcomes as the result of adopting different references points relative to which the outcomes are perceived and evaluated have been recognized as important in decision making research at least since Markowitz (1959) and in psychology more generally even earlier (Lewin, Dembo, Festinger, & Sears, 1944). Differences in the framing of an outcome that leads to its encoding as a relative gain or a relative loss, with the associated assumption that people's value functions for losses are of a different shape and slope than their value functions for gains, is an important component of prospect theory (Kahneman & Tversky, 1979) that allows it to describe choices that violate traditional expected utility theory. Thaler (1980) extended the domain of prospect theory's value function from risky prospects to riskless (consumer) choice.

Much of the J/DM literature on differences in subjective experience contains investigations on the effects of *concurrent* factors, such as the effect of the nature of the description of outcomes by the experimenter on the framing or encoding of outcomes (Slovic, Fischhoff, & Lichtenstein, 1982; Tversky & Kahneman, 1981). Equally important in predicting people's subjective experiences of an event, however, are *preceding* events; in particular, people's prior experiences with the same or similar judgments or decisions. Sunk cost effects (Staw, 1976) are a prominent example of the effects of prior experience. Past experience also plays a role in projecting one's future utility for outcomes (Elster & Loewenstein, 1992; Kahneman & Snell, 1992). When looking at the influence of prior experience on subjective encoding, it is important to consider not just the conscious but also the unconscious influence of prior events (Jacoby, Lindsay, & Toth, 1992; Jacoby et al., 1993), as a growing body of evidence in cognitive psychology suggests that unconscious memory of prior experiences can affect judgments and decisions. One example that has been of considerable interest in marketing is the mere exposure effect, that is, the phenomenon that familiarity (prior exposure) breeds liking (for a review, see Bornstein, 1989). Familiarity, especially when acquired in low-involvement processing tasks also increases the perceived truth value of (advertising) statements (Hawkins & Hoch, 1992). Yet another example is the false fame effect, that is, the fact that people misattribute familiarity resulting from prior exposure, of which they are unaware, to fame (for a review, see Jacoby et al., 1992).

Prior exposure of a more extended sort leads to the development of expertise in a domain, with attendant changes in the encoding of information. In fact, studies looking for the source of expert–novice performance differences have often found the main difference that distinguishes experts from novices is the way in which they encode domain-specific information. The pioneering work of DeGroot (1965) on expertise in chess suggested that differences in the structure of domain knowledge with resulting differences in information encoding (rather than differences in information processing strategies or depth of processing) lie at the root of the expert–novice distinction. As the result of practice and experience (Kleinmuntz, 1968), experts tend to encode and represent information more holistically, as integral parts of larger, meaningful units. Such differences in the representation of information have been demonstrated for expert versus novice players of chess (Chase & Simon, 1973), computer programmers (Adelson, 1984), and auditors (Libby & Frederick, 1990), and have been shown to permit faster, more automatic information processing. To model expert judgment and decision making, researchers may thus be well advised to give more thought to knowledge representation and memory processes. Fox (1980), for example, was able to simulate the (episodic) knowledge advantage of expert diagnosticians by supplementing an artificial intelligence expert system using nonprobabilistic inference processes with a memory mechanism reminiscent of Morton's (1970) logogen model of recognition, which provided concepts (e.g., diagnoses) that are activated more frequently with a higher level of standing activation.

2. Experiment 2: Selectivity and Simplification of Information

Although the simplification of stimulus information was explicitly included among the editing operations discussed by Kahneman and Tversky (1979), J/DM researchers have not devoted much attention to issues of information selection or simplification, with the notable exception of Reyna and Brainerd (1991; Brainerd & Reyna, 1992). We demonstrate the importance of these matters with an experiment in which we manipulated the order in which information was presented for a preferential choice task.

The effect of serial position has been well established for a broad range of memory tasks. That is, the impact of a given item of information depends crucially on *when* it is presented in a list of items. Serial position effects have been found to differ for memory and judgment tasks, with, for example, recency effects for the recall of adjectives but primacy effects for the adjectives' impact on likableness ratings (N. H. Anderson & Hubert, 1963). A variety of studies document such memory–judgment dissociations under different information and task conditions (e.g., Dreben, Fiske, & Hastie, 1979). Hogarth and Einhorn (1992) provide an extensive review and model of order effects in belief updating, with additional empirical support and model extension provided by Tubbs, Gaeth, Levin, and van Osdol (1993). Serial position effects have also been documented in the retrospective evaluation of ongoing experiences. Evaluations of aversive outcome streams (Kahneman, Fredrickson, Schreiber, & Redelmeier, 1993) as well as positive outcome streams (Hsee, Abelson, & Salovey, 1991) incorporate not only the value of outcomes at different points in time, but also changes in value, with strong preference for improvements in outcome at the end of the sequence.

Although serial position effects are well documented for judgment tasks, they have been little studied for choice tasks. It is not clear to us why the acquisition of information over time has been less of a concern for choice tasks. Outside of laboratory experiments, information received about choice

TABLE I

Instructions for Experiment 2

On each trial you will be asked to choose between two gambles, one called Gamble T and the other called Gamble B. The payoff produced by each gamble depends on the throw of a fair die. Here is an example. If you had to choose between the following two gambles (Gamble T vs. Gamble B), which would you choose? Tell the experimenter your choice.
If the number showing on the die equals 3, then
  you get +$8 by choosing Gamble T,
  you get −$7 by choosing Gamble B.
If the number showing on the die equals 5, then
  you get +$10 by choosing Gamble T,
  you get −$5 by choosing Gamble B.
If the number showing on the die equals 1, then
  you get +$3 by choosing Gamble T,
  you get −$2 by choosing Gamble B.
If the number showing on the die equals 2, then
  you get −$7 by choosing Gamble T,
  you get +$5 by choosing Gamble B.
If the number showing on the die equals 6, then
  you get −$9 by choosing Gamble T,
  you get +$10 by choosing Gamble B.
If the number showing on the die equals 4, then
  you get −$4 by choosing Gamble T,
  you get +$5 by choosing Gamble B.
The die is fair so that each of the integers (1, 2, 3, 4, 5, 6) are equally likely to be selected.
You can inspect the die if you wish. (Experimenter shows the die).
You will indicate your preference for gamble T or gamble B on a scale like the one below:

```
       Certain T          Indifferent          Certain B
       | --------------- | --------------- | --------------- | --------------- |
       100/0      75/25          50/50          25/75      0/100
```

This scale is used to instruct the computer how to make the choice for you. You will move a pointer to a position on this scale. If the pointer is placed on 100 at the right-hand side, then the computer will always choose Gamble B. If the pointer is placed on 75 at the right-hand side, then the computer will choose Gamble B on 75% of the trials and choose Gamble T on 25% of the trials. If the pointer is placed on 50, then the computer will choose Gamble B on 50% of the trials and choose Gamble T on 50% of the trials. If the pointer is placed on 75 at the left-hand side, then the computer will choose Gamble T on 75% of the trials and choose Gamble B on 25% of the trials. If the pointer is placed on 100 on the left-hand side, then the computer will always choose Gamble T. You can place the pointer anywhere you wish.
In the above example, the payoffs produced by each gamble for each die number were shown all at once on the computer screen. However, in this experiment, you will see the payoffs produced by each gamble for only one die number at a time. Here is an example. (Example is shown in which only the payoffs for one outcome of the die are shown on the screen at a time, for approximately 3 sec, followed by the payoffs for another outcome of the die, and so on)

(Continues)

TABLE I (*Continued*)

You begin the experiment with $6. (Experimenter hands over $6.) The entire experiment involves 16 choices. Each choice problem is like the example shown above. At the end of the experiment, the computer will randomly select one of these sixteen choice problems. Then you will throw the die and actually play out the gamble that you chose for the selected problem. The amount you win or lose will depend on your choice and on the die number. You take home whatever money you have left after playing out the gamble.

---

alternatives is rarely provided completely and simultaneously. Given the prevalence of choices in which people receive information about the outcomes of different choice alternatives over time (Lynch & Srull, 1982), it is surprising that not more is known about serial position effects for input into preferential choice. If the order in which information is received influences the way it is perceived or evaluated, there could be differences in choice as a function of the order in which information is received. In Experiment 2, conducted in collaboration with Jerome Busemeyer, we investigated people's preferences in a choice pair as a function of the order in which outcome information was received. The pattern of results strongly suggests that respondents were trying to reduce the difficulty of retaining information in memory by encoding it in a simplified manner.

Table I provides the task instructions, including a description of two choice alternatives, that is, monetary gambles whose payoffs depended on the role of a die. The potential payoffs of the two choice alternatives under each of the six possible states of the world (outcomes of the roll of the die) were displayed sequentially, one state of the world at a time, on a computer screen for approximately 3 sec, until all six potential payoffs had been shown. Die numbers defining the six different states of the world were randomly assigned to serial positions across subjects to ensure that the die number was not confounded with serial position. Each die number appeared with equal frequency at each serial position. Thus, serial position effects cannot be attributed to different subjective probabilities for particular numbers (e.g., "3" being a lucky number).

Thirteen students at Purdue University judged their relative preference for 16 choice pairs displayed in this fashion. As described in Table I, respondents earned $6 plus any win minus any loss they incurred when the preferred gamble of a randomly selected choice pair was played at the end of the session. There were 6 experimental pairs, randomly interspersed among 10 filler pairs. The six experimental pairs, shown in Table II, were identical in terms of outcomes, and all gambles had an expected value of $0. One gamble in each pair had four (smaller) negative outcomes and two (larger) positive outcomes, whereas the other gamble had two (larger)

TABLE II

CHOICE PAIRS USED IN EXPERIMENT 2

		Serial position of displayed outcomes					
Choice pair		1	2	3	4	5	6
1	T	+$2.50	+$2.50	−$5	−$5	+$2.50	+$2.50
	B	−$2.50	−$2.50	+$5	+$5	−$2.50	−$2.50
2	T	−$2.50	−$2.50	+$5	+$5	−$2.50	−$2.50
	B	+$2.50	+$2.50	−$5	−$5	+$2.50	+$2.50
3	T	+$5	+$5	−$2.50	−$2.50	−$2.50	−$2.50
	B	−$5	−$5	+$2.50	+$2.50	+$2.50	+$2.50
4	T	−$5	−$5	+$2.50	+$2.50	+$2.50	+$2.50
	B	+$5	+$5	−$2.50	−$2.50	−$2.50	−$2.50
5	T	−$2.50	−$2.50	−$2.50	−$2.50	+$5	+$5
	B	+$2.50	+$2.50	+$2.50	+$2.50	−$5	−$5
6	T	+$2.50	+$2.50	+$2.50	+$2.50	−$5	−$5
	B	−$2.50	−$2.50	−$2.50	−$2.50	+$5	+$5

negative outcomes and four (smaller) positive outcomes. The pairs differed from each other in the order in which participants received outcome information in a 2×3 factorial design that crossed the presentation of a gamble in the top (T) versus the bottom (B) row of the screen with the serial position in which the two extreme outcomes of the gambles were presented (at the beginning, middle, or end of the presentation sequence). Clearly, if the students saw the six gamble pairs as they are shown in Table II, that is, with all outcomes being displayed simultaneously, there is no reason why their preferences should be different in the six choice pairs. Thus, any differences in preference as a function of the serial presentation of outcomes must be a result of outcome integration processes that are not commutative. A plausible explanation of differential preference includes memory limitations and resulting differences in the encoding and/or retrieval of information as a function of the serial order of outcomes.

Overall, respondents preferred gamble G1 = (+2.5, +2.5, −5, −5, +2.5, +2.5) with its four smaller positive and two larger negative outcomes over its mirror image, gamble G2 = (−2.5, −2.5, +5, +5, −2.5, −2.5) which was of equal expected value: the overall choice proportion for G1 over all six order conditions was .61. Thus the *number* of positive and negative outcomes seemed to play a larger role than the magnitude of outcomes, consistent with the notion that, under naturalistic conditions of memory load, people seem to encode mostly the "gist" of outcomes (Brainerd & Reyna, 1992; Reyna & Brainerd, 1991). Furthermore, people's relative preferences for the two gambles showed strong serial position as well as spatial order (top/bottom) effects, with a significant interaction between the two factors ($F(2, 24) = 15.46$; MSE = 2.40; $p<.00001$). As shown in Fig. 2, the median strength of preference across the 13 respondents for gamble G1 was clearly different across the six different information order conditions. G1 was more preferred when its outcomes were displayed first in the top portion of the display (choice proportion for G1 was .63 across those three order conditions) than when they were listed second in the bottom portion of the display (choice proportion was only .58), suggesting that the features that made G1 more attractive to people were more salient when displayed in the top of the display. More interestingly, there were strong serial position effects for the order in which the different outcomes for the two gambles were received, the nature of which depended on whether gamble G1 or G2 was listed first. The four small advantages of G1 over G2 had greatest impact when they occurred as a "run" (i.e., as the first four or the last four outcomes), and were less effective when the series was interrupted by large advantages of G2 over G1, again suggesting that people were encoding the gist of the stimuli. There was mild evidence for such a run effect when the majority of outcomes in the top display row were positive; that is, the preference for G1 = (+2.5, +2.5, −5, −5, +2.5, +2.5) when it was listed as the top gamble was somewhat greater when the four positive outcomes occurred as the first four outcomes (pair 6: choice proportion for G1 was .65) or the last four outcomes (pair 4; choice proportion for G1 was .65)

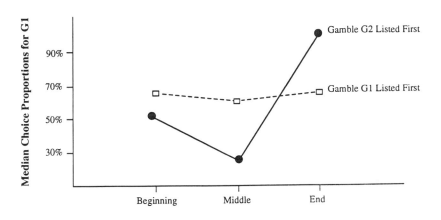

Fig. 2.   Median choice proportions for gamble G1 = (+$2.50, +$2.50, −$5, −$5, +$2.50, +$2.50) over gamble G2 = (−$2.50, −$2.50, +$5, +$5, −$2.50, −$2.50) as a function of which gamble was listed first (i.e., in the top portion of the display screen) and as a function of the position of the two larger outcomes (+/−$5, +/−$5) in the series of outcome presentations.

than when the run was broken up by the two intervening negative outcomes (pair 1: choice proportion was .60). This run effect was greatly magnified when the majority of outcomes in the top display row were negative, accounting for the significant interaction between top and bottom position and serial order of outcomes. Preference for G2 = (−2.5, −2.5, +5, +5, −2.5, −2.5) when it was listed in the top display row was lower when the four negative outcomes were presented as the first four outcomes (pair 5: choice proportion for G2 was .00) or as the last four outcomes (pair 3: choice proportion for G2 was .50) than when they were interrupted by the two positive outcomes (pair 2: choice proportion was .75). This run effect suggests that under conditions that put a strain on limited working memory, such as sequential information presentation, massed presentation of positive and, in particular, negative information will have maximum impact.

In summary, Experiment 2 establishes that serial position effects exist not just in judgment tasks but also in preferential choice. The results show that the order in which information is received in a sequential presentation choice task can have a strong effect on people's preferences for different choice alternatives, leading in our case to preference reversals between pairs that differed only in the sequence in which the same outcome information was provided. These preference reversals did not necessitate any change of strategy explanation, but instead seemed to implicate simplifying encoding processes as the source of the effect.

3. Information Elaboration and the Content of Memory

Asking people for reasons for decisions and/or to elaborate on provided information provides evidence about the way information is encoded and incorporated into existing knowledge structures. Looking at differences in argumentation or reasons for choice provides converging evidence that differences in the encoding or representation of the same set of information can be responsible for differences in preference or choice. Hogarth and Kunreuther (1995) studied the reasoning processes and arguments involved in a consumer decision, holding information about probabilities and outcomes constant. They found that people who provided different arguments in a decision used different decision strategies and arrived at different answers. The role of reasons for judgments and decisions has also been studied by Curley, Browne, Smith, and Benson (1993) and Shafir and Tversky (1993).

Getting more directly at the role of information representation in determining both choice and reasons for choice, Levin and collaborators used an information elaboration task in two domains: in decisions about public health intervention programs that differed in the number of leukemia versus

AIDS patients saved (Levin & Chapman, 1993) and in decisions about cars that differed in the number of foreign versus domestic workers involved in their production (Levin, Jasper, Mittelstaedt, & Gaeth, 1993). Elaboration in the public health program domain involved the generation of reasons for contracting either leukemia or AIDS. The fewer "personal responsibility" reasons people generated for contracting AIDS, the more favorably they rated those programs that (*ceteris paribus*) saved a larger proportion of AIDS than leukemia patients. Similarly in the car domain, elaborations about the respective qualities of foreign versus domestic workers and other expressions of nationalism predicted people's preferences for cars better than their expressed perceptions of car quality. In other words, in both domains, people's preferences could be predicted from the way they elaborated on the respective decision outcomes when asked to do so at a different point in time.

Information elaboration thus has the potential to provide yet another piece of converging evidence about the nature of information representation and its role in predicting differences in judgment and choice. Given the recent interest in reason-based choice, further investigation is needed into the relationships between information representation and decision arguments, and between decision arguments and choice. It would be interesting, for example, to understand why different respondents in Hogarth and Kunreuther (1995) provided different arguments for their decisions and used different processing strategies even though everybody received the same information about the choice alternatives. An information elaboration task would be useful to determine whether differences in choice arguments are associated with differences in prior knowledge or in value structures, and thus in encoding and evaluation of new information. (For further discussion of the effect of prior knowledge on decision processes, see Goldstein & Weber, 1995).

C. SUMMARY

In this section, we have tried to demonstrate the utility and even necessity of incorporating a more explicit consideration of memory structure and processes into models of judgment and choice. We argued that a new class of models about memory structure and processing should be considered by J/DM researchers. Experiment 1 demonstrated that the assumptions of distributed representation and parallel processing have the potential to change some basic conceptions about the relative effort of different processing strategies. We also argued that encoding differences, in addition to conventional framing effects, operate in J/DM tasks. Experiment 2 demonstrated that different serial presentation of the same informational input changed choices, most likely as the result of simplified encoding of outcomes resulting from memory limitations. Also, we argued that information elaboration tasks can help to reveal the organization of knowledge which is brought to bear on presented information. In summary, in this section we have made an argument for the integration of *memory concepts* into J/DM models. Section III tries to convince J/DM researchers that *memory techniques* are well suited (and probably underutilized) in testing J/DM models and their implicit encoding assumptions.

III. Use of Memory Techniques in J/DM

One postulate of behaviorism in psychology and logical positivism in economics and other social sciences has been that researchers should restrict themselves to studying observable phenomena. Differences in the way in which people encode information might seem as unobservable (and thus as metaphysical) to a behaviorist as claims about subatomic particles would be to an eighteenth century physicist. However, even though electrons, positrons, and neutrinos are not visible to the naked eye or even under a microscope, they can nevertheless be studied by means of the traces they leave: Nuclear physicists base much of their theories on photos of the trails left by particles as they traverse cloud chambers.

The trail that elementary particles leave in a cloud chamber can be taken as a metaphor for the trace that the cognitive processing of information leaves in memory. The basic notion underlying all memory techniques described in this section is that the encoding and utilization of information leaves a memorial residue. The nature of the trace or residue thus become evidence that information has been encoded or used in a particular way. For example, a basic question one can ask is whether information was encoded or utilized at all in a situation. As McClelland, Stewart, Judd, and Bourne (1987) point out, "if an attribute for an alternative is not processed, then it obviously cannot be remembered" (p. 238).

Memory as a research tool has a history in social cognition and consumer research, both areas of J/DM research that have been more aware than other areas of the prevalence of memory-based judgment and choice and of the importance of encoding processes. Much of the research in social cognition revolves around the question of how prior beliefs influence the way in which people interpret and thus encode information. As a result, studies frequently employ techniques such as clustering in free recall and priming manipulations. The memory tasks reviewed in this section include recognition and free recall.

We first describe a study that draws inferences about the initial encoding of information using the *speed* with which forced choice recognition judgments are made. The basic notion underlying this technique is that if information is encoded or recoded in a particular way at the time of initial processing, then people should be faster to make old–new discrimination judgments when information is presented in this previously encoded form than when it is presented in a different form.

A. EXPERIMENT 3: USE OF FORCED CHOICE RECOGNITION RT

Explanations based on encoding differences, for example, the evaluation of outcomes relative to different reference points as in Kahneman and Tversky's (1979) prospect theory, have successfully accounted for differences in judgments and choices made in different contexts or decision frames (Kahneman & Tversky, 1982). These differences are often well described by the shape of prospect theory's value function, both for risky decisions, the domain for which prospect theory was conceived, and for riskless decisions, the domain to which it was exported (e.g., Thaler, 1980, 1985). For decisions about gains, prospect theory's value function makes the same predictions as other theories, that is, expected utility with its predominant assumption of concave utility and Coombs and Avrunin's (1977) postulate that "good things satiate." Evidence has generally supported this common assumption. For decisions about losses, on the other hand, theories differ in their predictions. Prospect theory's value function is convex, making people risk-seeking for losses. Coombs and Avrunin (1977), however, assume a concave loss function and risk avoidance with their assertion that "bad things escalate." Here, the empirical evidence has been more equivocal. Schneider (1992) found people to be as frequently risk-averse as risk-seeking in the domain of losses. Linville and Fischer (1991) examined the predictions that an extension of prospect theory's value function would make about the aggregation versus segregation of (riskless) positive and negative events. They found that predictions held in the domain of gains (i.e., people preferred to segregate positive events), but failed to find the aggregation of losses that would follow from a convex value function in the domain of losses. Thaler and Johnson (1990) found that simple prospect theory predictions failed to describe people's risky choices after prior wins or losses and suggested additional assumptions about how people encode information in successive gambles.

If the encoding of information relative to some reference point has some psychophysical reality rather than just being a predictive as-if model (Arkes, 1991), then encoding differences should have consequences in addition to differences in the final judgment or choice. If the values of outcomes are encoded according to prospect theory's value function, which is steeper in the loss domain than in the gain domain, people should be able to discriminate differences between outcomes better in the loss domain than in the gain domain. The same objective difference in outcomes becomes a larger subjective difference when the outcomes are losses than when the outcomes are gains. With better discrimination, people should be more consistent when choosing between negatively framed prospects than between positively framed prospects, and they should also be faster. Consistency and speed of choices are, of course, affected by a variety of variables other than the psychophysical discriminability of the choice alternatives. Schneider (1992) found people to be less consistent in their choices across repeated trials when decision alternatives were negatively framed rather than positively framed, and attributed this result to the fact that emotional/motivational reasons for inconsistency (e.g., conflicting objectives) may overshadow and obscure the effects of psychophysical discriminability.

In the absence of such emotional/motivational reasons for inconsistency, however, consistency and RT measures may provide evidence not only about the difference in slope between the loss and gain functions, but also about the shape of the psychophysical discrimination function in the loss and gain domains. A concave, as opposed to convex, value function makes different predictions about the relative discriminability between members of different choice pairs, and thus about the relative consistency and speed of different choices. Experiment 3 was designed to test such psychophysical implications that follow from different assumptions about the shapes of people's value functions in the loss and gain domains. These results are described in Weber, Barlas, Wertenbrock, and Goldstein (1994). In summary, we found that RT and choice data were consistent with a value function that was steeper for losses than for gains. Evidence supported a concave value function in the gain domain, and, consistent with Coombsian predictions rather than with prospect theory predictions, also a concave value function for losses. In this chapter we describe another, related, objective of the study, namely to provide evidence for a specific information encoding, in particular for differences in encoding as the result of framing manipulations, by making use of the memorial residue of the initial encoding during a later task. We used RT measures for this purpose, in particular the time to respond to forced recognition memory questions.

As pointed out by Shanteau (1991), the use of RT as a dependent measure in decision research has been very limited, despite the fact that Donders (1868) used RT initially to analyze choice mechanisms. One notable exception is the work by Busemeyer, Forsyth, and Nozawa (1988) who showed that the use of RT allowed them to distinguish between Restle's (1961) suppression-of-aspects model and Tversky's (1972) elimination-by-aspects model, even though the two models make identical predictions about binary choice probability. Later in this chapter, we argue that RT measures should play a more important role in J/DM research, as they can help differentiate between different hypothesized processes that may lead to the same final decision or judgment.

1. Design and Instructions

In this microcomputer-administered experiment, respondents ($N = 384$) were asked to take the role of a salesperson in a large company and were told that management intended to change the current compensation system of its sales force. People in different groups received different expectations about the likely change in their salary and were asked to choose between pairs of compensation packages that differed in the amount of change in annual salary and in the number of vacation days. Precise scenario and task instructions that were designed to encourage people to use particular reference points when encoding the different salary offers are shown in Table III.

In a 2×2 between-subject design, we crossed whether the possible changes in compensation constituted an *actual* increase versus decrease in absolute salary level (real gain vs. real loss) with whether the changes constituted an increase versus a decrease in salary relative to respondents' *expectations*. Initial salary levels and possible choice alternatives were such that choices were comparable in the four different groups, in the sense that, for some choice pairs, the combination of starting salary and possible changes resulted in the same absolute levels of salary. Respondents in the real gain groups were told that their current salary was $40,000. One half of them were led to expect a $1,000 raise (for an absolute salary of $41,000), and the other half expected a $10,000 raise (for an absolute salary of $50,000). Both real gain groups saw choice pairs that involved actual increases in salary that ranged from $2,000 to $8,500. For the gain group that had been led to expect a $1,000 increase, all of these choice alternatives involved not only absolute gains but also gains relative to their expectation. For the gain group that had been led to expect a $10,000 increase, however, these choice alternatives were absolute gains but also relative losses if evaluated relative to their expectation. Respondents in the real loss groups were told that their current salary was $51,000. One half of them were led to expect a $1,000 reduction (for an absolute salary of $50,000), and the other half expected a $10,000 reduction (for an absolute salary of $41,000). Both real loss groups saw choice pairs that involved actual reductions in salary that ranged from $2,000 to $8,500. These choice pairs constituted both absolute and relative losses to the loss group that had been led to expect a $1,000 reduction in salary. For the loss group that had been led to expect a $10,000 reduction in salary, however, these choice alternatives

TABLE III

Scenario Description and Instructions for Choice Task in Experiment 3

This part of the experiment asks you to evaluate and choose between different compensation packages that are offered to you by the company that you work for as a traveling salesman or saleswoman. Take a minute to imagine the following scenario and answer all questions as you would if you actually held that job under the conditions described below:

You have worked for the Acme Widget company as a salesperson for the last 3 years. Your territory includes all of the Midwest and Southwest of the United States. You visit major industrial manufacturing companies to sell a variety of widgets produced by Acme. This means that your job takes you away from home 3 to 4 days out of each week, usually overnight. You generally like your job because it is challenging and has a lot of potential for growth and promotions, but being away from home so much sometimes gets to be a bit stressful. Up until now you received a fixed salary of $40,000 which you considered fair even though it was just about average by industry standards. You also get 10 working days of paid vacation a year.

In a leveraged buyout, your company has recently been taken over by a much larger widget manufacturing concern. The new management wants to increase the market share of Acme, and has decided that it needs to motivate its sales force more with a new incentive system that is more performance based. You were initially quite concerned about the takeover and the new compensation system. You know that you cannot increase your volume of sales very much, even if you tried harder. What will the new system do to your income in an average year if you maintained your current volume of sales? Will your salary go up or down?

You went to talk to your supervisor about it last week. He wasn't quite sure himself about the details of the new incentive system. However, he assured you that management intended to RAISE average salaries to keep its salesforce content and motivated. He told you that even though the new incentive system would make part of the salary dependent on your volume of sales, he could virtually guarantee you that—with your current volume of sales—the net effect of the changes would be an INCREASE in your annual income of about $10,000.

Today, management revealed their new compensation plans. Somewhat unexpectedly, they decided to combine FINANCIAL INCENTIVES that are tied to your volume of sales with ADDITIONAL VACATION TIME also tied to your volume of sales.

Because management is uncertain about the preferences of their sales force for additional money versus additional vacation days, they are passing out a questionnaire that asks you for your preferences between packages that differ in the relative amounts of money versus vacation days. Based on your answers and those of your colleagues, they will make a final decision on the composition of the new incentive system in a couple of weeks.

To help you make your decision, they customized the effect that each package would have on your annual income, given your current volume of sales. That is, they calculated how your income this past year would have been different under each of the new packages available to you now.

When you get the questionnaire containing the different compensation package options, you notice that all of the options actually increase your salary CONSIDERABLY LESS than the $10,000 that your supervisor had "virtually guaranteed" you last week. You had already

(Continues)

TABLE III *(Continued)*

made some plans about how to use the additional $10,000—just about the price of that new sailboat you have had your eyes on for a while. Needless to say, you are quite upset about getting less than expected.

Now please help management in their incentive system allocation by indicating for each pair of incentive packages shown to you which one you would prefer. Remember that your current annual salary is $40,000, with a total of 10 working days of paid vacation. Take your time and consider each pair of options carefully.

Instead of the promised $10,000 raise,

Package 1 will give you	Package 2 will give you
only a $5,000 raise	only a $6,000 raise
and	and
a total of 14 vacation days	a total of 10 vacation days

Would you prefer to get Package 1 or Package 2?

---

were absolute losses but also relative gains if evaluated relative to prior expectation. The computer recorded people's choices and measured their response latencies.

After having made their 18 pairwise choices between the different compensation packages, participants were given a surprise recognition-memory test. Presented with the description of two annual salaries, they had to decide as quickly as possible which of the two salaries they had previously seen during the pairwise choice task. For four recognition pairs, the "old" and "new" salaries were described in exactly the same way as they were described during the choice task (e.g., a $4,000 raise). For another four pairs, both salaries were expressed in terms of absolute salary (e.g., a raise that changed your annual salary to $44,000). For yet another set of four pairs, both salaries were expressed as deviations from people's prior expectations (e.g., a raise that was $6,000 less than a $10,000 raise). The 12 forced-choice recognition pairs were presented in random order. Respondents were encouraged to identify the previously seen salary level in each pair as quickly as possible while still being sure of their answer. Precise task instructions and an example of each of the three different formats in which the salary pairs were described are shown in Table IV. Again, people's responses as well as response latencies were recorded.

2. Results for Recognition Task

Figure 3 shows mean RT (top panel) and accuracy (bottom panel) for the forced-choice recognition judgments as a function of the initial framing condition (real gain groups vs. real loss groups, a between-subject variable)

TABLE IV

INSTRUCTIONS AND STIMULI FOR RECOGNITION-MEMORY TASK IN EXPERIMENT 3

We are interested in the impression that different compensation packages have made on you. To that end, we will ask you a variety of different questions that test your memory of these packages.

As in all other parts of this experiment, the computer times your responses. For this part in particular, it is important that you answer as quickly as possible while still being sure of your answer.

Each question will describe two packages, one that actually appeared on the questionnaire with all the different compensation packages you just saw and another one that did not. It is your task to indicate which of the two packages is the one that appeared on the questionnaire.

The packages will be described only in terms of the money component (i.e., annual income), leaving out the vacation days component. As you will see, the money component of the two packages will be described in different ways. Some of these ways may strike you as odd. You may have to do some simple calculations in addition to recalling what the packages were that you saw before. However, try to do your best to pick out the correct alternative as quickly as you can. Remember that your previous annual salary was $40,000 and that you expected to get a $10,000 raise. Now tell us which of the packages described below was actually offered to you as choice alternatives on the questionnaire.

Which of the following two packages appeared above as an option on the questionnaire?

"As-Shown" Item Format
(1) A package that gave you a $5,000 raise in your annual salary?
(2) A package that gave you a $2,000 raise in your annual salary?

"Absolute Salary" Item Format
(1) A package that changed your annual salary to $44,000?
(2) A package that changed your annual salary to $48,000?

"Deviation from Expectation" Item Format
(1) A package that gave you a raise that was $3,000 less than a $10,000 raise?
(2) A package that gave you a raise that was $1,000 less than a $10,000 raise?

---

and presentation format of the items to be discriminated (as shown, absolute salary, deviation from expectation; a within-subject variable). The results for the two gain and the two loss groups are not shown separately for the two prior-expectation levels (i.e., for relative gain vs. relative loss), as there was no (main nor interaction) effect of expectation level either on discrimination RT or accuracy.

The overall interaction between framing condition and item format was significant for accuracy ($z = 2.97$, $p < .005$) and marginally significant for RT ($F(2, 220) = 2.64$, $p < .07$). The as shown condition served as a baseline for the speed and accuracy with which people could make old–new discriminations between salaries that were shown to them in exactly the same format in which they had appeared before (i.e., on the basis of visual recognition). As shown in Fig. 3, people made their recognition judgments

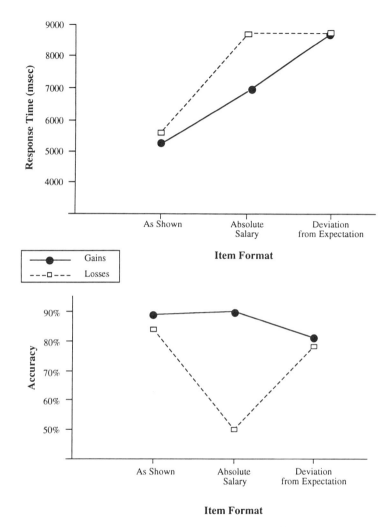

Fig. 3. Response time (top panel) and accuracy (bottom panel) for forced-choice recognition judgments for salary losses and salary gains as a function of the format in which items were presented (as shown during the previous judgment task vs. recoded in terms of absolute annual salary vs. recoded as deviation from prior expectation about salary change).

(including reading time) in the "as shown" condition in less than 6 sec (top panel), with an accuracy of close to 90% (bottom panel). Although judgments were somewhat slower and less accurate in the Real Loss than in the Real Gain groups, these differences were not significant.

Figure 3 also shows RT and accuracy of the discrimination judgments when item pairs were recoded to absolute salaries and to deviations from expectations. We assumed that people who recoded salaries during the choice task into absolute salary levels (i.e., recoded a $4,000 raise on a $40,000 salary as a new absolute salary of $44,000) would be faster and/or more accurate in detecting the "old" (i.e., previously seen) salary level during the discrimination task than people who did not do such recoding. In other words, we assumed that there would be some "saving" from the original recoding during the choice task. If people spontaneously recoded salary changes into absolute salaries during the choice task, this recoding should have left a memorial residue, and they should be able to do the old–new discrimination task by "recognition" based on their memory of the recoded information. On the other hand, people who did not spontaneously recode salary changes into absolute salaries during the choice task would have to do some recoding during the discrimination task, namely recoding absolute salary levels into changes in salary, in order to make the discrimination. Such recoding would presumably make their RT longer and/or their discrimination accuracy lower. The results in Fig. 3 show that respondents in the gain groups were both faster and more accurate in detecting the "old" item than respondents in the loss groups when salaries were presented in terms of absolute levels. Thus differences in RT between the two groups were *not* the result of any speed–accuracy trade-off. For respondents in the gain groups, accuracy was just as high for absolute salary discriminations as for as shown discriminations, and RT increased by less than 2 sec. For respondents in the loss groups, on the other hand, accuracy for absolute salary discriminations dropped to 50% (from a 90% baseline level), whereas RT increased by almost 4 sec.[1]

These results suggest that people in the gain groups were much more likely to recode salary changes into absolute salary levels during the initial choice task than people in the loss groups.[2] Calculating one's absolute salary

[1] These differences in difference between the as shown and absolute salary conditions were statistically significant for both RT and accuracy.

[2] An alternative explanation could be tested if we had included some additional control groups. One might argue that people in both the gain and loss groups recoded salary changes into absolute salary levels at the time of the recognition test and not during the initial choice task, and that the superior speed and accuracy observed for the gain groups resulted from the operation of addition (for the gain groups) being easier than the operation of subtraction (for the loss groups). Benchmarks to test this hypothesis could be obtained by including groups whose initial task, instead of preferential choice, had *required* them to perform recodings of the sort in question (e.g., addition and subtraction tasks). It would support our interpretation if respondents in our gain groups were as fast and accurate as people who had earlier performed the additions, and respondents in our loss groups were slower and less accurate than people who had earlier performed the subtractions. Additional benchmarks could be obtained by including groups whose initial tasks *prevented* them from performing the recodings in question. Although we don't have the data to draw definitive conclusions in this case, our main point is that the speed and accuracy of a surprise recognition test, compared with appropriate benchmarks, can be used to gather evidence concerning covert codings and recodings of information.

level for the different choice alternatives is, presumably, an emotionally much more rewarding task when all salary levels are larger than the status quo (in the gain groups) than when the absolute salary levels of all options are lower than one's current level (in the loss groups). The assumption that people try to maximize their hedonic experience of outcomes would predict the observed result of absolute salary recoding for the gain groups but not for the loss groups. Although this interpretation is post hoc, it is at least consistent with the hypothesis that the recoding of changes in outcomes into absolute outcome levels is under strategic control.

The same argument about savings of initial spontaneous recoding of information during the choice task can be made for the deviation from expectation condition of the discrimination task. We had hypothesized that, to maximize their hedonic experience of the choice alternatives, respondents in the loss group that expected a large $10,000 reduction in salary would recode subsequent smaller losses seen during the choice task as gains relative to their initial expectations. Respondents in the other loss group, who were led to expect a small $1,000 reduction in salary, however, should not recode subsequent larger losses seen during the choice task as losses relative to their initial expectations, as such recoding would lead to a double loss experience (i.e., an absolute as well as a relative loss). Similarly, we hypothesized that respondents in the gain group that were led to expect a large $10,000 salary increase would be unlikely to recode subsequent smaller gains as relative losses, but that respondents in the gain group with the small $1,000 salary increase expectation would be more likely to recode subsequent larger increases as relative gains. In summary, we predicted that recoding of outcomes as deviation from an expectation would occur when the recoding made the experience of the outcomes more positive, but not when it would make the experience more negative. As mentioned earlier, we did not find any significant main or interaction effects for the two prior expectation levels. Mean accuracy for the deviations-from-expectation condition was lower for the loss group, for whom recoding as deviation from expectation would have resulted in a relative loss, than for the other three groups, but this difference was not significant, especially when speed–accuracy trade-offs are taken into consideration. As shown in Fig. 3, the two gain and the two loss groups had very similar (long) RT and (lower) accuracy rates for the deviations-from-expectation condition. This absence of any significant difference in performance was contrary to our predictions, suggesting that our manipulation to get people to frame outcomes relative to their prior expectations failed. Although one could generate a range of post hoc explanations for this failure, the point that is important for the purposes of this chapter is not the absence of a framing effect, but our ability to diagnose this absence by means of people's performances on our surprise recognition memory test.

3. Discussion

The technique illustrated in Experiment 3, namely the speed of forced-choice recognition, is a useful tool if one wants to distinguish between decision or judgment models that predict the same final outcome but postulate different encoding and combination processes that lead up to that decision. There is an indeterminacy between models that postulate differences at the information encoding stage vs. differences at the information integration stage as being responsible for differences in final judgments or choices. Hogarth and Einhorn (1992), for example, show that certain characteristics of the way in which people update their beliefs that are usually attributed to different integration functions (i.e., additive vs. averaging functions) can be explained equally well by assuming different encoding strategies (encoding relative to a constant standard vs. encoding relative to a variable standard). The memory techniques discussed in this section are designed to provide "cloud-chamber evidence" for differences in encoding, and thus will help to discriminate between alternative explanations that cannot be discriminated by choice data alone. Similar indeterminacies exist among risky choice theories, for example, between change-of-process (i.e., integration rule) explanations of preference reversals (Mellers, Ordóñez, & Birnbaum, 1992), change-of-outcome-encoding explanations (Luce, Mellers, & Chang, 1993), and change-of-reporting explanations (Goldstein & Einhorn, 1987).

B. RECOGNITION TASKS TO INFER INFORMATION REPRESENTATION

In Experiment 3, the *speed* with which people were able to give recognition judgments served as evidence about the previous encoding and representation of information. Pennington and Hastie (1988) also used a surprise recognition-memory task to draw inferences about the representations that underlie people's judgments and choices. However, instead of looking at the *speed* with which people were able to give recognition judgments, they used the *pattern of false recognitions* to draw inferences about encoding and representation. Pennington and Hastie's goal was to provide evidence for their hypothesis that people spontaneously construct causal stories when hearing legal evidence. As discussed more extensively in Goldstein and Weber (1995), representation of information by fitting it into a "story" or some other schema has the property that information that has not been presented but that is a part of the story or schema may be inferred spontaneously by people, leading to "false" recognitions. Similar to hindsight, when people are unable to distinguish between elements of their knowledge structures that predate the revelation of the actual outcome and those that postdate it, Pennington and Hastie (1988) found that people were unable to distinguish between pieces of evidence that had actually been presented in testimony and pieces of evidence they had inferred as consistent with the case story. The recent legal controversy about whether memories of childhood sexual abuse that emerge late in life are false versus previously repressed revolves around the possibility that apparent recollections may not be recollections but constructions. Unfortunately, in real life the truth–value of recollections or recognitions is often undeterminable.

C. RECALL TASKS TO INFER STRATEGY USE

Higgins and Bargh (1987) draw a theoretical distinction between the availability and accessibility of information. *Availability* refers to whether information is stored in memory; *accessibility* refers to the ease with which stored information can be retrieved. In order to use memory information in judgments or decisions, it must not only be available, but also be accessible. Higgins and Bargh (1987) argue that recognition tests are sensitive indicators of what is stored in memory, that is, of availability, whereas free recall tests are better indicators of what can easily be retrieved, that is, of accessibility. If one is interested in showing the *existence* of some information in memory (e.g., the existence of a particular encoding), the use of recognition measures is appropriate. If, on the other hand, one is interested in demonstrating the *use* of some information from memory in a decision or judgment, recall measures may be more appropriate because recently used information is more accessible.

Hastie and Park (1986) based their distinction between on-line and memory-based processing in impression formation on evidence from a free recall task. In particular, they looked at the correlation between the favorability of information about a target that people recalled from memory and the favorability of their impression about the target. The absence of any significant correlation was shown to be characteristic of on-line processing, and the presence of a positive correlation was shown to be characteristic of memory-based processing. McGraw, Lodge, and Stroh (1990) argued that these two conclusions have different inferential strength; whereas the absence of a correlation between memory and judgment measures strongly suggests on-line processing, the presence of a positive correlation may not necessarily be the result of memory-based processing. In an experiment in which people were forewarned about a judgment task (promoting on-line impression formation), but not about a subsequent memory task, McGraw et al. found that the *type* of recall task influenced the magnitude of the correlation observed. In particular, cued recall of evidence (e.g., "recall as many of the pieces of evidence that you *liked*," followed by "recall as many of the pieces of evidence that you *disliked*") led to a stronger recall–impression relationship than standard free recall instructions (e.g., "recall as many of the pieces of evidence as you can"). As there was no difference in processing goals for the two conditions (memory task instructions were issued *after* the initial impression formation task), there was no reason why the evidence should have been encoded differently, an assumption that was confirmed by the absence of any difference in a subsequent recognition memory test. Thus, McGraw et al. argued that the positive memory-judgment correlation observed for the cued-recall group was an artifact of the cued-recall procedure (with favorability of the evidence acting as a retrieval cue), rather than evidence of memory-based processing. Their results suggest that researchers should stick to free recall tasks when assessing the accessibility of information.

McClelland et al. (1987) gave people a surprise memory task after a multiattribute choice task. Respondents had to choose either one or three cars from a set of 15 alternatives, with each alternative being described on three major and eight minor attributes. McClelland et al. used people's performances on a memory task described as cued recall, but perhaps closer to recognition (i.e., people had to decide whether each of the eight minor features had been present or absent in each car of the choice set), to infer what strategy they had used to make their multiattribute choices. In particular, McClelland et al. hypothesized that people used a lexicographic strategy that would allow them to winnow the full set of alternatives to a smaller set, using major attributes first and considering minor attributes only when necessary. This hypothesis predicted that minor attributes would be used more often when decisions were more difficult and consequently should be remembered better under those conditions. As predicted, memory for the minor car features was better in both conditions that made choice more difficult (in the choose-one vs. choose-three condition, and in a condition that had a dense set of good alternatives). Johnson and Russo (1984) used a free recall task to infer strategy use in judgments and choice. Free recall performance provided evidence for an elimination-based (i.e., noncompensatory) processing strategy used by people when making choices between automobiles that were described on multiple attributes but for more compensatory processing when making judgments of the desirability of individual cars. In particular, a much larger percentage of recalled attributes referred to the most preferred automobile in the choice task (35% belonged to the chosen car) than in the judgment task (18% belonged to the car with the highest desirability rating). These studies suggest that performance on free recall memory tasks may provide evidence about strategy use during judgment or choice tasks that is far easier to collect and analyze than other evidence, such as verbal protocols. Also, because memory tasks are administered as a surprise, after the judgment or choice task, there is no possibility that the diagnostic task can interfere with the task it is designed to diagnose.

In addition to using free recall to diagnose processing strategies, Johnson and Russo (1984) used people's free recall of product attributes to analyze their *organization of knowledge* about consumer products. Free recall does not guide or constrain people to generate previously seen items in any particular order. As a result, the way in which recalled information is clustered is diagnostic of the way the information is organized in memory. By analyzing clustering in free recall, Russo and Johnson (1980), for example, found clear evidence for brand-based rather than attribute-based organization of knowledge about consumer products. Johnson and Russo (1984) also found that brand-based organization became even more pronounced with increasing product familiarity.

D. SUMMARY

This section provided an overview and a demonstration of different ways in which memory tasks can be used to test the encoding and processing assumptions that are explicitly or implicitly made by J/DM models. Lynch and Srull (1982) lamented the mismatch between the proliferation of theoretical assumptions about cognitive processes in consumer research and the paucity of methodologies capable of diagnosing such processes. They advised researchers to adopt methods from cognitive psychology (in particular methods capitalizing on attention and memory processes) to supplement simple outcome measures (judgments or choices) as well as commonly used but difficult to analyze process-tracing methods. We offer our review of the recognition and free recall methods in that spirit. It is also noteworthy that all studies reviewed in this section at least implicitly acknowledge the strategic or goal-directed nature of information encoding and information usage by making the various memory tests used to diagnose encoding or strategy use a surprise task for their respondents.

IV. Conclusions

In this chapter, we considered the two main metatheoretical frameworks of J/DM research, that is, strategy selection and the perceptual framework (Payne et al., 1992), and for each one we discussed the potential contributions of memory research. With respect to strategy selection, we demonstrated that recent models of memory representation and memory processes have the potential to enlarge the set of explanatory constructs that J/DM researchers have available to account for information integration. Although information integration is usually thought to be accomplished by an effortful decision strategy, the formation of overall impressions may instead be the relatively effortless by-product of memory representations and storage operations (i.e., the superposition of distributed item representations). We also discussed the theoretical and methodological implications of distinctions based on the *content* of memory (i.e., episodic vs. semantic vs. procedural memory).

With respect to the perceptual framework, we showed strong effects of the order in which outcome information was serially received in a choice task, suggesting simplified "gist" encoding of information as the result of short-term memory limitations (see also, Brainerd & Reyna, 1992; Reyna & Brainerd, 1991). We also discussed the influence of prior events and experiences on the encoding of information and the use of information elaboration tasks to reveal the knowledge base that people use in encoding information. In addition, we also showed that memory tasks, such as free recall or forced-choice recognition, can provide innovative diagnostic tools to shed light on otherwise "invisible" cognitive processes. The speed and accuracy of performance on memory tasks can reveal the traces of prior mental representations and uses of information analogous to the way vapor trails in a cloud chamber reveal the passage of subatomic particles. As we show elsewhere (Goldstein & Weber, 1995), the representation of the information on which a decision is based is related to the content of the decision and can influence the process as well as the outcome of the decision.

What are the lessons and implications of the suggestions and demonstrations of this chapter? Beyond the use of memory techniques as a tool capable of diagnosing a particular form of information encoding and/or processing, our intention was to encourage decision theorists to show greater concern for the details of memory representation and processes in their models of judgment and decision making. As argued at various points of the chapter, most judgment and decision tasks involve elements of memory retrieval. Memory-based judgments and decisions and mixed tasks that involve the integration of retrieved information with information that is physically present are the norm rather than the exception in most domains, from consumer choice to medical diagnosis to social judgments. This chapter summarized much of the empirical evidence documenting the need to address memory-based processes.

In the course of this chapter, we touched on several directions for theory development that integrate memory processes and judgment or decision processes in different ways and at different levels of analysis. A prime example of one important direction is the work by Kahneman and associates on the way in which memories of past experiences are integrated to form preferences for events that extend and change over time (e.g., Kahneman et al., 1993). Models at this level of analysis consider selective encoding, storage, and retrieval of the substantive information, possibly providing psychological explanations and boundary conditions for the existence of any memory effects (e.g., neglect of the duration of aversive experiences in retrospective evaluations, or strong sequence effects). Another direction for theory extension at a more abstract level is exemplified by the work of Busemeyer and Townsend (1993). Their decision field theory attempts to describe, among other things, the dynamic process by which the anticipated consequences of different choice alternatives, assumed to be retrieved over time by associative memory processes, are integrated until preference for one alternative emerges strong enough to result in choice. Their stochastic–dynamic theory predicts the choice probability of different alternatives as a function of variables such as available information about past and present preferences, attentional manipulations, and length of deliberation time. Decision field theory models the results of the deliberation process over time, but makes no assumptions about the representation of information or structure of memory. A third direction for theory extension, namely consideration of specific microlevel assumptions about information repre-sentation and associated information storage and retrieval processes is exemplified by the work of Weber et al. (1991) and Kashima and Kerekes (1994), described earlier. Theory extensions for judgment and choice mod-els that address memory phenomena and processes at all of these levels of analysis will be necessary to predict real-world decisions and judgments that involve the evaluation and combination of new information, often obtained over time, in light of preexisting knowledge.

Researchers in other areas of cognitive psychology routinely acknowl-edge interconnections among different cognitive processes. Memory re-searchers, for example, have long incorporated attentional and decision processes into their models (e.g., Atkinson & Juola, 1973; Bernbach, 1967; Hockley, 1984; Hockley & Murdock, 1987; Ratcliff, 1978; Wickelgren & Norman, 1966). As reviewed by Elstein, Shulman, and Sprafka (1990), research in reasoning and, in particular, medical reasoning has in recent years addressed issues of memory organization, problem representation, and the structure of knowledge. We would like to reiterate the suggestion by Estes (1980) in Wallsten's (1980) predecessor to this volume that decision researchers can profit from following these examples. Explicit assumptions about the structure, processes, and content of memory ought to be incorpo-rated more into J/DM models. We believe that a broader range of theoretical constructs and dependent measures than traditionally used in decision research—but with a history in other branches of cognitive psychology—can make important theoretical contributions.

ACKNOWLEDGMENTS

We thank Jerome Busemeyer, Diederich Stapel, Thomas Wallsten, and Klaus Wertenbroch for discussions related to issues in this chapter. Thanks also go to Jerome Busemeyer, Arthur Elstein, Reid Hastie, William Hockley, Douglas Medin, and Joshua Klayman for editorial comments and suggestions.

REFERENCES

Adelson, B. (1984). When novices surpass experts: The difficulty of a task may increase with experience. *Journal of Experimental Psychology: Learning, Memory, and Cognition, 10,* 483–495.

Anderson, J. A. (1972). A simple neural network generating an interactive memory. *Mathematical Biosciences, 14,* 197–220.

Anderson, J. A., Silverstein, J. W., Ritz, S. A., & Jones, R. S. (1977). Distinctive features, categorical perception, and probability learning: Some applications of a neural model. *Psychological Review, 84,* 413–451.

Anderson, J. R. (1976). *Language, Memory, and Thought.* Hillsdale, NJ: Erlbaum.

Anderson, N. H. (1981). *Foundations of information integration theory.* New York: Academic Press.

Anderson, N. H., & Hubert, S. (1963). Effects of concomitant verbal recall on order effects in personality impression formation. *Journal of Verbal Learning and Verbal Behavior, 2,* 379–391.

Arkes, H. (1991). Costs and benefits of judgment errors: Implications for debiasing. *Psychological Bulletin, 110,* 486–498.

Atkinson, R. C., & Juola, J. F. (1973). Factors influencing speed and accuracy of word recognition. In S. Kornblum (Ed.), *Attention and performance IV.* New York: Academic Press.

Bargh, J. A. (1989). Conditional automaticity: Varieties of automatic influence in social perception and cognition. In J. S. Uleman & J. A. Bargh (Eds.), *Unintended thought* (pp. 3–51). New York: Guilford Press.

Barsalou, L. W. (1990). On the indistinguishability of exemplar memory and abstraction in category representation. In T. K. Srull & R. S. Wyer (Eds.), *Advances in social cognition* (Vol. 3, pp. 61–88). Hillsdale, NJ: Erlbaum.

Barsalou, L. W., & Ross, B. H. (1986). The role of automatic and strategic processing in sensitivity to superordinate and property frequency. *Journal of Experimental Psychology: Learning, Memory, and Cognition, 12,* 116–134.

Beach, L. R. (1993). Broadening the definition of decision making: The role of prechoice screening of options. *Psychological Science, 4,* 215–220.

Ben Zur, H., & Bresnitz, S. J. (1981). The effect of time pressure on risky choice behavior. *Acta Psychologica, 47,* 89–104.

Bernbach, H. (1967). Decision processes in memory. *Psychological Review, 74,* 462–480.

Böckenholt, U., & Kroeger, K. (1993). The effect of time pressure in multiattribute binary choice tasks. In O. Svenson & A. J. Maule (Eds.), *Time pressure and stress in human judgment and decision making* (pp. 195–214). New York: Plenum Press.

Bornstein, R. F. (1989). Exposure and affect: Overview and meta-analysis of research, 1968–1987. *Psychological Bulletin, 106,* 265–289.

Brainerd, C. J., & Reyna, V. F. (1992). Explaining "memory-free" reasoning. *Psychological Science, 3,* 332–339.

Brehmer, B. (1980). In one word: Not from experience. *Acta Psychologica, 45,* 223–241.

Brooks, L. R. (1978). Non-analytic concept formation and memory for instance. In E. Rosch and B. Lloyd (Eds.), *Cognition and categorization* (pp. 169–211). Hillsdale, NJ: Erlbaum.

Brooks, L. R., Norman, G. R., & Allen, S. W. (1991). Role of specific similarity in a medical diagnostic task. *Journal of Experimental Psychology: General, 120,* 278–287.

Bruce, D., Hockley, W. W., & Craik, F. I. M. (1991). Availability and category-frequency estimation. *Memory and Cognition, 19,* 301–312.

Busemeyer, J. R. (1985). Decision making under uncertainty: A comparison of simple scalability, fixed-sample, and sequential-sampling models. *Journal of Experimental Psychology: Learning, Memory, and Cognition, 11,* 538–564.

Busemeyer, J. R., Forsyth, B., & Nozawa, G. (1988). Comparisons of elimination-by-aspects and suppression of aspects choice models based on choice response time. *Journal of Mathematical Psychology, 32,* 341–349.

Busemeyer, J. R., & Townsend, J. T. (1993). Decision field theory: A dynamic-cognitive approach to decision making in an uncertain environment. *Psychological Review, 100,* 432–459.

Chandler, C. C. (1991). How memory for an event is influenced by related events: Interference in modified recognition tests. *Journal of Experimental Psychology: Learning, Memory, and Cognition, 17,* 115–125.

Chase, W. G., & Simon, H. A. (1973). Perception in chess. *Cognitive Psychology, 4,* 55–81.

Cohen, N. J. (1984). Preserved learning capacity in amnesia: Evidence for multiple memory systems. In L. R. Squire & N. Butters (Eds.), *The neuropsychology of memory* (pp. 419–432). New York: Guilford Press.

Coombs, C. H., & Avrunin, G. S (1977). Single-peaked functions and the theory of preference. *Psychological Review, 84,* 216–230.

Curley, S. P., Browne, G. J., Smith, G. F., & Benson, P. G. (1993). *Arguments in the practical reasoning underlying constructive probability responses.* Unpublished manuscript. University of Minnesota.

DeGroot, A. D. (1965). *Thought and choice in chess.* The Hague: Mouton.

Donders, F. C. (1868). Die Schnelligkeit psychischer Prozesse. *Archiv fuer Anatomie und Physiologie und Wissenschaftliche Medizin,* pp. 657–681.

Dreben, E. K., Fiske, S. T., & Hastie, R. (1979). The independence of evaluative and item information: Impression and recall order effects in behavior-based impression formation. *Journal of Personality and Social Psychology, 37,* 1758–1768.

Eddy, D. M. (1982). Probabilistic reasoning in clinical medicine: Problems and opportunities. In D. Kahneman, P. Slovic, & A. Tversky (Eds.), *Judgment under uncertainty: Heuristics and biases.* Cambridge, UK: Cambridge University Press.

Einhorn, H. J., & Hogarth, R. M. (1978). Confidence in judgment: The illusion of validity. *Psychological Review, 85,* 395–416.

Elstein, A. S., & Bordage, G. (1979). Psychology of clinical reasoning. In G. Stone, F. Cohen, & N. Adler (Eds.), *Health psychology: A handbook.* San Francisco: Jossey-Bass.

Elstein, A. S., Shulman, L. S., & Sprafka, S. A. (1990). Medical problem solving: A ten-year retrospective. *Evaluation and the Health Professions, 13,* 5–36.

Elster, J., & Loewenstein, G. (1992). Utility from memory and anticipation. In G. Loewenstein & J. Elster (Eds.), *Choice over time* (pp. 213–234). New York: Russell Sage Foundation.

Estes, W. K. (1980). Comments on directions and limitations of current efforts toward theories of decision making. In T. S. Wallsten (Ed.), *Cognitive processes in choice and decision behavior* (pp. 263–274). Hillsdale, NJ: Erlbaum.

Fischhoff, B. (1975). Hindsight ≠ foresight: The effect of outcome knowledge on judgment uncertainty. *Journal of Experimental Psychology: Human Perception and Performance, 1,* 288–299.

Fiske, S. T., & Neuberg, S. L. (1990). A continuum model of impression formation, from category-based to individuating processes: Influence of information and motivation on attention and interpretation. In M. P. Zanna (Ed.), *Advances in Experimental Social Psychology* (Vol. 23), (pp. 1–74). San Diego: Academic Press.

Fiske, S. T., & Taylor, S. E. (1991). *Social cognition* (2nd ed.). New York: McGraw-Hill.

Fox, J. (1980). Making decisions under the influence of memory. *Psychological Review, 87,* 190–211.

Friedrich, J. (1993). Primary error detection and minimization (PEDMIN) strategies in social cognition: A reinterpretation of confirmation bias phenomena. *Psychological Review, 100,* 298–319.

Frisch, D. (1993). Reasons for framing effects. *Organizational Behavior and Human Decision Processes, 54,* 399–429.

Frisch, D., & Clemen, R. T. (1994). Beyond expected utility: Rethinking behavioral decision research. *Psychological Bulletin, 116,* 46–54.

Gigerenzer, G., Hell, W., & Blank, H. (1988). Presentation and content: The use of base rates as a continuous variable. *Journal of Experimental Psychology: Human Perception and Performance, 14,* 513–525.

Goldstein, W. M., & Einhorn, H. J. (1987). Expression theory and the preference reversal phenomena. *Psychological Review, 94,* 236–254.

Goldstein, W. M., & Mitzel, H. C. (1992). The relative importance of relative importance: Inferring other people's preferences from relative importance ratings and previous decisions. *Organizational Behavior and Human Decision Processes, 52,* 382–415.

Goldstein, W. M., & Weber, E. U. (1995). Content and discontent: Indications and implications of domain specificity in preferential decision making. In J. R. Busemeyer, R. Hastie, D. L. Medin (Eds.), *The Psychology of Learning and Motivation, 32,* San Diego: Academic Press.

Hastie, R. (1988). A computer simulation model of person memory. *Journal of Experimental Social Psychology, 24,* 423–447.

Hastie, R., & Park, B. (1986). The relationship between memory and judgment depends on whether the judgment task is memory-based or on-line. *Psychological Review, 93,* 258–268.

Hawkins, S. A., & Hastie, R. (1990). Hindsight: Biased judgments of past events after the outcomes are known. *Psychological Bulletin, 107,* 311–327.

Hawkins, S. A., & Hoch, S. J. (1992). Low-involvement learning: Memory without evaluation. *Journal of Consumer Research, 19,* 212–225.

Higgins, E. T., & Bargh, J. A. (1987). Social cognition and social perception. *Annual Review of Psychology, 38,* 369–425.

Hockley, W. E. (1984). Analysis of response time distributions in the study of cognitive processes. *Journal of Experimental Psychology: Learning, Memory, and Cognition, 10,* 598–615.

Hockley, W. E., & Lewandowsky, S. (Eds.). (1991). *Relating theory and data: Essays on human memory in honor of Bennet B. Murdock.* Hillsdale, NJ: Erlbaum.

Hockley, W. E., & Murdock, B. B. (1987). A decision model for accuracy and response latency in recognition memory. *Psychological Review, 94,* 341–358.

Hogarth, R. M., & Einhorn, H. J. (1992). Order effects in belief updating: The belief-adjustment model. *Cognitive Psychology, 24,* 1–55.

Hogarth, R. M., & Kunreuther, H. (1995). Decision making under ignorance: Arguing with yourself. *Journal of Risk and Uncertainty, 10,* 15–36.

Holbrook, M. B. (1987). What is consumer research? *Journal of Consumer Research, 14,* 128–132.

Hsee, C. K., Abelson, R. P., & Salovey, P. (1991). The relative weighting of position and velocity in satisfaction. *Psychological Science, 2,* 263–266.

Huber, O. (1980). The influence of some task variables on cognitive operations in an information processing decision model. *Acta Psychologica, 45,* 187–196.

Humphreys, M. S., Bain, J. S., & Pike, A. R. (1989). Different ways to cue a coherent memory system: A theory for episodic, semantic, and procedural tasks. *Psychological Review, 96,* 208–233.

Jacoby, L. L., Lindsay, D. S., & Toth, J. P. (1992). Unconscious influences revealed: Attention, awareness, and control. *American Psychologist, 47,* 802–809.

Jacoby, L. L., Toth, J. P., & Yonelinas, A. P. (1993). Separating conscious and unconscious influences of memory: Measuring recollection. *Journal of Experimental Psychology: General, 122,* 139–154.

Johnson, E. J., & Russo, J. E. (1984). Product familiarity and learning new information. *Journal of Consumer Research, 11,* 542–550.

Joseph, G.-M., & Patel, V. L. (1990). Domain knowledge and hypothesis generation in diagnostic reasoning. *Medical Decision Making, 10,* 31–46.

Kahneman, D., Fredrickson, B. L., Schreiber, C. A., & Redelmeier, D. A. (1993). When more pain is preferred to less: Adding a better end. *Psychological Science, 4,* 401–405.

Kahneman, D., Slovic, A., & Tversky, A. (1982). *Judgment under uncertainty: Heuristics and biases.* Cambridge, UK: Cambridge University Press.

Kahneman, D., & Snell, J. (1992). Predicting a changing taste: Do people know what they will like? *Journal of Behavioral Decision Making, 5,* 187–200.

Kahneman, D., & Tversky, A. (1979). Prospect theory: An analysis of decision under risk. *Econometrika, 47,* 263–291.

Kahneman, D., & Tversky, A. (1982). The psychology of preference. *Scientific American, 246,* 163–169.

Kashima, Y., & Kerekes, A. R. Z. (1994). A distributed memory model of averaging phenomena in person impression formation. *Journal of Experimental Social Psychology, 30,* 407–455.

Klayman, J., & Ha, Y.-W. (1987). Confirmation, disconfirmation, and information in hypothesis testing. *Psychological Review, 94,* 211–228.

Kleinmuntz, B. (1968). The processing of clinical information by man and machine. In B. Kleinmuntz (Ed.), *Formal representation of human judgment* (pp. 149–186). New York: Wiley.

Kolodner, J. L., Simpson, R. L., & Sycara-Cyranski, K. (1985). A process model of case-based reasoning in problem solving. *Proceedings of the Ninth International Joint Conference on Artificial Intelligence.* Los Angeles, CA.

Kruschke, J. K. (1992). ALCOVE: An exemplar-based connectionist model of category learning. *Psychological Review, 99,* 22–44.

Levin, I. P., & Chapman, D. P. (1993). Risky decision making and allocation of resources for leukemia and AIDS programs. *Health Psychology, 12,* 110–117.

Levin, I. P., Jasper, J. D., Mittelstaedt, J. D., & Gaeth, G. J. (1993). Attitudes toward "buy American first" and preferences for American and Japanese cars: A different role for country-of-origin information. In L. McAlister & M. L. Rothschild (Eds.), *Advances in Consumer Research* (Vol. 20, pp. 625–629). Provo, UT: Association for Consumer Research.

Lewin, K., Dembo, T., Festinger, L., & Sears, P. S. (1944). Level of aspiration. In J. McV. Hunt (Ed.), *Personality and the behavior disorders: A handbook based on experimental and clinical research* (Vol. 1, pp. 333–378). New York: Ronald Press.

Libby, R., & Frederick, D. M. (1990). Experience and the ability to explain audit findings. *Journal of Accounting Research, 28,* 348–367.

Lichtenstein, S., Fischhoff, B., & Phillips, L. D. (1982). Calibration of probabilities: The state of the art to 1980. In D. Kahneman, P. Slovic, & A. Tversky (Eds.), *Judgment under uncertainty: Heuristics and biases.* Cambridge, UK: Cambridge University Press.

Lichtenstein, S., & Slovic, P. (1971). Reversal of preference between bids and choices in gambling decisions. *Journal of Experimental Psychology, 89,* 46–55.

Lingle, J. H., & Ostrom, T. M. (1979). Retrieval selectivity in memory-based impression judgments. *Journal of Personality and Social Psychology, 37,* 180–194.

Linville, P. W., & Fischer, G. W. (1991). Preferences for separating or combining events. *Journal of Personality and Social Psychology, 60,* 5–23.

Logan, G. D. (1988). Toward an instance theory of automatization. *Psychological Review, 95,* 492–527.

Lopes, L. (1994). Psychology and economics: Perspectives on risk, cooperation, and the marketplace. *Annual Review of Psychology, 45,* 197–227.

Luce, R. D., Mellers, B. A., & Chang, S. (1993). Is choice the correct primitive? On using certainty equivalents and reference levels to predict choices among gambles. *Journal of Risk and Uncertainty, 6,* 115–144.

Lynch, J. G., & Srull, T. K. (1982). Memory and attentional factors in consumer choice. *Journal of Consumer Research, 9,* 18–37.

Markowitz, H. (1959). *Portfolio selection: Efficient diversification of investment.* New York: Wiley.

McClelland, G. H., Stewart, B. E., Judd, C. M., & Bourne, L. E. (1987). Effects of choice task on attribute memory. *Organizational Behavior and Human Decision Processes, 40,* 235–254.

McGraw, K., Lodge, M., & Stroh, P. (1990). *Processes of candidate evaluation: On-line or memory based?* Unpublished manuscript, SUNY at Stonybrook.

Means, B., & Loftus, E. F. (1991). When personal history repeats itself: Decomposing memory for recurring events. *Applied Cognitive Psychology, 5,* 297–318.

Medin, D. L., & Edelson, S. (1988). Problem structure and the use of base-rate information from experience. *Journal of Experimental Psychology: General, 117,* 68–85.

Medin, D. L., & Schaffer, M. M. (1978). Context theory of classification learning. *Psychological Review, 85,* 207–238.

Mellers, B. A., Ordóñez, L., & Birnbaum, M. H. (1992). A change-of-process theory for contextual effects and preference reversals in risky decision making. *Organizational Behavior and Human Decision Processes, 52,* 331–369.

Melton, A. W., & Martin, E. (Eds.). (1972). *Coding processes in human memory.* Washington, DC: Winston.

Metcalfe Eich, J. (1982). A composite holographic associate recall model. *Psychological Review, 89,* 627–661.

Metcalfe, J. (1990). Composite holographic associate recall model (CHARM) and blended memories in eyewitness testimony. *Journal of Experimental Psychology: General, 119,* 145–160.

Miller, G. A. (1956). The magical number seven, plus or minus two: Some limits on our capacity for processing information. *Psychological Review, 63,* 81–96.

Montgomery, H. (1983). Decision rules and the search for a dominance structure: Toward a process model of decision making. In P. Humphreys, O. Svenson, & A. Vari (Eds.), *Analysing and aiding decision processes* (pp. 343–369). Amsterdam: North-Holland.

Morton, J. (1970). A functional model of memory. In D. A. Norman (Ed.), *Models of human memory* (pp. 203–260). San Diego: Academic Press.

Murdock, B. B., Jr. (1982). A theory for the storage and retrieval of item and associative information. *Psychological Review, 89,* 609–626.

Murdock, B. B., Jr. (1983). A distributed memory model for serial-order information. *Psychological Review, 90,* 316–338.

Murdock, B. B., Jr. (1989). Learning in a distributed memory model. In C. Izawa (Ed.), *Current issues in Cognitive Processes: The Tulane Floweree Symposium on Cognition* (pp. 69–106). Hillsdale, NJ: Erlbaum.

Murdock, B. B., Jr. (1993). TODAM2: A model for the storage and retrieval of item, associative, and serial-order information. *Psychological Review, 100,* 183–203.

Newell, A., & Simon, H. A. (1972). *Human problem solving.* Englewood Cliffs, NJ: Prentice-Hall.

Nisbett, R. E. (Ed.). (1993). *Rules for reasoning.* Hillsdale, NJ: Erlbaum.

Nosofsky, R. M. (1992). Exemplars, prototypes, and similarity rules. In A. F. Healy, S. M. Kosslyn, & R. M. Shiffrin (Eds.), *From learning theory to connectionist theory: Essays in honor of William K. Estes* (Vol. 1, pp. 149–167). Hillsdale, NJ: Erlbaum.

Payne, J. W. (1982). Contingent decision behavior. *Psychological Bulletin, 92,* 382–402.

Payne, J. W., Bettman, J. R., and Johnson, E. J. (1988). Adaptive strategy selection in decision making. *Journal of Experimental Psychology: Learning, Memory, and Cognition, 14,* 534–552.

Payne, J. W., Bettman, J. R., and Johnson, E. J. (1990). The adaptive decision maker: Effort and accuracy in choice. In R. M. Hogarth (Ed.), *Insights in decision making: A tribute to Hillel J. Einhorn.* Chicago: University of Chicago Press.

Payne, J. W., Bettman, J. R., and Johnson, E. J. (1992). Behavioral decision research: A constructive processing perspective. *Annual Review of Psychology, 43,* 87–131. Cambridge, UK: Cambridge University Press.

Payne, J. W., Bettman, J. R., and Johnson, E. J. (1993). *The adaptive decision maker.* Cambridge: Cambridge University Press.

Pennington, N., & Hastie, R. (1988). Explanation-based decision making: The effects of memory structure on judgment. *Journal of Experimental Psychology: Learning, Memory, and Cognition, 14,* 521–533.

Posner, M. I., & Keele, S. W. (1968). On the genesis of abstract ideas. *Journal of Experimental Psychology, 77,* 353–363.

Ratcliff, R. (1978). A theory of memory retrieval. *Psychological Review, 85,* 59–108.

Restle, F. (1961). *Psychology of judgment and choice.* New York: Wiley.

Reyna, V. F., & Brainerd, C. J. (1991). Fuzzy-trace and framing effects in choice: Gist extraction, truncation, and conversion. *Journal of Behavioral Decision Making, 4,* 249–262.

Roediger, H. L. (1990). Implicit memory: Retention without remembering. *American Psychologist, 45,* 341–357.

Rumelhart, D. E., & McClelland, J. L. (Eds.). (1986). *Parallel distributed processing: Explorations in the microstructure of cognition* (two volumes). Cambridge, MA: MIT Press.

Russo, J. E., & Johnson, E. J. (1980). What do consumers know about familiar products? In J. Olson (Ed.), *Advances in Consumer Research* (Vol. 7, pp. 417–423). Ann Arbor, MI: Association for Consumer Research.

Schneider, S. L. (1992). Framing and conflict: Aspiration level contingency, the status quo, and current theories of risky choice. *Journal of Experimental Psychology: Learning, Memory, and Cognition, 18,* 1040–1057.

Schneider, W., & Shiffrin, R. M. (1977). Controlled and automatic human information processing: I. Detection, search, and attention. *Psychological Review, 1984,* 1–66.

Shafir, E., & Tversky, A. (1992). Thinking through uncertainty: Nonconsequential reasoning and choice. *Cognitive Psychology, 24,* 449–474.

Shanteau, J. (1991). A functional measurement analysis of reaction times in problem solving. In N. H. Anderson (Ed.), *Contributions to integration theory* (Vol. 1). New York: Academic Press.

Simon, H. A. (1955). A behavioral model of rational choice. *Quarterly Journal of Economics, 59,* 99–118.

Simon, H. A. (1956). Rational choice and the structure of the environment. *Psychological Review, 63,* 129–138.

Slovic, P., Fischhoff, B., & Lichtenstein, S. (1982). Response mode, framing, and information-processing effects in risk assessment. In R. Hogarth (Ed.), *New directions for methodology of social and behavioral sciences: Question framing and response mode.* San Francisco: Jossey-Bass.

Smith, E. R. (1990). Content and process specificity in the effects of prior experience. In T. K. Srull & R. S. Wyer (Eds.), *Advances in Social Cognition* (Vol. 3, pp. 1–61). Hillsdale, NJ: Erlbaum.

Smith, J. F., Mitchell, T. R., Beach, L. R. (1982). A cost–benefit mechanism for selecting problem-solving strategies: Some extensions and empirical tests. *Organizational Behavior and Human Performance, 29,* 370–396.

Staw, B. (1976). Knee-deep in the big muddy: A study of escalating commitment to a chosen course of action. *Organizational Behavior and Human Performance, 16,* 27–44.

Thaler, R. (1980). Toward a positive theory of consumer choice. *Journal of Economic Behavior and Organization, 1,* 39–60.

Thaler, R. (1985). Mental accounting and consumer choice. *Marketing Science, 4,* 199–214.

Thaler, R., & Johnson, E. H. (1990). Gambling with the house money and trying to break even: The effects of prior outcomes on risky choice. *Management Science, 36,* 643–660.

Townsend, J. T. (1990). Serial versus parallel processing: Sometimes they look like tweedledum and tweddledee but they can (and should) be distinguished. *Psychological Science, 1,* 46–54.

Tubbs, R. M., Gaeth, G. J., Levin, I. P., & van Osdol, L. A. (1993). Order effects in belief updating with consistent and inconsistent evidence. *Journal of Behavioral Decision Making, 6,* 257–269.

Tulving, E. (1972). Episodic and semantic memory. In E. Tulving and W. Donaldson (Eds.), *Organization of Memory* (pp. 381–403). New York: Academic Press.

Tversky, A. (1972). Elimination by aspects: A theory of choice. *Psychological Review, 79,* 281–299.

Tversky, A., & Kahneman, D. (1973). Availability: A heuristic for judging frequency and probability. *Cognitive Psychology, 5,* 207–232.

Tversky, A., & Kahneman, D. (1981). The framing of decisions and the psychology of choice. *Science, 211,* 453–458.

Tversky, A., & Kahneman, D. (1986). Rational choice and the framing of decisions. *Journal of Business, 59,* S251–S278.

Tversky, A. Sattath, S., & Slovic, P. (1988). Contingent weighting in judgment and choice. *Psychological Review, 95,* 371–384.

Wallsten, T. S. (Ed.). (1980). *Cognitive Processes in choice and decision behavior* (pp. 263–274). Hillsdale, NJ: Erlbaum.

Wallsten, T. S. (1981). Physician and medical student bias in evaluating diagnostic information. *Medical Decision Making, 1,* 145–164.

Weber, E. U., Barlas, S., Wertenbrock, K., & Goldstein, W. M. (1994). The psychophysics of value functions. Unpublished manuscript. Center for Decision Research, University of Chicago.

Weber, E. U., Böckenholt, U., Hilton, D. J., & Wallace, B. (1993). Determinants of diagnostic hypothesis generation: Effects of information, base rates, and experience. *Journal of Experimental Psychology: Learning, Memory, and Cognition, 19,* 1151–1164.

Weber, E. U., Goldstein, W. M., Barlas, S., & Busemeyer, J. R. (1994). Memory representation and cognitive effort. Unpublished manuscript. Center for Decision Research. University of Chicago.

Weber, E. U., Goldstein, W. M., & Busemeyer, J. R. (1991). Beyond strategies: Implications of memory representation and memory processes for models of judgment and decision making. In W. E. Hockley & S. Lewandowsky (Eds.), *Relating theory and data: Essays on human memory in honor of Bennet B. Murdock.* Hillsdale, NJ: Erlbaum.

Whittlesea, B. W. A., Brooks, L. R., & Westcott, C. (1994). After the learning is over: Factors controlling the selective application of general and particular knowledge. *Journal of Experimental Psychology: Learning, Memory, and Cognition, 20,* 259–274.

Wickelgren, W., & Norman, D. (1966). Strength models and serial position in short-term recognition memory. *Journal of Mathematical Psychology, 3,* 316–347.

Young, A. W., & DeHaan, E. H. F. (1990). Impairment of visual awareness. *Mind and Language, 5,* 29–48.

CONTENT AND DISCONTENT: INDICATIONS AND IMPLICATIONS OF DOMAIN SPECIFICITY IN PREFERENTIAL DECISION MAKING

William M. Goldstein and Elke U. Weber

I. Introduction

Research on preferential decision making has been and largely continues to be dominated by the use of a particular kind of stimulus material: simple monetary gambles. Sometimes other highly structured stimuli are used (e.g., apartments described in terms of monthly rent and distance from work), but almost always the stimuli have an incomplete and schematic form that conveys a generic quality to the choice alternatives. Although research has also been conducted on moral decision making (Baron, 1993; Mellers & Baron, 1993), legal decision making (Hastie, 1993; Lloyd-Bostock, 1989), medical decision making (Bursztajn, Feinbloom, Hamm, & Brodsky, 1990; Schwartz & Griffin, 1986), and political decision making (Sniderman, Brody, & Tetlock, 1991), as well as some other content-specific forms of decision making, the fact remains that the vast majority of studies on preferential choice and judgment have employed simple monetary gambles or other highly structured and content-impoverished stimuli. This state of affairs contrasts sharply with several other areas of psychology, where the *semantic content* of the stimuli, that is, what the task is "about," has been found to influence behavior, and where energetic research has been under-taken to identify functionally distinct domains of content, to isolate the

THE PSYCHOLOGY OF LEARNING
AND MOTIVATION, VOL. 32

83

affected stages of psychological processing, and to delineate the responsible psychological mechanisms (Hirschfeld & Gelman, 1994).

Our impression is that decision researchers have regarded these developments in neighboring fields with considerable suspicion, but for reasons that may not be readily apparent to others. It may appear that decision researchers fear a loss of parsimony. It may indeed seem a poor trade to exchange familiar content-free taxonomies of decision problems (e.g., decisions under uncertainty, risk, and certainty) for an explosion of content-specific categories of decisions (e.g., career decisions, housing decisions, animal, mineral, and vegetable decisions, etc.), each of which may require a different theory. However, in addition to a desire for parsimony, we believe that decision researchers have reservations that are theoretically based. The prevalent use of simple gambles as stimuli is sanctioned by fundamental metatheoretical assertions about the "essence" of decision making, coupled with the belief that generalizability is enhanced by studying decision making in its "essential" form. If the metatheory of decision research has been underappreciated by others, we believe that decision researchers often reciprocate by failing to appreciate the reasons why many researchers have come to accept content specificity as a fact and as a research topic. Various areas of psychology have had their own metatheories to contend with, and have given up the dream of content-free accounts of behavior only when forced to by the data.

The purpose of this chapter is to critique the metatheory that guides most research on preferential judgment and choice, which we call the *gambling metaphor,* but to do so specifically with respect to the issue of content effects. Others have voiced concerns at the level of general metatheory, but these have related mainly to other issues (which will be discussed later). Some possible exceptions notwithstanding (Beach & Mitchell, 1987; Hastie, 1991), these criticisms need not be interpreted as questioning the content-impoverished nature of the stimuli that are used almost universally in studies of preferential decision making. Such a critique is the burden of this chapter.

It should be emphasized that we are restricting our scope to the study of preference and evaluation, that is, to decisions about what is "good." Although judgment and decision researchers collectively have devoted less attention to the possibility that behavior may depend on the semantic content of the stimuli than have researchers in other areas of psychology, within decision research, attention (or inattention) to the issue has been uneven. Researchers interested in learning have shown the most concern toward content, those studying probabilistic judgment have shown less (these areas of research will be discussed later), and investigators of preference and evaluation appear to have shown the least concern. Although research on probabilistic judgment has shifted from reliance on bookbag-and-poker-chip problems to word problems, an analogous shift has not taken place in research on preferential judgment and choice. In this area of decision research, simple monetary gambles remain as important to researchers as fruit flies to geneticists (Lopes, 1983).

The use of gambles as stimuli in psychological experiments is a reasonable extension of some time-honored lines of thought. We review this background to show how compelling the use of gambles can be. Then, we critique the gambling metaphor in two ways. First, we briefly review several areas of psychology in which the semantic content of stimuli has been found to be an important determinant of behavior: in memory, animal learning, categories and concepts, deductive reasoning, problem solving and expertise, and cognitive development. The psychological mechanisms underlying preferential decision making overlap sufficiently with those in other areas of psychology that decision researchers *should* draw from the substantive results concerning the effects of semantic content. We also find interesting historical parallels between developments in decision research and those in some of the other areas we discuss (especially memory), suggesting that thinking in decision research may evolve in similar ways. Our second line of criticism is more direct. We review the research on preferential decision making that bears on the issue of content dependence. We find a number of studies that might be interpreted as supporting the view that content effects are present and interesting, but they do not necessarily impugn the core theory of the gambling metaphor. Other recent studies, however, are much more damaging. They provide evidence that the central variables of the gambling metaphor—degree of belief and degree of desirability—cannot support generalizations at the level of analysis to which the gambling metaphor aspires. Finally, we sketch our views of what a theory of content effects in preferential decision making might look like if it is to maintain a reasonable degree of parsimony.

II. Metatheory of Preferential Decision Research: History of the Gambling Metaphor

In the late 1940s and 1950s, a number of psychologists became aware of work in economics and statistics that had direct implications for psychological measurement. The view that psychological measurement is central to the establishment of a scientific psychology goes back to Immanuel Kant, who concluded that psychological measurement was unattainable and that psychology therefore could never be more than a "merely" empirical science. Gustav Fechner (1860) proposed a method of psychological measurement, but because it relied on the prior measurement of response probabilities, it failed to achieve the goal of "fundamental" measurement, that is, measurement without any prior measurement of any kind. Nevertheless, Fechner's work was extremely influential and, as developed further (especially by Thurstone, e.g., 1927; see Thurstone, 1959), became the basis for much of the work on psychological measurement in the first half of this century.

In 1947, von Neumann and Morgenstern published the second edition of their book, *Theory of Games and Economic Behavior,* in which they listed conditions under which a person's choices among gambles could be used to infer a "utility function" for the outcomes of the gambles, which in turn could be used to describe the person's choices. That is, if the conditions were satisfied, people's choices could be described as if they were choosing so as to maximize the expected utility of choice outcomes. Expected utility was seen by psychologists as an interesting model of individual choice behavior, and they (and others) soon undertook to test it (Preston & Baratta, 1948; Mosteller & Nogee, 1951). Even more exciting was the fact that von Neumann and Morgenstern were a hair's breadth away from fundamental measurement of a psychological variable: utility. However, because von Neumann and Morgenstern required the prior measurement of the probabilities with which events occurred in the gambles offered to subjects, they did not quite achieve fundamental measurement. Nevertheless, von Neumann and Morgenstern's approach was quite different from Fechner's, and it generated much interest. By 1954, Leonard J. Savage had extended the von Neumann and Morgenstern approach to gambles whose payoffs depended on the results of uncertain events, for example, the result of an election or the weather, without prior measurement of the probabilities. In his book, *The Foundations of Statistics,* Savage provided conditions under which a person's choices could be used to infer a "subjective probability function" as well as a "utility function," and thus Savage spelled out conditions for true fundamental measurement of these psychological variables.

Psychologists then began to test whether these conditions were satisfied, and this stream of psychological research on decision making was off and running (Edwards, 1954; Thrall, Coombs, & Davis, 1954). In this research, one of the presuppositions that psychologists adopted is what we call the gambling metaphor. The examples in Savage's book make it clear that gambling decisions were believed to be prototypical of virtually *all* decisions. Almost any contemplated action, for example, where to go to school, what job to take, or whom to marry, will have consequences that cannot be predicted with certainty but which vary in their likelihood and desirability. In this sense, then, real-life decisions have the same structure as gambles. Moreover, because this applies to virtually all decisions, *life is a gamble.*

The generality of this metaphor leads directly to an argument for a simplification in research practice: if all interesting real-life decisions are fundamentally like gambling decisions, then real-life decision processes can be studied in the laboratory by asking people to make gambling choices. Bolstered by this argument, simple monetary gambles have become the primary stimulus material used in research on preferential decision making. Also, because of the appeal of the argument that all decisions can be reduced to the same structure, decision researchers have resisted the implications of recent findings on domain specificity, namely that *content* influences psychological processes.

Although the metaphor of life as a gamble apparently came to psychology via von Neumann and Morgenstern (1947) and Savage (1954), its origins are considerably older, dating back to Jakob Bernoulli's (1713) *Ars Conjectandi*. Discussions of gambling figured heavily in the mid-seventeenth century correspondence between Pascal and Fermat, but unlike Bernoulli, these early probabilists did not consider gambles to be representative of all decision problems. Rather, the very early probabilists turned to the law, both for a source of ideas (about degrees of certainty) and for a source of applications (e.g., aleatory contracts in matters of insurance, annuities, fair shares of uncertain profits, and games of chance; see Daston, 1988). By contrast Bernoulli made it clear that he was pursuing probability as "a general theory of rational decision under uncertainty, not just a mathematization of legal practice" (Daston, 1988, p. 44). He was seeking a theory that would apply to "choices about which witness (or creed) to believe, which venture to invest in, which candidate to elect, what insurance premium to charge, which scientific theory to endorse" (Daston, 1988, p. 50).

The generality of the gambling metaphor was reinforced by Bernoulli's interpretation of probability. Daston (1988) says:

> We owe to Bernoulli the classical interpretation of probability as a state of mind rather than a state of the world. . . . Bernoulli insists that the throw of a die is "no less necessary (*non minus necessario*)" than an eclipse. The only difference between the gambler and the astronomer lies in the relative completeness of their respective knowledge of dice and eclipses, and a people ignorant of astronomy might well gamble on the occurrence of eclipses. "Contingent" events only exist relative to our ignorance, so that one man's contingency might easily be another's necessity. (pp. 34–35)

This view of probability as a degree of knowledge is entirely consistent with Savage's (1954) notion (anticipated by Ramsey, 1931) of "personal probability" as a degree of belief. Moreover, by so enlarging the scope of events to which the concept of probability applies, this view strengthens the position that all of life's decisions have the same structure as games of chance.

The generality of the gambling metaphor was supported in an analogous way by Jakob Bernoulli's nephew, Daniel. Daniel Bernoulli (1738), although preceded by Gabriel Cramer (1728) as Bernoulli himself states, is usually credited with the idea that people do not (and should not) deliberate directly about the monetary amounts that might accrue to them in a game of chance (or from an insurance contract, etc.) (correspondence of Gabriel Cramer to Nicholas Bernoulli in a letter dated May 21, 1728.). Instead, people deliberate about the *worth* of that money to them, its *utility,* which depends on people's individual circumstances (e.g., their wealth). As Cramer (1728) put it, "Mathematicians value money in proportion to its quantity, commonsense men in proportion to its use" (quoted by Jorland, 1987, p. 159). Bernoulli's detailed examples referred to the utility of money, and the specific (logarithmic) utility function that Bernoulli proposed is only defined for a quantitative argument (e.g., money). Nevertheless, in his discussion, Bernoulli at least implied that the concept of utility was to be applied to other "items" as well, including the abstract notion of a person's "productive capacity" (D. Bernoulli, p. 25; see Daston, 1988, p. 74, for links to contemporary economic theory). In this way, Daniel Bernoulli's work can be seen as enlarging the scope of the "outcomes" that must be addressed by a theory of behavior under uncertainty. Whether a gamble paid off in monetary amounts or in another "currency" was immaterial. What mattered was the subjective *value* placed on the potential outcomes by the decision maker.

In laying out the logic and history behind the gambling metaphor's position that monetary gambles may be taken as emblematic of all of life's decisions, we have implicitly relied on another assumption. So far, the argument has proceeded roughly as follows. Monetary gambles are characterized by two sorts of variables: (1) the amounts of money that might be won or lost, and (2) the probabilities with which these outcomes actually occur. Through Daniel Bernoulli's treatment of utility, we are led to think of the monetary outcomes merely as representatives of any valued consequences that might result from the choice of an alternative. What counts is that people place more or less *value* (desire, want, hope, fear, etc.) on different outcomes. By using Jakob Bernoulli's interpretation of probability, we are led to think of the probabilities of the monetary gamble merely as representatives of the degrees of *belief* that a person might hold about the prospects that ensuing events will actually produce the valued outcomes. The implicit assumption in this approach, the gambling metaphor's *reductionist* aspect, is that all of the considerations involved in a decision can be reduced to two types of variables: (1) (degree of) value and (2) (degree of) belief.

The position that people evaluate their alternatives in terms of beliefs and values—that people take deliberate actions (and only those deliberate actions) that they *believe* will advance their *valued* goals—is a position that stretches back to antiquity. Schick (1991) traces this view to Aristotle in *De Motu Animalium* and *Nichomachean Ethics*. Some philosophers have held that it is necessary to assume some form of this view (characterized as assuming that people are rational in a very general sense) to be able to infer someone's beliefs from his or her behavior, or indeed to infer that the person has any beliefs at all (Cherniak, 1986; Davidson, 1973, 1974, 1975; Dennett, 1978, 1987; Stich, 1990, chap. 2, traces all variants of this idea to a passage in Quine, 1960). The view that people evaluate alternatives in terms of beliefs and values is so intuitive and so entrenched in Western culture that philosophers tend to refer to it as "folk psychology," and the connection to decision theory has not gone unnoticed (Pettit, 1991). (It should be noted that philosophers sometimes use the term in what seems to be a derogatory way. The claim is that a belief–value theory of behavior is a naive "folk" theory in much the same way that naive, intuitive, untutored physics is a "folk" theory, and moreover that both theories are empirically false. See Christensen and Turner, 1993, for papers on various aspects of these issues.)

The gambling metaphor is a special case of belief–value "folk" psychology that directs attention not to beliefs and values in themselves, but to the *degree* of belief and the *degree* of value. From this perspective, one's *reasons* for liking something or for thinking that an event is likely to happen, or more generally the *processes* by which one determines one's beliefs and values, are immaterial to the final choice among alternatives. Thus, the gambling metaphor is positioned at a level of analysis where the semantic content of the choice alternatives is irrelevant. It does not mandate the use of simple monetary gambles as stimuli, but it can be taken as theoretical justification.

It is important to note that the psychologists who drew inspiration from the work of von Neumann and Morgenstern (1947) and Savage (1954) didn't immediately, or unreflectively or exclusively, begin employing simple monetary gambles as stimuli. For example, Coombs and Beardslee (1954) reported an experiment in which the prizes in an imaginary lottery consisted of a rattan chair, an electric broiler, a typewriter, a radio, and a portable phonograph. Edwards commented in his well-known *Psychological Bulletin* paper (1954) that "Coombs is reluctant to use sums of money as the valuable objects in his experiments because of the danger that subjects will respond to the numerical value of the amount of dollars rather than to the psychological value. Therefore he used various desirable objects (e.g., a radio) as

stimuli, ..." Nevertheless, simple monetary gambles soon came to predominate.[1]

III. Content and Its Discontents

A. Nonsense Syllables and British Associationism

The prototypical example of the use of content-impoverished stimuli in
psychological research is provided by Ebbinghaus' (1964) study of memory.
Among the many important contributions for which he is remembered,
Ebbinghaus was the originator of stimulus materials known as "nonsense
syllables." Although the use of nonsense syllables has since lost its popularity, we think the use of nonsense syllables by memory researchers provides
an illuminating and provocative analogy to the use of simple monetary
gambles by decision researchers. This comparison is not meant to be dispar-
aging (to either party). On the contrary, we think this comparison helps to
illustrate why the use of content-impoverished stimuli can be so appealing.
For both nonsense syllables and monetary gambles, the choice of stimulus
materials was backed by theoretical frameworks that strongly suggested
that the generalizability of results would be enhanced, not limited, by the
use of these stimuli. In neither case were stimulus materials chosen lightly,
or merely for convenience. Moreover, their use enabled researchers to
make significant progress, discovering results and developing methods of
enduring importance. Nevertheless, in the case of memory research, as well
as in the other areas that we review later, the recurring finding is that
behavior is affected by the semantic content of the stimulus materials
employed. In these areas, the data force the conclusion that the exclusive
use of content-impoverished stimuli simply cannot support theory at the
level of generality implied by the metatheory. Similar data are beginning
to become available in work on preferential decision making.

Ebbinghaus (1964) described his reasons for employing content-impoverished materials as follows:

> The nonsense material, just described, offers many advantages, in part because of this
> very lack of meaning. First of all, it is relatively simple and relatively homogeneous. In
> the case of the material nearest at hand, namely poetry or prose, the content is now

---

[1] One of the present authors (W. M. G.) was a student of Coombs and recalls Coombs saying
that he gave up the use of nonmonetary objects because monetary amounts seemed not to present
the difficulty he had anticipated and because nonmonetary objects presented difficulties of their
own. As an example, Coombs described a subject who placed high value on a pair of binoculars
during football season, but low value on the binoculars after football season ended.

narrative in style, now descriptive, or now reflective; it contains now a phrase that is pathetic, now one that is humorous; its metaphors are sometimes beautiful, sometimes harsh; its rhythm is sometimes smooth and sometimes rough. There is thus brought into play a multiplicity of influences which change without regularity and are therefore disturbing. Such are associations which dart here and there, different degrees of interest, lines of verse recalled because of their striking quality or their beauty, and the like. All this is avoided with our syllables. (p. 23)

Ebbinghaus goes on to say that nonsense syllables can be used to generate an endless supply of new series that are comparable with each other, "while different poems, different prose pieces always have something incomparable" (p. 24). Also, series of nonsense syllables can be varied quantitatively, "whereas to break off before the end or to begin in the middle of the verse or the sentence leads to new complications because of various unavoidable disturbances of the meaning" (p. 24). Thus, Ebbinghaus used meaningless materials because they conferred certain practical advantages, and because their use reduced response variability caused by factors outside the main focus of his study.

It is good experimental practice to reduce error variance by careful selection of stimuli and by control of extraneous factors. However, this by itself is not enough to account for the popularity of nonsense syllables and gambles. In both cases, the stimulus materials were sanctioned by widely respected *theoretical frameworks* that (1) provided guidance about exactly which factors should be regarded as "extraneous" (e.g., meaningful content), and (2) provided a rationale for believing that the simplified stimuli retained exactly the structure required to get to the bottom of issues at the very foundation of psychology.

To understand this in the case of Ebbinghaus' meaningless materials and his experimental task of serial recall, one must consider a combination of the following beliefs: (1) empiricism (i.e., the assumption that all knowledge comes from experience), (2) sensationist atomism (i.e., the assumption that elementary sensations and memories of sensations form the indivisible "atoms" of experience which are combined to form "complex ideas" and which occur in sequences to form the "train of thought"), and (3) associationism (i.e., the assumption that ideas or sensations experienced in contiguity, at the same time or in quick succession, become "associated" and are thereby capable of eliciting one another in sequence or of coalescing into "complex ideas"). Given such a position, a study of the way that new materials without prior associations (e.g., nonsense syllables) come to be associated as a result of exposure to sequences (as in the serial recall task) is nothing less than a study of the ontogeny of mind. Titchener, who was perhaps the most outspoken and influential proponent of this theoretical position, considered "the recourse to nonsense syllables, as the means to the study of (conscious) association, . . . the most considerable advance in this chapter of psychology, since the time of Aristotle" (Titchener, 1909, pp. 380–381; quoted by Verhave & van Hoorn, 1987, p. 89). (To be fair, it should be noted that Ebbinghaus himself did not subscribe to any simple version of associationist theory; see Hoffman, Bamberg, Bringmann, & Klein, 1987; Verhave & van Hoorn, 1987. In fact, some of Ebbinghaus' own experiments demonstrated that a simple chaining of associations between adjacent items in a list could not account for the observed behavior. Moreover, Ebbinghaus *was* concerned with meaningful material as well as nonsense syllables; throughout his book, Ebbinghaus made comparisons between the learning of nonsense syllables and the learning of poetry.)

Simple gambles are as prevalent in decision research as nonsense syllables ever were in memory research (see Newman, 1987). In both cases, the content-impoverished stimuli, and the associated theoretical frameworks, have facilitated the discovery of many important phenomena and the development of many important methods. Our concern in this chapter, however, is with the limitations. Although neither early memory researchers nor current decision researchers have devoted all their efforts to the study of meaning-free materials, and although many insights have resulted from studies employing such materials, it is also true that the exclusive study of nonsense syllables would have prevented memory researchers from learning about such intrinsically content-based phenomena as: (1) the distinction between verbatim memory and memory for gist (Sachs, 1967), (2) distinctions among semantic, episodic, and procedural memory (Anderson, 1976; Tulving, 1972), (3) semantic priming effects (Meyer & Schvaneveldt, 1971), and (4) schema-based intrusions, deletions, and reorganizations (Bransford & Franks, 1971; Jenkins, 1974).

The point is not merely that the experimental practice of using content-impoverished stimuli would have failed to discover a number of interesting phenomena, but that the particular phenomena that would have been overlooked are those that *conflict* with the overarching theoretical framework. The demonstration that the *meaning* of material exerts a causal influence on psychological processing violates associationism. Fodor (1992) put it this way:

> . . . precisely because the mechanisms of mental causation were assumed to be associationistic (and the conditions for association to involve preeminently spatio-temporal propinquity), the [British] Empiricists had no good way of connecting the *contents* of a thought with the effects of entertaining it. They therefore never got close to a plausible theory of thinking, and neither did the associationistic psychology that followed in their footsteps. (p. 20, emphasis in original)

By analogy, our concern is not only that decision researchers may be overlooking a similarly rich set of phenomena, but that the gambling metaphor may be supporting an experimental practice that makes it impossible to detect its limitations. To be clear about this, we do not object to the use of gambles as stimuli per se, but we argue that the predominant use of these stimuli may impede the *theoretical* advance of recognizing the limited circumstances in which degree of belief and degree of value (rather than the beliefs and valued goals in themselves and the knowledge base in which they are embedded) suffice to account for behavior.

B. The General Climate in Psychology

In this section, we briefly review a number of areas of psychology in which initially content-independent accounts of behavior have been forced to change in the face of content-dependent effects. We believe these reviews are relevant for two reasons. First, we think decision researchers should draw from the substantive findings of researchers in related areas. Second, we think it is useful to see how researchers in neighboring fields have dealt with the often unwelcome prospect that behavior depends on the semantic content of the stimuli.

1. Learning

Contrary to Plato's doctrine of formal discipline, according to which study in abstract fields (e.g., arithmetic) provides general training for reasoning in all domains, early research on the transfer of learning (Thorndike & Woodworth, 1901) indicated remarkably little generality in the matter of *what* is learned. As a consequence, regularities in an organism's overt behavior were taken to depend on the historical accident of its specific experiences (i.e., its reinforcement history). No particular behavioral regularities could be expected on theoretical grounds to generalize across situations or organisms. Nevertheless, the matter of *how* learning takes place was considered to be entirely different. Behaviorists' refusal to distinguish among stimuli or responses on the basis of their content indicated a commitment to extremely general, abstract, content-independent laws of learning. However, the *how* of learning turned out to be not entirely independent of *what* was being learned, and the commitment to content-independent laws of learning could not be maintained. In a historical review of learning studies, Kimble (1985) chided himself for having failed to see this sooner. Commenting on his earlier opinion that "just about any activity of which the organism is capable can be conditioned, and these responses can be conditioned to any stimulus that the organism can perceive" (Kimble, 1956, p. 195), he remarked:

Kimble should have known better. As early as 1930, C. W. Valentine had reported being unable to repeat Watson's demonstration of fear conditioning in children, using a pair of opera glasses instead of a white rat as the conditioned stimulus. It was well-known laboratory lore that training a rat to press a bar or a pigeon to peck a key to turn off shock was next to impossible. More formal evidence along these lines was soon to accumulate to prove that the assumption of *equipotentiality* is wrong: animals are *prepared* to form certain associations and counterprepared to form others (Seligman & Hager, 1972). (Kimble, 1985, pp. 60–61, emphasis in original.)

Results indicating violations of equipotentiality (e.g., Garcia & Koelling, 1966) were slow to win acceptance (Lubek & Apfelbaum, 1987). However, behaviorists did eventually take steps toward content dependence in the laws of learning.

2. Categories and Concepts

Categories were classically conceived to be collections of entities that satisfy individually necessary and collectively sufficient conditions of membership (e.g., an "even" number is an integer that is divisible by 2 with no remainder). However, the discovery that natural categories have graded structure, that some members are considered "better" or more "typical" members than others, contradicted the classical conception, at least as a psychological model of category representation (Rosch & Mervis, 1975; Smith, Shoben, & Rips, 1974; people even discriminate among different examples of even numbers, see Armstrong, Gleitman, & Gleitman, 1983). In subsequent research conducted to account for typicality and related effects, debate has arisen as to whether categories are represented abstractly (e.g., by prototypes; Posner & Keele, 1968) or by storage of specific categorized instances (Brooks, 1978; Medin & Schaffer, 1978). Although it can be difficult to distinguish between prototype and exemplar models (Barsalou, 1990), the weight of evidence seems to favor the specific over the abstract (see Medin & Ross, 1989, for a review).

Exemplar models are specific in that they posit that categories are represented by memory traces of the particular instances encountered, and therefore they posit that regularities in people's categorization *behavior* depend on the historical accident of their specific experiences (i.e., history of encounters with exemplars). Nevertheless, they portray the matter of *how* categorization takes place as being entirely different, proceeding according to general, abstract, content-independent laws. However, a recent program of research on the coherence of people's categories appears to be forcing a modification of this view (Medin & Ortony, 1989; Murphy & Medin, 1985; Wattenmaker, Dewey, Murphy, & Medin, 1986; Wattenmaker, Nakamura, & Medin, 1988). These investigators found that the "structure" of encountered exemplars (i.e., the pattern of presences and absences among abstractly coded features of the exemplars) is insufficient to account for category learning. Rather, the identity of the features according to the cover story—and the activated knowledge structure—is crucial to the behavior. For example, Wattenmaker et al. (1986) found that they could facilitate the learning of linearly separable categories, or the learning of nonlinearly separable categories, depending on the knowledge structures they made salient. Wattenmaker et al. (1988) observed that "it is not the case that ease of learning can be specified in terms of the configuration of independent features inherent in the category structure" (p. 220). Rather, these investigators emphasize a knowledge-based approach to conceptual coherence and an explanation-based approach to categorization. In other words: (knowledge about) content matters.

3. Deductive Reasoning

Some of the earliest and most sustained interest in the role of semantic content has been shown by researchers who study deductive reasoning. One line of research concerns the effects of stimulus material that arouses people's emotions or prejudices (Janis & Frick, 1943; Kaufmann & Goldstein, 1967; Lefford, 1946). This research might be seen as a precursor to recent work on "motivated" cognition (Kunda, 1990; Larrick, 1993). A second line of research, stretching back nearly 70 years (Wilkins, 1928), compares the effect of material that is (1) abstract and symbolic, versus (2) concrete but unfamiliar, versus (3) concrete and familiar. A still energetic wave of research on this topic was begun some 23 years ago by Wason and Shapiro (1971) and by Johnson-Laird, Legrenzi, and Legrenzi (1972). These studies investigated Wason's (1966) well-known "four-card problem." Subjects are shown a deck of cards, each of which says on one side either "p" or "not p," and on the other side says either "q" or "not q." Four cards are dealt on the table so that the sides facing the subject read "p," "not p," "q," and "not q." Subjects are then asked to indicate exactly those cards that must be turned over in order to test whether the rule "if p then q" is satisfied by the deck. When the problem is given to people in the abstract form just described, they do spectacularly badly at it. However, the studies by Wason and Shapiro (1971) and by Johnson-Laird et al. (1972) showed that when the task is fleshed out with understandable content, there is remarkable improvement. Wason and Johnson-Laird (1972) commented that "Taken together, these two experiments force on us a radical reconsideration of the role of content in reasoning. The nature of the material would seem to be decisive in terms of whether the subjects exercise rational thought" (p. 193).

A great deal of research on the four-card problem ensued, and it was found that concrete stimulus materials did not always produce marked improvement in performance (e.g., Manktelow & Evans, 1979). This led to the proposal (Griggs & Cox, 1982) that it is not the concreteness of the material per se that improves performance, but sufficient *familiarity* with the domain to allow the recall of specific instances that could falsify the rule. Once more, people's behavior was described as depending on the historical accident of their specific experiences. Thus, *behavior* could be content-dependent while relying on general, abstract, content-independent *mechanisms* of memory storage and retrieval. This version of content independence was, however, also challenged. In papers that provided the source for much of our own interest in content effects, Cheng and Holyoak (1985; Cheng, Holyoak, Nisbett, & Oliver, 1986) argued that "people often reason using neither syntactic, context-free rules of inference, nor memory of specific experiences. Rather, they reason using abstract knowledge structures induced from ordinary life experiences, such as 'permissions,' 'obligations,' and 'causations'" (Cheng & Holyoak, 1985, p. 395). Cheng and Holyoak argued that people reason according to *pragmatic reasoning schemas* that stand at an intermediate level of abstraction and relate to people's goals.

In one striking example that shows that improvement on the four-card problem relies on the cuing of an appropriate *schema* which is neither purely syntactic nor bound to any particular domain-specific content, Cheng and Holyoak (1985, Experiment 2) asked subjects to imagine themselves as authorities checking to see whether people were obeying regulations of the form, "If one is to take action A, then one must first satisfy precondition P." In contrast with only 19% who correctly verified an arbitrary rule ("If a card has an *A* on one side, then it must have a 4 on the other side."), 61% of the subjects correctly verified the regulation. Although there is debate about the origin and identity of the reasoning schemas that people use (Cheng & Holyoak, 1989; Cosmides, 1989; Gigerenzer, in press; Gigerenzer & Hug, 1992), there seems to be consensus about the appropriateness of an intermediate level of abstraction.

4. Problem Solving and Expertise

In the 1960s and early 1970s, work on problem solving and expertise focused on general heuristics (e.g., means–ends analysis) by which a person could limit search through an abstract problem space (Newell, Shaw, & Simon, 1958; Newell & Simon, 1972). Soon thereafter, it became apparent that expertise was not driven by superior general-purpose search heuristics so much as by domain-specific knowledge that could enhance memory and promote specialized inference patterns within the domain (Anderson, 1987; Chase & Simon, 1973a, 1973b; Chi, Feltovich, & Glaser, 1981; Larkin,

McDermott, Simon, & Simon, 1980; however, see Holyoak, 1991, for an argument that superior domain knowledge does not explain all phenomena of expertise).

One particular line of research that directly addresses the role of content in the acquisition of expertise is concerned with the way that people access and use previously learned (base) problems in constructing analogies to help solve new (target) problems (for reviews, see Medin & Ross, 1989; Reeves & Weisberg, 1994). The evidence indicates that spontaneous transfer from base problems is affected by similarities and differences in both the overall content domains of the cover stories (Gick & Holyoak, 1980; B. H. Ross, 1984) as well as by the content of particular objects appearing in important relationships in the problems (Bassok, 1990; Holyoak & Koh, 1987). When people are told that the base problem is relevant to the target problem, so that the use and not the access of the base problem is the issue, people are affected by content in a way that appears to indicate a conflict between mapping structurally analogous objects from base to target, on the one hand, and mapping superficially similar objects to corresponding relational roles in the two problems, on the other hand (Bassok, 1990; Gentner & Toupin, 1986; B. H. Ross, 1987, 1989). Of course, if people *knew* which features of the base problem reflected structural (i.e., solution-relevant) properties and which reflected merely superficial content, they would map only the structural features. The apparent conflict is thought to result from the attempt to map as many features as possible, in the absence of knowledge about what really is and is not relevant.

This theoretical approach to content effects in analogical problem solving may or may not be yet another example in which content-dependent behavior is thought to depend on content-independent mechanisms. If the processes of feature matching are hypothesized to be domain-general, then this issue hinges on whether the primitive "features" themselves are thought to originate in ways that are independent of the content of the base and target problems. This matter is usually considered to be outside the scope of the theories, and in practice, the experiments are generally conducted under the assumption that the features are known. However, recent research by Bassok, Wu, and Olseth (1995) addresses this issue directly. Bassok et al. (1995) argue that naive subjects, who do not have the experimenter's understanding of the problem structure, use the content of the base problem together with its worked-out solution to abstract an *interpreted* structure which may or may not match the objective structure that the experimenter has in mind. Then subjects try to map from the base to the target problem on the basis of the features that are structural, given *their* interpretations.

To test their theory, Bassok et al. (1995, Experiment 2) first trained subjects on a base problem in which the manager of a country club assigned caddies at random to golfers and subjects had to compute the probability that the three most experienced caddies would be assigned to the three newest members, respectively. The correct answer depends on the total size of the "assigned" set (caddies) and not on the total size of the "receiving" set (golfers). Bassok et al. then tested subjects on target problems in which either carts were assigned to caddies (and so the correct answer depends on the number of carts) or caddies were assigned to carts (the correct answer depends on the number of caddies). If subjects transfer by mapping similar objects to similar roles, they should perform better on the caddies-assigned-to-carts problem because mapping caddies to caddies would give the correct answer. However, Bassok et al. predicted the reverse. They reasoned that the asymmetry in status between golfers and caddies would induce subjects to interpret the base problem in terms of a "get" relation rather than an "assign" relation: no matter who assigns what to whom, golfers "get" caddies and not the other way around. Likewise, for the target problems, caddies "get" carts (i.e., people "get" objects). Therefore, subjects should do better on the carts-assigned-to-caddies problem, because the "get" relation directs subjects to the number of to-be-gotten objects, carts, in this case the correct answer. In fact, 94% of the subjects answered correctly on the carts-assigned-to-caddies problem, and only 24% answered correctly on the caddies-assigned-to-carts problem. The results strongly support Bassok et al.'s argument that subjects map *what they interpret to be* structural features and that their interpretations are influenced by the *content* of the base problems.

5. Cognitive Development

Finally, we will briefly mention one more area of psychology in which content has come to be considered an important determinant of behavior. Because children begin as novices at virtually everything and become relative experts as they grow up, the literature on cognitive development has come to overlap that on the acquisition of expertise. In fact, the cognitive development literature shows a similar shift in emphasis from domain-general hypotheses (e.g., Piagetian stages of development, maturational increases in speed and capacity of the central processor) to an emphasis on the acquisition of knowledge. For example, Chi (1978) compared 10-year-olds and adults on two memory tasks: a digit-span task and a chess memory task of the sort studied by Chase and Simon (1973a, 1973b). The adults were superior to the children on the digit-span task, replicating a well-known result. However, the results of the chess task contradicted the hypothesis of a domain-general difference in memory capacity. The children, all experienced chess players, remembered the positions of more chess pieces than the adults, all of whom were chess novices. (See Chi & Ceci, 1987, for a review of the role of content knowledge in memory development.) More generally, as remarked by Carey (1990):

> It now seems unlikely that the grand simplifying description of universal developmental stages that Piaget proposed is correct—especially if the stages are interpreted as reflecting domain-general changes in the representational or computational capacity of the information processor. It seems that cognitive development is mainly the result of acquiring knowledge in particular content domains. (pp. 161–162)

(See also Hirschfeld & Gelman, 1994; Wellman & Gelman, 1992.)

6. Summary and Interpretation

It seems to us that a great deal of the reviewed research can be summarized in broad strokes as exhibiting one or more of four reactions to the prospect of content dependence, which can be arranged more or less in the following sequence. First, various areas of psychology initially sought to describe behavior at a level of analysis abstract enough to achieve generalizability across people, stimuli, conditions, and, in particular, semantic content (e.g., organisms strive to maximize reinforcement). However, because overt behavior and psychological mechanisms need not be analyzed at the same level of abstraction, it was a short step to the second stage. Specifically, by describing behavior in somewhat more concrete terms, researchers acknowledged that overt behavior depends on the individual, the stimuli, the conditions, and so on, while maintaining that this nongeneralizability of behavior was consistent with general, abstract, content-independent psychological mechanisms. Thus, differences in behavior were attributed to idiosyncratic factors of no particular interest to psychological theory (e.g., reinforcement histories, past encounters with exemplars, idiosyncratic utility functions, etc.). Third, particular psychological mechanisms of theoretical interest were deemed to be affected by content (e.g., encoding of stimulus information, retrieval of information, manipulation of encoded stimulus and/or retrieved information), but not the mechanisms considered to be of core interest (e.g., one could maintain that people employ content-independent rules of deductive inference, but that they systematically misinterpret the premises; see Henle, 1962.) Fourth, content effects were acknowledged as potential influences on core mechanisms, and research was undertaken to determine the mechanisms affected and to identify functionally distinct domains of content.

A succinct, if somewhat crude rendition of this sequence takes the following form: (1) behavior is thought to be content-independent, (2) behavior is acknowledged to be content-dependent for "uninteresting" reasons that can safely be ignored, (3) behavior is thought to be content-dependent for reasons that are somewhat interesting but not central to core theory, and (4) content-dependent phenomena are seen to have important implications for theory that cannot be ignored.[2] In the next section, we will see that research on preferential decision making can be characterized as mostly falling in the second or third stage of this sequence, but that there are some indications that it may be moving into the fourth stage.

IV.   Content Effects in Research on Preferential Judgment and Choice

Although simple monetary gambles have been the predominant stimulus material for studies in preferential decision research, the use of gambles has not been completely exclusive, and there is some research that is relevant to the issue of content effects. However, with the exception of a few studies to be discussed later, the issue of content has arisen only indirectly in (1) studies of phenomena that are attributed broadly to the way people encode decision inputs, and (2) studies of the way people deal with missing or degraded information.

A.   FRAMING EFFECTS

A number of phenomena attributed to encoding are sometimes referred to collectively as "framing" effects (Tversky & Kahneman, 1981). Studies of framing address the influence of people's perspectives, that is, whether, so to speak, it makes a difference to look at the glass as half empty or half full. To manipulate people's perspectives, the studies all involve manipulation of decision inputs apart from net final outcomes and probabilities, and can be viewed as manipulating (aspects of) content. However, as far as we are aware, only a few studies (Schneider, 1992; Wagenaar, Keren, & Lichtenstein, 1988; discussed later) have been concerned with semantic content as such. Probably the most studied issue concerns the coding of outcomes as losses or gains relative to different reference points or aspiration levels (e.g., Kahneman & Tversky, 1979; Levin & Gaeth, 1988; McNeil, Pauker, Sox, & Tversky, 1982; Payne, Laughhunn, & Crum, 1980; Schneider, 1992; see also Lopes, 1987). Related phenomena include sunk-cost effects

---

[2] It has been said that there is a typical sequence of reactions to most new ideas. First, it's not true. Later, it's true but unimportant. Finally, it's true and important but it's old news. (This joke may contain an important truth, but it's an old joke.)

(i.e., failure to restrict focus to future incremental outcomes without regard for unrecoverable costs already invested in particular alternatives; Arkes & Blumer, 1985; Staw, 1976), status quo effects (i.e., privileged standing accorded to whichever choice alternative represents the status quo or default alternative; Samuelson & Zeckhauser, 1988), endowment effects (i.e., greater value placed on an object that is "owned" rather than on an identical object that is not owned; Kahneman, Knetsch, & Thaler, 1990; Thaler, 1980), and loss aversion (subjective pleasure of gaining an object exceeded by the subjective pain of losing the same object; Tversky & Kahneman, 1991) (see Kahneman, Knetsch, & Thaler, 1991, for a review of the last three effects). A set of issues known collectively as *mental accounting* concerns people's preferences for and the effects of combining versus separating events (Linville & Fischer, 1991; Thaler, 1985; Thaler & Johnson, 1990) and decisions (Luce, in press; Redelmeier & Tversky, 1992). An additional issue that relates to the way people encode decision inputs concerns problem formats that make the applicability of a decision principle transparent versus opaque (Tversky & Kahneman, 1986).

Each of the above "perspectival" effects is well established, but contains little or no reference to content *domain,* that is, what the decision is "about." Possibly, content domain exerts an influence via perspectival effects by inducing people to look at things in a particular way (cf. Bassok et al., 1995, discussed earlier). None of the preceding studies systematically examined content domain in this way. The following effect, however, suggests that there may be some validity to this hypothesis: in choosing between a sure loss and the risk of incurring a larger loss, people are affected by whether the problem is described as a gambling decision or an insurance decision (Hershey, Kunreuther, & Schoemaker, 1982; Hershey & Schoemaker, 1980; Schoemaker & Kunreuther, 1979; Slovic, Fischhoff, Lichtenstein, Corrigan, & Combs, 1977). This effect is well known, but it seems to have been interpreted as demonstrating the general importance of framing, rather than as indicating a need to study the influence of content domain on preferential decision making.

B. MISSING OR DEGRADED INFORMATION

A good deal of research has been conducted on decision behavior in the face of incomplete or degraded information (e.g., Fischhoff, Slovic, & Lichtenstein, 1978; Slovic & MacPhillamy, 1974; Yates, Jagacinski, & Faber, 1978). One branch of this research examines whether, when, and how people draw inferences about the missing or degraded items of information (Davidson, Yantis, Norwood, & Montano, 1985; Einhorn & Hogarth, 1985; Ford & Smith, 1987; Huber & McCann, 1982; Jaccard & Wood, 1988;

Johnson & Levin, 1985; Levin, Chapman, & Johnson, 1988; Simmons & Lynch, 1991; Yamagishi & Hill, 1983). Also relevant is research on the construal of information (Griffin, Dunning, & Ross, 1990; L. Ross, 1987, 1989; L. Ross & Nisbett, 1991). Although most of this research has not directly addressed the content domain of the decision problem, inferences about missing or degraded information presumably rely on knowledge about the domain. Recent research by Sanbonmatsu, Kardes, and Herr (1992; see also Kardes & Sanbonmatsu, 1993) has shown that domain experts and novices respond differently to missing information. Experts are likelier to notice that information is missing and to infer likely values for the missing items.

In sum, although the research on perspectival effects and the processing of incomplete information is voluminous, and although these topics lend themselves to the study of content effects, scholars of preferential judgment and choice have given relatively little attention to content domain as such. Perspectives taken and inferences drawn are occasionally discussed as depending on the *amount* of knowledge or *aspects* of content, but even then it is rare to connect these aspects of knowledge to what the decision is about. Our impression is that decision researchers view these streams of research as efforts to flesh out rather than test the gambling metaphor; these studies are thought to indicate how people go about arriving at their degrees of belief and degrees of value, but they do not challenge the sufficiency of these variables to account for behavior. In this sense, we think these studies represent what we refer to as a "stage 3" reaction to content effects: interesting, but not of central importance to core theory (or metatheory). Of course, challenges to a content-independent metatheory cannot be discovered if researchers rely only on content-impoverished stimuli or stimuli from a single domain. Although the results of gambling studies may well replicate in other settings, and indeed often have, we think there is reason to be cautious about the generalizability of gambling studies, and therefore reason to be dubious of the gambling metaphor.

C.   CHALLENGES TO THE GENERALIZABILITY OF GAMBLING BEHAVIOR

Wagenaar et al. (1988) presented subjects with a variety of cover stories, all of which had the same deep structure, namely, versions of Tversky and Kahneman's (1981) well-known Asian disease problem. Manipulating such aspects as the identity of the potential victims (e.g., islanders subject to a disease vs. children held hostage by terrorists) and the role of the subject as decision maker (e.g., islander vs. public health officer for the islander version; parent vs. authority for the hostage version) had a profound effect on the choices of subjects who were all considering the "same" problem. In a sense, as Wagenaar et al. (1988) suggest, this result is a matter of framing (Tversky & Kahneman, 1981). In any case, generalizability across content domains is problematic, even when attempts have been made to hold constant the deep structure of the stimuli. Schneider (1992) obtained similar results, in that the magnitude of framing effects varied widely across scenarios that differed "only" in content (see also Frisch, 1993).

Heath and Tversky (1991) studied subjects' choices among gambles with identical potential outcomes, but whose payoffs were contingent on different sorts of events: a random event with stated probability, having one's answer to a general-knowledge question turn out to be correct, or giving a correct prediction for a football game or political election. Heath and Tversky (1991) found that subjects' choices were determined not solely by the perceived likelihood of the event yielding the favorable outcome and the precision with which this likelihood could be estimated, but also by the subject's self-perceived knowledge and "competence" in the domain of events. In one experiment, subjects predicted the results of various football games and the results of the (then future) 1988 presidential election in various states. Later, subjects rank ordered their preferences among gambles that were matched to have the same probability of winning on the basis of: (1) a chance device, (2) the subject's own prediction in his or her strong domain (politics or football), and (3) the subject's own prediction in his or her weak domain. Only when the probability of winning was 100% did subjects prefer to bet on the chance device. Otherwise, independent of the numerical probability of winning, subjects preferred to bet on their strong domain, the chance device, and their weak domain, in that order. In a sense, subjects were indicating that they had definite preferences among "identical" gambles; probabilities and outcomes did not capture all the relevant factors: domain still mattered.

Hogarth and Kunreuther (1995) asked subjects to assess the probability that they would buy 1-year maintenance contracts for various consumer durables (personal computer, stereo, VCR, CD player). Subjects were given the price of the product, the price of the maintenance contract, and a description of the manufacturer implying either high or low product reliability. After judging their purchase intentions for all four products, subjects considered each product again, this time judging their subjective probabilities and the likely costs of breakdowns should they occur. In a second session, subjects again rated their intentions to buy maintenance contracts for the same products, but this time subjects were given additional information about the probabilities and costs of breakdowns, specifically the same values that the subjects themselves previously had said were most likely. The result was that self-rated probability of purchase was reduced by the explicit information by approximately the same amount as increasing the price of the maintenance contract from 5 to 10% of the product price. Again, probabilities and outcomes did not capture all the relevant factors; subjects responded differently to "identical" gambles.

In addition to these results, indicating that subjects' purchase intentions did not generalize as one might have expected, Hogarth and Kunreuther (1995) also provided evidence that the decision *processes* did not generalize. At particular points in the experiment, they asked their subjects (1) to give free-form explanations of the reasons and arguments they had considered in judging their purchase intentions, and (2) to evaluate how much weight they had given to specific arguments listed by the experimenters. Hogarth and Kunreuther (1995) found that the kinds of arguments subjects reported depended on the information that was explicitly displayed in the problem description. Among other differences, the ratio of single-attribute arguments to multiple-attribute arguments was much smaller when probabilities and repair costs were explicitly displayed (in the neighborhood of 1.5) than when probabilities and repair costs were not explicitly displayed (approximately 3). Also, there was a subset of subjects whose arguments, independent of the display conditions, were insensitive to the attributes of the maintenance contracts or products (e.g., "I never buy these types of warranties."). Although subjects using these "meta" strategies, as Hogarth and Kunreuther called them, did not vary their strategies across display conditions, we speculate that subjects might vary their use of attribute-insensitive strategies across content domains.

In sum, despite numerous other areas of psychology in which content domain has been found to affect behavior, despite the evidence that neither behavior *nor* underlying processes may generalize from studies of gambling to other decisions, and with only a nod in the direction of "amount" of knowledge and "aspects" of content, decision researchers have continued to rely almost exclusively on simple monetary gambles or highly schematic stimuli that are just barely fleshed out with content, and to rely on the gambling metaphor as justification for this practice. It may not *always* be incorrect to think that decisions are mediated (only) by degree of belief and degree of desirability, but we think the evidence contradicts the universality to which the gambling metaphor aspires. Indeed, the gambling metaphor has proved inadequate even when applied to games of chance (Heath & Tversky, 1991).

D. INFLUENCE OF CONTENT DOMAIN ON JUDGMENT AND
    DECISION MAKING

In this section, we briefly summarize selected results from two experiments that we conducted for three purposes: (1) to gather additional evidence that semantic content influences the psychological processes underlying preferential judgment and choice, (2) to test some hypotheses about the way that processing is affected by content, and (3) to begin an exploration of the distinguishing characteristics of content domains that elicit different modes of processing. The experiments will be reported more fully elsewhere (Goldstein & Weber, in preparation).

In Experiment 1, we examined whether people would be differentially sensitive to an experimental manipulation when making evaluative judgments of stimuli from different content domains. We decided to contrast judgments about social relationships with judgments about inanimate objects (e.g., consumer items) in order to explore a broad distinction between the evaluation of people and things. Specifically, the two domains were (1) people with whom one might pursue a long-term romantic relationship potentially leading to marriage, and (2) compact disk (CD) players. We expected that people would evaluate CD players by weighing the advantages and disadvantages of the models. By contrast, for potential spouses, the work of Pennington and Hastie (1988, 1992, 1993; discussed later) suggested to us that people might try to construct stories or story fragments about what life might be like if they were to pursue the relationship.

It should be emphasized that we hypothesized the semantic content of the domain to affect only people's *preferred* mode of processing. We do not suppose that people are incapable of implementing unpreferred modes of processing. Certainly, people *could* evaluate potential spouses by enumerating and weighing their separate features, but doing so seems depersonalizing and inappropriate. Also, people *could* evaluate CD players by trying to imagine how life would unfold if the CD player were obtained, but this seems unlikely. The thrust of our hypothesis was that people have preferences for the type of decision strategy to be used, and that these preferences are affected by the semantic content of the decision domain. We hypothesized that people would tend to use the mode of processing they preferred in the content domain, unless we made it difficult for them to do so by our experimental manipulation, which is exactly what we tried to do.

A crucial difference between constructing a story and tallying up advantages and disadvantages is that story construction requires that one possess an overarching knowledge structure or schema (i.e., knowledge of what constitutes a coherent story; see Schank & Abelson, 1977; Stein & Glenn, 1979; Trabasso & van den Broek, 1985), which is used to draw inferences and to organize the information into a unified whole. That is, for people to construct a story, they must augment the presented information by filling in gaps and going "beyond the information given," to use Bruner's (1957) famous phrase. We expected people's inferences to be both semantically and evaluatively consistent with the information that was presented, thereby *accentuating* the attractiveness or unattractiveness of the stimuli relative to the evaluation produced by weighing (only) the presented information (without augmenting inferences). With this in mind, two stimuli in each content domain (marriage partners and CD players) were designed to be relatively attractive overall, and two were relatively unattractive.

Each stimulus was described by a set of "schema items," intended to promote the inference of interitem relations and the construction of an integrated representation, and a set of "nonschema items" that were more akin to isolated features. For the potential spouses, the nonschema items consisted of a list of personality traits. The schema items consisted of sentences describing how the decision maker had met the person, how the relationship had developed so far, and how things had been left. (To make it more plausible that the subject might be deciding which of several relationships to pursue, each relationship was described as having ended relatively amicably and on a somewhat ambiguous note.) For each potential spouse, we targeted a recognizable (stereotypical) story. The targeted stories could be labeled: (1) childhood sweetheart, (2) college friend turned lover, (3) intense and stormy romance, and (4) stagnant relationship.

To make the CD players a more comparable domain, we tried to design these stimuli with a structure parallel to that of the potential spouses. However, in a sense, the very difficulty of doing this helps to make our larger point: people are not inclined to use the same processes in evaluating CD players and potential spouses. People are capable of constructing a story of what life would be like with a CD player, but it seems unlikely that they would do so. More plausible, and still requiring the use of an overarching knowledge structure to draw inferences and organize the information, is that people would construct and decide on the basis of an image associated with a CD player (as in, "We don't sell a product, we sell an image") and/or a story of the act of purchasing the item. As with the potential spouses, we targeted a recognizable (stereotypical) image for each stimulus. The targeted images could be labeled: (1) Rolls Royce of CD players, (2) good-value-for-money model, (3) basic no-frills model, and (4) low-quality-but-cheap model. For each CD player, the schema items described the reputation/prestige of the brand, the reputation/prestige of the store and service, the reliability and standards of an acquaintance recommending the model, and the convenience of the store location. The nonschema items related the CD player's price, its capacity to hold multiple CDs, the manufacturer's warranty and availability of an extended warranty from the store, and the availability and features of a remote control.

Taking our cue from manipulations used by Pennington and Hastie (1988, 1992), we manipulated the order in which subjects received the items of information describing each stimulus. Specifically, we varied whether the schema items or the nonschema items were presented early in the description of each stimulus. The rationale for this manipulation is that people with foreknowledge of the task are likely to process the information on-line as they encounter each item of information (Hastie & Park, 1986). Presenting nonschema items early (personality traits for the potential spouses and product features for the CD players) encourages people to begin with an attribute-weighing decision strategy and may make it difficult for them to switch in midstream to a schema-based decision strategy when they later encounter the schema items, even if they are so inclined. Pennington and Hastie (1988, 1992) found analogous effects by presenting items in the sequence versus out of the sequence that would be required by a narrative.

As predicted, we found a three-way interaction between content domain, order of information, and attractiveness of stimuli. The differences in ratings given to attractive versus unattractive potential spouses were responsive to the order manipulation. When schema items were presented early, making it easy to implement the preferred (schema-based) mode of processing, we obtained a relatively large difference between attractive and unattractive spouses (4.91 rating points on a scale from −10 to +10). When the schema items were presented late, making it difficult to implement the preferred mode of processing, we obtained a relatively small difference between attractive and unattractive spouses (2.61 rating points). This difference between differences is as expected, because people using schemas (i.e., stories, images) to draw inferences beyond the information presented were predicted to accentuate the differences between attractive and unattractive stimuli. By contrast, the differences between ratings given to attractive and unattractive CD players were unresponsive to the order manipulation, presumably because subjects were *not* inclined to use schema-based (i.e., image) processing even when it was easy (mean differences of 3.21 and 4.02 rating points for schema items presented early and late, respectively). This pattern supports our hypothesis that people are inclined to employ schema-based processing when thinking about potential spouses, provided that conditions make it easy to do so (schema items early), but not when it is hard (schema items late). By contrast, when thinking about CD players, people seem predisposed to employ an attribute-weighing strategy of evaluation, irrespective of the order manipulation.

Experiment 2 was designed to compare the effect of content domain with another factor, apart from content per se, which might drive a shift in decision strategy. To state the obvious, choosing a spouse is more important than choosing a CD player. Payne, Bettman, and Johnson's (1993) theory of meta-decision making predicts that important decisions induce people to use decision strategies that are more effortful and more likely to reach the correct conclusion. Experiment 2 was designed in part to separate the effects of decision importance and content domain to see whether we could obtain evidence of a strategy shift that would be more clearly related to content per se.

In addition, we tried to push our notions about content domain and preferred decision strategy a bit further. In Experiment 1, we tested the hypothesis that decisions about social relationships tend to elicit a version of Pennington and Hastie's (1988, 1992, 1993) story model, in which people tell themselves story fragments about what life would be like if they were to pursue a course of action. Narratives describe events, actions, and reactions as they unfold over *time*. The basic temporality of narratives suggested to us that people might construct story fragments for a wider class of issues than social relationships. In some decisions, it is a salient fact that the chosen course of action will require monitoring and tending, unforeseeable subsidiary decisions and adjustments, all of which will evolve over time and be experienced as an ongoing stream of events and actions. For example, choosing a profession, weighing a permanent job offer, considering whether to have a child, all involve actions that will produce a flow of consequences to be experienced and managed over a lengthy period of time. In a sense, these are decisions about whether to embark on a "journey" or to undertake an "endeavor." For lack of a better label, we will refer to these as decisions about "endeavors," stressing the activity and ongoing experience that will follow after having made a choice, in contrast to decisions about "objects." We hypothesized that decisions about endeavors would tend to elicit the construction of story fragments. In contrast, for decisions about objects whose consequences do not require monitoring and tending, we predicted people to use schemas other than narratives, if they used schema-based processing at all, or to use a strategy in which attributes are weighed against each other directly, that is, without drawing inferences to construct an integrated, mediating representation of the alternative.

To test these ideas, we asked people their opinions about the strategies they thought they would use for various decision problems, and the strategies they thought typical, appropriate, and inappropriate. Despite concerns that people may not be in a position to report accurately on the decision strategies they would (or did) use (Ericsson & Simon, 1980; Nisbett & Wilson, 1977), inferring people's strategies from their decision patterns (as in Experiment 1) involves its own set of assumptions, and we thought we should seek converging evidence from a procedure with different assumptions. We constructed four decision problems in a 2 × 2 design. Two problems concerned matters that we thought undergraduates would construe as decisions about "endeavors" (roommates and jobs) and two concerned matters that we thought they would construe as decisions about "objects" (stereo systems and houses). Within each domain, one decision was more important than the other (jobs are more important than roommates, and houses are more important than stereo systems). This design let us examine the importance of the decision and the domain of the decision independently.

Each respondent was asked to consider all four decision problems, which were about: (1) a prospective roommate, (2) a postgraduation job offer, (3) the purchase of a house, and (4) the purchase of a stereo system. In each case, a short paragraph fleshed out a scenario to give some context to the decision problem. For example, in the roommate problem, respondents were asked to imagine that they were single, unattached, and continuing next year at the University of Chicago. After mentioning to a same-sex acquaintance, a fellow student, that an apartment would be needed, the acquaintance suggests looking for an apartment to share. The decision was whether or not to accept the suggestion.

After reading the description of a decision problem, people were shown descriptions of six decision "methods." (We avoided the word *strategy,* unsure of the connotations this word might have for undergraduates.) For each decision problem, people were asked to make four judgments about the listed decision methods. Specifically, they were asked to indicate the single decision method that best described: (1) the method they would use, (2) the most typical decision method for that problem, (3) the most appropriate method, and (4) the most inappropriate method. Although decision methods were described procedurally and not labeled for respondents, the six methods might be labeled: (1) follow gut feeling, (2) seek and follow advice, (3) social comparison, (4) feature-focused processing, (5) similarity to ideal, and (6) story-based processing. For our present purposes, we will concentrate on whether people said that they would use feature-focused processing ("Try to think it through 'rationally.' . . . See if the favorable points are more numerous and/or more important than the unfavorable points.") or story-based processing ("Try to think about what life would be like . . . . Picture how your life would unfold, and construct a story about the way things would go.").

The average respondent reported that he or she would use 2.3 distinct strategies across the four problems. Evidently, people believe that they would engage in considerable strategy shifting. For each decision problem, people most frequently said they would use the feature-focused strategy, with story-based processing running a not-too-distant second for the decisions involving endeavors (roommate and job decisions). Consistent with our hypothesis about domain-dependent processing, significantly more respondents said they would use story-based processing for at least one endeavor decision (roommate and job) than said they would use it for at least one object decision (stereo and house; 17/38 vs. 7/38 respondents; $p =$ .021 by binomial test for equality of correlated proportions). The popularity of the feature-focused strategy, however, was not so sensitive to the domain. The proportion of respondents saying they would use feature-focused processing for at least one endeavor decision (25/38) did not differ significantly from the proportion saying they would use this strategy for at least one object decision (28/38). Evidently, the greater popularity of the story-based strategy for the endeavors than for the objects comes at the expense of strategies other than feature-focused processing (see Goldstein & Weber, in preparation).

In contrast to the domain of the decision, the importance of the decision seemed to have little impact. Although there was a slightly greater tendency for the story-based approach to be used in the *more* important decision of each domain (job vs. roommate and house vs. stereo), the proportion of respondents saying they would use story-based processing for at least one relatively important decision (16/38) did not differ significantly from the proportion saying they would use it for at least one relatively unimportant decision (11/38). Neither did the proportion saying they would use the feature-focused strategy for at least one relatively important decision (30/38) differ from the proportion saying they would use it for at least one relatively unimportant decision (26/38). Thus, the content of these decisions seems to exert a greater influence on the decision strategy that people say they would use than does the importance of the decision.

In sum, Experiment 2 provides additional evidence that decision strategies are influenced by the content domain of the decision problem. Although story-based processing was never the most frequently selected strategy, people believed themselves more likely to use it for decisions involving endeavors rather than objects. The importance of the decision problem did not affect the strategies people thought themselves likely to use. (Both content domain and decision importance marginally affected the strategies that people thought were typical; see Goldstein & Weber, in preparation.)

V. Toward an Outline of a Theory of Domain-Specific Decision Making

A. Level of Analysis

The gambling metaphor represents an austere parsimony with its insistence that any decision whatsoever, in any content domain, can be explained with reference to only two relevant variables: degree of belief and degree of value. We have argued, however, that the evidence accumulated in neighboring fields of study, and in a number of studies specifically on judgment and decision making, demonstrates that psychological processing and overt responses are often sensitive to the semantic content of the stimuli used in the tasks. Therefore, we think that the gambling metaphor must be rejected as a general theory.

In defense, one might object that the issue is one of the level of analysis, and that choosing a level of analysis is to some extent a matter of strategy and of taste. It is legitimate to decide, for the sake of parsimony, to look first for highly general, content-independent results, and to put off until later the pursuit of more specialized content-specific phenomena. It is also legitimate to decide that one's scientific interests as a decision researcher focus on matters that transcend the semantic content of the choice alternatives and generalize across content domains.

Although we acknowledge the cogency of this objection as an argument in support of research at a content-independent level of analysis, we do not think it works as a defense of the gambling metaphor. The gambling metaphor does not merely assert that behavioral regularities are to be found at a content-independent level of analysis, but it also makes a powerful statement about the nature of those regularities, namely, that they depend only on degree of belief and degree of value. In fact, there is a trade-off to be faced between the *generality* or scope of a theory, that is, its applicability across people, alternatives, and conditions, and its *power* to make detailed statements about the cases to which it specifically applies (Coombs, 1983, chap. 5). Theories with extremely general applicability can be obtained at the price of vagueness and triviality (e.g., "people generally choose whatever seems best to them at the time"). Conversely, extremely rich and powerful descriptions may be obtained for the decision processes of particular individuals on specific occasions (e.g., President Kennedy's 1962 decision to impose a naval blockade on Cuba; see Allison, 1971), but the lessons to be drawn from these descriptions are unclear. It is entirely legitimate to choose a level of generality (e.g., content independence) and then pursue research to obtain the most powerful theory possible at that level. The gambling metaphor, however, presupposes a degree of power at the content-independent level of generality that we think is contradicted by the evidence (e.g., Heath & Tversky, 1991; Hogarth & Kunreuther, 1995).

If the gambling metaphor is rejected, then what? Do we have another metaphor or an alternative theoretical framework to offer? Unfortunately not. At present, we are in a position only to sketch what we see as possible directions and to take a few steps in a direction that seems promising. In very general terms, we see only two possibilities. On the one hand, one can continue the search for content-independent regularities of decision making, but do so with variables other than the two identified by the gambling metaphor's reductionist aspect, the degrees of belief and value. On the other hand, one can change the level of analysis and aim for a collection of theories of more limited scope.

Pursuing the first possibility, Shafir, Simonson, and Tversky (1993) have reviewed a number of studies that reveal violations of traditional models of value maximization, and they interpret these violations in terms of the reasons (e.g., *number* of reasons) that a person might offer in support of a decision. For example, a richly described alternative, with both good and bad aspects, provides many reasons why it should be chosen over a more neutral or sparsely described alternative. However, it also provides many reasons why it should be rejected. Shafir (1993) found that subjects instructed to choose, chose the rich alternative, and that subjects instructed to reject, rejected it. The concept of "number of reasons" can explain this effect. In another example, the fact that alternative A dominates alternative B, whereas alternative C does not, provides a reason for selecting A over C (Tversky & Shafir, 1992). Because the reasons under discussion by Shafir et al. (1993) are rather abstract and content-independent, we view them as shifting the focus away from degrees of belief and value as the key explanatory variables while retaining the goal of a content-independent level of analysis of the psychological mechanisms.

By contrast, we view the study of Hogarth and Kunreuther (1995), as pursuing the other alternative to the gambling metaphor, namely, changing the level of analysis. By shifting their focus toward a study of the *types* of reasons and arguments that subjects entertain, Hogarth and Kunreuther (1995) have opened the door for content to become a central matter in the explanation of psychological mechanisms. For the moment, we prefer to explore this latter possibility. However, we do not propose to go from one extreme to the other. The extreme opposite of content-independence, that is, the position that each decision is unique and cannot be explained without detailed information about the decision maker's content knowledge, is antithetical to the development of theoretical principles. Instead, we are seeking: (1) an intermediate level of analysis, neither content-free nor completely dependent on the minutiae of the content (cf. Cheng & Holyoak, 1985), and (2) a principled way of coordinating the various domain-specific theories that will result. To see how it might be possible to satisfy these criteria, we consider how content effects might exert their influence.

The semantic content of stimuli can affect psychological processing in various ways. In the literature we reviewed earlier, some of the content effects are attributed to the encoding and representation of information (e.g., Bassok et al., 1995). Some are attributed to the use of domain-specific rules for manipulating encoded information (e.g., Cheng & Holyoak, 1985).

Still others may be attributable to attentional mechanisms (e.g., Garcia & Koelling, 1966), in that people or animals may be predisposed to notice certain kinds of events or contingencies between certain kinds of events. One striking feature of the explanations that have been proposed for content effects, with the possible exception of innate mechanisms (Cosmides & Tooby, 1994), is the reliance on *prior knowledge* to guide the encoding, organization, and manipulation of information. In the remainder of this chapter, we explore the way that prior knowledge might affect psychological processes relevant to decision making.

B. DOMAIN KNOWLEDGE AND REPRESENTATION

Any theory of decision making, including the gambling metaphor, must leave room for domain knowledge to affect certain psychological processes. Knowledge is required for a person to identify and encode the relevant aspects of a situation, to extract the relevant implications, and to organize the information in a manner conducive for subsequent processing. From the perspective of the gambling metaphor, this is to say that people must use their knowledge to assess the subjective likelihood and desirability of possible events. It is even consistent with the gambling metaphor to assert that developing expertise in a content domain might change the way a person perceives this "deep structure" (i.e., subjective likelihood and desirability) in the domain (cf. Chi et al., 1981). Thus, domain knowledge might affect the reference points people use to frame outcomes as gains versus losses, or the manner in which people combine or separate events in their "mental accounting."

From our perspective, the undue limitation of the gambling metaphor is its assumption that all content domains are transduced through the same deep structure. We think that content knowledge permits people to organize situation-specific information in a variety of ways, and that different organizations of information are conducive to different modes of deliberation about the choice alternatives. We will consider next how processes of deliberation relate to different ways of representing and organizing knowledge. Then, we will discuss how semantic content influences knowledge representation and organization, thus constraining the applicable repertoire of decision strategies within the given circumstances. We will also consider how the semantic content of the decision problem might exert a direct influence on the selection of a decision strategy, in addition to its indirect influence via knowledge organization.

C. KNOWLEDGE STRUCTURES AND DELIBERATION

We briefly describe four broad categories of decision making, distinguished according to the way knowledge is used (or not used) to evaluate alternatives: nondeliberative, associative, rule-based, and schema-based. The boundaries between categories are not entirely sharp, however, and we acknowledge that hybrids and combinations of strategies from different categories are also possible.

1. Nondeliberative Decision Making

For a decision that is repeated and routinized (Ronis, Yates, & Kirscht, 1989), procedural memory might direct the overt behavior in much the same way that it directs overlearned motor tasks. For example, one might select the same brand of milk from the grocer's shelf time after time without so much as looking at the price. Habitual behavior may barely deserve to be called decision making, but it illustrates the fact that choices may be made in nondeliberative ways (cf. Langer, 1989). Additional examples of *nondeliberative* decision making include choosing at random or by whim, and "passing the buck" (i.e., giving decision making authority—and responsibility—to someone else). For an example of nondeliberative decision making that is driven by distributed representation of information and composite memory storage, see the chapter by Weber, Goldstein, and Barlas, this volume (see also Weber, Goldstein, & Busemeyer, 1991.)

A particularly noteworthy nondeliberative decision strategy draws on declarative memory. In a strategy we call *category-based* decision making, the decision maker recognizes the alternative or situation as a member of a category for which a judgment or action has already been stored. There may have been deliberation on previous occasions, but if judgment or action is required subsequently, it is only retrieved. For example, consider a decision maker who responds to others on the basis of stereotypes. In this case, a judgment is already stored in memory in association with the category (the stereotyped group), and if needed, it is retrieved rather than computed (cf. Fiske, 1982; Fiske & Pavelchak, 1986). Despite the negative connotations of stereotyping, having a large repertoire of categories whose members can be recognized quickly, together with associated and easily retrieved judgments or actions, is one way to characterize expertise (Chase & Simon, 1973a, 1973b). Such expertise could be driven by a rich episodic memory, in which the current situation reminds the expert of similar situations encountered in the past (i.e., situations in the same category), the actions taken then, and their consequences (Weber, Bockenholt, Hilton, & Wallace, 1993). If this reminding is unconscious (cf. Logan, 1988), episodic memory may provide a basis for the "intuitive" decision making of the expert.

2. Associative Deliberation

By *associative deliberation* we refer to a process of deliberation that was described by William James (1890):

At every moment of it [i.e., deliberation] our consciousness is of an extremely complex object, namely the existence of the whole set of motives and their conflict . . . Of this object, the totality of which is realized more or less dimly all the while, certain parts stand out more or less sharply at one moment in the foreground, and at another moment other parts, in consequence of the oscillations of our attention, and of the 'associative' flow of our ideas. (vol. II, pp. 528–529)

If habitual behavior barely deserves to be called decision making, it may be something of a stretch to refer to associative deliberation as a decision strategy. In associative deliberation, the decision maker is not actively guiding the process of deliberation by following a well-defined procedure so much as he or she is being buffeted by the stream of considerations that come to mind. Each successive consideration inclines the decision maker toward a particular course of action, either augmenting or counteracting the effects of previous considerations. The decision is resolved when the cumulative effects of the considerations sufficiently incline the decision maker toward a course of action.

When applied to very simple stimuli (e.g., monetary gambles), fluctuations in attention to the various probabilities and outcomes drive the fluctuations in the decision maker's inclinations. When applied to complex alternatives that are not completely described in explicit detail, the process of associative deliberation is driven by knowledge as represented in a semantic associative network and retrieved by spreading activation (Anderson, 1984). For these stimuli, the successive considerations can be regarded as inferences about the implications of a course of action, occurring in a stream-of-consciousness flow. A sophisticated mathematical model of associative deliberation that accounts for choice latency as well as choice probability has been offered by Busemeyer and Townsend (1993).

3. Rule-Based Deliberation

Whenever deliberation follows a plan, that is, a set of rules for acquiring and using relevant information, procedural memory is required to guide the implementation of the plan. For example, if a lexicographic strategy is to be implemented, the decision maker must have the procedural knowledge to direct his or her attention to the most important attribute of the alternatives, select the subset of alternatives that are tied at the best level of this attribute, examine the second most important attribute for alternatives in this selected subset, select the subset of these that are tied at the best level of this attribute, and so on, continuing until a single alternative remains or picking nondeliberatively from the tied set that remains after the attributes have been exhausted.

Several comments about this example are in order. First, we mean the example of lexicographic decision making to indicate behavior that is actually under the guidance and direction of a plan (i.e., following the plan) and not merely a sequence of behaviors that happens to be describable by a plan (see Smith, Langston, & Nisbett, 1992, for a discussion of this distinction). Second, it is clear in the example that the lexicographic strategy, as a generally applicable strategy, is not purely procedural. Declarative knowledge, namely the importance ordering of attributes and the relative desirability of levels within attributes, is required to implement the strategy. If the lexicographic strategy were applied repeatedly in a particular content domain, in which the orderings of attributes and levels could themselves be brought under the governance of rules, the entire strategy could be proceduralized or "compiled" (cf. Anderson, 1987). Thus, the experience and expertise of the decision maker is virtually certain to affect the interplay of declarative and procedural memory in following a plan. Third, especially if the plan has been proceduralized, the decision maker may have little conscious awareness of the rules that are being followed; experts are often unable to describe the procedures they follow. Following rules that are inaccessible to consciousness may be one of the bases for intuitive decision making. By contrast, the relatively slow, laborious following of rules that are stored in explicit declarative form is probably a large component of analytic decision making (see Weber et al., this volume).

So far, we have implied, perhaps, that our third category of decision processes consists of rule-following or plan-following decision making. However, upon thinking about how a person might select a decision strategy, it seems to us that it would be more useful to employ a somewhat broader notion. Suppose that a person focuses on each alternative and considers which procedures in his or her repertoire would sanction the selection of that alternative. Suppose also that the person chooses the alternative that is sanctioned by the plan the decision maker deems most satisfactory (rational, defensible, justifiable, explicable, etc.). In such a case, rules and plans have influenced the decision in more than an incidental way, and yet the rules have not been "followed" in a strict sense. To include such instances of rule-sanctioned, but not quite rule-followed, decision making in our third category of deliberation processes, we will use the term *rule-based* deliberation. Our purpose in including this strategy in our third category is to capture the collection of strategies that rely heavily on procedural memory or on declarative knowledge of procedures.

4. Schema-Based Deliberation

Our remaining category, *schema-based* deliberation, to which we alluded in describing our experimental results earlier, focuses more fundamentally on the uses of declarative knowledge in decision making. Much of our thinking about schema-based decision making was inspired by the work of Pennington and Hastie (1988, 1992, 1993) on explanation-based decision making. Explanation-based decision making, proposed by Pennington and Hastie and investigated intensively as applied to juror decisions in criminal trials, has three parts: (1) the decision maker constructs a causal model to explain available facts (e.g., a narrative story is constructed from witness testimony and attorney argument to explain the actions of the defendant and others in the case), (2) the decision maker endeavors to learn, create, or discover choice alternatives (e.g., the judge instructs the jury about the possible verdicts and the conditions for their appropriateness), and (3) the decision is made when the causal model is successfully matched to an available choice alternative.

The key property of explanation-based decision making is that it depends crucially on the construction of a mediating representation, namely, the causal model. The causal model organizes much (ideally all) of the information into a whole by promoting and guiding the inference of both supplemental items of information that were not presented explicitly (e.g., that the defendant formed a goal to harm the victim) and relations between items (e.g., various actions of the defendant are interpreted as efforts to achieve an overarching goal). Evidence for such inferences was provided by systematic intrusions into people's memories for presented items of information (Pennington & Hastie, 1988). Moreover, people's choices of action and the confidence they placed in those choices were shown to be mediated by their *evaluations of* the causal models they constructed (Pennington & Hastie, 1988, 1992, 1993). That is, causal models are subject to internal structural constraints (e.g., a story must be composed of related episodes that make reference to the goals and beliefs of the participants, the obstacles they face, their plans to overcome obstacles, etc.). The extent to which a person's causal model respects these constraints, accounts for a large portion of the information, and does so in the absence of competing causal models, affects both the likelihood that the person will accept the causal model as the basis for a choice and the confidence placed in that choice (Pennington & Hastie, 1988, 1992, 1993).

Our notion of schema-based decision making relaxes some of the restrictions that Pennington and Hastie explicitly place on explanation-based decision making, and some that are merely implicit in the studies they have conducted to date. We retain the central ideas of explanation-based decision making: (1) that judgments and choices proceed by fitting a preexisting knowledge structure to the available information and by fleshing it out with inferred information and relations, and (2) that the judgments and choices themselves depend partly on an assessment of the adequacy of the resulting instantiated structure as an organization of the information. (The requirements that inferences must fit into an overarching knowledge structure and that the assessed adequacy of the instantiated structure influences the decision, both distinguish schema-based processing from associative deliberation.) Our main relaxation of explanation-based decision making is that we do not require the mediating cognitive structure to be a *causal* model. Although Pennington and Hastie allow different sorts of causal models to be invoked in different content domains, they make it clear that they intend explanations to implicate causation, albeit with a liberal construal of causation. By referring to decision making as schema-based rather than explanation-based, we want to draw attention to the possibility that mediating cognitive structures may guide inferences and organize information by reference to relations that are typical, stereotypical, conventional, appropriate, meaningful, exemplary, ideal, and so on, as well as causal.[3]

We employ the notion of "schema" as an overarching or generic knowledge structure that provides the mental representation and organization of declarative information of all types. We regard as special cases the knowledge structures that represent categories (i.e., concepts; Smith & Medin, 1981),[4] events and activities (i.e., scripts, plans, and narratives; Schank & Abelson, 1977; Stein & Glenn, 1979; Trabasso & van den Broek, 1985), and various other physical and social structures (e.g., mental models; Johnson-Laird, 1983). Nevertheless, schemas are not completely unconstrained (Barsalou, 1992).

---

[3] Three additional differences between schema-based and explanation-based decision making should be mentioned briefly, although we think they may reflect matters of emphasis and interest rather than theoretical disagreement. First, Pennington and Hastie have used explanation-based decision making to account for people's constructions of belief (i.e., about "what really happened" in the matters concerning a criminal trial). By contrast, we are using the idea of schema-based decision making to account for people's constructions of value, that is, for preferential evaluations of various alternatives. Second, and related, Pennington and Hastie portray their subjects as constructing stories to explain events in the past. By contrast, we hypothesize that people instantiate schemas (including stories or story framents) to project events into the future (cf. Schoemaker, 1993). Third, Pennington and Hastie have examined their model in the context of choice among alternatives (i.e., selection of a verdict), whereas we apply the notion of schema-based decision strategies to evaluations of single stimuli as well as choice.

[4] The use of categories in schema-based decision making should not be confused with (nondeliberative) category-based decision making. The key property of category-based decision making is that an action or evaluation is merely retrieved from memory when an instance is categorized, and implemented or acted upon without deliberation. ("Oh, it's one of *those*. Well, I know how much I like *them*.") By contrast, categories may be used in schema-based decision making to guide nonevaluative inferences ("It's a sports car; it probably has a manual transmission."), to ground an assessment of one's understanding of the situation ("This thing is 'neither fish nor fowl.' I'm not sure *what* to do with it."), and to guide an assessment of gradation (via graded category membership).

D. SEMANTIC CONTENT, KNOWLEDGE REPRESENTATION, AND MODES OF DELIBERATION

1. Amount of Knowledge

Within each of the preceding categories of decision processes, there are ways of implementing particular strategies that require relatively more or less knowledge of the content domain of the decision problem. Category-based and schema-based decision making can be implemented with categories and schemas that are relatively abstract and content-general or relatively concrete and content-specific. Similarly, rule-based strategies can be geared to abstract attributes of alternatives (e.g., subjective probability and utility) or to relatively domain-specific aspects and relations (e.g., a prospective graduate student's glowing letters of recommendation should not be taken to compensate for mediocre grades or test scores unless you have personal knowledge of the recommenders' high standards).

We hypothesize, however, that the relative appeal of different categories of decision processes depends partly on the decision maker's experience and expertise in the content domain of the decision problem. Strategy selection clearly depends on a variety of factors. Nevertheless, category-based and schema-based strategies presumably are more attractive to decision makers who have rich, well-articulated sets of categories and schemas, whereas (non-category-based) nondeliberative strategies (e.g., passing the buck) and relatively abstract (and justifiable) rule-based approaches must appeal to less knowledgeable decision makers. Therefore, it is important to recognize that expertise in a content domain does not grow merely by increasing the number of facts in declarative memory, the number of associations in a semantic network, or the number of rules in procedural memory. Overarching knowledge structures emerge. New categories and schemas are developed. Because the various decision processes just discussed require knowledge to be represented and organized in different ways, growing expertise permits a broader array of strategies to be implemented and, we think, affects the relative attractiveness of the different strategies.

Given the prevalence within judgment and decision research of experiments that employ fairly abstract stimuli (e.g., explicit monetary gambles or sparsely described consumer items), it is not surprising that the typical findings indicate the use of rule-based strategies, albeit different rule-based strategies under different conditions. Even when the stimuli employed are not so abstract, the attributes of the stimuli are often varied orthogonally or otherwise without regard for the sorts of stimuli that people might experience outside the laboratory. This can easily create stimuli that appear "strange" and which cannot be approached with the categories and schemas that people have developed, with the result that people are forced to rely on less knowledge-demanding strategies than they might otherwise have preferred (cf. Brunswik, 1956). These considerations argue once more not only that researchers may have unwittingly conducted their experiments in a way that is likely to overlook interesting decision processes, but that the overlooked processes are exactly the ones that contradict the gambling metaphor by failing to reduce the problem (merely) to the variables of degree of belief and degree of value.

2. Semantic Content Per Se

If expertise in a content domain affects the variety of ways a person can represent information and thereby affects the relative attractiveness of different decision strategies, it does not necessarily follow that semantic content per se should be regarded as anything more than a variable that interacts with individual differences in expertise. One might take the position that content expertise produces variance akin to individual differences in the shapes of utility functions. These individual differences may be of some interest, but they are not of fundamental significance to core theory. By contrast, we argue that people's predilections for particular modes of deliberation in particular content domains are not idiosyncratic and are not merely the accidental product of idiosyncratic learning histories that have no bearing on core theory. We think the connections between semantic content, on the one hand, and representations of information and modes of deliberation, on the other hand, are more systematic and more significant than that. We have two classes of reasons for this belief.

First, there are intrinsic constraints on the types of content and the types of representations that are suited to each other. For example, story schemas have figured prominently in our earlier discussion. However, stories are necessarily about the way things unfold over *time*. This is the observation that led us to our notion of endeavors. Decision domains that do not involve a temporal dimension (e.g., aesthetic preferences for different styles of architecture) cannot be represented in story schemas. Because different decision processes require knowledge to be represented differently, constraints on the representations that *can* be used in particular content domains in turn constrain the repertoire of applicable decision processes.

Second, there is a cluster of considerations having to do with social norms and culture. In many domains, the nature of the knowledge that is considered expertise is socially constrained, or even socially constituted. Consequently, people do not become more idiosyncratic as they acquire expertise. Rather, they become socialized into a system of categories and schemas and rules, ways of organizing information about items in the domain, and ways of deliberating about items and options. Thus, experts may become *less* idiosyncratic in the ways they organize information and deliberate about alternatives. It is probably easiest to appreciate that experts may become more uniform in their decision processes (if not in their final decisions) in arcane areas of knowledge, where it is obvious to the novice that the expert has specialized ways of thinking about the issues. What may be overlooked by concentrating too much on arcane knowledge is that we are all relatively expert, that is, thoroughly socialized, in the ways of our culture. Culture provides us with ways of organizing information in spheres of life both large and small, with constraints on the applicability and relative attractiveness of different modes of deliberation. Beyond this, culture also carries prescriptions: (1) for *appropriate* ways of representing information for certain kinds of decisions in certain domains, thus indirectly constraining deliberation processes, and (2) for *appropriate* modes of deliberation, thus affecting these processes directly as well as indirectly. For example, in making personnel decisions, it may be mandated that job applicants be represented and evaluated "objectively," for example, via a profile of test scores, whereas it would be considered depersonalizing and inappropriate to represent and evaluate close personal relationships in this manner.

3. Construal

Despite the fact that we think semantic content is often connected in nonarbitrary ways to representation of information and to modes of deliberation, there is still room for people to *construe* domains and situations in ways that are sensitive to their idiosyncratic knowledge, preferences, and immediate goals (cf. Griffin, Dunning, & Ross, 1990; L. Ross, 1987, 1989). It is mainly for this reason that we emphasized earlier that we do not think people are compelled to use particular decision processes. We think that people's deliberations about decision alternatives, and the knowledge they bring to bear on these deliberations, are guided by the way they *interpret* the alternatives and the implications of the decision (Bassok et al., 1995). Within limits, intepretations themselves can be matters of choice, or habit, or whim. One may or may not be inclined to regard the purchase of a house, for example, as initiating a long-term flow of events and constraints to be understood in terms of a narrative. One could construct a story about what life would be like in the house. On the other hand, one could evaluate the house in terms of relevant features (e.g., cost, location, size), either with inferences drawn to flesh out a (nonnarrative) schematic understanding of the house (e.g., as a flawed example of the Second Empire style of architecture) or without drawing these sorts of inferences at all. It seems clear that some of these possibilities depend on the decision maker's expertise (e.g., knowledge about architecture), and that a decision maker's inclinations to interpret the decision one way or another may also depend on his or her resources (financial and otherwise) and goals (e.g., planning horizon).

In sum, by focusing on the relationships among semantic content, ways of representing and organizing information, and ways of deliberating, we think that room can be found for an approach to research on judgment and decision making that satisfies the criteria we listed earlier. Because the emphasis is on the *types* of representations and *modes* of deliberation that are related to content, the approach is positioned at an intermediate level of analysis, neither content-free nor completely dependent on the minutiae of the content. Moreover, by developing taxonomies of representation types and deliberation modes, researchers can avoid a chaotic proliferation of domain-specific theories. Rather, the taxonomies can provide a principled means of relating domain-specific theories to one another.

VI. Discussion and Conclusions

In the final paragraphs of this chapter, we would like to offer some additional context for the issues we have raised here by relating our concerns to the work of others in judgment and decision research and to some other research projects we have been involved with.

A. OTHER AREAS OF JUDGMENT AND DECISION RESEARCH

We have restricted our scope in this chapter to the study of preferential decision making. We did so because it is researchers in this area who have been particularly dedicated to the use of content-impoverished stimuli and to content-independent analyses. It seems only fair to point out that researchers who study learning and probabilistic judgment have not shown the same reluctance to address issues of semantic content. Studies of learning have examined the influence of content with tasks involving (1) multiple cue probability learning (e.g., Hammond & Brehmer, 1973; Miller, 1971; Sniezek, 1986; see Klayman, 1988, for a general review not limited to content effects), (2) covariation detection and estimation (e.g., Billman, Bornstein, & Richards, 1992; Chapman & Chapman, 1967, 1969; Jennings, Amabile, & Ross, 1982; Wright & Murphy, 1984; for general reviews see Alloy & Tabachnik, 1984; Crocker, 1981), and (3) induction (e.g., see Klayman & Ha, 1989, for investigation of a rule discovery task; see Nisbett, Krantz, Jepson, & Kunda, 1983, for investigation of a task requiring subjects to generalize from a sample to a population; see Holyoak & Nisbett, 1988, for a general review).

Research on probabilistic judgment has come into contact with issues of content in some indirect ways, all traceable to the seminal work of Tversky and Kahneman (1971, 1973, 1974; Kahneman & Tversky, 1972, 1973). First, work in this area has shifted away from content-impoverished bookbag-and-poker-chip tasks and toward the use of "word problems" about concrete situations. However, the typical use of word problems has been to demonstrate that a finding replicates across a variety of content domains—chosen intuitively for their diversity rather than for any theoretical distinction among the domains—suggesting that content domain is merely a nuisance variable that can safely be ignored. Second, Tversky and Kahneman's work prompted a search for the heuristics underlying judgments (Kahneman, Slovic, & Tversky, 1982). Although the hypothesized heuristics generally transcend any particular content domain as such, some of them do require knowledge of content. For example, the availability heuristic rests on a search of memory and therefore is affected by the organization of knowledge. The representativeness heuristic rests on a judgment of similarity or typicality, which itself is affected by knowledge about the domain (Tversky & Gati, 1978). In these ways, then, research on probabilistic judgment opened a door for the study of content-specific effects. Third, some researchers have stepped through this door. In particular, the phenomenon of base-rate neglect (Kahneman & Tversky, 1973) has led researchers to consider extrastatistical factors such as (1) the salience or concreteness of information (Borgida & Nisbett, 1977; Fischhoff et al., 1979; Nisbett, Borgida, Crandall, & Reed, 1976), (2) the "relevance" of the base rate or the specificity of the group to which it applies (Bar-Hillel, 1980; Carroll & Siegler, 1977), and (3) whether the event described by the base rate is perceived to be causally related to the target event (Ajzen, 1977; Tversky & Kahneman, 1980; see also Einhorn & Hogarth, 1986). Some investigators have argued explicitly that content domain is important to the use of base rates (Gigerenzer, Hell, & Blank, 1988).

It is evident that judgment and decision researchers have not all been equally averse to investigations of content effects. Nevertheless, it seems to us that judgment and decision researchers as a group are a few steps behind the rest of cognitive psychology in recognizing the importance of semantic content in influencing the processes by which people represent, retrieve, organize, and manipulate information.

B. Criticisms of Metatheory

Researchers who study preferential judgment and decision making have been the least concerned with issues of content effects. We think this is largely because the gambling metaphor offers a theoretical framework that encourages the belief that generalizability is enhanced by studying preferential decision making with simple monetary gambles or similar content-impoverished stimuli. We have argued at great length in this chapter against the general applicability of this metatheory and against this experimental practice. However, we are far from the first to argue that decision research should rethink its general metatheory.

For example, Simon's (1955, 1956) pioneering work on bounded rationality stressed the need for psychological theory to respect people's cognitive limitations. Payne et al. (1993) have emphasized the multiplicity of people's decision strategies and their ability to adapt them to the circumstances. Lopes (1987) has argued that research on risky decision making has overemphasized a psychophysical approach and neglected the way that stimuli raise motivational concerns and conflicts. Beach and Mitchell (1987) have argued that too much importance is placed on the selection of an optimal member of a choice set, as opposed to the way people screen individual alternatives for compatibility with their values, goals, and plans, and the way people monitor the progress of their ongoing plans-in-operation. Busemeyer and Townsend (1993) have urged researchers to put aside their static and deterministic perspectives and to face up to the time-dependent and inconsistent aspects of decision making with models that are dynamic and probabilistic. Tetlock (1991) criticizes the standard approach for its neglect of the social context of decision making. (For additional high-level reflections on decision research, see Hastie, 1991; Kahneman, 1991; Kleinmuntz, 1991.)

In view of the relatively large number of recent discussions about the general metatheory of decision research, it appears that the area is experiencing some dissatisfaction with the prospect of business as usual. We are sympathetic to many of the criticisms that have been offered. The criticism that we add implicates the prevalent use of content-impoverished stimuli and the general reliance on content-independent analyses (see also Beach & Mitchell, 1987; Hastie, 1991). We have argued that issues of semantic content should not be ignored in a rethinking of the metatheory of decision research, and we have tried to illustrate an approach that avoids the excesses of the opposite extreme.

C. SELECTION OF DECISION STRATEGIES

Elsewhere we have argued that researchers may have focused too narrowly on decision "strategy" as virtually the sole explanatory concept for a theory of judgment and decision making, and we urged that concepts drawn from the study of memory be included (Weber et al., this volume). To support that argument, we demonstrated that content-independent aspects of memory, specifically having to do with distributed representation of information and composite memory storage, may account for some phenomena that are usually attributed to information combination strategies (see also Weber et al., 1991). Our present emphasis that the repertoire of strategies (or modes of deliberation) is constrained by the way the decision problem is represented may seem to be inconsistent with our other arguments. However, we believe that the concepts of decision strategy and strategy selection should be supplemented, not replaced. For example, we have argued (Weber et al., this volume) that distributed representation and parallel processing have implications for processes which, in turn, influence strategy selection (e.g., the assessment of the cognitive "effort" that a particular strategy will require; see Payne et al., 1988, 1990, 1993). Thus, our contention that semantic content influences the selection of a decision strategy, both directly and indirectly via the organization of knowledge, is not inconsistent with the position taken in the chapter in this volume by Weber, Goldstein, and Barlas. In fact, because memory is the repository of knowledge about content, our current chapter also draws on concepts from memory research. Therefore, we view this chapter as complementing the other chapter, in that it attempts to bring additional aspects of memory within the orbit of decision research, specifically content-dependent aspects of the way that knowledge is represented, organized, stored, and retrieved.

D. History and Future

In closing, we would like to point out one more wrinkle in our historical analogy between associationism and the gambling metaphor: the robustness of these theoretical frameworks. Frederic Bartlett, the best-known early opponent of associationist psychology, the psychologist who characterized "every human cognitive reaction—perceiving, imaging, remembering, thinking and reasoning—as an *effort after meaning*" (Bartlett, 1932, p. 44, emphasis in original) once asked, "Why is it that, although everybody now admits the force of the criticism of associationism, the associationist principles still hold their ground and are constantly employed?" (Bartlett, 1932, p. 307). In summarizing his own answers to this question, Bartlett said, "It [associationism] tells us something about the characteristics of associated details, when they are associated, but it explains nothing whatever of the activity of the conditions by which they are brought together" (p. 308). In other words, laws of association help to describe the products of thought, if not the processes of thought. Bartlett concluded that "therefore, associationism is likely to remain, though its outlook is foreign to the demands of modern psychological science" (p. 308).

We foresee a similar robustness for the gambling metaphor, and for similar reasons. In broad strokes, people generally prefer alternatives that offer them higher probabilities of obtaining more highly valued outcomes; the gambling metaphor helps to describe people's final judgments and choices, at least approximately. However, we are also a bit more optimistic than Bartlett was about the prospects for the future. Most researchers who study judgment and decision making do feel the need to explain psychological processes as well as overt behavioral products. Although we think the gambling metaphor fails on both accounts, it is somewhat easier to make the case on process grounds that the gambling metaphor cannot be sustained: people do not transduce all their decision processes through the variables of degree of belief and degree of value. We have tried to outline an approach to decision research that would acknowledge this fact without opening a Pandora's box of unrelated domain-specific theories. We think this approach is promising.

ACKNOWLEDGMENTS

The authors thank Jerome Busemeyer, Jeanne Enders, Gerd Gigerenzer, Reid Hastie, Douglas Medin, and especially Miriam Bassok for valuable comments on an earlier draft of this chapter.

REFERENCES

Ajzen, I. (1977). Intuitive theories of events and the effects of base-rate information on prediction. *Journal of Personality and Social Psychology, 35,* 303–314.

Allison, G. T. (1971). *Essense of decision: Explaining the Cuban Missle Crisis.* Boston: Little, Brown.

Alloy, L. B., & Tabachnik, N. (1984). Assessment of covariation by humans and animals: The joint influence of prior expectations and current situational information. *Psychological Review, 91,* 112–149.

Anderson, J. R. (1976). *Language, Memory, and Thought.* Hillsdale, NJ: Erlbaum.

Anderson, J. R. (1984). Spreading activation. In J. R. Anderson & S. M. Kosslyn (Eds.), *Tutorials in learning and memory: Essays in honor of Gordon Bower* (pp. 61–90). San Francisco: W. H. Freeman.

Anderson, J. R. (1987). Skill acquisition: Compilation of weak-method problem solutions. *Psychological Review, 94,* 192–210.

Arkes, H. R., & Blumer, C. (1985). The psychology of sunk cost. *Organizational Behavior and Human Performance, 35,* 129–140.

Armstrong, S. L., Gleitman, L. R., & Gleitman, H. (1983). What some concepts might not be. *Cognition, 13,* 263–308.

Bar-Hillel, M. (1980). The base-rate fallacy in probability judgments. *Acta Psychologica, 44,* 211–233.

Baron, J. (1993). *Morality and rational choice.* Boston: Kluwer.

Barsalou, L. W. (1990). On the indistinguishability of exemplar memory and abstraction in category representation. In T. K. Srull & R. S. Wyer (Eds.), *Advances in social cognition: Vol. 3. Content and process specificity in the effects of prior experiences* (pp. 61–88). Hillsdale, NJ: Erlbaum.

Barsalou, L. W. (1992). Frames, concepts, and conceptual fields. In A. Lehrer & E. Kittay (Eds.), *Frames, fields, and contrasts: New essays in semantic and lexical organization.* Hillsdale, NJ: Erlbaum.

Bartlett, F. C. (1932). *Remembering: A study in experimental and social psychology.* Cambridge: Cambridge University Press.

Bassok, M. (1990). Transfer of domain-specific problem solving procedures. *Journal of Experimental Psychology: Learning, Memory, and Cognition, 16,* 522–533.

Bassok, M., Wu, L.-L., & Olseth, K. L. (1995). Judging a book by its cover: Interpretative effects of content on problem-solving transfer. *Memory and Cognition, 23,* 354–367

Beach, L. R., & Mitchell, T. R. (1987). Image theory: Principles, plans, and goals in decision making. *Acta Psychologica, 66,* 201–220.

Bernoulli, D. (1954). Specimen theoriae novae de mensura sortis. *Commentarii Academiae Scientarum Imperialis Petropolitaneae, 5,* (1730–1733) 175–192 (L. Sommer, Trans.). (Original work published 1738) [Exposition of a new theory on the measurement of risk.] *Econometrica, 22,* 23–36.

Bernoulli, J. (1969–1975). *Ars Conjectandi.* In *Die Werke von Jakob Bernoulli* (Vol. 3, pp. 107–259). Basel, Switzerland: Basel Naturforschende Gesellschaft. (Original work published 1713)

Billman, D., Bornstein, B., & Richards, J. (1992). Effects of expectancy on assessing covariation in data: "Prior belief" versus "meaning." *Organizational Behavior and Human Decision Processes, 53,* 74–88.

Borgida, E., & Nisbett, R. E. (1977). The differential impact of abstract versus concrete information. *Journal of Applied Social Psychology, 7,* 258–271.

Bransford, J. D., & Franks, J. J. (1971). The abstraction of linguistic ideas. *Cognitive Psychology, 2,* 331–350.

Brooks, L. R. (1978). Nonanalytic concept formation and memory for instances. In E. Rosch & B. B. Lloyd (Eds.), *Cognition and categorization* (pp. 169–211). Hillsdale, NJ: Erlbaum.

Bruner, J. S. (1957). Going beyond the information given. In H. Gruber, K. Hammond, & R. Jessor (Eds.), *Contemporary approaches to cognition* (pp. 41–70). Cambridge, MA: Harvard University Press.

Brunswik, E. (1956). *Perception and the representative design of psychological experiments* (2nd ed.). Berkeley and Los Angeles: University of California Press.

Bursztajn, H. J., Feinbloom, R. I., Hamm, R. M., & Brodsky, A. (1990). *Medical choices, medical chances.* New York: Routledge.

Busemeyer, J. R., & Townsend, J. T. (1993). Decision field theory: A dynamic–cognitive approach to decision making in an uncertain environment. *Psychological Review, 100,* 432–459.

Carey, S. (1990). Cognitive development. In D. N. Osherson & E. E. Smith (Eds.), *An Invitation to Cognitive Science: Vol. 3, Thinking* (pp. 147–172). Cambridge, MA: MIT Press.

Carroll, J. S., & Siegler, R. S. (1977). Strategies for the use of base-rate information. *Organizational Behavior and Human Performance, 19,* 392–402.

Chapman, L. J., & Chapman, J. P. (1967). Genesis of popular but erroneous diagnostic observations. *Journal of Abnormal Psychology, 72,* 193–204.

Chapman, L. J., & Chapman, J. P. (1969). Illusory correlation as an obstacle to the use of valid psychodiagnostic signs. *Journal of Abnormal Psychology, 74,* 271–280.

Chase, W. G., & Simon, H. A. (1973a). Perception in chess. *Cognitive Psychology, 4,* 55–81.

Chase, W. G., & Simon, H. A. (1973b). The mind's eye in chess. In W. G. Chase (Ed.), *Visual information processing.* New York: Academic Press.

Cheng, P. W., & Holyoak, K. J. (1985). Pragmatic reasoning schemas. *Cognitive Psychology, 17,* 391–416.

Cheng, P. W., & Holyoak, K. J. (1989). On the natural selection of reasoning theories. *Cognition, 33,* 285–313.

Cheng, P. W., Holyoak, K. J., Nisbett, R. E., & Oliver, L. M. (1986). Pragmatic versus syntactic approaches to training deductive reasoning. *Cognitive Psychology, 18,* 293–328.

Cherniak, C. (1986). *Minimal rationality.* Cambridge, MA: MIT Press.

Chi, M. T. H. (1978). Knowledge structures and memory development. In R. S. Siegler (Ed.), *Children's thinking: What develops?* (pp. 73–96). Hillsdale, NJ: Erlbaum.

Chi, M. T. H., & Ceci, S. J. (1987). Content knowledge: Its role, representation, and restructuring in memory development. *Advances in Child Development and Behavior, 20,* 91–142.

Chi, M. T. H., Feltovich, P. J., & Glaser, R. (1981). Categorization and representation of physics problems by experts and novices. *Cognitive Science, 5,* 121–152.

Christensen, S. M., & Turner, D. R. (Eds.). (1993). *Folk Psychology and the philosophy of mind.* Hillsdale, NJ: Erlbaum.

Coombs, C. H. (1983). *Psychology and mathematics: An essay on theory.* Ann Arbor: University of Michigan Press.

Coombs, C. H., & Beardslee, D. (1954). On decision-making under uncertainty. In R. M. Thrall, C. H. Coombs, & R. L. Davis (Eds.). *Decision processes* (pp. 255–285). New York: Wiley.

Cosmides, L. (1989). The logic of social exchange: Has natural selection shaped how humans reason? Studies with the Wason selection task. *Cognition, 31,* 187–276.

Cosmides, L., & Tooby, J. (1994). Origins of domain specificity: The evolution of functional organization. In L. A. Hirschfeld & S. A. Gelman (Eds.), *Mapping the mind: Domain specificity in cognition and culture* (pp. 85–116). New York: Cambridge University Press.

Crocker, J. (1981). Judgment of covariation by social perceivers. *Psychological Bulletin, 90,* 272–292.

Daston, L. (1988). *Classical probability in the enlightenment.* Princeton, NJ: Princeton University Press.

Davidson, A. R., Yantis, S., Norwood, M., & Montano, D. E. (1985). Amount of information about the attitudinal object and attitude–behavior consistency. *Journal of Personality and Social Psychology, 49,* 1184–1198.

Davidson, D. (1973). Radical interpretation. *Dialectica, 27,* 313–328.

Davidson, D. (1974). On the very idea of a conceptual scheme. *Proceedings and Addresses of the American Philosophical Association, 47,* 5–20.

Davisdon, D. (1975). Thought and talk. In S. Guttenplan (Ed.), *Mind and Language.* Oxford: Oxford University Press.

Dennett, D. (1978). *Brainstorms.* Cambridge, MA: MIT Press.

Dennett, D. (1987). *The intentional stance.* Cambridge, MA: MIT Press.

Ebbinghaus, H. (1964). *Memory: A contribution to experimental psychology.* (H. A. Ruger & C. E. Bussenius, Trans.), New York: Dover. (Reprint of book published in 1913, New York: Columbia University, Teacher's College; original work published 1885, Leipzig: Duncker and Humblot.)

Edwards, W. (1954). The theory of decision making. *Psychological Bulletin, 51,* 380–417. [Reprinted in W. Edwards and A. Tversky (Eds.). (1967). *Decision making* (pp. 13–64). Harmondsworth, UK: Penguin. Pagination taken from the reprinted article.]

Einhorn, H. J., & Hogarth, R. M. (1985). Ambiguity and uncertainty in probabilistic inference. *Psychological Review, 92,* 433–461.

Einhorn, H. J., & Hogarth, R. M. (1986). Judging probable cause. *Psychological Bulletin, 99*, 3–19.

Ericsson, K. A., & Simon, H. A. (1980). Verbal reports as data. *Psychological Review, 87*, 215–251.

Fechner, G. T. (1860). *Elemente der psychophysik.* Leipzig: Breitkopf and Hartel.

Fischhoff, B., Slovic, P., & Lichtenstein, S. (1978). Fault trees: Sensitivity of estimated failure probabilities to problem representation. *Journal of Experimental Psychology: Human Perception and Performance, 4*, 330–344.

Fischhoff, B., Slovic, P., & Lichtenstein, S. (1979). Subjective sensitivity analysis. *Organizational Behavior and Human Performance, 23*, 339–359.

Fiske, S. T. (1982). Schema-triggered affect: Applications to social perception. In M. S. Clark and S. T. Fiske (Eds.), *Affect and cognition: The seventeenth Annual Carnegie Symposium on Cognition* (pp. 55–78). Hillsdale, NJ: Erlbaum.

Fiske, S. T., & Pavelchak, M. A. (1986). Category-based versus piecemeal-based affective responses: Developments in schema-triggered affect. In R. M. Sorrentino & E. T. Higgins (Eds.), *Handbook of motivation and cognition: Foundations of social behavior* (pp. 167–203). New York: Guilford Press.

Fodor, J. A. (1992). Fodor's guide to mental representation: The intelligent auntie's vademecum. In J. A. Fodor, *A Theory of Content and Other Essays* (pp. 3–29). Cambridge, MA: MIT Press.

Ford, G. T., & Smith, R. A. (1987). Inferential beliefs in consumer evaluations: An assessment of alternative processing strategies. *Journal of Consumer Research, 14*, 363–371.

Frisch, D. (1993). Reasons for framing effects. *Organizational Behavior and Human Decision Processes, 54*, 399–429.

Garcia, J., & Koelling, R. (1966). Relation of cue to consequence in avoidance learning. *Psychonomic Science, 4*, 123–124.

Gentner, D., & Toupin, C. (1986). Systematicity and surface similarity in the development of analogy. *Cognitive Science, 10*, 277–300.

Gick, M. L., & Holyoak, K. J. (1980). Analogical problem solving. *Cognitive Psychology, 12*, 306–355.

Gigerenzer, G. (in press). Why social context matters to rationality. In P. B. Baltes & U. Staudinger (Eds.), *Interactive minds: Life-span perspectives on the social foundation of cognition.* Cambridge: Cambridge University Press.

Gigerenzer, G., Hell, W., & Blank, H. (1988). Presentation and content: The use of base rates as a continuous variable. *Journal of Experimental Psychology: Human Perception and Performance, 14*, 513–525.

Gigerenzer, G., & Hug, K. (1992). Domain-specific reasoning: Social contracts, cheating, and perspective changes. *Cognition, 43*, 127–171.

Goldstein, W. M., & Weber, E. U. (in preparation). Effects of content domain on preferential decision making. Unpublished manuscript. Center for Decision Research, Graduate School of Business, University of Chicago.

Griffin, D. W., Dunning, D., & Ross, L. (1990). The role of construal processes in overconfident predictions about the self and others. *Journal of Personality and Social Psychology, 59*, 1128–1139.

Griggs, R. A., & Cox, J. R. (1982). The elusive thematic-materials effect in Wason's selection task. *British Journal of Psychology, 73*, 407–420.

Hammond, K. R., & Brehmer, B. (1973). Quasi-rationality and distrust: Implications for international conflict. In L. Rappoport & D. A. Summers (Eds.), *Human judgment and social interaction* (pp. 338–391). New York: Holt, Rinehart, and Winston.

Hastie, R. (1991). A review from a high place: The field of judgment and decision making as revealed in its current textbooks. *Psychological Science, 2,* 135–138.

Hastie, R. (Ed.). (1993). *Inside the juror: The psychology of juror decision making.* Cambridge: Cambridge University Press.

Hastie, R., & Park, B. (1986). The relationship between memory and judgment depends on whether the judgment task is memory-based or on-line. *Psychological Review, 93,* 258–268.

Heath, C., & Tversky, A. (1991). Preference and belief: Ambiguity and competence in choice under uncertainty. *Journal of Risk and Uncertainty, 4,* 5–28.

Henle, M. (1962). On the relation between logic and thinking. *Psychological Review, 69,* 366–378.

Hershey, J. C., Kunreuther, H. C., & Schoemaker, P. J. H. (1982). Sources of bias in assessment procedures for utility functions. *Management Science, 28,* 936–954.

Hershey, J. C., & Schoemaker, P. J. H. (1980). Risk taking and problem context in the domain of losses: An expected-utility analysis. *Journal of Risk and Insurance, 47,* 111–132.

Hirschfeld, L. A., & Gelman, S. A. (Eds.). (1994). *Mapping the mind: Domain specificity in cognition and culture.* New York: Cambridge University Press.

Hoffman, R. R., Bamberg, M., Bringmann, W., & Klein, R. (1987). Some historical observations on Ebbinghaus. In D. S. Gorfein & R. R. Hoffman (Eds.), *Memory and learning: The Ebbinghaus centennial conference* (pp. 57–75). Hillsdale, NJ: Erlbaum.

Hogarth, R. M., & Kunreuther, H. (1995). Decision making under ignorance: Arguing with yourself. *Journal of Risk and Uncertainty, 10,* 15–36.

Holyoak, K. J. (1991). Symbolic connectionism: Toward third-generation theories of expertise. In K. A. Ericsson & J. Smith (Eds.), *Toward a general theory of expertise: Prospects and limits* (pp. 301–355). Cambridge: Cambridge University Press.

Holyoak, K. J., & Koh, K. (1987). Surface and structural similarity in analogical transfer. *Memory and Cognition, 15,* 332–340.

Holyoak, K. J., & Nisbett, R. E. (1988). Induction. In R. J. Sternberg & E. E. Smith (Eds.), *The psychology of human thought* (pp. 50–91). Cambridge: Cambridge University Press.

Huber, J., & McCann, J. (1982). The impact of inferential beliefs on product evaluations. *Journal of Marketing Research, 19,* 324–333.

Jaccard, J., & Wood, G. (1988). The effects of incomplete information on the formation of attitudes toward behavioral alternatives. *Journal of Personality and Social Psychology, 54,* 580–591.

James, W. (1890). *The principles of psychology.* New York: Henry Holt & Co. (Reprinted by Dover, 1950)

Janis, I. L., & Frick, F. (1943). The relationship between attitudes toward conclusions and errors in judging logical validity. *Journal of Experimental Psychology, 33,* 73–77.

Jenkins, J. J. (1974). Remember that old theory of memory? Well, forget it! *American Psychologist, 29,* 785–795.

Jennings, D. L., Amabile, T. M., & Ross, L. (1982). Informal covariation assessment: Data-based versus theory-based judgments. In D. Kahneman, P. Slovic, & A. Tversky (Eds.), *Judgment under uncertainty: Heuristics and biases* (pp. 211–230). Cambridge: Cambridge University Press.

Johnson, R. D., & Levin, I. P. (1985). More than meets the eye: The effect of missing information on purchase evaluations. *Journal of Consumer Research, 12,* 169–177.

Johnson-Laird, P. N. (1983). *Mental models.* Cambridge, MA: Harvard University Press.

Johnson-Laird, P. N., Legrenzi, P., & Legrenzi, M. (1972). Reasoning and a sense of reality. *British Journal of Psychology, 63,* 395–400.

Jorland, G. (1987). The Saint Petersburg paradox 1713–1937. In L. Kruger, L. J. Daston, & M. Heidelberger (Eds.), *The probabilistic revolution: Vol. 1. Ideas in history* (pp. 157–190). Cambridge, MA: MIT Press.

Kahneman, D. (1991). Judgment and decision making: A personal view. *Psychological Science, 2,* 142–145.

Kahneman, D., Knetsch, J. L., & Thaler, R. H. (1990). Experimental tests of the endowment effect and the Coase theorem. *Journal of Political Economy, 98*(6), 1325–1348.

Kahneman, D., Knetsch, J. L., & Thaler, R. H. (1991). The endowment effect, loss aversion, and status quo bias. *Journal of Economic Perspectives, 5,* 193–206.

Kahneman, D., Slovic, P., & Tversky, A. (Eds.). (1982). *Judgment under uncertainty: Heuristics and biases.* Cambridge: Cambridge University Press.

Kahneman, D., & Tversky, A. (1972). Subjective probability: A judgment of representativeness. *Cognitive Psychology, 3,* 430–454.

Kahneman, D., & Tversky, A. (1973). On the psychology of prediction. *Psychological Review, 80,* 237–251.

Kahneman, D., & Tversky, A. (1979). Prospect theory: An analysis of decision under risk. *Econometrica, 47,* 263–291.

Kardes, F. R., & Sanbonmatsu, D. M. (1993). Direction of comparison, expected feature correlation, and the set-size effect in preference judgment. *Journal of Consumer Psychology, 2,* 39–54.

Kaufmann, H., & Goldstein, S. (1967). The effects of emotional value of conclusions upon distortion in syllogistic reasoning. *Psychonomic Science, 7,* 367–368.

Kimble, G. A. (1956). *Principles of general psychology.* New York: Ronald.

Kimble, G. A. (1985). Conditioning and learning. In G. A. Kimble & K. Schlesinger (Eds.), *Topics in the history of psychology* (*Vol. 1,* p. 21–67). Hillsdale, NJ: Erlbaum.

Klayman, J. (1988). On the how and why (not) of learning from outcomes. In B. Brehmer & C. R. B. Joyce (Eds.), *Human judgment: The SJT view* (pp. 115–162). Amsterdam: North-Holland.

Klayman, J., & Ha, Y.-W. (1989). Hypothesis testing in rule discovery: Strategy, structure, and content. *Journal of Experimental Psychology: Learning, Memory, and Cognition, 15,* 596–604.

Kleinmuntz, D. N. (1991). Decision making for professional decision makers. *Psychological Science, 2,* 135, 138–141.

Kunda, Z. (1990). The case for motivated reasoning. *Psychological Bulletin, 108,* 480–498.

Langer, E. J. (1989). *Mindfulness.* Reading, MA: Addison-Wesley.

Larkin, J. H., McDermott, J., Simon, D., & Simon, H. A. (1980). Expert and novice performance in solving physics problems. *Science, 208,* 1335–1342.

Larrick, R. P. (1993). Motivational factors in decision theories: The role of self-protection. *Psychological Bulletin, 113,* 440–450.

Lefford, A. (1946). The influence of emotional subject matter on logical reasoning. *Journal of General Psychology, 30,* 127–151.

Levin, I. P., Chapman, D. P., & Johnson, R. D. (1988). Confidence in judgments based on incomplete information: An investigation using both hypothetical and real gambles. *Journal of Behavioral Decision Making, 1,* 29–41.

Levin, I. P., & Gaeth, G. J. (1988). How consumers are affected by the framing of attribute information before and after consuming the product. *Journal of Consumer Research, 15,* 374–378.

Linville, P. W., & Fischer, G. W. (1991). Preferences for separating or combining events. *Journal of Personality and Social Psychology, 59,* 5–21.

Lloyd-Bostock, S. M. A. (1989). *Law in practice: Applications of psychology to legal decision making and legal skills.* Chicago: Lyceum.

Logan, G. D. (1988). Toward an instance theory of automatization. *Psychological Review, 95,* 492–527.

Lopes, L. L. (1983). Some thoughts on the psychological concept of risk. *Journal of Experimental Psychology: Human Perception and Performance, 9,* 137–144.

Lopes, L. L. (1987). Between hope and fear: The psychology of risk. In L. Berkowitz (Ed.), *Advances in experimental social psychology (Vol. 20,* pp. 255–295). San Diego: Academic Press.

Lubek, I., & Apfelbaum, E. (1987). Neo-behaviorism and the Garcia effect: A social psychology of science approach to the history of a paradigm clash. In M. G. Ash & W. R. Woodward (Eds.), *Psychology in twentieth-century thought and society* (pp. 59–91). Cambridge: Cambridge University Press.

Luce, R. D. (in press). Joint receipt and certainty equivalents of gambles. *Journal of Mathematical Psychology.*

Manktelow, K. I., & Evans, J. St. B. T. (1979). Facilitation of reasoning by realism: Effect or noneffect? *British Journal of Psychology, 70,* 477–488.

McNeil, B. J., Pauker, S. G., Sox, H. C., & Tversky, A. (1982). On the elicitation of preferences for alternative therapies. *New England Journal of Medicine, 306,* 1259–1262.

Medin, D. L., & Ortony, A. (1989). Psychological essentialism. In S. Vosniadou & A. Ortony (Eds.), *Similarity and analogical reasoning* (pp. 179–195). Cambridge: Cambridge University Press.

Medin, D. L., & Ross, B. H. (1989). The specific character of abstract thought: Categorization, problem solving, and induction. In R. J. Sternberg (Ed.), *Advances in the psychology of human intelligence* (Vol. 5, pp. 189–223). Hillsdale, NJ: Erlbaum.

Medin, D. L., & Schaffer, M. M. (1978). A context theory of classification learning. *Psychological Review, 85,* 207–238.

Mellers, B. A., & Baron, J. (Eds.). (1993). *Psychological perspectives on justice: Theory and applications.* Cambridge: Cambridge University Press.

Meyer, D. E., & Schvaneveldt, R. W. (1971). Facilitation in recognizing pairs of words: Evidence of a dependence between retrieval operations. *Journal of Experimental Psychology, 90,* 227–234.

Miller, P. McC. (1971). Do labels mislead? A multiple-cue study, within the framework of Brunswik's probabilistic functionalism. *Organizational Behavior and Human Performance, 6,* 480–500.

Mosteller, F., & Nogee, P. (1951). An experimental measurement of utility. *Journal of Political Economy, 59,* 371–404. [Reprinted in W. Edwards and A. Tversky (Eds.). (1967). *Decision making* (pp. 124–169). Harmondsworth, UK: Penguin.]

Murphy, G. L., & Medin, D. L. (1985). The role of theories in conceptual coherence. *Psychological Review, 92,* 289–316.

Newell, A., Shaw, J. C., & Simon, H. A. (1958). Elements of a theory of human problem solving. *Psychological Review, 65,* 151–166.

Newell, A., & Simon, H. A. (1972). *Human problem solving.* Englewood Cliffs, NJ: Prentice-Hall.

Newman, S. E. (1987). Ebbinghaus' *On Memory:* Some effects on early American research. In D. S. Gorfein & R. R. Hoffman (Eds.), *Memory and learning: The Ebbinghaus centennial conference* (pp. 77–87). Hillsdale, NJ: Erlbaum.

Nisbett, R. E., Borgida, E., Crandall, R., & Reed, H. (1976). Popular induction: Information is not necessarily informative. In J. S. Carroll & J. W. Payne (Eds.), *Cognition and social behavior* (pp. 113–134). Hillsdale, NJ: Erlbaum.

Nisbett, R. E., Krantz, D. H., Jepson, D., & Kunda, Z. (1983). The use of statistical heuristics in everyday reasoning. *Psychological Review, 90,* 339–363.

Nisbett, R. E., & Wilson, T. D. (1977). Telling more than we can know: Verbal reports on mental processes. *Psychological Review, 84,* 231–259.

Payne, J. W., Bettman, J. R., & Johnson, E. J. (1988). Adaptive strategy selection in decision making. *Journal of Experimental Psychology: Learning, Memory, and Cognition, 14,* 534–552.

Payne, J. W., Bettman, J. R., & Johnson, E. J. (1990). The adaptive decision maker: Effort and accuracy in choice. In R. M. Hogarth (Ed.), *Insights in decision making: A tribute to Hillel J. Einhorn* (pp. 129–153). Chicago: University of Chicago Press.

Payne, J. W., Bettman, J. R., & Johnson, E. J. (1993). *The adaptive decision maker.* Cambridge: Cambridge University Press.

Payne, J. W., Laughhunn, D. J., & Crum, R. (1980). Translation of gambles and aspiration level effects in risky choice behavior. *Management Science, 26,* 1039–1060.

Pennington, N., & Hastie, R. (1988). Explanation-based decision making: The effects of memory structure on judgment. *Journal of Experimental Psychology: Learning, Memory, and Cognition, 14,* 521–533.

Pennington, N., & Hastie, R. (1992). Explaining the evidence: Tests of the story model for juror decision making. *Journal of Personality and Social Psychology, 62,* 189–206.

Pennington, N., & Hastie, R. (1993). Reasoning in explanation-based decision making. *Cognition, 49,* 123–163.

Pettit, P. (1991). Decision theory and folk psychology. In M. Bacharach and S. Hurley (Eds.), *Foundations of decision theory: Issues and advances* (pp. 147–175). Oxford: Basil Blackwell.

Posner, M. I., & Keele, S. W. (1968). On the genesis of abstract ideas. *Journal of Experimental Psychology, 77,* 353–363.

Preston, M. G., & Baratta, P. (1948). An experimental study of the auction value of an uncertain outcome. *American Journal of Psychology, 61,* 183–193.

Quine, W. (1960). *Word and object.* Cambridge, MA: MIT Press.

Ramsey, F. P. (1931). Truth and probability. In R. B. Braithwaite (Ed.), *The foundations of mathematics and other logical essays by Frank Plumpton Ramsey* (pp. 156–198). London: Kegan Paul, Trench, Trubner.

Redelmeier, D. A., & Tversky, A. (1992). On the framing of multiple prospects. *Psychological Science, 3,* 191–193.

Reeves, L. M., & Weisberg, R. W. (1994). The role of content and abstract information in analogical transfer. *Psychological Bulletin, 115,* 381–400.

Ronis, D. L., Yates, J. F., & Kirscht, J. P. (1989). Attitudes, decisions, and habits as determinants of repeated behavior. In A. R. Pratkanis, S. J. Breckler, & A. G. Greenwald (Eds.), *Attitude structure and function* (pp. 213–239). Hillsdale, NJ: Erlbaum.

Rosch, E., & Mervis, C. B. (1975). Family resemblances: Studies in the internal structure of categories. *Cognitive Psychology, 7,* 573–605.

Ross, B. H. (1984). Remindings and their effects in learning a cognitive skill. *Cognitive Psychology, 16,* 371–416.

Ross, B. H. (1987). This is like that: The use of earlier problems and the separation of similarity effects. *Journal of Experimental Psychology: Learning, Memory, and Cognition, 13,* 629–639.

Ross, B. H. (1989). Distinguishing types of superficial similarities: Different effects on the access and use of earlier problems. *Journal of Experimental Psychology: Learning, Memory, and Cognition, 15,* 456–468.

Ross, L. (1987). The problem of construal in social inference and social psychology. In N. E. Grunberg, R. E. Nisbett, J. Rodin, & J. E. Singer (Eds.), *A distinctive approach to psychological research: The influence of Stanley Schachter* (pp. 118–130). Hillsdale, NJ: Erlbaum.

Ross, L. (1989). Recognizing construal processes. In I. Rock (Ed.), *The legacy of Solomon Asch: Essays in cognition and social psychology* (pp. 77–96). Hillsdale, NJ: Erlbaum.

Ross, L., & Nisbett, R. E. (1991). *The person and the situation: Perspectives of social psychology.* New York: McGraw-Hill.

Sachs, J. D. S. (1967). Recognition memory for syntactic and semantic aspects of connected discourse. *Perception and Psychophysics, 2,* 437–442.

Samuelson, W., & Zeckhauser, R. (1988). Status quo bias in decision making. *Journal of Risk and Uncertainty, 1,* 7–59.

Sanbonmatsu, D. M., Kardes, F. R., & Herr, P. M. (1992). The role of prior knowledge and missing information in multiattribute evaluation. *Organizational Behavior and Human Decision Processes, 51,* 76–91.

Savage, L. J. (1954). *The foundations of statistics.* New York: Wiley.

Schank, R. C., & Abelson, R. (1977). *Scripts, plans, goals, and understanding.* Hillsdale, NJ: Erlbaum.

Schick, F. (1991). *Understanding action: An essay on reasons.* Cambridge: Cambridge University Press.

Schneider, S. L. (1992). Framing and conflict: Aspiration level contingency, the status quo, and current theories of risky choice. *Journal of Experimental Psychology: Learning, Memory, and Cognition, 18,* 1040–1057.

Schoemaker, P. J. H. (1993). Multiple scenario development: Its conceptual and behavioral foundation. *Strategic Management Journal, 14,* 193–213.

Schoemaker, P. J. H., & Kunreuther, H. C. (1979). An experimental study of insurance decisions. *Journal of Risk and Insurance, 46,* 603–618.

Schwartz, S., & Griffin, T. (1986). *Medical thinking: The psychology of medical judgment and decision making.* New York: Springer-Verlag.

Seligman, M. E. P., & Hager, J. L. (Eds.). (1972). *Biological Boundaries of Learning.* New York: Appleton-Century-Crofts.

Shafir, E. (1993). Choosing versus rejecting: Why some options are both better and worse than others. *Memory and Cognition, 21,* 546–556.

Shafir, E., Simonson, I., & Tversky, A. (1993). Reason-based choice. *Cognition, 49,* 11–36.

Simmons, C. J., & Lynch, J. G., Jr. (1991). Inference effects without inference making? Effects of missing information on discounting and use of presented information. *Journal of Consumer Research, 17,* 477–491.

Simon, H. A. (1955). A behavioral model of rational choice. *Quarterly Journal of Economics, 69,* 99–118.

Simon, H. A. (1956). Rational choice and the structure of the environment. *Psychological Review, 63,* 129–138.

Slovic, P., Fischhoff, B., Lichtenstein, S., Corrigan, B., & Combs, B. (1977). Preference for insuring against probable small losses: Implications for the theory and practice of insurance. *Journal of Risk and Insurance, 44,* 237–258.

Slovic, P., & MacPhillamy, D. (1974). Dimensional commensurability and cue utilization in comparative judgment. *Organizational Behavior and Human Performance, 11,* 172–194.

Smith, E. E., Langston, C., & Nisbett, R. E. (1992). The case for rules in reasoning. *Cognitive Science, 16,* 1–40.

Smith, E. E., & Medin, D. L. (1981). *Categories and concepts.* Cambridge, MA: Harvard University Press.

Smith, E. E., Shoben, E. J., & Rips, L. J. (1974). Structure and processes in semantic memory: A featural model for semantic decisions. *Psychological Review, 81,* 214–241.

Sniderman, P. M., Brody, R., & Tetlock, P. E. (1991). *Reasoning and choice: Explorations in political psychology.* Cambridge: Cambridge University Press.

Sniezek, J. A. (1986). The role of variable labels in cue probability learning tasks. *Organizational Behavior and Human Decision Processes, 38,* 141–161.

Staw, B. (1976). Knee-deep in the big muddy: A study of escalating commitment to a chosen course of action. *Organizational Behavior and Human Performance, 16,* 27–44.

Stein, N. L., & Glenn, C. G. (1979). An analysis of story comprehension in elementary school children. In R. O. Freedle (Ed.), *New directions in discourse processing* (Vol. 2, pp. 53–120). Norwood, NJ: Ablex.

Stich, S. P. (1990). *The fragmentation of reason.* Cambridge, MA: MIT Press.

Tetlock, P. E. (1991). An alternative metaphor in the study of judgment and choice: People as politicians. *Theory and Psychology, 1,* 451–475.

Thaler, R. (1980). Toward a positive theory of consumer choice. *Journal of Economic Behavior and Organization, 1,* 39–60.

Thaler, R. (1985). Mental accounting and consumer choice. *Marketing Science, 4,* 199–214.

Thaler, R. H., & Johnson, E. J. (1990). Gambling with the house money and trying to break even: The effects of prior outcomes on risky choice. *Management Science, 36,* 643–660.

Thorndike, E. L., & Woodworth, R. S. (1901). The influence of improvement in one mental function upon the efficiency of other functions. *Psychological Review, 8,* 247–261.

Thrall, R. M., Coombs, C. H., & Davis, R. L. (Eds.). (1954). *Decision Processes.* New York: Wiley.

Thurstone, L. L. (1927). A law of comparative judgment. *Psychological Review, 34,* 273–286.

Thurstone, L. L. (1959). *The measurement of values.* Chicago: University of Chicago Press.

Titchener, E. B. (1909). *A textbook of psychology.* New York: Macmillan.

Trabasso, T., & van den Broek, P. (1985). Causal thinking and the representation of narrative events. *Journal of Memory and Language, 24,* 612–630.

Tulving, E. (1972). Episodic and semantic memory. In E. Tulving & W. Donaldson (Eds.), *Organization of memory* (pp. 381–403). New York: Academic Press.

Tversky, A., & Gati, I. (1978). Studies of similarity. In E. Rosch & B. B. Lloyd (Eds.), *Cognition and categorization* (pp. 79–98). Hillsdale, NJ: Erlbaum.

Tversky, A., & Kahneman, D. (1971). The belief in the "law of small numbers." *Psychological Bulletin, 76,* 105–110.

Tversky, A., & Kahneman, D. (1973). Availability: A heuristic for judging frequency and probability. *Cognitive Psychology, 5,* 207–232.

Tversky, A., & Kahneman, D. (1974). Judgment under uncertainty: Heuristics and biases. *Science, 185,* 1124–1131.

Tversky, A., & Kahneman, D. (1980). Causal schemas in judgments under uncertainty. In M. Fishbein (Ed.), *Progress in social psychology* (Vol. 1, pp. 49–72). Hillsdale, NJ: Erlbaum.

Tversky, A., & Kahneman, D. (1981). The framing of decisions and the psychology of choice. *Science, 211,* 453–458.

Tversky, A., & Kahneman, D. (1986). Rational choice and the framing of decisions. *Journal of Business, 59* (No. 4, Pt. 2), S251–S278.

Tversky, A., & Kahneman, D. (1991). Loss aversion in riskless choice: A reference-dependent model. *Quarterly Journal of Economics, 107*(4, November), 1039–1061.

Tversky, A., & Shafir, E. (1992). Choice under conflict: The dynamics of deferred decision. *Psychological Science, 3,* 358–361.

Valentine, C. W. (1930). The innate bases of fear. *Journal of Genetic Psychology, 37,* 394–419.

Verhave, T., & van Hoorn, W. (1987). The winds of doctrine: Ebbinghaus and his reputation in America. In D. S. Gorfein & R. R. Hoffman (Eds.), *Memory and learning: The Ebbinghaus centennial conference* (pp. 89–102). Hillsdale, NJ: Erlbaum.

von Neumann, J., & Morgenstern, O. (1944, 1947, 1953). *Theory of games and economic behavior* (three editions). Princeton, NJ: Princeton University Press.

Wagenaar, W. A., Keren, G., & Lichtenstein, S. (1988). Islanders and hostages: Deep and surface structures of decision problems. *Acta Psychologica, 67,* 175–189.

Wason, P. C. (1966). Reasoning. In B. M. Foss (Ed.), *New horizons in psychology.* Harmondsworth, UK: Penguin.

Wason, P. C., & Johnson-Laird, P. N. (1972). *Psychology of reasoning: Structure and content.* London: B. T. Batsford.

Wason, P. C., & Shapiro, D. (1971). Natural and contrived experience in a reasoning problem. *Quarterly Journal of Experimental Psychology, 23,* 63–71.

Wattenmaker, W. D., Dewey, G. I., Murphy, T. D., & Medin, D. L. (1986). Linear separability and concept learning: Context, relational properties, and concept naturalness. *Cognitive Psychology, 18,* 158–194.

Wattenmaker, W. D., Nakamura, G. V., & Medin, D. L. (1988). Relationships between similarity-based and explanation-based categorization. In D. J. Hilton (Ed.), *Contemporary science and natural explanation* (pp. 204–240). Washington Square, NY: New York University Press.

Weber, E. U., Bockenholt, U., Hilton, D. J., & Wallace, B. (1993). Determinants of diagnostic hypothesis generation: Effects of information, base rates, and experience. *Journal of Experimental Psychology: Learning, Memory, and Cognition, 19,* 1151–1164.

Weber, E. U., Goldstein, W. M., & Barlas, S. (1995). And let us not forget memory: The role of memory processes and techniques in the study of judgment and choice. In J. R. Busemeyer, R. Hastie, & D. L. Medin (Eds.), *The Psychology of Learning and Motivation,* this volume.

Weber, E. U., Goldstein, W. M., & Busemeyer, J. R. (1991). Beyond strategies: Implications of memory representation and memory processes for models of judgment and decision making. In W. E. Hockley & S. Lewandowsky (Eds.), *Relating theory and data: Essays on human memory in honor of Bennet B. Murdock* (pp. 75–100). Hillsdale, NJ: Erlbaum.

Wellman, H. M., & Gelman, S. A. (1992). Cognitive development: Foundational theories of core domains. *Annual Review of Psychology, 43,* 337–375.

Wilkins, M. C. (1928). The effect of changed material on ability to do formal syllogistic reasoning. *Archives of Psychology, 16,* No. 102.

Wright, J. C., & Murphy, G. L. (1984). The utility of theories in intuitive statistics: The robustness of theory-based judgments. *Journal of Experimental Psychology: General, 113,* 301–322.

Yamagishi, T., & Hill, C. T. (1983). Initial impression versus missing information as explanations of the set-size effect. *Journal of Personality and Social Psychology, 44,* 942–951.

Yates, J. F., Jagacinski, C. M., & Faber, M. D. (1978). Evaluation of partially described multi-attribute options. *Organizational Behavior and Human Performance, 21,* 240–251.

AN INFORMATION PROCESSING PERSPECTIVE ON CHOICE

John W. Payne, James R. Bettman, Eric J. Johnson,
and Mary Frances Luce

I. Introduction

Imagine that you are a senior faculty member in the psychology department at a private university. One of your responsibilities is to participate in hiring new faculty for your department. One day, your department chairperson drops the files of five job applicants on your desk and tells you that she would like to know which one of the applicants you most prefer to invite for a job interview. The files contain information on each candidate's education, publications, research and teaching interests, teaching evaluations, and other information. Some of the applicants are better on some dimensions (e.g., their publication record), whereas others are better on different dimensions (e.g., teaching evaluations). How would you go about choosing a candidate? What information would you examine first? What information would you consider next? Would you try to simplify your task by eliminating some applicants from further consideration early in the process? Would you attempt to determine how much fit on research interests you would be willing to give up to get a better teacher? More generally, how would you conclude that one applicant is the one you prefer to bring in for the interview?

Choosing among alternative courses of action, as illustrated by the preceding scenario, lies at the heart of the decision-making process. Conse-

137

quently, the study of how people make preferential decisions has been of great interest for many years, with researchers embracing a variety of divergent perspectives. For example, choice has been addressed from the rational decision-making perspective of economic theory. Simon's (1955) "economic man" view of decision making includes the assumption that

> [the decision maker has] knowledge of the relevant aspects of his environment which, if not absolutely complete, is at least impressively clear and voluminous. He is assumed also to have a well-organized and stable system of preferences and a skill in computation that enables him to calculate, for the alternative courses of action that are available to him, which of these will permit him to reach the highest attainable point on his preference scale. (p. 99)

In psychology, substantial contributions to our understanding of choice behavior have been made by researchers adopting such conceptual structures as neural networks (Grossberg & Gutowski, 1987; Usher & Zakay, 1993) and elements of approach–avoidance motivational theories (Busemeyer & Townsend, 1993), as well as other perspectives (see, e.g., the chapters in this volume). Hammond, McClelland, and Mumpower (1980) provide a discussion and comparison of some of the many approaches taken to decision research.

Our purpose in this chapter, however, is more limited in scope. Rather than addressing a wide range of perspectives on choice, we discuss a program of decision research that adopts the information processing perspective pioneered by Simon and Newell (Simon, 1955; Newell & Simon, 1972). An extensive discussion of our program of research can be found in Payne, Bettman, and Johnson (1993); in this chapter, we emphasize the links between our program of behavioral decision research and cognitive psychology in general.

Roughly 40 years ago, Herbert Simon (1955) argued that understanding actual decision behavior would require determining how perceptual, learning, and cognitive factors cause human decision behavior to deviate from the predictions of the normative "economic man" model of judgment and choice. In addition, Simon argued that cognitive limits interact with complex decision environments to produce "bounded rationality," that is, decision behavior that reflects information processing limits. Thus, the idea that understanding decision making requires a link with cognitive psychology is an old one.

A little more than 20 years ago, Herbert Simon and Allen Newell (Newell & Simon, 1972) summarized a general approach to the study of human problem solving (cognition) called *information processing theory*. The information processing approach involved such theoretical concepts as the notion of limited processing capacity, the use of heuristics, and problem solving as the application of a sequence of mental operations. This information processing approach also stressed how the interaction between the limited cognitive capabilities of the individual and the complexity of task environments determined observed behavior. Simon (1990) has recently expressed that idea succinctly: "Human rational behavior is shaped by a scissors whose two blades are the structure of task environments and the computational capabilities of the actor" (p. 7).

In addition to theoretical concepts, Newell and Simon proposed a set of methodological tools to implement the information processing approach. They were among the first to attempt to simulate mental processes with computer programs and they argued for the use of methods such as verbal protocols and the monitoring of information acquisition behavior to trace the details of problem solving exhibited by specific individuals. Their emphasis on process tracing had a major impact on later research on choice using the information processing perspective.

Our program of research, described subsequently, emphasizes the use of concepts and methods drawn from this information processing approach and cognitive psychology to understand how people make preferential choices. Our major theme is that people use a variety of information processing strategies in making judgments and choices. For example, a decision maker would probably use different information processing strategies in choosing a candidate to invite for a job interview depending on whether the number of applicants was two, four, or a dozen or more (e.g., Payne, 1976). It is now well established that preferences and the information processing behaviors leading to an expressed judgment or choice are highly contingent on and predictable from task, context, and individual difference factors (Payne, Bettman, & Johnson, 1992). Task factors are general characteristics of a decision problem, such as the number of alternatives available (e.g., job applicants), which do not depend on the particular values of the alternatives. Context factors such as similarity of alternatives (e.g., similarity in terms of teaching and research interests), on the other hand, vary depending on the specific values of the alternatives. Task and context factors can evoke different strategies for combining information and lead to different preferences by causing different aspects of the problem to be salient. Finally, the solution to a decision problem may also be a function of individual difference factors such as processing capacities (Bettman, Johnson, & Payne, 1990) and prior knowledge or expertise (Shanteau, 1988).

We emphasize that cognitive effort considerations play a major role in determining contingent strategy use in decision making. In addition, we stress that preferences for and beliefs about objects or events are often constructed—not merely revealed—when responding to a judgment or choice task (Slovic, Griffin, & Tversky, 1990). March (1978) attributes the constructiveness of preferences to the limits on information processing capacity emphasized by Simon: "Human beings have unstable, inconsistent, incompletely evoked, and imprecise goals at least in part because human abilities limit preference orderliness" (p. 598). If preferences are constructed, then they do not result from reference to a master list in memory, nor are they generated by some consistent and invariant algorithm such as an expected value calculation (Tversky, Sattath, and Slovic, 1988). Therefore, whether different strategies exist based on training or experience, or whether they are constructed on the spot, we argue that decision makers have a repertoire of methods for identifying their preferences.[1]

II. An Information Processing Perspective on Choice

When facing a particular choice problem, how do people decide how to decide? What factors influence the use of one decision strategy rather than another in choosing among a set of alternatives such as job candidates? In trying to answer that question, we have made a number of assumptions about human decision making, which we discuss next.

A. THEORETICAL ASSUMPTIONS

1. The Concept of a Decision Strategy

What do we mean by the term *decision strategy?* We define a decision strategy as a sequence of mental and effector (actions on the environment) operations that transform some initial state of knowledge into a final knowledge state so that the decision maker perceives that the particular decision problem is solved. Cognitive operations used to transform knowledge states might include acquiring an item of information from the external environment (e.g., an applicant's teaching evaluations) or comparing two quantities (e.g., determining which applicant has more publications in top journals).

The initial state of knowledge includes facts about the problem and general goal statements regarding the task. For example, in the decision problem posed at the beginning of the chapter, there are five job candidates available, uncertainties must be considered (e.g., how well will a candidate interact with other faculty members), there is information available about such characteristics as teaching and research performance, and the goal is to choose the most preferred candidate for a job interview. Sometimes the initial problem state is not well defined; then, the decision maker must set

---

[1] The notion of constructive processes has been used in other areas of cognitive psychology as well. Neisser (1967), in one of the first texts on cognitive psychology, discussed constructive processes extensively, as did Cofer (1973). Bartlett (1932) espoused similar views even earlier.

up subgoals and accomplish subtasks such as generating new alternatives (see Keller & Ho, 1988; Keeney, 1992).

When the decision maker applies cognitive operators to states of knowledge, new intermediate states of knowledge are generated. For instance, the decision maker might acquire information and find that several job candidates have no prior teaching experience. As another example, after applying elimination operators to the faculty hiring problem, one might reach an intermediate state of knowledge in which the original problem has been transformed into a choice among a few candidates who have extensive prior publication records. This view of decision processing argues that the choice problem is constantly being redefined by the decision maker. Eventually, the application of additional operators will often lead to the final goal state and identification of the preferred alternative.

One important distinction between decision making and other types of problem-solving tasks is that decision problems are generally ill-defined about the exact characterization of the final goal. For example, when beginning to consider job candidates, the decision maker may not have a good sense of how to trade off research potential for teaching potential, or even if such trade-offs are required. Thus, the task of selecting a candidate often requires clarifying the goal state during the decision process.

Figure 1, adapted from Holland, Holyoak, Nisbett, and Thagard (1986), shows schematically how cognitive operations might be used to transform an initial state of knowledge into a final goal state of knowledge. S_I refers to the initial problem information given to the decision maker, and S_G refers to the goal state, which may be no more complex than "choose the most preferred alternative." S_{I^*} is the decision maker's internal representa-

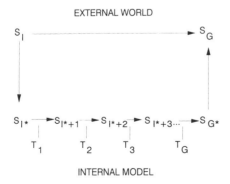

Fig. 1.   Decision making as a sequence of operations. (Adapted from Holland et al., 1986, p. 40.)

tion of the initial problem state, the S_{I^*+j} are intermediate internal states of knowledge, and S_{G^*} is the final internal goal state, which evolves as the problem is solved. The T_j terms represent application of cognitive operations to transform a decision maker's knowledge state. Thus, an intermediate state of knowledge might be that a particular option, for example, a particular faculty candidate in our example, does not meet some minimum requirement, such as having a published research article. The T_j terms or cognitive operations could be used to determine whether an option has a particular feature, for example, prior publications, or to determine which option has more of a feature, for example, more publications.

This view of decision strategies as a sequence of mental (and effector) operations is closely related to the views of Newell and Simon (1972) and Holland et al. (1986). In addition, other decision researchers view decision strategies in terms of cognitive operations (e.g., Huber, 1989).

2. Multiple Strategies with Benefits and Costs

One of our key assumptions is that people have a repertoire of strategies or decision heuristics, possibly acquired through formal training (e.g., Larrick, Morgan, & Nisbett, 1990), natural acquisition, or experience (Kruglanski, 1989). The availability of particular strategies is a function of the frequency and recency of prior use (Ginossar & Trope, 1987). The availability of particular strategies may also depend on the success associated with prior applications of the decision strategy. However, feedback on the success of a strategy may be delayed, sometimes unavailable, or biased (see Einhorn, 1980; Johnson & Payne, 1985), so that availability may not reflect perfectly the success of prior applications of a strategy. Thus, in our view, the decision maker has an "evoked set" of strategies potentially applicable to the current decision problem.

Another key assumption is that the available strategies have differing advantages (benefits) and disadvantages (costs) when both the decision maker's goals and the constraints associated with the structure and content of any specific decision problem are considered. More specifically, we argue that the major cost people consider when deciding how to decide is the amount of cognitive effort needed to execute the strategies. That is, the operators used in preferential choice tasks take cognitive resources to execute them and different operations may require different levels of cognitive resources (e.g., multiplying two numbers may require more resources than comparing two numbers). We also believe that people are generally motivated to use as little effort as necessary to solve a problem (Zipf, 1949); that is, a strategy is selected that ensures that minimum effort will be exerted to reach a specific desired result. This emphasis on the role of cognitive effort is a distinctive feature of our approach to decision research and builds directly on the pioneering ideas of Simon (1955).

When deciding how to decide, the major benefit considered is the accuracy of the various strategies in identifying the "best" alternative. For example, a strategy that eliminates some alternatives early in the process on the basis of just one piece of information, such as prior publication record, may result in not choosing an alternative that would in fact have been the most preferred option. Alternatively, a strategy that examines all the available information might reflect the decision maker's preferences more accurately. Given a desired effort level, we assume that a decision maker wants to maximize the chances of making the most accurate judgment or choice. Our emphasis on decision accuracy shares one focus of "economic man" approaches to decision research, although our assumptions about limited processing capacity clearly depart from such approaches.[2]

To explain why different decision strategies are used in different task environments, we make the additional assumption that decision environments have properties that affect the relative advantages and disadvantages of the various strategies. In other words, the structure of a particular decision environment can both (1) determine the likelihoods that various strategies yield a good solution to the decision problem, and (2) interact with the decision maker's cognitive capabilities to determine how much cognitive effort is required to execute various strategies in that environment. As a result, a given strategy may seem relatively more attractive than other strategies in some environments and relatively less attractive than those same strategies in other environments.

3. Trading Off Accuracy versus Effort

Finally, we assume that an individual selects the strategy that he or she anticipates will be best for the task. Strategy selection then becomes a multiattribute choice for which alternatives are strategies and the attributes are the benefits and costs of each strategy (Einhorn & Hogarth, 1981).[3]

---

[2] See Hammond (1990) for an interesting discussion of coherence versus correspondence theories of accuracy or "competence." Essentially, coherence involves the use of some model of rational behavior as a standard of comparison, for example, expected utility maximization. Correspondence theories of accuracy emphasize the actual outcomes experienced in the "real world."

[3] Such selections are sometimes conscious; however, individuals often may already know the accuracy and effort characterizing different strategies for a particular task (see Busemeyer & Myung, 1992, for possible mechanisms for learning such properties). Contingent strategy use might simply reflect pattern recognition of elements of the task and implementation of the previously learned appropriate strategy in such cases. Hence, strategy selection may not always involve a conscious, effortful decision about how to decide.

This idea that strategy selection is a compromise between the desire to make a correct decision and the desire to minimize effort is not unique to us (see, e.g., Beach & Mitchell, 1978; Klayman, 1983; Russo & Dosher, 1983; Shugan, 1980; Lipman, 1991, and the references therein). As noted earlier, the concept of decision making as bounded rationality is directly related to our view of strategy selection (Simon, 1955). The general view that strategy selection involves benefits and costs also allows one to maintain the assumption of calculated rationality on the part of the decision maker (March, 1978) once the computational and other costs of the decision process are included in the assessment of rationality. Even errors, such as intransitive preferences, can then be viewed as the outcome of a rational process (Tversky, 1969). De Palma, Myers, and Papageorgiou (1994) have explored the implications for issues in economics of the related idea of limits on information processing abilities in choice.

The concepts of strategy choice, effort, and performance just mentioned have also been used in a variety of applied problem domains. Wickens (1986), for example, discusses the implications of effort and accuracy in decision making for such domains as the diagnostic troubleshooting of complex electronic systems, arguing that when there are two or more strategies that may be employed to perform a task, the one that attains the desired performance level at the minimum cost in resources will be selected. Todd and Benbasat (1994) discuss the role of cognitive effort considerations in the design of computer-based decision aids.

In addition to the preceding theoretical assumptions, our approach to decision research is distinguished by the emphasis we place on detailed, information-processing level explanations for contingent decision behavior. As a result of this emphasis on understanding decision processes at a detailed level, we have developed an integrated methodology with two features: the ability to derive specific process-level predictions regarding contingent decision behavior, and the capability to gather the sort of detailed, process-tracing data necessary for testing those predictions. In the next section, we describe that methodology. We discuss how to model decision strategies with production systems using elementary information processes and then consider the use of computer simulations to derive predictions. Then, we discuss how to collect process-tracing data for testing those predictions and illustrate the methodology with some applications to understanding decision processing under time pressure and conflict.

B. AN INTEGRATED METHODOLOGY FOR STUDYING CONTINGENT DECISION MAKING

1. Production Systems

In the previous sections of this chapter, we offered a general definition of what we mean by a decision strategy and also emphasized the concept of cognitive effort. We have used production system representations to model decision strategies at a more precise level. A *production system* (Newell & Simon, 1972) consists of a set of productions, a task environment, and a working memory. The productions possessed by an individual are contained in long-term memory. The productions, expressed as (condition)–(action) pairs, specify a set of actions and the conditions under which they occur: the actions specified are performed (fired) only when the condition side matches the contents of working (active) memory. Working memory contains both information read from the environment and information deposited by the actions of other productions. The use of production systems to represent decision strategies is a key connection between our research and the efforts of cognitive psychologists to understand complex information processing behavior.

An example of a production might be "If there are more than four alternatives, then eliminate those alternatives that cost more than $100." The conditions can include goals, subgoals (e.g., If the goal is to please the chairperson, then . . .), and information on problem states. Including goals and subgoals on the condition side of productions induces a hierarchical structure to decision behavior. In addition, goals can be used to favor special modes of processing, such as efficiency (J. Anderson, 1983). Actions can include both actions on the choice task environment (e.g., then eliminate alternative X) and the creation of new states of knowledge (e.g., then candidate Y is better on teaching performance than candidate Z).

Production systems have a number of advantages for studying decision making. One of the foremost is that production systems, in combination with the notion of elementary information processes (EIPs), discussed next, provide a common language for describing a wide range of decision strategies. Production systems also represent a congenial metaphor for studying the adaptation of strategies with experience (Anderson, 1983) and the introduction of new strategies (Langley, Simon, Bradshaw, & Zytkow, 1987). Newell (1980) presents additional arguments for the value of production systems as representations of human cognitive processes. Holyoak and Spellman (1993) provide an interesting comparison of production system modeling and "connectionist" approaches; they emphasize networks of relatively simple processing units connected by links.

2. EIPs as Components of Choice Strategies

We have decomposed choice strategies into a set of EIPs. An EIP could be a cognitive operation such as reading a piece of information into working memory, comparing the attribute values of two alternatives to determine which is larger, or multiplying the probability and payoff of a gamble. EIPs are the operations used to transform the initial state of problem knowledge into the final goal state (i.e., the T_j terms in Fig. 1).

TABLE I

ELEMENTARY EIPs USED IN DECISION STRATEGIES

READ	Read an alternative's value on an attribute into STM (Short-Term Memory)
COMPARE	Compare two alternatives on an attribute
DIFFERENCE	Calculate the size of the difference of two alternatives for an attribute
ADD	Add the values of an attribute in STM
PRODUCT	Weight one value by another (multiply)
ELIMINATE	Remove an alternative or attribute from consideration
MOVE	Go to next element of external environment
CHOOSE	Announce preferred alternative and stop process

We have used the set of EIPs in Table I in our research on decision making. A particular decision strategy can be defined by a specific collection and sequence of EIPs. For example, a lexicographic choice strategy involves reading processes and comparison processes but no adding or multiplying EIPs. In contrast, an expected value maximization strategy would have reading processes, a number of adding and multiplying processes, and some (but fewer) comparison processes.

Newell and Simon (1972) have suggested that the number of EIPs needed to complete a task provides a measure of cognitive processing effort for that task. Russo and Dosher's (1983) definition of decision effort as the total use of cognitive resources to complete the task is similar. Empirically, this approach has been supported in areas of cognitive psychology other than decision making by showing a relationship between response times and the predicted number of EIPs used for a variety of tasks (Card, Moran, & Newell, 1983; Carpenter & Just, 1975). We adopt Newell and Simon's (1972) suggestion and propose that the number of EIPs required to execute a particular strategy in a particular task environment is a measure of the cognitive effort required to make a decision in that environment using that strategy. Decomposing strategies into sequences of EIPs allows us to examine effort in terms of the specific mix of EIPs as well as the total number of EIPs used (see Huber, 1989, for a similar view). We have shown (Bettman et al., 1990) that decision times can be modeled well using EIPs as predictors, which supports this general approach.[4]

The EIPs shown in Table I, which we use to model decision strategies, are similar to those postulated for other cognitive tasks, such as mental arithmetic (Dansereau, 1969) and problem solving (Newell & Simon, 1972).

[4] In most of our work, the options are fully described for the decision maker in terms of attributes and values. Thus, in our work, the READ operation usually refers to a retrieval from an external display of information or from a readily accessible memory trace. In other decision situations, the retrieval and evaluation of an item of information may itself be a more elaborate inference process that might require postulating additional EIPs.

To the extent that there exists a small set of EIPs common to a variety of tasks, decompositions using EIPs may provide a common framework for addressing a variety of issues in information processing. Chase (1978) provides a more general discussion about the role of EIPs in analyzing information processing.

3. Using Production Systems and EIPs to Model Decision Strategies

Table II contains a production system representation for the expected value maximization strategy for choice among gambles that uses the proposed set of EIPs. The system has three productions; each performs the actions on the right-hand side of the table only when the condition on the left-hand side is true. In the beginning of the choice process, only the third production would be true, so that production would READ the first alternative payoff into working memory, MOVE attention to that outcome's probability, READ it, and apply the PRODUCT operator to weight the payoff by its probability. This product is then ADDed to the option's running total, attention is MOVEd to the next payoff, and the production is applied until all outcomes have been examined. At this point, the second production fires, and the option just evaluated is COMPAREd to the best alternative found so far. The winner of this comparison is marked as the current best alternative. When this process has examined all of the alternatives, the condition side of the first production becomes true, then the current best alternative is chosen.

Expectation-based decision strategies are generally quite effortful. However, this strategy can be implemented without imposing large demands on working memory by combining partial results as soon as possible (see

TABLE II

A PRODUCTION SYSTEM REPRESENTATION OF THE EXPECTED VALUE
MAXIMIZATION STRATEGY

(If at the end of alternatives)	then (CHOOSE alternative that is currently the best)
(If at the end of the outcomes)	then (COMPARE the current alternative to the current best; winner becomes current best)
(If not at the end of the outcomes)	then (READ the outcome's payoff; MOVE to the probability; READ the outcome's probability; PRODUCT the probability times the payoff; ADD the result to the current alternative; MOVE to the next outcome's payoff)

From Johnson and Payne (1985, p. 399).

the ADD operation in Table II). All of the decision strategies we model use a working memory of eight cells (one holds the name of the chosen option) and do not store results in long-term memory. All of the production system representations are also designed to minimize the number of operations, so they represent lower bounds on the effort required to implement each strategy (i.e., human decision makers may not necessarily optimize in this way).

Several possible conflict resolution mechanisms might select which production to execute if more than one were true. For example, Holland et al. (1986) suggest that a matching process screens out those productions not matching the current state of knowledge and that each matched production rule has a "bid value" based on such factors as the history of past usefulness of the rule. A production is more likely to be executed the higher its bid value. Alternatively, productions could be selected on the basis of the degree to which their conditions are matched (Anderson, 1983). However, we simply assume that productions are examined in sequential order and the first production in the list whose condition side is matched fires.

Finally, although we recognize that decay, distortion, or confusion, or problems with intermediate computations are possible when executing a decision strategy (see Weber, Goldstein, & Busemeyer, 1991; Anderson, 1983), we assume as a useful first approximation that decision processes are implemented without error. We will have more to say about the issue of implementation error later in the chapter.

A particular EIP-based production system, such as the example in Table II, represents a theoretical judgment about the most appropriate level of decomposition for modeling decision strategies. We could model some of our operators at a more detailed level (e.g., decomposing the product operator into more elementary processes; Lopes, 1982). We could, on the other hand, try to depict decision processes using more aggregate components, such as a subprocess that would detect dominance relationships among alternatives (e.g., Coombs & Avrunin, 1977; Kahneman & Tversky, 1979; Montgomery, 1983). However, we believe that the level of decomposition shown in Table II provides a useful compromise between detail and aggregation and also allows meaningful comparisons of the cognitive effort among various decision strategies.

4. Computer Simulation of the Accuracy and Effort of Decision Strategies

It is reasonably straightforward to implement production systems like the one shown in Table II as computer programs. Then, we use Monte Carlo simulations to apply each strategy to sets of choice problems characterizing various task environments to generate counts of the average number of EIPs used by each strategy for that given set of choice problems. (For an example of the use of Monte Carlo simulation to study intuitive judgment strategies, see McKenzie, 1994.) Simultaneously, we calculate the average accuracy of the choices that are made (usually a normative strategy like expected value or weighted adding is used as a standard for defining accuracy, as described later). Such effort and accuracy estimates for various strategies across various decision environments yield insights into how the performance of decision strategies depends on task changes. On the basis of these insights, we can make predictions regarding how idealized adaptive decision makers might change their processing across different task environments if they attended to both effort and accuracy when selecting a strategy.

We will summarize work reported in Payne, Bettman, and Johnson (1988) to illustrate how we use computer simulation. The decision task used in the simulations was a risky choice in which each alternative has a different value for a given outcome, but the probability of that outcome is the same for all the alternatives. One major reason we used such problems is that subjects' choices among such gambles have real consequences if we have them play selected gambles for money.

To solve such choice problems, the decision maker must search among the probabilities for each outcome and the values of the outcomes for each alternative, and different decision strategies represent different ways for conducting that search. In Payne et al. (1988), we considered six strategies: weighted additive (expected value; WADD), elimination-by-aspects (EBA), lexicographic choice (LEX), satisficing (SAT), majority of confirming dimensions (MCD), and equal-weight (EQW) (see Svenson, 1979, or Payne et al., 1988, for definitions of these strategies).[5]

We characterize these choice strategies on three major aspects: the amount of processing, the degree to which processing is consistent or selective across alternatives and attributes, and the extent of alternative-based versus attribute-based processing. Different strategies examine different amounts of information ranging from exhaustive consideration of all available information to more limited examination of some subset of the information. One definition of a heuristic decision strategy is partial or limited

---

[5] Although the six decision strategies presented represent major types of compensatory (trade-offs) and noncompensatory strategies discussed in the literature, other models of decision making could be investigated. For example, in addition to the expected value model, one could consider models like the currently popular rank-dependent utility or decumulative weighting models (see Lopes, this volume). Such models seem to require additional operations, such as ordering the possible outcomes of the gamble. Thus, such models seem to imply even greater levels of cognitive processing effort than the standard forms of the expected value or expected utility strategies. In addition, criterion-dependent choice models could be addressed (Bockenholt, Albert, Aschenbrenner, & Schmalhofer, 1991).

use of the available information. Strategies also vary in the degree to which processing is consistent (i.e., the same amount of information is examined for each alternative or attribute) or selective (i.e., the amount of information considered varies across alternatives and attributes). Finally, some strategies are more alternative-based (several attributes of one option are considered before examining another alternative), whereas others are more attribute-based (values of several alternatives on a single attribute are processed before another attribute is considered).

We can characterize the preceding strategies in terms of these aspects. The WADD strategy examines all available information, is consistent, and is alternative-based. The EBA strategy is selective and attribute-based; the particular values of the alternatives and the cutoffs used affect the total amount of information considered. The LEX strategy is also selective, attribute-based, and the amount processed depends on the specific values of the alternatives. SAT is selective, alternative-based, and the extent of processing is contingent on the specific values of the options and the cutoffs used. The MCD strategy is consistent, attribute-based, and does not consider probability information. Finally, EQW is consistent, alternative-based, and also ignores probability information.

The effort required by each strategy was computed using counts of EIPs, as previously discussed (see Payne et al., 1988, for more details on parameter selection and other issues in implementing these strategies). The accuracy of each heuristic was measured by the performance of that heuristic relative to both the optimal choice using all relevant information given by the weighted additive rule (expected value for the gambles) and the choice involving no processing of information given by a random choice procedure (RAND). More precisely, we measured relative accuracy of a given strategy using expected values of the alternative chosen by each rule indicated: (given strategy-random)/(weighted adding-random).

We generated different choice environments by using several factors in the simulations which might have important effects on strategy effort or accuracy (e.g., see Thorngate, 1980; Beach, 1983; McClelland, 1978): the number of alternatives, the number of attributes, time pressure, the presence or the absence of dominated alternatives, and the degree of dispersion of probabilities across attributes (a four-outcome problem with low dispersion might have probabilities of .30, .20, .22, and .28, respectively, whereas a high-dispersion problem might have probabilities of .68, .12, .05, and .15 for the four outcomes, respectively).

There are three major conclusions from the simulations. First, in some decision environments, a decision maker could both significantly reduce the effort needed to make a decision and also obtain a high level of accuracy by using a simplifying strategy (e.g., the lexicographic rule). Therefore, using simplifying strategies may often make sense when the decision maker considers both accuracy and effort. Second, no one strategy was most efficient across all task environments. For example, the EQW strategy is quite accurate in an environment with low dispersion in which dominated alternatives can be present, even though EQW ignores probability information. In contrast, the LEX strategy is the most accurate in high-dispersion environments and substantially outperforms EQW. Thus, to achieve both reasonably high accuracy and low effort, a decision maker must select contingently from a repertoire of strategies based on task demands. Third, the accuracy of some decision strategies, such as the WADD (expected value) strategy, degrades rapidly under time pressure, but the accuracy of other strategies, such as the EBA and LEX strategies, show much smaller decrements in accuracy, with EBA often being the most accurate strategy under severe time pressure. Under time constraints, the best approach is to process some information about all of the alternatives as soon as possible, rather than process each alternative in depth. Eisenhardt (1989) reports that computer industry firms did better if they used a "breadth-not-depth" strategy for evaluating options when operating in rapidly changing environments.

Although these simulation results refer to particular strategies, we view the strategies in the simulation as prototypes that can be used to hypothesize how *aspects* of processing may change depending on properties of the choice environment. For example, inasmuch as selective and attribute-based strategies such as LEX and EBA performed quite well under time pressure in the simulation, we hypothesize that adaptive processing under greater time pressure will involve examining less information and being more selective and attribute-based. We describe such hypotheses further when we summarize some of our experimental work.

The simulation results allow us to generate detailed predictions about the nature of the processing individuals might exhibit when faced with a task factor such as time pressure. To test such predictions in experiments in which decision makers make actual choices, we must be able to examine such aspects as the amount, selectivity, and attribute-based versus alternative-based nature of processing. In the next section, we describe how process-tracing methods allow us to gather such data. Then we present two research applications using our integrated methodology in which we examine the extent to which actual decision behavior corresponds to the predictions of our accuracy/effort framework.

C. PROCESS-TRACING METHODS

Because decision strategies like WADD and EBA can be characterized in terms of such processing features as the amount of information utilized, the selectivity of processing, and whether processing is alternative-based or attribute-based, we need to go beyond standard input–output measures of analysis in order to be able to examine decision behavior in such detail (Payne, Braunstein, & Carroll, 1978). We require data collection methods that yield data on what information a decision maker obtains and how it is being processed. As noted earlier, Newell and Simon (1972) pioneered the collection of process-tracing data from individuals as a way to generate and test theories about human cognition. To borrow a phrase from Simon (1991), the idea behind process tracing is a "close, almost microscopic, study of how people actually behave" (p. 364).

Verbal protocols and monitoring information acquisition behavior are two especially valuable process-tracing methods, and we now briefly describe each (see Carroll & Johnson, 1990, for more details; see Ford, Schmitt, Schechtman, Hults, & Doherty, 1989, for a review of decision research using such methods). For a comparison of process versus "algebraic" approaches to modeling risky choice behavior, see the chapter by Lopes in this volume.

1.   Collecting Verbal Protocols

To collect verbal protocols, the subject is simply asked to "think aloud" and provide continuous verbal reports while making the decision. The researcher treats the verbal protocol as a record of the subject's ongoing choice behavior and interprets what is said as an indication of the subject's state of knowledge or the use of an operation (Newell & Simon, 1972).

The collection of verbal reports to obtain data on psychological processes of interest has a long (and sometimes controversial) history in experimental psychology. Wilhelm Wundt and Edward B. Tichener, for example, extensively used trained observation of mental processes and events under controlled conditions (introspection). Introspective methods, however, were virtually abandoned in twentieth century American psychology because of criticisms about objectivity by John B. Watson and other behaviorists (see Marx & Hillix, 1963, for a discussion of introspection and the behaviorist critique).

More recently, Nisbett and Wilson (1977) have argued that people have little or no ability to observe and verbally report on higher-order mental operations. They suggest that verbal data such as protocols may reflect the norms for behavior in a task more than the underlying processes used in carrying out the task. In addition, providing a verbal protocol, as a secondary task, may fundamentally alter the processes used in performing the primary task of interest (e.g., making a choice), because producing the verbal protocol requires at least some of the individual's cognitive resources.

Fortunately, Ericsson and Simon (1984, 1993) address these objections in their model of how people respond to instructions to think aloud. Ericsson and Simon provide compelling arguments that verbal protocols are valid and provide useful, high density observations on intermediate processing steps. They also discuss numerous examples of the successful use of verbal protocols to study cognitive processes (see Russo et al., 1989, and Payne, 1994, for further discussion).

We believe that verbal protocols can provide a valuable source of data on the processes used in solving complex tasks, but verbal protocol methods are difficult to use. They are usually labor intensive, require considerable transcription and coding effort, and involve difficult analysis. As a result, most verbal protocol studies of decision making use very few subjects. We report one application of verbal protocol methods later in the chapter; however, much of our work collecting process-level data has involved monitoring information acquisitions.

2. Monitoring Information Acquisitions

Monitoring information acquisition behavior is a popular process-tracing method in decision research (Ford et al., 1989). The decision task is set up so that the subject must seek information in a way that can be easily monitored. The researcher obtains data on what and how much information the subject seeks, in what order it is acquired, and how long it is examined.

Studies of decision making have utilized several methods for monitoring information acquisition behavior. Information boards were popular with many researchers in the 1970s and earlier (e.g., Jacoby, Chestnut, Weigl, & Fisher, 1976; Thorngate & Maki, 1976; Wilkins, 1967; Payne, 1976). Payne's (1976) information board was a matrix of envelopes attached to a sheet of cardboard. A subject pulled a card from the appropriate envelope to acquire the value of a particular alternative on a particular dimension when making a choice, turned the card around, and returned it to the envelope. The content, number, and sequence of cards pulled provided data on the information search process used to make the decision. Since the mid-1970s, information boards have been replaced to a large extent by a variety of computer-controlled information retrieval systems for presenting and recording information acquisition behavior (e.g., Dahlstrand & Montgomery, 1984; Jacoby, Mazursky, Troutman, & Kuss, 1984; Payne & Braunstein, 1978). The computer information retrieval systems monitor the time needed to acquire particular pieces of information, reduce the effort required to obtain the information by using pointing devices like a mouse, and some even provide information in a less structured form (Brucks, 1988).[6]

[6] One limitation of the MOUSELAB system is the use of a fairly well-structured decision environment. For a discussion of how people may respond to decision problems in which the options are not directly comparable on attributes, for example, choosing between a vacation trip or a new television set, see Johnson (1984) and Bettman and Sujan (1987).

The computer system we use to monitor information acquisitions in decision making is a program called MOUSELAB. The decision task is set up so that the subject must use a mouse to view or select information from matrix or other displays. In a matrix display, for example, there are closed boxes in each cell of the matrix which contain the value of a particular outcome for a particular alternative. When the mouse cursor is pointed at the box, it opens and the information is revealed. The box closes again when the cursor is moved out of the box. Figure 2 shows a typical MOUSE-LAB matrix display (for further details on MOUSELAB's capabilities, see appendix A of Payne et al., 1993). The program records data on the information the subject seeks, the order of acquisition, how much information is examined, and how long the information is examined. Such information allows us to develop direct measures of the amount, selectivity, and extent of alternative-based or attribute-based processing—the aspects of processing we discussed previously.

The recording of eye fixations is a sophisticated method for monitoring information acquisitions (e.g., Russo & Dosher, 1983) and studying other cognitive tasks such as reading (e.g., Just & Carpenter, 1984). One factor limiting more extensive use of eye movement recording is the complexity and expense of the equipment (Russo, 1978).

Verbal protocols and information monitoring acquisitions each have advantages and disadvantages. In general, verbal protocols provide the richest

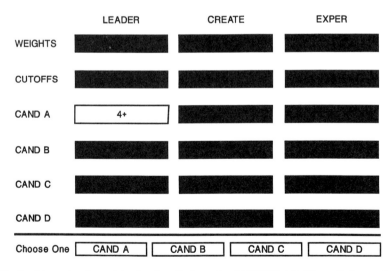

Fig. 2. Example of a matrix stimulus display using MOUSELAB. (From Bettman et al., 1990, p. 122.)

data but are difficult to analyze. Monitoring information acquisitions, on the other hand, is often less informative regarding the details of cognitive processes, but data collection and analysis are more straightforward. In the next section of the chapter, we illustrate the use of monitoring information acquisitions to collect process-tracing data. These data are then used to evaluate the predictions of our simulation studies of decision behavior.

III. Applications of Our Integrated Methodology

A. EFFECTS OF TIME PRESSURE AND DISPERSION IN WEIGHTS ON
     DECISION PROCESSES

Do people vary their choice processes as a function of context factors (e.g., the dispersion of probabilities) and task factors (e.g., time pressure)? If so, are the processing differences between choice environments in the directions suggested by our simulations? Payne et al. (1988) conducted a set of studies to address these questions.

We conducted experiments in which subjects made a series of choices from sets of four gambles, with four possible outcomes for each gamble. The probability for any given outcome was the same for all four gambles. After subjects completed their choices, one of the sets of gambles was chosen at random. Then, they actually played the gamble and received the amount of money corresponding to their chosen alternative. The gamble sets varied in terms of two within-subjects factors: (1) presence or absence of time pressure, and (2) high or low dispersion in probabilities. In addition, one half of the subjects had a 15-sec limit for the time pressure problems, whereas the other half had a 25-sec time limit (the average time taken under no time pressure was 44 sec). For time pressure trials, a clock on the display screen counted down to indicate the time remaining (see Fig. 3). MOUSELAB did not allow subjects to collect any information once the allotted time had expired. We monitored information acquisitions, response times, and choices using MOUSELAB.

Our earlier simulation results suggest that under high levels of time pressure there should be less information processed, greater selectivity in processing, and more attribute-based processing. Overall, the results validated these simulation-based predictions. Under severe time pressure (a 15-sec constraint), people accelerated their processing (e.g., spent less time per item of information), selectively focused on the more important information, and changed their processing to be relatively more attribute-based. Subjects with more moderate time pressure (a 25-sec constraint) showed some acceleration and some selectivity, but there was no evidence

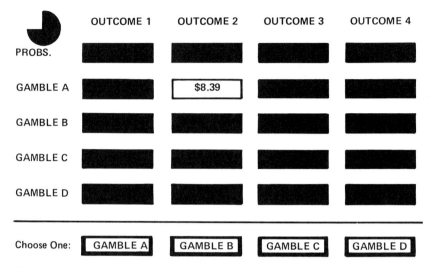

Fig. 3. Example of a MOUSELAB stimulus display with a time-pressure clock. (From Payne et al., 1988, p. 543. Copyright ©1988 by the American Psychological Association. Reprinted with permission.)

for a shift toward attribute-based processing. In combination, the results for the moderate and severe time pressure subjects suggest that there may be a hierarchy of responses to time pressure. Initially, people may respond to time pressure simply by working faster. If this is insufficient, they may selectively focus on a subset of the information. Finally, they may switch strategies to attribute-based processing if acceleration and selectivity do not suffice.

As the simulation also suggested, subjects processed less, were more selective, and processed more by attribute when dispersion in probabilities was high rather than low. Individuals who were more adaptive (i.e., who were relatively more selective and more attribute-based under high dispersion) also were relatively more accurate. Importantly, this increased performance did not require increased effort, so these *more adaptive decision makers were also more efficient.*

In the next section, we examine how another important context variable, the level of conflict among objectives, affects choice behavior.

B. CORRELATION, CONFLICT, AND CHOICE

Decision problems can vary in the degree to which the attribute values are positively or negatively correlated. If dominated options are included, for example, moderate positive correlations among attributes may result

(Einhorn, Kleinmuntz, & Kleinmuntz, 1979). If dominated options are removed from consideration (e.g., Coombs & Avrunin, 1977), then the correlation among attributes may become more negative. Attributes may also be negatively correlated for technological or other reasons (e.g., horsepower and gas mileage). In general, negative intercorrelations signal a higher degree of *conflict* in a choice: the more negative the correlation between two attributes, the more one must give up something on one attribute to obtain more on the other.

How do decision makers change their processing as interattribute correlation (conflict) varies? Bettman, Johnson, Luce, and Payne (1993) addressed this question using the same integrated methodological approach as just described (simulation followed by collection of process-tracing data). First, Bettman et al. (1993) used Monte Carlo simulation to explore how the performance of different choice strategies varies as a function of the level of interattribute correlations among the outcomes of gambles of the form previously described. The most striking characteristic of the simulation results was that simplifying decision strategies were generally less accurate in negatively correlated environments than in positively correlated environments (thus supporting the contention of Einhorn et al., 1979). For example, performance fell precipitously for MCD, EQW, and SAT in the negative correlation environment. From averages of .72 and .68 in positive correlation, low and high dispersion, MCD fell to .05 and $-.04$ and EQW dropped from .94 and .87 to .30 and .19; SAT decreased from .48 and .47 to .03 and $-.01$ in negative correlation, low and high dispersion. Although some simplifying strategies (e.g., LEX and EBA) maintained relatively good performance levels in both positive and negative environments, the *gap* between the performance of the best simplifying strategy and that of the WADD rule was still larger for negative than for positive correlation, especially under low dispersion (.40 for negative correlation, low dispersion vs. .06 for positive correlation, low dispersion; .20 for negative correlation, high dispersion vs. .13 for positive correlation, high dispersion). Given these results, the simulation suggested that individuals would need to use a strategy like WADD to obtain the highest levels of accuracy under negative correlation (i.e., as in the case of WADD, processing should be more extensive, less selective, and more alternative-based for the negative correlation environment, especially under low dispersion.).

Next, we conducted two experiments to examine how human decision makers adapt their processing to the degree of interattribute correlation and other factors. In particular, we examined whether individuals would vary their behavior in ways consistent with our accuracy–effort framework simulation predictions.

In the first experiment, subjects made choices among sets of four gambles with four outcomes, as in the previous studies. Subjects played one gamble after all choices were made and received the amount of money corresponding to the gamble they chose. The gamble sets varied in terms of two within-subjects factors: (1) positive or negative interattribute correlation, and (2) high or low dispersion in probabilities. We again used MOUSELAB to present the gamble sets and to monitor individuals' information acquisitions. As hypothesized on the basis of the simulation results, individuals used more processing and more alternative-based processing for negative correlation choices, especially under low dispersion. There was mixed evidence for lower selectivity, however. Individuals do change their processing in response to conflict, and the specific form of the adaptivity was generally in the directions predicted by our simulation work. These results support the idea that individuals attempt to confront conflict and do not support the notions that individuals either avoid conflict or do not notice the degree of correlation or conflict present. Although those individuals who were more adaptive to the correlation structure performed more accurately, they did not respond perfectly to correlation structure; performance was lower in the negative correlation environment, especially under low dispersion, despite the processing changes. Individuals may intend to be accurate but may not be able actually to implement the required mental calculations.

In our second experiment, we tested subjects' abilities to adapt to a more difficult environment involving correlation and conflict. In particular, we devised an environment in which a normally highly adaptive strategy (focusing on the most probable outcome under high dispersion) would backfire. We felt that if subjects respond in reasonable ways to such a "misleading" environment, this would constitute impressive evidence for adaptive decision making.

To implement this environment, we constructed 16 sets of gambles as 8 matched pairs. The probabilities had high dispersion for all gambles in all 16 sets. To construct the pairs, we arranged the payoffs on the most probable attribute in two different ways. For the eight "misleading cue" sets, we arranged the payoffs so that the ranking of outcome values on the most probable attribute was exactly opposite to the overall rank ordering of expected values for the gambles in that set (e.g., for these misleading sets, the gamble with the highest payoff on the most probable attribute had the lowest expected value). The control "twin" for each of these misleading sets was constructed by reordering the outcome values on the most probable attribute so that this ordering matched the ordering of expected values.

Subjects adapted to the misleading cues trials, either immediately or over time, by devoting more effort, being less selective, and being more alternative-based. Therefore, even in a situation specifically designed to put the implications of two context variables, dispersion and correlation structure, into conflict, individuals changed their processing in the direction predicted by our framework, and the more adaptive subjects were more accurate. This degree of adaptivity is highly impressive. However, subjects' adaptivity was not complete; the performance for the misleading choice problems was marginally poorer.

The results of these two experiments demonstrate that decision makers do adapt to correlation. In addition, our effort–accuracy perspective does a good job of predicting the directions in which individuals will shift their processing. However, although subjects in these experiments adapted their *processing* in response to correlation, performance did not always remain at high levels. In some choice environments, *implementation* of a strategy may have been highly difficult (i.e., difficult or extensive mental calculations). Hence, decision makers showed *intended adaptivity*. They apparently intended to achieve good results and switched processing to achieve these results, but they might not have been able to get them.

We have not yet considered the precision with which individuals can execute strategies within our effort–accuracy approach: It may be better to use a strategy that is theoretically less accurate than another strategy if that less-accurate strategy can be implemented more precisely (see Hammond, Hamm, Grassia, & Pearson, 1987, and Paquette & Kida, 1988, for related ideas). However, overconfidence in one's cognitive abilities is relatively common ("cognitive conceit"; Dawes, 1976), so individuals may tend to be overconfident concerning their abilities to execute decision strategies. For some empirical evidence on this issue, see Stone (1994). Thus, decision makers may try to undertake relatively difficult strategies that would have an unfavorable effort–accuracy trade off *if* an unbiased assessment of expected executional errors was undertaken. Research investigating effects related to errors in strategy implementation would be a significant extension of our current effort–accuracy approaches.

These two applications, to decisions characterized by time pressure and conflict, provide an overview of the research generated to date by our conceptual framework and process-tracing focus. In the next section, we outline two new research directions that extend our framework by exploring the process of constructing preferences in more detail and by examining the effects of negative emotion on choice processes.

IV. New Research Directions

Earlier in this chapter, we emphasized that preferences are often constructed—not merely revealed—while responding to a decision task. We have also stressed that one focus of an information-processing perspective on decision research is tracing the details of individuals' choice behaviors. To paraphrase a comment from Simon (1978), we are interested in the *process* of thought as well as its *product*. In this section of the chapter, we will briefly describe two new directions for our research on choice, both of which represent extensions to our work to date. First, we consider an important application of process tracing and the concept of constructive preferences to a topic of great practical interest, valuing environmental resources using the contingent valuation (CV) method. The second new direction extends our framework to consider the effects of negative emotion on information processing during choice.

A. INFORMATION PROCESSING AND CONTINGENT VALUATION OF ENVIRONMENTAL GOODS

Contingent valuation (Mitchell & Carson, 1989) is a method for measuring preferences that is increasingly being used to assess the value of environmental goods, both for the purpose of guiding policy decisions regarding environmental protection and for establishing liability in the case of environmental damages. The idea behind CV is to attempt to measure the values for environmental resources for which there are no relevant markets by creating hypothetical markets in which individuals directly express their willingness to pay (WTP) for changes in the supply of the environmental resource under specified contingencies. Proponents argue that CV methods can measure both *use* values (e.g., the value placed on using a wilderness area for hiking) and *non-use* values (e.g., an existence value, the value placed on simply knowing that a resource exists independent of any current or possible future use value; Krutilla, 1967).

To clarify the ideas underlying CV, consider the following scenario: Suppose you are told that 200,000 ducks, geese, and other migratory waterfowl were dying each year from contact with oil, gas, and other by-products of production and drilling operations in a distant region of the country.[7] A typical CV question might be What is the most your household would agree to pay in higher prices on oil and gas to prevent 200,000 of these birds from dying each year due to this problem? Thus, a respondent is asked to express his or her value for an environmental good by matching an option defined by a clearly specified level of an environmental good (e.g., the current number of waterfowl dying each year) and a current wealth level with a second option defined by a more preferred level of the environmental good (e.g., the number of birds saved) but a less preferred

---

[7] In an actual CV study, extensive details about the situation, proposed remedy, payment vehicle, and other relevant information would be provided (see Fischhoff & Furby, 1988).

wealth level (current wealth minus the WTP amount). The numbers elicited in a CV study are theorized to measure the economic value for the resource (Mitchell & Carson, 1989).[8]

Kahneman (1986) notes that the basic presumption underlying contingent valuation, whatever the question format, is that "there exists a set of coherent preferences for goods, including non-market goods such as clean air and nice views; that these preferences will be revealed by a proper market; and that these preferences can be recovered by CV" (p. 192). Studies have indeed shown that CV results can be reliable in a test–retest sense (e.g., Loomis, 1990). In addition, the obtained values generally correspond to the values obtained by other methods in the case of use values for familiar goods (see Cummings & Harrison, 1992, for a general review of literature on CV).

A growing body of research, however, suggests that the presumption of a coherent set of preferences is questionable, particularly in the case of non-use values for unfamiliar natural resources. More specifically, contingent valuation responses are sensitive to such task factors as response mode that some researchers argue should be theoretically irrelevant to the underlying value of the resource (e.g., Irwin, Slovic, Lichtenstein, & McClelland, 1993). In addition, CV responses are sometimes relatively insensitive to context factors that might reasonably be expected to influence WTP responses, such as whether a good such as a particular lake is evaluated on its own or as part of a more inclusive category, such as all lakes in a region (e.g., Kahneman & Knetsch, 1992). Such findings of task and context effects have led many researchers concerned with contingent valuation methods to speculate about the processes respondents use when answering WTP questions. Respondents may indeed be trading off an increase in the level of an environmental resource against a decrease in wealth, as is generally assumed. However, researchers have suggested that other considerations may be operating as well in determining a CV response and that these considerations might affect the interpretation given to that response. For instance, in addition to (or in place of) the value of the resource, respondents might be drawing an analogy to a contribution to a charity (Diamond & Hausman, 1992) or focusing on some aspect of the payment vehicle (e.g., whether it is a tax or an increased cost for a specified good) when constructing their WTP response. Other possibilities include making a symbolic response to a larger set of environmental issues (e.g., a large WTP might be given for the waterfowl example to express a general concern that something must be done about the environment, with the waterfowl

---

[8] Other types of CV questions include willingness-to-accept (i.e., what would one accept in return for accepting a reduction in environmental resources), choices between options, or votes on proposed referendums (see Cummings & Harrison, 1992, for more details on such methods).

serving as a symbol), expressing that one should "do their fair share" and other strategic behaviors (e.g., stating a low WTP because one feels that someone else will or should pay for it) (Mitchell & Carson, 1989).

We have argued that preferences are often constructed and that we can understand such construction processes by using process-tracing methods. In our work discussed earlier, we monitored information acquisitions to examine choice processes. To study what processes people use to formulate a WTP response, we used verbal protocols while subjects formulated their responses in a CV study (for more details on that study, see Schkade & Payne, 1994). This research extends our work to date by examining in more detail the process of constructing preferences for an unfamiliar but important environmental resource.

Schkade and Payne (1994) took an existing and previously tested contingent valuation questionnaire (see Desvousges et al., 1992) and studied it using verbal protocols. The scenario concerns protecting migratory waterfowl (e.g., ducks, geese) in the central flyway of the United States from the by-products of waste oil holding ponds. Three versions of the questionnaire were used in which the number of waterfowl expected to be killed without any action being taken was set at either 2,000, 20,000, or 200,000 birds per year (similar questionnaires were used by Desvousges et al.). Respondents were asked to state the most that their household would agree to pay each year in higher prices for oil and gas products in order to finance the installation of a protection device (wire net covers) to prevent approximately 2,000 (or 20,000, or 200,000, depending on the questionnaire version) migratory waterfowl from dying each year in waste oil holding ponds in the central flyway. Subjects were asked to "think aloud" as they responded to the questionnaire and to report everything that went through their minds as they responded to the questions.

The results provided interesting insights into the processes used to construct CV responses. First, and very importantly, Schkade and Payne obtained essentially the same stated WTP results with protocols as Desvousges et al. (1992) obtained in their much larger survey without protocols. Thus, there was no reason to believe on the basis of the actual WTP values that having respondents think aloud changed the way the responses were being generated in any substantial way.

Second, the analysis of the verbal protocols suggested that WTP responses are constructed on the basis of a wide variety of considerations other than trading off wealth for levels of the environmental good. For example, individuals generated their responses by signaling concern for a larger set of environmental issues, by reflecting an obligation to pay a fair share of the cost of the solution, and by using charity as a point of reference. The following excerpts illustrate such reasoning:

"I'm thinking like, um, I would pay $50, maybe even $100, $50 to $200 a year would sound about right to me. I think it's a little bit high, but I kind of think it's important because, um I feel it's important for us to preserve the wildlife, and not, not only ducks and geese, but other animals too. I feel like if we just continue to let things go, we're going to be paying money for other things that may not be quite as important, and when you're killing off all of these animals, and I don't think that's good. I'd like my children to see these animals one day . . . when I have them." (Respondent 2) (Schkade & Payne, 1994, p. 100)

"Um, this is very difficult to determine. You'd have to consider how many millions of people in the country would be contributing to this . . . as far as how much per family this would break down to and what is the cost of putting this netting over all the different ponds, and how many ponds there are, so that would be the cost. I mean, if it . . . comes out to be a couple dollars per household, then it seems reasonable. If it comes out to something more than that, um, it seems a little high. . . . So I'm going to say . . . $5." (Respondent 24) (Schkade & Payne, 1994, p. 99)

"I uh was just thinking about how I make a donation to like maybe the Fraternal Order of Police or to uh MADD or different types of, of things that are for the good of our society. . . ." (Respondent 83) (Schkade & Payne, 1994, p. 100)

Because the commodities that are judged in CV research are often unfamiliar, it seems natural for respondents to look for something familiar to them (e.g., charity) to serve as a point of reference for establishing their response. More generally, the use of analogies in problem solving is a common form of cognition (Holland et al., 1986).

Finally, to demonstrate that descriptions from the protocols, like those just described, are related to the stated WTP amounts, Schkade and Payne (1994) showed that a model using six variables representing coded protocol statements (concept of fair share, cost of solutions, charity, broader environmental concerns, guess, and family income) was able to explain 36% of the variation in WTP amounts, a substantial proportion of the variation for this type of study.

To summarize, the results of the Schkade and Payne (1994) study suggest that WTP numbers often reflect considerations other than trading off a change in wealth against a change in the provision of an environmental good. People appear to find contingent valuation questions difficult to answer, but if asked for a number, most people oblige with one, finding inventive and sometimes surprising mechanisms for doing so. Thus, CV questionnaires likely evoke constructed rather than well-articulated preferences. The preceding findings provide more details on this constructive process and are consistent with the findings of research in decision making and cognitive psychology on task sensitivity and the constructive nature of judgments.

One source of task sensitivity is that decisions like a CV response are often complex. For instance, CV tasks can involve environmental resources, payment vehicles, and diverse information on many dimensions. In addition, as noted by Gregory, Lichtenstein, and Slovic (1993), environmental resources are not normally thought of in quantitative (dollar) terms. Because decision makers typically simplify complex problems in many ways, the use of multiple methods to construct a CV response, contingent on task demands, may at least in part be explained by cognitive considerations of the type emphasized throughout this chapter. However, when considering such issues as how much it is worth to protect the lives of waterfowl or to have clean air and water, factors besides cognitive ones may be important determinants of how one goes about constructing a response. For example, it is quite likely that emotional responses will be evoked and will affect decisions in such a situation. In the next section of this chapter, we discuss how decision research might take into account emotional as well as cognitive concerns.

B.   INFORMATION PROCESSING UNDER NEGATIVE EMOTION

To date, we have explained decision processing largely as an interaction between the decision environment and one very important aspect of the decision maker, his or her resource limitations. We have recently begun some research that focuses on a second aspect of the decision maker, his or her propensity to experience feelings of conflict or related negative emotions. Like resource limitations, these experienced emotions may cause decision behavior to deviate from normative accuracy (Janis & Mann, 1977; Simon, 1987). However, explaining the influence of emotion on decision behavior will likely necessitate a broadening of our current theoretical approach to information processing during decision making. This broadening of our theoretical approach to include an understanding of emotion is consistent with recent movements in both psychology (e.g., Kunda, 1990; Lazarus, 1991; Zajonc, 1980) and behavioral decision research (e.g., Kahneman, 1993; Larrick, 1993; Lopes, 1987) toward understanding how emotion and motivation interact with cognition to determine processing and behavior.[9]

To illustrate how negative emotion may influence information processing during decision making, we ask you to once again imagine that you are deciding which of five faculty applicants your department will invite for a job interview. This time, also imagine that one applicant is currently a visiting member of your department and that she has become a close friend of yours. You believe that others of the five would be better hires, but you

[9] We concentrate on negative emotions because of the argument that decisions are often inherently negatively emotional (e.g., Festinger, 1957; Janis & Mann, 1977). That is, we concentrate on negative emotions because they seem to be much more common in complex decision situations than are positive emotions.

must personally relay the bad news to your friend if she does not get the interview. How would you go about choosing a candidate in this particular situation? More specifically, do you think your decision process would be influenced by how you feel about the potential implications of this decision for your friend?

The preceding decision involves one of three sources of emotion that may have an impact on decision processing. First, as in the preceding example, specific characteristics or aspects of decision alternatives may arouse emotion. These emotion-arousing context factors include the possible consequences or outcomes of alternatives, such as when a person making hiring decisions is concerned with the possible consequences for applicants who are not hired (e.g., Janis & Mann, 1977; Simon, 1987). They also include conflict among highly goal-relevant attributes, such as when an automobile purchaser feels she must give up safety in return for monetary savings (e.g., Festinger, 1957; Janis & Mann, 1977; Tversky & Shafir, 1992). Second, more general characteristics of decision problems, such as time pressure or the amount of information to be considered, may sometimes cause feelings of negative emotion or stress[10] (Hancock & Warm, 1989), especially when these factors are combined with a concern regarding decision outcomes or with a general desire to perform a decision well. Finally, ambient sources of emotion, for instance, an uncomfortable room temperature or a lingering negative mood, may influence decision processing. The bulk of the existing literature on decision processing and negative affect involves this third, ambient source of emotion (Isen, 1984; Lewinsohn & Mano, 1993; Mano, 1992); however, we are more interested in adaptation to emotion-arousing factors within the decision environment. Hence, we are interested in emotion aroused by context (e.g., potential decision consequences) and task (e.g., time pressure) variables. Two possible theoretical approaches to explaining the effects of these variables are discussed next.

We have developed two theoretical approaches to explain how decision makers may adapt to negative emotions aroused by characteristics of a decision problem. One approach involves the argument that individuals will alter their decision processing in order to satisfy goals related to coping with negative emotion, and the second involves the argument that negative emotion directly degrades processing efficiency. In considering these theoretical approaches, we derive predictions regarding two specific aspects of decision processing, namely the extent of processing and the degree to which processing is attribute-based.

---

[10] Following Lazarus (1991), we conceptualize psychological stress as part of the larger topic of emotions. Thus, we have drawn from the literature on decision making under stress, as well as from the more general psychological literature on emotion, in developing our theoretical framework.

One theoretical view for explaining the effects of negative emotion on decision processing, based on the work of Lazarus and Folkman (1984; Lazarus, 1991; Folkman & Lazarus, 1988), involves the idea that the goals guiding decision behavior may be altered under increasing negative emotion. That is, people may shift decision strategies in the interest of coping with or minimizing negative emotion. Thus, as emotion increases, decision strategies may be chosen by trading off three goals: maximizing accuracy, minimizing effort, and minimizing experienced negative emotion. This theoretical approach is difficult to incorporate into our paradigm of deriving processing hypotheses by simulating decision strategies; however, we have derived two specific predictions from the approach by considering the specific aspect of decision processing that each of two general methods of coping seems most likely to influence.

One way to cope with negative emotion is to attempt to solve or alleviate the environmental problem leading to that emotion. For instance, a person who is worried about having cancer may cope with her emotions by making an appointment to see a doctor (e.g., see Folkman & Lazarus', 1988, problem-focused coping). Consistent with this coping mechanism, decision makers adapting to negative emotion may devote increased attention and effort to the task, attempting to ensure that the best possible decision is made. This motivation seems likely to induce decision makers to work harder or to process a greater amount of information (i.e., making more acquisitions and taking more time) as a decision becomes more emotional. This effect seems particularly likely when emotion is directly tied to possible decision consequences, so that the decision maker's efforts may actually reduce the probability of the potential negative outcomes that are arousing stress (e.g., Eysenck, 1986).

At the same time that they try to solve environmental problems, indirectly minimizing emotion, decision makers may be motivated to minimize emotion more directly. For example, a person with health concerns may cope with the associated negative emotion by concentrating on a distracting hobby, as well as by visiting a doctor (see Folkman & Lazarus', 1988, emotion-focused coping). Consistent with this coping mechanism, it seems that decision makers may process in such a way that they avoid the most distressing aspect(s) of decision processing. Making explicit trade-offs between attributes is often considered to be particularly distressing (e.g., Hogarth, 1987), and simultaneously considering multiple attributes, as occurs when processing is alternative-based, may cause any conflict among attributes to be more salient. Thus, it seems that decision makers attempting to avoid experiencing negative emotion may shift to decision rules that are more attribute-based in form in order to shield themselves from the knowledge that trade-offs among attributes must be made and therefore that losses must be accepted. This shift to more attribute-based decision rules may occur at the same time that the decision maker "works harder" processing more information, consistent with Folkman and Lazarus' (1980, 1988) findings that both problem-focused and emotion-focused coping strategies tend to be brought to bear on any emotion-laden situation.

A second possible theoretical view builds on the literature on ambient emotion, in which a common proposition is that experienced emotion degrades cognitive performance, interfering with tasks such as decision processing. Thus, one may argue that each individual cognitive processing operation (i.e., each EIP) will both require more effort and contain more error as negative emotion increases (see Eysenck, 1986, for the related idea that anxiety reduces short-term storage capacity and attentional control). It would be possible to model this proposed effect in our simulations by attributing variable levels of effort to each EIP (according to levels of experienced emotion) and/or by respecifying our simulations of decision strategies to allow for error in strategy implementation (allowing for levels of error to vary with both the levels of emotion and the difficulty of the individual EIPs). Even without these modified simulations, however, it is possible to draw at least one prediction from this theoretical viewpoint. Specifically, a decrease in processing efficiency brought about by negative emotion may cause a shift to easier to implement decision strategies to compensate for emotion-induced decreases in cognitive efficiency. Thus, an efficiency argument implies that decision makers will shift to more attribute-based decision rules, as these rules are generally believed to be cognitively easier to implement than are more alternative-based rules (Russo & Dosher, 1983). This decreased efficiency could be associated with an increase in the extent of processing if one assumes that efficiency is so degraded by emotion that even simpler decision strategies require a greater amount of processing effort to execute, but it could also be associated with a decrease in the extent of processing if one considers only the proposed shift to more simplified decision rules. Thus, the implications of an efficiency argument for the extent of decision processing are unclear.

In general, the two possible theoretical approaches to decision processing under negative emotion yield overlapping predictions. By considering the specific aspects of processing that each of the problem- and emotion-focused coping motivations seems likely to influence most strongly, we predict that decision processing will become more extensive and more attribute-based under increasing negative emotion. The processing efficiency approach also indicates that decision processing will become more attribute-based under increased emotion. Thus, we make the relatively novel prediction that as a decision task becomes more negatively emotional, decision processing will become both more attribute-based (a processing characteristic typically associated with less normative decision processing) and more extensive (a characteristic typically associated with more normative processing). We have collected some preliminary data consistent with these two hypotheses, but much more research needs to be done before we can draw conclusions with any confidence. However, such an integration of concerns for accuracy, effort, and coping may be a fruitful approach for integrating cognitive and emotional considerations in other problem domains as well (see Luce, 1994, for further discussion and an application of these ideas to consumer choice).

V. Conclusion

Our conceptual framework and the preceding research lead to several conclusions about choice. People use a variety of strategies to solve decision problems, and which strategies they use depends on properties of the choice task. Selecting a particular strategy, or deciding how to decide, results from a trade-off between desires for maximal accuracy and minimal effort. Finally, although the use of simplifying strategies can sometimes lead to errors, people often are adaptive in their use of choice strategies: if not always optimal, they are often intelligent decision makers.

Our studies also support a theme of much recent decision research that preferences for objects of any complexity are often constructed—not merely revealed—in the generation of a response to a judgment or choice task. Preferences generally do not result from reference to a master list of values in memory, nor are they generated by some consistent and invariant algorithm. Our conceptual framework has emphasized the role of cognitive effort in the selection of a decision strategy and in the construction of preferences. However, we argued that how people make a decision or construct a choice also depends on how people cope with the emotions that are frequently associated with a decision task. In addition, we suggest that cognitive effort and coping with emotions play a role in understanding how people construct responses to contingent valuation questions, which are increasingly being used to guide public policy decisions.

Throughout this chapter, we have noted how our approach to decision research draws from and is related to cognitive psychology more generally. Now, we highlight important conceptual and methodological similarities. Several of our basic theoretical assumptions are shared with cognitive psychology in general. First, humans are subject to information processing limitations which lead to the need to conserve effort. In addition, the properties of the task interact with such limitations to influence strategy selection and behavior. Thus, we share Simon's (1990) view that behavior is shaped by both the structure of the task and the individual's cognitive capabilities. Third, strategies (one aspect of procedural knowledge) and strategy selection have been central to our work, and this focus is shared with other areas of cognitive psychology. For example, Anderson (1990) offers a rational analysis perspective that can be compared and contrasted with our own. Although both approaches agree that the nature of the task environment strongly influences strategy selection, we disagree about the level of adaptation. We argue that humans are reasonably adaptive but fallible decision makers, whereas Anderson maintains that assuming that cognitive systems have evolved in optimal ways provides a reasonable starting point for understanding cognitive functioning. Siegler and his colleagues (e.g., Siegler, 1988; Brown & Siegler, 1993) have also argued that children employ multiple strategies in solving arithmetic problems, although he argues that such contingent processing does not necessarily result from explicit consideration of strategies and their properties. Finally, Reder (1987) has examined the use of contingent strategies for answering questions.

At a more general level, Gagne (1984) has argued that good problem solving requires a third type of knowledge beyond procedural knowledge and declarative knowledge about facts. Gagne refers to this third type of knowledge as *strategic* knowledge (see also Greeno, 1978). People bring to their tasks "not only previously learned declarative knowledge and procedural knowledge but also some skills of *when and how to use this knowledge*" (Gagne, 1984, p. 381, emphasis added). Our theoretical framework clearly shares this emphasis of Gagne and others on the strategic aspects of decision processing.

As noted previously, there are also important methodological parallels between our work and that in many areas of cognitive psychology. We use production system models to represent decision strategies and focus on elementary information processes as the components for these productions. By adopting the production system architecture and EIPs as primitives, we model choice using terms and methods similar to those used in the study of other cognitive tasks. We also concentrate on the details of processing and use process-tracing methodologies such as protocol analysis and monitoring information acquisition behavior in our empirical work.

Our studies of decision behavior have been enriched by the concepts and methods of cognitive psychology. As cognitive psychologists ourselves, we hope that ideas about the topics of contingent strategy selection, constructive preferences, and the effects of emotion on information processing during choice can enrich research in other areas of cognition.

REFERENCES

Anderson, J. R. (1983). *The architecture of cognition.* Cambridge, MA: Harvard University Press.
Anderson, J. R. (1990). *The adaptive control of thought.* Hillsdale, NJ: Erlbaum.
Bartlett, F. C. (1932). *Remembering.* Cambridge: Cambridge University Press.
Beach, L. R. (1983). Muddling through: A response to Yates and Goldstein. *Organizational Behavior and Human Performance, 31,* 47–53.
Beach, L. R., & Mitchell, T. R. (1978). A contingency model for the selection of decision strategies. *Academy of Management Review, 3,* 439–449.
Bettman, J. R., Johnson, E. J., Luce, M. F., & Payne, J. W. (1993). Correlation, conflict, and choice. *Journal of Experimental Psychology: Learning, Memory, and Cognition, 19,* 931–951.
Bettman, J. R., Johnson, E. J., & Payne, J. W. (1990). A componential analysis of cognitive effort in choice. *Organizational Behavior and Human Decision Processes, 45,* 111–139.
Bettman, J. R., & Sujan, M. (1987). Effects of framing on evaluation of comparable and noncomparable alternatives by expert and novice consumers. *Journal of Consumer Research, 14,* 141–154.
Böckenholt, U., Albert, D., Aschenbrenner, M., & Schmalhofer, F. (1991). The effects of attractiveness, dominance, and attribute differences on information acquisition in multiattribute binary choice. *Organizational Behavior and Human Decision Processes, 49,* 258–281.
Brown, N. R., & Siegler, R. S. (1993). Metrics and mappings: A framework for understanding real-world quantitative estimation. *Psychologial Review, 100,* 511–534.
Brucks, M. (1988). Search monitor: An approach for computer-controlled experiments involving consumer information search. *Journal of Consumer Research, 15,* 117–121.
Busemeyer, J. R., & Myung, I. J. (1992). An adaptive approach to human decision making: Learning theory, decision theory, and human performance. *Journal of Experimental Psychology: General, 121,* 177–194.
Busemeyer, J. R., & Townsend, J. T. (1993). Decision field theory: A dynamic–cognitive approach to decision making in an uncertain environment. *Psychological Review, 100,* 432–459.
Card, S. K., Moran, T. P., & Newell, A. (1983). *The psychology of human–computer interaction.* Hillsdale, NJ: Erlbaum.
Carpenter, P. A., & Just, M. A. (1975). Sentence comprehension: A psycholinguistic processing model of verification. *Psychological Review, 82,* 45–73.
Carroll, J. S., & Johnson, E. J. (1990). *Decision research: A field guide.* Newbury Park, CA: Sage.
Chase, W. G. (1978). Elementary information processes. In W. K. Estes (Ed.), *Handbook of learning and cognitive processes* (Vol. 5, pp. 19–90). Hillsdale, NJ: Erlbaum.
Cofer, C. N. (1973). Constructive processes in memory. *American Scientist, 61,* 537–543.
Coombs, C. H., & Avrunin, G. S. (1977). Single-peaked functions and the theory of preference. *Psychological Review, 84,* 216–230.
Cummings, R. G., & Harrison, G. W. (1992). Identifying and measuring nonuse values for natural and environmental resources: A critical review of the state of the art. Unpublished technical report. Department of Economics, University of New Mexico.
Dahlstrand, U., & Montgomery, H. (1984). Information search and evaluative processes in decision making: A computer-based process tracing study. *Acta Psychologica, 56,* 113–123.
Dansereau, D. F. (1969). *An information processing model of mental multiplication.* Unpublished doctoral dissertation. Carnegie-Mellon University.

Dawes, R. M. (1976). Shallow psychology. In J. S. Carroll & J. W. Payne (Eds.), *Cognition and social behavior* (pp. 3–16). Hillsdale, NJ: Erlbaum.

De Palma, A., Myers, G. M., & Papageorgiou, Y. Y. (1994). Rational choice under an imperfect ability to choose. *American Economic Review, 84,* 419–440.

Desvousges, W., Johnson, R., Dunford, R., Boyle, K. J., Hudson, S., & Wilson, K. N. (1992). Using contingent valuation for natural resource damage assessments: An experimental evaluation of accuracy. Center for Economics Research monograph. Research Triangle Institute, North Carolina.

Diamond, P. A., & Hausman, J. A. (1992). On contingent valuation measurement of non-use values. In J. A. Hausman (Ed.), *Contingent valuation: A critical assessment* (pp. 3–38). Amsterdam: Elsevier.

Einhorn, H. J. (1980). Learning from experience and suboptional rules in decision making. In T. S. Wallsten (Ed.), *Cognitive processes in choice and decision behavior* (pp. 1–20). Hillsdale, NJ: Erlbaum.

Einhorn, H. J., & Hogarth, R. M. (1981). Behavioral decision theory: Processes of judgment and choice. *Annual Review of Psychology, 32,* 53–88.

Einhorn, H. J., Kleinmuntz, D. N., & Kleinmuntz, B. (1979). Linear regression and process-tracing models of judgement. *Psychological Review, 86,* 465–485.

Eisenhardt, K. M. (1989). Making fast strategic decisions in high-velocity environments. *Academy of Management Journal, 32,* 543–575.

Ericsson, K. A., & Simon, H. A. (1984). *Protocol analysis: Verbal reports as data.* Cambridge, MA: MIT Press.

Ericsson, K. A., & Simon, H. A. (1993). *Protocol analysis: Verbal reports as data* (rev. ed.). Cambridge, MA: MIT Press.

Eysenck, M. W. (1986). *A handbook of cognitive psychology.* London: Erlbaum.

Festinger, L. (1957). *A theory of cognitive dissonance.* Evanston, IL: Row, Peterson.

Fischhoff, B., & Furby, L. (1988). Measuring values: A conceptual framework for interpreting transactions with special reference to contingent valuations of visibility. *Journal of Risk and Uncertainty, 1,* 147–184.

Folkman, S., & Lazarus, R. S. (1980). An analysis of coping in a middle-aged community sample. *Journal of Health and Social Behavior, 21,* 219–239.

Folkman, S., & Lazarus, R. S. (1988). Coping as a mediator of emotion. *Journal of Personality and Social Psychology, 54,* 466–475.

Ford, J. K., Schmitt, N., Schechtman, S. L., Hults, B. M., & Doherty, M. L. (1989). Process tracing methods: Contributions, problems, and neglected research questions. *Organizational Behavior and Human Decision Processes, 43,* 75–117.

Gagne, R. M. (1984). Learning outcomes and their effects: Useful categories of human performance. *American Psychologist, 39,* 377–385.

Ginossar, Z., & Trope, Y. (1987). Problem solving in judgment under uncertainty. *Journal of Personality and Social Psychology, 52,* 464–474.

Greeno, J. G. (1978). Natures of problem-solving abilities. In W. K. Estes (Ed.), *Handbook of learning and cognitive processes: Vol. 5. Human information processing* (pp. 239–270). Hillsdale, NJ: Erlbaum.

Gregory, R., Lichtenstein, S., & Slovic, P. (1993). Valuing environmental resources: A constructive approach. *Journal of Risk and Uncertainty, 7,* 177–198.

Grossberg, S., & Gutowski, W. E. (1987). Neural dynamics of decision making under risk: Affective balance and cognitive-emotional interactions. *Psychological Review, 94,* 300–318.

Hammond, K. R. (1990). Functionalism and illusionism: Can integration be usefully achieved? In R. M. Hogarth (Ed.), *Insights in decision making: A tribute to Hillel J. Einhorn* (pp. 227–261). Chicago: University of Chicago Press.

Hammond, K. R., Hamm, R. M., Grassia, J., & Pearson, T. (1987). Direct comparison of the efficacy of intuitive and analytical cognition in expert judgment. *IEEE Transactions on Systems, Man, and Cybernetics, 17,* 753–770.

Hammond, K. R., McClelland, G. H., & Mumpower, J. (1980). *Human judgment and decision making: Theories, methods, and procedures.* New York: Praeger.

Hancock, P. A., & Warm, J. S. (1989). A dynamic model of stress and sustained attention. *Human Factors, 31,* 519–537.

Hogarth, R. M. (1987). *Judgement and choice* (2nd ed.). New York: Wiley.

Holland, J. H., Holyoak, K. J., Nisbett, R. E., & Thagard, P. R. (1986). *Induction: Processes of inference, learning, and memory.* Cambridge, MA: MIT Press.

Holyoak, K. J., & Spellman, B. A. (1993). Thinking. *Annual Review of Psychology, 44,* 265–315.

Huber, O. (1989). Information-processing operators in decision making. In H. Montgomery & O. Svenson (Eds.), *Process and structure in human decision making* (pp. 3–21). Chichester: Wiley.

Irwin, J. R., Slovic, P., Lichtenstein, S., & McClelland, G. H. (1993). Preference reversals and the measurement of environmental values. *Journal of Risk and Uncertainty, 6,* 5–18.

Isen, A. M. (1984). Toward understanding the role of affect in cognition. In R. S. Wyer, Jr. and T. K. Srull (Eds.), *Handbook of Social Cognition* (Vol. 3, pp. 179–236). Hillsdale, NJ: Erlbaum.

Jacoby, J., Chestnut, R. W., Weigl, K. C., & Fisher, W. (1976). Pre-purchase information acquisition: Description of a process methodology, research paradigm, and pilot investigation. In B. B. Anderson (Ed.), *Advances in consumer research* (Vol. 3, pp. 306–314). Chicago: Association for Consumer Research.

Jacoby, J., Mazursky, D., Troutman, T., & Kuss, A. (1984). When feedback is ignored: Disutility of outcome feedback. *Journal of Applied Psychology, 69,* 531–545.

Janis, I. L., & Mann, L. (1977). *Decision making.* New York: Free Press.

Johnson, E. J., & Payne, J. W. (1985). Effort and accuracy in choice. *Management Science, 31,* 394–414.

Johnson, M. D. (1984). Consumer choice strategies for comparing noncomparable alternatives. *Journal of Consumer Research, 11,* 741–753.

Just, M. A., & Carpenter, P. A. (1984). Using eye fixations to study reading comprehension. In D. E. Kieras & M. A. Just (Eds.), *New methods in reading comprehension research.* (pp. 151–182). Hillsdale, NJ: Erlbaum.

Kahneman, D. (1986). Comments on the contingent valuation method. In R. D. Cummings, D. S. Brookshire, & W. D. Schulze (Eds.), *Valuing environmental goods: An assessment of the contingent valuation method.* Totowa, NJ: Roman and Allen.

Kahneman, D. (1993, November). *J/DM president's address.* Paper presented at the meeting of the Judgment/Decision Making Society, Washington, DC.

Kahneman, D., & Knetsch, J. L. (1992). Valuing public goods: The purchase of moral satisfaction. *Journal of Economics and Environmental Management, 22,* 57–70.

Kahneman, D., & Tversky, A. (1979). Prospect theory: An analysis of decision making under risk. *Econometrica, 47,* 263–291.

Keeney, R. L. (1992). *Value-focused thinking.* Cambridge, MA: Harvard University Press.

Keller, L. R., & Ho, J. L. (1988). Decision problem structuring: Generating options. *IEEE Transactions on Systems, Man, and Cybernetics, 18,* 715–728.

Klayman, J. (1983). Analysis of predecisional information search patterns. In P. C. Humphreys, O. Svenson, & A. Vari (Eds.), *Analyzing and aiding decision processes* (pp. 401–414). Amsterdam: North-Holland.

Kruglanski, A. W. (1989). The psychology of being "right": The problem of accuracy in social perception and cognition. *Psychological Bulletin, 106,* 395–409.

Krutilla, J. V. (1967). Conservation reconsidered. *American Economic Review, 57*, 787–796.

Kunda, Z. (1990). The case for motivated reasoning. *Psychological Bulletin, 108*, 480–498.

Langley, P., Simon, H. A., Bradshaw, G. L., & Zytkow, J. M. (1987). *Scientific discovery.* Cambridge, MA: MIT Press.

Larrick, R. P. (1993). Motivational factors in decision theories: The role of self-protection. *Psychological Bulletin, 113*, 440–450.

Larrick, R. P., Morgan, J. N., & Nisbett, R. E. (1990). Teaching the use of cost–benefit reasoning in everyday life. *Psychological Science, 1*, 362–370.

Lazarus, R. S. (1991). Progress on a cognitive-motivational-relational theory of emotion. *American Psychologist, 46*, 819–834.

Lazarus, R. S., & Folkman, S. (1984). *Stress, appraisal, and coping.* New York: Springer.

Lewinsohn, S. & Mano, H. (1993). Multiattribute choice and affect: The influence of naturally occurring and manipulated moods on choice processes. *Journal of Behavioral Decision Making, 6*, 33–51.

Lipman, B. L. (1991). How to decide how to decide how to. . . . Modeling limited rationality. *Econometrica, 59*, 1105–1125.

Loomis, J. B. (1990). Comparative validity of the dichotomous choice and open-ended contingent valuation techniques. *Journal of Environmental Economics and Management, 18*, 78–85.

Lopes, L. L. (1982). Toward a procedural theory of judgment. Unpublished manuscript. University of Wisconsin.

Lopes, L. L. (1987). Between hope and fear: The psychology of risk. *Advances in Experimental Social Psychology, 20*, 255–295.

Luce, M. F. (1994). Emotion and consumer choice. Unpublished doctoral dissertation. Fuqua School of Business, Duke University.

Mano, H. (1992). Judgments under distress: Assessing the role of unpleasantness and arousal in judgment formation. *Organizational Behavior and Human Decision Processes, 32*, 216–245.

March, J. G. (1978). Bounded rationality, ambiguity, and the engineering of choice. *Bell Journal of Economics, 9*, 587–608.

Marx, M. H., & Hillix, W. A. (1963). *Systems and theories in psychology.* New York: McGraw-Hill.

McClelland, G. H. (1978). Equal versus differential weighting for multiattribute decisions. Unpublished manuscript. University of Colorado.

McKenzie, C. R. M. (1994). The accuracy of intuitive judgment strategies: Covariation assessment and Bayesian inference. *Cognitive Psychology, 26*, 209–239.

Mitchell, R. C., & Carson, R. T. (1989). *Using surveys to value public goods: The contingent valuation method.* Washington, DC: Resources for the Future.

Montgomery, H. (1983). Decision rules and the search for a dominance structure: Toward a process model of decision making. In P. C. Humphreys, O. Svenson, & A. Vari (Eds.), *Analyzing and aiding decision processes* (pp. 343–369). Amsterdam: North-Holland.

Neisser, U. (1967). *Cognitive psychology.* New York: Appleton-Century-Crofts.

Newell, A. (1980). Harpy, production systems, and human cognition. In R. Cole (Ed.), *Perception and production of fluent speech* (pp. 299–380). Hillsdale, NJ: Erlbaum.

Newell, A., & Simon, H. A. (1972). *Human problem solving.* Englewood Cliffs, NJ: Prentice-Hall.

Nisbett, R. E., & Wilson, T. D. (1977). Telling more than we can know: Verbal reports on mental processes. *Psychological Review, 84*, 231–259.

Paquette, L., & Kida, T. (1988). The effect of decision strategy and task complexity on decision performance. *Organizational Behavior and Human Decision Processes, 41*, 128–142.

Payne, J. W. (1976). Task complexity and contingent processing in decision making: An information search and protocol analysis. *Organizational Behavior and Human Performance, 16,* 366–387.

Payne, J. W. (1994). Thinking aloud: Insights into information processing. *Psychological Science, 5,* 241–248.

Payne, J. W., Bettman, J. R., & Johnson, E. J. (1988). Adaptive strategy selection in decision making. *Journal of Experimental Psychology: Learning, Memory, and Cognition, 14,* 534–552.

Payne, J. W., Bettman, J. R., & Johnson, E. J. (1992). Behavioral decision research: A constructive processing perspective. *Annual Review of Psychology, 43,* 87–131.

Payne, J. W., Bettman, J. R., & Johnson, E. J. (1993). *The adaptive decision maker.* Cambridge: Cambridge University Press.

Payne, J. W., & Braunstein, M. L. (1978). Risky choice: An examination of information acquisition behavior. *Memory & Cognition, 6,* 554–561.

Payne, J. W., Braunstein, M. L., & Carroll, J. S. (1978). Exploring predecisional behavior: An alternative approach to decision research. *Organizational Behavior and Human Performance, 22,* 17–44.

Reder, L. M. (1987). Strategy selection in question answering. *Cognitive Psychology, 19,* 90–138.

Russo, J. E. (1978). Eye fixations can save the world: Critical evaluation and comparison between eye fixations and other information processing methodologies. In H. K. Hunt (Ed.), *Advances in consumer research (Vol. 5,* pp. 561–570). Ann Arbor, MI: Association for Consumer Research.

Russo, J. E., & Dosher, B. A. (1983). Strategies for multiattribute binary choice. *Journal of Experimental Psychology: Learning, Memory, and Cognition, 9,* 676–696.

Russo, J. E., Johnson, E. J., & Stephens, D. M. (1989). The validity of verbal protocols. *Memory & Cognition, 17,* 759–769.

Schkade, D. A., & Payne, J. W. (1994). How do people respond to contingent valuation questions: A verbal protocol analysis of willingness-to-pay for an environmental regulation. *Journal of Environmental Economics and Management, 26,* 88–109.

Shanteau, J. (1988). Psychological characteristics and strategies of expert decision makers. *Acta Psychologica, 68,* 203–215.

Shugan, S. M. (1980). The cost of thinking. *Journal of Consumer Research, 7,* 99–111.

Siegler, R. S. (1988). Strategy choice procedures and the development of multiplication skill. *Journal of Experimental Psychology: General, 117,* 258–275.

Simon, H. A. (1955). A behavioral model of rational choice. *Quarterly Journal of Economics, 69,* 99–118.

Simon, H. A. (1978). Rationality as process and as product of thought. *American Economic Review, 68,* 1–16.

Simon, H. A. (1987). Making management decisions: The role of intuition and emotion. *Academy of Management Executive,* February, 57–64.

Simon, H. A. (1990). Invariants of human behavior. *Annual Review of Psychology, 41,* 1–19.

Simon, H. A. (1991). *Models of my life.* New York: Basic Books.

Slovic, P., Griffin, D., & Tversky, A. (1990). Compatibility effects in judgement and choice. In R. M. Hogarth (Ed.), *Insights in decision making: A tribute to Hillel J. Einhorn* (pp. 5–27). Chicago: University of Chicago Press.

Stone, D. N. (1994). Overconfidence in self-efficacy judgments: Effects on decision processes and performance. *Organizational Behavior and Human Decision Processes, 59,* 452–474.

Svenson, O. (1979). Process descriptions of decision making. *Organizational Behavior and Human Performance, 23,* 86–112.

Thorngate, W. (1980). Efficient decision heuristics. *Behavioral Science, 25,* 219–225.

Thorngate, W., & Maki, J. (1976). Decision heuristics and the choice of political candidates. Unpublished manuscript. University of Alberta.

Todd, P. A., & Benbasat, I. (1994). The influence of decision aids on choice strategies under conditions of high cognitive load. *IEEE Transactions on Systems, Man, and Cybernetics, 24,* 537–547.

Tversky, A. (1969). Intransitivity of preferences. *Psychological Review, 76,* 31–48.

Tversky, A., Sattath, S., & Slovic, P. (1988). Contingent weighting in judgment and choice. *Psychological Review, 95,* 371–384.

Tversky, A., & Shafir, E. (1992). Choice under conflict: The dynamics of deferred decisions. *Psychological Science, 6,* 358–361.

Usher, M., & Zakay, D. (1993). A neural network model for attribute-based decision processes. *Cognitive Science, 17,* 349–396.

Weber, E. U., Goldstein, W. M., & Busemeyer, J. R. (1991). Beyond strategies: Implications of memory representations and memory processes for models of judgment and decision making. In W. F. Hockley & S. Lewandowsky (Eds.), *Relating theory and data: Essays on human memory in honor of Bennett B. Murdock* (pp. 75–100). Hillsdale, NJ: Erlbaum.

Wickens, C. D. (1986). Gain and energetics in information processing. In G. Hockey, A. Gaillard, and M. Coles (Eds.), *Energetics and human information processing* (pp. 373–389). Dordrecht, The Netherlands: Martinus Nijhoff.

Wilkins, L. T. (1967). *Social deviance.* Englewood Cliffs, NJ: Prentice-Hall.

Zajonc, R. B. (1980). Feeling and thinking: preferences need no inferences. *American Psychologists, 35,* 151–175.

Zipf, G. K. (1949). *Human behavior and the principle of least effort.* Cambridge, MA: Addison-Wesley.

ALGEBRA AND PROCESS IN THE MODELING OF RISKY CHOICE

Lola L. Lopes

I. Introduction

There are two approaches to modeling risky choice. Some models focus on the algebraic pattern of people's risk preferences, others on the content of their choice processes. Although one might suppose that these two kinds of accounts are alternate ways of describing the same thing—indeed, that one kind of model might eventually be reducible to the other—the approaches have tended to be disjoint. Mathematical forms that have lent themselves to describing the algebraic pattern of sets of choices have not been particularly useful for describing the process of choosing. Conversely, the processes people appear to use for comparing alternatives lack the continuity and homogeneity required by algebraic accounts.

The aim of this chapter is to connect algebraic and process accounts of risky choice. I use the term "connect" advisedly in this context because it seems unlikely that either kind of account can replace the other. Instead, I shall argue that qualitative comparison operations applied at the level of the single trial produce aggregate data—pooled across replications, choice pairs, and (often) subjects as well—that have the quantitative structures that we associate with algebraic models.

I begin by tracing the evolution of algebraic models of risky choice from the seventeenth century to the present. Then, I examine a variety of tasks that have been used to study risky choice in the laboratory and identify

177

several important process models. Finally, I discuss how the process models relate to one another and how they look from an algebraic perspective. In the course of the latter exposition, I will show how the insights of process studies have been integrated into a new algebraic frame called SP/A (security-potential/aspiration) theory (Lopes, 1987, 1990).

II.   Algebraic Models of Risky Choice

A.   The Idea of Mathematical Expectation

Although it is common to trace the history of psychological thought back to the Greeks, it was not until the nineteenth century that psychological thought began to take on the exact and quantitative features that characterize modern theory. In the case of risky choice, however, theory in the modern sense began to emerge in the seventeenth century with the invention of the concept of mathematical expectation. Since then, the dominant strand in the three-plus centuries of risk theory has been the gradual modification of the idea that people choose among risks in order to maximize something analogous to expected value.

The idea of mathematical expectation first appeared in the writings of Blaise Pascal and Christian Huygens. Originally, the concept was understood in terms of the moral idea of a fair exchange or contract (Daston, 1980; Gigerenzer et al., 1989). Before long, however, the idea was applied to decision making under risk—Pascal's wager on heaven and hell is the prototype here—culminating in the normative proposition that one should choose among risks so as to maximize expected value:

$$\text{EV} = \sum_{i=1}^{n} p_i v_i, \tag{1}$$

where p_i is the probability of outcome i, v_i is its objective value, and n is the number of possible outcomes.

The normative application of the expected value criterion subsumes at least seven more elementary ideas:

1. Numerical representation: it is possible to express the value of a risky option numerically.
2. Unidimensional representation: a single number is sufficient to index the value of a risky option.
3. Probability/outcome combination: in calculating the value index, probabilities and outcomes are combined.

4. Probability/value independence: in calculating the value index, the impact of a probability is independent of the value to which it is attached and the impact of a value is independent of the probability of its occurrence.
5. Probability linearity: in calculating the value index, outcomes are weighted (i.e., multiplied) by their probability of occurrence.
6. Probability objectivity: probabilities are defined objectively and are the same for all people.
7. Value objectivity: outcome values are measured by the objective values assigned to outcomes and are the same for all people.

Although the first three ideas continue to figure in many modern theories of risky choice, the last four have been challenged one by one and have been replaced by less specific analogues.

B. DANIEL BERNOULLI AND THE ST. PETERSBURG PARADOX

The first challenge to the expected value criterion came in the form of a problem posed by Nicholas Bernoulli in a letter to Pierre de Montmort and published by de Montmort in 1713:

> Suppose that a fair coin is tossed until tails first appears, at which point the player is paid a sum equal to $\$2^n$, where n is the number of the toss on which tails appears. How much should a person be willing to pay for a single play of the game?

If we seek the counsel of the expected value criterion, we get a surprising answer:

$$EV = \tfrac{1}{2}(\$2) + \tfrac{1}{4}(\$4) + \tfrac{1}{8}(\$8) + \tfrac{1}{16}(\$16) + \ldots + \tfrac{1}{n}(\$2^n) \ldots$$
$$= 1 + 1 + 1 + 1 + \ldots + 1 \ldots$$
$$= \infty.$$

Though intuition whispers that the game is worth no more than a few dollars, expected value demands that one give all one has or hopes to have in exchange for a single play.

The patent folly of the expected value recommendation discomfited early probabilists because they considered probability theory to be a distillation of good sense rather than an independent mathematical theory (Gigerenzer et al., 1989). In 1738, however, Daniel Bernoulli published a solution in the annals of the Academy of St. Petersburg (Bernoulli, 1738/1967)[1] that

---

[1] Gabriel Cramer had hit on a similar resolution 10 years earlier and wrote to Nicholas Bernoulli about it in 1728. Daniel Bernoulli did not learn of Cramer's letter until after he had independently solved the problem. It is to Daniel Bernoulli's credit that he included the text of Cramer's letter in his monograph.

eliminated the difficulty. Bernoulli disputed the idea of value objectivity by pointing out that rich men value given increments in wealth less than poor men. He argued that if we acknowledge this state of affairs by assuming that the moral value (or utility) of wealth is logarithmic, we would expect people to maximize the expectation of utility, $u(v)$,

$$EU = \sum_{i=1}^{n} p_i u(v_i), \qquad (2)$$

rather than wealth, in which case the paradox disappears.

To understand how Bernoulli's solution works, recall that when we computed the game's expected value, the numerators (prizes) grew proportionally larger as the denominators (probabilities) shrank, so that each term in the infinite series reduced to 1. If logs are substituted for monetary values, however,

$$EU = \tfrac{1}{2} \log_2 (\$2) + \tfrac{1}{4} \log_2 (\$4) + \tfrac{1}{8} \log_2 (\$8) + \tfrac{1}{16} \log_2 (\$16) +$$
$$\ldots + \tfrac{1}{n} \log_2 (\$2^n) \ldots$$
$$= \tfrac{1}{2} (1) + \tfrac{1}{4} (2) + \tfrac{1}{8} (3) + \tfrac{1}{16} (4) + \ldots + \tfrac{1}{2^n}(n) \ldots$$
$$= \tfrac{1}{2} + \tfrac{2}{4} + \tfrac{3}{8} + \tfrac{4}{16} + \ldots + n/2^n \ldots$$
$$= 2,$$

the numerators in the series grow much more slowly than the denominators so that the expectation limits at 2 utility units (utiles), the monetary equivalent of which is $4.

Because negatively accelerated utility functions such as the log function have the general property of preferring sure things to gambles, they are commonly referred to as *risk averse* functions. Still, it is important to keep in mind that Bernoulli's proposal does not call on a directly realized concept of risk but resides instead in the subjective valuation of outcomes. Modern usage (particularly economic usage) has conflated the phenomenon (the rejection of gambles or "risk aversion") with the mechanism (what we today term *diminishing marginal utility*), making it difficult if not impossible to ask what it means for a gamble to be risky or how perceived riskiness figures in risk aversion.

Although other resolutions of the St. Petersburg paradox were eventually suggested (Samuelson, 1977; Todhunter, 1865), none had much impact on later thinking. Bernoulli's solution, on the other hand, set the pattern not only for the subsequent treatment of risk aversion but also for how later challenges to expected utility theory would be handled. Although modifications might be suggested for the more specific elements of the original expected value model, the more general characteristics would remain unchallenged and largely invisible.

C. MODERN AXIOMATIC UTILITY THEORY

By the twentieth century, Bernoulli's ideas about expected utility maximization had fallen into disfavor because of difficulties in measuring and comparing utilities across different people and because it was not clear that maximizing mathematical expectation made sense outside the context of repeated decisions. In the 1940s, however, von Neumann and Morgenstern (1947) invented a variant of expected utility theory in the course of developing a theory of rational behavior under competition. The new theory differed from the old in three critical ways. First, it provided an axiomatically based procedure for measuring cardinal utility—a term of somewhat unclear meaning (Anderson, Deane, Hammond, McClelland, & Shanteau, 1981) but suggesting something like Bernoulli's notion of subjective value. Second, it shifted the conception of a utility function from something that causes preferences to something that summarizes preferences. Third, it suggested, at least by default, that the reasoning underlying expected utility maximization applies as readily to single choices as to repeated choices.

The new theory stimulated an abundance of mathematical research, most of which had no impact on psychology. There were, however, two important exceptions. The first was a theoretical note from Friedman and Savage (1948) that illustrated how modern expected utility theory could be used to explain the well-known but theoretically uncomfortable fact that even though most people are sufficiently risk averse to buy insurance against large risks, they willingly participate in lotteries and other small risks. Friedman and Savage argued that if utility functions only summarize preferences, there is no reason why they cannot have both concave regions (capturing risk aversion) and convex regions (capturing risk seeking).

The second exception was a theoretical reformulation of expected utility theory by Savage (1954) that challenged the idea of probability objectivity by replacing measured or stated probabilities by their subjective counterparts. The new "subjectively expected utility theory" appealed strongly to psychologists who believed that probabilities are intrinsically personal and subjective. The same psychologists were also drawn to the idea that the formal laws governing subjective probability constitute a normative model for rational belief.

D. THE ALLAIS AND ELLSBERG PARADOXES

Although the new expected utility theories relaxed some of the assumptions of the old theory, they also increased the stringency of empirical tests by directing attention to the points at which the theories were most vulnerable. These were the axiomatic relations that were predicted to hold among preferences. A new round of theoretical challenges ensued, the first and ultimately the most devastating of which was leveled at the idea of probability linearity by the French economist, Maurice Allais (1952/1979a).

According to both expected and subjectively expected utility theory, if someone prefers a p chance of winning v to a p' chance of winning v', her preference should be unchanged even if p and p' are reduced by linear transformation. Allais was skeptical about this prediction, however, and argued that preferences might well shift if the transformation changed a sure option into an uncertain option. To demonstrate the point, he devised two problems, one involving probability differences and the other involving probability ratios. In both versions, subsequent research confirmed that Allais was right and that many people's preferences do, indeed, shift when probabilities are shifted. For example, most people who are asked to choose between having \$1 million for sure (option A) or having a .9 chance of winning \$2 million (option B) would prefer the safer option A. However, if the same people are offered a choice between a .009 chance of winning \$2 million (option D) and a .01 chance of winning \$1 million (option C), many switch their preferences to the slightly riskier option D despite the fact that the probabilities of winning in the two pairs are related by a constant ratio: .01 = 1.00/100 and .009 = .9/100.

A few years later, another challenge was aimed at the concept of subjective probability. Daniel Ellsberg (1961) asked people to consider an urn containing colored balls, some in known proportions (e.g., 30 red balls) and others in unknown proportions (e.g., 60 black and/or yellow balls). Ellsberg showed that depending on how payoffs are assigned to the different colors of balls, many people choose as if they consider the subjective probability of drawing a red ball to be sometimes greater than the subjective probability of drawing a black ball and sometimes less. For example, many people who prefer to bet on red over black also prefer to bet on black-or-yellow over red-or-yellow. If choices among risks are to be modeled by subjectively expected utility theory, the subjective probability of red cannot be both greater and less than the subjective probability of black.

Although the Allais and Ellsberg paradoxes (as they are now called) test features of different theories, they were defended in similar terms by their authors. Allais interpreted his results by proposing that people have a preference for security in the region of certainty that disappears as the certainty is reduced. Thus, people choose the sure thing when it is offered but trade off a little risk for a greatly increased payoff when certainty is low. Ellsberg also interpreted his problem in terms of the "security levels" that people justifiably seek when they face ambiguous (or vague) probabilities.

The Allais and Ellsberg paradoxes were both telling and compelling, capable of tripping up even the staunchest advocates of expected (or subjectively expected) utility theory. They were, in the best sense, critical tests that should have turned attention to the descriptive inadequacies of the two theories. The response in economics, however, was one of denial and distancing. For almost three decades, Allais and Ellsberg were mostly ignored, and when they were mentioned, it was typical to suggest that an adequate normative (i.e., theoretical) reading of their problems would forestall paradoxical choices and unacceptable yearnings.

E. WEIGHTED UTILITY AND PROSPECT THEORY

The situation in psychology was not much different. Although a strong interest in process accounts of risky choice developed in the 1970s, the differences that were observed between behavior and theory tended to be attributed to limitations in people's information processing capacity. Thus, when psychologists were finally ready to deal with the Allais and Ellsberg paradoxes descriptively, the theoretical language they chose was one of distortion and perceptual subjectivity rather than the language of "security" that Allais and Ellsberg had favored.

As early as 1962, Edwards (1962) suggested that it might be necessary to model the weight or impact of probability information in risky choice as a nonlinear function of its objective (or subjective) magnitude:

$$WU = \sum_{i=1}^{n} w(p_i)u(v_i). \tag{3}$$

Some years later, Karmarkar (1978, 1979) and Kahneman and Tversky (1979) independently proposed weighted utility theories that used nonlinear probabilities to account for the Allais paradox. Of these, the latter version (called *prospect theory*) dominated subsequent interest in the model.

Prospect theory proposed three major ways in which people's choice processes differ from the processes implied by expected utility theory or subjectively expected utility theory. One difference is that people are assumed to apply a set of "editing operations" in order to encode and (perhaps) simplify problem information before it is used. Although verification of the proposed editing operations offers a clear arena for further study, there has been surprisingly little research along this line.

The second difference is that the impact of probabilities on choice is nonlinear. Prospect theory predicts overweighting of small probabilities and underweighting of moderate and large probabilities. The weighting function is also discontinuous at both ends (as probability nears 1 and 0) and becomes steeper as it runs from small to large. Taken together, these properties provide an account of people's preferences in the Allais paradoxes and also provide additional sources of risk aversion (for gambles with large or moderate probabilities of winning) and risk seeking (for gambles with small probabilities of winning).

The third difference is that the value (or utility) function of prospect theory is S-shaped, predicting risk aversion in some cases and risk seeking in others. In contrast to Friedman and Savage (1948), however, the inflection occurs at the point that separates gains from losses. Kahneman and Tversky interpret the S-shape in terms of diminishing sensitivity to changes as one moves away from the currently adapted state or status quo. The function is also steeper for losses than for gains. This feature is needed to account for what Kahneman and Tversky call "loss aversion" (i.e., the fact that a loss of size k has greater impact than a gain of size k).

The idea of an S-shaped value function has garnered a great deal of attention from researchers who have worked at switching people's preferences from risk averse to risk seeking by changing the signs on outcomes (reflection) or by describing the same outcomes either as gains or losses (framing). However, the probability weighting function has been less well received, especially by economists, as it predicts that people will sometimes prefer obviously dominated alternatives. Although Kahneman and Tversky attempted to forestall the latter criticism by proposing that dominated alternatives are eliminated in editing, the problem is now considered to be indicative of a more fundamental inability of weighted utility to provide a descriptively and aesthetically acceptable account of risky choice.

F. DECUMULATIVE WEIGHTING FUNCTIONS

If one pauses a moment to consider the transformation of expected value into weighted utility, one can see that it has involved only three of the ideas underlying the expected value criterion: value objectivity, probability objectivity, and probability linearity. The most recent transformation in the series involves the somewhat more general idea that probabilities and values have independent impacts on gamble worth. To understand this new variation, consider that in the standard equation for expected value (Eq. 1), the index i is a nominal index: although the n probability-outcome terms are labeled by i, they have no intrinsic order. An equivalent equation in which i indexes terms in order of value from v_1 (the worst outcome) to v_n (the best outcome) can be written:

$$\text{EV} = v_1 + \sum_{i=2}^{n} \sum_{j=i}^{n} p_j(v_i - v_{i-1}) = v_1 + \sum_{i=2}^{n} D_i(v_i - v_{i-1}), \qquad (4)$$

where $D_i (= \sum_{j=i}^{n} p_j)$ is the decumulative probability of receiving at least the ith outcome.

The computational difference between the two expressions is easily understood by example. Consider a five-outcome gamble that pays $1 with probability .05, $25 with probability .15, $50 with probability .60, $75 with probability .15, and $99 with probability .05. If we compute the expected value of the gamble by Eq. 1, we proceed as follows: $(.05)($1) + (.15)($25) + (.60)($50) + (.15)($75) + (.05)($99) = 50. If we use Eq. 4, however, we proceed somewhat differently: $(1.00)($1) + (.95)($24) + (.80)($25) + (.20)($25) + (.05)($24) = 50. The latter "decumulative" computational scheme captures the sense that the gamble pays at least $1 for sure, with probability .95 pays another $24, with probability .80 pays yet another $25, with probability .20 pays yet another $25, and with probability .05 pays yet another $24.

In the standard computation, one can easily see the possibilities of transforming the values and raw probabilities. In the decumulative form, however, the apparent possibilities for psychological transformation shift. Although the option is still open to replace differences in values by differences in utility, $u(v_i) - u(v_{i-1})$, a transformation h on probability would now affect decumulative probabilities, $D_i = \sum_{j=i}^{n} p_j$, rather than raw probabilities:

$$\text{DWU} = u(v_1) + \sum_{i=2}^{n} h(D_i)(u(v_i) - u(v_{i-1})). \tag{5}$$

Transformations on decumulative probabilities differ critically from transformations on raw probabilities, because the magnitude of the transformed value in the former case depends on its position in the distribution.[2] For example, the preceding gamble has two outcomes ($1 and $99) that each occur with probability .05. If raw probabilities were transformed (as in weighted utility), the same transformation would apply to both. With decumulative weighting, however, quite different things can happen to the probability attached to the worst outcome and to the probability attached to the best outcome.

Decumulative weighting models are an attractive alternative to weighted utility models because they can handle the nonlinearities in probability weights that are suggested by the Allais and Ellsberg paradoxes while avoiding the problems with dominance that affect weighted utility models. The first applications of the model were independently proposed in economics by Quiggen (1982), Allais (1986), and Yaari (1987), followed in short order by many others (e.g., Chew, Karni, & Safra, 1987; Luce, 1988; Schmeidler, 1989; Segal, 1989). In psychology, decumulative weighting has

---

[2] The term *rank dependent* is also used to refer to theories with decumulative probability weights.

been used to capture individual differences in risky choice by Lopes (1987, 1990; Schneider & Lopes, 1986) and more recently by Tversky and Kahneman (1992) in a cumulative reformulation of prospect theory.[3]

Three different possibilities for the decumulative transformation function are shown in Fig. 1. The weighting patterns that they represent capture the relative importance to decision makers of avoiding bad outcomes (security) and achieving good outcomes (potential). On the abscissa of each graph are objective decumulative probabilities, $D_i = \sum_{j=i}^{n} p_j$, displayed right to left from $i = 1$ to $i = n$. A probability of 1.00 (at the far right) is the decumulative probability attached to the worst outcome (i.e., you get at least the worst outcome for sure). To the left are decumulative probabilities for successively better and better outcomes. These limit at zero, which is the probability of exceeding the best outcome. The ordinate shows psychologically transformed values, $h(D_i)$, under a particular weighting scenario.

The left panel displays what I call *security-mindedness*. The decumulative probability attached to the worst outcome (1.00) receives full weight. Successively better outcomes receive proportionally less and less of their objective weights (i.e., the weights they would receive in an expected value computation). Mild security-mindedness would entail a curve bowing only a little from the diagonal. Extreme forms of security-mindedness would entail a curve running tight against the graph's horizontal and vertical axes. A person displaying the security-minded pattern of probability weighting would appear to be risk averse even if his or her utility function were linear in money.

The middle panel shows the decumulative analogue to pure risk seeking. The decumulative probability attached to the worst outcome receives a weight of 1.00, but weights attached to successively better outcomes receive proportionally more and more weight than their objective weights warrant. I call this pattern *potential-mindedness*.

The pattern in the right panel, which I term *cautiously hopeful*, has been proposed by Allais (1986) and by me (Lopes, 1990)[4] to represent the weighting pattern of the average decision maker. The function is security-minded for low outcomes (i.e., proportionally more attention is devoted to worse outcomes than to moderate outcomes) but there is some over-weighting (extra attention) given to the very best outcomes. A person displaying the cautiously hopeful pattern would be basically security-minded but would consider potential when security differences were small.

---

[3] Somewhat earlier, Luce and Fishburn (1991) axiomatized a rank-dependent and sign-dependent representation for choices among uncertain alternatives that includes cumulative prospect theory as a special case.

[4] I have previously called this a "hybrid" function.

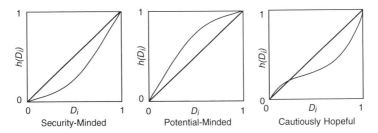

Fig. 1. Decumulative weighting functions representing three different attitudes toward risk.

The pattern is descriptively useful because it predicts the purchase of both insurance and lottery tickets (cf. Friedman & Savage, 1948) as well as handling both forms of the Allais paradox (Allais, 1986).[5]

G. STOCHASTIC CONTROL AND GOAL SEEKING

Although expectation models have dominated both normative and descriptive approaches to risky choice, there have been other views—at least one of which dates back to Bernoulli's time. Recall that Bernoulli's solution of the St. Petersburg game imposes a logarithmic transformation on monetary value that shrinks large values more than small values. Two other early contributors to probability theory, Jean d'Alembert and George Leclerc Buffon, disputed the focus on value and instead laid the blame on the tiny probabilities. Buffon, in particular, argued that probabilities smaller than .0001 were "moral impossibilities" and ought to be ignored, thus reducing the expected value of the gamble by an entirely different route (Daston, 1980).

There is, however, an important similarity between Bernoulli's utility-based analysis and the probability-based analyses of d'Alembert and Buffon. For all three, the psychological locus of effect lies at the high end: the expected utility of the game is made small by a mechanism that reduces the impact of terms having small probabilities of large payoffs. Additional solutions can be found, however, that exclude expectation entirely. One particularly interesting example also comes from Buffon (Todhunter, 1865), who hired a child to toss a coin 2000 times and record the sequence of outcomes. Buffon then used the data to estimate the worth of the gamble to the player and found it to be quite small. Some 230 years later, not knowing about Buffon, I ran a similar experiment involving hundreds of

[5] Tversky and Kahneman (1992) use a similar function to weight gains in cumulative prospect theory. But in keeping with the S-shaped utility function, they use a cumulative weighting function for losses that is roughly a mirror image of this.

millions of trials in a Monte Carlo simulation and confirmed that even at a price of $100, the game is a money maker for sellers and no bargain for buyers (Lopes, 1981; see also Lopes, 1995).

Experiments like mine and Buffon's argue that the worth of the St. Petersburg game appears very small for the good reason that it *is* very small most of the time. The argument is open to criticism, of course, on the grounds that the fact that a very, very rare event does not occur in a particular experiment does not mean that it cannot occur (see Samuelson, 1977, p. 51, on Buffon). One can, however, use the mathematically respectable "theory of ruin" to reach the same conclusion.

To understand how ruin enters the picture, suppose that someone worth a million dollars relies on the expected value criterion and pays her entire fortune for one play of the game. To avoid a net loss, she must toss at least 19 heads before a tail appears, an event that is expected to occur with probability $(1/2)^{20}$. Moreover, the most likely outcome is that she will reduce her fortune to a very small sum (e.g., $\leq$$100 with probability $1 - (1/2)^6 =$ .984). Someone owning a smaller fortune to start with would be less likely to lose money, of course, but even for a relative pauper whose total fortune is $1000, it would still be necessary to toss at least 9 heads before a tail appears, an event having probability $(1/2)^{10}$. Thus, consideration of ruin precludes all but the already destitute from giving all they have or hope to have for a single play of the game.

But there is more to the matter than this. Even if the player can buy the gamble so cheaply that she can purchase multiple trials, ruin is still the most likely outcome. According to Allais (1979b), a player with a bankroll of $1 million who is allowed to purchase plays of the game for $33 each will be ruined with probability .9999 if settlement is made after every game.[6] Allais used such calculations to defend the more general thesis that a prudent person will make decisions under risk in such a way as to balance the expectation of monetary gains (or utility gains) against the probability that he or she will fail to achieve some important goal.

Although Allais has had a profound impact on risk theory by reason of his paradoxes, it appears that no psychologist but myself has seen the interest and importance of his thoughts on the role that probabilistic thinking might play in risky choice. There is, however, an alternate route by which such a probabilistic account might have entered our collective consciousness. At about the time he published his esteemed book on subjectively expected utility theory, Savage became interested in a class of gam-

---

[6] This particular analysis assumes that the seller's bankroll is infinite. The result, however, would not be much changed by specifying a finite bankroll provided that it is sufficiently large (say $1 billion) to withstand some rare outcomes occurring early in the sequence of transactions.

bling problems of which the following is a prototype (Dubins & Savage, 1976):

> Imagine yourself at a casino with $1,000. For some reason, you desperately need $10,000 by morning; anything less is worth nothing for your purpose. . . . The only thing possible is to gamble away your last cent, if need be, in an attempt to reach the target sum of $10,000. . . . The question is how to play, not whether. (p. 1)

The solution that Savage and Dubins proposed is difficult to prove but easy to understand. What they discovered is that the hapless gambler, facing the unfair bets of a casino, cannot afford to play cautiously. If he wagers only small sums on each bet, he will allow the casino to chip away safely at his own small holding until it is gone. Instead, the gambler must play boldly, staking on each bet either everything he has or (if the target is not too far off) staking exactly as much as is necessary to meet his target with a single bet.

Dubins and Savage's book eventually stimulated a field of mathematics called stochastic control that focuses on how to maximize the probability that a desired state will be achieved (e.g., having $10,000 by morning) subject to stated constraints (e.g., starting with $1,000, facing the unfair bets offered in casinos, not being able to take out a loan, etc.). For the most part, however, researchers who study risky choice either do not know about this work or else consider it to be irrelevant. Indeed, Dubins and Savage (1976, p. 1) themselves thought that the gambling problems they were studying had no practical importance. Allais, in contrast, has argued for years (see, e.g., 1952/1979, p. 53), that the contexts in which risky choices are made fall along a strategic continuum on which expected utility maximization defines one pole and probability maximization defines the other. For situations in which risks are small in relation to one's assets, it is reasonable to be an expected utility maximizer. But as risks become larger, it becomes necessary to choose in ways that are sensitive to one's circumstances, trading off some expected utility against an increased probability of goal attainment.

H. SIMPLE RULES FOR ORDERING GAMBLES

One last class of approaches to risky choice also deserves mention. These are rules for ordering gambles that have appeared from time to time in economics and statistics as well as in psychology. Unlike the thoroughly algebraic rules in the expectation family, these rules do not yield a numerical measure of gamble attractiveness, nor do they allow one to maximize probabilities as in stochastic control theory. Instead, all these rules do—and that, only sometimes—is help one decide which of two gambles to choose.

One very simple rule is the maximin criterion. Under this rule, if two gambles have different "worst" outcomes, one should choose the gamble having the best (maximum) worst (minimum) outcome.[7] The maximin rule is often described as pessimistic because it chooses as if it expects the worst. A complementary (and thus optimistic) rule in the same family is the maximax criterion, under which one chooses the gamble that has the higher maximum. A weighted combination of maximin and maximax has also been suggested by Hurwicz (1951).

The maximin and maximax rules were originally suggested for choice under ignorance (i.e., for choosing in situations in which probabilities are unknown). Many consider these rules foolish for the case of risk because any small difference in minimum (or maximum) outcome, no matter how improbable, can outweigh large differences in the values and probabilities of other outcomes. Although the foolishness can be tempered by setting thresholds on the magnitudes of critical differences, one can always construct problems in which either rule recommends obviously poor choices.

A somewhat different rule is the minimax regret criterion discussed by Savage (1951). Regret is best understood in terms of the everyday sense that people experience regret when they would have chosen differently had they known what was going to happen. Thus, the criterion minimizes the maximum difference between the best that might happen and what actually happens. Normative interest in minimax regret eventually faded because the rule fails to exhibit independence from irrelevant alternatives,[8] but there has been considerable recent interest in incorporating regret into expectation models (Bell, 1982; Loomes & Sugden, 1982, 1987).

A third rule for ordering gambles is stochastic dominance. For illustration, consider a pair of two-outcome gambles having identical outcomes but different probabilities. Anyone who prefers more to less should prefer the gamble having the lower probability of the lesser outcome. This idea can be generalized to multioutcome or even continuous distributions by comparing the cumulative distributions of the offered gambles. We say that gamble B stochastically dominates gamble A if the cumulative distribution of B never exceeds that of A.

Dominance of this kind, technically called first-order stochastic dominance (FSD), has at least some relevance for economists because it is

---

[7] The term *minimax loss* is sometimes applied to situations in which the outcomes are losses as a synonym for maximin or maximin gain (Lee, 1971). In other cases, minimax loss is used as a synonym for minimax regret (Fishburn, 1985). It is possible that this confusion of terms stems from the fact that the earliest discussions of minimax loss were confined to cases in which there is no difference between minimax loss and minimax regret (Edwards, 1954a; Savage, 1951).

[8] For example, a person using the minimax regret criterion might choose *a* from the set {*a,b*} but choose *b* from the set {*a,b,c*}.

possible to show that if B dominates A, B will be preferred to A for any (monotone) utility function (Hadar & Russell, 1969). But FSD is a very strong condition, and it is unlikely to hold in many important decisions under risk. A weaker form of dominance called second-order stochastic dominance (SSD) is more useful. SSD holds whenever the area under one cumulative distribution is never greater than the area under the other. As it happens, SSD is implied by FSD, but the converse is not true. Thus, SSD allows one to order pairs in which FSD fails. This is important because it has been shown (Hadar & Russell, 1969) that if B dominates A in the sense of SSD, then B will be preferred given any risk averse utility function.

For most economists, interest in stochastic dominance ends with SSD. Borch (1979), however, has shown that stochastic dominance can be generalized to higher orders ($n > 2$) by applying the cumulation process recursively. Although the interpretation of higher-order stochastic dominance is not intuitive, it has two interesting properties. The first is that stochastic dominance can be used to get a complete ordering of any set of probability distributions provided that n is sufficiently large. The second is that, as n grows large, the ordering produced approaches the ordering that would be obtained by applying either the previously described maximin rule or, alternatively, by applying a decumulative weighting function with extreme security-mindedness. Thus, stochastic dominance, risk aversion, pessimism, and security-mindedness intertwine around a common theme: the simple idea suggested by a great many decision rules, each in its own mathematical way, that in choosing among risks, it is prudent to assign greater weight to the smaller outcome values.

III. Process Models of Risky Choice

The first process studies of risky choice were experiments on probability and variance preferences by Edwards (1953, 1954b), which suggested that people's choices among gambles were driven by factors other than those driving the normative model. Appearing only a few years after the first laboratory tests of expected utility theory, these studies were unmistakable harbingers of the view that normatively motivated experiments fail to ask "the question which logically ought to come first—how do people actually go about making decisions in gambling situations?" (Edwards, 1953, p. 351).

During the 1960s, all of psychology was pulled toward human information processing and cognitive psychology. Both paradigms would be commonplace in decision making research by the end of the decade. In describing how the movements advanced knowledge about risky choice, it is tempting to organize the story around the process-tracing methods that they spawned—techniques such as protocol analysis and eye movement record-ing. But examination of the literature makes it abundantly clear that the earliest and most important insights into the processes of risky choice came from experimental (i.e., non-process-tracing) studies showing that choice outcomes could be influenced in predictable ways by manipulations de-signed to affect choice processes. Although process-tracing techniques do provide a valuable new source of psychological data, risk researchers have used them primarily to verify experimentally derived hypotheses.

A. RISK DIMENSIONS AND DUPLEX BETS

One of the most important early influences on process studies of risky choice was an experiment in which Slovic and Lichtenstein (1968b) used regression analysis to measure the relative importance of four "risk dimen-sions" on judgments of gamble attractiveness. These dimensions were the probability of winning (P_W), the amount to be won ($\$_W$), the probability of losing (P_L), and the amount to be lost ($\$_L$). In order to vary the four dimensions independently, Slovic and Lichtenstein introduced a specialized kind of bet called a *duplex bet*. Duplex bets are represented schematically by a pair of spinners (pie diagrams), one displaying the win information and the other displaying the loss information (see, e.g., upper left panel of Fig. 2). Each spinner is spun once and the outcomes are summed to give the net payoff. For bets in which win and loss amounts differ in absolute

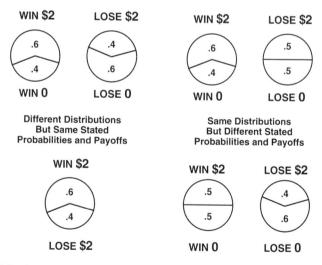

Fig. 2.   Stimulus types used to compare the effects of externally presented stimulus informa-tion and underlying distributions on choice.

value, the underlying distribution has four outcomes. If win and loss amounts have the same absolute value, the underlying distribution has only three outcomes because win/lose and zero/zero combinations both yield zero.

The subjects in Slovic and Lichtenstein's experiment either rated the attractiveness of duplex bets or made monetary bids for them, stating how much they would pay to play a bet or, if the bet was unattractive, stating how much they would charge to play the bet. At the end of the session, they also provided retrospective comments on the strategies they used. There were three general results. First, for many subjects, responses were overwhelmingly affected by one or two of the risk dimensions and were essentially unaffected by the others. Second, ratings and bids were differentially affected by the four risk dimensions. Third, subjects appeared to have considerable insight into their strategies as evidenced by the correspondence between what they reported and what individual regression analyses showed.

Slovic and Lichtenstein interpreted the results by proposing that the subjects had used a two-stage judgment process in which they first decided whether a bet was attractive or not and then quantified the binary attractiveness judgment by assigning a rating or bid. Detailed supplementary analyses of the data indicated that stage one (the like/dislike classification) was most heavily influenced by P_W for both rating and bidding groups. At stage two (the quantification step), the pattern for rating subjects was somewhat unclear but for bidding subjects, $\$_W$ was more important for attractive gambles and $\$_L$ was more important for unattractive gambles. Slovic and Lichtenstein explained the latter result in terms of what is nowadays called an "anchoring and adjustment" process in which subjects take a dollar amount as the starting point for the bid and then adjust the value in order to take other information into account.

Not long afterwards, the same authors (Lichtenstein & Slovic, 1971, 1973) showed that people's choices and bids can differ qualitatively, with higher bids sometimes being assigned to bets that are rejected in pairwise choice. This "preference reversal" phenomenon has had a major impact on thinking in both psychology and economics and has stimulated excellent research on judgment processes (Bostic, Herrnstein, & Luce, 1990; Goldstein & Einhorn, 1987; Mellers, Chang, Birnbaum, & Ordóñez, 1992; Mellers, Ordóñez, & Birnbaum, 1992; Tversky, Sattath, & Slovic, 1988). But as judgment processes are outside the present scope, I will set preference reversals aside and turn to a pair of studies that focused on how people choose among duplex bets.

As was mentioned earlier, there is a difference between the external display of duplex bets and their underlying distributions. One of the early process questions that was asked about these bets concerned the relative importance of the externally presented risk dimension information and the unseen distributional information. A pair of complementary experiments approached the question from different sides. Slovic and Lichtenstein (1968a) compared duplex bets to single bets having different underlying distributions but identical stated probabilities and payoffs (left panel of Fig. 2). Payne and Braunstein (1971) compared duplex bets having identical underlying distributions but different stated probabilities and payoffs (right panel of Fig. 2).

Both experiments showed that people's choices reflect stated probabilities and payoffs: preferences were the same for the distributionally different Slovic and Lichtenstein pairs but different for the distributionally identical Payne and Braunstein pairs. Payne and Braunstein proposed that both data sets could be described by an information processing model in which subjects first examine probability information and use it to exclude gambles having an unacceptable probability of winning. For the remaining cases, there is a second stage in which subjects try to maximize payoff. (The Payne and Braunstein model will be examined in greater detail later.)

In later years, duplex bets continued to exert a major influence on the experimental study of risky choice, but not primarily because of their pictorial characteristics. Instead, experimenters such as Payne and Braunstein (1978; see also Payne, Braunstein, & Carroll, 1978) would abstract from the pie diagrams their conceptual analysis of risky options into the four risk dimensions and present these to subjects in structured arrays that the subjects could then search however they chose.

B.   INTRANSITIVITY AND LEXICOGRAPHIC SEMIORDERS

Another very significant experimental study was conducted by Tversky (1969), who used specially constructed sets of gambles to demonstrate that subjects use a choice process—termed a *lexicographic semiorder* (LS)—that is qualitatively incompatible with expected utility maximization. Expected utility theory assumes that subjects choose among gambles by computing the expected utility for each gamble and then comparing values. Because expected utility values are transitive, preferences should also be transitive: if A is preferred to B, and B to C, then A should also be preferred to C. Tversky reasoned, however, that choices are more likely to reflect direct comparisons of probabilities and payoffs. He also reasoned that the importance of differences among values would be evaluated crudely so that adjacent values might be judged "about the same," whereas more widely separated values might be judged to be "clearly different."

Probability and payoff values for three of Tversky's gambles are given:

A	7/24	$5.00
B	8/24	$4.75
C	9/24	$4.50

The stimuli were represented as spinners with payoffs stated numerically but probabilities indicated only by a colored segment on the spinner. Tversky predicted that the lack of numerical values for probabilities would cause subjects to ignore small probability differences and choose between adjacent gambles (such as A and B, or B and C) on the basis of payoff. For gambles separated by larger probability steps (such as A and C), he predicted that the probability difference would sooner or later outweigh the difference in payoff, in which case the direction of the preference would be reversed.

The experiment had three main results. First, almost all subjects demonstrated the predicted intransitivities. Second, probability appeared to be processed before (or to be more important than) payoffs. And third, retrospective accounts given by subjects tended to confirm that they were explicitly and intentionally using an LS process. (Follow-up studies on intransitivity and lexicographic choice processes will be discussed later.)

C. EXPERIMENTS ON HISTOGRAMS AND
   MULTIOUTCOME DISTRIBUTIONS

The early studies on probability and variance preferences introduced the idea that distributional characteristics of risky options might affect preferences. Coombs later followed up his interest in the higher moments of distributions with a theory of risk perception called *portfolio theory* (Coombs, 1975; Coombs & Huang, 1970; Coombs & Lehner, 1981). Although most of this research used two-outcome gambles, Coombs and Bowen (1971) presented subjects with multiple-play games represented as 25-outcome distributions. Each distribution was represented twice, once as a histogram plotting net outcome against probability, and again as a list pairing each of the 25 possible outcomes with its probability of occurrence.

More recently, I have used multioutcome gambles to study how people's perceptions of risk and preferences among options relate to distributional shapes (Lopes, 1984, 1987). Examples of the gambles are shown in Fig. 3. Each display consists of a set of rows, at the left of which is an amount that might be won (or lost) and at the right of which is a row of tally marks representing probability. Subjects are instructed to think of the tally marks as lottery tickets, each one marked with the prize amount shown at the

```
200  I                 130  IIIIIIIIIIIIIIIIIIIIIIIIIII     200  IIIII
187  II                115  IIIIIIIIIIIIIIIIIIII            189  IIIII
172  III               101  IIIIIIIIIIIIII                 178  IIIII
157  IIII              86   IIIIIIIIII                      168  IIIII
143  IIIII             71   IIIIIII                         158  IIIII
129  IIIIII            57   IIIII                           147  IIIII
114  IIIIIII           43   IIII                            136  IIIII
99   IIIIIIIIII        28   III                             126  IIIII
85   IIIIIIIIIIIII     13   II                              116  IIIII
70   IIIIIIIIIIIIIIIIIIIIII  0  I                           105  IIIII
                                                            94   IIIII
        Riskless              Short Shot                    84   IIIII
                                                            74   IIIII
200  IIIIIIIIIII                                            63   IIIII
186  IIIIIIIIII                                             52   IIIII
172  IIIIIIIII                                              42   IIIII
159  IIIIIII                                                32   IIIII
146  IIIII                                                  21   IIIII
132  III                                                    10   IIIII
119  I                  439  I                              0    IIIII
106  I                  390  II
93   I                  341  III                                Rectangular
80   I                  292  IIII
66   III                244  IIIII
53   IIIII              195  IIIIII
40   IIIIIII            146  IIIIIIIIII
26   IIIIIIIII          98   IIIIIIIIIIIIII
13   IIIIIIIIIII        49   IIIIIIIIIIIIIIIIII
0    IIIIIIIIIII        0    IIIIIIIIIIIIIIIIIIIIIIIIIII

        Bimodal                Long Shot
```

Fig. 3. Examples of multioutcome lotteries. The numbers represent amounts that might be won (or lost) and the tally marks represent lottery tickets (100 total). The expected values of all lotteries are $100.

left. They are also told that each gamble has the same amount of prize money and tickets. Although the gambles have many possible outcomes, they are easy to understand because the shapes of the distributions are simple and the between-row spacing in a given gamble is roughly equal in terms of monetary outcome.

Schneider and Lopes (1986) used multioutcome gambles to study the influence of risk preference on the reflection effect. In the experiment, two groups of subjects were compared, one preselected for extreme risk aversion and the other for extreme risk seeking. The gamble preferences of the two groups differed substantially across gain and loss conditions. When risk averse subjects chose among gains, their preferences were essentially as would be predicted by classical risk aversion (diminishing marginal utility) or by security-minded decumulative weighting. For losses, however, their preferences were neither strictly risk averse (security-minded) nor risk seeking (potential-minded). In contrast, the preferences of the risk-seeking subjects were essentially as predicted by increasing marginal utility or potential-minded decumulative weighting for losses, but their preferences among gains were neither strictly risk seeking (potential-minded) nor risk averse (security-minded). The complex pattern of results plus retrospective comments from subjects suggested that the two groups used the same choice processes but assessed the trade-off between avoiding bad outcomes and seeking good outcomes very differently.

D. CHOICE BOARDS AND EYE MOVEMENT STUDIES

Although the algebraic models described earlier were not intended to describe the processes of choice, when they are taken seriously as candidate models of process, they make many interesting and testable predictions. Perhaps the most important such prediction concerns whether the choice involves holistic evaluations of individual alternatives or dimensional (i.e., attribute-based) comparisons that move back and forth between alternatives.[9] Holistic evaluation is implied, for example, by the idea that people choose among risks by comparing the expected utilities of the alternatives, whereas dimensional comparisons are implied by the LS model as well as by many other models that have been proposed for choice under risk (Payne, Bettman, & Johnson, 1990). Another important prediction concerns the amount of information that is used in the choice process. Holistic processes tend to call on all the available information, whereas dimensional processes usually shortcut search.

By far the most heavily used tool for studying information use is the choice board, in which information is offered to subjects in the form of an attribute-by-alternative array. Each cell in the array contains a single item of information that is hidden from sight until a subject "asks" to see it. Because a thorough review of research using choice boards is included in this volume (see the chapter by Payne, Bettman, & Johnson) there is no need to provide a detailed summary here. It suffices to say that the studies have consistently suggested that as the number of alternatives increases, the proportion of information searched per alternative decreases. In addition, variability of search within alternatives increases. This suggests that as task load increases, subjects tend to increase their use of (dimensional) strategies that allow them to process alternatives more efficiently. In addition, subjects also adapt their strategies to time pressure and to structural variations in problems, such as whether outcome probabilities are relatively homogeneous or not.

Eye movements have also been used to study information acquisition in risky choice. Subjects in a study by Rosen and Rosenkoetter (1976) chose between two-outcome gambles displayed on a computer screen. Each gam-

---

[9] Holistic processes are also called interdimensional, as search proceeds from dimension to dimension within a single alternative. Dimensional processes are also called intradimensional for obvious reasons.

ble was described by three pieces of information: the amount to be won, the probability of winning, and the amount to be lost. The (complementary) probability of losing was not shown. Subjects also chose between analogous pairs not involving risk (vacations, gift packages). The main result was that the stimulus environment had a major influence on choice strategy. The predominant search pattern for gambles was holistic: about one-third of the transitions were intradimensional and two-thirds were interdimensional. In contrast, the two varieties of transition were split almost evenly for choices between gift packages containing varying quantities of theater tickets, gasoline, and free groceries. Rosen and Rosenkoetter explained the predominance of holistic processing for gambles in terms of attribute interdependency. In their view, risk dimensions such as probability of winning or payoff have much less meaning in isolation than quantities of theater tickets, say, or gasoline.

Russo and Dosher (1983) also used eye movements to study risky choice. Their gambles were so-called "one outcome" gambles described only by probability of winning and payoff. Choice pairs were presented as 2 × 2 arrays. Unlike the previous eye movement study of Rosen and Rosenkoetter (1976), Russo and Dosher's data revealed a relatively even split between holistic and dimensional processing. One important task difference that may explain this is that dimensional strategies work well with one-outcome gambles. As Russo and Dosher pointed out, rough comparisons of gambles based on absolute dimensional differences come reasonably close to expected value computations but with considerably less effort.

E. VERBAL PROTOCOLS

As we have already seen (Slovic & Lichtenstein, 1968b; Tversky, 1969), it was not uncommon for the researchers who pioneered the use of experimental methods for studying risky choice processes to look to subjects' retrospective verbal accounts for confirmation of their ideas. However, some researchers have asked subjects to provide on-line ("think-aloud") protocols during choice that have later been subjected to detailed analysis (see, e.g., Payne et al., 1978; Payne, Laughhunn, & Crum, 1980). The results of such analyses have been useful as a source of converging data for validating conclusions drawn from experiments using other methods.

For example, Montgomery (1977) and Ranyard (1982) used protocols to study violations of transitivity. Montgomery's study used the same stimulus set as Tversky (1969) and supported the LS model. Ranyard's study differed in that it systematically varied the ranges on the probability and payoff dimensions. The results indicated that when either one of the ranges was large relative to the other, that dimension tended to dominate, but when differences on both dimensions were small, intransitivities occurred. The protocols in Ranyard's experiment also revealed that his subjects were paying attention to more of the information than Montgomery's subjects had seemed to use. This led Ranyard to suggest that the underlying choice rule is actually a nonlinear additive difference (NLAD) rule in which smaller differences receive less weight than larger differences.[10]

Other researchers have adapted protocol methods to settings in which choice times and comparison processes occur too quickly for on-line reporting. These methods ask subjects for retrospective accounts but move data collection closer to the choice process. For example, Russo and Dosher (1983) supplemented eye movement data with "prompted verbal protocols" in which real-time recordings of a subject's eye movements are replayed for the subject at the end of the experiment and subjects are asked to recall and report the thoughts that were occurring during the fixations. Alternatively, Lopes (1987) embedded occasional requests for written explication of the reasons for a current choice into the context of a larger choice set. Some of these protocols will be used for illustration in what follows.

IV. The Bridge between Process and Algebra

Our trek through the history of risky choice research has taken us across a variety of experimental terrains and up a series of theoretical peaks that may seem isolated and fundamentally unbridgeable. The isolation is more apparent than real, however, for there are points of connection everywhere—empirical outcroppings from which we can launch conceptual lines. In this section, we will examine four such lines, each one woven from several interrelated strands. The first connects the stepwise processes of lexicographic choice to the algebraic idea of decumulative weighting. The second contrasts several different algebraic approaches to modeling risk preference. The third discusses the relation between aspiration and conflict in risky choice, and the last shows how decumulative weighting and stochastic control can be incorporated into a single psychological model.

A. Lexicographic Processes and the Idea of Weighting

Lexicographic choice is rooted in the idea of priority: in order to apply the process, one needs to know what one values and in what order of importance. Glimmerings of lexicographic processes have surfaced repeatedly in studies of risky choice, all suggesting that probabilities are more important

---

[10] The LS model is a special case of NLAD in which differences that do not exceed a threshold are strictly ignored. Under NLAD, smaller probability differences receive less weight than larger differences but are still traded off against payoff differences.

than payoffs (Montgomery, 1977; Payne & Braunstein, 1971, 1978; Ranyard, 1982; Slovic & Lichtenstein, 1968b; Tversky, 1969). Still, it is not easy to prioritize probability and payoff in isolation (Rosen & Rosenkoetter, 1976; Schoemaker, 1979). Schoemaker, for example, tried to get a context-free measure of the relative importance of probabilities and payoffs by displaying an "urn" of unknown content and asking subjects to judge its worth. Before responding, however, subjects could request either information about the proportion of winning balls in the urn or about how much would be won if a winning ball were drawn. Although subjects complied with the task, their context-free requests were unrelated to the relative importance they later placed on probabilities and payoffs when choosing among duplex bets.

To resolve the apparent inconsistency between Schoemaker's result and the more typical finding, it is useful to study the mechanisms that mediated the enhanced influence of probability in three of the earlier experiments. Recall that in Slovic and Lichtenstein's (1968b) seminal study of duplex bets, subjects appeared to set bids in a two-stage process, first using P_W to determine whether a bet was attractive or not and then using $\$_W$ or $\$_L$ to establish a value. Given that the expected value of duplex bets reflects all four risk dimensions, why should subjects have given priority to probability when they decided whether or not a bet was attractive?

This question can be answered tentatively by examining the constraints in the task. Suppose that the subjects realized that all four dimensions contribute to attractiveness but did not know how to integrate them. They might have coped with the difficulty by looking for a one-dimensional cutting rule of the form "A gamble is attractive if it has the best level of X." Because $\$_W$ and $\$_L$ were already earmarked for use in the second stage, the only viable candidates for X would have been P_W and P_L.[11] Between these, approximately two-thirds of the subjects appeared to use P_W and one-third appeared to use P_L, a difference that could have been driven by a relatively minor task variable such as left-to-right reading habits or a tendency to imagine spinning the win pointer before the lose pointer. In either case, however, subjects appeared to use probability information (either P_W or P_L) to decide whether to accept an attractive bet (i.e., pay to play it) or to reject an unattractive bet (i.e., require payment to play it).

The study by Payne and Braunstein (1971) suggested that probabilities are also processed before payoffs when subjects choose between duplex bets. In their information processing model of the choice process, Payne and Braunstein proposed that subjects begin by determining the relation

---

[11] As it happens, each of these four rule variants is equivalent for the stimuli that Slovic and Lichtenstein used. The 9 attractive gambles under any of the variants yield a net expected value of $7, whereas the 18 unattractive gambles yield a net expected value of −$7.

between P_W and P_L.[12] If $P_W < P_L$ for both gambles, the most likely outcome is a loss. Given the unattractive situation, subjects choose so as to minimize P_L. If $P_W > P_L$ for both gambles, the most likely outcome is a win. Given the attractive situation, subjects maximize $\$_W$ if they can, or maximize P_W if not. If $P_W = P_L$, the situation is intermediate. Depending on type, one subject might choose pessimistically, opting to minimize P_L; another might choose optimistically, opting to maximize $\$_W$ or P_W. Thus, probability provides an initial screen on attractiveness just as it did in Slovic and Lichtenstein's (1968b) model of the bidding process. In the case of choice, however, attractiveness moderates the criterion that is used to differentiate between alternatives. When the alternatives are unattractive, the model applies a conservative rule aimed at reducing the probability of losing. When the alternatives are attractive, the model uses a less conservative approach focused on making the most of the opportunity for a win.

The studies of intransitivity by Tversky (1969) and others (Montgomery, 1977; Ranyard, 1982) also suggested that the relative attractiveness of (positive) two-outcome gambles is assessed initially in terms of probabilities, with payoffs figuring only secondarily. Thus, both choices and on-line protocols indicated that subjects choose conservatively when probability differences are large, opting for the gamble that gives them the smaller probability of losing. When probability differences are small, however, subjects switch their attention to payoffs, choosing the gamble with the more lucrative payoff.

Together, then, process models for three reasonably dissimilar tasks suggest that the apparently greater importance of probability information in risky choice is real and that it is driven by an inclination on the part of subjects to screen out gambles that offer an unacceptable probability of winning and to consider payoffs only for gambles that pass the initial screening. If this is so, however, we are left with explaining why Schoemaker's (1979) more direct assessment failed to confirm probability's enhanced relative importance. The explanation to be pursued here is that the extremely simple structure of the stimuli used in these older experiments has allowed the probability/payoff distinction to mask a more fundamental distinction. This is the difference between "worst-case" evaluations that are aimed at preventing bad outcomes and "best-case" evaluations that are aimed at exploiting opportunities for good outcomes.

The difference between the probability/payoff distinction and the worst-case/best-case distinction can be most easily appreciated with respect to multioutcome gambles. These gambles have many probabilities and many payoffs, making it difficult to imagine how a subject could use one class of

---

[12] In Payne and Braunstein's stimuli, there were only three possible relations: $P_W > P_L$ for both gambles, $P_W = P_L$ for both gambles, or $P_W < P_L$ for both gambles.

information while ignoring the other. However, it is easy to demonstrate how subjects evaluating multioutcome gambles can focus selectively on achieving security (a worst-case perspective) or on making the most of the potential for a big win (a best-case perspective). For example, when unselected subjects are offered a choice between the short shot and the long shot in Fig. 3, most appear to use a security-minded (or worst-case) weighting process, comparing lottery tickets from the "bottom up"[13] and choosing so as to maximize the probability of winning a prize of some sort:

> "I choose the [short shot] because there is only one chance of me losing and the best odds indicate a good chance of winning $71 or more. The [long shot] has too many opportunities to lose—it is too risky."

> "I'd rather have greater chances of winning a little something than greater chances for nothing. The triple jackpot [in the long shot] doesn't make me want to go for it cuz the odds are too great."

When the probabilities of winning appear similar, however, the same subjects may switch to a "top-down" (potential-minded or best-case) comparison of maximum payoffs. A particularly illuminating protocol is the following one in which a subject who is usually very security-minded nervously reverses an initial preference for the bimodal gamble (see Fig. 3) after realizing that it and the long shot are actually similar in probability of winning:

> "Chances of getting zero are greater in the [long shot]. On the other hand, there are better prizes in the [long shot] once you get a ticket with a prize. In fact, chances of getting a prize of less than 40 or 50 look about the same, and then the [long shot] has better prizes. I'm not sure I'm making a good decision here."

A process of the latter sort in which subjects switch from bottom-up (security-minded) to top-down (potential-minded) comparisons is functionally isomorphic to the "probabilities before payoffs" process that produces intransitivities in choices among two-outcome gambles. In other words, a

---

[13] "Bottom" here refers to the bottom (low or bad end) of the distribution and not necessarily to the bottom of the display. Displaying lotteries with bad outcomes on top does not affect subjects' preferences (Schneider & Lopes, 1986).

subject who chooses the two-outcome gamble with the larger probability of winning is—by virtue of that very act—also opting for security. Likewise, a subject who chooses the gamble with the larger payoff is also opting for potential.

The same bottom-up before top-down comparison strategy also predicts the sorts of nonlinearities that underlie the Allais paradoxes. For example, if the process is applied to the constant ratio problem described earlier, bottom-up comparison of gambles A and B quickly reveals that the gambles differ on the very first (i.e., worst) "ticket": B gets nothing, whereas A gets $1 million, so A is preferred. In comparing C and D, the bottom-most tickets all yield zero so neither gamble is favored. When a top-down comparison is engaged, however, D is favored, as its $2 million greatly exceeds the $1 million offered by C. Thus, a generalized lexicographic process operating on a comparison principle of bottom-up before top-down yields aggregate patterns that can be described by cautiously hopeful decumulative weighting. The same generalized emphasis on applying bottom-up criteria before other criteria also appears in algebraic rules that explain the Allais paradoxes by hybridizing maximin and expected utility (e.g., Gilboa, 1986; Jaffray, 1986).

Obviously, strict lexicographic choice is unlikely to hold up when differences in outcomes are very small; but the rule can be relaxed through two different psychological processes. The first involves some sort of discrimination function that discounts small differences among outcomes. If the size of the discountable difference were a function of outcome magnitude, the function would imply diminishing sensitivity. The second process involves changes in attention to differences as the comparison moves up or down the distribution. A process of the latter sort is what is captured quantitatively by decumulative weighting functions. The latter process also generalizes the NLAD process described by Ranyard (1982) to the case of multioutcome gambles and is, therefore, also a generalization of the LS process described by Tversky (1969).

In summary, it appears almost certain that lexicographic processes figure in risky choice. In each instance, importance judgments that are captured algebraically by the idea of *weight* express themselves in individual choices by the *order* in which operations are carried out. Nonetheless, there is ambiguity concerning what exactly is prioritized by the lexicographic rule. Studies based on one-outcome bets or duplex bets tend to suggest that probabilities are processed before payoffs. Studies with multioutcome bets tend to suggest that bottom-up (security-minded) analysis precedes top-down (potential-minded) analysis. And both kinds of studies suggest that subjects attempt to guarantee an acceptable outcome (maximize the probability of winning) before concerning themselves with the larger payoffs. As we have already seen, one of these ambiguities is easily resolved: when a bottom-up before top-down process is applied to simple gambles, the result is identical to a probabilities before payoffs process. But the ambiguity between security weighting and maximizing the probability of winning does not disappear. Instead, it is sharpened in the domain of losses and provides the key to understanding why gain and loss decisions are so often asymmetrical, being neither identical across domains nor reflected.

B. RISK ATTITUDE IN PROCESS AND ALGEBRA

Although the pattern of preferences that we call "risk aversion" has provided the predominant focus for behavioral models of risky choice, there have been important exceptions such as Friedman and Savage's (1948) suggestion concerning the purchase of lottery tickets. But the lottery ticket issue pales in comparison to the interest that Kahneman and Tversky generated by their suggestion (1979; also Tversky & Kahneman, 1992) that the utility function is S-shaped about the status quo, being concave (risk averse) for gains but convex (risk seeking) for losses.

Before examining the empirical evidence for and against the S-shaped function, it is worthwhile to examine its psychological rationale and to compare it with the Bernoullian rationale for a concave utility function. According to Tversky and Kahneman, the S-shaped function reflects a psychophysical principle of diminishing sensitivity by which "the impact of a change diminishes with the distance from the reference point" (1992, p. 303). Although diminishing sensitivity applies symmetrically to losses and to gains, Tversky and Kahneman also incorporate a principle of loss aversion into their utility function by which "losses loom larger than corresponding gains" (1992, p. 303). Loss aversion is needed to account for the fact that people typically reject gambles that give them a 50/50 chance at $\pm v$.

In psychophysics, sensitivity reflects the variance of responses to a stimulus of given intensity. Diminishing sensitivity corresponds to the case in which variance increases as a function of stimulus magnitude. As the concept is used by Tversky and Kahneman, it captures the intuition that—for either gains or losses—a difference of a constant magnitude (say $100) seems subjectively smaller when it is applied to large magnitudes ($4,200 vs. $4,300, for instance) than when it is applied to small magnitudes ($200 vs. $300). The intuition is clearly valid. Whether it accounts for risk attitude is another matter.

Diminishing marginal utility can also be linked to psychophysics: this time, to the shape of the psychophysical function that relates the physical magnitude of a stimulus to its psychological magnitude. In Bernoulli's conception, increasing the asset level of a poor person by some objective increment v produces a much greater increase in subjective well-being than would be gotten by increasing the asset level of a rich person by the same increment. This idea suggests a saturation phenomenon: inputs to the system can increase indefinitely, but the output of the system cannot.

"Psychophysical shape" and "sensitivity" may seem to be different names for the same thing, but the two are empirically and conceptually distinct. For example, just-noticeable-differences increase (i.e., sensitivity decreases) as a function of stimulus magnitude for both brightness and line length, but the psychophysical function for brightness is concave, whereas the function for line length is linear. Thus, although it is possible that diminishing marginal utility and diminishing sensitivity both play a role in people's evaluations of gamble outcomes, it is not possible for the utility function to be both Bernoullian and S-shaped.

For reasons of history, Bernoulli's function was the first to face empirical scrutiny. It was also the first to fail, most obviously because people do buy lottery tickets and are also willing to take risks in order to avoid losses (Fishburn & Kochenberger, 1979; Williams, 1966). But the Bernoullian failure did not ensure that the S-shaped function succeeded when it was tested empirically. In fact, evidence from three different kinds of experiments suggests the contrary.

Reflection studies compare people's preferences among gambles involving gains with their preferences among corresponding gambles in which the outcomes are losses. In general, S-shaped utility predicts that the preference order should be reversed (reflected) across the two domains.[14] In many cases, however, studies that have tested the reflection hypothesis across parametric variations of probability and value have found that preferences among gain gambles demonstrate strong risk aversion, whereas preferences for losses are weaker (nearer to risk neutrality) or more variable than the corresponding pattern for risk aversion (Cohen, Jaffray, & Said, 1987; Hershey & Schoemaker, 1980; Schneider & Lopes, 1986; Weber & Bottom, 1989; Experiment 3; see also Luce, Mellers, & Chang, 1993).

In framing studies, the gambles that are presented in gain and loss frames are numerically the same, but outcomes are described in complementary terms that reflect different reference points. Thus, if a treatment may save some members of a doomed group, one may describe either the number who will be saved if the treatment is applied or the number who will die despite treatment. The original demonstrations of framing effects were

---

[14] Small differences in the slopes of the utility and weighting functions may cause there to be some pairs of gambles in which reflection is not predicted. Which gambles these are depends critically on the details of the two functions and would, therefore, differ from person to person. However, situations of nonreflection are uncommon and would tend to be restricted to particular sorts of gambles.

shown in the work of Tversky and Kahneman (1981; also Kahneman & Tversky, 1982, 1984). Since then, however, there have been several systematic studies using a variety of different problems in which framing effects have been inconsistent. Although the predominant pattern for choice in the positive frame has been risk aversion, choices in the loss frame have tended to be variable across problems (Fagley & Miller, 1987; Maule, 1989; Miller & Fagley, 1991; Schneider, 1992) and people's expressed preferences for frames have not predicted their choices (Fischhoff, 1983).

The final approach to testing the S-shaped utility hypothesis focuses on its effects on higher-order phenomena. A study by Budescu and Weiss (1987) illustrates the type. The object was to test whether the sorts of intransitive cycles that were demonstrated by Tversky (1969) would be reflected if outcomes were switched from gains to losses. Three basic results were obtained. First, gain/loss reflection was supported. Second, the clear majority of subjects were either transitive in both domains or intransitive in both domains. Third—and contrary to expectation—intransitive cycles were not reflected.

Given the support for reflection across gain and loss choices, the lack of reflection for intransitive cycles was surprising. However, a closer look at the data suggests how it may have happened. For the most part, Budescu and Weiss's results are counts of the numbers of subjects who show particular effects. A subject who reversed his or her majority preferences across the 12 gain/loss comparisons was (properly) scored as confirming reflection. Whether the subject was equally consistent in the two domains is not generally indicated. The authors do, however, include raw data for one intransitive subject (Budescu & Weiss, 1987, Table 3, p. 192). Although this subject is risk averse for gains and risk seeking for losses by the majority rule, the subject's preferences are highly reliable for gain pairs (scores of 11/12, 12/12, 0/12, or 1/12 account for 10 out of 12 table entries) and much less reliable for loss pairs (none of the scores was more extreme than 10/12 or 2/12). Thus, although reflection occurred in terms of majority counts, the pattern for losses may have been less reliable, thus decreasing the likelihood that higher-order patterns (such as intransitivities) would be reflected in toto.

Although the most studied explanations for risk aversion have been based on the idea of convexity in the utility function, other alternatives exist. Yaari (1987) was the first to suggest that one could explain risk aversion without diminishing marginal utility by the use of a decumulative weighting function like the security-minded function of Fig. 1. Lopes (1990) later took a similar tack but preferred the cautiously hopeful function that also explains the purchase of lottery tickets. Other approaches (e.g., Allais, 1986; Quiggen, 1982; Tversky & Kahneman, 1992) have combined convexity with decumulative weighting. Despite the shifts in modeling strategy, however, most theories of risk taking either accept risk aversion as an empirical fact or base the shape of the utility function on psychological assumptions (diminishing marginal utility, diminishing sensitivity) that imply risk aversion at least for gains. Risk seekers have been out in the cold because no theories have provided a principled reason for expecting their existence.

With the growth of interest in decumulative weighting models, however, the situation could change. Not only is there a function (the potential-minded function of Fig. 1) that can describe risk-seeking choices algebraically, the psychological basis of the function is also easily argued. One interpretation is that risk seekers are optimistic. Another is that they value opportunity (potential) over safety (security). In either case, the psychological mechanism can be operationalized as a top-down (or top-down before bottom-up) comparison sequence that affects the relative attention that is paid to bad and good outcomes.

The clearest evidence favoring such an attentional or value-directed concept is seen in the protocols of the subjects who consistently prefer riskier options. For illustration, here are the protocols of two subjects who preferred the long shot to the short shot (see Fig. 3):

"The chance for winning nothing is small with the [short shot] but since the dollar amount in the [long shot] is attractive I run the risk of losing and go for the [long shot]."

"I'll take the added risks of losing it all or getting a lower number for the chance of the higher prizes."

Although these subjects are seemingly as aware of the bad outcomes in the long shot as the security-minded subjects who were profiled previously, they willingly trade security for the enhanced potential of the riskier gamble.

Although less is known about people who choose risky options than is known about people who choose safe options, there have been occasional suggestions of an individual difference factor involving the relative attention that people pay to preventing bad outcomes versus enabling good outcomes. In the Payne and Braunstein (1971) model described earlier, for instance, an individual difference factor intervenes whenever a gamble pair cannot be categorized as either attractive or unattractive. The factor determines whether the subject chooses to minimize P_L (a security-based decision) or to maximize either $\$_W$ or P_W (both potential-based decisions). Similarly, in a study of duplex bets incorporating protocols, Schoemaker (1979) found that of the 16 subjects who said that they focused solely on loss dimensions (P_L or $\$_L$), 94% were risk averse in an unrelated coin flipping task. In contrast, of the 14 subjects who said that they focused solely on win dimensions (P_W or $\$_W$), 57% were risk seeking in the coin flipping task.

In summary, there are several ways to describe when risks will be taken and who will take them. The popular hypothesis of the S-shaped utility function suggests that risk seeking will occur about as often and about as consistently for losses as risk aversion occurs for gains. The data, however, reveal a considerable asymmetry across the two domains in the strength and reliability of preferences. In contrast, theories that locate risk attitude in decumulative weighting functions (e.g., Yaari, 1987) do not distinguish between gains and losses. Although such theories may predict well for gains, they cannot handle the sometimes unreliable but still relatively high levels of risk seeking that occur for losses.

C. ASPIRATION AND CONFLICT

An alternate route to explaining risk seeking for losses is suggested by the observation that subjects are not only less predictable when choosing among losses, they also complain more often about the difficulties of choosing. The following, for example, are protocols from two subjects choosing between the rectangular and the short-shot loss lotteries (see Fig. 3). Although they choose differently, both are conflicted.

"Another difficult one. I chose the [rectangular] lottery because the odds are equal on each dollar amount, whereas the [short shot] shows the odds in favor of a loss of $70 or more, and very good odds of losing $130. The [rectangular] seems to be a safer risk despite the potential for a higher loss, i.e., $200 max."

"Chances of losing ≤$100 are about the same for both, but [rectangular] has higher possible loss, so I picked [short shot]. I realize [shot shot] gives less chance of a very low loss, which reduces my certainty about choice."

Protocols such as these suggest that subjects facing losses are often torn between a desire to take the lottery offering the better chance of losing little or nothing and the inescapable fact that the lottery doing so is usually the more dangerous. The latter consideration is recognizable as the routine output of a bottom-up comparison process that focuses on the differences in the gambles' worst outcomes. Given either a security-minded or a cautiously hopeful weighting process, the choice should be settled immediately in favor of the short shot. In contrast, the apparent desire to lose little or nothing is reminiscent of the kinds of aspiration-driven risk taking that figure in bold play and other forms of stochastic control.

The existence and operation of aspiration levels in choice has long been acknowledged in the form of criteria that function as cutoffs in noncompensatory decision models. In the case of risky choice, however, aspiration levels have slipped in by the back door as kinks in the utility function (Friedman & Savage, 1948), utility functions with discrete steps (Simon, 1955), and shifts in the reference point defining gains and losses (Kahneman & Tversky, 1979). Thus, the idea of achieving an aspiration level has been folded into the idea of maximizing expected utility, a move that saves the expected utility model but only at the theoretical price of defining away the experience of conflict in risky choice.

SP/A (security-potential/aspiration) theory (Lopes, 1987, 1990) has pursued an alternative course by proposing that aspiration level functions as an additional basis for choice, one whose recommendations sometimes conflict with the recommendations of a decumulative comparison process. For illustration, consider a security-minded subject who has a modest aspiration level for gains (perhaps winning $50 or more) but who hopes to give up little or nothing (perhaps $50 or less) for losses. If this subject is presented with the rectangular and the short-shot gambles for gains (see Fig. 3), both security and aspiration favor the short shot (upper left panel of Fig. 4). Choice should be easy and unconflicted. For losses, however, security favors the short shot because it has a better worst outcome ($-\$130$ vs. $-\$200$),

Short Shot Vs. Rectangular

Security-Minded Pattern				Potential-Minded Pattern		
	Security	Aspiration			Potential	Aspiration
Gains	Short Shot	Short Shot		Gains	Rectangular	Short Shot
Losses	Short Shot	Rectangular		Losses	Rectangular	Rectangular

Short Shot Vs. Riskless

Security-Minded Pattern				Potential-Minded Pattern		
	Security	Aspiration			Potential	Aspiration
Gains	Riskless	Riskless		Gains	Riskless	Riskless
Losses	Short Shot	Short Shot		Losses	Short Shot	Short Shot

Fig. 4. SP/A predictions of security-minded (left panels) and potential-minded (right panels) decision makers. SP/A predicts reversed preferences for these two types of decision makers for the short-short versus rectangular comparison and identical preferences for the short-shot versus riskless comparison.

whereas aspiration favors the rectangular gamble because it offers the greater chance of losing less than $50 (25% vs. 10%). The result is psychological conflict, reduced confidence, and inconsistent choices. Thus, the theory predicts that security-minded subjects will demonstrate reliable security seeking for gains but will have mixed preferences for losses, exactly as Schneider and Lopes (1986) found with subjects preselected for extreme degrees of risk aversion.

The opposite pattern is predicted for potential-minded subjects. To see this, first consider the response of such subjects to losses (upper right panel of Fig. 4). In this case it is assumed that potential-minded subjects (like everyone else) hope to lose little or nothing (perhaps $50 or less), which makes them favor the rectangular gamble. Because their top-down comparison process favors the same gamble, choice is easy and unconflicted. A pattern of consistent potential seeking for losses should result, exactly as Schneider and Lopes (1986) found with subjects preselected for extreme risk seeking. For gains, however, potential continues to favor the rectangular gamble because of its high maximum. But aspiration level can produce a conflict if the subject adopts the goal of not coming up empty (say, winning $50 or more), a goal that is more likely met with the short shot. Thus, SP/A predicts mixed preferences for gains, as Schneider and Lopes (1986) also found.

SP/A theory also predicts the choices on which security-minded and potential-minded subjects agree. For example, offered the riskless and the short-shot gain lotteries (see Fig. 3), both groups overwhelmingly prefer the riskless lottery (see lower left panel of Fig. 4). Moreover, they do so for similar reasons, as can be seen in the following protocols, the first from a security-minded subject and the second from a potential-minded subject:

"The [riskless lottery] has (1) a higher jackpot and (2) greater chance of winning a larger amount *under* $100. I look at the highest amount I could lose rather than the highest amount I could win."

"I picked the [riskless lottery] because both the minimum and the maximum amounts are more, and because for both there's a good chance of getting around $100."

Although these subjects ordinarily disagree about gains, they agree here because the riskless gamble effectively satisfies each of their dominant criteria. Likewise, for losses, both groups of subjects strongly prefer the short shot (lower right panel of Fig. 4), as can be seen in protocols given, respectively, by the same two subjects:

"[Took short shot because] (1) there is a greater chance of losing $130 or more with the [riskless lottery]. (2) There is a greater chance of losing less than $70 in the [short shot]."

"I pick the short shot because the maximum loss is less and because you may be able to hit as low as zero loss. No matter what, you lose $70 and possibly $200 in the [riskless] lottery—too much risk."

The reflection of preferences from gains to losses is complete and identical for both subjects because the recommendations of both the security (or potential) factor and the aspiration factor are reflected completely and identically for both groups.

The issue of when and how reflection occurs is interesting and depends critically on the distributional characteristics (that is, the "shapes") of the gambles being compared. To see this, recall for a moment the protocol from the ordinarily security-minded subject who convinced himself that choosing the long shot over the bimodal gamble was warranted by the fact that "chances of getting a prize of less than 40 or 50 look about the same [for both]." This is exactly the kind of shift that LS and NLAD models predict when probability differences are small. When the same subject was confronted with the two gambles defined as losses, however, the bimodal was chosen with dispatch:

"The bimodal has a lower ceiling with the same chances of paying $100 or less."

Although this subject reflected his preference from the long shot to the bimodal, he did not reflect his reasoning process. Instead, his routine bottom-up comparison process suggested that the bimodal and long shot gambles are similar in security for gains but are unequivocally dissimilar in security for losses.

Evidence of reflection across gains and losses has ordinarily been interpreted as evidence favoring an S-shaped utility function. But the S-shaped utility hypothesis also predicts reflection in reasoning, as Hershey and Schoemaker (1980) pointed out in their parametric comparison of subjects' choices for gains and losses. When they examined subjects' stated rationales, however, they found no evidence of reflectivity in reasoning. Similarly, the failure of Budescu and Weiss (1987) to find reflection in intransitive cycles suggests that the process that generates intransitivity for gains has a different result when it operates on losses.

The difference can be illustrated by revisiting the gambles used earlier to illustrate Tversky's (1969) transitivity experiment. Figure 5 shows the three gain gambles and corresponding loss gambles laid out schematically so that bad outcomes are on the bottom and good outcomes are on the top. The inequalities show how a person using the bottom-up before top-down comparison process might evaluate the various possible pairs. For gains, a bottom-up analysis would reveal that A and B are similar: there is only a small difference (4.1%) in the proportion of "tickets" resulting in zero and this occurs relatively "far up" in the comparison. If the person switches to a top-down process, the result would favor A. A similar analysis would hold for B versus C. In the case of A versus C, however, the bottom-up process would discover a larger difference (8.2%) that also becomes evident sooner (i.e., nearer the bottom). Although a three-gamble sequence might not be long enough to elicit intransitivity from every subject, anyone using the proposed process would eventually switch from top-down (potential-driven) choices to bottom-up (security-driven) choices given longer sequences.

For losses, however, the situation is different. A bottom-up process would discover right away—with the very first "ticket"—that A is worse than B ($-\$5.00 < -\$4.75$), that B is worse than C ($-\$4.75 < -\$4.50$), and that A is worse than C ($-\$5.00 < -\$4.50$), and would consequently prefer B to A, C to B, and C to A. Thus, although the outcomes of the gambles have

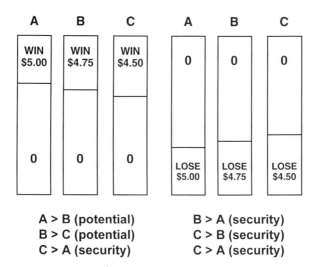

Fig. 5. Illustration of how lexicographic processing of security and potential predicts intransitivity for gains but not for losses.

been reflected, the operations and recommendations of the comparison process have not. Whether a person is choosing between gains or between losses, the comparison process is still bottom-up before top-down, producing intransitivity for gains but transitivity for losses.

Of course, what Budescu and Weiss (1987) actually found when they looked at intransitivity for losses was a little more complicated than this. Their subjects' preferences displayed an unsystematic mixture of transitivity and intransitivity along with a reasonable amount of risk seeking. But this is exactly what one would expect when aspiration level is considered as it is in SP/A theory: although security alone might argue that $C > B > A$ for losses, aspiration level pulls in the opposite direction because maximizing the probability of no loss argues that $A > B > C$.

D. SP/A AND DUAL-CRITERION DECISION MAKING

Having journeyed this far and constructed some bridges between distant theoretical viewpoints, it is time to take stock of our present surroundings. Although algebraic models and process models of risky choice seem miles apart conceptually, they can be easily reconciled by recognizing that algebraic models describe patterns of preference across option sets, whereas process models describe the sequence and content of comparison processes that underlie individual acts of choosing. What in algebra is expressed as "importance" or "weight" is expressed in process by temporal "priority" or by relative "attention." And what in process is expressed as strategy or criterion shift is expressed in algebra by nonlinearity. Although there is no conflict between algebraic and process descriptions, they are not the same thing.

SP/A theory represents the terminus (if only temporary) of my own intellectual meandering—back and forth, from algebra to process, from judgment to choice—over the last 20 years. It embodies a variety of process/algebra connections that have already been discussed. These include noncompensatory processes, lexicographic semiorders, attentional mechanisms, and aspiration levels on the process side, along with compensatory processes, nonlinear averaging, decumulative weighting, and stochastic control on the algebraic side. There remains, however, one additional feature that characterizes the theory: this is the fact that SP/A is a dual-criterion model.

If an algebraic expression for SP/A is written that covers everything discussed thus far, it would look something like this:

$$\text{SP/A} = F[\text{SP,A}] = F\left[v_1 + \sum_{i=2}^{n}h(D_i)(v_i - v_{i-1}), \sum_{i=1}^{n}\alpha_i p_i\right]. \quad (6)$$

The model states that there are two basic inputs to the choice process. The first input, SP, represents the aggregate effect of a comparison process that can be operationalized for most people as bottom-up before top-down. The weighting function (h), which transforms the decumulative probabilities $(D_i = \sum_{j=i}^{n} p_j)$, captures the relative importance to the decision maker of avoiding bad outcomes (security) and achieving good outcomes (potential).

Because the SP process can be modeled algebraically with a cautiously hopeful weighting function, it can be classed with the family of weighted averaging models that evolved from the expected value criterion of the sixteenth century. However, it is important to remember that the SP term describes aggregate patterns of data across trials rather than behavior on single trials. Thus, someone who compares gambles lexicographically using only rough assessments of security and potential will produce patterns of choices that suggest cautiously hopeful weighting even though no decumulative weighted value is ever computed.

The second input, A, represents the aggregate effect of a process that evaluates risky options in terms of the likelihood that the payoff will exceed an aspiration level. The variable α_i (multiplying the individual values of p_i) takes a value between 1 and 0 depending on whether the associated v_i meets the aspiration level. If the aspiration level is discrete, α_i is an index variable taking only the values 1 or 0; if the aspiration level is fuzzy, α_i will vary continuously between 1 and 0.

The A process is cousin at least to the concepts of bold play and stochastic control first studied by Dubins and Savage (1976). By including the stochastic control term in the model, SP/A theory challenges yet another of the basic elements underlying the expected value criterion, this being the idea that probabilities and outcomes are combined in the index of gamble value. Although combination of probability and value does occur in the bottom-up before top-down SP process, it does not occur in assessing whether the aspiration level will be met.

The function F combines two inputs that are logically and mathematically distinct, much as Allais (1952/1979) proposed long ago. Because SP and A provide conceptually independent assessments of a gamble's attractiveness, one possibility is that F is a weighted average in which the relative weights assigned to SP and A reflect their relative importance in the current decision environment. Another possibility is that F is multiplicative. In either version, however, F would yield a unitary value for each gamble, in which case SP/A would be unable to predict the sorts of intransitivities demonstrated by Tversky (1969) and others.

The existence of intransitivities suggests that the various inputs to the choice process may not be combined into a unitary value, in which case SP/A theory may also need to challenge the higher-order idea that a single index is sufficient to describe the value of a risky option. For example, SP and A (and even S and P) might be assessed sequentially and evaluated according to the sorts of context-sensitive lexicographic processes that figure in the LS and NLAD models proposed by Tversky (1969) and Ranyard (1982). Indeed, I called on a sequential process of just this sort in Fig. 5 to "explain" the existence of intransitivities for gains in the Budescu and Weiss (1987) experiment.

Alternatively, it may be that SP and A assessments are themselves subject to context effects that depend on the particular pair of gambles being compared. Luce, Mellers, and Chang (1994), for example, recently showed that intransitivity can result if the process of choosing among gambles involves a "reference level" that itself changes as a function of the gambles being compared. Previous work with SP/A theory has also suggested that aspiration levels may be affected by the gambles in the immediate choice set (Lopes, 1987). For example, if one of the gambles offers a sure amount (such as the $70 minimum in the riskless lottery of Fig. 3), that value is likely to serve as the aspiration level in evaluating an alternative gamble provided that no other aspiration level is operating.

As it stands, SP/A theory does not include a utility transformation. This is not because the concept of subjective value seems wrong or unnecessary. Instead, the omission signals some theoretical uneasiness at inserting a free function into the theory without knowing what purpose the function will serve. It seems at present that most experimental results involving "risk aversion" and "risk seeking" can be handled by SP/A theory without this additional complication. But even if new results suggest conclusively that something akin to utility needs to be considered, it remains to be seen whether that something extra should be diminishing marginal utility (as might be operating in problems that span very wide outcome ranges) or diminishing sensitivity (as might be operating if subjects evaluate gambles superficially without considering the impact of outcomes on living standards). A good case could be made for either logically, but data must show the way.

SP/A theory sprang from the desire to construct an algebraic model of risky choice that incorporates the subjective reality of the chooser. As experience with SP/A has accumulated, the model has demonstrated its ability to provide qualitative accounts of data that appear anomalous from more standard perspectives. For example, when Schneider and Lopes (1986) tested preselected groups of risk-averse and risk-seeking subjects on preferences for gain and loss lotteries, the results were highly complex across the two groups and failed to support any of the commonly proposed forms of utility function (concave, convex, or S-shape). In SP/A terms, however, the complexity in the data signaled a single difference between groups: whether the subjects were security-minded or potential-minded.

SP/A theory has also been able to explain differences in the degree to which decision makers experience conflict during the choice process and to account for seemingly anomalous patterns of risk preference such as those underlying the St. Petersburg paradox (Lopes, 1995), both forms of the Allais paradox, and both occurrences and nonoccurrences of intransitivity as observed by Budescu and Weiss (1987). That it does so without invoking either nonlinear utility or sign-dependent weighting functions (i.e., weighting functions that differ for gains and losses) testifies to the value of doing algebraic modeling with process in mind. Although there are limits to what we can learn about process experimentally, the descriptive successes of SP/A theory suggest that in exploring the psychological world of risky choice, it is simpler and more certain to travel from process to algebra than to go the other way around.

ACKNOWLEDGMENTS

I am indebted to Gregg Oden, Jerry Busemeyer, Reid Hastie, and Ward Edwards for their insights and encouragement on earlier drafts of this chapter.

REFERENCES

Allais, M. (1979a). The foundations of a positive theory of choice involving risk and a criticism of the postulates and axioms of the American School. In M. Allais & O. Hagen (Eds.), *Expected utility hypotheses and the Allais Paradox* (pp. 27–145). Dordrecht, Holland: Reidel. (Original work published 1952)

Allais, M. (1979b). The so-called Allais paradox and rational decisions under uncertainty. In M. Allais & O. Hagen (Eds.), *Expected utility hypotheses and the Allais Paradox* (pp. 437–681). Dordrecht, Holland: Reidel.

Allais, M. (1986). *The general theory of random choices in relation to the invariant cardinal utility function and the specific probability function.* Working Paper No. C4475. Centre d'Analyse Economique, École des Mines, Paris, France.

Anderson, B. F., Deane, D. H., Hammond, K. R., McClelland, G. H., & Shanteau, J. C. (1981). *Concepts in judgment and decision research.* New York: Praeger.

Bell, D. E. (1982). Regret in decision making under uncertainty. *Operations Research, 30,* 961–981.

Bernoulli, D. (1967). *Exposition of a new theory on the measurement of risk* (L. Sommer, Trans.). Farnsborough Hants, UK: Gregg Press. (Original work published 1738)

Borch, K. (1979). Utility and stochastic dominance. In M. Allais & O. Hagen (Eds.), *Expected utility hypotheses and the Allais Paradox* (pp. 193–201). Dordrecht, Holland: Reidel.

Bostic, R., Herrnstein, R. J., & Luce, R. D. (1990). The effect on the preference-reversal phenomenon of using choice indifferences. *Journal of Economic Behavior and Organization, 13,* 193–212.

Budescu, D., & Weiss, W. (1987). Reflection of transitive and intransitive preference: A test of prospect theory. *Organizational Behavior and Human Decision Processes, 39,* 184–202.

Chew, S.-H., Karni, E., & Safra, S. (1987). Risk aversion in the theory of expected utility with rank dependent probabilities. *Journal of Economic Theory, 42,* 370–381.

Cohen, M., Jaffray, J.-Y., & Said, T. (1987). Experimental comparison of individual behavior under risk and under uncertainty for gains and for losses. *Organizational Behavior and Human Decision Processes, 39,* 1–22.

Combs, C. H. (1975). Portfolio theory and the measurement of risk. In M. F. Kaplan & S. Schwartz (Eds.), *Human judgment and decision processes.* New York: Academic Press.

Coombs, C. H., & Bowen, J. N. (1971). A test of VE-theories of risk and the effect of the central limit theorem. *Acta Psychologica, 35,* 15–28.

Coombs, C. H., & Huang, L. (1970). Tests of a portfolio theory of risk preference. *Journal of Experimental Psychology, 85,* 23–29.

Coombs, C. H., & Lehner, P. E. (1981). Evaluation of two alternative models for a theory of risk: I. Are moments of distributions useful in assessing risk? *Journal of Experimental Psychology: Human Perception and Performance, 7,* 1110–1123.

Daston, L. J. (1980). Probabilistic expectation and rationality in classical probability theory. *Historia Mathematica, 7,* 234–260.

Dubins, L. E., & Savage, L. J. (1976). *Inequalities for stochastic processes: How to gamble if you must* (2nd. ed.). New York: Dover.

Edwards, W. (1953). Probability-preferences in gambling. *American Journal of Psychology, 66,* 349–364.

Edwards, W. (1954a). The theory of decision making. *Psychological Bulletin, 51,* 380–417.

Edwards, W. (1954b). Variance preferences in gambling. *American Journal of Psychology, 67,* 441–452.

Edwards, W. (1962). Subjective probabilities inferred from decisions. *Psychological Review, 69,* 109–135.

Ellsberg, D. (1961). Risk, ambiguity, and the Savage axioms. *Quarterly Journal of Economics, 75,* 643–669.

Fagley, N. S., & Miller, P. M. (1987). The effects of decision framing on choice of risky versus certain options. *Organizational Behavior and Human Decision Processes, 39,* 264–277.

Fischhoff, B. (1983). Predicting frames. *Journal of Experimental Psychology: Learning, Memory, and Cognition, 9,* 103–116.

Fishburn, P. C. (1985). Utility theory and decision theory. In J. Eatwell, M. Milgate, & P. Newman (Eds.), *The New Palgrave: Utility and probability* (pp. 303–312). New York: Norton.

Fishburn, P. C., & Kochenberger, G. A. (1979). Two-piece von Newmann–Morgenstern utility functions. *Decision Sciences, 10,* 503–518.

Friedman, M., & Savage, L. J. (1948). The utility analysis of choices involving risk. *Journal of Political Economy, 56,* 279–304.

Gigerenzer, G., Swijtink, Z., Porter, T., Daston, L., Beatty, J., & Kruger, L. (1989). *The empire of chance: How probability changed science and everyday life.* New York: Cambridge University Press.

Gilboa, I. (1986). A Combination of Expected Utility and Maximin Decision Criteria. Working Paper No. 12-86. Tel Aviv University.

Goldstein, W. M., & Einhorn, H. J. (1987). Expression theory and the preference reversal phenomena. *Psychological Review, 94,* 236–254.

Hadar, J., & Russell, W. R. (1969). Rules for ordering uncertain prospects. *American Economic Review, 59,* 25–34.

Hershey, J. C., & Schoemaker, P. J. H. (1980). Prospect theory's reflection hypothesis: A critical examination. *Organizational Behavior and Human Performance, 25,* 395–418.

Hurwicz, L. (1951). *Optimality criteria for decision making under ignorance* (No. 370). Cowles Commission Discussion Paper.

Jaffray, J.-Y. (1986). *Choice under risk and the security factor: An axiomatic model.* Unpublished manuscript. Laboratorie d'Econometrique, University Paris VI.

Kahneman, D., & Tversky, A. (1979). Prospect theory: An analysis of decision under risk. *Econometrica, 47,* 263–291.

Kahneman, D., & Tversky, A. (1982). The psychology of preferences. *Scientific American, 248,* 163–169.

Kahneman, D., & Tversky, A. (1984). Choices, values, and frames. *American Psychologist, 39,* 341–350.

Karmarkar, U. S. (1978). Subjectively weighted utility: A descriptive extension of the expected utility model. *Organizational Behavior and Human Performance, 21,* 61–82.

Karmarkar, U. S. (1979). Subjectively weighted utility and the Allais paradox. *Organizational Behavior and Human Performance, 24,* 67–72.

Lee, W. (1971). *Decision theory and human behavior.* New York: Wiley.

Lichtenstein, S., & Slovic, P. (1971). Reversals of preference between bids and choices in gambling decisions. *Journal of Experimental Psychology, 89,* 46–55.

Lichtenstein, S., & Slovic, P. (1973). Response-induced reversals of preference in gambling: An extended replication in Las Vegas. *Journal of Experimental Psychology, 101,* 16–20.

Loomes, G., & Sugden, R. (1982). Regret theory: An alternative theory of rational choice under uncertainty. *Economic Journal, 92,* 805–824.

Loomes, G., & Sugden, R. (1987). Some implications of a more general form of regret theory. *Journal of Economic Theory, 41,* 270–287.

Lopes, L. L. (1981). Decision making in the short run. *Journal of Experimental Psychology: Human Learning and Memory, 7,* 377–385.

Lopes, L. L. (1984). Risk and distributional inequality. *Journal of Experimental Psychology: Human Perception and Performance, 10,* 465–485.

Lopes, L. L. (1987). Between hope and fear: The psychology of risk. *Advances in Experimental Social Psychology, 20,* 255–295.

Lopes, L. L. (1990). Remodeling risk aversion. In G. M. von Furstenberg (Ed.), *Acting under uncertainty: Multidisciplinary conceptions* (pp. 267–299). Boston: Kluwer.

Lopes, L. L. (1995). When time is of the essence: Averaging, aspiration, and the short run. *Organizational Behavior and Human Decision Processes,* in press.

Luce, R. D. (1988). Rank-dependent, subjective expected-utility representations. *Journal of Risk and Uncertainty, 1,* 305–332.

Luce, R. D., & Fishburn, P. C. (1991). Rank- and sign-dependent linear utility models for finite first-order gambles. *Journal of Risk and Uncertainty, 4,* 29–59.

Luce, R. D., Mellers, B. A., & Chang, S.-J. (1993). Is choice the correct primitive? On using certainty equivalents and reference levels to predict choices among gambles. *Journal of Risk and Uncertainty, 6,* 115–143.

Maule, A. J. (1989). Positive and negative decision frames: A verbal protocol analysis of the Asian disease problem of Tversky and Kahneman. In H. Montgomery & O. Svenson (Eds.), *Process and structure in human decision making.* London: Wiley.

Mellers, B., Chang, S., Birnbaum, M. H., & Ordóñez, L. D. (1992). Preferences, prices, and ratings in risky decision making. *Journal of Experimental Psychology: Human Perception and Performance, 18,* 347–361.

Mellers, B. A., Ordóñez, L. D., & Birnbaum, M. H. (1992). A change-of-process theory for contextual effects and preference reversals in risky decision making. *Organizational Behavior and Human Decision Processes, 52,* 331–369.

Miller, P. M., & Fagley, N. S. (1991). The effects of framing, problem variations, and providing rationale on choice. *Personality and Social Psychology Bulletin, 17,* 517–522.

Montgomery, H. (1977). A study of intransitive preferences using a think-aloud procedure. In H. Jungermann & G. dr Zeeuw (Eds.), *Decision making and change in human affairs* (pp. 347–362). Dordrecht, Holland: Reidel.

Payne, J. W., Bettman, J. R., & Johnson, E. J. (1990). The adaptive decision maker: Effort and accuracy in choice. In R. M. Hogarth (Ed.), *Insights in decision making: A tribute to Hillel J. Einhorn.* Chicago: University of Chicago Press.

Payne, J. W., & Braunstein, M. L. (1971). Preferences among gambles with equal underlying distributions. *Journal of Experimental Psychology, 87,* 13–18.

Payne, J. W., & Braunstein, M. L. (1978). Risky choice: An examination of information acquisition behavior. *Memory & Cognition, 6,* 554–561.

Payne, J. W., Braunstein, M. L., & Carroll, J. S. (1978). Exploring predecisional behavior: An alternative approach to decision research. *Organizational Behavior and Human Performance, 22,* 17–44.

Payne, J. W., Laughhunn, D. J., & Crum, R. (1980). Translation of gambles and aspiration level effects in risky choice behavior. *Management Science, 26,* 1039–1060.

Quiggin, J. (1982). A theory of anticipated utility. *Journal of Economic Behavior and Organization, 3,* 323–343.

Ranyard, R. (1982). Binary choice patterns and reasons given for simple risky choice. *Acta Psychologica, 52,* 125–135.

Rosen, L. D., & Rosenkoetter, P. (1976). An eye fixation analysis of choice and judgment with multiattribute stimuli. *Memory & Cognition, 4,* 747–752.

Russo, J. E., & Dosher, B. A. (1983). Strategies for multiattribute choice. *Journal of Experimental Psychology: Learning, Memory, and Cognition, 9,* 676–696.

Samuelson, P. A. (1977). St. Petersburg paradoxes: Defanged, dissected, and historically described. *Journal of Economic Literature, 15,* 24–55.

Savage, L. J. (1951). The theory of statistical decision. *Journal of the American Statistical Association, 46,* 55–67.

Savage, L. J. (1954). *The foundations of statistics.* New York: Wiley.

Schmeidler, D. (1989). Subjective probability and expected utility without additivity. *Econometrica, 57,* 571–587.

Schneider, S. L. (1992). Framing and conflict: Aspiration level contingency, the status quo, and current theories of risky choice. *Journal of Experimental Psychology: Learning, Memory, and Cognition, 18,* 1040–1057.

Schneider, S. L., & Lopes, L. L. (1986). Reflection in preferences under risk: Who and when may suggest why. *Journal of Experimental Psychology: Human Perception and Performance, 12,* 535–548.

Schoemaker, P. J. H. (1979). The role of statistical knowledge in gambling decisions: Moment versus risk dimension approaches. *Organizational Behavior and Human Performance, 24,* 1–17.

Segal, U. (1989). Axiomatic representation of expected utility with rank-dependent probabilities. *Annals of Operations Research, 19,* 359–373.

Simon, H. H. (1955). A behavioral model of rational choice. *Quarterly Journal of Economics, 69,* 99–118.

Slovic, P., & Lichtenstein, S. (1968a). Importance of variance preferences in gambling decisions. *Journal of Experimental Psychology, 78,* 646–654.

Slovic, P., & Lichtenstein, S. (1968b). Relative importance of probabilities and payoffs in risk taking. *Journal of Experimental Psychology Monograph, 78,* (No. 3, Pt. 2), 1–18.

Todhunter, I. (1865). *A history of the mathematical theory of probability from the time of Pascal to that of Laplace.* Bronx, NY: Chelsea.

Tversky, A. (1969). Intransitivity of preferences. *Psychological Review, 76,* 31–48.

Tversky, A., & Kahneman, D. (1981). The framing of decisions and the psychology of choice. *Science, 211,* 453–458.

Tversky, A., & Kahneman, D. (1992). Advances in prospect theory: Cumulative representation of uncertainty. *Journal of Risk and Uncertainty, 5,* 297–323.

Tversky, A., Sattath, S., & Slovic, P. (1988). Contingent weighting in judgment and choice. *Psychological Review, 95,* 371–384.

von Neumann, J., & Morgenstern, O. (1947). *Theory of games and economic behavior* (2nd ed.). Princeton, NJ: Princeton University.

Weber, E. U., & Bottom, W. P. (1989). Axiomatic measures of perceived risk: Some tests and extensions. *Journal of Behavioral Decision Making, 2,* 113–132.

Williams, C. A. (1966). Attitudes toward speculative risks as an indicator of attitudes toward pure risks. *Journal of Risk and Insurance, 33,* 577–586.

Yaari, M. E. (1987). The dual theory of choice under risk. *Econometrica, 55,* 95–115.

UTILITY INVARIANCE DESPITE
LABILE PREFERENCES

Barbara A. Mellers, Elke U. Weber, Lisa D. Ordóñez, and
Alan D. J. Cooke

I. Introduction

For over two decades, researchers in decision theory have been puzzled by inconsistencies in human judgment and choice known as *preference reversals*. Preference reversals were first demonstrated in studies of risky decision making by Lichtenstein and Slovic (1971) and Lindman (1971). In these studies, subjects were presented with pairs of gambles matched on expected value. One gamble, referred to as the P-Bet, had a large probability of winning a relatively small amount, and the other gamble, referred to as the $-Bet, had a small probability of winning a relatively large amount. Subjects selected the gamble they preferred from each pair. Then, they assigned selling prices to each separate gamble. The surprising result was that their preferences for gambles derived from choices differed from those derived from selling prices. Subjects chose the P-Bet over the $-Bet, but they assigned a higher selling price to the $-Bet than the P-Bet. Furthermore, the opposite reversal rarely occurred, so the rank order changes could not be attributed to noise or random error.

What do these reversals imply about the measurement of preference? When the weights of objects are measured, one does not expect to find two different orderings depending on whether a balance scale or a digital scale is used. If the digital scale gave systematically higher readings, one

221

would assume the scales were poorly calibrated. But if one object weighed more than another on the balance scale, and the opposite order was obtained with the digital scale, one would worry about the usefulness of the scales. Similarly, when preferences reverse depending on the response mode, it leads one to wonder about the methods of elicitation and the construct itself.

We begin this chapter by examining the robustness of preference reversals. Then, we discuss research in the domain of risky decision making that goes beyond simple demonstrations of preference reversals based on a few pairs of gambles. We show how the entire preference order over a large set of gambles changes with the response mode. In addition, we examine preference reversals in a riskless domain in which subjects state their preferences for apartments using choices and ratings of attractiveness. We propose a two-pronged theory of preference reversals. In the risky domain, we attribute preference reversals to different decision strategies across tasks. In the riskless domain, we argue that preference reversals are caused by weight changes across tasks, a variation of a theory proposed by Tversky, Sattath, and Slovic (1988): The attribute judged more important has a greater effect in choices than in ratings. Finally, we show how this two-pronged theory, which assumes that subjects change either strategies or weights across tasks, gives a coherent account of many important properties of the data while allowing the elicitation of utilities or psychological values to remain constant across tasks. We demonstrate that, with the appropriate models, utilities are stable and have meaning over and beyond the task from which they are derived.

II.   Robustness of Preference Reversals

The first experiments on preference reversals gave rise to a large number of studies that tested the robustness of the phenomenon in both risky and riskless domains. Although preference reversals in risky domains were demonstrated primarily with gambles, other stimuli were also used. Mowen and Gentry (1980) presented subjects with products having either high probabilities of success or high expected profits. Subjects chose products with high probabilities of success, but assigned higher selling prices to products with higher expected profits. Reversals of preference were also found in financial settings. Tversky, Slovic, and Kahneman (1990) showed that people chose the short-term investment with a lower yield over the long-term investment with the higher yield, but they assigned a higher price to the long-term investment.

Preference reversals were also demonstrated in the riskless domain. Bazerman, Loewenstein, and White (1992) showed that people reversed their preferences for reward allocations using choices and ratings. Subjects chose the allocation of $600 for oneself and $800 for the other person over the allocation of $500 for both parties, but they rated the latter as more desirable than the former. Irwin, Slovic, Lichtenstein, and McClelland (1993) demonstrated the reversals with public policy questions. They asked people about their willingness to pay for improvements in air quality and improvements in consumer goods (e.g., a better camera or VCR). Irwin et al. found that, in a choice task, people paid more for improvements in air quality than for improvements in consumer goods; but in a pricing task, people assigned a higher value to improvements in consumer goods. Finally, Chapman and Johnson (1993) obtained preference reversals with health items and commodities. Health items were judged as more valuable when measured with life expectancy evaluations, but commodities were judged more valuable with monetary evaluations.

Not only have preference reversals been found in risky and riskless domains, they also occur with different response modes. In addition to selling prices and choices, preference reversals were demonstrated with choices and attractiveness ratings (Goldstein & Einhorn, 1987), attractiveness ratings and buying prices (Goldstein & Einhorn, 1987), and buying prices and selling prices (Birnbaum & Sutton, 1992), among other combinations.

Numerous attempts have been made to reduce preference reversals or eliminate them entirely. Financial incentives have had either limited effects (Pommerehne, Schneider, & Zweifel, 1982) or no effect at all (Lichtenstein & Slovic, 1971; Grether & Plott, 1979). Even when subjects used their *own* money to gamble in a casino in Las Vegas, preference reversals continued at approximately the same rate as found in laboratory studies (Lichtenstein & Slovic, 1973). Extensive instructions have also been used to reduce preference reversals with mixed success. Lichtenstein and Slovic (1971) gave "lengthy and careful" instructions to their subjects, but the phenomenon continued to occur. Reilly (1982), however, taught subjects about expected values and significantly reduced the rate of preference reversals. Other researchers have examined the effects of multiple plays on preference reversals. Wedell and Böckenholt (1990) told people to assume that they were playing each gamble 100 times and found that preference reversals with choices and selling prices were significantly reduced, but not eliminated.

Experimental markets, where buyers and sellers make trades using specified rules of communication, have had more success at reducing preference reversals (Cox & Grether, 1992). A particularly powerful technique is a money pump. With a money pump, people are caught in a cycle of exchanges in which they eventually end up with their initial option *and* less money.[1] Berg, Dickhaut, and O'Brien (1985) found that subjects still made preference reversals after one cycle of a money pump. However, Chu and Chu (1990) showed that preference reversals were completely extinguished after three cycles. In sum, certain types of feedback from the market may correct the inconsistencies, but very few decisions have such immediate and obvious feedback.

III.   Comparing Preference Orders

We conducted several experiments designed to compare preference orders across a variety of different tasks. In Mellers, Chang, Birnbaum, and Ordóñez (1992) and Mellers, Ordóñez, and Birnbaum (1992), we used 36 two-outcome gambles of which one outcome was a positive payoff and the other outcome was zero. The probabilities, payoffs, and expected values for these gambles are presented in Fig. 1. Probabilities and payoffs were selected so that gambles along the diagonals would have the same expected values.

In this section we focus on responses from three tasks: selling prices (minimum amounts that people would accept to sell the gambles), attractiveness ratings, and strength of preference judgments (choices, followed

PAYOFF

		$3.00	$5.40	$9.70	$17.50	$31.50	$56.70
	0.05	0.15	0.27	0.49	0.88	1.58	2.84
	0.09	0.27	0.49	0.87	1.58	2.84	5.10
PROBABILITY	0.17	0.48	0.86	1.55	2.80	5.04	9.07
	0.29	0.87	1.57	2.81	5.08	9.14	16.44
	0.52	1.56	2.81	5.04	9.10	16.38	29.48
	0.94	2.82	5.08	9.12	16.45	29.61	53.30

Fig. 1.   Expected values for two outcome gambles with some probability (rows) of winning a specified amount (columns), or otherwise zero.

---

[1] Given a choice between a P-Bet and a $-Bet, subjects often choose the P-Bet. Subjects then pay to exchange the P-Bet for the $-Bet (as the buying price for the $-Bet is higher than the P-Bet). When given the choice, subjects then trade the $-Bet for the P-Bet. The result is that subjects have incurred a loss to regain the initially owned gamble.

by judgments of the magnitude of preference). In each task, we derived preference orders, which are shown in Fig. 2. The numbers 1 and 36 represent the least preferred and most preferred gambles, respectively. Arrows indicate the direction of preference for pairs of gambles with equal expected values. Arrows pointing upward show pairs for which the P-Bet (having the larger probability of winning) was ranked higher than the $-Bet (having the larger amount to win). Arrows pointing downward highlight pairs for which the $-Bet was ranked higher than the P-Bet.

As Fig. 2 shows, there are numerous reversals of preference across tasks. For example, people rate the gamble with a 94% chance of winning $3.00 as more attractive than the gamble with a 5% chance of winning $56.70. Rank orders are 31 versus 13. But those same people assign a *lower* selling price to the gamble with a 94% chance of winning $3.00 than to the one with a 5% chance of winning $56.70. Rank orders are 13 and 23. Furthermore, the entire pattern of preferences differs across tasks. For attractiveness ratings (A), almost all of the arrows point up; P-Bets are more attractive than $-Bets. People have risk averse preferences because, holding expected value constant, gambles with lower variance or less variability in the outcomes (P-Bets) are judged more attractive than gambles with higher variance ($-Bets). For the pricing task (C), almost all of the arrows point down; $-Bets are worth more than P-Bets. In this task, preferences are risk seeking; people assign greater worth to gambles with higher variance than to gambles with lower variance. In the strength of preference task (B), arrows point down when the probabilities of winning are small and up when the probabilities increase. Preferences are risk seeking when the probabilities of winning are small and risk averse when the probabilities increase. This pattern of preference has been well documented (Kahneman & Tversky, 1979). To summarize, preference orders are strikingly different across tasks.

Do preference orders vary when subjects are financially motivated? We ran versions of the experiments with students who were paid a flat fee to

A

PAYOFF

PROBABILITY	3.00	5.40	9.70	17.50	31.50	56.70
.05	1	2.5	6	6	6	13
.09	2.5	6	9	11	16	16
.17	6	11	11	16	19	21
.29	16	16	20	23	23	26
.52	25	23	27	28.5	28.5	30
.94	31	32	33	34	35	36

B

PAYOFF

	3.00	5.40	9.70	17.50	31.50	56.70
.05	1	3	6	9	14	18
.09	2	4	8	13	17	20
.17	5	7	12	16	24	25
.29	10	11	15	23	27	30
.52	19	21	26	29	32	33
.94	22	28	31	34	35	36

C

PAYOFF

	3.00	5.40	9.70	17.50	31.50	56.70
.05	1	2.5	6	9	17	23
.09	2.5	6	10.5	15	21	26
.17	4	8	13	19	24.5	30
.29	6	13	18	24.5	29	33
.52	10.5	16	22	28	32	35
.94	13	20	27	31	34	36

Fig. 2. Preference orders for attractiveness ratings (A), strength of preference (B), and selling price judgments (C). Larger numbers refer to more preferred gambles. Arrows show the direction of preference for pairs of gambles with equal expected values.

participate and, at the end of the experiment, were allowed to play a gamble from each task. With attractiveness ratings and selling prices, students were told that two gambles would be randomly selected from the entire set, and the gamble to which they assigned a higher rating or selling price was the gamble they would be allowed to play. With the strength of preference task, one pair was randomly selected and the gamble to which they had assigned a higher strength of preference judgment was played. Payoffs were 25% of the stated outcomes. Results were virtually identical to those shown in Fig. 2.

What happens when outcomes are losses rather than gains? We conducted another version of the experiment in which positive outcomes were converted to negative outcomes. People rated the unattractiveness of the gambles, assigned avoidance prices to the gambles (or amounts of money they would be willing to pay to avoid playing the gambles), and rated the strength of their preference for one gamble over another (i.e., the better of two evils). Preference orders in the domain of losses were the reflection of those in the domain of gains. Preferences were risk seeking with unattractiveness ratings (P-Bets were rated more unattractive than $-Bets), risk averse with avoidance prices ($-Bets had higher avoidance prices than P-Bets), and strength of preference judgments were a mixture of both risk attitudes: when the probabilities of losing were small, preferences were risk averse; but when the probabilities increased, preferences were risk seeking.

Kahneman and Tversky (1979) and others have shown that choices between risky options often reflect around the status quo. Except with small probabilities, preferences are characterized as risk averse in the gain domain and risk seeking in the loss domain. We compared preference orders for gambles based on strength of preference judgments in the gain and loss domains and found that our data also showed this pattern of reflection.

Expected values in the preceding studies ranged from $0 to $53.30 (in the gain domain) and $0 to −$53.30 (in the loss domain). These expected values are relatively small, and preference orders might differ if expected values were larger. Casey (1991) discovered that when expected values of the gambles were approximately $100, *unexpected* preference reversals occurred with choices and buying prices. That is, subjects chose the $-Bet over the P-Bet, but they assigned a higher buying price to the P-Bet than to the $-Bet.

To investigate Casey's results, we ran a version of the experiment with expected values ranging from $0.15 to $1000. Preference orders are displayed in Fig. 3; arrows connect gambles with equal expected values. Arrows point up in the attractiveness rating task (A), as found earlier (Fig. 2); P-Bets are rated more attractive than $-Bets. In the strength of preference task (B), arrows also tend to point up for all levels of probability; P-Bets

A

PROBABILITY	PAYOFF					
	3.00	9.70	31.50	102	330	1070
.05	1	3	3	6	8	11.5
.09	3	5	11.5	11.5	11.5	19.5
.17	7	11.5	15.5	17	19.5	24
.29	11.5	15.5	19.5	19.5	24	24
.52	24	24	27.5	27.5	29	30.5
.94	30.5	32	33	34.5	34.5	36

B

PROBABILITY	PAYOFF					
	3.00	9.70	31.50	102	330	1070
.05	1	4	7	9	15	21
.09	2	5	9	14	20	25
.17	3	8	13	19	23	28
.29	6	12	18	23	27	31
.52	9	17	25	29	32	34
.94	16	22	30	33	35	36

C

PROBABILITY	PAYOFF					
	3.00	9.70	31.50	102	330	1070
.05	1	4.5	10	16	16	21
.09	2	7	12	19	23	24
.17	3	7	14	21	26	30
.29	4.5	11	18	26	28	33
.52	7	13	21	29	31	35
.94	9	16	26	32	34	35

Fig. 3. Preference orders for attractiveness ratings (A), strength of preference (B), and buying price judgments (C) for gambles with a wider range of expected values. Arrows show the direction of preference for pairs of gambles with equal expected values.

are ranked higher than $-Bets. Finally, in the buying price task (C), arrows tend to point down for smaller payoffs and up for larger payoffs. Thus, preference orders based on the wider range of expected values are somewhat different from those based on the smaller range, from $0.15 to $53.30, for strength of preference judgments and pricing judgments.

In the lower right-hand corner of each table, expected values are approximately $100 or greater. In this region, we find no evidence of unexpected reversals. The preference order for these gambles does not seem to differ notably from those in the rest of the table for both strength of preference judgments and buying prices. If anything, there are fewer preference reversals. We find preference orders for gambles with larger expected values to be similar to those with smaller expected values, but larger stakes appear to produce more risk averse preferences in both strength of preference and pricing tasks. There is no evidence of unexpected reversals.

IV. Violations of Strong Transitivity

Preference reversals are sometimes interpreted as violations of transitivity. This interpretation, although incorrect, does not exclude the possibility that transitivity violations could occur in choices. Research on violations of strong stochastic transitivity is summarized next.

Preference reversals often involve choices, and there is an extensive literature on theories of probabilistic choice. Tests of theories are often based on stochastic transitivity (Coombs, 1983). In binary choice, a stochastic preference for gamble i over gamble j is said to occur when $P(i,j)$, the proportion of times i is chosen over j, exceeds .5. According to weak stochastic transitivity, if $P(i,j) \geq .5$ and $P(j,k) \geq .5$, then $P(i,k) \geq .5$. Moderate stochastic transitivity requires that $P(i,k) \geq \min [(P(i,j), P(j,k)]$, and strong stochastic transitivity states that $P(i,k) \geq \max [(P(i,j), P(j,k)]$.

Strength of preference judgments can also be used to test properties of transitivity. On any trial, subjects are asked to state not only the direction of their preference but also the magnitude. Assume that a judgment of 0 represents indifference on a strength of preference scale, and $S(i,j) \geq 0$ represents a judged preference for gamble i over gamble j. Suppose that $S(i,j) \geq 0$ and $S(j,k) \geq 0$. The deterministic forms of transitivity are easy to specify. Weak transitivity states that $S(i,k) \geq 0$, moderate transitivity implies that $S(i,k) \geq \min [S(i,j), S(j,k)]$, and strong transitivity states that $S(i,k) \geq \max [S(i,j), S(j,k)]$.

Empirical investigations with both animals and humans indicate that weak and moderate stochastic transitivity are often satisfied, with a few notable exceptions (Tversky, 1969). However, strong stochastic transitivity is frequently violated (Busemeyer, 1985; Rumelhart & Greeno, 1971; Tversky & Russo, 1969; Becker, DeGroot, & Marschak, 1963; Krantz, 1967; Sjöberg, 1975, 1977; Sjöberg & Capozza, 1975; Battilio, Kagel, & MacDonald, 1985). Empirical tests of these properties in strength of preference judgments also show that weak and moderate transitivities are usually satisfied, but strong transitivity often fails (Mellers & Biagini, 1994; Mellers, Chang, Birnbaum, & Ordóñez, 1992). In the experiments described previously, the median percentage of weak transitivity violations over individuals was 5%. The median percentage of moderate transitivity violations was approximately 20%. Strong transitivity violations were much more frequent, ranging from approximately 50% to 60%. This pattern occurred in choices involving both gains and losses, with large and small stakes, regardless of whether subjects were financially motivated.

Is there a pattern to the triplets that violates strong transitivity? Violations tended to occur in triplets that had at least one gamble pair with similar levels of probabilities or payoffs. When levels on one dimension were similar, differences in levels on the other dimension seemed to be enhanced, causing violations of strong transitivity. To illustrate, consider the following three gambles with equal expected values. Gamble a has a 52% chance of winning $3.00, otherwise $0; gamble b has a 5% chance of winning $56.70, otherwise $0; and gamble c has a 9% chance of winning $17.50, otherwise $0. With these gambles, people prefer a to b, b to c, and a to c, thus satisfying weak transitivity. The median strength of preference judgment for a over b was 10 (on a scale from 0, representing indifference, to 80, representing a very strong preference), and the median strength of preference judgment for b over c was 22. To satisfy strong transitivity, the strength of preference judgment for a over c should have exceeded 22, but it was only 12. The majority of subjects displayed this pattern in their judgments. Either the preference for gamble b over c was too large, or the preference for a over c was too small, according to strong transitivity.

In this example, gambles *b* and *c* have similar levels of probability, but different levels of payoffs. Probabilities are .05 and .09, respectively, and payoffs are $56.70 and $17.50, respectively. The similarity of probabilities may enhance differences in payoffs, making the strength of preference judgment for *b* over *c* too large, relative to the other judgments. Similar patterns are found in other triplets that violate strong transitivity.

V. Psychological Theories of Preference Reversals

Results from the preceding experiments show systematically different orders, depending on the procedure used to elicit preferences. The challenge is to discover what, if anything, remains invariant across tasks. An additional constraint on any theory of preference reversals that involves choices is that it must be able to predict the violations of strong transitivity.

We begin our discussion of invariance by representing judgment as a composition of functions, as shown in Fig. 4. In this framework, attractiveness ratings and pricing judgments can be decomposed into three processes, represented by the functions H, C, and J. Physical values of the stimuli—objective probabilities and payoffs—are represented as subjective values. Objective probabilities are transformed into subjective probabilities, and payoffs are converted to utilities. The functions that relate subjective values to physical values are H_P and H_A for probabilities and amounts, respectively.

As Weber, Goldstein, and Barlas (this volume) point out, much of psychology concerns itself with how physical values are mapped onto subjective values, and this concern dates back to research from the 1800s. As early as 1860, Fechner, a pioneer in the field of psychophysics, proposed that the physical world was related to the subjective world by means of a logarithmic relationship. Furthermore, in his classic book, Elements of Psychophysics, Fechner (1860/1966) argued that the logarithmic function had been proposed as the link between physical and subjective values 100 years earlier by Daniel Bernoulli, who used it to describe the relationship between *fortune morale* (moral wealth) and *fortune physique* (physical wealth). Although there is still controversy about the shape of the H function in a variety of different tasks, there is no disagreement about the need to postulate subjective values.

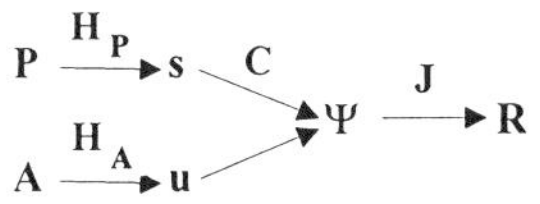

Fig. 4. Framework for analysis of judgment.

Subjective values of probabilities and payoffs, denoted s and u, are combined by means of a function, C, to form a subjective impression of the gamble, represented as Ψ. When the dependent variable is an attractiveness rating, Ψ represents the composite attractiveness of the gamble. When the dependent variable is a pricing judgment, Ψ represents the composite worth of the gamble. These subjective impressions are then transformed to numerical responses, R, such as a number on a category rating scale or a dollar amount, by means of a judgment function, J. This function represents the response transformation and is typically assumed to be monotonic.

First, we consider three psychological theories of preference reversals: contingent-weighting theory (Tversky et al., 1988), reference-level theory (Luce, Mellers, & Chang, 1992), and expression theory (Goldstein & Einhorn, 1987). Then, we discuss a fourth possibility, the change-of-process theory, in more detail.

A. CONTINGENT-WEIGHTING THEORY

Tversky et al. (1988) proposed a hierarchy of contingent trade-off models to account for discrepancies between judgment and choice. A special case is the contingent-weighting model, which Tversky et al. proposed to account for preference reversals between buying price judgments and attractiveness ratings of two-outcome gambles with some probability p of winning amount A, otherwise winning nothing. According to this model, the weights associated with the attributes depend on their compatibility with the response scale. Tversky et al. assumed that the value of a gamble is the product of probability and payoff, with each attribute weighted by a power function that depends on its relationship to the response scale. Using additive, linear multiple regression on the logarithms of the responses, they argued that the relative weight for payoffs is greater in the pricing task than in the rating task because, in a pricing task, the independent variable (payoffs in terms of dollars) is more compatible with the response scale (dollars).

According to this account, preference reversals are caused by changes in the weights of the attributes. Differential weighting might be attributed to changes in the C function; however, the aggregation rule does not vary. Furthermore, Tversky et al. did not have independent estimates of weights and scales. For these reasons, we prefer to treat contingent weighting as a theory that attributes preference reversals to changes in the H function. Tversky et al. (1988) presented a more general contingent trade-off model in which both scales and processes can vary with the task, but this more general model makes no predictions about when scales or processes should vary.

B. REFERENCE-LEVEL THEORY

Luce et al., (1992) proposed a theory of preference reversals for certainty equivalents (CEs) and choices. Certainty equivalents (in this case, selling prices) are assumed to be the basic primitive, and choices are derived from comparisons of CEs. When confronted with a pair of gambles and asked to make a choice, people assess the monetary worth, or CE, of each gamble relative to a reference level that is unique to each pair of gambles. If either of the two CEs is positive, the reference level is the smaller of the two CEs. If both of the CEs are losses, the reference level is the smallest CE. Before making a choice, subjects are assumed to recode the outcomes of the gambles relative to the reference level. This recoding reflects the fact that even gains can feel like losses when expectations are higher than positive outcomes. Finally, gambles are evaluated by means of their rank- and sign-dependent utility (Luce, 1991; Luce & Fishburn, 1991). In this account, preference reversals also occur as the result of changes in the H function that vary systematically for each pair of gambles.

C. EXPRESSION THEORY

Goldstein and Einhorn (1987) proposed another account, called *expression theory,* in which preference reversals occur in the J function. Although this function is typically assumed to be monotonic, Goldstein and Einhorn postulated a nonmonotonic function that differs systematically for each gamble. This transformation presents gambles in terms of their "proportional worth." The proportional worth of the gamble on a pricing scale is defined with respect to the gamble's best and the worst outcomes. Similarly, the proportional worth of the gamble on a rating scale is defined with respect to the highest and lowest permissible ratings. Subjects convert gambles to their proportional worths, and those proportional worths should be monotonically related across tasks.

   Mellers, Ordóñez, and Birnbaum (1992) present evidence inconsistent with contingent-weighting theory and expression theory, and Luce et al. (1992) discuss the pros and cons of reference-level theory. Additional dis- cussions of these theories can be found elsewhere. Now, a fourth theory, referred to as *change-of-process* theory will be presented in more detail.

D. CHANGE-OF-PROCESS THEORY

Mellers, Chang, Birnbaum, and Ordóñez (1992) and Mellers, Ordóñez, and Birnbaum (1992) have suggested using a change-of-process theory to describe preference reversals. In this account, decision strategies by which subjects combine information vary across tasks and subjective values of the payoffs remain constant. That is, the combination rule (C in Fig. 4) depends on the response mode, but the psychophysical function (H) remains constant. A number of researchers (Payne, 1982; Payne, Bettman, & Johnson, 1992, 1993; Smith, Mitchell, & Beach, 1982) discuss the possibility that decision makers use different decision strategies depending on the effort required, the accuracy needed, and the cost of decision errors. Some have theorized that preference reversals should be attributed to different decision strategies across tasks (Lichtenstein & Slovic, 1971; Schkade & Johnson, 1989; Johnson, Payne, & Bettman, 1988). Change-of-process theory extends these ideas by postulating specific models for ratings, prices, and strength of preference judgments. In the strength of preference judgments, weights depend not on compatibility but rather on the similarity of the attribute levels under consideration. Furthermore, the change-of-process theory has the additional assumption of utility invariance; that is, the utilities associated with monetary outcomes are assumed to be invariant across response modes (Birnbaum, 1974; Birnbaum & Veit, 1974).

The importance of this assumption cannot be overstated. Utility invariance has theoretical consequences because it implies that preference measurements have meaning over and beyond the task in which they are derived. This constraint increases the psychological validity and usefulness of the measurements and helps create a more solid theoretical framework in which both models and measurements contribute to our understanding of preference reversals.

Consider gamble a, with some probability p of winning an amount x or otherwise winning nothing. The change-of-process theory asserts that under some conditions, the attractiveness rating of gamble a can be described by an additive combination of utility and subjective probability, and scales are equated by means of a constant, k, as follows:

$$A(a) = J_A[k \, s_a + u_a], \tag{1}$$

where A is the attractiveness rating of gamble a. J_A is a monotonic response function, k is the scaling constant, s_a is the subjective probability associated with probability p, and u_a is the utility associated with amount x. The selling price for gamble a is described by a multiplicative model:

$$P(a) = J_P[s_a \, u_a], \tag{2}$$

where P is the selling price of gamble a, J_P is the response function, and s_a and u_a are the subjective probability and utility, respectively. Finally, strength of preference judgments are described by both operations. That is, the strength of preference for one gamble over another is a monotonic function of the difference between the two subjective products, with one additional assumption: contrast weighting. This assumption, which is necessary to account for violations of strong transitivity, is that people focus attention primarily on attributes that differ. Utilities and subjective probabilities are weighted according to the contrast between levels along a dimension. For example, if gambles have similar probabilities of winning, the weight given to the probability dimension is smaller than if probabilities differ. Likewise, if gambles have similar payoffs, the weight given to the payoff dimension is smaller than if payoffs differ. Contrast weights may represent an attentional focus (Nosofsky, 1986). The discounting of dimensions that are not terribly diagnostic may be one way to simplify the task and minimize effort (Payne, 1976; Payne et al., 1992).

The contrast-weighting model is expressed as follows:

$$S(a,b) = J_S[u_a{}^\alpha \, s_a{}^\beta - u_b{}^\alpha \, s_b{}^\beta], \tag{3}$$

where $S(a,b)$ is the strength of preference for gamble a over gamble b, J_S is the judgment function, α is the contrast weight for utilities, β is the contrast weight for probabilities, and the other symbols are as defined earlier. To fit this model to any set of data, it is necessary to define the terms *similar* and *dissimilar*. Mellers, Chang, Birnbaum, and Ordóñez (1992) used a simple proxy for similarity; adjacent levels of probability and payoffs in the experimental design (e.g., $3.00 and $5.40, $5.40, and $9.70 in Fig. 1) were treated as similar and received one contrast weight, and nonadjacent levels were treated as dissimilar and received a different contrast weight. Thus, two contrast weights were allowed for each dimension, one when contrasts were small and the other when contrasts were large.

This proxy for similarity is undoubtedly too simple; Goldstone, Medin, and Gentner (1991) show that similarity is often relational. That is, the degree to which a shared feature affects similarity depends on the other features shared by those objects. Nonetheless, the proxy used by Mellers, Chang, Birnbaum, and Ordóñez (1992) worked well at describing the patterns of strong transitivity violations described earlier. That is, the similarity of levels on one attribute intensifies differences on other attributes.

Fits of the change-of-process theory to the experiments described earlier have been quite promising. The theory can describe the changing preference orders with little residual variance. Estimated contrast weights for similar levels along a dimension are smaller than weights for dissimilar levels. Furthermore, the theory accurately predicts the violations of strong transitivity in strength of preference judgments. Finally, the assumption of stable utilities is satisfied. That is, utilities are invariant despite labile preferences.

In sum, change-of-process theory gives an excellent description of judgments and choices in the domain of risky decision making.

VI. Deciding How to Decide

If subjects actually use different strategies to evaluate gambles, what factors determine strategy selection for a particular task? One factor that appears to influence the choice of a decision strategy is the stimulus context. We have found that when subjects rate the attractiveness of gambles, attractiveness ratings appear parallel, consistent with the interpretation that subjects combine probabilities and payoffs additively. However, the additive model makes some implausible predictions. According to this model, payoffs and probabilities should make independent contributions to the overall attractiveness of the gamble. If subjects are shown gambles with varying probabilities of winning $0, the attractiveness of the gamble should *increase* as the probability of winning *increases*. Similarly, if subjects are shown a set of gambles with a 0% chance of winning various amounts, the attractiveness of the gambles should increase as the amount to win increases.

We examined whether people show this peculiar behavior by presenting them with a set of gambles, some of which had zero probabilities of winning various amounts or varying probabilities of winning $0. For the majority of subjects, attractiveness ratings were no longer parallel. Instead, ratings showed a bilinear interaction consistent with a multiplicative combination rule of probability and payoff. It is likely that the inclusion of these unusual gambles highlighted the problems of an additive strategy, and therefore subjects switched to a multiplicative strategy. The process by which subjects combine information may depend not only on the response mode, but also on the surrounding stimulus context.

Payne et al. (1992, 1993) argued that people have a repertoire of decision strategies from which they select a particular strategy, depending on the task, the context, the cost of decision errors, the accuracy required, and the effort required. This framework implies that preference reversals will diminish when the cost of a decision error increases or effort decreases. Most tests of this hypothesis have focused on the cost of decisions. Studies that build in financial incentives increase the costs of decision errors, yet preference reversal rates are often unaffected by financial incentives, a finding that runs counter to the effort–accuracy framework for selecting strategies.

Johnson et al. (1988) examined the level of effort required of the decision maker by manipulating the display of probabilities. They reasoned that simple probability displays should produce fewer preference reversals than more complex displays; and, in fact, they found a somewhat lower rate of preference reversals when probabilities were presented in a simple form (e.g., .88 or 7/8) compared with a more complex form (399/456). They argued that people expend less effort and can more easily perform expected-value computations with simple displays than with more complex displays. Johnson et al. reasoned that if subjects use expected-value computations, their preferences would be more consistent across tasks.

However, in another study, González-Vallejo and Wallsten (1992) varied the display of probabilities by using numerical and verbal forms and found that preference reversals were significantly reduced with verbal probabilities. It seems unlikely that verbal probabilities encouraged expected-value computations. Thus, the evidence supporting the effort–accuracy framework for preference reversals appears mixed. As Payne, Bettman, and Johnson point out, many factors presumably influence the decision about how to decide, and the effects of these factors do not appear to be simple.

VII. Which Preference Order Represents "True" Preferences?

The change-of-process theory asserts that people use different decision strategies for combining information, and those decision strategies produce different preference orders. Does one of those preference orders better reflect people's "true" preferences? This question presupposes a set of "true" preferences, a somewhat controversial assumption. Perhaps an easier question to answer is whether any of the preference orders derived from pricing judgments, attractiveness ratings, or strength of preference judgments is more stable and robust than the others. Ordóñez, Mellers, Chang, and Roberts (1994) pointed out that a common thread runs through almost all of the past research on preference reversals: subjects perform the tasks *sequentially*. That is, they evaluate a set of gambles with one response mode and later reevaluate the same set with a second response mode. By using this procedure, subjects are never directly confronted with their own inconsistencies.

We attempted to make subjects aware of their preference reversals by asking them to perform two tasks *simultaneously*. In this case, they evaluated pairs of gambles with both response modes before continuing to the next pair of gambles. Pairs of response modes were selected from three possible tasks (attractiveness ratings, selling prices, and strength of preference judgments). We thought that this procedure might motivate subjects to produce more consistent responses. We provided additional motivation for consistency by telling subjects that at the end of the experiment we would randomly select a trial that contained a pair of gambles. If their responses in the two tasks were consistent (e.g., they priced gamble *a* higher than gamble *b* and they also rated gamble *a* as more attractive than gamble *b*), they would be allowed to play the preferred gamble. If their responses were inconsistent, the experimenter would select the gamble to be played, and that gamble might not be the one they preferred.

If this procedure yields a single preference order across tasks, there are at least three different ways in which preferences could become more consistent. First, preference orders for gamble pairs could be determined on the basis of the first task performed; the preference order for the second task would always be identical to the preference order for the first task. Second, the preference order for one of the two tasks could dominate the preference order for the other task. For example, if selling prices dominated the other tasks, the preference orders for the other tasks would resemble that of selling prices, regardless of task order. Third, preference orders from the two tasks could merge into a new preference order. This order presumably would be some composite of the original two preference orders.

When financially motivated subjects made responses to the two tasks simultaneously, preference reversals were not only reduced but they were actually eliminated for two of the three task pairs. The derived preference order for each task appeared to merge into a new, compromise order that differed depending on the pair of tasks. For attractiveness ratings and selling prices, the merging was incomplete (i.e., the two tasks still had somewhat different preference orders) and reversals continued to occur.

Does one of these preference orders represent subjects' true preferences? No single preference order appeared across the relevant task combinations. It seems unlikely that a true preference order exists, as subjects were presumably just responding to the procedure and incentives in the experiment. They appeared to construct their preferences as some compromise of the preference orders from each separate task. Another procedure and incentive structure might have produced a different set of consistent preference orders. Results from this study suggest that subjects can give consistent responses when motivated to do so, but these preferences do not necessarily reflect true preferences, and the concept of "true preference" is, itself, somewhat dubious.

VIII.   Preference Reversals in Riskless Domains

Goldstein and Weber (this volume) argue that decision researchers have been excessively drawn to the gambling metaphor. It is easy to see why this seductive tool has been so widely used. It contains the main elements of a risky decision, namely, alternative actions controlled by the decision maker, states of nature that constitute the environment, and outcomes that are the results of actions and states of nature. Furthermore, with gambles, these elements are easy to manipulate. Goldstein and Weber argue that because of this simplicity, the central assumption of the gambling metaphor, that decisions depend on some combination of degree of belief and degree of desirability, may not generalize to other types of decisions. If so, our theories of decisions based on gambles may not generalize to nongambling contexts. Therefore, it seems reasonable to ask whether the change-of-process theory can also describe preference reversals outside the domain of gambles. Do people use different decision strategies in riskless domains?

To answer this question, Mellers and Cooke (1994) examined preference reversals using apartments described by monthly rent and distance to campus. One group of students rated the attractiveness of apartments, and another group made choices between pairs of apartments. Figure 5 shows the preference orders for the two tasks. Arrows connect pairs of nondominated apartments that differ in rent and distance; one apartment is closer to campus, and the other apartment is cheaper. Downward arrows represent preferences for closer apartments over cheaper apartments. Upward arrows show preferences for cheaper apartments over closer apartments. In the rating task (A), most of the arrows point down: closer apartments are more attractive than cheaper apartments. In the choice task (B), all of the arrows point up: cheaper apartments are chosen over closer apartments.

Why might these reversals occur? It seems quite reasonable that students would rate closer apartments as more attractive. Closer apartments are usually more convenient. However, if closer apartments are more attractive, why are they not chosen? Perhaps students want to save their money; they prefer to spend less. But if they want to save money, then why do they not rate cheaper apartments as more attractive? These two tasks may highlight different features of the apartments: one task may represent preferences under no constraints and the other may represent preferences with realistic

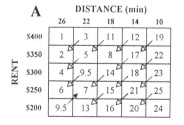
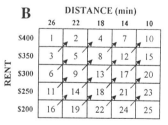

Fig. 5.   Preference orders for attractiveness ratings (A) and choices (B) for apartments described by monthly rent and distance to campus. Arrows show the direction of preference for pairs of apartments differing in rent and distance.

aspirations. However, nothing in the task instructions guided subjects to take different points of view.

Mellers and Cooke (1994) did *not* find evidence to support the change-of-process theory. Both attractiveness ratings and choices were consistent with a single decision strategy. If changes in decision strategies cannot account for preference reversals, then what can?

Tversky et al. (1988) proposed two hypotheses to describe why subjects weight attributes differently across tasks. *Compatibility,* described earlier, focuses on the similarity of the attribute and response scales. The second hypothesis, *prominence,* states that the more prominent attribute weighs more heavily in choices than in matching tasks. People tend to make choices according to the more important dimension(s), but they match options by comparing trade-offs along two or more dimensions. If rent is more prominent than distance in evaluations of apartments, rent will receive relatively more weight in the choice task than in the rating task.

Although Tversky et al. (1988) proposed the prominence hypothesis to account for discrepancies between choice and matching tasks, this hypothesis can also be tested for choice and rating tasks. If people assign greater weight to the more important attribute in choice tasks than in rating tasks, one would expect preference reversals to be different for people who differ in their opinion about the more important attribute. In particular, people who say that distance is more important might choose closer apartments over cheaper apartments, but rate cheaper apartments as more attractive. Those who say that rent is more important might choose cheaper apartments over closer apartments, but rate closer apartments as more attractive.

To test this hypothesis, Mellers and Cooke (1994) investigated preferences for apartments using a within-subject design in which students assigned ratings to apartments and chose between pairs of apartments. After completing each task, they indicated which attribute, rent or distance, was more important by allocating 100 points between the two attributes to reflect their relative importance. A few individuals reversed their relative importance judgments for the two tasks. A few others said the attributes were equally important in one or both tasks. The remaining students fell into two groups, those who said that rent was more important than distance and those who said that distance was more important than rent.

Figure 6 shows the patterns of preference for the two groups. Comparisons were made over both subjects and apartment pairs. Entries are percentages from 4900 comparisons in panel A and 6000 comparisons in panel B. Panel A shows results for people who said that rent was more important than distance. These people chose cheaper apartments more frequently than closer apartments in 66% of the pairs (18% + 48%). They also rated cheaper apartments as more attractive than closer apartments in 56% of

A

RATINGS	CHOICES: Closer	CHOICES: Cheaper
Closer	27	18
Cheaper	8	48

B

RATINGS	CHOICES: Closer	CHOICES: Cheaper
Closer	66	9
Cheaper	10	15

Fig. 6. Patterns of preference for subjects who assigned ratings and made choices between pairs of apartments. Preferences are shown for those who say that rent is more important than distance (A) and for those who say that distance is more important than rent (B).

the pairs. Panel B shows data for people who said that distance was more important than rent. In 76% of the pairs, these subjects chose closer apartments more often than cheaper apartments, and in 75% of the pairs, they rated closer apartments as more attractive. Thus, preferences in the two groups differed in the expected directions, consistent with their judged importance weights.

What about preference reversals? Students who thought rent was more important picked cheaper apartments over closer apartments and rated closer apartments as more attractive significantly more often than the opposite preference reversal (18% vs. 8%). On the other hand, students who thought distance was more important chose the closer apartment in the choice task, and rated the cheaper apartment as more attractive slightly more often than the opposite reversal (10% vs. 9%). Although these latter two preference reversals are very similar, they are in the direction predicted by the prominence hypothesis, suggesting that preference reversals depend on which attribute is judged to be more important.

If preference reversals interact with judged importance weights, students in both groups who have extreme judged weights should show even stronger preference reversals. Results were consistent with this prediction; subjects with more extreme judged weights demonstrated more pronounced reversals across choices and ratings. For example, those who assigned 75 points or more to rent chose the cheaper apartment, but rated the closer apartment as more attractive 22% of the time. The opposite reversal occurred only 4% of the time. Subjects who assigned 75 points or more to distance chose the closer apartment, but rated the cheaper apartment as more attractive 11% of the time, and the opposite reversal occurred in only 4% of the cases. These results suggest that, at least in some cases, the prominence hypothesis can account for differing orders in choice and rating tasks, and the attribute judged more important is weighted more heavily in choices.

To investigate other similarities between risky and riskless domains, we constructed 100 triplets of the form $p(a,b), p(b,c)$, and $p(a,c)$ from apartment choice pairs in the within-subject experiment. For both groups, weak stochastic transitivity was always satisfied, moderate stochastic transitivity was almost always satisfied, and violations occurred in only 8% of the triplets for both groups. However, strong stochastic transitivity failed in more than one-third of the triplets; violations occurred in 36% and 37% of the triplets for the groups who said that distance was more important and rent was more important, respectively.

To account for preference reversals and violations of strong stochastic transitivity, we proposed that (1) subjects average information about rent and distance in both tasks, (2) attribute weights can vary with tasks and subjects assign greater weight to the more important dimension in choices than in ratings, (3) weights in the choice task also vary depending on the similarity of levels along an attribute, and (4) utilities remain invariant across tasks. We will now show how each of these assumptions is incorporated into a change-of-weight theory that formalizes the prominence hypothesis for a riskless domain, applies it to choices and ratings, and adds two important new assumptions—contrast weighting and utility invariance.

Averaging. In the rating task, subjects are assumed to average attribute information about monthly rent and distance as follows:

$$R(a) = J_R[w \ r_a + (1 - w) \ d_a], \qquad (4)$$

where $R(a)$ is the attractiveness rating of apartment a, J_R is a linear function, w is the weight of rent, r_a is the utility of rent, and d_a is the utility of distance. In the choice task, attributes are also averaged and then compared by means of a subtractive operation:

$$P(a,b) = J_P[(w^* \ r_a + (1 - w^*) \ d_a) - (w^* \ r_b + (1 - w^*)d_b)], \qquad (5)$$

where $P(a,b)$ is the proportion of subjects who choose apartment a over apartment b, J_P is a logistic function with one slope parameter, w^* is the weight of rent in the choice task that varies depending on the similarity of rents for apartments a and b, r_a and r_b are the rent utilities for apartments a and b, and d_a and d_b are the distance utilities for apartments a and b.

Change-of-weight. Weights in Eq. 4 and Eq. 5 are represented as

$$w = w_r / \ (w_r + w_d) \qquad (6)$$

and

$$w^* = w_r^* / (w_r^* + w_d^*) \tag{7}$$

in the rating and choice tasks, respectively. These weights are allowed to differ across tasks. Subjects assign greater weight to the more important dimension in choices than in ratings. If rent is judged to be the more important dimension, then w_r^* is greater than w_r, and if distance is judged to be more important, w_d^* is greater than w_d.

Contrast weighting. Attribute weights in choice are allowed to vary with the similarity of attribute levels. Thus, in the choice task, there are two sets of weights for each attribute (or two values for each w_r^* and w_d^*), one for when attribute levels are similar (levels that are adjacent in the experimental design), and one for when attribute levels are dissimilar.

Utility invariance. The utilities of rent and distance, r and d, are assumed to be identical in the two tasks (Eqs. 4 and 5).

We fit this change-of-weight theory to mean attractiveness ratings and choice proportions separately for each group of subjects. Predicted preference reversals closely resembled the observed orderings. In addition, estimated weights of rent and distance were in the predicted direction. The estimated weight of rent for subjects who said that rent was more important than distance was greater in the choice task than in the rating task. The estimated weight of distance for those who said that distance was more important than rent was also greater in the choice task than in the rating task. Furthermore, contrast weights were in the predicted direction; similar levels along an attribute received less weight than dissimilar levels. Finally, the theory described the observed violations of transitivity in choice proportions.

In summary, the change-of-weight theory provides a good account of preference reversals in a riskless domain. The direction of preference reversals systematically differs depending on the attribute judged more important. Rent has a greater effect on choices than on ratings when rent is judged more important, and distance has a greater effect on choices than ratings when distance is judged more important. Furthermore, violations of strong stochastic transitivity can be described by contrast weighting. When two apartments have similar levels along an attribute, that attribute receives less weight than when levels differ. These weight changes allow the model to capture both preference reversals and violations of strong stochastic transitivity. Last, but not least, all of this is accomplished while maintaining the assumption of utility invariance. The utilities of rent and distance are invariant across tasks. Thus, even though preferences are labile, measurements of utilities need not be. With the proper model of preference reversals, utilities remain stable and have meaning beyond the task from which they were derived.

IX.   A Two-Pronged Explanation of Preference Reversals

Preference reversals do not *always* occur. There are many instances in which we are perfectly clear about what we want, regardless of how the question is asked. These situations are ones in which one option dominates another, one option has a decisive advantage, or when conflicts between attribute trade-offs have been resolved. However, preference measurement is much more complicated when trade-offs are difficult, when uncertainties are hard to specify, and when our preferences themselves are unstable (March, 1978). In these cases, preferences can be influenced by a variety of seemingly irrelevant factors (Payne et al., 1992).

Why do preferences reverse across response modes? Results from the preceding studies in risky and riskless domains suggest that they reverse for at least two reasons: (1) subjects appear to change either strategies or weights across tasks, and (2) they appear to change decision strategies in risky domains and attribute weights in riskless domains. Why might the introduction of risk change the decision strategies used in ratings, prices, and choices? In risky alternatives, probability is an attribute, and probabilities may be conducive to different interpretations. In attractiveness ratings of monetary lotteries, probability is often treated as an independent variable that contributes to the overall attractiveness of the lottery in an additive fashion. For pricing judgments, however, probability is treated as a discount factor, moderating outcome information in a multiplicative fashion. Other attributes (e.g., price or rent) do not have similar interpretative ambiguity. However, even though different mechanisms appear to be responsible for preference reversals, stable measures of utility can be found across a variety of different tasks.

Several studies have shown that it *is* feasible to maintain utility invariance across tasks. Birnbaum, Coffey, Mellers, and Weiss (1992) accounted for differences between buying and selling prices of risky options by assuming that buyers and sellers have identical utilities for monetary payoffs but differ in the decision weights associated with outcomes. Buyers tended to be more pessimistic and weighted lower-valued outcomes more heavily, whereas sellers tended to be more optimistic and weighted higher-valued outcomes more heavily. The question of whether utilities vary in risky versus riskless decisions has been a longstanding controversy (see Bell & Raiffa, 1988; Dyer & Sarin, 1982; von Winterfeldt & Edwards, 1986). Birnbaum and Sutton (1992) managed to preserve utility invariance for monetary payoffs across risky and riskless domains by assuming that differences between risky and riskless choices were the result of different decision weights that depended on the rank order of the outcome, with lower-valued outcomes being weighted more heavily than higher-valued outcomes. Finally, Weber, Anderson, and Birnbaum (1992) described attractiveness ratings and risk ratings for the same gambles by assuming that the utilities of the payoffs were identical across the two tasks. Differences between tasks, and even differences among individuals, were explained solely by changes in decision weights.

Although there are still many unanswered questions, the results from these studies suggest that preference reversals can occur from either changes in weight or changes in process. Understanding the mechanisms that produce both types of changes and investigating how they are affected by memory, attention, and emotional states are fruitful areas for future research. In the meantime, it is encouraging and of considerable practical usefulness that we can obtain stable measures of utility despite labile preferences. With appropriate models of judgment and choice, we *can* estimate utilities that do not depend on the method used to infer preference.

ACKNOWLEDGMENTS

This research was supported by National Science Foundation Grant SES-9023160 to B. A. Mellers, National Science Foundation Grant SES-9022192 to E. U. Weber with financial support from the Graduate School of Business, University of Chicago, and a Ford Foundation Fellowship to L. D. Ordóñez. Preparation of the manuscript occurred while the E. U. Weber was a Fellow at the Center for Advanced Study in the Behavioral Sciences, Stanford, CA. The authors thank Jerry Busemeyer and Doug Medin for helpful comments.

REFERENCES

Battilio, R. C., Kagel, J. H., MacDonald, D. N. (1985). Animals' choices over uncertain outcomes: Some initial experimental results. *American Economic Review, 75,* 597–613.

Bazerman, M. H., Loewenstein, G. F., & White, S. B. (1992). Reversals of preference in allocation decisions: Judging an alternative versus choosing among alternatives. Unpublished manuscript. Northwestern University.

Becker, G. M., DeGroot, M. H., & Marschak, J. (1963). Stochastic models of choice behavior. *Behavioral Science, 8,* 41–55.

Bell, D. E., & Raiffa, H. (1988). Marginal value and intrinsic risk aversion. In D. Bell, H. Raiffa, & A. Tversky (Eds.), *Decision making: Descriptive, normative, and prescriptive interactions.* New York: Wiley.

Berg, J. E., Dickhaut, J. W., & O'Brien, J. R. (1985). Preference reversal and arbitrage. In V. Smith (Ed.), *Research in Experimental Economics* (Vol. 3, pp. 31–32). Greenwich, CT: JAI Press.

Birnbaum, M. H. (1974). The nonadditivity of personality impressions. *Journal of Experimental Psychology, 102,* 543–561. (Monograph)

Birnbaum, M. H., Coffey, G., Mellers, B. A., & Weiss, R. (1992). Utility measurement: Configural-weight theory and the judge's point of view. *Journal of Experimental Psychology: Human Perception and Performance, 18,* 331–346.

Birnbaum, M. H., & Stegner, S. E. (1979). Source credibility in social judgment: Bias, expertise, and the judge's point of view. *Journal of Personality and Social Psychology, 37,* 48–74.

Birnbaum, M. H., & Sutton, S. E. (1992). Scale convergence and utility measurement. *Organizational Behavior and Human Decision Processes, 52,* 331–346.

Birnbaum, M. H., & Veit, C. (1974). Scale convergence as a criterion for rescaling: Information integration with difference, ratio, and averaging tasks. *Perception and Psychophysics, 15,* 7–15.

Busemeyer, J. R. (1985). Decision making under uncertainty: A comparison of simple scalability, fixed-sample, and sequential-sample models. *Journal of Experimental Psychology: Learning, Memory, and Cognition, 11,* 538–564.

Casey, J. (1991). Reversal of the preference reversal phenomenon. *Organizational Behavior and Human Decision Processes, 48,* 224–251.

Chapman, G. B., & Johnson, E. J. (1993). Preference reversals in monetary and life expectancy evaluations. Unpublished manuscript. University of Illinois.

Coombs, C. (1983). *Psychology and mathematics.* Ann Arbor: University of Michigan Press.

Cox, J., & Grether, D. (1992). *The preference reversal phenomenon: Response mode, markets, and incentives.* Social Science Working Paper 810. California Institute of Technology.

Chu, Y., & Chu, R. (1990). The subsidence of preference reversals in simplified and market-like experimental settings. A note. *The American Economic Review, 80,* 902–911.

Dyer, J. S., & Sarin, R. K. (1982). Relative risk aversion. *Management Science, 28,* 875–886.

Fechner, G. (1966). *Elements of psychophysics.* D. H. Howes & E. G. Boring (Eds.). H. E. Alder (Trans.). New York: Holt, Rinehart, and Wilson. (Original work published 1860)

Goldstein, W. M., & Einhorn, H. J. (1987). Expression theory and the preference reversal phenomenon. *Psychological Review, 94,* 236–254.

Goldstein, W. M., & Weber, E. U. (1995). Content and discontent: Indications and implications of domain specificity in preferential decision making. In J. R. Busemeyer, R. Hastie, D. L. Medin (Eds.), *The Psychology of Learning and Motivation,* this volume.

Goldstone, R. L., Medin, D. L., & Gentner, D. (1991). Relational similarity and the nonindependence of features in similarity judgments. *Cognitive Psychology, 23,* 222–262.

González-Vallejo, C., & Wallsten, T. (1992). Effects of probability mode on preference reversals. *Journal of Experimental Psychology: Learning, Memory, and Cognition, 18,* 855–864.

Grether, D. M., & Plott, C. R. (1979). Economic theory of choice and the preference reversal phenomenon. *American Economic Review, 69,* 623–638.

Irwin, J. R., Slovic, P., Lichtenstein, S., & McClelland, G. H. (1993). Preference reversals and the measurement of environmental values. *Journal of Risk and Uncertainty, 6,* 5–18.

Johnson, E. J., Payne, J. W., & Bettman, J. R. (1988). Information displays and preference reversals. *Organizational Behavior and Human Decision Processes, 42,* 1–21.

Krantz, D. (1967). Rational distance functions for multidimensional scaling. *Journal of Mathematical Psychology, 4,* 226–245.

Kahneman, D., & Tversky, A. (1979). Prospect theory: An analysis of decision under risk. *Econometrica, 47,* 263–291.

Lichtenstein, S., & Slovic, P. (1971). Reversals of preference between bids and choices in gambling decisions. *Journal of Experimental Psychology, 89,* 46–55.

Lichtenstein, S., & Slovic, P. (1973). Response-induced reversals of preference in gambling: An extended replication in Las Vegas. *Journal of Experimental Psychology, 101,* 16–20.

Lindman, H. R. (1971). Inconsistent preferences among gambles. *Journal of Experimental Psychology, 89,* 390–397.

Luce, R. D. (1991). Rank- and sign-dependent linear utility models for binary gambles. *Journal of Economic Theory, 53,* 75–100.

Luce, R. D., & Fishburn, P. C. (1991). Rank- and sign-dependent linear utility models for finite first-order gambles. *Journal of Risk and Uncertainty, 4,* 29–59.

Luce, R. D., Mellers, B. A., & Chang, S. (1992). Is choice the correct primitive? On using certainty equivalents and reference levels to predict choices among gambles. *Journal of Risk and Uncertainty, 6,* 115–143.

March, J. G. (1978). Bounded rationality, ambiguity, and the engineering of choice. *Bell Journal of Economics, 9,* 587–608.

Mellers, B. A., & Biagini, K. (1994). Similarity and choice. *Psychological Review, 101,* 505–518.

Mellers, B. A., Chang, S., Birnbaum, M. H., & Ordóñez, L. D. (1992). Preferences, prices, and ratings in risky decision making. *Journal of Experimental Psychology: Human Perception and Performance, 18,* 347–361.

Mellers, B. A., & Cooke, A. D. J. (in press). The role and task and context in preference measurement. Psychological Science.

Mellers, B. A., Ordóñez, L. D., & Birnbaum, M. H. (1992). A change-of-process theory for contextual effects and preference reversals in risky decision making. *Organizational Behavior and Human Decision Processes, 52,* 331–369.

Mowen, J. C., & Gentry, J. W. (1980). Investigation of the preference reversal phenomenon in a new product introduction task. *Journal of Applied Psychology, 65,* 715–722.

Nosofsky, R. (1986). Attention, similarity, and the identification-categorization relationship. *Journal of Experimental Psychology: General, 115,* 39–57.

Ordóñez, L., Mellers, B., Chang, S., & Roberts, J. (in press). Are preference reversals reduced when made explicit? Organizational Behavior and Human Decision Processes.

Payne, J. W. (1982). Contingent decision behavior. *Psychological Bulletin, 92,* 382–402.

Payne, J. W., Bettman, J. R., & Johnson, E. J. (1992). Behavioral decision research: A constructive processing perspective. *Annual Review of Psychology, 43,* 87–131.

Payne, J. W., Bettman, J. R., & Johnson, E. J. (1993). *The adaptive decision maker.* New York: Cambridge University Press.

Pommerehne, W. W., Schneider, F., & Zweifel, P. (1982). Economic theory of choice and the preference reversal phenomenon: A reexamination. *American Economic Review, 72,* 569–574.

Reilly, R. J. (1982). Preference reversal: Further evidence and some suggested modifications in experimental design. *American Economic Review, 72,* 576–584.

Rumelhart, D., & Greeno, J. (1971). Similarity between stimuli: An experimental test of the Luce and Restle choice models. *Journal of Mathematical Psychology, 8,* 370–381.

Schkade, D. A., & Johnson, E. J. (1989). Cognitive processes in preference reversals. *Organizational Behavior and Human Decision Processes, 44,* 203–231.

Sjöberg, L. (1975). Uncertainty of comparative judgments and multidimensional structure. *Multivariate Behavioral Research, 10,* 207–218.

Sjöberg, L. (1977). Choice frequency and similarity. *Scandinavian Journal of Psychology, 18,* 103–115.

Sjöberg, L., & Capozza, D. (1975). Preference and cognitive structure of Italian political parties. *Italian Journal of Psychology, 2,* 391–402.

Smith, J. F., Mitchell, T. R., & Beach, L. R. (1982). A cost–benefit mechanism for selecting problem-solving strategies: Some extensions and empirical tests. *Organizational Behavior and Human Performance, 29,* 370–396.

Tversky, A. (1969). Intransitivity of Preferences. *Psychological Review, 76,* 31–48.

Tversky, A., & Kahneman, D. (1992). Advances in prospect theory: Cumulative representations of uncertainty. *Journal of Risk and Uncertainty, 5,* 297–323.

Tversky, A., & Russo, J. (1969). Substitutability and similarity in binary choice. *Journal of Mathematical Psychology, 6,* 1–12.

Tversky, A., Sattath, S., & Slovic, P. (1988). Contingent weighting in judgment and choice. *Psychological Review, 95,* 371–384.

Tversky, A., Slovic, P., & Kahneman, D. (1990). The causes of preference reversal. *American Economic Review, 80,* 204–217.

von Winterfeldt, D., & Edwards, W. E. (1986). *Decision analysis and behavioral research.* New York: Cambridge University Press.

Weber, E. U. (1994). From subjective probabilities to decision weights: The effect of asymmetric loss functions on the evaluation of uncertain outcomes and events. *Psychological Bulletin, 115,* 228–242.

Weber, E. U., Anderson, C. J., & Birnbaum, M. H. (1992). A theory of perceived risk and attractiveness. *Organizational Behavior and Human Decision Processes, 52,* 492–523.

Wedell, D. H., & Böckenholt, U. (1990). Moderation of preference reversals in the long run. *Journal of Experimental Psychology: Human Perception and Performance, 16,* 429–438.

COMPATIBILITY IN COGNITION AND DECISION

Eldar Shafir

I. Introduction

The experimental study of decision making, which has developed in parallel with the field of cognitive psychology, emphasizes the role of human information processing in describing the ways in which people arrive at their decisions. Of particular interest are explanatory psychological principles that relate the characteristics of the tasks and stimuli under study to the ways in which people interpret and code the information and generate a response. Our behavior consists largely of selected responses to environmental stimuli. Performance on complex manual tasks, for example, requires that the stimulus be efficiently coded and an appropriate action produced; successful communication requires that incoming information be appropriately interpreted and the response efficiently translated into an outgoing message; decision making requires that options be appropriately evaluated to lead to the formulation of a distinct choice.

The stimuli that we encounter are often complex, consisting of multiple attributes of varying importance to the required response. Auditory messages, for example, include source information and semantic content, which are usually relevant to the recipient; intonation and pitch, which tend to be of lesser interest; and various pauses and noises that often can be ignored. Likewise, choice between candidates for a graduate program relies to a greater degree on undergraduate performance and letters of recommendation, to a lesser degree on the candidates' hobbies and ease with foreign

247

languages, and not at all on their marital status or height. Just as the various attributes of an auditory or visual message are accorded different degrees of attention in generating a response, in decision-making, the various dimensions of options need to be assigned adequate weights in the process of evaluation and choice.

An important principle that relates the characteristics of input stimuli to the ways in which people code the information and produce a response is the principle of compatibility. This principle states that when stimuli and responses are mentally represented, the weight of a stimulus attribute is enhanced to the extent that it is compatibile with the required response. Thus, for example, in the realm of perceptual-motor performance, a pointing response is faster than a vocal response if the stimulus is presented visually (relative to an auditory presentation), but a vocal response is relatively faster than pointing if the stimulus is presented in an auditory mode. An implication of compatibility is that some stimulus components tend to be more salient than others and some tasks are easier to perform than others because of the particular sets of stimuli and responses that are being considered and because of the ways in which these stimuli and responses interact with each other.

The significance of compatibility between input and output has recently been evoked by cognitive psychologists and by students of judgment and decision making to account for a series of surprising yet systematic patterns of behavior. In what follows, the compatibility hypothesis is considered as it relates to findings in areas ranging from choice and prediction to similarity and social judgment. It is suggested that compatibility is a psychological principle that characterizes human performance in numerous domains, and whose import into the study of decision making helps explain systematic patterns of behavior that are puzzling from a normative perspective.

The chapter is organized as follows. Section II discusses the notion of stimulus-response compatibility, central to work in perception and motor performance. Section III reviews scale compatibility, particularly as it relates to persistent discrepancies between judgment and choice, known "preference reversal phenomena." Section IV discusses the notion of relative prominence, regarded as a special instantiation of the compatibility principle, and Section V reviews strategy compatibility, which can be viewed as a generalization of the prominence effect. Section VI reviews semantic compatibility, which is seen to influence human performance in tasks ranging from choice and social judgment to visual estimation tasks and judgments of similarity. Some remarks about confirmation bias, and a brief discussion regarding the normative and prescriptive implications of the aforementioned studies, are presented in the concluding section.

II. Stimulus–Response Compatibility

Stimulus–response (S-R) compatibility refers to the fact that some tasks are easier or more difficult than others because of the particular sets of stimuli and responses that are used, and because of the ways in which individual stimuli and responses are paired with each other. The significance of S-R compatibility has long been recognized by students of human perceptual and motor performance, who observed that responses were fastest when there was a direct correspondence between stimulus and response locations. For example, responses to visual displays of information, such as an instrument panel, are faster and more accurate if the response structure is spatially compatible with the arrangement of the stimuli (Fitts & Seeger, 1953; Wickens, 1984). Thus, a square array of four burners on a stove is easier to control with a corresponding square array of knobs than with a linear array. Similarly, the response to a pair of lights is faster and more accurate if the left light is assigned to the left key and the right light to the right key.

It has been shown that these effects cannot be attributed simply to a correspondence based on anatomical features, because the same pattern of response times is obtained when the left and right hands are crossed, placing the left hand at the right response location, and the right hand at the left location (Anzola, Bertoloni, Buchtel, & Rizzolatti, 1977; Wallace, 1972). In this crossed-hands condition, responses are still faster when there is a direct correspondence between the stimulus and response locations, even though the opposing hand is used to make the response. It appears, furthermore, that it is not the position of the hands but rather that of the response key that determines compatibility. In one study, for example, subjects were required to manipulate response keys by using sticks that were either uncrossed or crossed at body midline, and the size of the compatibility effect was equivalent in the crossed and uncrossed conditions (Riggio, Gawryszewski, & Umilta, 1986). Indeed, it is not even the absolute or egocentric locations of stimuli and response keys that determine the degree of compatibility, but their relative locations. The standard spatial compatibility effect occurs, for example, when both stimuli are in the same hemispace, and when both response keys are located on one side of the body midline (Nicoletti, Anzola, Luppino, Rizzolatti, & Umilta, 1982).

With spatial location stimuli, S-R compatibility is a function of the extent to which the assignment of stimulus locations to response locations maintains some direct correspondence. More generally, however, for S-R compatibility effects to occur, the correspondence need not be strictly spatial. Although spatial compatibility is the most prevalent in the experimental literature, S-R compatibility can also be observed among stimuli and responses that share no physical spatial dimensions. Stimulus–response compatibility has been evoked, for example, to account for the fact that a pointing response is faster than a vocal response when the stimulus is visual, whereas a vocal response is faster than pointing when the stimulus is presented in an auditory mode (Brainard, Irby, Fitts, & Alluisi, 1962). For another example, compatibility effects based on phonetic features have been documented (Gordon & Meyer, 1984) where responses were faster when a speech stimulus and a speech response shared a voicing feature (e.g., *tuh* and *puh,* both unvoiced) than when they did not (e.g., *duh* and *puh,* the former voiced). Finally, reaction times are shorter when stimuli such as the written words *left* and *right,* or left- and right-pointing arrows, are assigned to left and right physical responses, or when "left" and "right" vocal responses are assigned to corresponding stimulus locations (Magliero, Bashore, Coles, & Donchin, 1984; Weeks & Proctor, 1990).

It appears that S-R compatibility effects do not require actual physical correspondence, but merely a "conceptual correspondence" (Alluisi & Warm, 1990). In this vein, various S-R compatibility effects have been observed that were due to dimensional overlap across different modalities. In one study (Marks, 1987), for example, subjects' discrimination of pitch, brightness, and tactile stimuli was faster and more accurate when stimuli in one modality were paired with "matching" values in another modality (e.g., high pitch paired with bright lights) than when paired with "nonmatching" values in the other modality (e.g., high pitch paired with dim lights). (See Kornblum, Hasbroucq, & Osman, 1990, for a review). Compatibility effects tend to occur whenever physical or conceptual correspondences exist among the stimuli and responses. An S-R mapping is compatible if the codes are physically or conceptually similar between stimuli and their assigned responses, and it is incompatible if they conflict.

It is noteworthy that some features of stimuli appear to be psychologically more salient than others. Thus, for example, letter identity is more salient than letter size (Proctor, Reeve, & Van Zandt, 1992), and the left–right dimension is more salient than the above–below dimension (Nicoletti & Umilta, 1984). Stimuli and responses are coded in terms of their salient features; translation from one to the other is fastest, thus leading to greatest compatibility effects, when salient features correspond. (Indeed, highly salient features may sometimes affect a response even when they are formally irrelevant to the task at hand, which can lead to stroop-like effects; see, e.g., Dyer, 1973, and Simon & Small, 1969, for the related "Simon effect".)

Compatibility between stimulus and response ensembles has been proposed to account for results obtained in a wide variety of perceptual and motor performance tasks (see, e.g., Kornblum et al., 1990; see also Proctor & Reeve, 1990, for related discussion), and plays an important role in the design and engineering of systems and the display of information (Wickens, 1984). Stimulus–response compatibility effects are prevalent and robust. In addition to occurring with normal adults, they occur with children (Ladavas, 1990), as well as with aging adults (Simon & Pouraghabagher, 1978), and they persist despite extended practice (Dutta & Proctor, 1992).

The rationale for such effects is that a translation stage intervenes between the presentation of stimuli and the selection of responses: the greater the compatibility between stimuli and responses, the less time is required and the lower the likelihood of error. When a person is required to execute a particular response on the basis of some stimulus information, three general processing stages are typically presumed to intervene. These are labeled differently by various researchers, but generally reflect stimulus identification, stimulus–response (S-R) translation, and response execution (Hasbroucq, Guiard, & Ottomani, 1990; Proctor, Reeve, & Weeks, 1990). Stimulus–response compatibility effects are typically attributed to the intermediate stage, namely, S-R translation, which is presumed to involve a translation between codes that are used to represent the stimuli and the responses. The contribution of this stage to reaction time and error is greater when a direct correspondence between stimuli and responses is lacking, thus involving an incompatibility, then when the required S-R translation is minimal, making the stimuli and responses compatible and thus reducing time and error.

In what follows, the notion of compatibility is used to explain people's behavior in numerous domains. Because there is neither a formal definition of compatibility nor a general procedure for its assessment, the analysis in terms of compatibility remains informal and incomplete. However, just as a control panel is clearly more compatible with some information displays than others, so can the compatibility ranking in the context of choice or judgment be sufficiently clear to allow experimental investigation and insight.

III. Scale Compatibility

Recent work in the areas of judgment and decision making has extended the notion of compatibility and proposed that the weight of stimulus attributes in judgment or in choice is enhanced by their compatibility with the particular scale that is being used to provide the response (Slovic, Griffin, & Tversky, 1990; Tversky, Sattath, & Slovic, 1988). The rationale for this principle is that the specific nature of the response scale tends to focus attention on the compatible features of the stimulus. For example, setting the price of a gamble is likely to emphasize payoffs more than probabilities, because both the price and the payoffs are in monetary units (e.g., dollars). When a stimulus attribute and the response scale do not match, additional steps are required to map one into the other. As with the spatial mapping between stimulus and response ensembles, noncompatibility between a stimulus attribute and the response scale requires additional mental operations, which often increase effort and error and reduce impact.

A. PREDICTION

A simple demonstration of scale compatibility in a prediction task was provided by Slovic et al. (1990), who asked subjects to predict the performance of 10 students in a course (e.g., history) on the basis of the students' performances in two other courses (say, philosophy and english). For each of the 10 students, the subjects saw a letter grade (from A+ to D) in one course, and a class rank (from 1 to 100) in the other course. One half of the respondents were asked to predict a grade; the other half were asked to predict class rank. Scale compatibility implies that a given predictor (e.g., grade in philosophy) will be weighted more heavily when the predicted variable is expressed on the same scale (e.g., grade in history) than when it is expressed on a different scale (e.g., rank in history). The relative weight of grades to ranks, in other words, is predicted to be higher for the group that predicts grades than for the group that predicts ranks. This is precisely what was found, as is described in more detail next.

Let (r_i, g_j) denote a student with rank i in the first course and grade j in the second, and let r_{ij} and g_{ij} denote, respectively, the rank and grade predicted for that student. Tversky et al. (1988) developed a hierarchy of "contingent trade-off models" intended to accommodate the various compatibility effects observed in studies of judgment and choice. We can use the simplest and most restrictive of Tversky et al.'s formulations (with additive representation of multiattribute options and linearity) to model the preceding respondents' predictions:

$$r_{ij} = \alpha_r r_i + \beta_r g_j \text{ and } g_{ij} = \alpha_g r_i + \beta_g g_j.$$

The constants α_i and β_i represent the weights assigned, respectively, to a student's known rank and grade, with i = r and g when rank and grade are predicted, respectively. By regressing the predictions of each respondent against the predictors, r_i, g_j, one obtains for each respondent in the rank condition an estimate of $\theta_r = \beta_r/\alpha_r$, and for each respondent in the grade condition an estimate of $\theta_g = \beta_g/\alpha_g$. These estimates reflect the relative weight of grades to ranks in the two prediction tasks. In the absence of a compatibility effect, that is, if ranks and grades were equally weighted in the two tasks, θ_r and θ_g would be roughly equal. Instead, as implied by compatibility, the values of θ_g—the relative weight of grades to ranks when grades are predicted—were significantly higher than the values of θ_r, which captures the relative weight of grades to ranks when ranks are predicted ($p < .001$). A further, ordinal test of respondents' data revealed that the differential weighting induced by compatibility leads to frequent reversals in the implied ordering of students. Thus, within student pairs, the student with the higher grade was expected to perform better 58% of the time by respondents who predicted grades, but only 42% of the time by respondents who predicted rank ($p < .001$).

B. PREFERENCE REVERSAL

Scale compatibility also accounts for the *preference reversal phenomenon,* one of the more robust and counternormative phenomena discovered in recent research into decision behavior. The preference reversal phenomenon was first demonstrated by Lichtenstein and Slovic (1971, 1973), who presented subjects with two prospects of similar expected value. One typical prospect, the H bet, offers a high chance to win a relatively small payoff (e.g., 8 chances in 9 to win $4), whereas the other prospect, the L bet, offers a lower chance to win a larger payoff (e.g., a 1 in 9 chance to win $40). When asked to choose between these prospects, most subjects choose the H bet over the L bet. Subjects are also asked, on a separate occasion, to price each prospect by indicating the smallest amount of money for which they would be willing to sell this prospect if they owned it. Here, most subjects assign a higher price to the L bet than to the H bet. In a recent study that used this particular pair of bets, for example, 71% of the subjects chose the H bet over the L bet, whereas 67% priced L above H (Tversky, Slovic, & Kahneman, 1990).

Preference reversal typically occurs when subjects choose a lottery that offers a greater chance to win over another that offers a higher payoff but then assign a higher price to the lottery offering the higher payoff than to the one with the greater chance to win. This pattern of preferences has been replicated in numerous experiments using a variety of prospects and incentive schemes, including a version conducted for real payoffs equivalent to months' worth of the subjects' salaries (Kachelmeier & Shehata, 1992). It has also been observed in a study involving professional gamblers, conducted on the floor of the Four Queens Casino in Las Vegas (Lichtenstein & Slovic, 1973).

The classical analysis of choice assumes that people's preferences can be elicited through any of a number of normatively equivalent methods. Thus, people can be asked to indicate which option they prefer; alternatively, they can be asked to price each option. The standard assumption, known as *procedure invariance,* requires that normatively equivalent elicitation procedures should give rise to the same preference order: if one option is chosen over another, it is also expected to be priced higher. Procedure invariance is essential for the interpretation of psychological measurement, as it is for physical measurement. The ordering of objects with respect to mass, for example, can be established either by placing each object separately on a scale or by placing two objects on two sides of a pan balance; the two procedures yield the same ordering, within the limit of measurement error. Analogously, the classical theory of choice assumes that each individual has a well-defined preference order (or a utility function) that can be elicited either by choice or by pricing. These alternative methods of elicitation, in turn, should give rise to the same ordering of preferences. The preceding preference reversal phenomena, however, constitute apparent violations of procedure invariance: people choose one bet over another, but price the second bet above the first.

What is the cause of preference reversal? Why do people assign a higher monetary value to the low probability bet, but choose the high probability gamble more often? To capture the phenomenon more precisely, let us introduce some notation.

Let C_H and C_L denote, respectively, the stated cash equivalents (or minimum selling prices) of bets H and L, and let $>$ and $\approx$ denote strict preference and indifference, respectively. Preference reversal can then be described as the following pattern of responses (Tversky, Slovic, & Kahneman, 1990):

$$H > L \text{ and } C_L > C_H,$$

where H is preferred over L, but L is priced above H. (Note that $>$ refers to preference between bets, whereas $>$ refers to the ordering of cash amounts. It is assumed that $x > y$ implies $x > y$, i.e., more money is preferred to less).

As long as procedure invariance holds, a decision maker will be indifferent between a bet and his or her stated price for that bet, that is, $B \approx X$ iff $C_B = X$. Thus, as long as procedure invariance holds, $C_H \approx H$ and $C_L \approx L$, and preference reversal implies the following intransitive pattern:

$$C_H \approx H > L \approx C_L > C_H.$$

However, if procedure invariance does not hold, then preference reversal can result not from a cyclical pattern of preferences, but rather from a discrepancy between choice and pricing, in particular, from an inappropriate pricing of one or both bets. Thus, a decision maker who chooses H over L, could exhibit preference reversal if she overpriced L or if she underpriced H (the terms overpricing and underpricing merely identify a discrepancy between pricing and choice; they are not meant to imply that the bias resides solely in pricing.) Overpricing of L is evident if the decision maker prefers her stated price for the bet over the bet itself when offered a choice between them on another occasion, that is, $C_L > L$; underpricing of H occurs when $H > C_H$.

Tversky, Slovic, and Kahneman (1990; see also Tversky & Thaler, 1990, for a concise review) conducted a study specifically designed to discriminate between alternative causes of the preference reversal phenomenon. Whereas approximately 10% of preference reversals observed by these researchers were accounted for by intransitivity (as expected if procedure invariance holds), the remaining 90% violated procedure invariance. More-over, nearly two-thirds of the observed patterns of preference reversal were the result of the overpricing of the L bet (see also Bostic, Herrnstein, & Luce, 1990.)

It appears that a major cause of people's tendency to overprice the low-probability high-payoff bets is the compatibility between prices and payoffs. Because the price that the subject assigns to a lottery is expressed in dollars, compatibility implies that the bet's payoffs, which are also expressed in dollars, will be weighted more heavily in pricing than in choice. Further-more, because the payoffs of the L bets are much larger than the payoffs of the H bets, the major consequence of this scale compatibility effect is an overpricing of the L bet. As a consequence, the L bet is evaluated more favorably in pricing than in choice, which gives rise to preference reversals.

This account of preference reversal in terms of scale compatibility is further supported by the observation that the incidence of reversal is greatly reduced for bets involving nonmonetary outcomes. Slovic et al. (1990), for example, presented subjects with H (high probability) and L (low probabil-ity) bets involving outcomes such as a 1-week pass for all movie theaters in town or a dinner for two at a local restaurant. Note that here the outcomes are no longer expressed in the same units as the prices generated by subjects and are therefore less compatible. If preference reversals are due primarily to the compatibility between prices and payoffs, their incidence should be substantially reduced by the use of nonmonetary outcomes. Indeed, the prevalence of preference reversal was reduced by one-half.

Finally, although most replications of the preference reversal phenome-non involve risky prospects, the compatibility hypothesis does not depend on the presence of risk. Indeed, it implies a similar discrepancy between choice and pricing in the context of riskless options that have a monetary component. Thus, consider a long-term prospect L, which pays $2,500 5 years from now, and a short-term prospect S, which pays $1,600 in 1 1/2 years. Tversky et al. (1990) asked subjects to choose between L and S and to price both prospects by stating the smallest immediate cash payment for which they would be willing to exchange each prospect. Because the payoffs and the prices again are expressed in the same units, compatibility suggests that the long-term prospect (offering the higher payoff) will be overvalued in pricing relative to choice. In accord with the compatibility hypothesis, subjects chose the short-term prospect 74% of the time but priced the long-term prospect above the short-term prospect 75% of the time.

These observations indicate that the preference reversal phenomenon is another instance of compatibility-induced weighting, not a peculiar phenomenon of choice between bets. It appears that the major cause of preference reversal is the compatibility between response modes—choice or pricing—and the attributes of the gambles, which are weighted differentially depending on the response. Additional evidence for the role of scale compatibility in preference reversals is provided by Delquie (1993) and by Schkade and Johnson (1989). The latter, using a computer-controlled experiment, were able to show that subjects spend more time on (and thereby presumably focus more attention on) the stimulus components that are most compatible with the scale of the response mode.

Naturally, compatibility effects are limited in their ability to influence decision. When one option is overwhelmingly preferred over another, a slight difference in the relative weighting of dimensions is unlikely to alter a person's choice. Yet, in many instances, when the decision is difficult and the options are of otherwise comparable worth, compatibility can have a decisive effect on the determination of preference.

IV. Relative Prominence

The compatibility effects illustrated in the previous section occur in the context of a comparison between two alternative procedures for eliciting preference: choice and pricing. Related violations of procedure invariance have been documented between choice and another procedure known as *matching*. An early study of this type was conducted by Slovic (1975), who was interested in the ancient philosophical puzzle of how decision makers would choose between two equally attractive options. To investigate this question, Slovic first had subjects equate pairs of alternatives and later asked them to choose between the equally valued alternatives in each pair. One pair, for example, was gift packages consisting of a combination of cash and coupons. For each pair, one component of one alternative was missing, as shown, and subjects were asked to determine the value of the missing component that would match between the two alternatives (hence, "matching"), rendering them equally attractive. (In the following example, the matching value volunteered by the subject may be, say, $10.)

	Gift package A	Gift package B
Cash	—	$20
Coupon book worth	$32	$18

One week later, subjects were asked to choose between the two equated alternatives. They were also asked, independently, which dimension—cash or coupons—did they consider to be more important. Classical theory predicts that the two alternatives, explicitly equated for value, are equally likely to be selected. In contrast, in the choice between the preceding gift packages, 88% of the subjects who had equated these alternatives for value, then proceeded to choose the alternative that was higher on the dimension that they considered more important. Slovic (1975) replicated this pattern in numerous domains, including in choices between college applicants, auto tires, baseball players, and routes to work. All the results were consistent with the hypothesis that people do not choose between the equated alternatives at random. Instead, they resolve the conflict by selecting the alternative that is superior on the more important dimension, which seems to provide a more compelling reason for choice (for further discussion of the role of reasons in choice, see Shafir, Simonson, & Tversky, 1993).

The general mechanism underlying the preceding pattern involves the notion of relative prominence, and is known as the *prominence effect* (Tversky et al., 1988). In many instances, people agree that one attribute (e.g., safety) is more prominent than another (e.g., cost). Although the interpretation of this claim is not entirely clear, the prominence effect refers to the observation that the attribute that is judged more prominent looms larger in choice than in matching or in pricing. To illustrate this notion, consider two programs designed to reduce the number of fatalities caused by traffic accidents, characterized by the expected reduction in the number of casualties and an estimated cost. Because human lives are regarded as more important than money, the prominence effect predicts that the casualties dimension will be given more weight in choice than in matching. Indeed, when given a choice between programs X and Y, the great majority of respondents favored X, the more expensive program that saves more lives (Tversky et al., 1988).

	Expected number of casualties	Cost
Program X	500	$55 million
Program Y	570	$12 million

However, when the cost of one of the programs was removed and subjects were asked to determine the missing cost so as to make the two programs equally attractive, nearly all subjects assigned values that imply a preference for Y, the less expensive program that saves fewer lives. For example, when the cost of program X is removed, the median estimate of the missing cost that renders the two programs equally attractive was $40 million. This implies that at $55 million, program X should not be chosen over program Y, contrary to the aforementioned choice. Thus, in accord with the prominence effect, the prominent attribute (saving lives) tends to dominate the choice but not the pricing. (Note that, according to this effect, different public policies may be supported depending on whether people are asked which policy they prefer or how much, in their opinion, each policy ought to cost.)

Additional applications of the prominence effect were reported in a study of people's responses to environmental problems (Kahneman & Ritov, 1993). Several pairs of issues were selected. In each case, one issue involved human health or safety and the other concerned protection of the environment. Each issue included a brief statement of a problem, along with a suggested form of intervention, as illustrated here.

> *Problem:* Skin cancer from sun exposure is common among farm workers.
> *Intervention:* Support free medical checkups for threatened groups.
>
> *Problem:* Several Australian mammal species are nearly wiped out by hunters.
> *Intervention:* Contribute to a fund to provide safe breeding areas for these species.

One group of subjects was asked to choose which of the two interventions they would rather support; a second group of subjects was presented with one issue at a time and asked to determine the largest amount they would be willing to pay for the respective intervention. Because the treatment of cancer in humans is generally viewed as more important than the protection of Australian mammals, the prominence effect predicts that the former will receive greater support in direct choice than in independent evaluation. This prediction was confirmed. When asked to evaluate each intervention separately, subjects, who might have been moved by these animals' plight, were willing to pay more, on average, for safe breeding of Australian mammals than for free checkups for skin cancer. However, when faced with a direct choice between these options, most subjects favored free checkups for humans over safe breeding for mammals. Irwin, Slovic, Lichtenstein, and McClelland (1993) report related findings in settings in which improvements in air quality were compared with improvements in consumer commodities. In general, people may evaluate one alternative more positively than another when each is evaluated independently, but then reverse their evaluation when the alternatives are directly compared, which tends to accentuate the prominent attribute.

Setting a gamble's cash equivalent is essentially a matching procedure: the person needs to determine that amount of cash which, if obtained for certain, "matches" or is as attractive as, the probabilistic amount. A number of studies have suggested, moreoover, that in choice situations, people generally perceive probability as more important than payoffs (see, e.g., Goldstein & Einhorn, 1987; Shafir, Osherson, & Smith, 1993; Slovic & Lichtenstein, 1968; Tversky et al., 1988). Thus, if pricing is a special case of matching and probabilities are more prominent then payoffs, then the reversals of preference between bets documented in the preceding section can be thought of as special cases of the prominence effect in which the probability of winning is the prominent attribute that gets weighted more heavily in choice than in matching.

The prominence effect, moreover, can be viewed as a type of compatibility effect. In particular, it is seen to arise out of the compatibility between a particular task—choice versus matching—and the strategies that the task invokes. Consider, in this context, the difference between quantitative and qualitative choice strategies. Quantitative strategies, likely to be evoked by matching, are based on trade offs or the relative weighting of dimensions. Qualitative strategies (like dominance), on the other hand, are based on purely ordinal criteria regarding ordering by attribute importance. In line with compatibility, the qualitative strategy of selecting the option that is superior on the more important dimension, that is, the prominence effect, is more likely to arise in the qualitative method of choice, whereas quantitative considerations regarding trade-offs between dimensions are more likely to arise in the quantitative method of matching.

V.   Strategy Compatibility

We concluded the previous section by suggesting that the prominence effect can be viewed as a type of compatibility effect. In line with compatibility, the qualitative strategy of selecting the option that is superior on the more important dimension is more likely to arise in the qualitative method of choice than in the quantitative method of matching. As a result, the qualitative nature of choice is more likely than the quantitative nature of matching to lead to a preference for the alternative that is superior with respect to the prominent attribute. Note that unlike scale compatibility, this explanation of the prominence effect depends not on the particular correspondence between stimuli attributes and the response scale, but rather on the general distinction between qualitative and quantitative response methods and the compatible strategies that they evoke. This latter notion has been called the *strategy compatibility hypothesis* (Fischer & Hawkins, 1993).

Strategy compatibility generalizes the prominence effect from choice versus matching to any comparison between qualitative and quantitative preference tasks. Fischer and Hawkins (1993) conducted studies using a number of different response modes and found, for example, that strength-of-preference ratings, unlike matching, evoked essentially identical preferences as choice. This, despite the fact that both matching and strength-of-preference ratings require a response on a numerical scale whereas choice does not. In these studies, the critical feature appears to be whether the response task requires subjects to consider quantitative trade-offs, as required by matching, or allows for a direct ordinal comparison between the alternatives, which characterizes both choice and strength-of-preference ratings. Fischer and Hawkins (1993) found the expected prominence effects when either ordinal strategy—choice or strength-of-preference rating—was employed.

It is interesting to note that different compatibility effects do not always work in tandem. One can construct cases, for example, in which scale compatibility and strategy compatibility work in opposing directions. Consider, for example, a choice between options that consist of two dimensions, salary and vacation time. For most people, salary is the prominent attribute in this case (Fischer & Hawkins, 1993). Thus, strategy compatibility implies that the prominence effect, which involves attaching a greater weight to salary than to vacation time, will be observed in choice rather than in pricing. Scale compatibility, on the other hand, implies that people will attach a greater weight to salary in the pricing task than in choice. Fischer and Hawkins (1993) presented subjects with these types of stimuli and observed both scale compatibility effects in the pricing tasks as well as strategy compatibility effects in choice, although in their studies, strategy compatibility proved considerably stronger than scale compatibility.

VI. Semantic Compatibility

Compatibility effects can also be induced by a simple semantic correspondence between the instructions given to subjects and particular features of the stimuli under consideration; those features of a stimulus that are more compatible with the given instructions are likely to be weighted more heavily than features of the stimulus that are less compatible with the instructions. An early example of semantic compatibility was provided in the context of similarity judgments, and other examples have since been documented in decision making and in social judgment, as well as in a visual estimation task. These are briefly described in turn.

A. SIMILARITY JUDGMENTS

In his contrast model of similarity, Tversky (1977) presents a set-theoretical approach to similarity, in which objects are represented as collections of features and similarity between objects is expressed as an increasing function of the features that they have in common and a decreasing function of the features that each object has and the other does not. Thus, each object a is characterized by a set of features, denoted A, and the similarity between objects a and b, denoted $s(a, b)$, is expressed as a function of three arguments: $A \cap B$, the features shared by a and b; $A\text{-}B$, the features of a that are not shared by b; and $B\text{-}A$, the features in b that are not in a. The first argument is assumed to increase similarity, whereas the latter two are assumed to decrease it.

Judgments of dissimilarity, or difference, between objects a and b, denoted $d(a, b)$, are commonly assumed to be complementary to similarity judgments: dissimilarity is an increasing function of distinctive features and a decreasing function of common features. Tversky suggests, however, that due to a change in focus, judgments of similarity and dissimilarity may not be mirror images. In the assessment of similarity between stimuli, the subject—as suggested by semantic compatibility—may attend more to their common features, whereas in the assessment of difference, the subject may attend more to their distinctive features. As a result of semantic compatibility, common features are predicted to loom larger in judgments of similarity than in judgments of dissimilarity, whereas distinctive features are predicted to loom larger in judgments of dissimilarity than in judgments of similarity.

Along with a function f defined on the relevant feature space, the contrast model assumes that there exist two non-negative constants, θ and λ, such that

$$s(a, b) > s(c, e) \text{ iff } \theta f(A \cap B) - f(A - B) - f(B - A)$$
$$> \theta f(C \cap E) - f(C - E) - f(E - C),$$

and

$$d(a, b) > d(c, e) \text{ iff } f(A - B) + f(B - A) - \lambda f(A \cap B)$$
$$> f(C - E) + f(E - C) - \lambda f(C \cap E).$$

The weights associated with distinctive features can be set to 1. (Although the contrast model allows for the two sets of distinctive features to differ in importance, this does not affect the following analysis). Hence, θ and λ reflect the relative weight assigned to the common features in the assessments of similarity and difference, respectively. Note that if θ is very large, then similarity ordering is determined primarily by the common features. On the other hand, if λ is very small, then difference ordering is essentially determined by distinctive features. This leads to a straightforward but surprising prediction, namely, that both $s(a, b) > s(c, e)$ and $d(a, b) > d(c, e)$ could obtain whenever $f(A \cap B) > f(C \cap E)$ and $f(A - B) + f(B - A) > f(C - E) + f(E - C)$. In other words, a pair of objects with many common and many distinctive features could be judged as more similar, as well as more dissimilar, than another pair of objects with fewer common and fewer distinctive features.

Tversky and Gati (1978) observed this pattern in the comparison of pairs of well-known countries with pairs of countries that were less well-known. They had one group of subjects—the similarity group—select from each two pairs of countries the pair that were more similar. The second group of subjects—the difference group—selected between the two pairs the pair of countries that were more different.

Let P_s and P_d denote, respectively, the percentage of subjects who selected the prominent pair in the similarity task and in the difference task. If similarity and difference are complementary (i.e., $\theta = \lambda$), then the sum of $P_s + P_d$ should equal 100 for all pairs. On the other hand, if common features are weighted more in similarity than in difference judgments (i.e., $\theta > \lambda$), then the prominent pair should be selected more often and this sum should exceed 100. Indeed, in line with the semantic compatibility hypothesis, the average share obtained by Tversky and Gati for the more prominent pairs (113.5) was significantly greater than 100. For example, most subjects in the similarity condition selected East Germany and West Germany (the prominent pair) as more similar to each other than Ceylon and Nepal (the nonprominent pair), whereas most subjects in the dissimilarity condition selected East Germany and West Germany as more different from each other than Ceylon and Nepal. Related findings are reported in Medin, Goldstone, and Gentner (1990; see also Medin, Goldstone, & Markman, 1994, for discussion). The results demonstrate that, in line with compatibility, the relative weight of common and distinctive features varies with the nature of the task. In particular, common features, which contribute to the perceived similarity between objects, are weighted more heavily in similarity judgments than in judgments of difference.

B. Choosing and Rejecting

The occurrence of semantic compatibility has been documented in decision making, where the reasons for choosing or rejecting an option can be more or less compatible with the particular task at hand. The advantages of options provide compelling reasons for choice, making the decision easier to determine and to justify to oneself and to others. Relative disadvantages, on the other hand, provide natural reasons for rejecting options, and thus make rejection easier to determine and to justify. Semantic compatibility suggests that positive dimensions will be weighted more when choosing than when rejecting, whereas negative dimensions will be emphasized more when rejecting than when choosing.

Consider having to choose one of two options or, alternatively, having to reject one of two options. Logically, the tasks are identical. According to the assumption of procedure invariance, in a binary choice situation, it should not matter whether people are asked which option they prefer, or which they would rather reject. If people prefer the first, they will reject the second, and vice versa. Naturally, the more positive features an option has the more likely it is to be chosen and the less likely it is to be rejected; conversely, the more negative features it has the more likely it is to be rejected and the less likely it is to be chosen. Let each option a be characterized by a set of positive and a set of negative features, denoted A^+ and A^-, respectively, and assume a value function, v, defined on these sets of features. Thus, a's overall value increases with $v(A^+)$ (a positive number) and decreases with $v(A^-)$ (a negative number). The relative weights assigned to positive and negative features, however, may differ between when choosing and when rejecting. People are likely to focus on reasons for choosing an option when asked to choose and they are likely to focus on reasons for rejecting an option when asked to reject. Thus, the positive features of options (their pros) are expected to loom larger when choosing, whereas the negative features of options (their cons) are expected to weigh more heavily when rejecting. Assume, therefore, that there exist non-negative constants δ and λ such that

a is chosen over b iff $v(A^+) + \delta v(A^-) > v(B^+) + \delta v(B^-)$, and
$\quad a$ is rejected in favor of b iff $v(A^+) + \lambda v(A^-) < v(B^+) + \lambda v(B^-)$.

Thus, δ and λ reflect the relative weight of negative features in the decisions to choose and to reject, respectively. Note that if δ is very small, then preference is essentially determined by the positive features, and if λ is very large, then preference is determined primarily by the negative features. This hypothesis leads to a straightforward prediction, namely, that a situation may arise in which a is chosen over b, and a is also rejected in favor of b whenever

$$v(A^+) > v(B^+) \text{ and } v(A^-) < v(B^-).$$

That is, if—in line with compatibility—positive features are weighted more heavily when choosing than when rejecting, than an option with greater positive and greater negative features could be chosen over, as well as rejected in favor of, another option with lesser positive and lesser negative features.

The preceding prediction was tested and corroborated by Shafir (1993a), who presented subjects with a choice between two options: an option with more positive and more negative features (henceforth, the *enriched* option) and an option with fewer positive and fewer negative features (henceforth, the *impoverished option*). Let P_c and P_r denote, respectively, the percentages of subjects who choose and who reject the enriched option. If choosing and rejecting are complementary (i.e., $\delta = \lambda$), then the sum $P_c + P_r$ should equal 100. According to the semantic compatibility rationale, on the other hand, this sum should exceed 100.

> Imagine that you serve on the jury of an only-child sole-custody case following a relatively messy divorce. The facts of the case are complicated by ambiguous economic, social, and emotional considerations, and you decide to base your decision entirely on the following few observations. [To which parent would you award sole custody of the child?/Which parent would you deny sole custody of the child?]

Parent		Award	Deny
A	Average income		
	Average health		
	Average working hours		
	Reasonable rapport with the child	36%	45%
	Relatively stable social life		
B	Above-average income		
	Very close relationship with the child	64%	55%
	Extremely active social life		
	Lots of work-related travel		
	Minor health problems		

Consider the above problem which was presented in two versions that differed only in the bracketed questions. One half of the subjects received the *award* version, the other half the *deny* version.

Parent A, the impoverished option, is quite plain, with no striking positive or negative features. Parent B, the enriched option, on the other hand, has very positive features that provide good reasons for being awarded custody (a very close relationship with the child and high income), but also has negative features that constitute reasons to be denied sole custody (such as health problems and extensive absences due to travel). To the right of the options are the percentages of subjects who chose to award and to deny custody to each of the parents. Parent B is the majority choice, both for being awarded custody of the child and for being denied it. As predicted, $P_c + P_r$ for Parent B ($64 + 55 = 119$) is significantly greater than the 100 that would be expected if choosing and rejecting were complementary. Contrary to procedure invariance, Parent B's likelihood of obtaining custody is significantly greater when subjects decide whom to award than when they ask themselves whom to deny. This pattern is attributed to the fact that the enriched option provides more features compatible with either the choosing or rejecting tasks; features compatible with choosing weigh more when we choose than when we reject, and features compatible with rejection matter more when we reject than when we choose. This pattern has been replicated in hypothetical choices between bets, college courses, and political candidates (Shafir, 1993a). Similar results are reported in Ganzach and Schul, (in press).

C. SOCIAL JUDGMENT

Semantic compatibility effects stemming from the discrepancy between enriched and impoverished options can also be observed in judgmental tasks in which people tend to seek out information that is compatible with their hypotheses, for example, to focus on a person's most compatible attributes when asked to evaluate him or her on a particular dimension. Downs and Shafir (1995), for example, presented subjects with the descriptions of two people; the description of one—the enriched personality— was filled with instances characteristic of immoral and of moral behavior (e.g., flirting with employees and giving to charity), and the description of the other—the impoverished personality—consisted of information largely irrelevant on the morality dimension. One half of the subjects were asked which of the two people they considered more moral; the others were asked which of the two seem more immoral. In line with compatibility, subjects were inclined to judge the enriched personality, who presented instances of both types of behaviors, as both more moral (52%) and more immoral

(72%) than the impoverished personality, who presented fewer instances of either.

Note that the enriched–impoverished discrepancy need not be created in the laboratory and is bound to arise naturally between personalities about whom we know a lot and others about whom we know little. All else being equal, a person who is well known and to whom we can attribute positive as well as negative features is likely to constitute an "enriched" option, whereas a person who is less well known naturally presents an "impoverished" option. Downs and Shafir (1995) presented subjects with names of famous public figures. The "enriched" figures (e.g., Ronald Reagan and Woody Allen) were very well known to most subjects; the "impoverished" figures (e.g., John Major and Federico Fellini) were recognizable but less well known to most subjects. To facilitate comparison, enriched and impoverished figures with similar occupations were paired and subjects were than asked to indicate which of the two in the pair was better described by each of a number of opposite adjectives, such as moral versus immoral, or confident versus insecure.

Let P_a and $P_\hat{a}$ denote the percentages of subjects who chose the enriched figure as being better described by an adjective (e.g., confident) and by it's opposite (insecure), respectively. If the applicability to a person of one adjective is roughly complementary to the applicability of its opposite; that is, if a person who is widely regarded as insecure is rarely considered confident, then the sum $P_a + P_\hat{a}$ should equal roughly 100. If, on the other hand, subjects tend to assign relatively more weight to the features of a person that are more compatible with the adjective in question, then this sum should exceed 100. As predicted, the average sum of $P_a + P_\hat{a}$ was 110%, significantly greater than 100. In line with semantic compatibility, when asked who is more confident, subjects appear to focus on instances of confidence, whereas when contemplating who is more insecure, subjects weigh more heavily features diagnostic of insecurity.

Note that unlike the earlier examples in which information was explicitly presented to subjects, this last study involved items for which the relevant information needed to be retrieved from memory. Thus, in addition to affecting the weights assigned to explicitly mentioned features, semantic compatibility is also likely to facilitate the retrievability from memory of compatible as opposed to less compatible features (see Snyder & Cantor, 1979, for related discussion in the context of confirmation biases).

D. Visual Estimation

A recently documented "region salience" bias in a visual estimation task can also be interpreted in terms of semantic compatibility. Goldstone (1993) presented people with two displays composed of a mixture of 60 black and white squares. In one of the displays the squares were randomly distributed, whereas the second display was designed to have clusters of black and white squares. One half of the subjects were asked to choose the display with a higher percentage of black squares; the others were asked to choose the one with a higher percentage of white squares. The results show that clustered displays were judged to have a higher percentage of both kinds of squares. Thus, when asked to select the display with a greater percentage of white squares, the clustered display was chosen about 56% of the time, and when asked to select the display with the greater percentage of black squares, the clustered display was again chosen 56% of the time. These results are consistent with the hypothesis that subjects have a tendency to selectively focus on areas that have a high concentration of instruction-compatible features. Because the percentage of instruction-compatible features in these salient areas is high, the prevalence of those features tends to be overestimated.

VII. Discussion

The tendency to focus entirely on features of a stimulus that are compatible with the given instructions has been observed in choice behavior of young children. Falk (1983) presented children (about 6 years old) with two urns containing different proportions of blue and yellow beads; one urn contained more of both colored beads than the other (e.g., one urn had 6 blue and 4 yellow beads; the other had 2 blue and one yellow). In each round, the children were told which color (blue or yellow) was the winning color and were invited to draw from either urn at random. The dominant error that characterized the children's choices was to select the urn with the greater number of beads of the winning color. Thus, whether told that the winning color was blue or yellow, these children would reach into the same urn, namely, the one containing the larger absolute number of winning color beads (see also Falk, Falk, & Levin, 1980; Piaget & Inhelder, 1975).

Selective focusing on features that are compatible with a currently held hypothesis or with the given instructions may be seen to underlie numerous studies reporting what have variously been called confirmatory biases (Barsalou, 1992; Skov & Sherman, 1986; Snyder & Swann, 1978), congruence biases (Baron, 1994), verification biases (Johnson-Laird & Wason, 1970), and matching biases (Evans & Lynch, 1973; Evans, 1984, 1989), among other names. In most of these cases, performance that violates certain normative principles of deductive or inductive reasoning, social inference, or contingency judgments is not simply attributed to a lack of understanding of the relevant normative rules. Rather, the various biases are presumed to arise out of people's tendency to focus selectively on "confirming," "matching," or "congruent" instances, usually those that are more compatible with the terms that appear in the instructions or with the hypotheses under consideration.

Selective focusing on compatible instances has been shown to occur also in memory search. Snyder and Cantor (1979), for example, had subjects read a story about a woman who behaved in ways that could be characterized either as extroverted or introverted. Two days later, these subjects were asked to assess the woman's suitability for an "extroverted" occupation (real estate agent) or for an "introverted" occupation (librarian). The results showed that subjects considering the extrovert occupation recalled more extrovert items, whereas those considering the introvert occupation recalled more introvert items, each group recalling with greater ease those items that were compatible with its underlying hypothesis. A related mood-induced focusing on compatible instances has been suggested, in which people's good or bad moods appear to increase the availability of "mood-congruent" thoughts and information, thus biasing retrievability and affecting judgments of subjective well-being (Bower, 1981; Isen, Shalker, Clark, & Karp, 1978; although see Schwarz & Clore, 1983, for an alternative interpretation). The proneness to focus selectively on compatible instances has clear implications for people's tendency to confirm hypotheses and detect covariation, as it is always possible to encounter compatible (i.e., positive) instances and thus detect relationships between things even when there is no relationship at all (see, e.g., Gilovich, 1991, chap. 3).

Finally, certain aspects of decision problems are more compatible with one perspective on the problem than with another. Redelmeier and Tversky (1990), for example, investigate whether physicians make different judgments when evaluating an individual patient as compared with considering a group of such patients. Their data suggest that, in fact, physicians give more weight to the personal concerns of patients when considering them as individuals and relatively more weight to aggregate criteria, such as general effectiveness and cost, when considering them as a group. This is, of course, problematic, as physicians normally treat each patient as a unique case but over time are likely to encounter many such patients. Similar shifts in the perspective that decision makers adopt may arise as a result of temporal variations. As pointed out by Bursztajn et al. (1991), for example, clinicians make treatment decisions prospectively, with the hope of improving the patient's health, whereas judges hearing malpractice cases must address such decisions retrospectively, after harm has occurred. Thus, the potential harms of a treatment are more salient from the court's perspective, relative to the doctors for whom the potential benefits are more compatible with the task of finding a cure despite the risk of harm.

As suggested in this review, diverse aspects of stimuli and responses may enhance their compatibility. These include spatial and perceptual organization, the use of similar units on a scale, an evaluation in qualitative versus quantitative terms, a reliance on shared versus distinctive attributes, the specific instructions that guide the decision, and the particular hypothesis or perspective that motivate the evaluation. Although there is no general procedure for assessing compatibility, it is evident that some stimulus–response configurations are more compatible than others. In the performance of various perceptual and motor tasks, such as a pointing response to a visual display, compatibility predicts that some arrangements of stimuli and responses will yield better performance (in terms of shorter reaction times and fewer errors) than others. In various judgment and decision making tasks, on the other hand, compatibility entails that the decisions people make will often depend on the particular form in which a problem is presented, or the mode in which responses are provided. This, in turn, is likely to generate systematic violations of some of the fundamental requirements of the classical analysis of rationality (Tversky & Kahneman, 1986).

Perhaps the most basic assumption of the rational theory of choice is the principle of procedure invariance, which requires strategically equivalent methods of elicitation to yield the same preference order. As observed in this chapter, however, compatibility effects lead to violations of procedure invariance in a systematic and predictable manner. For example, asking people to choose between two lotteries or, alternatively, asking them to state their price for each of these lotteries often lead to different preference orders: the monetary payoffs of lotteries weigh more heavily when setting a (monetary) price than when choosing, and the relative prominence of the chance to win looms larger when making a choice than when setting a price. In a similar fashion, asking people to choose one of two options or, alternatively, to reject one of two options can lead to different preference orders: advantages are weighted more heavily when choosing than when rejecting, and disadvantages weigh more heavily when rejecting than when choosing.

Because invariance is normatively indispensable, no normative theory of decision making can be reconciled with these findings. More importantly, perhaps, these findings may not be easily reconcilable with our own intuitions. Although compatibility can have a powerful effect on the expression of preference, people are generally unaware of its influence, operating as it does at an elementary level of information processing (see Slovic et al., 1990, for discussion). Furthermore, it is doubtful whether the compatibility bias can be eliminated by careful instructions or monetary rewards, as is indicated, for example, by the failure of incentives to affect the prevalence of preference reversals (Kachelmeier & Shehata, 1992; Slovic & Lichtenstein, 1983).

The lability of preferences that results from compatibility, as from other framing and elicitation effects, raises difficult questions concerning the assessment of values and preferences. We typically think of people's choices as reflecting their underlying values, and regard most elicitation methods as neutral means by which to translate these subjective values into explicit and meaningful expressions. But if one option is both chosen over and rejected in favor of another, or if one is priced over the other but the second is chosen over the first, in what sense can we speak about subjective values? Are people's true preferences exhibited when they reject or when they choose? when they choose or when they price? In contrast with the classical analysis, which assumes stable and well-defined preferences, the experimental evidence suggests that preferences are actually constructed, not merely revealed, during the elicitation procedure, and that these constructions depend on the context, the framing of the problem, and the method of elicitation, among other factors (see, e.g., Payne, 1982, Shafir & Tversky, in press, and Tversky & Kahneman, 1986, for further discussion).

Because the expression of preferences is strongly sensitive to the elicitation procedure, no method of elicitation can be assumed to yield a person's "true" preference ordering without its particular influence on the way information is processed. With this in mind, some researchers have tried to combine alternative decision frames in the presentation of problems (e.g., McNeil, Pauker, & Tversky, 1988), and others have called for more interactive methods in which multiple elicitation techniques are employed in helping the respondent create and enunciate preferences (Irwin et al., 1993; Slovic, Fischhoff, & Lichtenstein, 1982).

What seems commonplace or surprising about behavior is largely a function of our understanding of how the organism processes information and interacts with its environment (see Shafir, 1993b, for further discussion). Hence, an understanding of compatibility and its influence on information processing helps make sense of various phenomena that appear puzzling from a normative perspective. Additional theoretical analysis and empirical investigation will likely clarify the nature of compatibility and its role in decision making processes. Whatever future investigation reveals, it is clear that compatibility, a fundamental principle of human cognition, plays an important role in the making of decisions.

ACKNOWLEDGMENTS

This work was supported by U.S. Public Health Service Grant 1-R29-MH46885 from the National Institute of Mental Health. It was partly prepared while the author was a Visiting

Scholar at the Russell Sage Foundation, and later a Fellow at The Institute for Advanced Studies of The Hebrew University.

REFERENCES

Alluisi, E. A., & Warm, J. S. (1990). Things that go together: A review of stimulus–response compatibility and related effects. In R. W. Proctor & T. G. Reeve (Eds.), *Stimulus–response compatibility: An integrated perspective.* Amsterdam: North-Holland.

Anzola, G. P., Bertoloni, G., Buchtel, H. A., & Rizzolatti, G. (1977). Spatial compatibility and anatomical factors in simple and choice reaction times. *Neuropsychologia, 15,* 259–302.

Baron, J. (1994). *Thinking and deciding* (2nd ed.). New York: Cambridge University Press.

Barsalou, L. W. (1992). *Cognitive psychology: An overview for cognitive scientists.* Hillsdale, NJ: Erlbaum.

Bostic, R., Herrnstein, R. J., & Luce, R. D. (1990). The effect on the preference reversal phenomenon of using choice indifferences. *Journal of Economic Behavior and Organization, 13*(2), 193–212.

Bower, G. H. (1981). Mood and memory. *American Psychologist, 36,* 129–148.

Brainard, R. W., Irby, T. S., Fitts, P. M., & Alluisi, E. (1962). Some variables influencing the rate of gain of information. *Journal of Experimental Psychology, 63,* 105–110.

Bursztajn, H., Chanowitz, B., Kaplan, E., Gutheil, T. G., Hamm, R. M., and Alexander, V. (1991). Medical and judicial perceptions of the risks associated with use of antipsychotic medication. *Bulletin of the American Academy of Psychology and the Law, 19*(3), 271–275.

Delquie, P. (1993). Inconsistent trade-offs between attributes: New evidence in preference assessment biases. *Management Science, 39*(11), 1382–1395.

Downs, J., & Shafir, E. (1995). Why Ronald Reagan is more confident and more insecure than John Major: Enriched and impoverished options in social judgment. Unpublished manuscript. Princeton University.

Dutta, A., & Proctor, R. W. (1992). Persistence of stimulus–response compatibility effects with extended practice. *Journal of Experimental Psychology: Learning, Memory, and Cognition, 18*(4), 801–809.

Dyer, F. N. (1973). The Stroop phenomenon and its use in the study of perceptual, cognitive, and response processes. *Memory & Cognition, 1,* 106–120.

Evans, J. St. B. T. (1984). Heuristic and analytic processes in reasoning. *British Journal of Psychology, 75,* 451–468.

Evans, J. St. B. T. (1989). *Bias in human reasoning: Causes and consequences.* Hillsdale, NJ: Erlbaum.

Evans, J. St. B. T., & Lynch, J. S. (1973). Matching bias in the selection task. *British Journal of Psychology 64,* 391–397.

Falk, R. (1983). Children's choice behavior in probabilistic situations. *Proceedings of the First International Conference on Teaching Statistics* (Vol. 2, pp. 714–726). University of Sheffield, UK.

Falk, R., Falk, R., & Levin, I. (1980). A potential for learning probability in young children. *Educational Studies in Mathematics, 11,* 181–204.

Fischer, G. W., & Hawkins, S. A. (1983). Strategy compatibility, scale compatibility, and the prominence effect. *Journal of Experimental Psychology: Human Perception and Performance, 19*(3), 580–597.

Fitts, P. M., & Seeger, C. M. (1953). S-R compatibility: Spatial characteristics of stimulus and response codes. *Journal of Experimental Psychology, 46,* 199–210.

Ganzach, Y., & Schul, Y. (in press). The influence of quantity of information and goal framing on decision. *Acta Psychologica.*

Gilovich, T. (1991). *How we know what isn't so: the fallibility of human reason in everyday life.* New York: The Free Press.

Goldstein, W. M., & Einhorn, H. J. (1987). Expression theory and the preference reversal phenomena. *Psychological Review, 94*(2), 236–254.

Goldstone, R. L. (1993). Feature distribution and biased estimation of visual displays. *Journal of Experimental Psychology: Human Perception and Performance, 19,* 564–579.

Gordon, P. C., & Meyer, D. E. (1984). Perceptual-motor processing of phonetic features in speech. *Journal of Experimental Psychology: Human Perception and Performance, 10,* 153–178.

Hasbroucq, T., Guiard, Y., & Ottomani, L. (1990). Principles of response determination: Thelist-rule model of S-R compatibility. *Bulletin of the Psychonomic Society, 28,* 327–330.

Irwin, J. R., Slovic, P., Lichtenstein, S., & McClelland, G. H. (1993). Preference reversals and the measurement of environmental values. *Journal of Risk and Uncertainty, 6,* 5–18.

Isen, A. M., Shalker, T. E., Clark, M., & Karp, L. (1978). Affect, accessibility of material in memory, and behavior: A cognitive loop? *Journal of Personality and Social Psychology, 36,* 1–12.

Johnson-Laird, P. N., & Wason, P. C. (1970). A theoretical analysis of insight into a reasoning task. *Cognitive Psychology, 1,* 134–148.

Kachelmeier, S. J., and Shehata, M. (1992). Examining risk preferences under high monetary incentives: Experimental evidence from the People's Republic of China. *American Economic Review, 82,* 1120–1141.

Kahneman, D., & Ritov, I. (1993). Determinants of stated willingness to pay for public goods: A study in the headline method. Unpublished manuscript. University of California, Berkeley.

Kornblum, S., Hasbroucq, T., & Osman, A. (1990). Dimensional overlap: Cognitive basis for stimulus-response compatibility—A model and taxonomy. *Psychological Review, 97*(2), 253–270.

Ladavas, E. (1990). Some aspects of spatial stimulus-response compatibility in adults and normal children. In R. W. Proctor & T. G. Reeve (Eds.), *Stimulus-response compatibility: An integrated perspective.* Amsterdam: North-Holland.

Lichtenstein, S., & Slovic, P. (1971). Reversals of preference between bids and choices in gambling decisions. *Journal of Experimental Psychology, 89,* 46–55.

Lichtenstein, S., & Slovic, P. (1973). Response-induced reversals of preference in gambling: An extended replication in Las Vegas. *Journal of Experimental Psychology, 101,* 16–20.

Magliero, A., Bashore, T. R. Coles, M. T. H., & Donchin, E. (1984). On the dependence of P300 latency on stimulus evaluation processes. *Psychophysiology, 21,* 171–186.

Marks, L. E. (1987). On cross-modal similarity: Auditory-visual interactions in speeded discrimination. *Journal of Experimental Psychology: Human Perception and Performance, 13,* 384–394.

McNeil, B. J., Pauker, S. G., & Tversky, A. (1988). On the framing of medical decisions. In D. Bell, H. Raiffa, & A. Tversky (Eds.), *Decision making: descriptive, normative, and prescriptive interactions* (pp. 562–568). New York: Cambridge University Press.

Medin, D. L., Goldstone, R. L., & Gentner, D. (1990). Similarity involving attributes and relations: Judgments of similarity and differences are not inverses. *Psychological Science, 1*(1), 64–69.

Medin, D. L., Goldstone, R. L., & Markman, A. B. (1994). Comparison and choice: Relations between similarity processes and decision processes. Manuscript in preparation.

Nicoletti, R., Anzola, G. P., Luppino, G., Rizzolatti, G., & Umilta, C. (1982). Spatial compatibility effects on the same side of the body midline. *Journal of Experimental Psychology: Human Perception and Performance, 8,* 664–673.

Nicoletti, R., & Umilta, C. (1984). Right–left prevalence in spatial compatibility. *Perception and Psychophysics, 35,* 333–343.

Payne, J. W. (1982). Contingent decision behavior. *Psychological Bulletin, 92,* 382–402.

Piaget, J., & Inhelder, B. (1975; Orig. 1951). *The origin of the idea of chance in children.* L. Peake, Jr., P. Burrell, & H. D. Fishbein (Trans.). New York: Norton.

Proctor, R. W., & Reeve, T. G. (Eds.). (1990). *Stimulus-response compatibility: An integrated perspective.* Amsterdam: North-Holland.

Proctor, R. W., Reeve, T. G., & Van Zandt, T. (1992). Salient-features coding in response selection. In G. E. Stelmach & J. Reguin (Eds.), *Tutorials in Motor Behavior* (Vol. 2). Amsterdam: North-Holland.

Proctor, R. W., Reeve, T. G., & Weeks, D. J. (1990). A triphasic approach to the acquisition of response-selection skill. In G. H. Bower (Ed.), *The psychology of learning and motivation* (Vol. 26, pp. 207–240). San Diego: Academic Press.

Redelmeier, D. A., & Tversky, A. (1990). Discrepancy between medical decisions for individual patients and for groups. *New England Journal of Medicine, 322*(16), 1162–1164.

Riggio, L., Gawryszewski, L. G., & Umilta, C. (1986). What is crossed in crossed-hand effects? *Acta Psychologica, 62,* 89–100.

Schkade, D. A., & Johnson, E. J. (1989). Cognitive processes in preference reversals. *Organizational Behavior and Human Decision Processes, 44,* 203–231.

Schwarz, N., & Clore, G. L. (1983). Mood, misattribution, and judgments of well-being: Informative and directive functions of affective states. *Journal of Personality and Social Psychology, 45*(3), 513–523.

Shafir, E. (1993a). Choosing versus rejecting: Why some options are both better and worse than others. *Memory & Cognition, 21*(4), 546–556.

Shafir, E. (1993b). Intuitions about rationality and cognition. In K. I. Manktelow & D. E. Over (Eds.), *Rationality: Psychological and philosophical perspectives* (pp. 260–283). New York: Routledge.

Shafir, E., Osherson, D. N., & Smith, E. E. (1993). The advantage model: A comparative theory of evaluation and choice under risk. *Organizational Behavior and Human Decision Processes, 55*(3), 325–378.

Shafir, E., Simonson, I., & Tversky, A. (1993). Reason-based choice. *Cognition, 49*(2), 11–36.

Shafir, E., & Tversky, A. (in press). Decision making. In E. E. Smith & D. N. Osherson (Eds.), *Invitation to Cognitive Science* (2nd ed.). Cambridge, MA: MIT Press.

Simon, J. R., & Pouraghabagher, A. R. (1978). The effect of aging on the stages of processing in a choice reaction time task. *Journal of Gerontology, 33,* 553–561.

Simon, J. R., & Small, A. M. (1969). Processing auditory information: Interference from an irrelevant cue. *Journal of Applied Psychology, 53,* 433–435.

Skov, R. B., & Sherman, S. J. (1986). Information-gathering processes: Diagnosticity, hypothesis-confirmatory strategies, and perceived hypothesis confirmation. *Journal of Experimental Social Psychology 22,* 93–121.

Slovic, P. (1975). Choice between equally valued alternatives. *Journal of Experimental Psychology: Human Perception and Performance, 1,* 280–287.

Slovic, P., Fischhoff, B., & Lichtenstein, S. (1982). Response mode, framing, and information-processing effects in risk assessment. In R. Hogarth (Ed.), *New directions for methodology of social and behavioral science: Question framing and response consistency.* (No. 11, pp. 21–36). San Francsico: Jossey-Bass.

Slovic, P., Griffin, D., & Tversky, A. (1990). Compatibility effects in judgment and choice. In R. Hogarth (Ed.), *Insights in decision making: Theory and applications* (pp. 5–27). Chicago: University of Chicago Press.

Slovic, P., & Lichtenstein, S. (1968). Relative importance of probabilities and payoffs in risk taking. *Journal of Experimental Psychology Monograph 78*(Pt. 2), 1–18.

Slovic, P., & Lichtenstein, S. (1983). Preference reversals: A broader perspective. *American Economic Review, 73,* 596–605.

Snyder, M., & Cantor, N. (1979). Testing hypotheses about other people: The use of historical knowledge. *Journal of Experimental Social Psychology, 15,* 330–342.

Snyder, M., & Swann, W. B. (1978). Behavioral confirmation in social interaction: From social perception to social reality. *Journal of Experimental Social Psychology, 14,* 148–162.

Tversky, A. (1977). Features of similarity. *Psychological Review, 84,* 327–352.

Tversky, A., & Gati, I. (1978). Studies of similarity. In E. Rosch & B. Lloyd (Eds.), *Cognition and categorization* (pp. 79–98). Hillsdale, NJ: Erlbaum.

Tversky, A., & Kahneman, D. (1986). Rational choice and the framing of decisions. *Journal of Business, 59* (4, Pt. 2), 251–278.

Tversky, A., Sattath, S., & Slovic, P. (1988). Contingent weighting in judgment and choice. *Psychological Review, 95*(3), 371–384.

Tversky, A., Slovic, P., & Kahneman, D. (1990). The causes of preference reversal. *American Economic Review, 80,* 204–217.

Tversky, A., & Thaler, R. H. (1990). Preference reversals. *Journal of Economic Perspectives, 4*(2), 201–211.

Wallace, R. J. (1972). Spatial S-R compatibility effects involving kinesthetic cues. *Journal of Experimental Psychology, 93,* 163–168.

Weeks, D. J., & Proctor, R. W. (1990). Compatibility effects for orthogonal stimulus-response dimensions. *Journal of Experimental Psychology: General, 119,* 355–366.

Wickens, C. D. (1984). *Engineering psychology and human performance.* Columbus, OH: Merrill.

PROCESSING LINGUISTIC PROBABILITIES: GENERAL PRINCIPLES AND EMPIRICAL EVIDENCE

David V. Budescu and Thomas S. Wallsten

I. Overview

How do people use and understand linguistic expressions of probability? Is information processing, choice behavior, or decision quality more optimal in any well-defined sense when subjective uncertainty is expressed linguistically or numerically? Do people communicate with each other better in one modality or another? These and related questions are of considerable practical and theoretical importance. Practical issues arise because weighty decisions often depend on forecasts and opinions communicated from one person or set of individuals to another. Examples of decisions that depended on the communication of expert judgment include the Bay of Pigs invasion (Wyden, 1979, pp. 89–90), safety assessments regarding components of the space shuttle (Marshall, 1986, 1988) or of nuclear power plants (Vesely & Rasmusen, 1984), or simply one's own selection of investments or medical treatments. The standard wisdom (e.g., Behn & Vaupel, 1982; Moore, 1977; von Winterfeldt & Edwards, 1986) has been that numerical communication is better than linguistic, and therefore, especially in important contexts, it is to be preferred. But a good deal of evidence suggests that (1) this advice is not uniformly correct, and (2) it is inconsistent with strongly held preferences. A theoretical understanding of the preceding questions is an important step toward the development of means for improving communication, judgment, and decision making under uncertainty.

The theoretical issues concern how individuals interpret imprecise linguistic terms, what factors affect their interpretations, and how they combine those terms with other information (itself vague or imprecise to some degree) for the purpose of taking action. The action may be a discrete choice, an evaluation of options, or the communication of one's own opinion to other people. In this chapter, we review the relevant literature in order to develop a theory of how linguistic information about imprecise continuous quantities is processed in the service of decision making, judgment, and communication. We restrict ourselves almost entirely to research on qualitative expressions of subjective uncertainty, where we have done most of our work on the topic. However, without much effort, the theoretical ideas can be extended to and tested in other domains. The theory that we will present has evolved over the years as our research has progressed, and pieces of it in one form or another can be found in our and our colleagues' publications. We take advantage of this chapter to present our current view, which has evolved inductively, to substantiate it where the data allow, and to suggest where additional research is needed.

The relevant literature is a rich one; indeed, it dates back at least half a century to Simpson's (1944) paper on relative frequency terms. The literature has moved in many directions, but to keep this chapter focused, we do not review research on frequency, quantity, or amount terms and their use in questionnaires and surveys (see Bass, Cascio, & O'Connor, 1974; Bradburn & Miles, 1979; Hammerton, 1976; Mosier, 1941; Newstead, 1988; and Pepper, 1981, for some key representative examples). Nor do we discuss the empirical literature comparing verbal and numerical representations of other (i.e., nonprobability) attributes of options in decision situations (e.g., Schkade & Kleinmuntz, 1994; Stone & Schkade, 1991; Svenson & Karlsson, 1986).

In the next section, we set the stage by presenting a useful three-way taxonomy of sources of vagueness. This typology leads naturally to a pair of background assumptions that underlie our review. The third section then summarizes the research on meanings of qualitative probability expressions, and the fourth section compares judgments and decisions made on the basis of vague and precise (generally linguistic and numerical) probabilities. Each section consists of a review of the empirical regularities that have emerged, followed by a theoretical statement in the form of general principles that can explain the regularities, and, when available, a summary of research supporting the principles. The final section brings the background assumptions and the empirical principles together into a unified theoretical statement and provides some concluding remarks.

II. Setting the Stage

A. STIMULUS AND TASK CONSTRAINTS

Any theory of how people process information about uncertain events must be constrained by stimulus and task considerations. The former refers to the type of event in question, the nature of the uncertainty about it, and the manner in which that uncertainty is represented. The latter concerns the purpose for which the information is being processed. Indeed, specifying those constraints goes a long way toward developing the structure of the theory. Therefore we must consider stimulus and task characteristics before laying out our theoretical principles.

Zwick and Wallsten (1989) proposed and Wallsten (1990) somewhat modified a useful three-way taxonomy according to the nature of the event, the uncertainty about that event, and the manner in which the uncertainty is represented. Each of the three ways is a continuum that ranges from absolute precision at one end to absolute vagueness at the other. Considering events first, the distinction between those that are precise and those that are vague is straightforward. For example, the event of *noontime temperature exceeding 75°F* is precise, whereas the event of *a warm noontime* is vague. More generally, an event is precise if it is defined such that any outcome in the universe of discourse either is or is not an exemplar of it (for any day, the noontime temperature either does or does not exceed 75°F). All other events are vague to some degree. In set-theory terms, an event is precise if all outcomes in the universal set unequivocally have membership of either 0 or 1 in the subset that is defined by that event. If membership of 0 or 1 cannot be definitively assigned to each outcome, then the event is vague to some extent. For example, the event of a warm noontime is somewhat but not absolutely vague, because some temperatures, say below 40°F and above 110°F, are definitely outside the concept *warm.* It is vague to some degree because individuals will consider some temperatures between those two extremes more worthy of the designation *warm* than others. (Murphy & Brown, 1983, and Murphy, Lichtenstein, Fischhoff, & Winkler, 1980, provide additional illustrations of the distinction between vague and precise events.)

The notion that uncertainty varies from vague to precise is more subtle and less easily described. Generally, uncertainty is precise if it depends on external, quantified random variation; and it is vague if it depends on internal sources related to lack of knowledge or to judgments about the nature of the database. But regardless of the source of the uncertainty, we say that it is precise if the judge can place the event in question within a total likelihood ordering of a sufficiently rich set of events. Specifically,

David V. Budescu and Thomas S. Wallsten

consider the set of canonical events $\{E_0, E_1, \ldots, E_i, \ldots, E_{N-1}, E_N\}$, defined as the radial sectors of a perfectly balanced spinner with relative areas of i/N for any positive integer N. E_0 is the null event, E_N is the universal event, and the events are ordered such that

$$E_0 < E_1 < \ldots < E_i < \ldots < E_{N-1} < E_N, \qquad (1)$$

where $<$ means "is less likely than."[1] The uncertainty of event A can be considered absolutely precise if for any N there exists two successive events, E_i and E_{i+1}, such that the judge agrees that

$$E_i < A < E_{i+1}. \qquad (2)$$

For virtually any event A in a real situation, there will exist a sufficiently large N that an individual will not feel comfortable judging Eq. 2 to hold for any E_i. In that sense, subjective uncertainty is rarely, if ever, absolutely precise; but in a practical sense, people often will judge Eq. 2 to hold for reasonably large values of N and we would deem the event uncertainty to be precise. Thus, defining A as the event of a coin landing heads up, one might, after a sufficient number of test flips, be willing to state for $N = 99$ that

$$E_{49} < A < E_{50}.$$

The subjective uncertainty in that case would be very precise.

More often, the uncertainty is relatively vague. For example, defining the event A as noontime temperature exceeding 75°F, a weather forecaster might be unwilling to endorse Eq. 2 with any E_i for N as small as 10, but would be willing to assert for $N = 5$ that

$$E_3 < A < E_4. \qquad (3)$$

Our goal here is not to develop an index of vagueness, but rather to develop the important intuition that the degree to which a judge can place events in a connected, transitive likelihood ordering varies as a function of the nature and source of the supporting information. Note that this conception of subjective uncertainty differs markedly from a common viewpoint that vague uncertainties (generally misleadingly called ambiguous

[1] Canonical events of this sort, with the assumption that $P(E_i) = i/N$, are included in some axiom systems leading to subjective probability representations (e.g., DeGroot, 1970, chap. 6). We are concerned here with qualitative likelihood judgments, not with numerical representations, but want to convey the idea of precise events that would be judged equally spaced in likelihood.

probabilities) can be represented by second-order probability distributions, that is, precise probabilities over all possible probability distributions (see, e.g., the review by Camerer & Weber, 1992). As Gärdenfors and Sahlin (1982) have suggested, there are psychological and epistemological differences between unspecified, or unspecifiable, probabilities and those that are given in the form of a distribution. The former are vague to some degree and the latter are precise. The distinction matters for some purposes and not for others, but to represent both types of uncertainty by second-order probability distributions is to miss the problems for which it is important.

Finally, representations of uncertainty vary from precise to vague. Probability theory provides a language for precise representation. Imprecise portrayals include numerical intervals, quantified numbers (e.g., *approximately* .6), and linguistic probabilities of the sort we are considering in this chapter. An advantage of numerical intervals is that they signal both location and degree of imprecision. Verbal expressions do not have this benefit, but they compensate by conveying greater nuances of meaning. Their rich semantic structure allows one to convey not only approximate location and degree of imprecision, but also relative weights over levels of uncertainty within an implied range, and perhaps also other aspects of the communicator's knowledge or opinions beyond degrees of uncertainty.

The three continua along which stimulus vagueness can vary—event type, uncertainty type, and representation type—are distinct but not fully independent (Budescu & Wallsten, 1987). That is, a representation can be no more precise than the underlying uncertainty, which in turn can be no more precise that the event in question. The converse, however, does not hold: The uncertainty of an event can be vague to any degree, as can the representation of that uncertainty. Thus it would be perfectly natural for a television weather forecaster to (1) consider the precise event that the temperature at noon will exceed 75°F, (2) judge its uncertainty as vaguely as indicated by Eq. (3), and (3) say, "There is a good chance that the noontime reading will be above 75°F." On the other hand, it would be very strange for him or her to say, "There is a 70% chance that the temperature at noon will be warm," because a precise probability of a vague event is meaningless.

Tasks are not so easily taxonomized. They may involve making choices, rating or ranking alternatives, forming judgments for later use or for communication to other people, or any of a myriad of other possibilities. We should be mindful, however, that the manner in which the task is carried out depends on the nature of the information, and, correspondingly, the way in which the information is processed depends on the purpose to which it is being put.

B. BACKGROUND ASSUMPTIONS

Our goal is to explain how humans process vague, especially linguistic, information about uncertainty and how they combine it with and trade it off against information about other stimulus dimensions. The theory consists of two background assumptions and five principles. Some of the principles are no more than restatements of robust empirical regularities in theoretical terms, whereas others have further testable consequences. They are presented at the conclusion of the relevant review sections, along with supporting data where they are available. Here, we focus on the two background assumptions. Both are falsifiable, but they strike us as reasonable and we are treating them without evidence as true. These assumptions have, however, testable corollaries and we will summarize the relevant results.

1. Background Assumption B1

Except in very special cases all representations are vague to some degree in the minds of the originators and in the minds of the receivers. This assumption builds the logical constraints previously discussed into our theory of how humans process information about uncertain events. It implies that to the extent possible people consider the event definition and the data base both when deciding how to represent their own uncertain judgment and when interpreting a representation that they have received from someone else.

2. Background Assumption B2

People use the full representation whenever feasible, but they narrow it, possibly to a single point, if the task requires them to do so. This assumption expresses the idea that the task determines whether and how an individual resolves representational vagueness. Thus, for example, people treat separate judgments in their vague form when receiving and combining them, but they restrict attention to a narrow range of uncertainty or to a single point value when making specific decisions. Put crudely, one can have imprecise opinions, but one cannot take imprecise actions.

III. Meanings of Qualitative Probability Expressions

As already mentioned, probability phrases have rich semantic structures and it is likely that we use them to communicate more information than simply an approximate location on a [0,1] scale (Moxey & Sanford, 1993; Teigen & Brun, 1993). Nevertheless, most behavior studies of probability terms have focused on their numerical referents; and on this topic, there is a voluminous literature. The representations investigated vary from a single number (e.g., Beyth-Marom, 1982), through a range of numerical values (e.g., Hamm, 1991), to functions representing acceptability (Mosteller & Youtz, 1990; Reagan, Mosteller, & Youtz, 1989) or membership (Wallsten, Budescu, Rapoport, Zwick, & Forsyth, 1986) over the [0,1] interval. Among the elicitation methods used are words-to-numbers translation (e.g., Lichtenstein & Newman, 1967), numbers-to-words conversion (e.g., Reagan et al., 1989), comparison of the appropriateness of various numbers to describe a word and of various words to describe a given numerical value (Wallsten, Budescu, Rapoport, Zwick, & Forsyth, 1986), and elicitation of numerical and verbal responses to identical events (Budescu, Weinberg, & Wallsten, 1988). We review the empirical literature in four subsections, each focusing on distinct issues related to communication with these terms: intra-individual vagueness of probability terms, interindividual variance in the understanding and use of probability phrases, intra-individual sensitivity to context, and preferences for various modes of communicating degrees of uncertainty.

A.   INTRA-INDIVIDUAL VAGUENESS OF PROBABILITY TERMS

One important aspect of our work in this domain was to establish that a probability term within a context can be modeled by means of membership functions over numerical values.[2] We think of a probability phrase as a vague or fuzzy concept whose members are the numerical probabilities in the [0,1] interval. A membership function assigns to each numerical probability a real number, which we refer to as its *membership* in the concept defined by the phrase (in that context). In principle, these membership values are ratio scaled and range from 0, for probabilities that are absolutely not included in the concept, to a maximum value, arbitrarily fixed at 1, for probabilities that are ideal or perfect exemplars of the concept being considered; intermediate values represent intermediate degrees of membership. There are no special constraints on the shape, or any other property, of these functions. In particular, a membership function is not a

[2] It should be clear that phrases are always considered within a context of some sort, even if that context is no more than the single phrase in isolation or within a list, as has sometimes been the case in research. A simple list or individual phrase may be as close to a "null" context as one can get, or it may be an invitation for subjects to provide their own idiosyncratic frame of reference, as Moxey and Sanford (1993) suggest, but it is nevertheless a context. Thus, when we speak of representing the meaning of a probability phrase by a membership function, we are always referring to its meaning in a particular context regardless of whether or not we explicitly say so. Unfortunately, we have not been sufficiently careful to stress this point in the past. Indeed, as will become apparent, an important question is whether membership functions of phrases change systematically across contexts.

density function. It need not be continuous and the area under it need not integrate to 1. For example, precise (crisp) terms are characterized by a membership function with only two values (1 for all probabilities that are ideal exemplars of the concept, and 0 for all other values).

The concept of a membership function provides a useful generalization of simpler, perhaps more intuitive representations of linguistic uncertainties, such as a best probability and a range of probabilities. Presumably, the best point representation of a term characterized by a membership function is some central measure of that function. Of the various measures possible, a natural choice is the probability with the highest membership (or if the value is not unique, a summary, such as the mean of all of the probabilities with maximal membership). Another measure, analogous to the mean, was proposed by Yager (1981) as

$$W_e = \frac{\int\limits_0^1 \mu_e(p)\, p \, dp}{\int\limits_0^1 \mu_e(p)\, dp},\qquad (4)$$

where $\mu_e(p)$ represents the membership value of p in expression e. W_e is simply an average of the probabilities in the [0,1] interval, weighted by their normalized (forced to sum to unity) membership values. A discrete version of Eq. (4) is straightforward. Other location measures have been proposed in the fuzzy sets literature (see Bortolan & Degani, 1985, for a review), and an interesting empirical question is which, if any, of these measures is the best.

The range of acceptable probabilities for a term within a particular context, usually called the support of the membership function, consists of all of the values with positive membership. A convenient measure of spread, which we have used occasionally, is analogous to the variance of a density. Making use of W_e in Eq. (4), this measure is

$$V_e^2 = \frac{\int\limits_0^1 \mu_e(p)\, (p - W_e)^2\, dp}{\int\limits_0^1 \mu_e(p)\, dp}.\qquad (5)$$

Finally, membership functions implicitly define subsets of probabilities that are members of the concept implied by the phrase to specified degrees. This definition is accomplished by restricting subset membership to probabilities with membership values above some threshold, v, where $0 < v < 1$. Subsets monotonically decrease (become narrower) as v increases. The notion of thresholds provides a convenient quantitative way to theorize about probabilities that are "sufficiently well described by a phrase," and we will use it subsequently. Figure 1 presents hypothetical examples of some membership functions of verbal expressions.

Wallsten, Budescu, Rapoport, Zwick, and Forsyth (1986) and Rapoport, Wallsten, and Cox (1987) have shown that membership functions of the sort shown in Fig. 1 can be empirically derived and validated at the individual subject level. For each phrase used in these studies, the subjects were asked to compare various pairs of probabilities (represented by spinners) and to indicate which member of the pair better represents the meaning of the given term and how much better it does so. The graded pair-comparison judgments were reliable over replications. Conjoint measurement techniques showed that the functions satisfied the ordinal properties of a difference or a ratio representation (see also Norwich & Turksen, 1984), and goodness of fit measures indicated that both metrics scaled the judgments equally well. Rapoport et al. (1987) showed that the scales derived from the pair-comparison judgments can be approximated well by simpler and quicker direct rating techniques, which we have applied successfully in

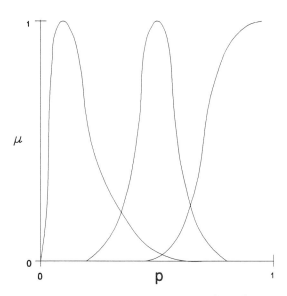

Fig. 1.   Generic membership functions for three phrases.

several subsequent papers (e.g., Budescu & Wallsten, 1990; Fillenbaum, Wallsten, Cohen, & Cox, 1991; Jaffe-Katz, Budescu, & Wallsten, 1989; Tsao & Wallsten, 1994; Wallsten, Budescu, & Zwick, 1993).

Most derived membership functions are single-peaked and a sizeable minority are monotonic, decreasing from probabilities close to 0 for low terms and increasing to probabilities close to 1 for high terms. (In many cases, these monotonic functions may actually be single-peaked, but just appear to be monotonic because we failed to include probabilities sufficiently close to the end points. See also Reagan et al.'s, 1989, footnote on this topic.) Single-peaked functions may be considerably skewed in one direction or another. Most functions cover a relatively large range of values, indicating that the terms are vague to individuals. Calculations of the spread measure, V_e^2 in Eq. (2), confirms this impression (e.g., Fillenbaum et al., 1991; Tsao & Wallsten, 1994). Only a small minority of the functions can be classified as relatively "crisp" (i.e., having a narrow support with uniformly high membership). Relatively crisp functions generally represent terms such as *toss-up* or *even odds,* which tend to convey specific values.

It is important to realize that because membership functions are derived from temporally stable judgments at the level of individual subjects, they indicate that phrases are *intra-individually vague.* Reagan et al. (1989) present similarly appearing functions, but they are relative frequency distributions of acceptable or best probability judgments aggregated over individuals. There are two problems in interpreting the Reagan et al. functions. First, as Rubin (1979) pointed out in a different domain of vague terms, such response distributions are just as easily interpreted in terms of error variance as in terms of vagueness or fuzziness. Second, regardless of whether the functions represent noise or vagueness, they relate to inter- not intra-individual differences in translating phrases to numbers.

Returning to single-subject data, other procedures, which require fewer judgments than needed to establish membership functions and therefore are simpler for respondents, also indicate that terms are vague to individuals. The simplest procedure is just to ask for a range—a lower and an upper probability—that the phrase represents. Wallsten, Budescu, Rapoport, Zwick, and Forsyth (1986) posed that question prior to eliciting membership functions. The results are summarized in Fig. 2, reproduced from their article. Median within-subject ranges were substantial, varying from approximately .1 for the terms *almost impossible* and *almost certain* to more than .5 for *possible.* Hamm (1991) also asked subjects to provide lower and upper bounds for 19 terms. The median range (taken across 65 subjects) for 14 of these terms was greater than .10, and it was 0 only for the anchor terms *absolutely impossible, toss-up,* and *absolutely certain.*

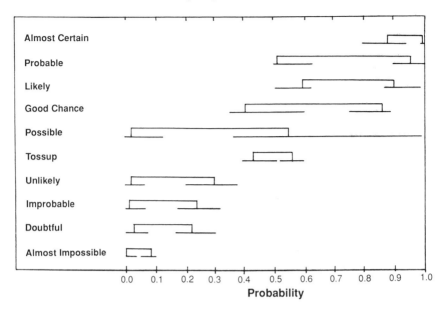

Fig. 2.   First, second, and third quartiles over subjects of the upper and lower probability limits for each phrase in Experiment 1 of Wallsten, Budescu, Rapoport, Zwick, and Forsyth (1986).

If probabilities belong in varying degrees to the concept defined by a phrase, one might expect subjects to give differing probability ranges for a particular phrase, depending on the degree of acceptability they deem necessary to include the probability in its concept. In membership function terms, subjects respond to the task of giving a lower and an upper probability by setting an acceptability level, v, and reporting the lower and upper probabilities, p_* and p^*, respectively, for which

$$\mu\,(p_*) = \mu\,(p^*) = v, \tag{6}$$

assuming single-peaked functions. In the case of truly monotonic functions, one of the limits would be either 0 or 1. Presumably, v would be sensitive to instructions, payoffs, or other factors, and would be constant over all phrases within a particular context. To our knowledge, this interesting prediction has not been checked. However, it would explain why when Weber and Hilton (1990) and Wallsten, Fillenbaum, and Cox (1986, Experiment 1) gave their subjects the opportunity to use a range of values, rather than a single number, only a few subjects chose to do so. Perhaps, because they were simply allowed but not required to give a range, they eased their task as much as possible by setting $v = 1$.

Other data relevant to intra-individual vagueness come from studies in which subjects are asked for point numerical translations on more than one occasion. As already indicated, the problem with such data from our perspective is that one cannot determine the degree to which nonperfect replicability reflects error variance rather than vagueness. Following our membership function theme, if people set $v = 1$ for purposes of providing point estimates, then any differences in replication are the result of random error. In fact, standard words-to-numbers translations within a fixed (or in the absence of any) context appear to yield relatively narrow (although clearly greater than 0) ranges of values within each individual (e.g., Beyth-Marom, 1982; Clarke, Ruffin, Hill, & Beamen, 1992). Similar results, but with other summary measures, have been reported by Bryant and Norman (1980), Budescu and Wallsten (1985), Johnson (1973), Mullet and Rivet (1991), and Sutherland et al. (1991).

Yet another was to assess the intra-individual vagueness of a phrase is to determine the range of probabilities for when an individual uses it. In the first stage of the experiment of Budescu et al. (1988), 20 subjects judged probabilities of 11 spinners six times. The procedure provided subjects with the opportunity to invoke the same word to describe different displays, and provided us with a convenient way to quantify the considerable within-subject variability of probabilities which can be described by any given term. On the average this variance was larger than in the case of numerical judgments, and in approximately one-half of the cases, the within-subject variance exceeded the between-subject component.

We have assumed (assumption B1) that all representations are vague to some degree. A somewhat counterintuitive corollary of this statement is that the scale meanings of numbers should also show imprecision. This prediction has been sustained by at least two studies, which have established that the meanings of numbers are both imprecise and subject to context effects. We concentrate here only on the imprecision and consider context effects later. Mullet and Rivet (1991) had children and adolescents rate the meanings of various sentences (in French) that described the chances of certain children passing or failing in school the next year. The sentences included both numerical (e.g., *one-in-four chance*) and verbal (e.g., *doubtful*) phrases. Ratings were made on a continuous (unnumbered) response scale. Between- and within-subject variances in the ratings of each sentence were not substantially different in the verbal and numerical cases. Shapiro and Wallsten (1994) had subjects rate verbal and numerical probabilities both in isolation and in the context of forecasts. On an unnumbered response scale, they provided a best, a highest, and a lowest rating in each case. The measured difference between the highest and lowest ratings is an index of vagueness. Numbers were less vague than words, but not completely precise. Finally, Budescu et al. (1988) also found in the first stage of their study that both numerical and verbal expressions were applied to describe more than a single graphical display, although numerical expressions were used less than verbal expressions.

Despite the evidence just reviewed that people treat numbers as vague, we assume they would believe numbers to be relatively more precise if they knew the values represented extensive relative frequency data rather than other individuals' judgments. But, to our knowledge, this fact has not been established.

To summarize, a vast array of data at the individual subject level must be interpreted not as error variance, but as indicating that phrase (and number) meaning extends over a range of probabilities. Moreover, the data strongly suggest that a given expression represents a set of probabilities to varying degrees, a point that we formalize below as Principle P1. After considering this principle, we turn to the questions of how these vague meanings differ over people and contexts.

B. PRINCIPLE P1

Membership functions can be meaningfully scaled. Membership functions, $\mu_3(p)$, over the probability interval $[0,1]$ can be used meaningfully to scale interpretations of numerical or verbal probability expressions or of other subjective representations of uncertainty. The operative term in this statement is *meaningful*. As reviewed earlier, numerous procedures have been devised to establish such scales; our assumption is that they capture subjective meanings and interpretations in a manner that allows prediction of independent behavior.

The first test of meaningfulness in this sense was reported by Wallsten, Budescu, Rapoport, Zwick and Forsyth (1986). In that study, we scaled membership functions for individual phrases by having subjects judge the degree to which a given phrase better represented one spinner probability than another. We then used those scaled values to predict successfully judgments in which pairs of phrases were shown with single probabilities and subjects had to indicate how much more descriptive one of the phrases was than the other.

This could be viewed as a weak test, as the two types of judgments are fundamentally similar, but membership functions have passed stronger hurdles as well. One such test was that of Jaffe-Katz et al. (1989), who examined the semantic congruity and semantic distance effects (e.g., Holyoak, 1978) as applied to verbal (V) and numerical (N) expressions of uncertainty. One goal of that work was to show that the two modes of expression represent the same underlying construct of subjective uncertainty and therefore operate identically and (given the right model) interchangeably in such comparisons. Subjects performed speeded paired comparisons of terms under instructions to choose the larger (or the smaller) term. We used both single mode (VV, NN) and mixed (NV) pairs. The time required for a decision exhibited identical qualitative patterns in all three conditions. Consistent with the symbolic distance effect obtained in other domains, the closer were two terms, the longer it took to compare them; and consistent with semantic congruity effects observed elsewhere, the larger (smaller) of two large (small) terms was identified faster than the larger (smaller) of two small (large) terms. The NN comparisons were made more rapidly than the NV and VV, which did not differ significantly from each other. Important to this discussion is that membership functions were obtained and successfully used in an expanded reference point model that performed 70% better than did the basic version (Holyoak, 1978). Thus, it is fair to conclude that the membership functions predicted well the complex reaction time patterns obtained in speeded magnitude comparisons. In another study, Wallsten, Budescu, and Erev (1988) used membership functions to predict the stochastic properties of repeated choices between lotteries for constant amounts of money based on the outcomes of events described verbally or numerically. As this study provides the underpinning for a subsequent principle, we defer discussion of it here.

Finally, relative membership values were successfully predicted in a bidding study by Budescu and Wallsten (1990, Experiment 2). In that experiment, decision makers bid for lotteries with chance events that had been described verbally and numerically by independent forecasters. The decision makers also provided judgments from which their membership functions for the forecaster's phrases could be inferred. In 23% of the cases, the decision makers' membership values were in fact 1.0 at the forecasters' estimated probability. In another 27% of the cases, the membership was below 1.0 but still higher than the memberships of all of the competing phrases of that probability. Thus, on approximately one half of the occasions, we can conclude on the basis of membership values that the decision makers considered the same particular phrase to be better than any other used by the forecaster for the intended probability. This is a remarkable result, considering the tremendous range of vocabulary the forecasters used.

Given all of the preceding results, we feel justified in concluding that when membership values are properly scaled by means of pair comparison or by suitably constrained magnitude estimation procedures, they provide meaningful representations of an individual's understanding of a phrase within the context that it is being used. Therefore, these membership values can be used in quantitative model testing.

C. INTERINDIVIDUAL VARIANCE IN THE UNDERSTANDING AND USE OF PROBABILITY PHRASES

A widely accepted generalization is that people differentially understand probability phrases (e.g., Clark, 1990). Consequently, different individuals use diverse expressions to describe identical situations and understand the same phrases differently when hearing or reading them. The data strongly support both of these statements and show that people have surprisingly rich and individualized lexicons of uncertainty.

For example, consider the range of expressions people use in identical situations. In the Budescu et al. (1988) experiment, 20 subjects spontaneously generated 111 distinct phrases to describe 11 different graphically displayed probabilities. Similarly, 40 forecasters in a study by Tsao and Wallsten (1994, Experiment 5) freely selected 148 unique phrases to describe 11 probabilities of drawing balls of specific colors from urns. Zwick and Wallsten (1989) report an experiment in which 20 individuals used an average of over 35 distinct expressions to represent the uncertainty of 45 real-world events. Many subjects in a revision of opinion experiment (Rapoport, Wallsten, Erev, & Cohen, 1990) used over 30 phrases despite a request to limit the number to 15. Wallsten, Budescu, and Zwick (1993) asked 21 subjects to create a vocabulary for expressing degrees of confidence in the truth of almanac-type statements. Each respondent was required to include the anchor terms *certain, toss-up,* and *impossible* and to select 8 additional phrases from a list of 64 such that he or she considered the whole [0,1] probability interval to be covered. Overall, 60 distinct phrases were selected, of which only 8 were chosen by more than 5 subjects and 20 were each selected by only a single individual. Finally, in a study by Erev and Cohen (1990), four experts each freely generated between 10 and 17 distinct terms in making probability judgments about 27 basketball events. Thus, without question, people have different working vocabularies for expressing degrees of confidence or uncertainty and create different lexicons for themselves when given the opportunity to do so.

To investigate the flip side of the problem of how people understand phrases when they receive them, it is necessary to compare individuals' responses to distinct expressions. Numerous studies of phrase-to-number conversion have reported vary large degrees of between-subject variability in the assessments of the same terms in a fixed context or in the absence of a specified context. The list of studies and replications is too long to be reproduced here. Johnson and Huber (1977) using Army personnel, Budescu and Wallsten (1985) using psychology graduate students and faculty, and Mullet and Rivet (1991) using children between the ages of 9 and 15 all found that variability between subjects far exceeded that within. Other studies finding considerable interpersonal variability in interpreting probability phrases among either lay people or experts within their professional domains include Beyth-Marom (1982), Brackner (1985), Bryant and Norman (1980), Chesley (1985), Clarke et al. (1992), Farkas and Makai-Csasar (1988), Hamm (1991), Kong, Barnett, Mosteller, and Youtz (1986), Lichtenstein and Newman (1967), Merz, Druzdzel, and Mazur (1991), Murphy et al. (1980), Nakao and Axelrod (1983), and Sutherland et al. (1991). Two exceptions of interest include a study by Brun and Teigen (1988, Study 2) that demonstrated greater consensus among physicians than among parents of young children in assigning numerical meanings to linguistic probabilities. The other is by Timmermans (1994), who noted that experienced and resident internists and surgeons interpreted probability terms similarly when applied to describe symptoms.

Of course, the degree of interindividual variance is not identical for all terms. Consensus regarding the meaning of phrases tends to be greatest near the ends of the continuum (e.g., *almost certain* or *practically impossible*) or in the vicinity of 0.5 (e.g., *even odds*), and to be least between these anchor points. An interesting result, especially from a linguistic perspective, is that negation (e.g., Reyna, 1981) and symmetric reversals (e.g., Clarke et al., 1992; Reagan et al., 1989; Lichtenstein & Newman, 1967) do not necessarily lead to complementary numerical estimates.

The phenomenon is not an artifact of the differential use of a numerical scale. Budescu and Wallsten (1985) elicited rankings of various terms and found interindividual rank reversals (see also Moore & Thomas, 1975). Using somewhat different methodology, Reagan et al. (1989) asked 115 subjects to provide words-to-numbers translations, words-to-numbers (range) acceptability functions, and numbers-to-words acceptability functions using 18 probability phrases and 19 numerical values (from .05 to .95 in steps of .05), and analyzed the joint results. They found large variance across subjects in all the tasks. They were also able to demonstrate high levels of consistency (mean correlations above .85 for all pairs of tasks compared) in the distribution of responses across individuals.

All of the studies just reviewed demonstrate extreme variation over individuals when people are required to translate phrases into numerical equivalents or to indicate which numbers are acceptable translations or expressions. Analysis of individual membership funtions carries this result a step further. We have shown (Wallsten, Budescu, Rapoport, Zwick, and Forsyth, 1986; Rapoport et al., 1987; Budescu & Wallsten, 1990) that the location and spread of functions representing any given term vary considerably across subjects. Even more impressive is the fact that the shape of these functions is not universal. For example, Budescu and Wallsten (1990) report that 25% of the functions describing *unlikely* are monotonically decreasing and 67% are single-peaked; of the functions describing *very good chance,* 44% are single-peaked and the same proportion are monotonically increasing. Thus, not only do phrases differ over individuals in their central meaning, but they also differ in the extent and nature of their vague referents. To the degree that membership functions carry implications for the semantics of terms, such semantics vary considerably over individuals.

D. Intra-individual Sensitivity to Context

One obvious solution to potential communications problems raised by intra-individual vagueness and interindividual variability in understanding probability phrases is to standardize the language. That is, develop a verbal scale by identifying a reasonably small subset (7 to 13 members) of frequently used terms, impose a ranking, and associate a range of probabilities with each of the terms on the list. It is a little known fact that the National Weather Service (NWS) has done just that with respect to probability of precipitation (POP) forecasts (National Weather Service, 1984, Chapter C-11). In issuing POP forecasts, NWS meteorologists can translate .10 and .20 only to the term *slight chance;* .30, .40, and .50 only to *chance,* and .60 and .70 only to *likely.* Other terms are not allowed in POP forecasts.

The general argument for a standardized probability language is best articulated by Mosteller and Youtz (1990) (comments by other researchers for and against their proposals plus their rejoinder immediately follow their article, and we refer readers to the entire interesting discussion). Too many scales have been proposed to mention all of them here, but representative examples include Beyth-Marom (1982), who grouped 19 terms into seven categorical ranges; Hamm (1991), who suggested a single best term for each of the 19 intervals of width 0.05 in the .05 to .95 range; and Kadane (1990), who proposed 11 terms to label 11 intervals. And, of course, there is the infamous scale used by NASA engineers that was linked (Marshall, 1986, 1988) to the space shuttle accident.

In a similar spirit, artificial intelligence researchers who need to incorporate uncertainty in expert systems have suggested that a selected subset of terms be represented by a family of partially overlapping membership functions. For example, Bonissone, Gans, and Decker (1987), in an expert system named RUM, suggested using nine terms from Beyth-Marom's (1982) list and describing each one by a trapezoidal function; Degani and Bortolan (1988) proposed triangular membership functions for 13 terms; and López de Mántaras, Meseguer, Sanz, Sierra, and Verdaguer (1988) described a medical diagnostic expert system (MILORD) in which uncertainty is captured by nine terms represented by trapezoidal functions.

A standardized scale is feasible if: (1) people can suspend or suppress the meanings they normally associate with particular terms, and (2) meanings and representations of selected terms are invariant over all contexts in which they are applied. The former condition has not been studied extensively. In fact, the only study that has addressed this issue was reported by Wallsten, Fillenbaum, and Cox (1986, Experiment 1). They showed that weather forecasters were subject to base-rate effects in a domain outside of their expertise with the very phrases that had been endowed with standardized meaning in the context of POP forecasts. The effects were substantial. For example, *chance* was interpreted on average as indicating a probability of .39 when referring to the likelihood that an ankle twisted in a soccer game was sprained rather than broken, but as .18 when referring to the likelihood that severe life-threatening effects would accompany a flu shot. This result strongly suggests that meanings cannot be legislated.

The second condition is the primary subject of this section. As it turns out, most empirical results obtained to date show that this condition is systematically violated in interesting ways. Just as with terms of frequency (e.g., Pepper, 1981) and quantity (e.g., Newstead, 1988), probability phrases tend to change their meanings according to the context in which they are used.

The first result of note is simply that context matters. In Beyth-Marom's (1982) study, a group of political forecasters translated 14 common probability terms to numbers on two occasions. The phrases first were presented in isolation and then embedded in paragraphs from reports published by their organization. Interestingly, the second administration lead to greater interindividual variance for most expressions. This pattern of increased variability in specific contexts was replicated in two studies reported by Brun and Teigen (1988). Mapes (1979) reported a study in which physicians assigned different distributions of numerical values to probability (and frequency) terms when used to describe likelihood (and frequency) of side effects in response to different medications. Beyth-Marom (1982) speculated that there were three reasons why interindividual variance may have increased with the context she supplied, (1) because the context included other vague terms (e.g., *hostile activities* or *severe illness*) that also required interpretation so that the subjects perceived the nominally identical frames differently, (2) because individuals imposed their own judgments on the contexts rather than just interpreting the phrases, or (3) because perceived outcome values influenced the interpretations of the phrases. Whatever the cause, and it may have been all three, the results certainly demonstrate that the interpersonal variability in translating phrases to numbers commonly observed in laboratory settings does not result from the *absence* of a specified context as has been occasionally suggested (e.g., Moxey & Sanford, 1993; Parduci, 1968).

Context, of course, is not a well-defined unidimensional concept. To reach more specific generalizations, we review next a few situational variables that have been shown to affect systematically probability phrase meanings. We first consider perceived *base rates*. Following Pepper's (1981; see also Pepper & Prytulak, 1974) lead with frequency expressions, Wallsten, Fillenbaum, and Cox (1986) have shown that the numerical interpretation of a term used to describe the chances of a given event occurring depends on whether the context implies a high or a low base rate. For example, the numerical translation of *probable* when referring to the likelihood of snow in the North Carolina mountains is higher when the statement specifies the month of December than when it specifies October. In an elaborate study (Wallsten, Fillenbaum, & Cox, 1986, Experiment 2), the average effect size due to base rate exceeded .11 over the nine probability terms used, but was considerably stronger for the high (e.g., *likely*) and neutral (e.g., *possible*) terms than for the low (e.g., *improbable*) terms. Detailed analyses at the group level suggested that the meaning assigned to any given term may be a weighted combination of its meaning in isolation and the perceived scenario base rate.

Recently, Shapiro and Wallsten (1994) replicated the effect with a different set of scenarios covering a wider range of base rates and also with numerical as well as verbal expressions. Because they had the same subjects both judge base rates and interpret numbers and phrases, they were able to analyze data at the individual level. It appeared on this basis that the averaging may have been an artifact of analyzing group rather than individual data. Shapiro and Wallsten suggested that relatively few people rely on base rates when interpreting low expressions because base rates generally are used only in the narrow range below some "neutral" level and therefore are only associated with those probabilities. The range is narrow because neutral points are never greater than .5, and often are much less. That is, when a phrase is used to describe the chances of an event within a context in which only two alternative events are possible, neutral is naturally taken as .5. If there are four possible outcomes, neutral is .25.

A few studies have looked at phrase meaning directly as a function of the *number of possible alternatives, n.* Tsao and Wallsten (1994, Experiments 1–4) encoded subjects' membership functions for low, neutral, and high phrases when n equaled 2 or 4. The functions tended to shift left when $n = 4$ relative to when $n = 2$ for probabilities from 0 to roughly .60. As a consequence, the function for the neutral term *even chance* tended to peak at .50 and .25 for $n = 2$ and $n = 4$, respectively; functions for high terms, which increased monotonically in the 0 to .60 range, described lower probabilities better when $n = 4$ than when $n = 2$; and functions for low terms, which tended to decrease monotonically in that range, did the opposite. These are sensible results on the assumption that low, neutral, and high are assessed relative to $1/n$.

Teigen (1988a) obtained parallel results when he examined how the number and relative likelihoods of alternatives affect people's understanding and use of (Norwegian) probability phrases in real-world contexts. He showed that the number of alternatives did not affect the fraction of subjects who indicated that high rather than low terms (e.g., *great chances* vs. *small chances; not improbable* vs. *improbable*) more appropriately described the likelihood of specific outcomes. Teigen interpreted this result as showing that people's tendencies to overestimate probabilities increase as the number of alternatives increases. We prefer the interpretation that meanings of high phrases depend on a perceived neutral point, $1/n$. As n increases (and $1/n$ decreases), high phrases are increasingly appropriate for lower probabilities. If this is so, then their continued use as n increases is not surprising.

Teigen (1988b) did find, however, that the source of the uncertainty dramatically affected phrase selection. The pattern of results suggested subtle semantic effects not understood simply in terms of implied probabilities. Recently, Gonzales and Frenck-Mestre (1993) reported a series of experiments in which various groups of subjects read short scenarios about probabilistic events. The various versions of these vignettes differed with respect to the type and nature of information provided (base rate, trend, global and local weight, etc.), but, in most cases, the event's (objective) probability remained fixed. They showed that the verbal responses (in French) were more sensitive than the numerical ones to variability in base rates and local weight. Both papers emphasize the importance of semantic concerns beyond those captured by simple numerical translations, but their results may depend to some degree on idiosyncratic aspects of the scenarios considered (only a fraction of the results were significant) and/or on the special nature of the response mechanism used (only a small number of phrases were used and subjects were asked to rate their appropriateness by using scales with two to seven categories).

Weber and Hilton (1990) investigated base-rate effects but also *outcome severity* in the context of medical scenarios. In three experiments (using some of the scenarios used by Wallsten, Fillenbaum, & Cox, 1986), subjects judged the meanings of probability phrases associated with each scenario, the case's severity, and its prevalence (base rate). Weber and Hilton replicated the base-rate effect, but also found that on average the phrases were interpreted to imply greater probabilities when associated with events of more severe consequence. The authors correctly pointed out that event severity and prevalence are negatively correlated in medical contexts (serious illnesses are generally less common than mild ones) and therefore their separate effects on meanings of probability terms are hard to disentangle. This correlation can explain the results reported by Merz et al. (1991), who found that the numerical values associated with some expressions decreased when associated with more severe outcomes. Severity effects are not universal. Sutherland et al. (1991) report that cancer patients responded similarly to verbal descriptions of different ("death" vs. "illness") side effects of blood transfusion.

Closely related to the notion of outcome salience is that of *outcome valence,* whether the outcome is positively or negatively valued. Mullet and Rivet (1991) compared scale values assigned to 24 French expressions used in predictions of children's chances of passing or failing a test. On average, the positive context induced higher estimates. A similar pattern was found in two experiments described by Cohen and Wallsten (1992), in which subjects compared pairs of lotteries whose (positive or negative) payoffs depended on the outcomes of binary probability spinners. For most subjects and most words in both studies the inferred probability of an expression was higher when associated with a positive than a negative outcome.

Yet another context effect relates to the *characteristics of the available uncertainty vocabulary* (such as its length, composition, and structure) when judging particular expressions. Hamm (1991) found less interindividual variance and better discrimination among the meanings of 19 phrases when they were presented in ordered rather than random lists. Clarke et al. (1992) found similar results. Fillenbaum et al. (1991) elicited membership functions for a list of core expressions (*likely, probable, possible, unlikely,* and *improbable*) and for the same words when embedded in longer lists including modified expressions (such as *very likely, quite probable,* etc.) or anchor terms (such as *toss-up* and *almost certain*). The additional terms did not affect the shape, location (W), or scatter (V^2) of the core phrases, but they did decrease the degree to which these words were judged to be most appropriate for certain events.

Finally, a particularly important factor in determining phrase meaning concerns one's *role in a dialogue or exchange.* The recipient of a communication may understand a probability expression differently than intended by the originator because the two individuals differentially interpret the base rates, valences, or severities or outcomes, or because meaning depends more generally on the direction of communication. We are not aware of any research that has compared recipients' and originators' perceptions of context, but a number of studies have looked at the overall effects of communication direction.

In a study of dyadic decision making (Budescu & Wallsten, 1990), one member of the dyad (the forecaster, F) saw a probability spinner and communicated the chances of the target event to another subject (the decision maker, DM) who used this information to bid for a gamble. The DM had no direct access to the spinner and the F was not informed of the amounts to be won or lost. Both subjects provided numerical translations for all of the words used. A clear pattern emerged: The recipients of the verbal forecasts generally assigned values closer to 0.5 than originally intended by the communicators. Fillenbaum et al. (1991) obtained analogous results with elicited membership functions. Functions were located closer to 0.5 (in terms of their W values) and were broader (in terms of V^2) for phrases selected by others than for those selected by the subjects themselves for communication. Thus, both the Budescu and Wallsten and the Fillenbaum et al. studies suggested that people interpret phrases more broadly and more centrally when receiving them than when selecting them.

To summarize, context effects on the interpretation of probability terms are pervasive. Individual differences in assigning numerical values to expressions are greater when the expressions are used in discourse than when they appear alone. More specifically, perceived base rate, number of alternatives, valence and severity of outcomes, and direction of communication all have been shown to have large and systematic effects on phrase meaning. To a lesser degree, meanings may also depend on the available vocabulary and on the order in which phrases are seen. It is interesting to note that studies have been carried out in many languages and in many cultures with no appreciable differences in the magnitudes or directions of results. Nevertheless, in view of the cultural differences in probabilistic thinking documented in other domains (Wright et al., 1978; Yates, Zhu, Ronis, Wang, Shinotsuka and Toda (1989), it would be of interest to search carefully for any differences that might exist.

E. PRINCIPLE P2

The location, spread, and shape of membership functions vary over individuals and depend on context and communication direction. This principle implies that the individual differences summarized in section III(B) and the systematic effects on phrase meaning described in section III(C) can be represented by membership function location, spread, and shape. Individual differences in membership functions are already well documented and were discussed in section III(C). But the representation of context and communication effects on such terms has not been directly tested.

A particularly interesting implication of principle P2, should it be correct, is that membership functions may provide the quantitative handle necessary for theorizing about the semantic features of probability expressions. Moxey and Stanford (1993), in their very selective review, suggest that the use of membership functions or other quantitative measures is inconsistent with understanding the semantic functions of such phrases, because, among other reasons, phrase meaning is affected by context. That is a very pessimistic view. An alternative one is that each expression in an individual's lexicon can be represented by a basic membership function, which is operated upon by the particular context, communication direction, and communication intention. Parsimonious theory development along such lines requires that a particular context, direction, or intention affect all basic membership functions in a similar way. Research testing this idea remains to be done.

F.   COMMUNICATION MODE PREFERENCES

Do people prefer verbal or numerical communications, and to what degree do any such preferences depend on the properties of language that we have previously documented? A corollary of background assumption B1, that all representations are vague, is that people generally prefer to communicate their opinions verbally because this mode conveys the underlying vagueness. The general folklore is consistent with this expectation and so are the empirical results. Erev and Cohen (1990) had basketball experts give their opinions of the likelihood of future basketball events. Three of the four experts spontaneously used verbal rather than numerical probabilities for almost every prediction. Subsequently, 21 students who had used these judgments were asked to provide their own judgments for future decision makers. Of these, 14 (67%) spontaneously did so verbally. In a medical context, Brun and Teigen (1988) found that 50 of 66 physicians (76%) preferred conveying their likelihood judgments in a verbal fashion. The suggestion that these results occurred simply because it is easier for people to communicate verbally rather than numerically is not a criticism. Rather, it is a natural explanation for this pattern if one assumes that it is easier to communicate in the modality that provides the most accurate representation of the underlying opinion.

This interpretation and related findings are supported in a survey of 442 respondents (undergraduate, graduate nursing, and MBA students) by Wallsten, Budescu, Zwick, and Kemp (1993). Overall, 77% thought that most people prefer communicating verbally rather than numerically and 65% indicated that mode as their initial personal preference. An analysis of reasons given for the preferences suggested that verbal communications generally are preferred unless the underlying opinions are based on solid evidence and are therefore relatively precise or unless the importance of the occasion warrants the effort to attempt greater precision.

Assumption B1 provides less guidance about what to expect about people's preferences for receiving judgments of uncertainty, but the data are clear: most people prefer receiving such judgments numerically. In the Erev and Cohen (1990) study, 27 (75%) of the decision makers always chose to look at numerical rather than verbal information and only 4 (11%) always did the reverse. Brun and Teigen (1988) found that 38 of 64 patients (60%) preferred receiving numerical rather than verbal judgments. In the Wallsten, Budescu, Zwick, and Kemp (1993) survey, 70% of the respondents expressed an initial personal preference for receiving information numerically. The same reasons were given as for communicating to others. Those who preferred verbal judgments did so because they are more natural, more personal, and easier; and those who preferred numerical judgments did so because they are more precise.

The fact that most people have initial preferences for communicating to others verbally and for receiving from others numerically means that there must be some people who have both preferences simultaneously. The Wallsten et al. survey found this pattern for 35% of their respondents, and Erev and Cohen found it for 47% of the decision makers. The reverse preference pattern, to communicate numerically to others and to receive verbally from others, virtually never appeared.

In a series of papers, Teigen and Brun have shown that linguistic probabilities have connotations that are not captured by their numerical counterparts, which provides another reason why their use often is preferred. Among these connotations are "affective intensity" (Brun & Teigen, 1988) and "directionality" (Teigen, 1988b; Teigen & Brun, 1993). Another indication of people's sensitivity to the vagueness of probability terms is the fact that many experts insist on communicating their opinions verbally. The evidence is primarily anecdotal but quite convincing (see Behn & Vaupel, 1982, and Wallsten, 1990, for some interesting examples). Beyth-Marom (1982) speculates that this preference is related to the perception that (because of their vagueness) linguistic forecasts cannot be verified and evaluated as can their numerical counterparts (but see the recent method proposed by Wallsten, Budescu, and Zwick, 1993).

G. PRINCIPLE P3

Communication mode choices are sensitive to the degrees of vagueness inherent in the events being described, the source of the uncertainty, and the nature of the communication task. This principle is really a corollary of background assumption B2, but it also summarizes the main results of the previous section. It captures the idea that most people prefer the communication mode that they can use most easily and accurately for the task at hand. Thus, they communicate their opinions to others in a verbal rather than numerical form because it is the easiest way to convey different locations and nuances of imprecision. On the other hand, even when recognizing that opinions are not precise, people prefer to receive information numerically because they know that individuals differ greatly in their phrase selection. Therefore, people believe they can more easily and accurately obtain a fix on the rough uncertainty location another individual intends to communicate when he or she does so numerically rather than verbally.

One implication of this principle was developed and tested by Erev, Wallsten, and Neal (1991). They suggested that in many contexts vague communications promote the well-being of a society to a greater extent than do precise ones, and that people will select their communication modes accordingly. Vague language is beneficial because it is more likely to result in heterogeneous rather than homogeneous actions, which in turn increase the chances that at least some individuals will be successful and the society as a whole will survive. Their experiment involved groups (societies) of seven subjects each. On each trial, one subject was the F, three were DMs, and the remaining three were passive participants. Subjects' roles rotated over trials. The F alone saw a probability spinner partitioned into three sectors and communicated to the group the probability of its landing on each one. The F had the option of selecting numerical or verbal terms to communicate these assessments. The DMs then individually and privately chose one of the three events to bet upon. Two different groups were run with different payoff structures. In the first condition, the group's total outcome was maximized if all subjects agreed in their choices; but in the second group, the total outcome was maximized by a pattern of heterogeneous selections. As predicted, the proportion of cases in which Fs used verbal terms increased systematically across trials in the second group but remained stable in the first. The clear implication is that subjects realized the condition in which vagueness was beneficial and precision harmful, and chose to use linguistic terms in that case.

IV. Judgment and Decision with Verbal and Numerical Probabilities

The picture that emerges from the previous section is that linguistic terms are imprecise and subject to multiple interpretations by different individuals and under different conditions. Therefore, they are problematic in communication and should be avoided for important decisions. We (Budescu & Wallsten, 1985) have referred to the possible "illusion of communication" induced by the use of these terms, and decision analysts routinely have recommend avoiding them (e.g., Behn & Vaupel, 1982; Moore, 1977; von Winterfeldt & Edwards, 1986). In this section, we review empirical results comparing judgmental accuracy and decision quality given probabilistic information in verbal and numerical form. Most of these studies involved within-subject comparisons of judgments and decisions performed with the two modes of information. The next subsection focuses on studies of probabilistic judgments and inferences, and the following subsection is concerned with experiments in which subjects made choices, gave bids, or in some way took action on the basis of verbal or numerical information.

A. ACCURACY OF JUDGMENTS

According to background assumption B1, all representations are vague to some degree. On this basis, contrary to intuition, verbal judgments are not necessarily less accurate than their numerical counterparts. Indeed, Zimmer (1983, 1984) argued persuasively that they should be more accurate. Beginning with the premise that the mathematics of uncertainty (probability theory) developed only in the seventeenth century, whereas the language of uncertainty is ubiquitous and much older, Zimmer (1983) wrote, "It seems unlikely that the mathematically appropriate procedures with numerical estimates of uncertainty have become automatized since then. It is more likely that people handle uncertainty by customary verbal expressions and the implicit and explicit rules of conversation connected with them" (p. 161). He continued the argument in another article by writing,

> It seems plausible to assume that the usual way humans process information for predictions is similar to putting forward arguments and not to computing parameters. Therefore, if one forces people to give numerical estimates, one forces them to operate in a "mode" which requires "more mental effort" and is therefore more prone to interference with biasing tendencies (Zimmer, 1984, p. 123)

To evaluate these claims, Zimmer (1983, 1984) ran experiments (in German) in which he tested for biases with verbal responses that typically are found with numerical ones (overconfidence in judgment and conservatism in revision of opinion). The data appear to substantiate his prediction of greater accuracy in the verbal mode, but more thorough tests are required. As Clark (1990) pointed out, both studies employed very coarse response scales (median number of categories approximately five), and lacked appropriate direct comparisons with numerical responses. Recently, we tested Zimmer's thesis by allowing subjects a much richer vocabulary (in English) and comparing the results with closely matched numerical controls.

In one study, Zimmer (1983, 1984) had subjects use verbal responses to estimate posterior probabilities in a simple two-alternative Bayesian revision of opinion paradigm. His subjects saw items, bricks or balls, as they were sampled from one of two bins. They knew that sampling was a priori equally likely to be from either bin and they knew the compositions of both bins. After each item was sampled, the subject provided an updated verbal judgment of "the chance of getting a brick or a ball the next time from the bin" (Zimmer, 1983, p. 177). It appears from the description that subjects were limited to approximately five phrases and that for purposes of comparing the responses to the optimal Bayesian values, each was converted to the central probability with the maximum empirically determined membership value for that phrase. The resulting judgments were more accurate (i.e., closer to the predicted Bayesian response) than generally found in studies using numerical responses (e.g., Edwards, 1968).

Rapoport et al. (1990) replicated the study with certain crucial differences. For each problem, subjects saw two urns containing specified proportions of red and white balls. Prior sampling probabilities were always equal, but the urn compositions changed from problem to problem. A within-subject design was used in which each subject provided verbal and numerical judgments in different sessions and a payoff scheme was used to motivate careful responding. Subjects constructed their own vocabularies, and individual membership functions were established for the 14 to 16 phrases each subject used most frequently. Verbal terms were quantified in two ways, by the probability with the highest membership value and by the location measure, W. The results indicated near equivalence in the quality of verbal and numerical judgments. That is, verbal judgments were more variable than numerical, as Budescu and Wallsten (1990) had also found, and consequently were less accurate when measured by mean absolute deviation from optimal. However, on average, verbal judgments were more accurate than numerical ones when the verbal responses were quantified by peak values. To complicate matters, the two modes yielded equal degrees of conservatism when the phrases were quantified by W.

In a related Bayesian revision opinion problem, Hamm (1991) also found very little difference between verbal and numerical modes. In contrast, Timmermans (1994) claimed in a medical context using physician subjects that probability judgments were more accurate (closer to the Bayesian posterior probabilities) in response to the numerical information than the verbal information. Some of Timmermans' conclusions are particularly hard to evaluate, as it is not clear that (1) the "objective" Bayesian values calculated and the estimates provided by the physicians pertain to the same events, or (2) the numerical meanings of the terms, which were elicited in the absence of any context, can be generalized to the diagnostic problems.

Thus, although the data do not support Zimmer's strong claim that reasoning is better in the revision of opinion context when people can respond verbally rather than numerically, neither do they show the opposite to be true. Rather, it appears that reasoning is about equivalent in these tasks given the two modes of responding. The same seems to be true in the case of judgment, in which the usual finding with numerical responses is that people are overconfident. Zimmer (1983) reported results of a study in which 90 soldiers answered 150 political science questions and assessed their chances of being correct by means of verbal expressions. Unfortunately, the description of the experiment is too sparse to properly evaluate it, but the calibration curve that is presented (based on the median value of the words) is closer to the identity line than generally occurs with numerical responses (e.g., Lichtenstein, Fischhoff, & Phillips, 1982). The implication is that subjects are less overconfident and more accurate when their judgments are verbal than when they are numerical. We recently replicated and extended this study and arrived at somewhat different conclusions.

Wallsten, Budescu, and Zwick (1993) asked 21 subjects to report their confidence in the truth of 600 factual items (in the domains of geography, demography, and history) consisting of 300 true statements and their semantically identical false complements. Subjects selected their own vocabularies (in addition to three specified anchor terms). They provided verbal and numerical judgments in separate sessions and encoded individual membership functions for each linguistic term. Verbal and numerical judgments correlated very highly within individual subjects and behaved very similarly in most aspects analyzed. The only differences we observed between the two modes were that the central numerical response (0.5) was used more frequently than its verbal counterpart (*toss-up*) and that the level of overconfidence (excluding the middle category) was higher for the verbal terms. A possible interpretation of these differences is that judges may use the central category more frequently in the numerical than in the verbal mode to represent imprecise judgments, because that category is equally defensible regardless of the outcome. In contrast, the verbal mode allows more honest representations of vaguely formed opinions without resort to the central category. If this is true, then overconfidence, as usually measured, may actually be greater than observed when subjects respond numerically.

Two points must be added in summarizing this evidence and its relation to background assumption B1. First, recent developments by Erev, Wallsten, and Budescu (1994) suggest that the underconfidence common in opinion revision studies and overconfidence common in judgment studies may both arise from one set of processes, leading to data that researchers analyze differently in the two paradigms. Erev et al. (1994) noted that when objective probabilities are independently defined, as in Bayesian revision of opinion studies, researchers analyze mean subjective estimates as a function of objective values and generally find underconfidence. In contrast, when objective probabilities are not independently definable, they analyze percentage correct as a function of the subjective estimates and generally find overconfidence. Erev et al. (1994) applied both types of analyses to three data sets and found that judgments appeared underconfident when analyzed one way and overconfident when analyzed the other way. They generated simple models that assumed well-calibrated underlying true judgment plus an error function and showed that such models yield the full range of observed results under standard methods of analysis. Erev et al. were concerned only with situations of numerical responses, but there is every reason to believe that their conclusions apply to verbal responding as well: that is, verbal probabilities imply underconfidence in one case and overconfidence in the other at least in part because they are an errorful representation of underlying judgment. Furthermore, because the degrees of under- and overconfidence are equivalent in the verbal and numerical cases, we can assume that so is the extent of error. Erev et al. (1994) concluded that questions of true under- and overconfidence cannot be properly addressed without a substantive and an error theory relating responses to judgment. The same applies, of course, to verbal responses. Moreover, this approach suggests that the same theories should apply in both cases.

The second point to make in concluding this summary is that although no systematic evidence has accrued thus far indicating that one mode of responding is more accurate than another, many avenues remain to be explored. For example, Zimmer (1983) suggested that the type of information subjects think about in making forecasts or predictions depends on the mode in which they must respond. He claims that people focus more strongly on qualitative data when they can respond verbally and on quantitative data when they can respond numerically. This is an intriguing idea that is consistent with the "compatibility effect" (Tversky, Sattath, & Slovic, 1988) and deserves follow-up.

Nevertheless, the available data provide no indication that the one mode of representation systematically leads to more accurate judgments than does the other. This conclusion is not implied by assumption B1, but it is eminently consistent with it, and no further summary principle is required.

B. CHOICE AND DECISION QUALITY

Although Knight (1921) and Keynes (1921) distinguished between various types of uncertainty, it was Ellsberg's (1961) famous paradox that made decision theorists pay closer attention to the effects of vagueness (or ambiguity, as it is often, but incorrectly, described) on preference (see Budescu & Wallsten, 1987, and Camerer & Weber, 1992, for reviews). Ellsberg's results, and subsequent empirical studies (e.g., Curley & Yates, 1985; Einhorn &

Hogarth, 1985) seem to indicate that, everything else being equal, most people prefer precise probabilities over vague (ambiguous) representations of uncertainty. This pattern of "avoidance of ambiguity" is consistent with findings, described previously, indicating that people prefer receiving numerical rather than verbal information. As phrases are relatively more vague than numbers, one would expect that choices and overt decisions (as operationalized by bids, attractiveness ratings, or rankings of risky options) reflect this preference. On the other hand, Zimmer's argument (1983, 1984) regarding the superiority of the verbal mode makes just the opposite predictions. Next, we describe a series of studies in which these two conflicting predictions were tested empirically.

Budescu et al. (1988) reported two experiments comparing the quality of decisions based on verbal and numerical probabilities. In the first stage of the study, we determined the single best numerical and verbal representations for 11 distinct spinners for each subject. Next, we used these representations to describe lotteries (some involving gains and others losses), which the subjects evaluated either by bidding for the lotteries (Experiment 1) or rating their attractiveness (Experiment 2). Although, on the average, subjects won more (by 1.2.%) and lost less (by 4.7%) with numerical probabilities, the bids, attractiveness ratings and decision times (after eliminating the possibility of calculations) were almost identical under the three presentation modes. Because the results may reflect the high level of intra-individual consistency in the use of words (further reinforced by the initial judgment stage), Budescu and Wallsten (1990) replicated the study with dyads. The F saw probability spinners and communicated the probabilities of the target events in either numerical or verbal form to the DM who had to bid for gambles. The DM could not see the spinner and the F was not informed of the amounts to be won or lost for each specific gamble. Yet, the mean bids, and the expected gains, were identical under the two modes of communication.

Erev and Cohen (1990) used a more realistic version of this dyadic paradigm. Four expert sportscasters provided numerical and verbal forecasts for 27 basketball events (e.g., one player will score more points than another) in a randomly chosen game from a group of games identified by the experimenters. Then, 36 students were asked to rate the attractiveness of gambles whose outcome probabilities were given by the experts' forecasts. The actual events were disguised, forcing the subjects to rely on the expert judgments and not on their own knowledge. The gambles were presented in sets consisting of eight events (with verbal or numerical probabilities and monetary outcomes) that the subjects ranked from the most to the least attractive under a payoff scheme that motivated careful responding. Subjects' ratings and expected payoffs were well above chance level but did not vary as a function of the mode of communication.

In a recent experiment (Gonzáles-Vallejo, Erev, and Wallsten, 1994), Fs made predictions about video games in which the event probabilities were controlled. Fs observed events on the computer screen and provided simultaneous verbal and numerical estimates of the event probabilities. Each DM subsequently was presented with sets of six monetary gambles, whose probabilities were the numerical or verbal forecasts of a particular F, and had to rank the gambles from the most to the least attractive under a payoff structure similar to that used by Erev and Cohen (1990). Once again, the DMs' expected profits were practically identical under the two modes of forecasting.

The single exception to this line of results is Experiment 5 of Tsao and Wallsten (1994). Fs provided numerical and verbal estimates of event chances when the number of possible outcomes was $n = 2$ or $n = 4$. On the basis of these estimates, DMs subsequently estimated (under a payoff scheme designed to promote accuracy) how many times out of 100 the event would occur. Estimates based on verbal and numerical judgments were equally accurate when $n = 2$, but not when $n = 4$. In the latter case, quality suffered in the verbal mode. This task differed from the other decision tasks in that it required the estimate of a sample statistic, rather than a choice or a bid for a gamble. Nevertheless, this suggests that more careful work is needed in contexts in which $n > 2$.

To summarize, with the single exception just noted, all of the experiments described here agree that, on the average, decision quality is unaffected by the mode in which the probability information is provided. To say the least, the result is puzzling in light of the material discussed in section III. In part, it may be a result of the fact that judgmental accuracy is roughly equivalent given verbal and numerical information, as described in section IV(A). But that explanation alone will not do, as it still does not explain the approximately equal decision quality given the wide interpersonal variability in interpreting phrases and the considerably greater imprecision of verbal versus numerical expressions. However, the next principle provides the link that in conjunction with the findings of section IV(A) brings together the two otherwise contradictory sets of results. We propose one more principle that suggests a subtle but important way in which the two modes, verbal and numerical, do differentially affect trial by trial decision behavior while generally leaving average results unaffected.

C. PRINCIPLE P4

The question we must address is How are imprecise assessments of uncertainty resolved for the purpose of taking action? (Assumption B2 asserts that such resolution takes place, but does not specify the mechanism.) A natural answer would be to assume that when faced with an expression covering a wide range of probabilities—but representing some values within that range better than others—one restrict attention to the best-described values. An extreme version of this assumption would be that for purposes of making a decision, one treats a phrase as equivalent to that probability (or to the mean of those probabilities) for which the membership function, $\mu_e(p)$ is maximal. If this were true, however, then decision variability would be equal under verbal and numerical information conditions, and it generally is not. For example, Budescu and Wallsten (1990) found, on a within-subject basis, that the variance of bids based on verbal probabilities was larger than the variance of numerical bids by a factor of 2.44. Thus, a weaker assumption is needed. We propose, instead, that **when combining, comparing, or trading-off information about uncertainty with information about other dimensions, such as outcome values, the uncertainty representation, $\mu_e(p)$, is converted from a vague interval to a point value by restricting attention only to values of p with membership above a threshold v, that is, for which $\mu_e(p) \geq v$.** A specific point value p^* is then selected probabilistically according to a weighting function proportional to the $\mu_e(p) \geq v$. Expressed formally, p^* is selected for expression e according to the density $f_e(p^*)$ defined by

$$f_e(p^*) = \frac{\mu_e(p^*)}{\int_x^y \mu_e(p)\, dp}, \qquad (7)$$

where

$$x = \begin{bmatrix} 0 \text{ if } \mu_e(p) \text{ monotonically decreases} \\ \text{Min}(p|\mu_e(p) = v) \text{ otherwise,} \end{bmatrix}$$

and

$$y = \begin{bmatrix} 1 \text{ if } \mu_e(p) \text{ monotonically increases} \\ \text{Max}(p|\mu_e(p) = v) \text{ otherwise,} \end{bmatrix}$$

Equation (7) says that membership values above the threshold v are converted to (proportional) choice probabilities.

Good but limited support for this principle comes from a study by Wallsten et al. (1988), in which subjects chose between two gambles, (a, p, 0) and (a, q, 0). That is, one gamble offered outcome a with probability p, and outcome 0 with probability $1-p$; and the other offered the same outcomes with probabilities q and $1-q$, respectively. The value, p, was easily estimated as the relative area of a visible spinner; whereas the value q was conveyed by means of a probability phrase. For each of the 10 probability phrase–outcome value combinations (five phrases by two outcomes), subjects made nine choices at each of six levels of p. Subsequent to the choice phase of the study, each subject provided membership functions for each phrase used. Finally, a single threshold parameter v was sought for each subject that provided for the best prediction of his or her tendency to choose the gamble with the visible spinner by converting membership values greater than or equal to the threshold to sampling weights. Although the model did not fit perfectly, the mean deviation between predicted and observed choice probabilities was very small, .01, for 9 of the 10 subjects.

We have replicated these results in unpublished work,[3] but have not pursued the obvious question of what factors control the placement of v. Various hypotheses are reasonable. One might argue, for example, that as decision importance increases, so too does motivation to consider the full range of possible meanings conveyed by an expression. Consequently, v should decrease with decision importance. Thus, as we argued earlier, when subjects are allowed but not required to give a probability range in situations of vague uncertainties, and the response is of no real consequence, they simplify their task to the greatest extent possible by setting $v = 1$. Presumably, they would set v lower for more important decisions. An alternative line of reasoning, however, suggests that v increases with decision importance, because, as illustrated earlier, people typically prefer precise information for important decisions; that is, as the stakes increase, so too does the necessity to make a clear decision. These competing conjectures remain to be tested. Along another dimension, assuming that the greater v, is the easier and more rapidly can the decision be made, one might expect that v increases with time pressure. Again, we have no data.

Principle P4 provides a qualitative explanation of Budescu and Wallsten's (1990) dyadic decision results, which were discussed previously, but has not been further tested. Clearly, additional evaluation is required. Nevertheless, assuming the principle's validity, we are in a position to understand why average decision quality is unaffected by probability mode. Note first that when a phrase is converted to a probability value, p^*, for decision purposes, its expected value, $E_e(p^*)$, is equivalent to W_e defined for $\mu_e(p)$ restricted

---

[3] Wallsten and Erev ran an additional nine subjects in essentially the same design, but with more observations per point, and obtained equivalent results.

to values greater than or equal to v. This fact can be seen by using Eq. (7) to obtain $E_e(p^*)$ and comparing the result to Eq. (1). Moreover, for symmetric single-peaked functions, W_e equals the peak probability, that is, the value p^{**} such that $\mu_e(p^{**}) = 1$. However, regardless of the shape of the membership function, as v increases $E_e(p^*)$ approaches p^{**} (or the mean of the p^{**}, should the value not be a single point). Therefore, we can claim that in general, when making decisions, people interpret phrases as equivalent to probabilities in the neighborhood ranging from their central value, W, to their peak value(s), p^{**}.

Two more steps are needed to complete the explanation of why average decision quality is unaffected by probability mode. Recall, first, that people treat numbers received from others as vague at least to some degree. Therefore, we can assume that just as occurs with phrases, DMs interpret numbers somewhat more broadly and centrally than the F intended. Second, recall from section IV(A) that verbal and numerical information is processed with roughly equivalent accuracy. On that basis, we can deduce that for a given DM, there is no systematic difference between W_e or p^{**} of the phrase selected by a F and the interpreted meaning of the numerical probability communicated by that F. Given this entire train of argument, it is not surprising that average decision quality was unaffected by probability mode in the experiments reviewed in section IV(B), while, simultaneously, decision variance was somewhat greater when communication was verbal than when it was numerical.

D. Principle P5

Decision patterns differ in more than just variance given verbal and numerical information, although the additional difference is sufficiently subtle that it eluded us for some time. We express this result as the following principle: **When combining, comparing, or trading-off information across dimensions, the relative weight accorded to a dimension is positively related to its precision.** In other words, the narrower $\mu_e(p)$ is, the more weight is accorded to p^*.

The finding leading to this principle was first evident in the data of a pilot study run by González-Vallejo et al. (1994). The effect was replicated in a second, much more substantial experiment, which we now consider. In the first phase, Fs observed uncertain events in a video game and expressed their judgments of the probabilities both verbally and numerically. These events were then used as the basis for gambles of the form (a, p, 0). DMs saw the gambles in sets of six and rank-ordered them from most to least preferred under a payoff scheme. DMs never saw the actual probabilities but only the Fs' numerical estimates for some sets and verbal estimates for others. The sets all were constructed such that the outcomes and probabilities were negatively correlated, and that the gambles' expected values agreed in rank order with the outcomes for one half of the sets, and with the probabilities for the other half. When the probabilities were expressed verbally, subjects' rankings correlated positively with the payoffs. In contrast, when the probabilities were expressed numerically, the subjects' rankings were positively related to the probabilities. Consequently, when ranking gamble sets in which outcomes were positively correlated with expected value, subjects made more money given the verbal probabilities than the numerical probabilities; and when ranking gamble sets with the opposite structure, the reverse occurred. This result is consistent with Tversky et al.'s (1988) contingent weighting model, suggesting that the relative weight given to the probability and the outcome dimensions depended on the information format. Thus, we see that *on the average* subjects can do equally well under either mode, but not given a particular stimulus structure.

Principle P5 also motivated, in part, a study by Gonzáles-Vallejo and Wallsten (1992) on preference reversals. Six subjects, acting as Fs, provided verbal and numerical probability judgments of events in video displays. These events served as the basis for gambles (a, *p*, 0) shown to 60 DMs, who saw only the outcomes, a, and the verbal or numerical estimates of *p*. They, in turn, bid twice for individual gambles and chose twice from pairs of gambles, once in each task given the numerical expressions and once given the verbal expressions. The regular pattern of reversals between choices and bids (e.g., Grether & Plott, 1979) was found in both modes, but its magnitude was much smaller in the verbal case. Looked at differently, bids were very similar given the verbal and numerical representations, but the choices were not. Considerably greater risk aversion was shown in the numerical case than in the verbal case.

This entire pattern of results is expected, given the conjunction of P5 and the oft-repeated generalization that "probabilities loom larger in choice than in bidding" (Tversky et al., 1988). That is, when bidding for gambles, people tend to focus relatively more strongly on the outcomes than on the probabilities. Therefore, an additional decrease in the weight accorded the probability dimension resulting from vagueness in the verbal condition has little effect on the bids. In contrast, this weight decrease strongly affects choice, where probabilities are in primary focus.

V. Recapitulation and Conclusions

A. ASSUMPTIONS AND PRINCIPLES

For ease of reference, it is useful to repeat here the two background assumptions and the five principles. We will then consider the epistemological status of each and their joint implications.

B1. Except in very special cases, all representations are vague to some degree in the minds of the originators and in the minds of the receivers.

B2. People use the full representation whenever feasible, but they narrow it, possibly to a single point, if the task requires them to do so.

P1. Membership functions can be meaningfully scaled.

P2. The location, spread, and shape of membership functions vary over individuals and depend on context and communication direction.

P3. Communication mode choices are sensitive to the degrees of vagueness inherent in the events being described, the source of the uncertainty, and the nature of the communication task.

P4. When combining, comparing, or trading-off information about uncertainty with information about other dimensions, such as outcome values, the uncertainty representation, $\mu_e(p)$, is converted from a vague interval to a point value by restricting attention to values of p with membership above a threshold v, that is, for which $\mu_e(p) \geq v$. A specific point value p^* is then selected probabilistically according to a weighting function proportional to the $\mu_e(p) \geq v$.

P5. When combining, comparing, or trading off information across dimensions, the relative weight accorded to a dimension is positively related to its precision.

Our story is straightforward. Rarely is one's opinion or judgment precise (B1), although one acts upon precise values when action is called for (B2). The nature and extent of one's vague representation depends on various individual, situational, and contextual factors (P2), and is measureable in a meaningful fashion (P1). One converts vague opinion to a point value for purposes of action by a probabilistic process that is sensitive to the form of the opinion and to the task (P4). However, despite this conversion, the degree of attention one accords to a dimension depends on its underlying vagueness (P5). Somewhat outside this stream that travels from opinion to action is the issue of communication mode preferences, which are systematically affected by degrees of vagueness (P3). Finally, also important but not formulated as a principle because it does not have theoretical content, is the fact that judgment is approximately equally accurate given verbal and numerical expressions of probability.

These assumptions and principles are not epistemologically equivalent. We have simply asserted assumption B1, but numerous corollaries that can be inferred from it are empirically supported. Similarly, there are no data to sustain assumption B2 in its full generality, but a particular instantiation of it, principle P4, is well supported. Principles P1 and P5 are well buttressed by data; whereas, in contrast, principle P3 describes a range of results, but does not have independent post hoc support. Finally, principle P2 is at this point a reasonable conjecture that is consistent with a good deal of related evidence.

B. Concluding Comments

We have attempted to review a substantial portion of the literature on linguistic probability processing, to develop a coherent theory of such processing in the form of a small set of principles, and to suggest additional necessary research. In this final section, we summarize and extend remarks relating to the third goal that have been sprinkled throughout the chapter.

An important missing link in the present development is firm support for principle P2, that membership function characteristics vary systematically with individuals and contexts. Two major obstacles must be overcome in order to achieve this goal, one technical and the other substantive. On the technical end, a relatively large number of repetitive judgments are required to obtain accurate and reliable empirical membership functions. The task is boring, it is unlikely that successive judgments are independent, and the very judgments being elicited may cause perceived meanings to change during the course of long sessions. One possible solution is to rely more heavily on parametric curve fitting for the various membership functions. In the past, we have used cubic polynomials (Wallsten et al., 1988; Zwick, 1987), but other approaches (splines, piecewise logistics) may work just as well. These techniques may require fewer points and the effects of the various factors may be detected by examining trends in the parameters of the fitted functions.

More important, however, may be the lack of a good theory of context and an appropriate framework within which to deal with individual differences. With one exception (the unequivocal distinction between the two directions of communication), most variables that have been examined (perceived base rate, severity, etc.) are continuous and their levels rely on subjective judgments. Moreover, the classification of cases into discrete "contexts" is all too often after the fact and invariably arbitrary. (Are medical scenarios describing a fractured ankle or wrist following a friendly game of tennis or basketball different or indentical contexts?) Similarly, the notion that different people may have different membership functions for the same terms in a given context, as intuitive and reasonable as it may seem, requires a good theoretical foundation. The problem is not simply to show that *likely* is understood differently by different people, but to show that this variance is systematically related to other meaningful variables. For example, Weber (1988) proposed and Weber and Bottom (1989) tested descriptive risk measures for risky prospects involving precise numerical probabilities. It would be interesting to relate these measures to parameters of membership functions for verbal probabilities involved in similar prospects.

Related to issues of context and individual differences is the intriguing possibility that membership functions will provide a means of quantifying the semantic content of probability phrases and become standard tools for dealing with important psycholinguistic problems. That goal will be reached when quantitative models of context and individual differences are developed that predict meaning as represented by membership functions. Reyna's (1981) work on negation, Reagan et al.'s (1989) analysis of complementary symmetry, and Cliff's (1959) well-known study on adjective–adverb combinations are examples of other issues that might be addressed more fully if the (point numerical) representations of the verbal stimuli were to be replaced by appropriate membership functions. An example of the possible applications of these functions is provided in a study by Zwick, Carlstein, and Budescu (1987). Subjects judged the degree of similarity between pairs of terms (say, *likely* and *good chance*) and also provided judgments for membership functions of each term. Then, a large number of mathematical measures of similarity between functions were calculated and used to predict the empirically determined proximities. The results of this study could, for example, be used to determine a mathematical definition of synonymity.

Crucial to our approach is the assumption embodied in B2, that representations are treated in their vague form whenever possible and reduced to precise values only when necessary. The idea is so reasonable, and seems so adaptive, that we would argue it must be correct at some level. The underlying processes, however, are very much open to question. We provided a stochastic mechanism in the form of principle P4 and offered limited evidence in support of it, but more research is needed to establish its credibility. Particularly important is the question of how the threshold, v, is set when making decisions based on vague inputs. In work to date (Wallsten et al., 1988), v has been left as a free parameter, but for the theory to be useful, we must learn how it depends on context, task, or individual variables.

Another topic requiring additional work concerns the relationships between decision quality, preference patterns, and linguistic processing when the number of possible outcomes exceeds two. In our judgment, we understand these issues fairly well now in the case of two alternatives. The Tsao and Wallsten (1994) data, however, suggest that matters are much more complicated in the general case.

Finally, we point out that our treatment of the role of linguistic information processing in judgment and preference is incomplete in another important way. That is, we must consider how people combine multiple inputs (say, judgments from two or more experts or consultants) to arrive at their own opinion. In section II(B), we amplified assumption B2 by stating that "people treat separate judgments in their vague form when receiving *and combining them,* but they restrict attention to a narrow range of uncertainty or to a single point value when making specific decisions" (emphasis added here). Subsequently, we amplified the latter part of that statement and ignored the former. That issue is treated to some degree, however, in a recent chapter by Wallsten, Budescu, and Tsao (1994).

ACKNOWLEDGMENTS

The order of authors is arbitrary; both authors contributed equally. Preparation of this chapter was facilitated by an Arnold O. Beckman Research Award from the Research Board of the University of Illinois and by National Science Foundation Grant SBR-9222159. We acknowledge the contribution of many students and colleagues who have been involved in various stages and aspects of the work summarized in this chapter. In particular, we thank Brent Cohen, Jim Cox, Ido Erev, Sam Fillenbaum, Claudia González-Vallejo, Amnon Rapoport, Chen-Jung Tsao, Andrea Shapiro, and Rami Zwick for their help in shaping our thinking about these issues over the years.

REFERENCES

Bass, B. M., Cascio, W. F., & O'Connor, E. J. (1974). Magnitude estimation of expressions of frequency and amount. *Journal of Applied Psychology, 59,* 313–320.

Behn, R. D., & Vaupel, J. W. (1982). *Quick analysis for busy decision makers.* New York: Basic.

Beyth-Marom, R. (1982). How probable is probable? A numerical translation of verbal probability expressions. *Journal of Forecasting, 1,* 257–269.

Bonissone, P. P., Gans, S. S., & Decker, K. S. (1987). RUM: A layered architecture for reasoning with uncertainty. In *Proceedings of IJCAI* (pp. 373–379). Milan, Italy.

Bortolan, G., & Degani, R. (1985). A review of some methods for ranking fuzzy subsets. *Fuzzy Sets and Systems, 15,* 1–19.

Brackner, J. W. (1985). How to report contingent losses in financial statements? *Journal of Business Forecasting, 4*(2), 13–18.

Bradburn, N. M., & Miles, C. (1979). Vague quantifiers. *Public Opinion Quarterly, 43,* 92–101.

Brun, W., & Teigen, K. H. (1988). Verbal probabilities: Ambiguous, context-dependent, or both? *Organizational Behavior and Human Decision Processes, 41,* 390–404.

Bryant, G. D. & Norman G. R. (1980). Expressions of probability: Words and numbers. *New England Journal of Medicine, 302,* 411.

Budescu, D. V., & Wallsten, T. S. (1985). Consistency in interpretation of probabilistic phrases. *Organizational Behavior and Human Decision Processes, 36,* 391–405.

Budescu, D. V., & Wallsten, T. S. (1987). Subjective estimation of precise and vague uncertainties. In G. Wright & P. Ayton (Eds.), *Judgmental forecasting* (pp. 63–81). Sussex, UK: Wiley.

Budescu, D. V., & Wallsten, T. S. (1990). Dyadic decisions with verbal and numerical probabilities. *Organizational Behavior and Human Decision Processes, 46,* 240–263.

Budescu, D. V., Weinberg, S., & Wallsten, T. S. (1988). Decisions based on numerically and verberbally expressed uncertainties. *Journal of Experimental Psychology: Human Perception and Performance, 14,* 281–294.

Camerer, C., & Weber, M. (1992). Recent developments in modeling preferences: Uncertainty and ambiguity. *Journal of Risk and Uncertainty, 5,* 325–370.

Chesley, G. R. (1985). Interpretation of uncertainty expressions. *Contemporary Accounting Research, 2,* 179–199.

Clark, D. A. (1990). Verbal uncertainty expressions: A review of two decades of research. *Current Psychology: Research and Reviews, 9,* 203–235.

Clarke, V. A., Ruffin, C. L., Hill, D. J., & Beamen, A. L. (1992). Ratings of orally presented verbal expressions of probability by a heterogeneous sample. *Journal of Applied Social Psychology, 22,* 638–656.

Cliff, N. (1959). Adverbs as multipliers. *Psychological Review, 66,* 27–44.

Cohen, B. L., & Wallsten, T. S. (1992). The effect of constant outcome value on judgments and decision making given linguistic probabilities. *Journal of Behavioral Decision Making, 5,* 53–72.

Curley, S. P., & Yates, J. F. (1985). The center and range of the probability interval as factors affecting ambiguity preferences. *Organizational Behavior and Human Decision Processes, 36,* 273–287.

Degani, R., & Bortolan, G. (1988). The problem of linguistic approximation in clinical decision making. *International Journal of Approximate Reasoning, 2,* 143–162.

DeGroot, M. H. (1970). *Optimal statistical decisions.* New York: McGraw-Hill.

Edwards, W. (1968). Conservatism in human information processing. In B. Kleinmuntz (Ed.), *Formal representations of human judgment* (pp. 17–52). Wiley, NY.

Einhorn, H. J., & Hogarth, R. M. (1985). Ambiguity and uncertainty in probabilistic inference. *Psychological Review 92,* 433–461.

Ellsberg, D. (1961). Risk, ambiguity, and the Savage axioms. *Quarterly Journal of Economics, 75,* 643–669.

Erev, I., & Cohen, B. L. (1990). Verbal versus numerical probabilities: Efficiency, biases, and the preference paradox. *Organizational Behavior and Human Decision Processes, 45,* 1–18.

Erev, I., Wallsten, T. S., & Budescu, D. V. (1994). Simultaneous over- and underconfidence: The role of error in judgment processes. *Psychological Review, 101,* 519–527.

Erev, I., Wallsten, T. S., & Neal, M. (1991). Vagueness, ambiguity, and the cost of mutual understanding. *Psychological Science, 2,* 321–324.

Farkas, A., & Makai-Csasar, M. (1988). Communication or dialogue of deafs: Pitfalls of use of fuzzy quantifiers. In *Second Network Seminar of the International Union of Psychological Science.* Amsterdam: North-Holland.

Fillenbaum, S., Wallsten, T. S., Cohen, B., & Cox, J. A. (1991). Some effects of vocabulary and communication task on the understanding and use of vague probability expressions. *American Journal of Psychology, 104,* 35–60.

Gärdenfors, P., & Sahlin, N. E. (1982). Unreliable probabilities, risk taking, and decision making. *Synthese, 53,* 361–386.

Gonzales, M., & Frenck-Mestre, C. (1993). Determinants of numerical versus verbal probabilities. *Acta Psychologica, 83,* 33–51.f

González-Vallejo, C. C., Erev, I., & Wallsten, T. S. (1994). Do decision quality and preference order depend on whether probabilities are verbal or numerical? *American Journal of Psychology, 107,* 157–172.

González-Vallejo, C. C., & Wallsten, T. S. (1992). Effects of probability mode on preference reversal. *Journal of Experimental Psychology: Learning, Memory, and Cognition, 18,* 855–864.

Grether, D. M., & Plott, C. R. (1979). Economic theory of choice and the preference reversal phenomenon. *American Economic Review, 69,* 623–638.

Hamm, R. M. (1991). Selection of verbal probabilities: A solution for some problems of verbal probability expression. *Organizational Behavior and Human Decision Processes, 48,* 193–223.

Hammerton, M. (1976). How much is a large part? *Applied Ergonomics, 7,* 10–12.

Holyoak, K. J. (1978). Comparative judgments with numerical reference points. *Cognitive Psychology, 10,* 203–243.

Jaffe-Katz, A., Budescu, D. V., & Wallsten, T. S. (1989). Timed magnitude comparisons of numerical and nonnumerical expressions of uncertainty. *Memory & Cognition, 17,* 249–264.

Johnson, E. M. (1973). *Numerical encoding of qualitative expressions of uncertainty.* Technical Paper No. 250. U.S. Army Research Institute for the Behavioral and Social Sciences.

Johnson, E. M., & Huber, G. P. (1977). The technology of utility assessment. *IEEE Transactions on Systems, Man, and Cybernetics, SMC-7,* 311–325.

Kadane, J. B. (1990). Comment: Codifying chance. *Statistical Science, 5,* 18–20.

Keynes, J. M. (1921). *A treatise on probability.* London: Macmillan.

Knight, F. H. (1921). *Risk, uncertainty, and profit.* Chicago: University of Chicago Press.

Kong, A., Barnett, G. O., Mosteller, F., & Youtz, C. (1986). How medical professionals evaluate expressions of probability. *The New England Journal of Medicine, 315,* 740–744.

Lichtenstein, S., Fischhoff, B., & Phillips, L. D. (1982). Calibration of probabilities: The state of the art to 1980. In D. Kahneman, P. Slovic, & A. Tversky (Eds.), *Judgment under uncertainty: Heuristics and biases* (pp. 306–334). Cambridge: Cambridge University Press.

Lichtenstein, S., & Newman, J. R. (1967). Empirical scaling of common verbal phrases associated with numerical probabilities. *Psychonomic Science, 9,* 563–564.

López de Mántaras, R., Meseguer, P., Sanz, F., Sierra, C., & Verdaguer, A. (1988). A fuzzy logic approach to the management of linguistically expressed uncertainty. *IEEE Transactions on Systems, Man, and Cybernetics, 18,* 144–151.

Mapes, R. E. A. (1979). Verbal and numerical estimates of probability terms. *Journal of General Internal Medicine, 6,* 237.

Marshall, E. (1986). Feynman issues his own shuttle report, attacking NASA's risk estimates. *Science, 232,* 1596.

Marshall, E. (1988). Academy panel faults NASA's safety analysis. *Science, 239,* 1233.

Merz, J. F., Druzdzel, M. J., & Mazur, D. J. (1991). Verbal expressions of probability in informed consent litigation. *Journal of Medical Decision Making, 11,* 273–281.

Moore, P. G. (1977). The manager's struggle with uncertainty. *Journal of the Royal Statistical Society, 140,* 129–165.

Moore, P. G., & Thomas, H. (1975). Measuring uncertainty. *International Journal of Management Science, 3,* 657.

Mosier, C. I. (1941). A psychometric study of meaning. *Journal of Social Psychology, 39,* 31–36.

Mosteller, F., & Youtz, C. (1990). Quantifying probabilistic expressions. *Statistical Science, 5,* 2–16.

Moxey, L. M., & Sanford, A. J. (1993). *Communicating quantities: A psychological perspective.* Hove, UK: Erlbaum.

Mullet, E., & Rivet, I. (1991). Comprehension of verbal probability expressions in children and adolescents. *Language and Communication, 11,* 217–225.

Murphy, A. H., & Brown, B. G. (1983). Forecast terminology: Composition and interpretation of public weather forecasts. *Bulletin of the American Meteorological Society, 64,* 13–22.

Murphy, A. H., Lichtenstein, S., Fischhoff, B., & Winkler, R. L. (1980). Misinterpretations of precipitation probability forecasts. *Bulletin of the American Meteorological Society, 61,* 695–701.

Nakao, M. A., & Axelrod, S. (1983). Numbers are better than words: Verbal specifications of frequency have no place in medicine. *American Journal of Medicine, 74,* 1061.

National Weather Service (1984). *Weather service operations manual.* Silver Spring, MD: National Oceanic and Atmospheric Administration.

Newstead, S. E. (1988). Quantifiers as fuzzy concepts. In T. Zetenyi (Ed.), *Fuzzy sets in psychology* (pp. 51–72). North-Holland: Elsevier.

Norwich, A. M., & Turksen, I. B. (1984). A model for the measurement of membership and the consequences of its empirical implementation. *Fuzzy Sets and Systems, 12,* 1–25.

Parducci, A. (1968). How often is often. *American Psychologist, 23,* 828.

Pepper, S. (1981). Problems in the quantification of frequency expression. In D. W. Fiske (Ed.), *New directions for methodology of social and behavioral science.* New York: Jossey-Bass.

Pepper, S., & Prytulak, L. S. (1974). Sometimes frequently means seldom: Context effects in the interpretation of quantitative expressions. *Journal of Research in Personality, 8,* 95–101.

Rapoport, A., Wallsten, T. S., & Cox, J. A. (1987). Direct and indirect scaling of membership functions of probability phrases. *Mathematical Modeling, 9,* 397–417.

Rapoport, A., Wallsten, T. S., Erev, I., & Cohen, B. L. (1990). Revision of opinion with verbally and numerically expressed uncertainties. *Acta Psychologica, 74,* 61–79.

Reagan, R. T., Mosteller, F., & Youtz, C. (1989). Quantitative meanings of verbal probability expressions. *Journal of Applied Psychology, 74,* 433–442.

Reyna, V. F. (1981). The language of possibility and probability: Effects of negation on meaning. *Memory & Cognition, 9,* 642–650.

Rubin, D. C. (1979). On measuring fuzziness: A comment on "a fuzzy set approach to modifiers and vagueness in natural language." *Journal of Experimental Psychology: General, 108,* 486–489.

Schkade, D. A., & Kleinmuntz, D. N. (1994). Information displays and choice processes: Differential effects of organization, form, and sequence. *Organizational Behavior and Human Decision Processes, 57,* 319–337.

Shapiro, A. J., & Wallsten, T. S. (1994). *Base-rate effects on interpreting verbally and numerically communicated probabilities.* Unpublished manuscript. University of North Carolina.

Simpson, R. H. (1944). The specific meanings of certain terms indicating differing degrees of frequency. *Quarterly Journal of Speech, 30,* 328–330.

Stone, D. N., & Schkade, D. A. (1991). Numeric and linguistic information representation in multiattribute choice. *Organizational Behavior and Human Decision Processes, 49,* 42–59.

Sutherland, H. J., Lockwood, G. A., Tritchler, D. L., Sem, F., Brooks, L., & Till, J. E. (1991). Communicating probabilistic information to cancer patients: Is there "noise" on the line? *Social Science and Medicine, 32,* 725–731.

Svenson, O., & Karlson, G. (1986). Attractiveness of decision alternatives characterized by numerical and non-numerical information. *Scandinavian Journal of Psychology, 27,* 74–84.

Teigen, K. H. (1988a). When are low-probability events judged to be 'probable'? Effects of outcome-set characteristics on verbal probability estimates. *Acta Psychologica, 67,* 157–174.

Teigen, K. H. (1988b). The language of uncertainty. *Acta Psychologica, 68,* 27–38.

Teigen, K. H., & Brun, W. (1993). Yes, but it is uncertain: Direction and communicative intention of verbal probabilistic terms. Presented at *Subjective Probability, Utility, and Decision Making (SPUDM) 14,* Aix-en Provence, France.

Timmermans, D. (1994). The roles of experience and domain of expertise in using numerical and verbal probability terms in medical decisions. *Medical Decision Making, 14,* 146–156.

Tsao, C. J., & Wallsten, T. S. (1994). Effects of the number of outcomes on the interpretation and selection of verbal and numerical probabilities in dyadic decisions. Unpublished manuscript.

Tversky, A., Sattath, S., & Slovic, P. (1988). Contingent weighting in judgment and choice. *Psychological Review, 95,* 371–384.

Vesely, W. E., & Rasmuson, D. M. (1984). Uncertainties in nuclear probabilistic risk analysis. *Risk Analysis, 4,* 313–322.

von Winterfeldt, D., & Edwards, W. (1986). *Decision analysis and behavioral research.* Cambridge: Cambridge University Press.

Wallsten, T. S. (1990). Measuring vague uncertainties and understanding their use in decision making. In G. M. von Furstenberg (Ed.), *Acting under uncertainty* (pp. 377–398). Norwell: Kluwer.

Wallsten, T. S., Budescu, D. V., & Erev, I. (1988). Understanding and using linguistic uncertainties. *Acta Psychologica, 68,* 39–52.

Wallsten, T. S., Budescu, D. V., Rapoport, A., Zwick, R., & Forsyth, B. H. (1986). Measuring the vague meanings of probability terms. *Journal of Experimental Psychology: General, 115,* 348–365.

Wallsten, T. S., Budescu, D. V., & Tsao, C. J. (1994). *Combining linguistic probabilities.* Paper presented at the Symposium on Qualitative Aspects of Decision Making, Universität Regensburg, Regensburg, Germany, July 20, 1994.

Wallsten, T. S., Budescu, D. V., & Zwick, R. (1993). Comparing the calibration and coherence numerical and verbal probability judgments. *Management Science, 39,* 176–190.

Wallsten, T. S., Budescu, D. V., Zwick, R., & Kemp, S. M. (1993). Preference and reasons for communicating probabilistic information in numerical or verbal terms. *Bulletin of the Psychonomic Society, 31,* 135–138.

Wallsten, T. S., Filenbaum, S., & Cox, J. A. (1986). Base-rate effects on the interpretations of probability and frequency expressions. *Journal of Memory and Language, 25,* 571–587.

Weber, E. U. (1988). A descriptive measure of risk. *Acta Psychologica, 69,* 185–203.

Weber, E. U., & Bottom, W. P. (1989). Axiomatic measures of perceived risk: Some tests and extensions. *Journal of Behavioral Decision Making, 2,* 113–131.

Weber, E. U., & Hilton, D. J. (1990). Contextual effects in the interpretations of probability words: Perceived base rate and severity of events. *Journal of Experimental Psychology: Human Perception and Performance, 16,* 781–789.

Wright, G. N., Phillips, L. D., Whalley, P. C., Choo, G. T., Ng, K. O., Tan, I., & Wisudha, A. (1978). Cultural differences in probabilistic thinking. *Journal of Cross-Cultural Psychology, 9,* 285–299.

Wyden, P. (1979). *Bay of Pigs.* New York: Simon & Schuster.

Yager, R. R. (1981). A procedure for ordering fuzzy sets on the unit interval. *Information Sciences, 24,* 143–161.

Yates, J. F., Zhu, Y., Ronis, D. L., Wang, D.-F., Shinotsuka, H., & Toda, M. (1989). Probability judgment accuracy: China, Japan, and the United States. *Organizational Behavior and Human Decision Processes, 43,* 145–171.

Zimmer, A. C. (1983). Verbal versus numerical processing of subjective probabilities. In R. W. Scholz (Eds.), *Decision making under uncertainty.* Amsterdam: Elsevier.

Zimmer, A. C. (1984). A model for the interpretation of verbal predictions. *International Journal of Man and Machine Studies, 20,* 121–134.

Zwick, R. (1987). *Combining stochastic uncertainty and linguistic inexactness: Theory and experimental evaluation.* Unpublished doctoral dissertation. University of North Carolina at Chapel Hill.

Zwick, R., Carlstein, E., & Budescu, D. V. (1987). Measures of similarity among fuzzy concepts: A comparative analysis. *International Journal of Approximate Reasoning, 1,* 221–242.

Zwick, R., & Wallsten, T. S. (1989). Combining stochastic and linguistic inexactness: Theory and experimental evaluation of four fuzzy probability models. *International Journal of Man and Machine Studies, 30,* 69–111.

COMPOSITIONAL ANOMALIES IN THE SEMANTICS OF EVIDENCE

John M. Miyamoto, Richard Gonzalez, and Shihfen Tu

I. Introduction

Semantic theory plays a central role in the normative and descriptive theory of deductive inference, but its role in the study of inductive inference has been much less prominent. The disparity is both odd and understandable. It is odd because deductive and inductive reasoning both rely heavily on linguistic representations, and semantic theory is the natural tool for investigating inference within propositional structures. It is understandable because the logical approach to induction, as championed by Lambert, Keynes, and Carnap, to name only a few, was eclipsed by important developments in the theory of subjective probability, following the work of De Finetti, Savage, and others. From a semantical perspective, the basis for subjective probability theory is very elementary, namely, that there exist Boolean algebras of events that are ordered by how strongly one believes that they are true (the belief strength ordering). The axiomatic theory of subjective probability specifies further properties of belief strength that characterize so-called coherent beliefs; if strength of belief is coherent in this sense, then there exist numerical probabilities that represent the belief strength ordering and satisfy the mathematical laws of probability (Fine, 1973; Krantz, Luce, Suppes, & Tversky, 1971).[1]

---

[1] There is, of course, an alternative approach to formalizing subjective probability in terms of preferences among uncertain options or *acts* (Fine, 1973). This approach, due to Savage (1954), will not be discussed here because the phenomena in this paper concern strength of belief only, and not preferences for risky or uncertain options.

THE PSYCHOLOGY OF LEARNING
AND MOTIVATION, VOL. 32

319

Historically, the study of natural language semantics has been closely linked to theories of deductive inference because deductive relations among propositions serve as clues to semantic structure (Davidson & Harman, 1975a; Quine 1960). A theory of semantics relates three aspects of language: (1) the syntactic structure of propositions, that is, a specification of how complex propositions are built from simpler parts; (2) the semantic structure of propositions, that is, a specification of the relation between propositional structure, reference, and truth values; and (3) inference rules that define inferential relations in terms of syntactic and semantic structure. Together these three aspects constitute a compositional theory of inference, a theory of the relationship between deductive inference and the compositional structure of propositions. A classical example of this line of analysis is the inference rule called *modus ponens,* according to which the truth of a proposition *Q* may be inferred, given that *if P, then Q* and *P* are true. The truth table for the material conditional (the if–then statement of the propositional calculus) is a semantic hypothesis concerning the meaning of conditional statements. It serves as part of the explanation for why inferences of the form of modus ponens are valid. Of course, this hypothesis is open to debate—the truth table for the material conditional is widely accepted as a semantic analysis of if–then statements in mathematical proofs, but it is quite debatable as an analysis of conditionals in ordinary (nonmathematical) discourse (Traugott, ter Meulen, Reilly, & Ferguson, 1986). Our point is simply that deductive relations between conditionals and other statements constitute evidence for the semantics of conditionals, and, more generally, deductive relations among diverse natural language statements constitute evidence for theories of the semantic structure of natural language (Davidson & Harman, 1975b; McCawley, 1993).

What we hope to show in this chapter is that there are many empirical phenomena that exhibit interesting interactions between the compositional structure of propositions and inferences drawn inductively from evidence. Just as deductive relations serve as clues to the semantic structure of propositions, relations between belief strength, propositional structure, and evidence serve as further clues to semantic structure. We begin by describing five empirical phenomena that exemplify interactions between propositional structure, evidence, and judgments of belief. We then describe the basic elements of a semantic approach to the theory of evidence. A semantic theory of evidence is a theory of how strength of belief is affected by two factors: (1) the structure of the evidence, and (2) the compositional structure of propositions. What we present is a framework for studying the interaction between propositional structure, evidence, and belief strength. Next, we consider a variety of empirical results that illustrate concretely the relationship between strength of belief, propositional structure, and the structure of evidence. Some of these results are well known in the literature; for example, we will discuss conjunction and disjunction errors in probability judgment from the perspective of a semantic theory of evidence. Other results are less well known; for example, aspects of counterfactual reasoning can be treated as problems in the semantics of evidence. What we hope to show is that the concept of a semantic theory of evidence provides a unifying framework for seeking general answers to the question of how belief strength is affected by natural language representations and the structure of evidence.

Many of the phenomena discussed in this chapter can be characterized as compositional anomalies—they are cases in which observed relations in belief strength conflict with the semantic structure of propositions, or at least with well-established theories of this semantic structure. The term *compositional* is deserved, because the conflicts arise in the relationship between the belief strengths of complex propositions and their component propositions. One reason for thinking that semantic theories of evidence will have something new to say about language structure is that compositional anomalies demonstrate the existence of perplexing inconsistencies between inductive and deductive inference. We will return to this point after presenting examples of such inconsistencies.

II. Five Compositional Anomalies in Probability Judgment

We present five examples of compositional anomalies in probability judgment. These examples serve as illustrations in a later section where a theoretical framework for the semantics of evidence is presented.

The first two examples are no doubt very familiar, namely, the occurrence of conjunction and disjunction errors in probability judgment. A *conjunction error* is said to occur if an individual judges $P(A \cap B) > P(A)$ or $P(A \cap B) > P(B)$. A *disjunction error* is said to occur if an individual judges $P(A \cup B) < P(A)$ or $P(A \cup B) < P(B)$. Many experiments have demonstrated the occurrence of conjunction and disjunction errors (Carlson & Yates, 1989; Morier & Borgida, 1984; Tversky & Kahneman, 1983; Yates & Carlson, 1986). The famous Linda problem of Tversky and Kahneman (1983) can be used to elicit both types of errors. Tversky and Kahneman (1983) presented subjects with the following description of a fictitious individual:

Linda is 31 years old, single, outspoken and very bright. She majored in philosophy. As a student, she was deeply concerned with issues of discrimination and social justice, and also participated in antinuclear demonstrations

Subjects were asked to rank order a series of statements according to the likelihood that they were true. Among these were statements (2), (3), and (4) in Table I. Tversky and Kahneman (1983) found that the majority of subjects ranked the probabilities in the order: $P(FM) > P(BT \cup FM) > P(BT)$. Morier and Borgida (1984) replicated the Tversky and Kahneman (1983) study with various alterations, one of which was to add the disjunctive statement (5) to the set of statements (see Table I). They found that mean probability estimates were ordered as follows:

$$P(FM) > P(BT \cup FM) > P(BT \cap FM) > P(BT). \tag{1}$$

In these comparisons, judgments of $P(BT \cap FM)$ were significantly greater than judgments of $P(BT)$, and judgments of $P(FM)$ were significantly greater than judgments of $P(BT \cup FM)$. Although Morier and Borgida (1984) did not report a statistical test for $P(FM)$ versus $P(BT \cup FM)$, one can infer that $P(FM)$ was significantly greater than $P(BT \cup FM)$ from the reported proportion of "union errors" and sample sizes ($z = 2.88, p < .005$, two-tailed sign test). These results demonstrate the occurrence of conjunction and disjunction errors with the Linda problem. Numerous other instances of conjunction and disjunction errors have been documented (Bar-Hillel & Neter, 1993; Carlson & Yates, 1989; Tversky & Kahneman, 1983; Wells, 1985; Yates & Carlson, 1986).

Conjunction and disjunction errors are anomalies of propositional composition because probability judgments for conjunctions and disjunctions are inconsistent with logical relations that are implied by the compositional

TABLE I

Statement	Probability of event	Propositional notation
2. Linda is a bank teller.	$P(BT)$	BT
3. Linda is active in the feminist movement.	$P(FM)$	FM
4. Linda is a bank teller and is active in the feminist movement.	$P(BT \cap FM)$	$BT \wedge FM$
5. Linda is a bank teller or is active in the feminist movement.	$P(BT \cup FM)$	$BT \vee FM$
6. Suppose that in addition to the other information about Linda, you are told that she is active in the feminist movement. What is the probability that she is a bank teller?	$P(BT \mid FM)$	$BT \mid FM$

structure of these propositions. Later, we will analyze these errors more carefully; but first, we present other examples of compositional anomalies.

Shafir, Smith, and Osherson (1990) discovered an interesting variant on the conjunction error. Suppose that one conducts a survey of people who are shopping in a large mall. Among the people contacted in the survey are young bankers, older bankers, and many other types of people. Now consider the two statements:

Statement	Probability of event
7. Every single banker in the group is conservative.	$P[(\forall x)(x \in B \to x \in C)]$
8. Every single young banker in the group is conservative.	$P[(\forall x)(x \in Y \cap B \to x \in C)]$

If every banker in a group is conservative, then every young banker in the group is conservative, but not vice versa. Consequently, the probability that (8) is true must be equal or greater than the probability that (7) is true, or symbolically, it must be the case that

$$P[(\forall x)(x \in Y \cap B \to x \in C)] \geq P[(\forall x)(x \in B \to x \in C)], \qquad (9)$$

where $\to$ denotes the material conditional (if–then) and $(\forall x)$ denotes the universal quantification (for all x). Let us say that an individual commits a *quantificational conjunction error* (QCE) if he or she judges $P[(\forall x)(x \in Y \cap B \to x \in C)] < P[(\forall x)(x \in B \to x \in C)]$ for some choice of events Y, B, and C. Shafir et al. (1990) demonstrated empirically that QCEs occur in statements that are structurally analogous to (7) and (8). The key feature of these statements is that a prototypical B is a C, but a prototypical $Y \cap B$ is not a C; for example, a prototypical banker is conservative, but a prototypical young banker is not. QCEs appear to result from the fact that the more inclusive category (e.g., "bankers") is more typical of the predicate (e.g., "conservative") than the less inclusive category (e.g., "young bankers").

Miyamoto, Lundell, and Tu (1988) discovered another anomaly in the relation between conjunctive and conditional probabilities. Note that if $1 > P(X) > 0$ and A is any other event, then $P(A \cap X)/P(X) > P(A \cap X)$. Applying the definition of conditional probability, we have

$$P(A \mid X) > P(A \cap X). \qquad (10)$$

If A = "Linda is a bank teller" and X = "Linda is active in the feminist movement," then (10) shows that, normatively, Linda is more likely to be a bank teller given that she is a feminist than she is likely to be a bank teller and a feminist. We will say that a *conditionalization error* has occurred if a subject judges $P(A \mid X) < P(A \cap X)$. Miyamoto et al. (1988) had subjects read the description of Linda and then rate the probability of various statements. Different samples of subjects rated the probabilities of statements (4) and (6), which were intermixed with other statements that did not pertain to bank tellers or feminists. Not surprisingly, subjects gave significantly higher ratings to the conjunctive probability (4) than to the conditional probability (6) (Mann-Whitney $U = 7,233.5$, $n = 134$, 167, $p < .001$, two-tailed).

In a second problem, subjects were asked to rate the probability of various weather conditions in Seattle, among which were included statements (11) and (12):

Statement	Probability of event
11. Suppose it is an overcast day in mid-November. Rate the probability that it rains and the temperature remains below 38 degrees.	$P(RN \cap TM)$
12. Suppose it is an overcast day in mid-November and it has begun to rain. Rate the probability that the temperature remains below 38 degrees.	$P(TM \mid RN)$

Subjects were University of Washington undergraduates who presumably knew that rain is common in Seattle during the month of November, but the combination of near freezing weather and rain is rare but not impossible. Different samples of subjects rated statements (11) and (12) along with other filler statements. Once again, the conjuctive probability (11) received a significantly higher rating than the conditional probability (12) (Mann-Whitney $U = 8,377.0$, $n = 172$, 154, $p < .001$, two-tailed). These results demonstrate the occurrence of conditionalization errors. We will describe analogous conditionalization errors in counterfactual reasoning later in this chapter and discuss a psychological explanation for this phenomenon at that time.

Consider next a comparison of conditional and unconditional probabilities that is motivated by the following relationships.

$$P(A \mid X) \geq P(X \mid A) \quad \text{iff} \quad \frac{P(A \cap X)}{P(X)} \geq \frac{P(A \cap X)}{P(A)} \tag{13}$$

$$\text{iff} \quad P(A) \geq P(X) \tag{14}$$

Therefore, the relative ordering of the conditional probabilities, $P(A \mid X)$

versus $P(X \mid A)$, should be the same as the relative ordering of the unconditional probabilities, $P(A)$ versus $P(X)$. Let us say that *conditionals are inconsistent with priors* if an individual judges $P(A \mid X) > P(X \mid A)$ and $P(A) < P(X)$, or vice versa. A simple example illustrates how conditionals could be inconsistent with priors. Suppose that Frank and Billy are two exconvicts who meet at a Chicago bar. Subjects were asked to rate the probability of the following statements:

Statement	Probability of event
15. What is the probability that Frank pulls a knife on Billy while in the Star Bar?	$P(K)$
16. What is the probability that Billy makes an insulting ethnic comment to Frank while they are in the Star Bar?	$P(I)$
17. Suppose Billy makes an insulting ethnic comment to Frank sometime while they are together in the Star Bar. What is the probability that Frank pulls a knife on Billy sometime while in the Star Bar?	$P(K \mid I)$
18. Suppose Frank pulls a knife on Billy sometime while in the Star Bar. What is the probability that Billy makes an insulting ethnic comment to Frank sometime while they are together in the Star Bar?	$P(I \mid K)$

The results for a sample of University of Washington undergraduates are shown in the following table (K = knife, I = insult). Subjects with tied ratings were dropped from the analysis because their inclusion complicates the picture without changing it substantially.

	$P(K) < P(I)$	$P(K) > P(I)$
$P(K \mid I) < P(I \mid K)$	42 (51%)	10 (12%)
$P(K \mid I) > P(I \mid K)$	22 (27%)	8 (10%)

The conditionals were consistent with the priors of 50 (61%) subjects, and inconsistent with the priors of 32 (39%) subjects.

Each of the phenomena described here is a compositional anomaly in the sense that probability judgments are inconsistent with logical relations deriving from the compositional structure of propositions. The phenomena are listed in Table II along with the propositions whose judged probabilities constitute the anomalies. The conjunction and disjunction errors, the QCE, and the conditionalization error have been found to occur in a significant majority of subjects, at least with particular choices of propositions. In the

TABLE II

Compositional anomaly	Probabilities to be compared
Conjunction error	$P(A)$, $P(B)$, $P(A \cap B)$
Disjunction error	$P(a)$, $P(B)$, $P(A \cup B)$
QCE	$P[(\forall x)(x \in A \rightarrow x \in C)]$, $P[(\forall x)(x \in B \rightarrow x \in C)]$, $P[(\forall x)(x \in A \cap B \rightarrow x \in C)]$
Conditionalization error	$P(A \cap B))$, $P(A \mid B)$, $P(B \mid A)$
Inconsistency between conditionals and priors	$P(A \mid B)$, $P(B \mid A)$, $P(A)$, $P(B)$

fifth case, the inconsistency between conditionals and priors, it is possible that only a minority of individuals produce the inconsistent pattern. The purpose of the present discussion, however, is not to establish the prevalence of these anomalies, but rather to raise the question of whether the relationship between compositional structure and strength of belief can be the focus of a fruitful scientific inquiry. The phenomena listed in Table II exemplify the interaction of compositional structure with inductive inference. What we seek is a theoretical framework that promotes the systematic study of the relationship between evidence, propositional structure, and strength of belief. In the next section, we propose such a framework, and then turn to specific examples that illustrate the difficulties and rewards of this enterprise.

III. Semantic Theories of Evidence

A semantic theory of evidence must coordinate a theory of language with a theory of how evidence affects belief strength for propositions in a language. To discuss these relationships, it will help to define some notation for formal structures. Let L be a formally defined language, like a propositional calculus, predicate calculus, or intensional logic (Lewis, 1972; Montague, 1974; Quine, 1972). We assume that L is defined syntactically by specifying the symbols that comprise the language, together with rules that define well-formed expressions within the language. Deductive inference in L can be specified in terms of syntactic rules of inference or semantic definitions of reference and truth (or by types of rules) (van Fraassen, 1971). The former rules determine a relation of deductive consequence; the latter rules determine a relation of logical consequence. Let $\mathcal{P}$ be the set of propositions in L. Let $\mathcal{E}$ be a set of possible bodies of evidence. The fundamental relation of a semantic theory of evidence is the ordering of proposition/evidence pairs according to strength of belief. Stated formally, for any propositions $p, q \in \mathcal{P}$ and evidence $e, f \in \mathcal{E}$, let $(p, e) \geq (q, f)$ signify that the strength of belief for p given e is at least as great or greater than the strength of belief for q given f. For example, if p is the proposition that a patient has a cancerous tumor, q is the proposition that a patient has a noncancerous tumor, e is an x-ray picture, and f is a pathology report based on a biopsy, then $(p, e) \geq (q, f)$ indicates that one would be more certain of a cancerous tumor given the x-ray picture (and no other evidence) than one would be of a noncancerous tumor given the pathology report (and no other evidence).

We will refer to $\geq$ as the *belief strength order,* or more simply, the *belief order.* When we want to emphasize that the belief order is an ordering of proposition/evidence pairs, we will refer to the pairs as *p/e pairs* and the ordering as the *p/e order.* We assume that $\geq$ has the properties of an order relation.[2] There are several empirical procedures that might be used to determine a belief order. One could ask individuals to make paired comparison judgments of belief strength, that is, present individuals with p/e pairs, (p, e) versus (q, f), and ask, which is more believed? The notation, $(p, e) > (q, f), (p, e) \sim (q, f)$, or $(p, e) < (q, f)$, would indicate whether belief in p given e was judged to be strictly stronger, equally strong, or strictly weaker than belief in q given f. Alternatively, one could ask individuals to rate the degree of belief that particular propositions are true given a body of evidence. Let $R(p, e)$ be the rated belief strength for p given e. Operationally, one could measure $R(p,e)$ by asking the individual to place a mark on a line labeled 0 at one end and 100 at the other end, letting the position of the marked indicate the relative degree of belief. The belief order would then be inferred from the ratings under the assumption:

$$(p, e) \geq (q, f) \text{ iff } R(p, e) \geq R(q, f). \tag{19}$$

There are other methods for determining a belief order, including methods based on willingness to bet, which we will not attempt to describe here. As psychologists, we must recognize that alternative, logically equivalent methods for determining a belief order might lead to inconsistent orders (Slovic & Lictenstein, 1983), but we will not attempt to compare different methods in this chapter.

We assume that the belief order is consistent with the existence of an underlying scale of belief strength, denoted S, that satisfies the condition:

$$(p, e) \geq_1 (q, f) \text{ iff } S(p, e) \geq S(q, f). \tag{20}$$

---

[2] Technically, by an order relation we mean a relation that is transitive and connected. Transitive: For every $(p, e), (q, f)$, and (r, g), if $(p, e) \geq (q, f)$ and $(q, f) \geq (r, g)$, then $(p, e) \geq (r, g)$. Connected: For every (p, e) and $(q, f), (p, e) \geq (q, f)$ or $(p, e) \leq (q, f)$ or both.

The belief function S is not directly observable, but the $\geq$ order is observable through paired comparisons or ratings, and the existence of the scale S is guaranteed if the $\geq$ order is transitive and connected.[3] In effect, we are assuming the existence of a belief scale S that is at least an ordinal scale, but a goal of research is to discover further properties of belief strength that would establish interval or ratio-scale uniqueness of S (cf. Krantz, 1991). Conditions (19) and (20) imply that $R(p, e)$ is a strictly increasing function of the unobserved belief strength $S(p, e)$. In other words, ratings and belief strengths are related by the equation:

$$R(p, e) = M[S(p,e)], \qquad (21)$$

for some response function M about which we assume only that it is strictly increasing.[4] Equation (21) is plausible because one assumes that the individual perceives her own strengths of belief, and hence, can produce larger ratings whenever the belief strengths are in fact larger.

Given these definitions, we now define an *evidence structure* to be an ordered quadruple of the form $(L, P, E, \geq)$, where L is a formally defined language, P is the set of propositions in L, E is a set of different bodies of evidence, and $\geq$ is an ordering of $P \times E$. A semantic theory of evidence is a theory of the relationship between belief strength, semantic and syntactic properties of propositions in P, and properties of the evidence in E. A central goal of the semantic theory of evidence is to discover properties of evidence structures that constrain the form of a belief function S that satisfies Condition (20); specifically, can we discover empirical properties of belief strength $\geq$ that determine how the mathematical form of S is related to the compositional structure of propositions and properties of evidence? Of course, to pose and solve problems in the semantic theory of evidence, it will be necessary to give more details about the structure of the language L, its propositions P, the bodies of evidence in E, and the empirical belief order $\geq$.

To clarify the motivation for this formulation, we will sketch a concrete example. Suppose that Mr. A was found dead from a knife wound in his hotel room. Mr. X is accused of the crime. Two issues in the trial of Mr. X would be whether he had a motive for the crime and an opportunity to commit the crime. Let u be the proposition that Mr. X had a motive to murder Mr. A, let v be the proposition that Mr. X had the opportunity to

---

[3] Technically, the existence of S also requires the assumption of a countable dense subset in the belief order, but this assumption is plausible on conceptual grounds. For the definition of transitivity and connectedness, see footnote 2; for the definition of a countable dense subset, see Krantz et al. (1971).

[4] M is strictly increasing provided that $S(p, e) > S(q, f)$ iff $M[S(p, e)] > M[S(q, f)]$.

murder Mr. A in the manner in which he was killed, and let $u \wedge v$ be the conjunctive proposition that Mr. X had both the motive and the opportunity to murder Mr. A (see Table III). Let f_1, f_2, and f_3 be alternative versions of the evidence. For example, f_1 might be a scenario in which witnesses testify that Mr. X had strong reasons for revenge against Mr. A, and independent witnesses saw Mr. X in the vicinity of Mr. A's room. The evidence f_2 might be like f_1 except that the reasons given for Mr. X's desire for revenge are less plausible. The evidence f_3 might be like f_1 except that the witnesses are unsure whether Mr. X was the person that they saw near Mr. A's room. One can imagine many alternative bodies of evidence, varying in the strength of the putative motives for murder, the presence and quality of an alibi, the certainty of witnesses, the existence of other suspects, and so forth.

The central problem in a semantic theory of evidence is to explain how properties of p and e affect belief strength $S(p, e)$. Krantz (1991) proposed an analysis of belief for conjunctions that illustrates our approach to this problem. In the murder example, the evidence decomposes naturally into evidence for u (X had a motive to kill A) and evidence for v (X had the opportunity to kill A). One can imagine evidence that goes specifically to the question of motive without pertaining in any way to opportunity. At one extreme, imagine a scenario in which Mr. X had strong reasons to want revenge against Mr. A, or a strong financial interest in Mr. A's death. At the other extreme, imagine evidence that Mr. X had a minor disagreement with Mr. A of a type that rarely produces violent consequences. Let $\mathcal{E}_1$ denote the set of all such bodies of evidence, varying from very strong to very weak. Similarly, one can imagine different bodies of evidence pertaining to opportunity. Let $\mathcal{E}_2$ denote the set of bodies of evidence pertaining to opportunity, varying also from the very strong to the very weak. We assume that $\mathcal{E}_1$ is restricted to evidence that pertains only to motive without carrying information about opportunity, and that $\mathcal{E}_2$ is restricted to evidence that pertains only to opportunity without carrying information about mo-

TABLE III

Rated strength of belief			State of evidence
u	v	$u \wedge v$	
$R(u, f_1)$	$R(v, f_1)$	$R(u \wedge v, f_1)$	f_1
$R(u, f_2)$	$R(v, f_2)$	$R(u \wedge v, f_2)$	f_2
$R(u, f_3)$	$R(v, f_3)$	$R(u \wedge v, f_3)$	f_3

tive. For any $e_1 \in \mathcal{E}_2$ and $e_2 \in \mathcal{E}_2$, let e_1e_2 denote the combination of the evidence, e_1 pertaining to motive and e_2 to opportunity; the cartesian product, $E = \mathcal{E}_1 \times \mathcal{E}_2$ is the set of all such evidence combinations.

How do $S(u, e_1)$, $S(v, e_2)$, and $S(u \wedge v, e_1e_2)$ vary as a function of e_1 and e_2? Shafer (1976) and Krantz (1991) suggested that when u and v are supported by independent bodies of evidence, the belief for $u \wedge v$ should be a product of the strengths of each conjunct, that is,

$$S(u \wedge v, e_1e_2) = S(u,e_1) \cdot S(v,e_2) \tag{22}$$

for every $e_1 \in \mathcal{E}_1$ and $e_2 \in \mathcal{E}_2$. Applying Eq. (21) to Eq. (22) yields

$$R(u \wedge v, e_1e_2) = M[S(u \wedge v, e_1e_2)] = M[S(u,e_1) \cdot S(v,e_2)]. \tag{23}$$

Equations (22) and (23) are examples of compositional hypotheses in the semantic theory of evidence; they describe how belief for a conjunction $u \wedge v$ might be related to the strength of its components. Testable assumptions that are sufficient for the validity of Eqs. (22) and (23) are described in Krantz et al. (1971). The point of this example is to show how a testable empirical hypothesis can be developed to describe belief strength for a specified propositional structure, conjunctions of propositions, and a specified class of evidence, namely, combinations of independent evidence.

A general goal of the semantic theory of evidence would be to consider a variety of propositional structures, disjunctions, negations, conditionals, statements with quantifiers, statements with complex clausal structures, counterfactual conditionals, propositional attitudes, and so forth, and to model belief strengths for this ensemble of propositions with respect to diverse evidence states. What one would seek in this investigation would be testable hypotheses, like Eqs. (22) and (23), that describe belief for complex propositions as a function of the structure of the propositions and properties of the evidence. An ultimate goal in this endeavor would be to account for belief across a wide spectrum of natural language expressions and evidence states. A more accessible, proximal goal would be to investigate belief for relatively simple propositional and evidential structures. As we hope to demonstrate, even modest goals are challenging, but also revealing of relationships that have theoretical interest.

Before continuing, we must clarify several issues that were omitted from the preceding discussion. First, we should mention that in the following discussion we will treat judgments of probability as ordinal measures of belief strength. In other words, when individuals are asked to judge the probability of events or propositions, or to rank propositions in terms of their relative probability, we interpret the data from such tasks as indicators of the ordering of these events or propositions by degree of belief. We do not assume that degree of belief has the properties of a probability measure, even when the ordering of belief is inferred from judgments that purport to pertain to the probability of the events. We use the expression "probability judgment" as if it were synonymous with "judgment of belief strength" under the assumption that individuals typically judge strength of belief when asked to judge the probability of events. This assumption seems reasonable because it is well established that judgments of probability do not conform to the laws of probability. Hence, what subjects consult when they were asked to judge probability is not a subjective probability representation that satisfies the laws of probability, but rather a nonprobabilistic psychological representation that we are calling the belief order.

Second, we suggested earlier that belief strength is an ordering of p/e pairs, where the propositions are elements in a formalized language. But if belief strengths are determined by asking subjects to rate natural language statements, the propositions in question would appear to be statements of natural language, and not propositions in a formalized language. The response to this is that the propositions in $\mathcal{P}$ are intended to serve as semantic representations for natural language statements. We assume that a linguistic theory specifies the mapping from natural language statements into propositions in $\mathcal{P}$, as well as referential relations between propositions in $\mathcal{P}$ and states of the world. Admittedly, in our present state of knowledge, the specification of this mapping may be controversial or poorly understood. Nevertheless, for a particular research problem, it may be possible to adopt working hypotheses concerning this mapping; for example, one might assume that a natural language conjunction corresponds to a formal conjunction that satisfies the truth conditions and inference rules governing conjunctions in a propositional calculus. One can investigate consequences of this working hypothesis even if it is not embedded within a more developed linguistic theory. Of course, investigations into the semantics of evidence would advance more rapidly if there existed a widely accepted and well-established theory of the mapping from natural language statements to semantic representations, but even before such a theory is developed, it may be fruitful to adopt heuristic working hypotheses concerning this mapping and to study belief strength under these working hypotheses.

The rationale for postulating formal propositions in a theory of evidence is analogous to the rationale for postulating underlying formal structures in a theory of natural language inference. It is simpler to hypothesize a mapping from natural langauage statements to propositions in a formalized language and to formulate deductive relations with respect to these propositions, than it is to describe deductive relations directly with respect to natural language statements. We propose to develop a theory of belief in which the objects of belief are propositions in a formal language rather than statements of natural language, because the syntactic and semantic relations that affect belief are more easily represented in a formal language. Of course, correspondences between natural language statements and formal propositions are empirical claims that are falsifiable, as are other aspects of a theory of belief.

Third, although our previous example ignored the existence of semantic and syntactic structure internal to propositions, for example, decompositions of propositions into subject and predicate, or quantified statements, or complex clausal structures, we recognize the likelihood that finer aspects of propositional structure affect the belief order. Indeed, it is our hope that belief strength will be sensitive to many aspects of propositional structure, for only if this is the case will the investigation of belief lead to deeper theories of the compositional structure of propositions. The examples to be discussed are confined to compositions of propositions without analysis of structure below the level of the proposition; this limitation reflects only our ignorance of the relation between belief strength and finer levels of grammatical analysis, and not some necessary limitation on the scope of a semantic theory of evidence.

Finally, we should comment briefly on the relation between the semantics of evidence and other research in philosophy and psychology. Our conceptualization of the semantics of evidence was greatly influenced by Davidson's proposal that a semantic theory of natural language should take the form of a Tarski-style truth definition (Davidson, 1967, 1970; Davidson & Harman, 1975a). In other words, Davidson proposed that a theory of natural language semantics should explain how the truth conditions for complex propositions depend on the referential relations and truth conditions of more elementary components, and on the way these components are combined. The semantics of evidence is analogous to a truth theory for natural language. Whereas a truth theory attempts to explain the relation between states of the world and the truth of propositions, a semantic theory of evidence attempts to explain the relation between states of evidence and degrees of belief for propositions. In both types of theory, propositional structure mediates the connection between language judgments and a nonlinguistic reality. In a truth theory for natural language, propositional structure is an explanatory construct for intuitions of reference and truth; and in a semantic theory of evidence, propositional structure is an explanatory construct for judgments of belief strength.

Our interest in the semantics of evidence originated in an investigation into the foundations of Shafer's (1976) theory of evidence undertaken by the first author, John Miyamoto, and David Krantz during the early 1980s. Unlike the Bayesian theory in which evidence (data) and hypotheses are both treated as propositions in a probability space, evidence in Shafer's theory is ontologically distinct from the propositions that constitute objects of belief. The role of evidence is to induce degrees of belief for the propositions in a logical space. Shafer posits a mathematical structure for belief that is different from and more general than that of a probability measure. The precise structure of Shafer's (1976) theory need not concern us here because our formulation of the semantic theory of evidence adopts only a few general features of Shafer's (1976) theory, specifically, the fundamental assumption that belief strength is an ordering of p/e pairs and the assumption that the structure of inductive inference can be discovered by investigating how this ordering varies as a function of evidence and propositions (see also, Krantz, 1991). We depart from Shafer's theory in that our goals are descriptive and not prescriptive or normative, and for this reason, we have proposed a framework that allows for non-normative as well as normative patterns of belief. In particular, Shafer's (1976) theory of belief functions and the Dempster/Shafer rule for the combination of evidence play no role in our formulation of the semantics of evidence. Moreover, our approach emphasizes the interaction between belief strength and the compositional structure of propositions, a concern that is secondary in Shafer's research program (Shafer, 1976, 1981; Shafer & Tversky, 1985).

As will be apparent from our ensuing discussion of empirical research, the semantics of evidence is intended to serve as a framework for thinking about a number of research problems that already exist in the judgment literature. Thus, research on conjunctive probabilities (Morier & Borgida, 1984; Tversky & Kahneman, 1983; Wells, 1985; Yates & Carlson, 1986), on disjunctive probabilites (Bar-Hillel & Neter, 1993; Carlson & Yates, 1989), on verbal (non-numerical) labels for probabilities (Wallsten, Budescu, Rapoport, Zwick, & Forsyth, 1986), on inductive argument strength (Osherson, Smith, Wilkie, Lopez, & Shafir, 1990), and on counterfactual inference (Miyamoto & Dibble, 1986; Miyamoto, Lundell, & Tu, 1989) can all be regarded as problems in the semantics of evidence. This is not to say that previous investigations were intended as contributions to the semantic theory of evidence, for historically, these investigations have focused on the theory of probability judgment without attempting to coordinate this theory with a theory of propositional structure. Perhaps Wallsten et al.'s investigations of verbal probability quantifiers and Osherson et al.'s studies of categorical arguments are closest to our interest in the relation between language structure and strength of belief. In general, however, research in probability judgment and inductive inference has not attempted a systematic study of how evidence and propositional structure jointly affect strength of belief.

In the next section of this chapter, we take a closer look at conjunction errors in probability judgment. Tversky and Kahneman (1983) proposed that conjunction errors result from the use of a representativeness heuristic in probability judgment. From the perspective of a semantic theory of evidence, a representativeness explanation of conjunction errors raises the issue of the compositional structure of concepts, an issue that is also raised in the theory of typicality and concept structure (Medin & Shoben, 1988; Smith & Osherson, 1984). We attempt to point out the parallels between compositional theories of typicality and inductive inference. Next, we turn to an alternative theory of conjunction errors, according to which these errors result from the application of improper mental rules for the combination of subjective probabilities (Gavanski & Roskos-Ewoldsen, 1991; Yates & Carlson, 1986). We review arguments for this theory and then present new experimental results that cannot be explained by these improper rules. In a subsequent section, we discuss compositional anomalies in counterfactual reasoning. We show that theories of counterfactual reasoning due to Braine and O'Brien (1991), Stalnaker (1968), and Lewis (1973) incorporate a strategy for conditional reasoning, called a Ramsey test, that predicts relationships between the compositional structure of counterfactuals and the belief strength of counterfactuals. We then present experimental evidence to show that the predicted relationships are systematically violated in intuitive reasoning. We propose a modification of the Ramsey test strategy that appears to account for the pattern of counterfactual reasoning observed in our experiments.

Although our discussion of probabilistic and counterfactual reasoning errors attempts to evaluate the evidence for different theories of the errors, our purpose is not to provide a definitive explanation for these phenomena. Indeed, we will argue that further research is needed before adequate explanations can be found. Rather, our purpose is to show that empirical studies of the relationship between propositional structure, evidence, and belief strength are viable and productive for theory construction. Hence, our primary goal is not to resolve the question of why reasoning errors occur, but rather to use reasoning errors as illustrations of theoretically interesting interactions between propositional structure and belief strength, that is, to use them as illustrations of interesting problems in the semantics of evidence.

IV. A Normative Principle Linking Deduction and Induction

Before discussing empirical examples of compositional anomalies, we must introduce a fundamental normative principle that influences this discussion. The principle may be stated as follows.

Principle 1 (Consistency of Belief with Logical Consequence): For any evidence e, the ordering of propositions by belief strength ought to be the same as the ordering of propositions by the relation of logical consequence.

What Principle 1 says is that if q is a logical consequence of p, then normatively, the belief strength for q should equal or exceed the belief strength for p no matter what evidence e is available. Letting $p \models q$ symbolize the relation that q is a logical consequence of p, Principle 1 asserts that for any propositions p and q, and evidence e, if $p \models q$, then $(q, e) \succeq (p, e)$.

The rationale for Principle 1 is that if q is a logical consequence of p, then any evidence supporting p also supports q, but there could be evidence supporting q that does not support p. Because q has as much or more evidence supporting it than does p, belief strength ought to be equal or greater for q than for p. If the ordering of belief strength satisfies Principle 1, we will say that belief is consistent with logical consequence. Suppes proved that Principle 1 is satisfied in a Bayesian system of subjective probabilities (cf. Suppes, 1966, Theorem 1), and Adams (1975) proposed a similar hypothesis: *"If an inference is truth-conditionally sound than the uncertainty of its conclusion cannot exceed the sum of the uncertainties of its premises* (where *uncertainty* is here defined as probability of falsity. . . .)" (p. 2) (italics in the original). We propose that it ought to be satisfied by any normative theory of deduction and induction, whether Bayesian or non-Bayesian. Principle 1 is closely related to the principle of extensionality as discussed in Tversky and Kahneman (1983): "If the extension of A includes the extension of B (i.e., $A \supset B$), then $P(A) \geq P(B)$." (p. 294) Principle 1 differs from the extensionality principle in that Principle 1 states a relation between belief strength and logical consequence, and the extensionality principle states a relation between probability and set inclusion among events. Even if belief strength and (subjective) probability are equated as in a Bayesian system, relations of logical consequence do not necessarily reduce to inclusion relations among events (cf. our discussion of counterfactual semantics later in this chapter.)

In the following discussion, examples will be presented in which human judgment violates Principle 1. Because Principle 1 is proposed as a normative principle and not as a psychological law, empirical violations of it need not cast doubt upon its validity. Violations do bring into question, however, the relation between deductive and inductive reasoning. After examining a number of ways that Principle 1 is violated descriptively, we will discuss the implications of such violations for the semantics of evidence.

V. Conjunction and Disjunction Errors in Probability Judgment

In this section, we examine conjunction and disjunction errors more carefully from the perspective of the semantics of evidence. If p and q are any propositions, let $p \wedge q$ represent the conjunction of p and q, and let $p \vee q$ represent the inclusive disjunction of p and q. (The inclusive disjunction of p and q is the proposition that is true if p is true, q is true, or both p and q are true.) The third column of Table I shows the propositional notation for the statements in the Linda problem. In this notation, a conjunction error occurs whenever an individual judges

$$(p \wedge q, e) > (p, e) \text{ or } (p \wedge q, e) > (q, e), \tag{24}$$

and a disjunction error occurs whenever an individual judges

$$(p, e) > (p \vee q, e) \text{ or } (q, e) > (p \vee q, e). \tag{25}$$

In the Linda problem, the typical conjunction error is of the form $(BT \wedge FM, L) > (BT, L)$, and the typical disjunction error has the form $(FM, L) > (BT \vee FM, L)$, where the evidence L is the initial description of Linda.

Conjunction and disjunction errors are basic examples of violations of Principle 1. Conjunction errors violate Principle 1 because q is a logical consequence of $p \wedge q$ but it is observed that $(p \wedge q, e) > (q, e)$. Disjunction errors violate Principle 1 because $p \vee q$ is a logical consequence of p but it is observed that $(p, e) > (p \vee q, e)$. Because the semantic properties of conjunctions and disjunctions are central to logical theory, inconsistencies between strength of belief and the logical properties of conjunctions and disjunctions pose a fundamental difficulty for any theory of reasoning that incorporates deductive and inductive modes. Before discussing the implications of such errors, we should first examine more carefully the evidence for their existence.

A. Pragmatic Objections to Conjunction and Disjunction Errors

A number of authors have questioned whether conjunction errors are truly errors. Perhaps they are simply cases in which subjects interpret statements differently from the interpretation intended by the experimenters. Specifically, Marcus and Zajonc (1985) and Pennington (1984) suggested that subjects may contrast statement (2), "Linda is a bank teller," to statement

(4), "Linda is a bank teller and is active in the feminist movement," and infer that statement (2) implicitly means that

---

26. Linda is a bank teller who is not active in the feminist movement. $(BT \wedge \neg FM)$

(The expression $\neg FM$ is the negation of the FM.) Under this analysis, the apparent tendency to judge $P(BT \wedge FM) > P(BT)$ is actually a tendency to interpret (2) as (26), together with a belief that $P(BT \wedge FM) > P(BT \wedge \neg FM)$. Because the ordering, $P(BT \wedge FM) > P(BT \wedge \neg FM)$, does not violate any laws of probability, this hypothesis would imply that the so-called conjunction error is not a true reasoning error.

Several counterarguments can be made to this suggestion. In one of their control conditions, Tversky and Kahneman (1982a, 1983) asked one sample of subjects to rank the likelihoods of a set of statements that included (2) and (3) but not (4), and asked a different sample of subjects to rank a set of statements that included (4) and excluded (2) and (3). Because the subjects who saw the constituent propositions BT and FM were different from those who saw the conjunction $BT \wedge FM$, there was no pragmatic reason for the subjects to interpret BT as $BT \wedge \neg FM$. Nevertheless, the ranking of $BT \wedge FM$ with respect to the filler statements was significantly greater than the ranking of BT with respect to the same filler statements. In addition, Tversky and Kahneman asked a third sample of subjects to rank the likelihoods of the same statements with (4) excluded, and with (2) replaced by the following statement (2*):

2*. Linda is a bank teller whether or not she is active in the feminist movement. (BT^*)

The mean ranking of statement (4), $BT \wedge FM$, was also significantly higher than the mean ranking of (2*). Thus, clarifying the meaning of the statement that Linda is a bank teller did not eliminate the conjunction error.

Morier and Borgida (1984) asked subjects to estimate the probabilities of statements that included (2), (3), (4), and (26).[5] Presumably the presence of (26), $BT \wedge \neg FM$, among the stimuli would suppress any tendency to interpret (2), BT, as $BT \wedge \neg FM$. Nevertheless, a majority of subjects produced conjunction errors (77.4% errors, $n = 30$, $p<.01$ by a sign test). In addition to the Linda problem, Morier and Borgida (1984) studied

[5] The exact wording of the statement used by Morier and Borgida was "Linda is a bank teller who is not a feminist" rather than statement (26), but we assume that this difference in wording is unimportant.

another problem with an analogous logical structure. For this second problem, Morier and Borgida found that subjects who rated statements analogous in form to (2), (3), (4), and (26) produced significantly fewer conjunction errors than subjects who rated only the statements that were analogous to (2), (3), and (4) (48.7% errors, $n = 39$, vs. 76.7% errors, $n = 30$; $p<.05$ by a chi-squared test). Thus there is some evidence that clarifying the meanings of statements can reduce the frequency of conjunction errors with particular statements and stories, but the results for the Linda problem displayed a high proportion of conjunction errors even after clarifying the meaning of the statements.

Wells (1985) raised the issue whether disjunction errors occur because subjects interpret disjunctive statements as exclusive disjunctions, that is, whether subjects interpret statement (5) to mean that

---

27. Either Linda is a bank teller or she is active in the $(BT \wedge \neg FM) \vee (\neg BT \wedge FM)$
feminist movement, but not both.

No laws of probability are violated if someone judges $P(FM)$ to be greater than $P[(BT \wedge \neg FM) \vee (\neg BT \wedge FM)]$. Under this analysis, the apparent disjunction error is actually a tendency to interpret (5) as (27), together with the belief that $P(FM) > P[(BT \wedge \neg FM) \vee (\neg BT \wedge FM)]$. To test this objection, Wells (1985) added the phrase "or both" to disjunctive statements that were analogous to (5). Nevertheless, a large proportion of disjunction errors was still observed. Carlson and Yates (1989) had subjects rank order the probability of statements that were analogous in form to statements (2) through (5). For some of the subjects, the phrase "or both" was appended to the disjunctive statements, whereas the phrase was omitted for the remaining subjects. No significant differences were found in the proportions of disjunction errors of subjects who saw or did not see disjunctive statements with "or both" appended to them, and the overall proportion of disjunction errors was quite high (80% disjunction errors when averaged over reasoning problems; Carlson & Yates, 1989, Study 2).

We conclude that clarifying the meaning of the statements, either by revising the wording or by eliminating contrasts between statements that suggest an unintended interpretation, does not eliminate the occurrence of conjunction and disjunction errors. Although our discussion has focused primarily on the Linda problem, conjunction and disjunction errors have been observed with many different reasoning problems (Agnoli & Krantz, 1989; Bar-Hillel & Neter, 1993; Carlson & Yates, 1989; Shafir, Smith, & Osherson, 1990; Tversky & Kahneman, 1983; Wells, 1985; Yates & Carlson, 1986). Finally, we note that the conditionalization error, the tendency to judge $P(A \wedge B) > P(A \mid B)$, is not subject to the same pragmatic criticisms as conjunction problems, because both propositions A and B appear in the critical statements. In particular, $A \mid B$ cannot be misinterpreted as $A \wedge \neg B \mid B$. Therefore, the tendency to judge $P(A \wedge B) > P(A \mid B)$ is consistent with the view that conjunctions are sometimes overweighted in probability judgment. This evidence is not conclusive, however, because it may show that the conditional $A \mid B$ is sometimes underweighted. One may conclude, however, that either conjunctions are sometimes overweighted, or conditionals are sometimes underweighted, or both.

B. REPRESENTATIVENESS, TYPICALITY, AND CONJUNCTION ERRORS

In the remainder of this chapter, we focus on investigations of conjunction errors because the research on disjunction errors is less extensive. Tversky and Kahneman (1983) undertook the investigation of conjunction errors in the context of their famous studies of a general reasoning strategy, which they call the *representativeness heuristic* (Kahneman & Tversky, 1972, 1973; Tversky & Kahneman, 1971, 1974, 1982a, 1983). To illustrate this heuristic, suppose that Ms. A is described to have characteristics $A_1, A_2, \ldots, A_n$. A person who employs the representativeness heuristic judges the probability that Ms. A is in category X as a function of the similarity between the given characteristics of Ms. A and the typical characteristics of category X. For example, it is hypothesized that people evaluate the probability that Linda is a bank teller as a function of the similarity between the given characteristics of Linda and bank tellers in general. By the *similarity hypothesis,* we mean the hypothesis that people judge the probability of an event by its similarity to the given information. Judging probability in terms of similarity is one of the main characteristics of the representativeness heuristic; there are other aspects that we will not discuss here because they are not relevant to conjunction errors.

Juding the probability of an event by its similarity to the given information may often be a reasonable heuristic. As Kahneman and Tversky have repeatedly pointed out, however, the intuition of similarity differs structurally from the mathematical properties of a probability measure, and where it differs, judgments of probability can systematically diverge from normative patterns of probability judgment (Kahneman & Tversky, 1973; Tversky & Kahneman, 1982a, 1983). Specifically, a conjunction of properties can be more similar to a standard than one of the properties in isolation; for example, a feminist bank teller is more like the initial description of Linda than a bank teller whose attitudes towards feminism are left unspecified. Not only is this intuitively clear, it is easily established empirically. Tversky and Kahneman (1983) had subjects rank order the categories, feminist, bank teller, feminist bank teller, and other filler categories, in terms of "the degree to which [Linda] resembles the typical member of that class." The majority of subjects (85%, $n = 88$) ranked the similarity of the categories in the order: feminist, feminist bank teller, and bank teller. Thus, the preferred rank order of the similarity between Linda and these categories coincides exactly with the preferred rank order of the probability of these categories, which is what the similarity hypothesis predicts. There is no fallacy in ordering the similarity of these categories in this fashion. The fallacy lies in equating the probability order to the similarity order.

Shafir et al. (1990) carried out a more thorough test of the similarity hypothesis. The stimuli in Shafir et al. (1990) were 14 brief personality sketches, one of which was the Linda sketch and others of which were new. For each sketch, they constructed an incompatible conjunction, $p \wedge q$, and a compatible conjunction, $p \wedge r$, such that p was the same representative outcome for both conjunctions (e.g., Linda is a feminist), q was an unrepresentative outcome (e.g., Linda is a bank teller), and r was a representative outcome (e.g., Linda is a teacher). In terms of the Linda example, $p \wedge q$ would be "Linda is a feminist bank teller" and $p \wedge r$ would be "Linda is a feminist teacher." One sample of subjects rated the *typicality* of the propositions q, r, $p \wedge q$, and $p \wedge r$, and a different sample of subjects rated the *probability* of these same propositions. There were 14 personality sketches, 4 propositions per sketch, and 2 types of ratings per proposition. Over the 56 propositions, the correlation between mean typicality rating and mean probability rating was .93 ($p < .001$).[6] The high correlation between the typicality of a category and its probability supports the similarity hypothesis.

The high correlation between typicality and judged probability also suggests that typicality ratings should predict the locus of conjunction errors, and this is indeed the case. The incompatible conjunctions ($p \wedge q$) were significantly more typical and also significantly more probable than the unrepresentative category (q). The compatible conjunctions ($p \wedge r$) were neither significantly more typical nor significantly more probable than the representative category (r). Furthermore, typicality ratings also predicted the magnitude of conjunction errors in the following sense. Let $p \wedge x$ stand for any of the conjunctions used in the Shafir et al. experiment, where x is either q or r. The difference in mean typicality between $p \wedge x$ and x was moderately correlated with the difference in mean probability between $p \wedge x$ and x (the correlation was .83, $n = 28$, $p < .01$). Thus, differences in typicality predicted the magnitude of differences in probability between

---

[6] This correlation was not reported by Shafir et al. (1990), but it can be computed from the statistics that they did report.

$p \wedge x$ and x. One might object that a request to judge the typicality of an outcome has the same meaning as a request to judge the probability of that outcome, and thus the results are unsurprising. To do so, however, is to concede the validity of the similarity hypothesis in the guise of objecting to it. The objection would have teeth, so to speak, if the intuition of typicality conformed to the mathematical laws of probability but the finding of Shafir et al. was rather to the contrary—estimates of probability conformed to the psychological laws of typicality (cf. Osherson, 1990, and Tversky & Kahneman, 1982a, for elaboration on this point).

In the cognitive theory of typicality, the problem of determining the typicality of conjunctive categories is referred to as the problem of conceptual combination (Medin & Shoben, 1988; Osherson & Smith, 1982; Smith & Osherson, 1984, 1989; Smith, Osherson, Rips, & Keane, 1988). Perhaps the most complete model of conceptual combination is the prototype combination model (Smith & Osherson, 1984, 1989; Smith et al., 1988); in this model, categories are represented as lists of attribute–value combinations, with each attribute value weighted by its diagnosticity and salience. The attribute values for a category are not regarded as necessary and sufficient features; rather, they define a prototype or most typical member of the category. The typicality of instance X in category A is determined by the similarity of X to the category A prototype, where the measure of similarity is a variant of Tversky's (1977) feature contrast rule.

To determine the prototype for a combined category like "feminist bank teller," the Smith/Osherson theory proposes that the category prototype of "bank teller" serves as a default representation. Attributes and values of the noun that are unspecified by the adjective remain unchanged in the combined category, but attributes and values of the noun that differ from those of the adjective are modified to conform more closely to the adjective. We will not describe the precise mathematical rule that governs conceptual combination in the Smith/Osherson theory other than to note that its effect is to increase the diagnosticity of attributes and the salience of values that are specified by the adjective. Smith et al. (1988) have shown that their model is able to predict conditions under which an instance is more typical of a combined category than of a constituent category (e.g., Linda is more typical of "feminist bank teller" than of "bank teller"), as well as cases in which it is not (e.g., Linda is less typical of "uninformed teacher" than of "teacher").[7]

---

[7] The example of "uninformed teacher" versus "teachers" does not appear in Smith and Osherson (1989) or Smith et al. (1988). Their experiments concern combinations of fruit and vegetable categories with color and shape adjectives. The claim that Linda is more typical of "teacher" than of "uniformed teacher" has not been verified empirically, although it is plausible based on intuition and also on the Smith et al. (1988) results.

A thorough discussion of typicality is beyond the scope of this chapter, but we wish to point out the analogy between issues in the theory of typicality and the concern in the present chapter with compositional models of belief. The central problem in the semantics of evidence is to predict relations in belief strength from the compositional structure of propositions and from properties of evidence. If belief strength is determined by a representativeness heuristic, and if this heuristic reduces to judgments of typicality in questions of category membership, then for propositions asserting category membership, a compositional theory of belief must be based on a compositional theory of typicality. The theory of typicality is obviously not a finished product, but rather a theory under construction with many viewpoints and empirical phenomena to take into account (Hampton, 1987a, 1987b; Huttenlocher & Hedges, 1994; Medin & Shoben, 1988; Murphy, 1988; Osherson & Smith, 1982; Smith & Medin, 1981; Smith & Osherson, 1984; Smith et al., 1988; Zadeh, 1982). What we can look for in the near future are not ultimate answers to questions concerning the compositional structure of concepts, but rather informative ways to investigate this structure and its relation to strength of belief.

C. PROBABILITY COMBINATION MODELS FOR CONJUNCTION ERRORS

The main competitors to the representativeness explanation of conjunction errors are various probability combination models. For example, let $R(A, e)$ denote a rating of the probability of A given evidence e. A weighted averaging model asserts that

$$R(A \land B, e) = \frac{v_1 R(A, e) + v_2 R(B, e)}{v_1 + v_2}, \qquad (28)$$

where v_1 and v_2 are positive weights (Wyer, 1976). We are interested in more general models in which the combination process occurs at the level of belief strength rather than at the level of ratings. For example, an averaging model for belief strength asserts that

$$S(A \land B, e) = \frac{w_1 S(A, e) + w_2 S(B, e)}{w1 + w_2}, \qquad (29)$$

where w_1 and w_2 are positive weights. The difference between models (28) and (29) is that (28) hypothesizes a relation between ratings of probability, whereas (29) hypothesizes a similar relation between the unobserved belief strengths. Weighted averaging models like (28) and (29) are natural models for conjunctive probability judgments because they predict that $R(A,$

$e) > R(A \wedge B, e) > R(B, e)$, if A is the more probable and B is the less probable outcome given e.

Our discussion will focus on combination models for belief strength, like model (29), rather than on combination models for ratings, like model (28), but our analysis will be equally relevant to both types of models. To see how this could be, recall that ratings and belief strengths are related by the condition $R(p, e) = M[S(p, e)]$. Thus, model (29) is equivalent to the hypothesis that

$$R(A \wedge B, e) = M \left[\frac{w_1 S(A, e) + w_2 S(B, e)}{w_1 + w_2} \right]. \qquad (30)$$

If one assumes that M is linear, then model (30) reduces to model (28). Model (30) allows for the possibility that M is nonlinear. We will present several probability combination models of belief strength, as in (29) and (30), and derive ordinal predictions from these models. These predictions are also implied by corresponding models that assume a linear response function, like (28). If empirical findings contradict an ordinal prediction derived from these models, all versions of the model, those that assume a linear response function and those that do not, are equally rejected.

Probability combination models are models, like (28), (29), and (30), that treat the belief strengths of conjunctions as functions of the belief strengths of the components. Their essential characteristic is that the component propositions contribute to the belief strength of the conjunction only through their belief strengths and not through semantic or conceptual relations between the components. A formal definition of the class of probability combination models is given with Eqs. (42) and (43). Although probability combination models for conjunctions had been proposed as early as Wyer (1976), interest in these models was stimulated by the finding of Yates and Carlson (1986) that conjunction errors occur even among conjunctions of conceptually unrelated propositions. For example, consider the propositions:

---

31. Governor Blanchard will succeed in raising the Michigan state income tax. A
32. Bo Derek will win an Academy Award for the movie that she is currently B
    making.

At the time of the Yates and Carlson (1986) study, Governor Blanchard was lobbying to raise the Michigan state income tax, and his chances were generally regarded as good. Bo Derek was a well known, sexy but untalented actress whose chances of winning an Academy Award were widely recognized to be slight. Subjects were asked to rank the probability of a series of propositions, among which were included A, B, and $A \wedge B$. Of 78 subjects, 44 (56.4%) ranked the probability of $A \wedge B$ higher than the probability of B alone. Because the component propositions, A and B, are obviously unrelated semantically, it is difficult to see how the judged probability of $A \wedge B$ could be based on the representativeness of the conjunction, that is, the typicality of the conceptual combination of Blanchard's success and Bo Derek's winning. This finding suggests that conjunction errors may result simply from the combination of particular belief strengths, without regard to semantic relations between the component propositions.

Let us define zero, single, and double conjunction errors by the conditions:

Zero: $(A, e) \geq (A \wedge B, e)$ and $(B, e) \geq (A \wedge B, e)$
Single: $(A, e) \geq (A \wedge B, e) > (B, e)$ or $(A, e) < (A \wedge B, e) \leq (B, e)$
Double: $(A \wedge B, e) > (A, e)$ and $(A \wedge B, e) > (B, e)$

Yates and Carlson (1986) factorially combined events that were either low or high in probability according to public opinion of the time with events that were either conceptually related or unrelated. Conceptually related events pertained to interrelated political events or interrelated sports events, whereas conceptually unrelated problems were like the preceding Governor Blanchard/Bo Derek example. Subjects rank ordered the probabilities of conjunctions and their component propositions, and the frequencies of zero, single, and double conjunction errors were counted.

The results in Table IV are a reanalysis of the results in Table III of Yates and Carlson (1986). The top half of Table IV shows the percentage of zero, single, and double conjunction errors in conjunctions of related and unrelated events. High/high, high/low, and low/low refer to the combination of high and low probabilities in the particular conjunction. The bottom half of Table IV shows the number of problems and sample sizes that contributed to the percentages in the top half of the table. The most striking feature of Table IV is the systematic relation between the probabilities of the component events and the types of conjunction errors that were most common in those problems. For both related and unrelated events, zero conjunction errors occurred most frequently in the low/low problems, single conjunction errors occurred most frequently in the high/low problems, and double conjunction errors occurred most frequently in the high/high problems. The similarity in the pattern of conjunction errors produced by problems with related and unrelated events lends credibility to the

TABLE IV

PERCENTAGE OF ZERO, SINGLE, AND DOUBLE CONJUNCTION ERRORS

	Related events			Unrelated events		
	0	1	2	0	1	2
High/High	38.7	15.2	46.1	40.7	29.4	30.0
High/Low	31.0	67.7	1.3	42.7	54.8	4.5
Low/Low	58.0	27.3	14.8	58.5	35.7	5.8
High/High	2 problems in study 4, $N = 105$			4 problems in study 4, $N = 105$		
High/Low	3 problems in study 2, $N = 46$			3 problems in study 2, $N = 46$		
	3 problems in study 3, $N = 33$			3 problems in study 3, $N = 33$		
Low/Low	2 problems in study 4, $N = 105$			3 problems in study 4, $N = 105$		

Note. Percentages are averaged over problems in Yates and Carlson's (1986) Studies 2, 3, and 4. Within any study, the problems were administered within subject. (From Yates & Carlson, 1986, Table 3.)

conjecture that the causes of conjunction errors are similar in the two types of problems.

We will shortly present evidence that is inconsistent with all probability combination models, but we first note that the data from Yates and Carlson (1986) are sufficient to rule out the weighted averaging model as a model of conjunctive probabilities. An averaging model like (28) or (29) predicts that single conjunction errors should always occur, because an average of two numbers is always between the numbers in magnitude (Yates & Carlson, 1986). Clearly the data in Table IV rejects this prediction, as do the data reported in other studies (Tversky & Kahneman, 1983; Wells, 1985). A modified version of the averaging model allows for the occurrence of all three patterns—zero, single, and double conjunction errors—for different conjunctions.

$$S(A \wedge B, e) = \frac{w_0 S_0 + w_1 S(A, e) + w_2 S(B, e)}{w_0 + w_1 + w_2}. \tag{33}$$

In this model, s_0 is an initial impression or default level of belief for an arbitrarily chosen conjunction. Model (33) will be referred to as the *initial impression averaging model*. Model (33) is equivalent to the model

$$S(A \wedge B, e) = p_0 S_0 + (1 - p_0)[p_1 S(A, e) + (1 - p_1)S(B, e)], \tag{34}$$

where $p_0 = w_0/(w_0 + w_1 + w_2)$, and $p_1 = w_1/(w_1 + w_2)$. Equation (34) makes it clear that zero or single conjunction errors should occur whenever s_0 is less than the smaller of $S(A, e)$ and $S(B, e)$, single conjunction errors should occur whenever s_0 is between $S(A, e)$ and $S(B, e)$, and single or double conjunction errors should occur whenever s_0 is greater than the larger of $S(A, e)$ and $S(B, e)$. Thus, the initial impression averaging model predicts that zero conjunction errors should be most prevalent when $S(A, e)$ and $S(B, e)$ are both large, and double conjunction errors should be most prevalent when $S(A, e)$ and $S(B, e)$ are both small. This is precisely opposite to the pattern of conjunction errors displayed in Table IV. To test the statistical reliability of this pattern, we treated the percentage of double conjunction errors for each problem in the high/high and low/low conditions as the data in a two-factor analysis of variance. The factors were relatedness (related events vs. unrelated events) and probability levels (high/high vs. low/low). The percentages from the high/low condition were excluded because they came from Yates and Carlson's Studies 2 and 3, whereas the high/high and low/low percentages were from a single study, Study 4. The main effect of probability level was highly significant ($F(1, 7) = 41.9$, $M_{se} = 46.4$, $p<.001$). On the average, the double conjunction errors were 27.7 percentage points more common in the high/high problems. We conclude that an initial impression averaging model is inconsistent with the data in Yates and Carlson (1986), and must be rejected.

Yates and Carlson (1986) proposed a *signed summation* model that correctly predicts the qualitative pattern of conjunction errors in Table IV. According to this model, the belief strength of a conjunction is a sum of the strengths of its components:

$$S(A \wedge B, e) = S(A, e) + S(B, e), \tag{35}$$

where the belief strength scale S is allowed to take on either positive or negative values. Let $\neg A$ denote the negation of A, and let us say that A is "likely" if $S(A, e) > S(\neg A, e)$, "unlikely" if $S(A, e) < S(\neg A, e)$, and "neutral" if $S(A, e) = S(\neg A, e)$. The essence of the signed summation rule is the assumption that $S(A, e) > 0$ if A is likely, $S(A, e) = 0$ if A is neutral, and $S(a, e) < 0$ if A is unlikely. Given these assumptions, the signed summation model predicts that double conjunction errors will occur when A and B are both likely, single conjunction errors will occur when one proposition is likely and the other is unlikely, and zero conjunction errors will occur when A or B are both unlikely. This is precisely the qualitative pattern in Table IV.

One defect of the signed summation model is that it predicts the occurrence of single conjunction errors for any self-contradictory conjunction. $A \wedge \neg A$. Thus, "Jones will win the race and Jones will lose the race" should be judged more probable than the less likely outcome. This criticism can be avoided if one assumes that individuals detect self-contradictions and apply some other reasoning rule to them. One might also object that it is counterintuitive to have negative values of belief strength. This criticism is also easily avoided. From the standpoint of ordinal predictions of belief strength, the signed summation model (35) is equivalent to a multiplicative model,

$$S(A \wedge B, e) = S(A, e) \cdot S(B, e), \tag{36}$$

where the belief scale S ranges from 0 to $+ \infty$. The qualitative equivalence of signed summation (35) and the multiplicative model (36) is readily seen if one takes logarithms of both sides of Eq. (36), yielding Eq. (35) after resetting log $(S) \rightarrow S$.

It could be objected that Yates and Carlson's (1986) experiment confounded the distinction between related/unrelated events with the specific propositions used to instantiate this distinction. In other words, the problems with related events were constructed from different positions than those used in the problems with unrelated events. Perhaps the similarity of the results for related and unrelated events is merely a coincidence resulting from a particular choice of propositions. Gavanski and Roskos-Ewoldsen (1991) provided evidence against this objection, as well as a sharper test of the generality of probability combination methods. They selected propositions A_1, A_2, B_1, and B_2 such that A_1 and A_2 pertained to the same issue, and B_1 and B_2 pertained to some other issue. Let us call $A_1 \wedge A_2$ and $B_1 \wedge B_2$ the conceptually related conjunctions, and let us call $A_1 \wedge B_1$ and $A_2 \wedge B_2$ the conceptually unrelated conjunctions, or more simply, the related and unrelated conjunctions, respectively.[8] For example,

---

37. Linda is both a bank teller [A_1] and extremely fashion conscious [A_2]. $A_1 \wedge A_2$
38. Jason is both a computer programmer [B_1] and is very shy [B_2]. $B_1 \wedge B_2$
39. Linda is a bank teller [A_1] and Jason is a computer programmer [B_1]. $A_1 \wedge B_1$
40. Linda is extremely fashion conscious [A_2] and Jason is very shy [B_2]. $A_2 \wedge B_2$

For conjunctions of the form (37) through (40), probability combination models predict the following equivalence, which we prove in Appendix 2:

$$S(A_1 \wedge A_2, e) > S(A_1 \wedge B_1, e) \text{ iff } S(B_1 \wedge B_2, e) < S(A_2 \wedge B_2, e), \tag{41}$$

that is,

[8] Our notation differs from that of Gavanski and Roskos-Ewoldsen (1991) in order to be consistent with the notation used later in this chapter.

Related > *Unrelated* iff *Related* < *Unrelated*.

Thus, a probability combination model predicts that unrelated conjunctions will be neither systematically stronger nor weaker in strength of belief than the corresponding related conjunctions. Gavanski and Roskos-Ewoldsen (1991) did not test (41) directly, although it is a testable condition, but rather they tested a consequence of (41), namely, that the average number of conjunction errors should be about the same for related and unrelated conjunctions. Gavanski and Roskos-Ewoldsen (1991) found no significant differences in the frequency of conjunction errors produced by related and unrelated conjunctions. The statistics reported in their study do not permit one to evaluate the power of their tests, but the fact that the null result was found in experiments with samples of 180 and 153 subjects, respectively, suggests that statistical power was sufficient to detect differences of moderate size. Thus, conjunctions of related and unrelated events appear to produce conjunction errors equally often when the components of the conjunctions are drawn from the same set of propositions. This result supports the hypothesis that the same processes underly conjunction errors in related and unrelated conjunctions.

Representativeness does not provide a straightforward explanation for conjunction errors among unrelated events. Therefore, if conjunction errors are produced by the same process in conjunctions of related and unrelated events, the most plausible explanation would seem to be that they result from improper probability combination rules. Reasoning along these lines, Gavanski and Roskos-Ewoldsen (1991) boldly advanced the hypothesis that probability combination models could account for all types of conjunction errors, including those involving conceptually related events.

> To what extent does judgment by representativeness contribute to the conjunction fallacy? Our results support a surprising answer: The only contribution of representativeness stems from its effects on a conjunction's component events. Conjunction fallacies, even in exemplar representativeness problems, stem primarily from the incorrect rules people use to combine probabilities. These rules are likely to yield the fallacy with certain combinations of component probabilities, regardless of whether these probabilities are arrived at by means of assessments of representativeness. (p. 190)

We construe this remark as implying the following hypothesis: For any propositions p and q and evidence e,

$$R(p \wedge q, e) = F[R(p, e), R(q, e)], \qquad (42)$$

where F is a function specified in a particular probability combination model, for example, averaging in an averaging model or addition in the signed summation model. Model (42) formalizes the intuition expressed in the remark from Gavanski and Roskos-Ewoldsen (1991) that the conjunctive probability $R(p \wedge q, e)$ is simply a function of component probability ratings $R(p, e)$ and $R(q, e)$. Representativeness influences the conjunctive probability $R(p \wedge q, e)$ only by affecting the component ratings. In particular, the conjunctive probability does not depend on any semantic or conceptual relationship between the components. Assuming that $R(p, e) = M[S(p, e)]$, and that M and F are continuous and strictly increasing, Equation (42) is equivalent to the hypothesis that there exists a continuous, strictly increasing function G such that

$$S(p \wedge q, e) = G[S(p, e), S(q, e)] \tag{43}$$

for every proposition p and q, and every body of evidence e.[9] Equation (43) implies that belief strength of a conjunction depends only on the belief strengths of the components, and not on any relationship between the components. Thus, the essential feature of the probability combination models, as characterized by either Eq. (42) or (43), is that they deny that semantic or conceptual relations *between* the components can affect the belief strengths of conjunctions.

Equation (43) implies four simple predictions that every probability combination model must satisfy. First, for any propositions A, C, D, and X, and any evidence e,

$$(C, e) > (D, e) \text{ iff } (A \wedge C, e) > (A \wedge D, e) \tag{44}$$

and

$$(C, e) > (D, e) \text{ iff } (C \wedge X, e) > (D \wedge X, e) \tag{45}$$

The intuition behind (44) and (45) is that if the belief strength of a conjunction is unaffected by conceptual relations between the components, then the belief order between C and D should predict the belief order after they are conjoined with any other proposition, A or X. For example, if "Linda is a teacher" seems more probable than "Linda is a bank teller," then "Linda is a teacher and wears bifocals" should seem more probable than "Linda is a bank teller and wears bifocals." Equation (43) also predicts that for any propositions A, B, C, D, X, and Y, and any evidence e,

$$(A \wedge C, e) > (A \wedge D, e) \text{ iff } (B \wedge C, e) > (B \wedge D, e) \tag{46}$$

and

[9] Proof: Eq. (42) is true iff $S(p \wedge q, e) = M^{-1}[F\langle M(S(p, e)), M(S(q, e))\rangle]$ iff Eq. (43) is true.

$$(C \wedge X, e) > (D \wedge X, e) \text{ iff } (C \wedge Y, e) > (D \wedge Y, e). \qquad (47)$$

The intuition behind (46) and (47) is that if the belief strength of a conjunction is unaffected by conceptual relations between the components, then the belief order between conjunctions that share a common component should not change if that common component is replaced by some other proposition. For example, if "Linda is a teacher and wears bifocals" seems more probable than "Linda is a bank teller and wears bifocals," then "Linda is a teacher and walks to work" should seem more probable than "Linda is a bank teller and walks to work." The proof that conditions (44) through (47) follow from Eq. (43) is given in Appendix 2.

In the terminology of the analysis of variance, conditions (44) through (47) assert that crossover interactions should not occur if one changes the component shared by a pair of conjunctions. Crossover interactions are excluded by probability combination models because these models deny that relations between the components of a conjunction can have interactive effects on belief strength. The analysis of variance will not be used to test Eqs. (44) through (47) because ordinal tests have greater generality of interpretation, but the intuition of crossover versus no crossover is appropriate. Conditions (44) through (47) are independence assumptions in the sense of conjoint measurement theory (Krantz et al., 1971). As shown in conjoint measurement, ordinal tests of independence assumptions are preferable to the analysis of variance because one is not forced to assume interval scale responses and the linearity of the response function (the function M in our notation).

Our strategy for testing (44) through (47) is straightforward. To test (45), choose C, D, and X such that C and X are conceptually compatible and C and X are conceptually incompatible, and C is less believed than D given evidence e, that is, $(C, e) < (D, e)$. If conceptual relations actually affect the judged probability of conjunctions, then the ordering $(C \wedge X, e) > (D \wedge X, e)$ might be observed, in violation of condition (45). To test (47), choose C, D, and X as before, and in addition, choose some other Y such that C and Y are conceptually incompatible and D and Y are conceptually compatible. With appropriately chosen propositions, it should be possible to find $(C \wedge X, e) > (D \wedge X, e)$ and $(C \wedge Y, e) < (D \wedge Y, e)$ in violation of condition (47). Violations of (44) and (46) might be obtained by analogous constructions. The following experiment tests the validity of conditions (44) through (47).

Experiment 1

Subjects: Subjects were 422 undergraduates at the University of Washington who received credit in a psychology course for participation in the experiment. Subjects were tested in large groups.

Stimulus materials: The experimenters wrote 10 vignettes and 10 statements that pertained to the events in each vignette.[10] The vignettes and statements are contained in Appendix 1. For any vignette, the statements were of the following types: two filler statements, four simple propositions (A_1, A_2, B_1, B_2), and four conjunctions $(A_1 \wedge A_2, A_1 \wedge B_2, B_1 \wedge A_2, B_1 \wedge B_2)$. The statements were written such that A_1 and A_2 were conceptually compatible, as were B_1 and B_2, whereas A_1 and B_2 were conceptually incompatible, as were B_1 and A_2. (See the following examples and Appendix 1).

Procedure: The 10 vignettes were arbitrarily divided into five pairs of vignettes. Subjects were randomly assigned to one of these pairs. The vignettes and statements were presented to subjects in the form of a questionnaire. Subjects were taught to rate the probability of a statement by placing a mark on a response line labeled "Absolutely Impossible" at one end and "Absolutely Certain" at the other end. They then read a first vignette, rated the 10 statements for that vignette, read a second vignette, and rated the 10 statements for that vignette. The statements for each vignette were presented in one of two randomly selected orders. The data were converted to a 30-point scale by measuring the position of the marks on the response line; a rating of 1 indicated the lowest probability, and 30 the highest probability.

Results: Because of the relations of compatibility and incompatibility among the stimulus statements, we predicted that

$$(A_1 \wedge A_2, e) > (B_1 \wedge A_2, e) \text{ and } (A_1 \wedge B_2, e) <1 (B_1 \wedge B_2, e) \quad (48)$$

in contradiction to condition (46), and

$$(A_1 \wedge A_2, e) > (A_1 \wedge B_2, e) \text{ and } (B_1 \wedge A_2, e) < (B_1 \wedge B_2, e) \quad (49)$$

in contradiction to condition (47). For example, in Problem 4-1 (Appendix 1), a high school senior, Joe B, had applied for admission to Harvard, Princeton, Oklahoma, and Texas. The statements were: (A_1) Joe is accepted at Harvard, (A_2) Joe is accepted at Princeton, (B_1) Joe is rejected at Oklahoma, and (B_2) Joe is rejected at Texas. Acceptance at Harvard and Princeton $(A_1 \wedge A_2)$ should appear more probable than rejection at Oklahoma and acceptance at Princeton $(B_1 \wedge A_2)$, because rejection at Oklahoma is diagnostic of characteristics that lower chances of acceptance at Princeton, and acceptance at Princeton is diagnostic of characteristics that reduce the chance of rejection at Oklahoma. Therefore, one predicts that $A_1 \wedge A_2 > B_1 \wedge A_2$. However, acceptance at Harvard and rejection at Texas $(A_1 \wedge B_2)$ should seem less probable than rejection at Oklahoma and Texas

---

[10] We would like to thank Rob Flaherty for his able assistance in constructing stimulus materials and running subjects.

$(B_1 \wedge B_2)$. Thus, $A_1 \wedge B_2 < B_1 \wedge B_2$. Hence, condition (48) should be observed. Similarly, acceptance at Harvard and Princeton $(A_1 \wedge A_2)$ should appear more probable than acceptance at Harvard and rejection at Texas $(A_1 \wedge B_2)$, but rejection at Oklahoma and acceptance at Princeton $(B_1 \wedge A_2)$ should seem less probable than rejection at Oklahoma and Texas $(B_1 \wedge B_2)$. Hence condition (49) should be observed.[11]

Tables V and VI show the results of tests of (44) through (47). Problem k-j refers to the jth vignette ($j = 1$ or 2) in condition k ($k = 1$–5). The same subjects rated the statements for Problems k-1 and k-2. We will explain the format of Table V in detail; the format of Table VI is analogous. Each cell displays the proportion of times that the first proposition was rated higher than the second proposition in the column heading (ties were dropped). For example, in Problem 1-1, A_2 received a higher rating than B_2 in 68% of the untied responses, and $A_1 \wedge A_2$ was rated higher than $A_1 \wedge B_2$ in 78% of the untied responses. Asterisks and daggers indicate the p-values of the proportions as calculated by two-tailed sign tests. Conditions

TABLE V

TESTS OF CONDITIONS (44) AND (46)

	A_2 vs. B_2	$A_1 \wedge A_2$ vs. $A_1 \wedge B_2$	$B_1 \wedge A_2$ vs. $B_1 \wedge B_2$	Pattern
Problem 1-1	.68*	.78	.67*	◆◆◆
Problem 1-2	.43	.80††	.03††	◁◖◆◀
Problem 2-1	.92††	.89††	.74††	◆◆◆
Problem 2-2	.84††	.91††	.60	◆◆◇
Problem 3-1	.45	.56	.35*	◁◇◆
Problem 3-2	.51	.71†	.28††	◇◆◆
Problem 4-1	.73††	.71†	.39	◆◆◇
Problem 4-2	.87††	.93††	.38*	◆◆◆
Problem 5-1	.12††	.42	.11††	◀◇◆
Problem 5-2	.71†	.69†	.65*	◆◆◆

Note. All proportions refer to the proportion of times the first proposition was rated higher than the second proposition in the column heading (ties were dropped). *P*-values are for two-tailed sign tests: * $p<.05$; ** $p<.01$; † $p<.005$; †† $p<.001$. Pattern column: The triples of arrows indicate the direction of greater belief strength in the three comparisons; solid black arrows indicate significant comparisons ($p<.05$) and open white arrows indicate nonsignificant comparisons.

---

[11] Experiment 1 and the example of Joe B were inspired by the following remark of Tversky and Kahneman (1983, p. 305): "it is more representative (as well as more probable) for a student to be in the upper half of the class in both mathematics and physics or to be in the lower half of the class in both fields than to be in the upper half in one field and in the lower half in the other. Such observations imply that the judged probability (or representativeness) of a conjunction cannot be computed as a function (e.g., product, sum, minimum, weighted average) of the scale values of its constituents. This conclusion excludes a large class of formal models that ignore the relation between the constitutents of a conjunction."

TABLE VI

Tests of Conditions (45) and (47)

	A_1 vs. B_1	$A_1 \wedge A_2$ vs. $B_1 \wedge A_2$	$A_1 \wedge B_2$ vs. $B_1 \wedge B_2$	Pattern
Problem 1-1	.68**	.57	.47	→ ⇒ ⇐
Problem 1-2	.55	.99††	.18††	⇒ → ←
Problem 2-1	.82††	.76††	.61	→ → ⇒
Problem 2-2	.63*	.63*	.20††	→ → ←
Problem 3-1	.44	.66**	.44	⇒ ← ⇒
Problem 3-2	.38	.58	.13††	⇐ ⇒ ←
Problem 4-1	.70	.67†	.33†	→ → ←
Problem 4-2	.64*	.89††	.12††	→ → ←
Problem 5-1	.37*	.76††	.24††	← → ←
Problem 5-2	.36*	.48	.28†	← ⇐ ←

Note. The notation is the same as for Table V.

(44) and (46) predict that in every row of Table V the proportions will all be greater than .5, or all less than .5. We will say that condition (44) or (46) is significantly violated if a row of Table V contains at least one proportion that is significantly greater than .5 and at least one proportion that is significantly less than .5 ($p<.05$ in both cases).

The arrows in the far right column indicate whether the proportions in a row are consistent with or in violation of conditions (44) and (46). The arrows point in the direction from the higher to the lower rated probability; bold arrows indicate proportions that are significantly different from .5 ($p<.05$), and non-bold arrows indicate proportions that are not significantly different from .5. For example, Problem 1-1 of Table V displays the pattern → → → indicating that every proportion in the row was significantly greater than .5, and that they were consistent with each other as predicted by (44) and (46). Problem 4-2 displays the pattern → → ← indicating significant violations of conditions (44) and (46); the proportions in the first and third data columns violate (44), and the proportions in the second and third data columns violate (46). Problem 4-1 displays the pattern → → ⇐ indicating that the last proportion in the row was inconsistent with the first two proportions, but that the proportion .39 was not significant. The format and notation of Table VI is exactly the same as that of Table V, except that the results test conditions (45) and (47) rather than (44) and (46).

The probability combination models predict that conditions (44) through (47) should be satisfied by every row in Tables V and VI. Even one violation of one of the conditions, (44) through (47), is sufficient to reject this class of models, provided that one can establish that the apparent violation is not due to sampling error. An examination of the arrow patterns in Tables

V and VI indicates that there were five significant violations of conditions
(44) and (45) (Problem 4-2 of Table V; Problems 2-2, 4-1, 4-2, and 5-1
of Table VI), and eight significant violations of conditions (46) and (47)
(Problems 1-2, 3-2, and 4-2 of Table V; Problems 1-2, 2-2, 4-1, 4-2, and 5-
1 of Table VI). All of the violations were in the predicted direction, that
is, an incompatible conjunction was rated below a corresponding compatible
conjunction where condition (44), (45), (46), or (47) would require the
opposite ordering.

We also tested whether conjunction errors occurred in the probability
ratings of these reasoning problems. We will not describe this analysis in
detail because it simply replicates the findings of other experiments, but
the point to be made here is that conjunction errors did occur among
the same problems that produced significant violations of conditions (44)
through (47). Specifically, conjunction errors occurred in the comparisons
of A_1 to $A_1 \wedge A_2$, and B_1 to $B_1 \wedge B_2$ in Problem 1-2; in the comparison of
B_2 to $B_1 \wedge B_2$ in Problem 2-2; and in the comparisons of A_2 to $A_1 \wedge A_2$,
and B_2 to $B_1 \wedge B_2$ in Problems 4-2 and 5-1. All of these comparisons were
statistically significant by two-tailed sign tests ($p < .05, .01, .005, .001, .001$,
and .05, respectively). Note that these problems also produced violations
of conditions (44) through (47) (see Tables V and VI). If violations of
probability combination models occurred in a different class of problems
from those that produce conjunction errors, one could retain probability
combination models as explanations of conjunction errors, leaving the violations of (44) through (47) to be explained by a different theory pertaining
to this other class of problems. This defense of probability combination
models is not viable, however, for violations of (44) through (47) occurred
among the same problems that produced conjunction errors, and hence,
they must be explained by any theory of conjunction errors.

D. Conclusions from Conjunction and Disjunction Errors in Probability Judgment

Both the representativeness hypothesis and probability combination models
have difficulty accounting for all results on conjunction errors. For the
representativeness theory, the main difficulty is to explain conjunction errors with conceptually unrelated propositions (Gavanski & Roskos-Ewoldsen, 1991; Yates & Carlson, 1986). According to this theory, conjunction
errors occur because the conjunction evokes a composite representation
that is more similar to the given information than the less representative
component. It is not obvious what mechanisms would lead to a composite
representation of conceptually unrelated components, especially one that
is more similar to the given information than the less probable component.

Another potential difficulty for the representativeness theory are the disjunction errors (Carlson & Yates, 1989; Morier & Borgida, 1984; Wells, 1985). The problem for the representativeness theory lies in explaining how a disjunction of propositions is represented cognitively, and how its similarity to the given information is evaluated.

The results of Experiment 1 demonstrate that conceptual relations between the components of a conjunction affect belief for the conjunction in ways not predicted by the strengths of the components. Conceptual compatibility enhances the belief strength of a conjunction and conceptual incompatibility reduces belief strength. The violations of conditions (44) through (47) establish that probability combination models cannot account for judgments of conjunctive probabilities in general. Thus, weighted averaging, weighted averaging with initial impression, signed summation, multiplicative combination, min, and max can all be rejected as models for conjunctive probabilities in general. The results of Experiment 1 do not eliminate the possibility that conjunctions of conceptually unrelated components are evaluated by a probability combination model, because all of the problems in Experiment 1 involved conjunctions of conceptually related events. Indeed, the construction of counterexamples to the probability combination models was based on conceptually related events that varied in compatibility. Therefore, we cannot exclude the possibility that a probability combination model governs judgments of likelihood for conjunctions of conceptually unrelated components, and representativeness governs judgments of likelihood for conjunctions of conceptually related components.

We should mention several lines of inquiry that deserve further attention. First, can probability combination models explain judgments of probability for disjunctions? The finding that the probability of disjunctions correlates with the representativeness of disjunctions suggests that probability combination models will also fail as a general account of the belief strength of disjunctions. Perhaps an experiment analogous to Experiment 1 can be devised to test whether conceptual relations between the components affect the belief strengths of disjunctions. Second, we need to explore how models of representativeness can be extended to conjunctions of unrelated events and to disjunctions of events, whether related or unrelated. Third, we need to see how the belief strength of conjunctions varies as a function of variation in the evidence. Oddly, most studies that we are aware of (our own included) confound propositions with evidence, in the sense that a given proposition is always presented with the same, possibly implicit body of evidence. Experiments that hold propositions constant while varying the evidence can be contrasted with experiments that hold evidence constant while varying the semantic properties of the propositions. Such contrasts might permit us to identify the independent contributions of propositional structure and evidence structure. Fourth, we believe that the relationship between compositional theories of typicality and compositional theories of belief deserves continued investigation. The theory of typicality is arguably the best developed theory of the representations and mechanisms underlying judgments of representativeness. Accordingly, the attempt to establish the relationship between belief strength and typicality constitutes an important test of representativeness explanations of belief.

VI. Anomalous Compositions in Counterfactual Reasoning

In this section, we extend the discussion to the semantics of evidence for counterfactual conditionals. Counterfactual conditionals are statements of the form.

50. If A were the case, then X would be the case.

where A and X are propositions. Typically, the antecedent of a counterfactual, A, is a proposition that is known to be false, and the consequent, X, is a proposition whose truth is related to the truth of the antecedent. For example, the following is a counterfactual.

51. If Richard Nixon had not resigned from the presidency, he would have been impeached.

The semantic properties of counterfactuals have been the focus of philosophical investigations because important, yet problematic, questions appear to depend on the analysis of counterfactual inference (Chisholm, 1946; Gardenfors, 1988; Goodman, 1947; Harper, Stalnaker, & Pearce, 1981; Lewis, 1973; Sosa, 1975; Stalnaker, 1984).

Let $A \mapsto X$ stand for a counterfactual like statement (50). A theory of evidence for counterfactuals must account for the belief strengths of p/e combinations, $(A \mapsto X, e)$, as a function of the semantic content of A and X, properties of the evidence e, and other beliefs that are not explicitly represented in the propositions or evidence. In the Nixon example, implicit beliefs would include beliefs concerning Richard Nixon, his political situation, and the conditions that would have influenced events had Nixon not resigned. Although we will not attempt to discuss philosophical issues pertaining to counterfactuals in this chapter, we would like to point out that the theory of evidence provides a new perspective on counterfactuals. Whereas previous studies have tended to ask the questions, what are the truth conditions for counterfactuals, and what are the logical entailments of counterfactuals, the theory of evidence focuses on the question of how belief strength for $(A \mapsto X, e)$ varies as a function of A, X, and e. This is a natural question psychologically because many counterfactuals produce degrees of belief that are intermediate between certainty of truth or falsity. The theory of evidence attempts to model these intermediate degrees of belief as well as the special cases in which belief is at the extremes of certainty.[12]

What we examine in this section are compositional anomalies in counterfactual reasoning, in other words, inconsistencies between the propositional structure of counterfactuals and the belief strengths of counterfactuals. We first discuss the Ramsey test, a schema for conditional inference that was proposed by the English philosopher Frank Ramsey (1931). Next, we consider the Theory of IF due to Braine and O'Brien (1991). The Theory of IF includes a theory of counterfactual reasoning as part of a larger theory of conditional reasoning. We show that the Theory of IF incorporates a Ramsey test as part of a psychological model of conditional reasoning, and from the properties of the Ramsey test, one can derive implications among counterfactuals. In combination with Principle 1, these implications predict relations in belief strength among counterfactuals. We also consider alternative theories of counterfactual inference that embody versions of the Ramsey test. These theories also predict relations in belief strength among counterfactuals. We then slow empirically that belief strengths are inconsistent with the predictions that were derived from the hypothesis of a Ramsey test. We conclude from this that the Ramsey test, which has influenced many modern theories of conditional reasoning, is incorrrect as a descriptive model of counterfactual inference. We will attempt to pinpoint how actual reasoning with counterfactuals differs from the pattern of the Ramsey test.

A.   THE RAMSEY TEST HYPOTHESIS

The semantic properties of counterfactual conditionals are quite different from the properties of the material conditional, the if–then construction of the propositional calculus (Quine, 1972). A material conditional, "if A, then X," is true if A is false or if X is true, or both. Interpreted as material conditionals, the following conditionals are both true because their antecedents are both false:

52. If $2 + 2 = 5$, then the moon is made of cheese.
53. If $2 + 2 = 5$, then the moon is not made of cheese.

---

[12] The observation that counterfactuals vary through intermediate levels of belief is not new: "Between subjunctive conditionals in a reasonably dispositional spirit and subjunctive conditionals at their wildest there is no boundary, but only a gradation of better and worse" (Quine, 1960, pp. 225). What is new is the proposal to use these gradations of belief as the data for a semantic theory.

Because a material conditional is true when its antecedent is false, material conditionals with self-contradictory antecedents are always true. The same is not the case for counterfactual conditionals. Consider the following example (from Goodman, 1947). Suppose that a match is sitting dry and unused in a box, and one says of this match:

54. If that match had been scratched, it would have lighted.

Clearly, this statement is not intended as a material conditional for if it were, the following would also be true (because (54) and (55) both have false antecedents):

55. If that match had been scratched, it would not have lighted.

Statements (54) and (55) illustrate the fact that the truth of a counterfactual depends on semantic relations between the antecedent and consequent beyond whether they are true or false. Rather, a counterfactual asserts or presupposes that some sort of relation obtains between antecedent and consequent, and the problem for philosophical analysis is to elucidate the nature of this relation (Chisholm, 1946; Goodman, 1947). To interpret (54) and (55), one assumes the validity of causal laws (flammable materials ignite when heated; scratching heats materials) and background conditions (oxygen was present; temperatures were not too cold; the surroundings were dry). In the context of these laws and background conditions, the scratching of a match results in the lighting of the match. The basic schema of counterfactual inference would thus seem to be that in the context of implicit background conditions and natural laws, the antecedent of a counterfactual implies the consequent of the counterfactual. Essentially, this schema was proposed by Ramsey (1931), in his influential analysis of conditional statements:

> In general we can say with Mill that "if p, then q" means that q is inferrible from p, that is, of course, from p together with certain facts and laws not stated but in some way indicated by the context.

As Goodman (1947) pointed out, one cannot evaluate the truth of a counterfactual simply by inferring the consequences of the antecedent in the context of one's current beliefs because the antecedent typically contradicts other propositions that are currently believed. For example, the antecedent of (51) contradicts the belief that Nixon did resign. If the premises of a counterfactual inference consisted of current beliefs supplemented by the antecedent, then, typically, the antecedent would contradict other current beliefs, and from these contradictory premises, any conclusion whatsoever could be inferred.

To avoid these difficulties, let us amend the proposal by supposing that after adding the antecedent of a counterfactual to one's current beliefs, one temporarily suspends belief in propositions that contradict the antecedent. Stalnaker (1968) expressed this strategy as follows:

> First, add the antecedent (hypothetically) to your stock of beliefs; second, make whatever adjustments are required to maintain consistency (without modifying the hypothetical belief in the antecedent); finally, consider whether or not the consequent is then true. (p. 102)

The adjustments in beliefs made in the second step have the effect of eliminating beliefs that are inconsistent with the antecedent, and adding beliefs that are consequences of the antecedent and other consistent beliefs. A counterfactual is true, according to this theory, if the consequent is among the propositions that are believed after existing beliefs are modified to accomodate the hypothetical truth of the antecedent.

We will say the truth of a counterfactual is evaluated by a *Ramsey test* if the evaluation proceeds through the three steps described in the Stalnaker quotation (Harper, 1981). By the *Ramsey test hypothesis* we mean the hypothesis that counterfactuals are evaluated by a Ramsey test in actual reasoning. Neither Ramsey (1931) nor Stalnaker (1968) proposed their theories as descriptive psychological theories, for their primary interests were normative. We will see, however, that psychologists and researchers in artificial intelligence have proposed Ramsey tests as part of descriptive theories of conditional inference.

B. Braine and O'Brien's Theory of IF

The Theory of IF is part of a descriptive theory of deductive reasoning developed by Braine and his colleagues in a series of publications (Braine, 1978, 1990; Braine, Reiser, & Rumain, 1984; Braine & Rumain, 1981). The general theory describes a set of inference schemata, and a reasoning program that characterizes how people select and apply the schemata in the construction of deductive sequences. The Theory of IF is the subtheory of the general theory that pertains to natural inferences with conditionals. In the Theory of IF, the truth of a conditional is evaluated by means of a Ramsey test:

> To derive or evaluate *if p then* . . ., first suppose *p;* for any proposition *q* that follows from the supposition of *p* taken together with other information assumed, one may assert *If p then q*. (Braine & O'Brien, 1991, p. 183)

Braine and O'Brien call this the *Schema for Conditional Proof.* An important difference between the Theory of IF and standard propositional logic lies in the treatment of contradictory premises. Whereas by standard logic, inconsistent premises imply that every proposition is true, in the Theory of IF, nothing follows from inconsistent premises other than the conclusion that at least one premise is false. This restriction on deduction is called the *Constraint on Conditional Proof:*

> A supposition can be the antecedent of a conditional conclusion reached via Schema 2 [Schema for Conditional Proof] only if it is consistent with prior assumptions (i.e., premise assumptions plus any previously made suppositions). [Furthermore] an assumption reiterated into a conditional argument cannot contradict the supposition that is to be the antecedent of the conditional. (Braine & O'Brien, 1991, p. 185)

The Constraint on Conditional Proof implies that one cannot infer "if p, then q" when p is inconsistent with other premises.

It might seem that the Constraint on Conditional Proof would prevent Braine and O'Brien from giving an analysis of counterfactuals, for the antecedent of a counterfactual is typically inconsistent with other beliefs of the discourse participants. This is not the case, however, for Braine and O'Brien (1991) draw a distinction between the totality of beliefs that the reasoner holds and the premises that the reasoner introduces into a deduction that originates in a counterfactual supposition:

> In this case of a deliberate counterfactual supposition, the premise assumptions can never be a record of an actual state of affairs. For example, if we wished to argue from the supposition *If Dukakis had won the 1988 election,* our premise assumptions could not be a record of the actual events of 1988; for example, they could not include the fact the Bush had won. (p. 184)

Thus, to infer the consequences of a counterfactual supposition, A, the reasoner cannot take the totality of propositions believed to be true as premises. Rather, the reasoner adopts as premises only the propositions that are consistent with A that would have been true had A been true. We note in passing that Braine and O'Brien (1991) are vague concerning the criteria or process by which these auxiliary premises are selected, but our critique of the Theory of IF can be given without explicitly spelling out these criteria.

In summary, Braine and O'Brien (1991) propose that a counterfactual, $A \mapsto X$, is evaluated by supposing that A is true and attempting to derive X from this supposition. Other propositions can be introduced as premises in this derivation provided that these propositions are consistent with A. Every inference in the derivation must be an instance of a basic inferential schema in Braine's general theory of inference.

We now state two implications of the Theory of IF. If an individual reasons in accordance with the Theory of IF, then he or she will satisfy the following hypotheses:

Hypothesis 1: Let *p, q,* and *r* be any three propositions. If the reasoner believes that "if *p* were the case, then *q* and *r* would be the case," then she must also believe that "if *p* were the case, then *q* would be the case" and "if *p* were the case, then *r* would be the case." In other words, $p \mapsto q \wedge r$ implies $p \mapsto q$ and $p \mapsto r$.

Hypothesis 2: Let *p, q,* and *r* be any three propositions. If the reasoner believes that "if *p* were the case, then *q* and *r* would be the case," then she must also believe that "if *p* and *q* were the case, then *r* would be the case" and "if *p* and *r* were the case, then *q* would be the case." In other words, $p \mapsto q \wedge r$ implies $p \wedge q \mapsto r$ and $p \wedge r \mapsto q$.

The proof that these hypotheses are implied by the Theory of IF is given in Appendix 2.

The Theory of IF was not proposed as a theory of belief strength; thus, it would be improper to claim that it predicts relations in belief strength on its own. In combination with Principle 1, however, Hypothesis 1 implies that

$$(p \mapsto q \wedge r, e) \leq (p \mapsto q, e) \text{ and } (p \mapsto q \wedge r, e) \leq (p \mapsto r, e), \quad (56)$$

and Hypothesis 2 implies that

$$(p \mapsto q \wedge r, e) \leq (p \wedge q \mapsto r, e) \text{ and } (p \mapsto q \wedge r, e) \leq (p \wedge r \mapsto q, e) \quad (57)$$

for all propositions *p, q,* and *r,* and evidence *e.* Condition (56) is analogous to the probability relation $P(B \cap C \mid A) \leq P(B \mid A)$; violations of (56) are analogous to conjunction errors in probability judgment. Condition (57) is analogous to the probability relations $P(B \cap C \mid A) \leq P(C \mid A \cap B)$; violations of (57) are analogous to conditionalization errors in probability judgment. If judgments of belief strength violate (56), we call this a *counterfactual conjunction error,* and if they violate (57), we call this a *counterfactual conditionalization error.*

C. Alternative Approaches to Counterfactual Inference

Perhaps the most influential among current theories of counterfactual inference is a model-theoretic analysis due to Stalnaker (1968) and Lewis (1973).

We will refer to this theory as the Stalnaker/Lewis theory, because Lewis's (1973) theory is a generalization of the basic principles proposed by Stalnaker (1968). The Stalnaker/Lewis theory is based on the concept of a *possible world*. Possible worlds are abstract entities relative to which propositions have truth values. The actual world is a possible world, but there are infinitely many possible worlds that differ from the actual world in a multitude of ways. According to the Stalnaker/Lewis theory, to evaluate whether $A \mapsto X$ is true, one considers alternative possible worlds where A is true, and tests whether X is true in these worlds (a Ramsey test). In carrying out the Ramsey test, it is proposed that one considers only those worlds that are as similar as possible to the actual world, subject to the constraint that A is true in those worlds. If X is true in these maximally similar alternative worlds where A is true, then $A \mapsto X$ is true. For example, to decide whether statement (51) is true, consider alternative possible worlds in which Nixon did not resign, subject to the constraint that these worlds should otherwise be as similar to the actual world as possible. If Nixon was impeached in all of these worlds, then (51) is true; if Nixon was not impeached in at least some of these worlds, then (51) is false.

Our description of the Stalnaker/Lewis theory attempts to convey the intuition behind the theory without delving into the formal structure of the theory. A more precise, mathematical formulation was given in Miyamoto et al. (1989) and, of course, in Stalnaker (1968) and Lewis (1973). The point we want to make here is that the Stalnaker/Lewis theory implies Hypotheses 1 and 2 (Miyamoto et al., 1989); hence, in combination with Principle 1, it predicts conditions (56) and (57). We should hasten to add that the Stalnaker/Lewis theory was proposed as a normative theory, and therefore empirical tests of (56) and (57) cannot refute it. Nevertheless empirical tests of these predictions may shed light on the relationship between reasoning norms and actual reasoning processes.

The Stalnaker/Lewis theory also implies another logical relation among counterfactuals:

> *Hypothesis 3:* Let p, q, and r be any three propositions. If the reasoner believes that "if p were the case, then q would be the case" or "if p were the case, then r would be the case," then he or she must also believe that "if p were the case, then q or r would be the case." In other words, $p \mapsto q$ implies $p \mapsto q \vee r$ and $p \mapsto r$ implies $p \mapsto q \vee r$.

In combination with Principle 1, Hypothesis 3 predicts that

$$(p \mapsto q, e) \leq (p \mapsto q \lor r, e) \text{ and } (p \mapsto r, e) \leq (p \mapsto q \lor r, e). \quad (58)$$

Formal derivations of Hypotheses, 1, 2, and 3 from the Stalnaker/Lewis theory are given in Miyamoto et al. (1989). The reason we did not attempt to derive Hypothesis 3 from the Theory of IF is that the inference schema, p implies $p \lor q$, is not a basic inference schema in the Theory of IF. Thus, it could be argued that in the Theory of IF, the inference of $p \lor q$ from p involves greater cognitive complexity than the inferences by which Hypotheses 1 and 2 were derived.

Beginning with Ginsberg (1986), researchers in artifical intelligence (AI) have investigated the relation between the intuitions underlying the Stalnaker/Lewis theory and knowledge representations in large databases (see Eiter & Gottlob, 1992, for a review). In the AI literature, counterfactual reasoning is treated as a problem of resolving inconsistencies in a database when new, contradictory information is added to it (so-called non-monotonic reasoning). A counterfactual is evaluated as true if the consequent is a logical consequences of the database after adding the antecedent and updating the database. The updating process is constrained to maximize the similarity between the initial and updated database (Ginsberg, 1986) or to minimize the changes from the initial database (Eiter & Gottlob, 1992). Without attempting to explore the formal details of the AI approach, we note that these models incorporate Ramsey tests in the evaluation of counterfactuals (Eiter & Gottlob, 1992; see also Gardenfors, 1988, for similar ideas in epistemic logic); consequently, the AI analyses of counterfactuals imply Hypotheses 1, 2, and 3.

Rips and Marcus (1979) proposed a theory of conditional reasoning that combined the intuitive structure of the Stalnaker/Lewis theory with explicit assumptions concerning the representation and processing of propositions in working memory. The Rips and Marcus (1979) theory can be viewed as a precursor of the AI database update models discussed in Eiter and Gottlob (1992). Once again, we will not describe the details of Rips and Marcus (1979) other than to note that their theory incorporates a Ramsey test in the evaluation of conditionals, and, as such, it implies Hypotheses 1, 2, and 3. The simulation heuristic proposed by Tversky and Kahneman (1982b) is essentially a Ramsey test, although it was not presented as a logical analysis of counterfactual inference, but rather as a study of the situational factors that inspire counterfactual reasoning.

Before turning to empirical studies of belief strength for counterfactuals, we should mention that the mental modes theory of conditional reasoning due to Johnson-Laird (1986) has some of the flavor of a Ramsey test theory, but it differs from it in an important way. We will discuss this theory and its relation to the Ramsey test hypothesis after presenting empirical findings for counterfactuals.

D. EMPIRICAL TESTS OF HYPOTHESES 1, 2, 3

Miyamoto and Dibble (1986) tested conditions (56) and (58), and Miyamoto et al. (1989) tested (56), (57), and (58). We will describe the latter study. Miyamoto et al. constructed counterfactual statements that exemplified the propositional structures in (56), (57), and (58). The statements pertained to the vacation plans of the Conley's, as described in the following story.

Vacation Plans

When Bill and Lucy Conley were planning their vacation last year, they had a friendly disagreement over what to do.

Bill wanted to go hiking and camping in the Canadian Rockies. He collected brochures showing the beauty of the lakes and mountains, spectacular ice fields, and magnificent forests. Lucy wanted to visit New York City where she had never been. She argued for the cultural advantages of New York City—the great art museums, theaters on and off Broadway, elegant and exotic restaurants, and famous stores.

Bill had to admit that New York had a lot to offer. He shared Lucy's taste for culture. His main concern was that New York would cost a lot more than camping and hiking in the Canadian Rockies. Food and lodging were much more expensive in New York. Theater tickets were very expensive and hard to get. The opera was also extremely expensive, but this didn't matter because they didn't like opera.

Of course, some things were not expensive even in New York. For example, the price of admission to art museums was very reasonable, and they both loved to see great art. It wouldn't cost anything to browse in the stores, as long as they didn't buy anything. Some friends had told them where they could hear good, live jazz for under $5 apiece.

When the Conley's gave careful consideration to the cost of visiting New York, however, they decided that they really couldn't afford it this year. They briefly considered a compromise solution, a vacation in Denver, where they could combine city amusements with outdoor activities. It was quickly obvious, however, that neither Bill nor Lucy would be happy in Denver, so they scrapped that idea. In the end, they went camping in the Canadian Rockies and had a lot of fun for relatively little money. They promised themselves that they would save money for a vacation in New York someday.

Table VII lists the critical statements for tests of (56), (57), and (58). In addition to these statements, there were 15 other statements that were irrelevant to our present discussion. These 25 statements were presented to subjects in one of four random orders.

Subjects were 70 University of Washington undergraduates. None of the subjects had had a course in logic and all were native English speakers. Subjects read the story and rated the statements for "how true or false they seem based on the information in the preceding story and whatever else you know about the world." Ratings were made by placing a mark on a horizontal line labeled "Absolutely True" at one end and "Absolutely

TABLE VII

Statements: Topic 1	Form	Median
59. If the Conley's had vacationed in New York, they would have visited art museums.	$A \mapsto X$	26.0
60. If the Conley's had vacationed in New York, they would have attended the opera.	$A \mapsto Y$	3.0
61. If the Conley's had vacationed in New York, they would have visited art museums, and they would have attended the opera.	$A \mapsto X \wedge Y$	11.0
62. If the Conley's had vacationed in New York, they would have visited art museums, or they would have attended the opera, or both.	$A \mapsto X \vee Y$	18.0
63. If the Conley's had vacationed in New York and visited art museums, they would also have attended the opera.	$A \wedge X \mapsto Y$	5.0

Statements: Topic 2		
64. If the Conley's had vacationed in New York, they would have heard outstanding live jazz.	$A \mapsto X$	24.0
65. If the Conley's had vacationed in New York, they would have gone for late evening walks in Central Park.	$A \mapsto Y$	15.0
66. If the Conley's had vacationed in New York, they would have heard outstanding live jazz, and gone for late evening walks in Central Park.	$A \mapsto X \wedge Y$	19.0
67. If the Conley's had vacationed in New York, they would have heard outstanding live jazz, or gone for late evening walks in Central Park, or both.	$A \mapsto X \vee Y$	21.0
68. If the Conley's had vacationed in New York and had heard outstanding live jazz, they would have gone for late evening walks in Central Park.	$A \wedge X \mapsto Y$	15.0

False" at the other end. Numerical ratings were derived by measuring the position of the mark on a scale from 1 (= maximum falsity) to 30 (= maximum truth). Median ratings for the 10 statements are listed next to the statements. Note that the ordering of the medians violated statements (56), (57), and (58) for both topics: $A \mapsto X \wedge Y$ received a higher median rating than $A \mapsto Y$ in violation of (56); $A \mapsto X \vee Y$ received a lower median rating than $A \mapsto X$, in violation of (58); and $A \mapsto X \wedge Y$ received a higher median rating than $A \wedge X \mapsto Y$, in violation of (57). Table VIII shows the results of two-tailed sign tests for the critical comparisons. Each cell shows the percentage of times the first counterfactual in the column heading was rated higher than the second counterfactual (ties were dropped). As one can see, the violations of (56), (57), and (58) in Topics 1 and 2 were all significant.

As with probabilistic conjunction errors, it can be objected that counterfactual conjunction errors result from subjects and experimenters having

TABLE VIII

Counterfactuals in the Comparison

	$A \mapsto X \wedge Y$ $A \mapsto Y$	$A \mapsto X \vee Y$ $A \mapsto X$	$A \mapsto X \wedge Y$ $A \wedge X \mapsto Y$
Topic 1	87.9, $p < .001$	9.7, $p < .001$	91.1, $p < .001$
Topic 2	70.0, $p < .01$	27.8, $p < .005$	80.0, $p < .001$

different interpretations of the stimulus statements. Specifically, subjects might contrast $A \mapsto Y$ to $A \mapsto X \wedge Y$, leading them to interpret $A \mapsto Y$ as $A \mapsto Y \wedge \neg X$ (cf. Marcus & Zajonc, 1985, and Pennington, 1984). One way to counter this objection is to have different subjects rate $A \mapsto Y$ and $A \mapsto X \wedge Y$. We conducted such an experiment using the Vacation Plans story. Approximately half the subjects rated $A \mapsto X$ and $A \mapsto Y$ for Topic 1, and $A \mapsto X \wedge Y$ for Topic 2. The remaining subjects rated $A \mapsto X \wedge Y$ for Topic 1 and $A \mapsto X$ and $A \mapsto Y$ for Topic 2. For both topics, $A \mapsto X \wedge Y$ received significantly higher ratings than $A \mapsto Y$ ($U = 6,642.5$ $p<.001$ for Topic 1; $U = 8,008.5$, $p<.001$ for Topic 2; $n = 158, 157$). Thus, counterfactual conjunction errors occurred even when the subject did not have an opportunity to contrast $A \mapsto Y$ and $A \mapsto X \wedge Y$ for the same topic, which was the rationale for interpreting $A \mapsto Y$ as $A \mapsto Y \wedge \neg X$. It appears that counterfactual conjunction errors do not result from this kind of miscommunication.

We conclude that belief strengths for counterfactuals violate Principle 1. The violations have the form:

Counterfactual conjunction error:	$(A \mapsto X \wedge Y, e) > (A \mapsto Y, e)$
Counterfactual disjunction error:	$(A \mapsto X, e) > (A \mapsto X \vee Y, e)$
Counterfactual conditionalization error:	$(A \mapsto X \wedge Y, e) > (A \wedge X \mapsto Y, e)$

E. The Ramsey Test Hypothesis and Anomalies of Counterfactual Belief

The experimental results demonstrate the occurrence of counterfactual conjunction, disjunction, and conditionalization errors. We will argue that these results suggest a modification of the Ramsey test in which judgments of similarity replace judgments of truth in a model. The argument applies to many versions of the Ramsey test, not only to the Theory of IF and the Stalnaker/Lewis semantics, but also to the AI theories reviewed in Eiter and Gottlob (1992) and to Rips and Marcus's (1979) theory of conditionals.

The following argument attempts to identify the features of the Ramsey test that are questionable from a descriptive standpoint.

First, let us introduce some notation. Suppose that $A \mapsto X$ is a counterfactual, and that $\mathcal{B}(e)$ represents the current state of belief. Depending on the theoretical framework, $\mathcal{B}(e)$ might be a propositional network, possible world, or a knowledge base. We treat current belief as a function of the evidence e because it is natural to expect belief to be influenced by evidence. It is likely that belief is also affected by other factors, such as learning history, but such factors remain implicit in our notation because we are not attempting to model them at this time. Let $\mathcal{W}[A, \mathcal{B}(e)]$ denote the revision of $\mathcal{B}(e)$ to accomodate the hypothetical truth of A. For purposes of our critique, we need not specify the criteria that $\mathcal{W}[A, \mathcal{B}(e)]$ must satisfy other than that $\mathcal{W}[A, \mathcal{B}(e)]$ is a set of one or more representations that are a function of $\mathcal{B}(e)$ and A.

In any theory that embodies a Ramsey test, the truth of $A \mapsto X$ is evaluated by testing whether X is true in $\mathcal{W}[A, \mathcal{B}(e)]$. Hypothesis 1 is derived from the fact that in any such theory, $X \wedge Y$ implies Y and, hence, Y is true in $\mathcal{W}[A, \mathcal{B}(e)]$ if $X \wedge Y$ is true in $\mathcal{W}[A, \mathcal{B}(e)]$. In most such theories, X implies $X \vee Y$, and Hypothesis 3 results from the fact that $X \vee Y$ is true in $\mathcal{W}[A, \mathcal{B}(e)]$ if X is true in $\mathcal{W}[A, \mathcal{B}(e)]$. Hypothesis 2 was derived from the fact that in the Theory of IF and in the Stalnaker/Lewis semantics, if X is true in $\mathcal{W}[A, \mathcal{B}(e)]$, then $\mathcal{W}[A \wedge X, \mathcal{B}(e)] = \mathcal{W}[A, \mathcal{B}(e)]$ (see Appendix 2 and Miyamoto et al., 1989). Although we do not have a general proof that this must hold in every version of a Ramsey test, this equation is plausible because if X is true in $\mathcal{W}[A, \mathcal{B}(e)]$, then a situation in which $\mathcal{B}(e)$ represents one's beliefs and A is posited to be true must be very similar to a situation in which $\mathcal{B}(e)$ represents one's beliefs and $A \wedge X$ is posited to be true. If $X \wedge Y$ is true in $\mathcal{W}[A, \mathcal{B}(e)]$, and $\mathcal{W}[A \wedge X, \mathcal{B}(e)] = W[A, B(e)]$, then Y is true in $\mathcal{W}[A \wedge X, \mathcal{B}(e)]$, implying Hypothesis 2. The purpose of these arguments is to show that Hypotheses 1, 2, and 3 follow from the general structure of the Ramsey test. Therefore, most versions of the Ramsey test will combine with Principle 1 to yield the predictions, (56), (57), and (58) that were found to be violated empirically.

To see what psychological mechanisms would produce the observed pattern of belief strengths, consider first the representativeness explanation of conjunction errors. According to the respresentativeness hypothesis, the similarity of a conjunction to a standard of comparison can be greater than the similarity of a single component. Applying this idea to the Ramsey test, one could argue that the procedure for testing the truth of a conjunctive consequent, $X \wedge Y$, against the revised beliefs, $\mathcal{W}[A, \mathcal{B}(e)]$, is also a judgment of similarity. From this, we infer that the conjunction $X \wedge Y$ could be more similar to $\mathcal{W}[A, \mathcal{B}(e)]$ than a single component, Y alone, and that these differences in similarity could account for counterfactual conjunction errors. The essence of our proposal is to alter the "test" in the Ramsey test from a test of truth of the consequent in a revision of current beliefs to a judgment of similarity between the consequent and these revised beliefs.

Let us say that counterfactuals are evaluated by a *modified Ramsey test* if the evaluation of belief strength for $(A \mapsto X, e)$ follows these four steps: first, add the antecedent A to one's current beliefs $\mathcal{B}(e)$; second, construct a revised belief representation $\mathcal{W}[A, \mathcal{B}(e)]$ that modifies $\mathcal{B}(e)$ to accomodate the hypothetical truth of A; third, evaluate the similarity of X to $\mathcal{W}[A, \mathcal{B}(e)]$; fourth, let the belief strength for $(A \mapsto X, e)$ be an increasing function of this similarity. The revised representation constructed at the second stage may satisfy some criterion of maximal similarity to currrent belief, as in the Stalnaker/Lewis theory, or a criterion of minimal change from current belief, as in the AI theories reviewed in Eiter and Gottlob (1992). The modified Ramsey test differs from the original Ramsey test at step 3, where a judgment of similarity replaces a judgment of truth, and at step 4, where belief strength is evaluated. Step 4 is omitted from the original Ramsey test because the original Ramsey test only allows for counterfactuals to be true or false without qualification.

To explain how $A \mapsto X \wedge Y$ could have greater belief strength than $A \mapsto Y$, one must postulate a cognitive representation in which $X \wedge Y$ is more similar to $\mathcal{W}[A, \mathcal{B}(e)]$ than is Y alone. Given such a representation, it follows that $(A \mapsto X \wedge Y, e) > (A \mapsto Y, e)$ because belief strength is an increasing function of similarity. In effect, the representativeness explanation for conjunction errors in probability judgment has a straightforward generalization to counterfactual conjunction errors. It is not clear how a modified Ramsey test could explain counterfactual disjunction errors, but the difficulty here is much like the problem of providing a representativeness explanation for disjunction errors in probabilistic reasoning. As yet, it is not clear how to represent the typically or similarity of a disjunction. A representativeness account of counterfactual conditionalization errors seems to be quite promising. If the belief strength of $A \mapsto X$ is high, then X and $\mathcal{W}[A, \mathcal{B}(e)]$ must be highly similar. But if X and $\mathcal{W}[A, \mathcal{B}(e)]$ are highly similar, then $\mathcal{W}[A, \mathcal{B}(e)]$ must be highly similer to $\mathcal{W}[A \wedge X, \mathcal{B}(e)]$. Therefore, it is possible for $X \wedge Y$ to be more similar to $\mathcal{W}[A, \mathcal{B}(e)]$ than Y alone is to $\mathcal{W}[A \wedge X, \mathcal{B}(e)]$. Hence, the belief strength for $A \mapsto X \wedge Y$, which is a function of the similarity of $X \wedge Y$ to $\mathcal{W}[A, \mathcal{B}(e)]$, could be higher than the belief strength for $A \wedge X \mapsto Y$, which is a function of the similarity of Y to $\mathcal{W}[A \wedge X, \mathcal{B}(e)]$.

Elsewhere, we attempted to explain compositional anomalies in counterfactual reasoning by means of a mechanism that is structurally different from the modified Ramsey test (Miyamoto et al., 1989). The essence of this alternative theory is to propose that people compare two different representations, $\mathcal{W}[A, X, \mathcal{B}(e)]$ and $\mathcal{W}[A, \neg X, \mathcal{B}(e)]$, when evaluating the truth of $A \mapsto X$. The former, $\mathcal{W}[A, X, \mathcal{B}(e)]$, is the most similar world in which A and X are both true, and the latter, $\mathcal{W}[A, \neg X, \mathcal{B}(e)]$, is the most similar world in which A is true and X is false. For example, in deciding whether statement (51) is true, one compares the most plausible scenario in which Nixon does not resign and Nixon is impeached to the most plausible scenario in which Nixon does not resign and Nixon is not impeached. Statement (51) is believed to be true to the degree that the former scenario is more plausible than the latter. In effect, $\mathcal{W}[A, X, \mathcal{B}(e)]$ is the most plausible example, and $\mathcal{W}[A, \neg X, \mathcal{B}(e)]$ is the most plausible counterexample to $A \mapsto X$. $A \mapsto X$ is judged to be true to the extent that the most plausible example is more plausible than the most plausible counterexample to the counterfactual hypothesis.

This approach to counterfactual judgments is similar to the role of examples and counterexamples in Johnson-Laird's theory of deductive reasoning (Johnson-Laird, 1983; Johnson-Laird & Byrne, 1991), and especially to his proposal that for certain classes of counterfactuals, the truth of a counterfactual is judged in terms of "[whether] the consequent is true with respect to the model based on the antecedent and any relevant beliefs (*including those triggered by the consequent*)." (p. 72) (Johnson-Laird, 1986; the italics are ours). It is this last point that separates Johnson-Laird's (1986) theory of counterfactuals from the various Ramsey test theories and our own modified Ramsey test theory. In a Ramsey test, the consequent of $A \mapsto X$ has no influence over the construction of a revised belief representation, $\mathcal{W}[A, \mathcal{B}(e)]$. In contrast, Johnson-Laird's (1986) theory proposes that the consequent can influence the construction of a mental model of the antecedent. Similarly, the relative plausibility theory of Miyamoto et al. (1989) proposes that the consequent could influence the construction of a model, $\mathcal{W}[A, X, \mathcal{B}(e)]$, and countermodel, $\mathcal{W}[A, \neg X, \mathcal{B}(e)]$, upon which the judgment of relative plausibility is based. We will not attempt to compare the modified Ramsey test theory presented here to the relative plausibility theory presented in Miyamoto et al. (1989), for our discussion is already lengthy and at present there are no data that distinguish between these theories.

VII.   Conclusions

The semantic theory of evidence attempts to integrate two domains of research, the semantic theory of natural language and the study of inductive inference. To be sure, theorists have long envisaged a marriage of these disciplines (Keynes, 1921; Carnap, 1952), but their conceptualizations focused on normative theories of deductive and inductive inference. Our proposal is to integrate these theories at the descriptive level of the psychology of reasoning. Since the linguistic revolution of the late 1950s and 1960s, there has been an explosion of studies of natural language inference and the semantic structure of natural language. At the same time, but without strong interconnections to linguistic research, the study of the Bayesian theory and expected utility theory stimulated enormous progress in the psychology of inductive reasoning. We believe there exists the potential for a productive interchange between these lines of research.

The theory of natural language semantics emphasizes the idea that the semantic structure of propositions is a compositional structure—complex expressions are built from more elmentary parts by means of syntactic rules, and the semantic properties of expressions are determined by this compositional structure. In a sense, what the theory of inductive inference brings to this enterprise is a new dependent variable, namely, the study of relations in belief strength. Whereas the principal objects of classical semantic studies are referential relations, truth conditions, and relations of logical consequence, we suggest that the study of belief strength will provide additional insights into language structure and the role of this structure in reasoning. The theory of inductive inference also contributes a new independent variable to the study of language, namely, variations in the evidence with respect to which the belief strengths of propositions are evaluated. Table IX summarizes the propositional structures that have been discussed in this chapter along with the p/e pairs that enter into a particular structure. Many of these structures were only briefly discussed in this chapter; we included them here to emphasize the variety of research problems

TABLE IX

Compositional structure	Comparison of P/E combinations
Conjunctions	$(A \wedge B, e)$, (A, e), (B, e)
Disjunctions	$(A \vee B, e)$, (A, e), (B, e)
Quantificational conjunctions	$[(\forall x)(x \in A \rightarrow x \in C), e]$, $[(\forall x)(x \in B \rightarrow x \in C), e]$,
	$[(\forall x)(x \in A \cap B \rightarrow x \in C), e]$
Conditionalization	$(A \wedge B, e)$, $(A \mid B, e)$ $(B \mid A, e)$, (A, e), (B, e)
Conditionals and priors	(A, e), (B, e), $(A \mid B, e)$, $(B \mid A, e)$
Counterfactual conjunctions	$(A \mapsto X \wedge Y, e)$, $(A \mapsto X, e)$, $(A \mapsto Y, e)$
Counterfactual disjunctions	$(A \mapsto X \vee Y, e)$, $(A \mapsto X, e)$, $(A \mapsto Y, e)$
Counterfactual conditionalization	$(A \mapsto X \wedge Y, e)$, $(A \wedge X \mapsto Y, e)$, $(A \wedge Y \mapsto X, e)$,
	$(A \mapsto X, e)$, $(A \mapsto Y, e)$

that will emerge in a semantic theory of evidence. As these examples show, it is not so much the belief strengths of individual p/e pairs that require explanation when taken in isolation, rather, it is the relations in belief strength among different p/e pairs that are the main objects of study.

The interaction between compositional structure and belief strength is richly illustrated in the study of conjunctive propositions. Conjunction is one of the most basic forms of semantic composition. An interesting point that emerged from the investigation of conjunctions was the finding that the belief strength of a conjunction is not simply a function of the strengths of its components. Contrary to the predictions of probability combination models, the belief strength of a conjunction is a function of conceptual relations between the component propositions as well as their respective belief strengths. For the sake of brevity, we did not explore the details of a representativeness theory of conjunctive probabilities, but it, too, can be viewed as a compositional theory (Medin & Shoben, 1988; Osherson & Smith, 1982; Smith & Osherson, 1984, 1989; Smith et al., 1988). In a representativeness theory, what are composed are the property structures and prototype representations of categories, not the belief strengths of propositions. The belief strength of a conjunction derives from the conceptual combination of its components, and the psychological similarity of this combination to a target event or population. It is still too early to evaluate whether this program will succeed in explaining the belief strengths of conjunctions in general, but the point we wish to make is that in the case of conjunctive propositions, the attempt to explain belief strength is leading towards a more refined analysis of the internal structure of propositions and concepts.

We conjecture that for many, perhaps all, propositional structures, the attempt to explain relations in belief strength will lead to a more refined theory of the cognitive representation of semantic structure, and the processes that access or transform this structure. We did not attempt to survey the work on belief for disjunctive propositions, but it should be clear even from our superficial discussion that the modeling of belief strength for disjunctions presents an interesting challenge for both the representativeness theory and probability combination models. We proposed the study of counterfactual conditionals as another domain in which compositional structure is likely to interact in interesting ways with evidence and strength of belief. Experimental results suggest that the Ramsey test, which has served as a paradigm for many theories of counterfactual reasoning, is descriptively inadequate. Where the Ramsey test tests the truth of a consequent in a model of the antecedent, or the proof of a consequent under the supposition of the antecedent, we propose that intuitive reasoning tests the representativeness of the consequent in a model of the antecedent.

Kahneman and Tversky have often emphasized that the properties of similarity are structurally different from the properties of a probability measure, and, we would add, they are also structurally different from the properties of logical consequence. It remains to be shown, however, that this intuitively appealing approach to counterfactual beliefs can develop into a well-articulated theory. The point we make here is merely that the semantic theory of evidence is likely to be productive because there are a number of research problems in this area that have interesting structure.

Another feature of the semantic theory of evidence that was implicit in our treatment of conjunctive propositions is the central role of conjoint measurement theory in theory construction. Conjoint measurement theory is a theory of qualitative or ordinal assumptions that are implied by quantitative models of judgment like the probability combination models for conjunctions. In many cases, it has been possible to axiomatize psychological models in the conjoint measurement framework, in other words, to discover qualitative assumptions that are jointly sufficient for the validity of a particular model. The axiomatic analysis of subjective probability and utility are among the most famous examples of the conjoint measurement methodology (Luce & Suppes, 1965; Wallsten, 1977), but the methodology can now be applied quite generally to the analysis of psychological models (Falmagne, 1985; Krantz et al., 1971; Luce, Krantz, Suppes, & Tversky, 1990; Suppes, Krantz, Luce, & Tversky, 1989). The value of an axiomatic analysis is that it identifies critical ordinal predictions of a psychological model. For example, the analysis of probability combination models presented in this chapter was essentially an axiomatic analysis. The critical predictions derived in this analysis, conditions (46) and (47), are independence assumptions, a very common form of axiom in conjoint measurement analyses (Krantz et al., 1971; Falmagne, 1986). We used a standard line of measurement theoretic reasoning to discover predictions whose empirical testing lead to the rejection of the probability combination models for conjunctions. The rejection of probability combination models does not lead away from an axiomatic analysis, however, for the similarity theory that underlies the representativeness account is equally amenable to an axiomatic analysis (Osherson, 1987; Tversky, 1977).

Conjoint measurement theory should be an effective tool in the semantic theory of evidence because it is well adapted to attacking the kinds of research problems that arise in this area. Whereas physical measurement systems are largely (but not exclusively) based on concatenations of objects, psychological measurement of the rigorous axiomatic variety has been based more often on trade-offs between different orderings that arise within structured sets of objects (Krantz et al., 1971; Luce et al., 1990). If we are correct in supposing that belief strength is systematically related to the compositional structure of propositions, as suggested by the examples in Table IX, then the belief orderings between related propositions are likely candidates for conjoint measurement analysis. We have not attempted a full-blown measurement analysis of belief in this chapter, but the examples that we have discussed are suggestive of the kinds of relationships that can be investigated effectively in the conjoint measurement framework (see also Krantz, 1991).

Finally, we must ask what the anomalies discussed in this chapter tell us about the semantics of evidence. Belief strength was found to be inconsistent with relations of logical consequence among conjunctive and disjunctive propositions, and among counterfactuals with conjunctive or disjunctive consequents. We also noted that conditionalization, the shifting of a proposition from a conjunctive consequent into the antecedent, reduced the belief strength of counterfactuals, whereas a logical analysis would require that belief should stay constant or increase. Evidently, Principle 1 is descriptively invalid, that is, relations in belief strength are inconsistent with logical consequence. This would seem to show that deductive reasoning plays a limited role in the formation of belief strength, although this may be an overgeneralization. Perhaps it plays a role in specific contexts that are different from the contexts that have been studied in the experiments discussed here. In view of the clear evidence demonstrating that naive reasoning violates norms of probability theory (Kahneman, Slovic, & Tversky, 1982) and norms of deductive inference (Evans, 1982; Johnson-Laird & Byrne, 1991), it is not surprising that inconsistencies should be found between deductive and inductive reasoning.

What may be less obvious, however, is that these findings cast doubt upon the proposal that the study of belief strength will contribute to a compositional theory of natural language semantics. This pessimistic view can be argued as follows. Much of what we know about semantic structure derives from studying intuitions of reference, truth and logical consequence, and inferring propositional structures as explanatory hypotheses for these intuitions. At least, such is the explicit strategy in the Davidson program for natural language semantics (cf. Davidson & Harman, 1975b, and other references therein), and something very like it motivates the work of theorists as diverse as McCawley (1993), Montague (1974), and Quine (1972).[13] If belief strength is inconsistent with logical consequence, then it is unlikely that the study of belief strength can contribute to a theory of compositional structure, for this structure has been inferred from intuitions of logical consequence and the postulated structure is intended to explain these intuitions.

---

[13] Semantic theory in the Chomskian tradition is less closely tied to referential semantics, although it is by no means independent from it (cf. Chomsky, 1986; Jackendoff, 1990).

An optimist might reply that the inconsistency between belief strength and logical consequence gives us reason to hope that belief strength is sensitive to aspects of semantic structure to which logical consequence is insensitive. Specifically, belief strength appears to be sensitive to psychological representations of similarity and typicality that run counter to truth functional operations like conjunction and disjunction (Tversky & Kahneman, 1982a, 1983), and to the test of truth in a model that is at the heart of the Ramsey test for conditionals. To develop a representativeness theory of belief strength, it will be necessary to determine the conceptual representations of composite categories and propositions, and to describe the computations of similarity or typicality that apply to these representations. We hope that this endeavor will discover aspects of semantic structure that could never be revealed solely by the study of reference, truth, and logical consequence.

ACKNOWLEDGMENTS

Many of the ideas concerning the semantic theory of evidence were developed in discussions between John Miyamoto and David Krantz while Miyamoto was a graduate student at the University of Michigan. We acknowledge Krantz's invaluable influence on this work. We thank Jay Lundell for his contributions to the work on conjunctions and counterfactuals reported here.

Appendix 1:   Vignettes and Statements for Experiment 1

PROBLEM 1-1

Background Information.   Tracy is 35 years old. She works in a major hospital. She has always been a very happy person, who enjoys life a great deal and has lots of friends. She likes to travel; her most recent trips were to Tahiti and Bali.

Statements

A1	Tracy has never been married.
A2	Tracy's boyfriend is a devout Catholic.
B1	Tracy is divorced.
B2	Tracy has two children.
A1 $\wedge$ A2	Tracy has never been married and her boyfriend is a devout Catholic.
A1 $\wedge$ B2	Tracy has never been married and has two children.
B1 $\wedge$ A2	Tracy is divorced and her boyfriend is a devout Catholic.
B1 $\wedge$ B2	Tracy is divorced and has two children.
filler	Tracy is afraid to fly in airplanes.
filler	Tracy earns over $20,000 per year.

PROBLEM 1-2

Background Information. The choices presented below represent different possible forms that a seven-letter word might take. For example, "-----i-" represents a seven-letter word with "i" as the sixth letter. "Acclaim" and "abstain" are examples of words that fit this form. Consider each of the forms described below. For each form, rate the probability that a seven-letter word randomly chosen from the dictionary would have that form.

Statements

A1	-----n-
A2	------g
B1	-----l-
B2	------y
A1 $\wedge$ A2	-----n g
A1 $\wedge$ B2	-----n y
B1 $\wedge$ A2	-----l g
B1 $\wedge$ B2	-----l y
filler	------s
filler	------x

PROBLEM 2-1

Background Information. Joan W. is a highly ambitious woman whose professional career is the single most important interest in her life. Eight years ago, Joan graduated in the top 3% of her class at a prestigious law school. She works many long hours and most of her friends are associated in some way with her professional life. Her principal indulgence is that she enjoys buying expensive, fashionable clothing.

Statements

A1	Joan is a highly respected corporate lawyer.
A2	Joan's husband is the chairman of a powerful banking conglomerate.
B1	Joan is a well-known criminal lawyer.
B2	Joan's husband is a rather macho police captain.
A1 $\wedge$ A2	Joan is a highly respected corporate lawyer and is married to the chairman of a powerful banking conglomerate.
A1 $\wedge$ B2	Joan is a highly respected corporate lawyer and is married to a rather macho police captain.
B1 $\wedge$ A2	Joan is a well-known criminal lawyer and is married to the chairman of a powerful banking conglomerate.
B1 $\wedge$ B2	Joan is a well-known criminal lawyer and is married to a rather macho police captain.
filler	Joan knows how to type.
filler	Joan watches soap operas for at least 2 hours each day.

PROBLEM 2-2

Background Information. Jane is a sophomore in the University of Washington and her cumulative GPA is 3.4. She is taking Psych 101 this quarter. Please predict her performance in this course.

Statements

A1	Jane gets a 3.7 on her first test.
A2	Jane gets a 3.9 for the class at the end of the quarter.
B1	Jane gets a 3.1 on her first test.
B2	Jane gets a 2.9 for the class at the end of the quarter.
A1 $\wedge$ A2	Jane gets a 3.7 on her first test and gets a 3.9 for the class at the end of the quarter.
A1 $\wedge$ B2	Jane gets a 3.7 on her first test and gets a 2.9 for the class at the end of the quarter.
B1 $\wedge$ A2	Jane gets a 3.1 on her first test and gets a 2.9 for the class at the end of the quarter.
B1 $\wedge$ B2	Jane gets a 3.1 on her first test and gets a 3.9 for the class at the end of the quarter.
filler	Jane drops out of Psych 101.
filler	Jane passes Psych 101.

PROBLEM 3-1

Background Information. Susan is a quiet girl and spends a great deal of her time in the school library. She is shy and does not like parties. Most of her energies are directed toward her school work, and her grades are very good. She has only a few friends, most of whom are students as well.

Statements

A1	Susan is a music student.
A2	Susan plays the saxophone for relaxation.
B1	Susan is a business administration student.
B2	Susan reads the Wall Street Journal every morning at breakfast.
A1 $\wedge$ A2	Susan is a music student and plays the saxophone for relaxation.
A1 $\wedge$ B2	Susan is a music student and reads the Wall Street Journal every morning at breakfast.
B1 $\wedge$ A2	Susan is a business administration student and plays the saxophone for relation.
B1 $\wedge$ B2	Susan is a business administration student and reads the Wall Street Journal every morning at breakfast.
filler	Susan always cheats on her exams.
filler	Susan's GPA is above 3.0.

PROBLEM 3-2

Background Information. Edward L. is married and has four children. He has a good income. Due to the nature of his job, he often needs to work nights and weekends. He dislikes this aspect of his job because it keeps him from spending time with his family.

Statements

A1	Edward works in a noisy factory.
A2	Edward is becoming prematurely deaf.
B1	Edward is a policeman who patrols a rough neighborhood.
B2	Edward was stabbed last year by a drug addict.

A1 ∧ A2	Edward works in a noisy factory and is becoming prematurely deaf.
A1 ∧ B2	Edward works in a noisy factory and was stabbed last year by a drug addict.
B1 ∧ A2	Edward is a policeman who patrols a rough neighborhood and is becoming prematurely deaf.
B1 ∧ B2	Edward is a policeman who patrols a rough neighborhood and was stabbed last year by a drug addict.
filler	Edward is under 20 years old.
filler	Edward is over 20 years old.

PROBLEM 4-1

Background Information. Joe B. is a high school senior. He is a good student who is extremely active in extracurricular activities, especially football, rugby, school theatricals, and school politics. His high school GPA is 3.4. Joe has applied to four universities: Harvard, Princeton, Oklahoma and Texas at Austin.

Statements

A1	Joe is accepted at Harvard.
A2	Joe is accepted at Princeton.
B1	Joe is rejected at Oklahoma.
B2	Joe is rejected at Texas.
A1 ∧ A2	Joe is accepted at Harvard and accepted at Princeton.
A1 ∧ B2	Joe is accepted at Harvard and rejected at Texas.
B1 ∧ A2	Joe is rejected at Oklahoma and accepted at Princeton.
B1 ∧ B2	Joe is rejected at Oklahoma and rejected at Texas
filler	Joe will go to college.
filler	Joe will take an extra year to finish high school.

PROBLEM 4-2

Background Information. The following problems ask you to evaluate the likelihood of various conditions that might affect the price of oil and gasoline in 1991[14].

Statements

A1	Oil exports from Saudi Arabia are severely restricted during 1991, due to military conflicts between Iran and its neighbors.
A2	The price of gasoline rises over $2.50 per gallon in 1991.
B1	In 1991, Dow Chemicals discovers an inexpensive way to manufacture synthetic gasoline.
B2	The price of gasoline drops below $.50 per gallon in 1991.
A1 ∧ A2	Oil exports from Saudi Arabia are severely restricted during 1991, due to military conflicts between Iran and its neighbors, and the price of gasoline rises over $2.50 per gallon.
A1 ∧ B2	Oil exports from Saudi Arabia are severely restricted during 1991, due to military conflicts between Iran and its neighbors; nevertheless the price of gasoline drops below $.50 per gallon.

[14] The experiment was conducted during January to March of 1989. Iraq invaded Kuwait on August 2, 1990.

B1 ∧ A2	In 1991, Dow Chemicals discovers an inexpensive way to manufacture synthetic gasoline; nevertheless, the price of gasoline rises over $2.50 per gallon.
B1 ∧ B2	In 1991, Dow Chemicals discovers an inexpensive way to manufacture synthetic gasoline, and the price of gasoline drops below $.50 per gallon.
filler	Saudi Arabia is a major oil producer in 1991.
filler	Japan is a major oil producer in 1991.

PROBLEM 5-1

Background Information.   The following problems ask you to evaluate the likelihood of various events that might affect the space shuttle program in 1990[15]. Read each statement carefully. Place a vertical mark on the rating line indicating how sure you are that the statement is true or false.

Statements

A1	During 1990, another space shuttle blows up during lift-off.
A2	During 1990, Congress votes to eliminate the space shuttle program.
B1	During 1990, the Soviet Union launches a successful manned spaceflight to Mars.
B2	During 1990, Congress votes to divert $4 billion from the defense budget to the space shuttle program.
A1 ∧ A2	During 1990, another space shuttle blows up during lift-off, and Congress votes to eliminate the space shuttle program.
A1 ∧ B2	During 1990, another space shuttle blows up during lift-off, and Congress votes to divert $4 billion from the defense budget to the space shuttle program.
B1 ∧ A2	During 1990, the Soviet Union launches a successful manned spaceflight to Mars, and Congress votes to eliminate the space shuttle program.
B1 ∧ B2	During 1990, the Soviet Union launches a successful manned spaceflight to Mars, and Congress votes to divert $4 billion from the defense budget to the space shuttle program.
filler	During, 1990, a space shuttle flight sets a record for the most number of orbits by a manned space vehicle.
filler	During 1990, a robot is sent into outer space along with human crew members.

PROBLEM 5-2

Background Information.   Tom is currently retired. He was born in a small town in the Midwest, and has returned to his hometown after retirement. Tom has made enough money in his working days to retire comfortably. He spends his time fishing and playing card games with his friends.

Statements

A1	Tom was a professional football player.
A2	Tom has knee problems.
B1	Tom is a cigarette smoker.

[15] The experiment was conducted during January to March of 1989. The space shuttle Challenger exploded during take off on January 28, 1986.

B2	Tom has had lung cancer, which is presently in remission.
A1 ∧ A2	Tom was a professional football player, and has knee problems.
A1 ∧ B2	Tom was a professional football player, and he has had lung cancer, which is presently in remission.
B1 ∧ A2	Tom is a cigarette smoker, and has knee problems.
B1 ∧ B2	Tom is a cigarette smoker, and he has had lung cancer, which is presently in remission.
filler	Tom is under 40 years old.
filler	Tom is at least 50 years old.

Appendix 2

Proof that Eq. (43) implies conditions (44)–(47): Choose any propositions C, D, and X, and evidence e. Then,

$$(C, e) > (D, e) \text{ iff } S(C, e) > S(D, e) \tag{69}$$

$$\text{iff } G[S(C, e), S(X, e)] > G[S(D, e), S(X, e)] \tag{70}$$

$$\text{iff } S(C \wedge X, e) > S(D \wedge X, e) \tag{71}$$

$$\text{iff } (C \wedge X, e) > (D \wedge X, e), \tag{72}$$

where (70) follows from (69) because G is strictly increasing in both of its arguments, and (71) follows from (70) by Eq. (43). Therefore (45) follows from (43). But this shows that $(C, e) > (D, e)$ iff $(C \wedge Y, e) > (D \wedge Y, e)$ for any other Y. Hence $(C \wedge X, e) > (D \wedge X, e)$ iff $(C \wedge Y, e) > (D \wedge Y, e)$ as required by (47). Therefore (47) follows from (43). The proof that Eq. (43) implies conditions (44) and (46) is analogous and is therefore omitted.

Proof that probability combination models predict condition (41):

$$S(A_1 \wedge A_2, e) > S(A_1 \wedge B_1, e) \text{ iff } S(A_2, e) > S(B_1, e) \tag{73}$$

$$\text{iff } S(A_2 \wedge B_2, e) > S(B_1 \wedge B_2, e) \tag{74}$$

where (73) follows by (44), and (74) follows by (45).

Proof that the Theory of If implies Hypotheses 1 and 2: The derivation of Hypothesis 1 is straightforward. Le $\Sigma(p)$ denote the set of propositions that can be introduced as premises in an inference based on the supposition of p. According to the Theory of IF, if $p \mapsto q \wedge r$ is true, then $q \wedge r$ can be derived from $\Sigma(p)$ and p. But then q can be derived from $q \wedge r$ and r can be derived from $q \wedge r$. Therefore q can be derived from p and $\Sigma(p)$, and similarly for r. Hence, $p \mapsto q$ and $p \mapsto r$ are true, so the Theory of IF implies Hypothesis 1. To derive Hypothesis 2, if $p \mapsto q \wedge r$ is true, then $q \wedge r$ can be derived from p and $\Sigma(p)$. Therefore p, $\Sigma(p)$, q, and r must be consistent, for if not, the Constraint on Conditional Proof would be violated. But then $\Sigma(p)$ and $p \wedge q$ must be consistent, so $\Sigma(p) = \Sigma(p \wedge q)$. Hence, $q \wedge r$ can be derived from $p \wedge q$ and $\Sigma(p \wedge q)$, so r can be derived from $p \wedge q$ and $\Sigma(p \wedge q)$; hence, $p \wedge q \mapsto r$ is true. This establishes that $p \mapsto q \wedge r$ implies $p \wedge q \mapsto r$. A similar argument shows that $p \mapsto q \wedge r$ implies $p \wedge r \mapsto q$. Thus, the Theory of IF implies Hypothesis 2.

References

Adams, E. W. (1975). *The logic of conditionals*. Dordrecht, The Netherlands: Reidel.

Agnoli, F., & Krantz, D. H. (1989). Suppressing natural heuristics by formal instruction: The case of the conjunction fallacy. *Cognitive Psychology, 21,* 515–550.

Bar-Hillel, M., & Neter, E. (1993). How alike is it versus how likely is it: A disjunction fallacy in probability judgments. *Journal of Personality and Social Psychology, 65,* 1119–1131.

Braine, M. D. S (1978). On the relation between the natural logic of reasoning and standard logic. *Psychological Review, 85,* 1–21.

Braine, M. D. S. (1990). The "natural logic" approach to reasoning. In W. F. Overton (Ed.), *Reasoning, necessity, and logic: Developmental perspectives* (pp. 133–157). Hillsdale, NJ: Erlbaum.

Braine, M. D. S., & O'Brien, D. P. (1991). A theory of IF: A lexical entry, reasoning program, and pragmatic principles. *Psychological Review, 98,* 182–203.

Braine, M. D. S., Reiser, B. J., & Rumain, B. (1984). Some empirical justification for a theory of natural propositional logic. In G. H. Bower (Ed.), *The psychology of learning and motivation: Advances in research and thinking* (Vol. 18, pp. 317–371). New York: Academic Press.

Braine, M. D. S., & Rumain, B. (1983). Logical reasoning. In J. H. Flavell & E. M. Markman (Eds.), *Carmichael's handbook of child psychology: Vol. 3. Cognitive development.* San Diego: Academic Press.

Carlson, B. W., & Yates, J. F. (1989). Disjunction errors in qualitative likelihood judgment. *Organizational Behavior and Human Decision Processes, 44,* 368–379.

Carnap, R. (1952). *The continuum of inductive methods.* Chicago: University of Chicago Press.

Chisholm, R. M. (1946). The contrary-to-fact conditional. *Mind, 55,* 289–307.

Chomsky, N. (1986). *Knowledge of language: Its nature, origin, and use.* New York: Praeger.

Davidson, D. (1967). Truth and meaning. *Synthèse, 17,* 304–323.

Davidson, D. (1970). Semantics for natural languages. *Linguaggi nella Società e nella Tecnica,* 117–188. (Reprinted in D. Davidson & G. Harman (Eds.). (1975b). *The logic of grammar.* Encino, CA: Dickenson.)

Davidson, D., & Harman, G. (1975a). Introduction. In D. Davidson & G. Harman (Eds.), *The logic of grammar* (pp. 1–14). Encino, CA: Dickenson.

Davidson, D., & Harman, G. (Eds.). (1975b). *The logic of grammar.* Encino, CA: Dickenson.

Eiter, T., & Gottlob, G. (1992). On the complexity of propositional knowledge base revision, updates, and counterfactuals. *Artificial Intelligence, 57,* 227–270.

Evans, J. St. B. T. (1982). *The psychology of deductive reasoning.* London: Routledge and Kegan Paul.

Falmagne, J. C. (1985). *Elements of psychophysical theory.* New York: Oxford University Press.

Fine, T. L. (1973). *Theories of probability: An examination of foundations.* New York: Academic Press.

Gardenfors, P. (1988). *Knowledge in flux.* Cambridge, MA: MIT Press.

Gavanski, L., & Roskos-Ewoldsen, D. R. (1991). Representativeness and conjoint probability. *Journal of Personality and Social Psychology, 61,* 181–194.

Ginsberg, M. L. (1986). Counterfactuals. *Artificial Intelligence, 30,* 35–79.

Goodman, N. (1947). The problem of counterfactual conditionals. *Journal of Philosophy, 44,* 113–128.

Hampton, J. A. (1987a). Inheritance of attributes in natural concept conjunctions. *Memory & Cognition, 15,* 55–71.

Hampton, J. A. (1987b). Overextension of conjunctive concepts: Evidence for a unitary model of concept typicality and class inclusion. *Journal of Experimental Psychology: Learning, Memory, and Cognition, 14,* 12–32.

Harper, W. L. (1981). A sketch of some recent developments in the theory of conditionals. In W. L. Harper, R. Stalnaker, and G. Pearce (Eds.), *IFS: conditionals, belief, decision, chance, and time.* Dordrecht, The Netherlands: Reidel.

Harper, W. L., Stalnaker, R., & Pearce, G. (Eds.). (1981). *IFS: conditionals, belief, decision, chance, and time.* Dordrecht, The Netherlands: Reidel.

Huttenlocher, J., & Hedges, L. V. (1994). Combining graded categories: Membership and typicality. *Psychological Review, 101,* 157–165.

Jackendoff, R. (1990). *Semantic structures.* Cambridge, MA: MIT Press.

Johnson-Laird, P. N. (1983). *Mental models: Toward a cognitive science of language, inference, and consciousness.* Cambridge, MA: Harvard University Press.

Johnson-Laird, P. N. (1986). Conditionals and mental models. In E. C. Traugott, A. ter Meulen, J. S. Reilly, & C. A. Ferguson (Eds.), *On conditionals.* Cambridge: Cambridge University Press.

Johnson-Laird, P. N., & Byrne, R. M. J. (1991). *Deduction.* Hillsdale, NJ: Erlbaum.

Kahneman, D., Slovic, P., & Tversky, A. (Eds.). (1982). *Judgment under uncertainty: Heuristics and biases.* Cambridge: Cambridge University Press.

Kahneman, D., & Tversky, A. (1972). Subjective probability: A judgment of representativeness. *Cognitive Psychology, 3,* 430–454.

Kahneman, D., & Tversky, A. (1973). On the psychology of prediction. *Psychological Review, 80,* 237–251.

Keynes, J. M. (1921). *A treatise on probability.* London: Macmillan.

Krantz, D. H. (1991). From indices to mappings: The representational approach to measurement. In D. R. Brown & J. E. K. Smith (Eds.), *Frontiers of mathematical psychology: Essays in honor of Clyde Coombs.* New York: Springer-Verlag.

Krantz, D. H., Luce, R. D., Suppes, P., & Tversky, A. (1971). *Foundations of measurement* (Vol. 1). New York: Academic Press.

Lewis, D. K. (1972). General semantics. In D. Davidson & G. Harman (Eds.), *Semantics of natural language.* Dordrecht, The Netherlands: Reidel.

Lewis, D. K. (1973). *Counterfactuals.* Cambridge, MA: Harvard University Press.

Luce, R. D., Krantz, D. H., Suppes, P., & Tversky, A. (1990). *Foundations of measurement* (Vol. 3). San Diego: Academic Press.

Luce, R. D., & Suppes, P. (1965). Preference, utility, and subjective probability. In R. D. Luce & E. Galanter (Eds.), *Handbook of mathematical psychology* (Vol. 3). New York: Wiley.

Marcus, H., & Zajonc, R. (1985). The cognitive perspective in social psychology. In G. Lindzey & E. Aronson (Eds.), *Handbook of social psychology* (3rd ed.). Reading, MA: Addison-Wesley.

McCawley, J. D. (1993). *Everything that linguists have always wanted to know about logic but were ashamed to ask* (2nd ed.). Chicago: University of Chicago Press.

Medin, D. L., & Shoben, E. J. (1988). Context and structure in conceptual combination. *Cognitive Psychology, 20,* 158–190.

Miyamoto, J. M., & Dibbe, E. (1986). Counterfactual conditionals and the conjunction fallacy. *Proceedings of the Eighth Annual Conference of the Cognitive Science Society.*

Miyamoto, J. M., Lundell, J. W., & Tu, S. (1988). Conditional fallacies in probability judgment. *Bulletin of the Psychosomatic Society, 26,* 516.

Miyamoto, J. M., Lundell, J. W., & Tu, S. (1989). Anomalous conditional judgments and Ramsey's thought experiment. *Proceedings of the Eleventh Annual Conference of the Cognitive Science Society* (pp. 212–220). Hillsdale, NJ: Erlbaum, 1989.

Montague, R. (1974). *Formal philosophy: Selected papers of Richard Montague.* Edited and with an introduction by R. H. Thomason. New Haven, CT: Yale University Press.

Morier, D. M., & Borgida, E. (1984). The conjunction fallacy: A task-specific phenomenon? *Personality and Social Psychology Bulletin, 10,* 243–252.

Murphy, G. L. (1988). Comprehending complex concepts. *Cognitive Science, 12,* 529–562.

Osherson, D. N. (1987). New axioms for the contrast model of similarity. *Journal of Mathematical Psychology, 31,* 93–103.

Osherson, D. N. (1990). Judgment. In D. N. Osheron & E. E. Smith (Eds.), *Thinking: An invitation to cognitive science* (Vol. 3). Cambridge, MA: MIT Press.

Osherson, D. N., & Smith, E. E. (1982). Gradedness and conceptual combination. *Cognitive Science, 12,* 299–318.

Osherson, D. N., Smith, E. E., Wilkie, O., Lopez, A., & Shafir, E. (1990). Category-based induction. *Psychological Review, 100,* 254–278.

Pennington, N. (1984). *Technical note on conjunctive explanations.* Center for Decision Research, Graduate School of Business, University of Chicago, February, 1984.

Quine, W. V. (1960). *Word and object.* Cambridge, MA: M.I.T. Press.

Quine, W. V. (1972). *Methods of logic.* New York: Holt, Rinehart, and Winston.

Ramsey, F. P. (1931). *The foundations of mathematics and other logical essays.* London: Kegan Paul, Trench, Trubner.

Rips, L. J., & Marcus, S. L. (1979). Suppositions and the analysis of conditional sentences. In M. A. Just & P. A. Carpenter (Eds.), *Cognitive processes in comprehension* (pp. 185–220). Hillsdale, NJ: Erlbaum.

Savage, L. J. (1954). *The foundations of statistics.* New York: Wiley.

Shafer, G. (1976). *A mathematical theory of evidence.* Princeton, NJ: Princeton University Press.

Shafer, G. (1981). Constructive probability. *Synthèse, 48,* 1–60.

Shafer, G., & Tversky, A. (1985). Languages and designs for probability judgment. *Cognitive Science, 9,* 309–339.

Shafir, E. B., Smith, E. E., & Osherson, D. N. (1990). Typicality and reasoning fallacies. *Memory & Cognition, 18,* 229–239.

Slovic, P., & Lichtenstein, S. (1983). Preference reversals: A broader perspective. *American Economic Review, 73,* 596–605.

Smith, E. E., & Medin, D. L. (1981). *Categories and concepts.* Cambridge, MA: Harvard University Press.

Smith, E. E., & Osherson, D. N. (1984). Conceptual combination with prototype concepts. *Cognitive Science, 8,* 337–361.

Smith, E. E., & Osherson, D. N. (1989). Similarity and decision making. In S. Vosniadou & A. Ortony (Eds.), *Similarity, analogy, and thought.* New York: Cambridge University Press.

Smith, E. E., Osherson, D. N., Rips, L. J., & Keane, M. (1988). Combining prototypes: A selective modification model. *Cognitive Science, 12,* 485–527.

Sosa, E. (Ed.). (1975). *Causation and conditionals.* New York: Oxford University Press.

Stalnaker, R. C. (1968). A theory of conditionals. In N. Rescher (Ed.), *Studies in logical theory.* Oxford: Blackwell. (ApQ Monograph No. 2. Reprinted in E. Sosa, *Causation and conditionals.* Oxford: Oxford University Press, 1975.)

Stalnaker, R. C. (1984). *Inquiry.* Cambridge, MA: MIT Press.

Suppes, P. (1966). Probabilistic inference and the concept of total evidence. In J. Hintikka & P. Suppes (Eds.), *Aspects of inductive logic* (pp. 49–65). Amsterdam: North-Holland.

Suppes, P., Krantz, D. H., Luce, R. D., & Tversky, A. (1989). *Foundations of measurement* (Vol. 2). San Diego: Academic Press.

Traugott, E. C., ter Meulen, A., Reilly, J. S., & Ferguson, C. A. (Eds.). (1986). *On conditionals.* Cambridge: Cambridge University Press.

Tversky, A. (1977). Features of similarity. *Psychological Review, 84,* 327–352.

Tversky, A., & Kahneman, D. (1971). Belief in the law of small numbers. *Psychological Bulletin, 2,* 105–110.

Tversky, A., & Kahneman, D. (1974). Judgment under uncertainty: Heuristics and biases. *Science, 185,* 1124–1131.

Tversky, A., & Kahneman, D. (1982a). Judgments of and by representativeness. In D. Kahneman, P. Slovic, & A. Tversky (Eds.), *Judgment under uncertainty: Heuristics and biases.* Cambridge: Cambridge University Press.

Tversky, A., & Kahneman, D. (1982b). The simulation heuristic. In D. Kahneman, P. Slovic, & A. Tversky (Eds.), *Judgment under uncertainty: Heuristics and biases.* Cambridge: Cambridge University Press.

Tversky, A., & Kahneman, D. (1983). Extensional versus intuitive reasoning: The conjunction fallacy in probability judgment. *Psychological Review, 90,* 293–315.

van Fraassen, B. C. (1971). *Formal semantics and logic.* New York: Macmillan.

Wallsten, T. S. (1977). Measurement and interpretation of beliefs. In H. Jungermann & G. de Zeeuw (Eds.), *Decision making and changes in human affairs* (pp. 369–393).

Wallsten, T. S., Budescu, D. V., Rapoport, A., Zwick, R., & Forsyth, B. (1986). Measuring the vague meanings of probability terms. *Journal of Experimental Psychology: General, 115,* 348–365.

Wells, G. L. (1985). The conjunction error and the representativeness heuristic. *Social Cognition, 3,* 266–279.

Wyer, R. S. (1976). An investigation of the relations among probability estimates. *Organizational Behavior and Human Performance, 15,* 1–18.

Yates, J. F., & Carlson, B. W. (1986). Conjunction errors: Evidence for multiple judgment procedures, including "signed summation." *Organizational Behavior and Human Decision Processes, 37,* 230–253.

Zadeh, L. A. (1982). A note on prototype theory and fuzzy sets. *Cognition, 12,* 291–297.

VARIETIES OF CONFIRMATION BIAS

Joshua Klayman

I. Introduction

Since about 1960, there has been considerable interest among cognitive and social psychologists in the idea that people tend to hang on to their favored hypotheses with unwarranted tenacity and confidence. This tendency has been referred to as perseverance of beliefs, hypothesis preservation, and confirmation bias. Research in this area presents a rather heterogeneous collection of findings: a set of confirmation biases, rather than one unified confirmation bias. There are often substantial task-to-task differences in the observed phenomena, their consequences, and the underlying cognitive processes. Moreover, there is no consensus about such basic questions as what is a "favored hypothesis," against what norm is a belief "unwarranted," and under what circumstances are people susceptible or not susceptible to a bias.

In this chapter, I review research concerning a variety of confirmation biases and discuss what they have in common and where they differ. The overall picture is one of heterogeneous, complex, and inconsistent phenomena, from which it is nevertheless possible to discern a general direction, namely a general tendency for people to believe too much in their favored hypothesis. I offer some thoughts about how to reconcile the apparent heterogeneity and the apparent generality of confirmation biases.

A. What Is Confirmation and What Is Bias?

There are almost as many operational definitions of *confirmation bias* as there are studies. It is useful to distinguish two general senses here. Some authors use the term to mean looking for the presence of what you expect, as opposed to looking for what you do not expect. I prefer to call this *positive hypothesis testing* (Klayman & Ha, 1987), and to reserve the confirmation bias label to refer to an inclination to retain, or a disinclination to abandon, a currently favored hypothesis. Although these two senses of confirmation are certainly connected, the relation between them can be complex, as will be discussed later. In addition, there is ambiguity regarding the implied motivational status of confirmation in either sense. Does one simply *tend to* search for the expected over the unexpected (e.g., because the expected comes to mind more easily), or is one deliberately selective (e.g., because the unexpected events are thought to be irrelevant)? Does one *tend to* favor one's focal hypothesis (e.g., because alternatives do not come to mind), or does one take action to attempt to preserve one's beliefs (e.g., by avoiding unequivocal tests)?

It is also useful to distinguish several different meanings of "bias." In one, evaluatively neutral sense, bias refers to a tendency or inclination. (For example, in signal detection theory, a bias is simply an overall tendency to favor one response over another.) Bias can also refer to a systematically flawed judgment process that is ultimately deleterious to the interests of the actor or society (as in "racial bias"). Finally, a sort of moral middle ground has been suggested (e.g., by Funder, 1987, and Anderson, 1990, 1991), akin to Simon's (1957) concept of bounded rationality. People may deviate systematically from theoretical standards, but may still be behaving optimally when broader concerns are taken into account (mental effort, cognitive capacity, emotional well-being, multiplicity of goals, etc.).

B. WHERE DO CONFIRMATION BIASES COME IN?

The development of beliefs entails a complex set of cognitive processes. These include accessing prior beliefs and knowledge, generating hypotheses, searching for evidence to test the hypotheses, interpreting the evidence received, and the subsequent revision of beliefs and generation of new hypotheses (Klayman, 1991; cf. Millward & Wickens, 1974). These are not discrete, sequential steps, however, but a highly interconnected system of processes: Initial beliefs affect the interpretation of data; the way alternative hypotheses are generated affects how one searches; data provide information about how effective the search process is; and all stages are tied to more general knowledge about how the world works. I will refer to this system of processes collectively as *hypothesis development.*

There is potential for confirmation biases of different sorts in each component of hypothesis development. For example:

1. You might start out overconfident in an initial belief. If you do, and are a proper Bayesian otherwise, you will remain overconfident after you receive additional evidence.

2. You may search for evidence in a way that biases the data to favor your hypothesis, for example, by avoiding tests that you think likely to contradict your hypothesis.
3. Your interpretation of the information you receive might be biased in favor of your hypothesis. For example, you may regard hypothesis-confirming data as trustworthy and disconfirming data as dubious.
4. You might revise your confidence in your hypothesis insufficiently given your beliefs about the strength of the data.
5. You may have trouble generating viable new hypotheses even when you do feel like abandoning an old one.

There is evidence for all of these sorts of confirmation biases. However, many of these phenomena have proven to be more complex and less ubiquitous than they seem to be at first. Moreover, consistent with the view of hypothesis development as a system, many phenomena cannot be attributed to any one cognitive process, but are better understood in terms of interactions among different processes. In this chapter, I focus on the search for evidence to test hypotheses, the interpretation of the evidence received, and the connections between them. I consider the nature of possible biases, how and when they occur, and what their consequences may be.

II. The Search for Evidence

A large proportion of the research on hypothesis development is concerned with how people search for information to test their hypotheses. Most studies demonstrate that people's hypothesis testing differs significantly and systematically from norms of optimality. Usually, the standard for optimality is, either implicitly or explicitly, based on the Bayesian concept of the expected value of information. The expected value of information is a fairly complex matter. Suppose you are considering just one hypothesis, which might be true or false. For each potential test, you need to know the range of possible outcomes of that test and the probability of each outcome if the hypothesis is true and if the hypothesis is false. From these estimates, you can calculate the diagnosticity (or more precisely, the likelihood ratio) of each possible outcome, $p(D|H)/p(D|-H)$, the probability of observing the outcome (datum) D given that hypothesis H is true, divided by the probability of observing D if H is false. That tells you how much to change your belief in H should the test produce outcome D. Obviously, you must select a test before you know its outcome, so the expected value of a test also depends on the a priori probability of each possible outcome. You can derive that from your estimates of $p(D|H)$ and $p(D|-H)$ and your a priori belief in H. You also need to consider the relative costs of Type

I and Type II errors. From all of that, then, you can in principle calculate which test is most likely to reduce the expected cost of errors, and you can also discern when it no longer pays to conduct any further tests. Such calculations are more complex when there are more than two hypotheses, when the diagnosticity of results from different tests are not independent, and if you want to plan out an optimal series of tests before you start.

Needless to say, it is unlikely that people approximate this Bayesian approach very closely. Even most researchers use simpler metrics for the expected information from different tests (see Baron, 1985, chap. 4; Klayman, 1987; Klayman & Ha, 1987; Kleinmuntz, 1985). Two natural questions, then, are how do people select tests for their hypotheses and how do their information search strategies affect the development of their beliefs. From time to time, debates have broken out in the literature over whether people's information gathering is guided by appropriate (e.g., Bayesian-like) considerations or by other, normatively irrelevant or improper factors. Such a dichotomy is artificial: Subjects' test strategies are influenced by multiple task characteristics, some of which correspond nicely to normative influences, some of which do not. In the next sections, I discuss the evidence concerning three major determinants of how people test hypotheses: positive test strategy, extremity preference, and attention to diagnosticity (Slowiaczek, Klayman, Sherman, & Skov, 1992). Following that, I discuss the extent to which all of this adds up to a systematically biased (in the sense of flawed) information gathering process.

A. POSITIVE TEST STRATEGIES

The concept of positive testing has its origin in one of the earliest, best known, and most obsessively studied of all hypothesis-testing tasks, the "rule discovery" paradigm of Wason (1960), popularly known as "the 2-4-6 task." The basic method is as follows: The experimenter has in mind a rule that generates sets of three numbers (triples). The subject must try to discover the generating rule by proposing triples, which the experimenter identifies as fitting or not fitting the rule. To begin, the experimenter tells the subject that the triple 2, 4, 6 fits the generating rule. From that point on, the subject proposes triples one at a time, with the experimenter responding yes or no. In the original version of this rule-discovery task, subjects were told to stop proposing triples when they were "highly confident" they had the correct rule.

Wason found that subjects often developed considerable confidence in a hypothesis on the basis of inconclusive data. When subjects formed a hypothesis about the rule that generated the triples (e.g., increasing by two), they most often tested instances that fit their hypothesis (e.g., 5, 7,

9; 10, 12, 14; 106, 108, 110). All these triples received "yes" responses, and subjects became convinced that they had quickly found the rule. In most cases, they did not discover that Wason's rule was in fact more general, namely "numbers in ascending order." Wason referred to this as confirmation bias, because subjects performed tests that were aimed at confirming a current belief. To find the correct rule, subjects had to test triples that did not fit the rule they thought correct, such as 1, 2, 3.

The basic finding of a preference for positive tests has been replicated in a number of different studies using other rule-discovery tasks (see Evans, 1989; Friedrich, 1993; Klayman & Ha, 1987). Corresponding patterns of behavior have also been documented in studies of social inference. When asked to determine whether a person is an extrovert, for example, people prefer questions with extroversion as the premise, such as What would you do if you wanted to liven things up at a party? (Snyder & Swann, 1978). People testing a hypothesis of introversion choose different questions, such as What factors make it hard for you to really open up to people? Similarly, in studies of covariation perception, there is widespread evidence that people rely most heavily on information about what happens when the presumed cause is present, and much less on information about what happens in its absence (see Kao & Wasserman, 1993; Klayman & Ha, 1987; McKenzie, 1994; Wasserman, Dormer, & Kao, 1990).

The history of the positive testing phenomenon provides a good illustration of how confirmation biases can be trickier than they seem. For one thing, Wason associated confirmation in the positive testing sense with confirmation in the perseverence-of-beliefs sense. Indeed, in the specific situation Wason set up, the two often coincided, but that is not necessarily the case (see Klayman & Ha, 1987). Positive hypothesis tests can reveal errors in a hypothesis: Testing things you think will work is how you discover false positives (cases that your hypothesis predicts will have the desired property but that in fact do not). They are useless, however, for uncovering false negatives (cases that you hypothesize will not have the desired property but that actually do.) If your hypothesis is too broad, then it is prone to a lot of false positives, and positive hypothesis testing is the best way to discover where you are wrong. If your hypothesis is too narrow, then it is prone to false negatives, and positive hypothesis testing will reveal few errors and may leave you falsely believing you have just about hit the nail on the head. The latter is the case in Wason's task, because subjects' early hypotheses are almost always more specific than the correct rule of "any increasing sequence." More generally, a tendency toward positive hypothesis testing implies that the errors people make will be predominantly in the direction of holding overly restricted hypotheses. It does not mean, however, that subjects favor positive hypothesis tests because they wish to prove their hypothesis right. Analyses of the tests subjects use and their expressed intentions for them often suggest deliberate attempts to falsify hypotheses while positive testing. For example, subjects often test unusual or extreme instances of the hypothesis (e.g., testing the "ascending" rule with the triple −100, 0, 105; Klayman & Ha, 1989; see also Farris & Revlin, 1989).

B. PREFERENCE FOR EXTREMITY

A series of studies by Skov and Sherman (1986) and Slowiaczek et al. (1992) demonstrate that, in addition to a preference for positive tests, people want information about features that are either extremely likely or extremely unlikely under the focal hypothesis. In some of their experiments, for example, subjects were told that they were about to visit a distant planet, inhabited by equal populations of two (and only two) types of creatures, *Gloms* and *Fizos*. For each type of creature, information was available about the percentage of the population that possessed each of eight different features. For example, 50% of Gloms exhale fire, whereas only 10% of Fizos do so. Some subjects were told that it is important to determine quickly whether or not the creature was a Glom; others were told to determine whether or not the creature was a Fizo. This proved sufficient to establish either Gloms or Fizos as the focus.

Subjects were then asked to indicate which features would be best to check upon encountering a creature. Skov and Sherman (1986) and Slowiaczek et al. (1992) found, as expected, that subjects preferred positive tests, asking about features that were more common in the target group than the alternative. However, they preferred some positive tests over others. For example, subjects with "Glom" as their focal hypothesis preferred to ask about a feature present in 90% of Gloms and 50% of Fizos over one percent in 50% of Gloms and 10% of Fizos. Among negative tests, these subjects indicated a preference for one present in 10% of Gloms and 50% of Fizos over one present in 50% of Gloms and 90% of Fizos. (Statistically, each of these questions is of equal expected value a priori, given two equal, mutually exclusive, and exhaustive populations.) Slowiaczek et al. (1992) also found the same kind of extremity preference in a task presented as a series of choices among pairs of medical tests.

C. DIAGNOSTICITY

While researchers were documenting the non-normative aspects of information gathering in hypothesis testing, others were protesting that subjects were not so far off the mark as those studies made them look. For example, Trope and colleagues (e.g., Trope & Bassok, 1982, 1983; Trope & Mackie,

1987) demonstrated that subjects, when given the chance, showed a clear preference for tests that better distinguished the alternatives (e.g., asking a possible extrovert "Do you prefer big or small parties?"). They argued, therefore, that people used a "diagnosing strategy" rather than a "confirmation strategy." Trope et al. were right in that previous research had not demonstrated that people actually were motivated to protect their hypotheses from possible disconfirmation or that they acted in a way that would necessarily do so. On the other hand, many of the studies Trope et al. criticize did legitimately demonstrate that something other than diagnosticity was driving people's choices of tests (particularly, a preference for positive tests).

Diagnosticity is not the only determinant of people's hypothesis testing, but it is a major one. Skov and Sherman (1986) provide a straightforward demonstration of this in their Glom-and-Fizo experiments. Given the chance to test for feature A, present in 90% of Gloms and 50% of Fizos, or equally diagnostic feature B, present in 50% of Gloms and 90% of Fizos, subjects with Gloms as their target group prefer the positive test A. However, they would still rather test feature B than a less diagnostic feature C, present in 55% of Gloms and 85% of Fizos.

It was noted earlier that the a priori expected value of a test is actually a fairly complex thing to calculate. How is it, then, that subjects' intuitions seem to track the diagnostic value of different tests pretty well, when more basic Bayesian principles seem difficult to fathom (Fischhoff & Beyth-Marom, 1983)? Slowiaczek et al. (1992) offer an explanation: More complex measures of diagnosticity, such as the a priori expected increase in one's probability of making a correct true–false judgment about the focal hypothesis (Baron, 1985, chap. 4), can be closely approximated by something very simple, namely, the difference between the probability of the feature under the hypothesis and the probability of the feature under the alternative. If 80% of extroverts and 50% of introverts go to rock concerts, and 42% of introverts and 12% of extroverts fall asleep in class, those features are just about equally valuable to find out about when trying to classify the respondent. A simple subtraction will provide a very good guide to the expected value of asking a question.[1] Here, then, is a case in which simple intuitions do provide a pretty good match to statistical norms.

As I will discuss later, responding appropriately to diagnosticity when devising tests of hypotheses is not the same as responding appropriately to diagnosticity when revising beliefs in the light of new evidence. In the

[1] This assumes that the cost of false positives and the cost of false negatives are similar, and that the prior probability of the alternative is close to that of the hypothesis. The difference-in-proportions measure can deviate more from Bayesian expected value under other conditions.

latter case, there may not be so felicitous a congruence between normative and intuitive judgments.

D. Do People's Hypothesis Testing Strategies Produce Bias?

To what extent do preferences for positive testing or for extreme features lead to suboptimal performance in hypothesis development? To answer that question requires knowing the environment, the goals, and the mental and physical resources of the person with the hypotheses. Authors are very seldom clear and specific about these things, so this very basic question remains largely a matter of opinion. Nevertheless, there are several interesting dimensions to consider here.

To begin with, biases in information search alone produce only inefficiency, not biased belief. The potential for bias exists only if one also fails to appreciate the consequences of one's search strategy. Take positive hypothesis testing, for example. If I stop testing my hypothesis after conducting only some positive tests, have I done anything wrong? Only if I fail to realize that I have checked only for false positive errors and have left open the possibility of false negatives. Wason's (1960) subjects were mistaken not in choosing positive tests, but in pronouncing themselves very certain they had the correct rule on that basis.

A similar analysis applies to the preference for extreme features. From a statistical norm, there is nothing wrong with choosing features with high and low probabilities given the hypothesis. If that preference causes me to pass up some more diagnostic tests that are available, then I am guilty of inefficiency because I am not selecting strictly according to the tests with the greatest expected value. But having chosen a test, if I use a proper method, such as Bayes' equation, to evaluate the data I get, I will remain unbiased in my beliefs.

What if subjects prefer positivity and extremity in their hypothesis tests because they think that this is what makes the tests more diagnostic? This seems plausible, although there is surprisingly little direct evidence on this point. If subjects overestimate the diagnosticity of these types of tests, it will lead to errors in interpretation of the data received from them. However, those errors might be in favor of the focal hypothesis or against it, depending on the results of the test. For a systematic confirmation bias to result there must be other processes involved, as I discuss later.

What about *really* biased search? For example, some studies suggest that people tend to think of facts, experiences, and arguments that support a current hypothesis more readily than those that refute it (Hoch, 1985; Koriat, Lichtenstein, & Fischhoff, 1980; Kunda, Fong, Sanitioso, & Reber, 1993; Snyder & Cantor, 1979), but even this would not, *by itself,* lead to biased beliefs. If I knew that my search process tended to be imbalanced, then I would be very impressed by any piece of negative evidence that did happen to enter my head, and not very impressed with the preponderance of supportive thoughts. This may be a less efficient and more error prone process than if I naturally generated a balanced or random sampling of mental evidence. For the imbalance to produce bias, however, there must also be a misconstrual of the evidence retrieval process, such as the belief that my memory supplies me with a representative sampling of evidence pro and con.

In conclusion, people's strategies for gathering information to test their hypotheses deviate systematically from theoretical norms of efficiency. As Friedrich (1993) argues, goals appropriate to real life, such as minimizing the costs of errors, need not match the goals set in laboratory tasks, such as determining truth values (see also Anderson, 1990, 1991; Payne, Bettman, & Johnson, 1993). In evaluating hypothesis-testing strategies, it is important to keep in mind the multiplicity of goals that people are attempting to meet, including minimization of time, effort, and boredom, and maintenance of self-image and social standing. Nonetheless, laboratory studies have identified some fundamental characteristics of people's hypothesis-testing strategies that have the potential to cause trouble for them, in the sense of keeping them from efficiently attaining their goals. These strategies are not in themselves directly responsible for confirmation biases. However, as I will discuss later, they can be important contributing factors when people are unaware of the consequences of their search strategies.

III. Interpretation of Evidence

A number of the suggested mechanisms behind confirmation biases lie not in the process of generating tests of hypotheses, but in the process of interpreting the evidence received. There are many phenomena of interest in this realm that concern how people combine information from different sources (statistical base rates, prior beliefs, new data, etc.; see, e.g., Fischhoff & Beyth-Marom, 1983; Yates, 1990). The intriguing findings in this line of research (e.g., conservatism, overconfidence, base-rate neglect) seem to be just as complex and situation-dependent as any in the confirmation bias literature. I will not attempt to review the whole research literature on people's responses to data here, but I will discuss several phenomena that are closely associated with concepts of confirmation bias.

A. INTERPRETING AMBIGUOUS EVIDENCE

Many laboratory tasks, like the 2-4-6 task described earlier, provide subjects with precise data, such as yes and no. Real data are seldom like that; they

are prone to error (i.e., vague) and often subject to different interpretations (i.e., ambiguous). Suppose you have just returned home from a
party. Did you have a good time? The data with which to answer that
question are vague in that you have imprecise perception and memory
for the cognitive and physiological states you went through at the party.
Indeed, numerous studies associated with self-perception theory (e.g.,
Bem, 1972) suggest that we have such imperfect access to our own
mental states that we have to infer them from our actions. (I know I
had fun because I laughed so much.) Some data from the party are
also ambiguous: Some aspects of the party could be counted as positive
or negative, depending on our interpretation. (Was that affectionate
teasing or thinly disguised criticism?)

    Research indicates that vague and ambiguous data are fertile ground for
confirmation bias, because when faced with such evidence, people tend to
give the hypothesis the benefit of the doubt. For instance, an advertisement
for a less popular brand might suggest to you that you try the product to
see whether you think it is as good as the well-known, higher-priced brand.
If you then examine different brands, will you be influenced by the ad's
suggestion? You will if the products are ones for which quality, durability,
and other features are hard to measure precisely (e.g., polo shirts), but not
if the product qualities are clearly perceptible (e.g., paper towels). Once
the ad puts the hypothesis in the consumer's head, interpretations of vague
or ambiguous evidence are biased toward the hypothesis (Hoch & Ha,
1986). A similar psychological mechanism has been implicated in the endowment effect in economic transactions (Kahneman, Knetsch, & Thaler,
1990). A number of studies have found that people seem to value an item
or a risky prospect more if they own it than if they do not. Part of the
explanation for this is that there is a zone of ambiguity around people's
estimates of how much they value something, and that people tend to give
the items they possess the benefit of the doubt, valuing them nearer the
high end of the range of plausible values.

B. HYPOTHESIS-PRESERVING EVALUATIONS OF CREDIBILITY

Another way in which interpretations can be biased toward the hypothesis
is if the hypothesis tester tends to believe information that is consistent
with the hypothesis and discount disconfirming evidence. Probably the best
known example of this process is the study by Lord, Ross, and Lepper
(1979) in which advocates and opponents of capital punishment received
mixed evidence about the efficacy of that practice. The two sides ended
up farther apart than when they began, apparently having been influenced
by supportive evidence more than by contradictory evidence. A related

effect was found by Koehler (1993) in a study of professional scientists. He surveyed members of an organization that advocates the scientific study of parapsychology (e.g., ESP) and also members of a society dedicated to refuting claims of parapsychological phenomena. Respondents evaluated the methodological soundness of studies with stated results either supporting or refuting the existence of a parapsychological effect. Koehler found that people thought better of the methodology of studies whose results were consistent with their beliefs than studies whose findings contradicted their beliefs (see also Mahoney, 1976, and Mahoney and DeMonbreun, 1977). Laboratory studies with various hypothesis-testing tasks (Gorman, 1986, 1989; Koehler, 1993) also indicate that when data are believed to be subject to error, disconfirming data are more likely to be discounted than are confirming data.

It is clear that confirmation bias will result if people believe only those data that conform to their prior beliefs. Koehler (1993) found that subjects knew this, and most endorsed the idea that their evaluation of the soundness of a study's methodology was not, and should not be, influenced by knowledge of the results. However, as Koehler points out, subjects were wrong both when they said they were not influenced *and* when they said they should not be. From a Bayesian point of view, the fact that a study gives a surprising result does constitute valid probabilistic evidence that the study was done incorrectly. Lord et al. (1979) give the example of a physicist who would be justified to judge the appropriateness of a new method for measuring the speed of light according to whether the number it produced conformed to expectations. In the same spirit, some recent treatments of reasoning explicitly recognize that the relation between datum and hypothesis is a mutual one when both are uncertain (e.g., Thagard, 1989). How much distrust of disconfirming results is appropriate and how much is too much? The normative issues here are complex and remain unresolved.

C. Feature-Positive Effects

A number of discrimination learning studies over the last three decades have found that subjects (people and pigeons) learn more easily when discrimination is based on the presence of a feature than on its absence. Hearst and Wolff (1989), for example, put pigeons in a situation in which they had to learn that food was available only when a certain light or tone was present. For another group, food was available only when the light or tone was absent. The latter group took roughly twice as long to achieve a given level of discrimination. Similar results have been observed with human discrimination learning (e.g., Newman, Wolff, & Hearst, 1980; Agostinelli, Sherman, Fazio, & Hearst, 1986).

The possible impact of this "feature-positive effect" on hypothesis development is illustrated in a study by Fazio, Sherman, & Herr (1982). They found that the self-perceptions of human subjects were more affected by actions they took than by actions they failed to take. In their study, for example, preference ratings were changed more by the act of nominating an item as a good one than they were by having passed over an item for nomination. A parallel may exist in the tendency to find errors of commission more blameworthy than errors of omission (Spranca, Minsk, & Baron, 1991). Slowiaczek et al. (1992) also found evidence that subjects revised their beliefs more when learning that an asked about feature was present than when learning it was absent, independent of whether presence or absence favored the focal hypothesis.

The feature-positive effect conforms to the saying that one cannot learn what an elephant is by being told what it is not. Basic cognitive processes may come into play here, but it must also be noted that the set of features that elephants lack is much larger and more varied than the set of features they possess. It seems plausible to say that this imbalance is true of most categorical concepts. If so, there is generally more information about category membership in a feature that is observed than in one that is not observed. Nevertheless, there can be important exceptions, such as when one hypothesis is distinguishable from a set of competitors by an absent feature (e.g., an infectious disease that produces no fever). Feature-positive effects, like other cognitive processes, may represent mis- or overapplications of cognitive processes that have a legitimate ecological basis.

D. DIAGNOSTICITY

As with information search, people's use of the information they receive is not out of touch with reality. People do show some conformity to statistical notions of diagnosticity in responding to information, as they do in searching for it. For example, people request more information before making a decision if the information is less diagnostic (e.g., Van Wallendael & Guignard, 1992), although they do not follow normative stopping rules. The fact that people respond differently to ambiguous versus unambiguous data implies a degree of sensitivity to differences in the diagnosticity of information. Well-known phenomena such as base-rate neglect, hindsight bias, overconfidence, and conservatism document deviations from Bayesian norms, but researchers almost always also find a positive correlation between diagnosticity of information and subjects' judgments. At the same time, there are also some interesting ways that people's ideas about diagnosticity differ qualitatively from what a Bayesian would think.

1. Pseudodiagnosticity

Doherty, Mynatt, Tweney, and Schiavo (1979) published a series of studies showing that people fundamentally misunderstand one of the most basic concepts of diagnosticity, namely, that it depends on a comparison of conditional probabilities given the hypothesis and given the alternative. Instead, subjects in these studies seemed to believe that the evidentiary force of a datum could be determined by knowing $p(D|H)$ alone, or what Doherty et al. call "pseudodiagnosticity." In a typical pseudodiagnosticity study, the subjects' task is to determine the category membership of an instance (the source of an archeological find [Doherty et al., 1979; Doherty, Schiavo, Tweney, & Mynatt, 1981] or the ailment of a patient [Kern & Doherty, 1982]), given some known features. For example, a pot with a narrow mouth and curved handles might come from either Shell Island or Coral Island. What information would you need to help you determine the probability that the pot came from Shell Island? Subjects often choose to ask about the proportion of Shell Island pots with narrow necks and with curved handles, and are less interested in the proportion of those characteristics on Coral Island. In other words, people feel that they need to know the typicality or representativeness (Kahneman & Tversky, 1972; Tversky & Kahneman, 1982) of the feature, but not the likelihood ratio. (See also Beyth-Marom & Fischhoff, 1983; Doherty & Mynatt, 1990; Mynatt, Doherty, & Dragan, 1993).

2. Question Diagnosticity versus Answer Diagnosticity

Suppose there were two large urns full of red and white marbles. One urn contained 90% red marbles and 10% white, the other contained 50% red and 50% white. As is traditional with such problems, suppose you do not know which urn is which, and you reach into a randomly chosen one and pull out a marble. Suppose the marble you get is red; how confident would you now be about which urn you had drawn from? And what if the marble were white? For most people, intuition suggests that the two draws should be about equally informative: It seems as though the roles of red and white in the problem are symmetric. However, practiced Bayesians note that the likelihood ratio for a red datum is .9/.5, whereas for a white datum it is .1/.5. Given equal priors, then, there are 9:5 odds (a 64% chance) that a red marble comes from the mostly red urn, but 5:1 odds (an 83% chance) that the white marble comes from the half-and-half urn.

Using similar urn problems, plus Glom-and-Fizo problems, Slowiaczek et al. (1992) demonstrated that people are insufficiently sensitive to the difference between the diagnosticities of different answers to the same question. With the urns-and-balls problem described in the previous paragraph, for example, subjects who were told that a white ball was drawn were, on average, 77% sure of the identity of the urn. Those who were told that a red ball was drawn also expressed 77% confidence. Similar responses were observed for a variety of different probability combinations and for estimates of relative frequencies in a population as well as for confidence in individual judgments.

E. DO PEOPLE'S EVIDENCE INTERPRETATION PROCESSES LEAD TO BIAS?

In some ways, there seem to be more direct connections between bias and evidence interpretation than there are between bias and information search. A tendency to resolve ambiguity in favor of the focal hypothesis, for example, seems like a proximal cause of confirmation bias. Even here, however, there must be the additional assumption that people do not anticipate this aspect of their cognitive processes, and thus do not take it into account. Otherwise, arbitrary focus on one hypothesis over another, or introduction of a hypothesis by an interested party such as an advertiser, would not influence the interpretation of subsequent data. Similarly, the tendency to credit sources of confirming evidence over sources of disconfirmation leads to confirmation bias only to the extent that people do so more than the appropriate amount—whatever that is.

In other cases, evaluation processes may lead to systematic errors, but not necessarily in favor of the focal hypothesis. Present features may be overweighted relative to absent ones, but those features could favor the hypothesis or its alternative. A feature that is pseudodiagnostic of the focal hypothesis might prove to be nondiagnostic, or even diagnostic against the hypothesis, but the opposite could just as well be true.

Parallel to the conclusions drawn earlier about information gathering processes, data evaluation processes differ in systematic and interesting ways from what we might expect from theoretical norms, but are not completely detached from reality. As we move from the search to the interpretation phase of hypothesis development, we seem to be moving closer to the sources of confirmation bias, but there are still a number of missing links.

IV. Combinations of Search and Interpretation

It is clear that quite a few of the putative sources of confirmation bias do not directly imply any consistent bias toward the focal hypothesis. The hypothesis testers' preference for positivity or extremity may lead to inefficient search, but not to biased conclusions. The hypothesis evaluators' bias toward positive features and their misreadings of diagnosticity may misrepresent the impact of certain data, but that misrepresentation could work against the focal hypothesis as well as for it. Processes that are innocent of direct responsibility for confirmation bias may, however, be guilty as accomplices or conspirators; that is, there may be some forms of confirmation bias that derive from neither search processes nor interpretation processes, alone, but only from an unfortunate combination of the two. Here are some examples.

A. POSITIVE TESTING AND FEATURE-POSITIVE EFFECTS

Positive testing means that people tend to test features that are expected to be present if the hypothesis is true. Thus, the presence of a feature tends to support the hypothesis, and its absence tends to counter it. Feature-positive effects suggest that people tend to be more influenced by the presence of a feature than by its absence. Neither positive testing nor feature-positive effects alone favors the focal hypothesis, but together they do. For example, Hodgins and Zuckerman (1993) asked subjects to generate questions to find out whether a target person possessed a given trait (e.g., if they were optimistic). Subjects predominantly asked questions for which a positive answer favored the focal hypothesis (i.e., positive tests) and on average they gave more credence to the focal hypothesis following positive tests than following negative tests. It seems that, in line with the feature-positive effect, yes answers to either type of test had more impact than no answers. Yes answers to positive tests confirm the hypothesis; yes answers to negative tests disconfirm. Thus, where positive tests predominate, hypothesis-confirming evidence has an overall advantage.

B. POSITIVE TESTING AND ACQUIESCENCE BIAS

Zuckerman, Knee, Hodgins, and Miyake (1995) demonstrate another interaction between a positive search tendency and the interpretation of information. They point out that social psychologists have documented an "acquiescence bias." That is, people are biased toward saying yes to questions posed to them in social interactions. This may result in part from deference to the question-asker or to a tendency to look for and find evidence consistent with the hypothesis framed in the question. In social interaction, then, the following series of events can occur: (1) the questioner tests a hypothesis by, as usual, asking a question to which a yes answer favors the hypothesis (e.g., "Do you like to spend time alone?" for introversion); (2) the respondent is biased toward answering yes, thus confirming the hypothesis; (3) the questioner either does not know about the acquiescence bias or else fails to take it into account; (4) hypothesis-confirming data are, on average, overweighted, not because they confirm the hypothesis, but because they tend to be yes answers and the questioner fails to discount them for bias and/or fails to be sufficiently impressed by the occasional against-the-grain no.

C. EXTREMITY PREFERENCE AND INSENSITIVITY TO DIFFERENTIAL DIAGNOSTICITY

Another interaction between search and interpretation processes was documented by Slowiaczek et al. (1992). As discussed earlier, they found that subjects failed to appreciate the potential for differences in diagnosticity between different answers to the same questions, giving them too nearly equal weight. This could result in errors in favor of the hypothesis or against it, depending on which answer confirmed the hypothesis and which was in fact more diagnostic. However, Slowiaczek et al. point out that people's search preferences tend to favor questions for which the hypothesis-confirming answer is less diagnostic than the disconfirming answer, and thus the tendency to treat the two as nearly equal produces a bias toward confirmation. Specifically, subjects favor questions about features that are either extremely common or extremely uncommon given the hypothesis. They are less concerned with extremity with regard to the alternative. Thus, people tend to select questions for which the probability given the hypothesis is more extreme than the probability given the alternative. In general, this means that the answer that favors the hypothesis will be less diagnostic.[2]

D. WHAT'S GOING ON HERE?

The interactive processes described here illustrate the importance of thinking about processes of hypothesis development as a system and not in

[2] Slowiaczek et al. offer the following proof: Assume that there are two answers and two hypotheses such that answer A favors the hypothesis α and answer B favors the alternative β. The more diagnostic answer is always the one that has the less extreme probability given the hypothesis it favors. The diagnosticity of A answers can be taken as the likelihood ratio $LR_A = p(A|\alpha)/p(A|\beta)$, and for B answers, $LR_B = p(B|\beta)/p(B|\alpha)$.

$$\frac{p(A|\alpha)}{p(A|\beta)} < \frac{p(B|\beta)}{p(B|\alpha)} \leftrightarrow p(A|\alpha) \cdot p(B|\alpha) < p(B|\beta) \cdot p(A|\beta)$$
$$\leftrightarrow p(A|\alpha) \cdot [1\text{-}p(A|\alpha)] < p(B|\beta) \cdot [1\text{-}p(B|\beta)],$$

which is true if (and only if) $p(A|\alpha)$ is more extreme (further from .5) than $p(B|\beta)$. If subjects select questions for which $p(A|\alpha)$ is more extreme than $p(B|\beta)$, the confirming answer (A) will be less diagnostic than the disconfirming answer (B).

isolation from one another. First, the effects of a given search strategy or evaluation process cannot be determined apart from their connections to other components of the hypothesis development process. Second, the complexity of such interconnected effects argues against any simple, direct motivation toward confirmation. Do we think that subjects intuit that choosing extreme features will make them less diagnostic, a fact which they can then ignore, producing the hypothesis-preserving effect they seek? On the other hand, it is also hard to believe that all of these combination effects happen to produce confirmation bias just by coincidence. I will discuss some possible ways of resolving this dilemma later. First, however, I discuss some of the conditions under which confirmation bias does not prevail.

V. When Do Confirmation Biases Go Away?

After years of research, it is clear that sometimes you see confirmation bias and sometimes you don't. Some have taken this inconsistency as a failure to replicate, that is, that confirmation bias is not a robust finding. However, if it is possible to make sense of the conditions of appearance and disappearance, this lack of robustness can reveal a lot about the nature of the phenomena. In the case of confirmation biases, there do seem to be some consistent and interpretable patterns to the comings and goings.

A. A FRIENDLY ENVIRONMENT

Whether or not a strategy produces biases depends on how well suited it is to the environment in which it is used. Some environments are rather lenient, providing little punishment for less-than-ideal judgment and providing ample opportunity for low-cost corrections and adjustments (Hogarth, 1981; Hogarth, Gibbs, McKenzie, & Marquis, 1991). In the case of positive testing, for example, consequences depend greatly on the options open to the hypothesis tester. Klayman and Ha (1987) suggest that people actually favor two kinds of positive testing. In addition to favoring tests of things that are expected to work, people think of examining things that are *known to work* (e.g., "How have people managed this in the past?"). This is the equivalent of asking the experimenter for a sample of different triples that fit the rule, or asking the possible introvert to list some of his or her frequent social behaviors. Such "positive target tests" supplement positive hypothesis tests nicely: They find false negatives (things that were not expected to fit, but do). This type of positive testing isn't possible in most rule discovery or social hypothesis studies, but is often an option in real life.

It may also be the case that a theoretically suboptimal heuristic provides a close approximation to optimal performance under many conditions. No one to my knowledge has followed Brunswik's example (e.g., Brunswik, 1956) and representatively sampled people's hypothesis testing in vivo, but there has been some analysis and much speculation on the topic. Klayman and Ha (1987), for example, show that false positives are indeed more frequent than false negatives under common conditions (i.e., when the phenomenon about which you are hypothesizing is relatively rare and your hypothesis gets the base rate of occurrence about right). McKenzie (1994) simulates a wide range of contingency relations to show that many simplified heuristics for judging causal relations correlate well with accepted statistical methods across the universe of possible data.

At the same time, it is important to recognize that a strategy that performs well in the general environment may perform poorly in many specific subenvironments. A strategy can be well adapted, without being completely *adaptable* (Klayman & Brown, 1993). That is, people may fail to recognize and respond appropriately to the environmental variables that determine how any given strategy performs. For example, it has been suggested that positive testing's focus on false positives rather than false negatives is well adapted, because false positive errors are generally more costly than false negatives in "real life." Both Klayman and Ha (1989) and Friedrich (1993) cite the example that it is better to pass up some perfectly good cars than to buy a lemon. At the same time, positive testing is not as good a strategy when false negatives are more costly, when the phenomenon of interest is common rather than exceptional, and when the best available hypothesis underpredicts the phenomenon. How good is people's ability to adapt their strategies appropriately to such unusual conditions? Friedrich's 1993 review provides strong circumstantial evidence that people respond appropriately to shifts in the relative cost of false positive and false negative errors. However, there is little direct evidence to date concerning the adaptability of people's hypothesis development processes to specific task characteristics.

B.   KNOWLEDGE AND EXPERIENCE

Almost from the beginning, hypothesis-testing research has documented the importance of context and content in reasoning. For example, logic problems framed in concrete terms are often much easier to solve than a structurally equivalent abstract problem. One of the most striking contrasts is the difference in performance on two forms of the "selection task" of Wason (1966), presented by Griggs and Cox (1982). An abstract form of the selection task uses the rule "If a card has a vowel on one side, then it has an odd number on the other." Subjects are provided with four cards, showing, respectively, an A, a D, a 4, and a 7. They are then asked to indicate which cards need to be turned over in order to find out if the rule is true. A concrete, isomorphic version uses the rule "If a person is drinking beer, then that person must be over 19 years of age." Both rules indicate "p implies q," and thus require checking p (the card with the vowel, the person drinking beer) and $not\text{-}q$ (the card with the 4, the person under age 19). In both versions, most subjects see the relevance of the p card (the vowel, the beer drinker). In the abstract task, most subjects also indicate that the q card (the odd number) should be checked and most fail to indicate the $not\text{-}q$ (the even number). In the beer version, the great majority of subjects correctly identify beer drinkers and underage persons as the relevant cases to check.

At first, the prevailing theory was that having a concrete context was the critical facilitating element, but that turned out not to be the case (see Evans, 1989, chap. 4). Some contexts facilitate, and others do not. In cases in which the commonsense meaning conflicts with the underlying logic, concrete content can even make matters worse. Content seems to help most when the problem solver has had direct experience in the domain of the problem. For example, Nisbett, Krantz, Jepson, and Kunda (1983) studied the statistical reasoning of students who had experience in sports or in acting. They found that subjects showed better statistical intuitions (e.g., about the effects of sample size and regression toward the mean) when thinking about events in the domain in which they had experience, even though the problems in both domains were formally identical. Smith and Kida (1991) conducted a meta-analysis of studies of various cognitive biases among professional auditors. They found that most cognitive biases (including confirmation biases) were absent when experienced auditors were given problems of a sort they themselves solved frequently. On the other hand, biases reappeared when the auditors were presented with problems from domains that were job-relevant and familiar, but in which they had little practice. Feltovitch, Johnson, Moller, and Swanson (1984) provide another example of the effects of experience on reasoning skills within a domain. They found that experienced physicians were less prone to pseudo-diagnostic reasoning than were residents, who had completed their schooling but who lacked much clinical experience.

Studies like these suggest that people can learn domain-specific rules and procedures that help with reasoning and hypothesis development. However, the same people who have learned good reasoning skills in their area of expertise may be no better than anyone else when it comes to, say, rearing their children or fixing their cars. At the same time, there do seem to be some ways in which knowledge and experience can have broader effects on reasoning. For example, people may sometimes be able to tap into general schemas that facilitate hypothesis testing by indicating what events are and are not consistent with the schema. Likely candidates include schemas for "permission" and "obligation" (Cheng & Holyoak, 1985; Cheng, Holyoak, Nisbett, & Oliver, 1986), and for other forms of "social exchange" (Cosmides, 1989; Cosmides & Touby, 1992). For instance, a rule such as "If the check is over $50, it must have the manager's signature on the back" may not have been experienced before by subjects, but is easily mapped onto a schema whereby permission is required for some, but not all actions. The permission schema includes the knowledge that there is a risk of noncompliance when the restricted action has taken place (p) and when some action has been taken without authority (not-q), with little concern for permissions obtained superfluously (not-p and q). More subtle contextual changes can also facilitate deduction by highlighting the relevance and irrelevance of different states. Hoch and Tschirgi (1983, 1985), for example, show that subjects find it easier to solve Wason's selection task when on the other side of each letter there is either an even number or a blank face. This seems to tap into a sort of something-missing schema that makes salient the need to check items that are supposed to have a feature and items that are lacking the feature (here, cards with vowels and cards with blanks). Similar facilitation was found for rules that used a cutoff along a continuum, like ". . . then it has a number greater than 10 . . . ," which presumably tapped into a minimum-requirements schema.

Does training in general principles of reasoning help hypothesis testing? Brief instructions (e.g., in Popperian falsification principles, as in Tweney et al., 1980) do not seem to help much, but there is evidence that more thorough education and training may. Hoch and Tschirgi (1985) found that masters-level subjects did significantly better on variants of Wason's selection task than did bachelors-level subjects, and the latter outperformed high school students when facilitating cues were provided. In statistical reasoning, Nisbett and colleagues (see Nisbett, 1993) report that training in various basic principles generalized to new domains, and the beneficial effects persisted. There are questions, however, about how specific the training needs to be in order to have a significant effect on reasoning. A number of studies by Nisbett and colleagues find that the benefits of training on different kinds of reasoning vary with the field of study (see Nisbett, 1993); and in a recent review of laboratory studies of deductive reasoning, Evans, Newstead, and Byrne (1993) conclude that there is weak evidence for the beneficial effects of general education on laboratory deduction tasks, but better evidence for the benefits of training in technical and scientific fields (pp. 107–109). In one of the few field studies of scientific reasoning, Dunbar (1995) reports that neophyte members of molecular biology research teams are prone to confirmation biases but have that trained out of them by more senior researchers who engage in vigorous efforts to falsify their junior colleagues' hasty inferences. Dunbar's study illustrates the efficacy of on-the-job training, but it also suggests that the new researchers' graduate training did not completely succeed in imbuing appropriate hypothesis-development skills. It is clear that people can learn to improve their hypothesis-development skills, but it is unclear how specific the training must be and how well newly trained skills generalize to different tasks.

C. CONSIDERING ALTERNATIVES

Another important mitigating factor is the production of specific alternatives. Often, we are not testing the truth value of one specific hypothesis against the generalized "other." Rather, people often think of (or are confronted with) competing alternative explanations. In many cases, people do better when contrasting two viable alternatives than when evaluating the truth of a single hypothesis. For example, just reframing the 2-4-6 task as dividing the universe into "Dax" and "Med" triples, instead of "fits" and "does not fit," greatly facilitates solution (Tweney et al., 1980; see Wharton, Cheng, & Wickens, 1993, for a summary of subsequent studies). In their expanded version of that task, Klayman and Ha (1989) found that mention of specific alternatives was three times more common among successful than unsuccessful subjects. When subjects thought of an alternative to their current best hypothesis, they almost always generated a test triple that was a positive test of one hypothesis (usually the new one) and simultaneously a negative test of the other. Thus, considering specific alternatives broadened the domain in which tests were conducted. Moreover, Fratianne and Cheng (1993) find that subjects can reencode past data according to its implications for a new hypothesis, so they do not have to start their evaluation of each new alternative from scratch.

There is reason to believe that training and world knowledge can facilitate the consideration of alternatives. In familiar situations, people may learn certain natural sets of competing hypotheses that must be distinguished, rather than having to think of suitable alternatives on the spot. In such situations, people may pay more attention to features that distinguish the alternative hypotheses. The reduction in pseudodiagnostic thinking with experience in physicians, for example, has been attributed to their learning to contrast hypothesized diagnoses with likely alternatives (Feltovich et al., 1984). Klayman and Brown (1993) show that errors resulting from pseudodiagnosticity can be greatly reduced in novices, as well, if they are provided with information in a way that facilitates comparisons of the symptom patterns for competing diagnoses.

Hypothesis development can also be facilitated by others' ability to generate alternatives, should one be reluctant to do so oneself. In the laboratories studied by Dunbar (1995), for example, researchers were quick to point out neglected alternative explanations for any overenthusiastic colleague. Journal reviewers serve a similar function for many of us.

It is also important to acknowledge the critical role of luck and mistakes in hypothesis development. I suspect that many of the alternatives people do test are arrived at by accident. A favorite legend along these lines concerns the invention of the Norwegian delicacy of *lutefisk,* an unusual sort of cured fish. On one of their excursions, the Vikings were about to raid an Irish fishing village. Having caught wind of the impending invasion, and wishing to deny sustenance to the invaders, the local fishermen poured lye over their recent catch, thinking that this would render it inedible. The Vikings mistook the ruined catch for an exotic Irish preparation and developed a taste for it.

Similarly, you might discover a new low-fat cake recipe when you accidentally forget to put in the second stick of butter. You might discover it is easier to take the train to work than to drive when your car breaks down and has to spend a week in the shop. In each case, it might never occur to you to test alternatives to your established hypotheses, but accidental occurrences may lead you to do so.

VI.   Does Confirmation Bias Exist, and If So, What Is It?

Despite all the complexities, hedges, fudges, and caveats presented so far, the corpus of evidence does support the basic idea of confirmation bias: When people err, it tends to be in a direction that favors their hypotheses. Such tendencies are by no means universal, nor do they seem to arise from any single, unifying cognitive process. Nevertheless, the net effect of it all is in the direction of confirmation. If confirmation bias is really a collection of various and sundry processes, some operating in some situations and some in others, why would a general direction emerge? A logical place to start is with general principles of motivation and cognition. A number of possibilities have been suggested, although the ratio of speculation to data is very high.

A number of investigators have based explanations of confirmation bias on the presence of cognitive limitations. The general idea is that people have limited resources with which to accomplish all the cognitive tasks they face. Thus, they tend to follow courses of action that are easier. Within this general framework, several general themes have been suggested.

Evans (1989) attributes many cognitive biases to people's "widespread cognitive difficulty in thinking about any information which is essentially negative in its conception" (p. 63):

> The phenomena associated with studies of confirmation bias reflect not a motivational bias but a set of cognitive failures . . . . The cognitive failure is caused by a form of selective processing which is very fundamental indeed in cognition—a bias to think about positive rather than negative information . . . . In support of the existence of such a positivity bias are many studies showing profound difficulties experienced by subjects in comprehending and processing linguistic and logical negations (see, for example, Evans, 1982, chap. 2). (p. 42)

Indeed, several processes in hypothesis development seem to have positiveness as a feature, such as positive testing, feature-positive effects, and acquiescence bias. Processing advantages for positive information have been noted in other contexts as well. For example, positive correlations between cues are easier to learn than negative (see Klayman, 1988a). Thus, greater facility with positive information seems to be a factor in various stages of hypothesis development.

A second theme in cognitive limitations explanations is that people often fail to give proper consideration to alternative hypotheses. Positive testing, for example, implies that search is guided by what is expected under the focal hypothesis, without equivalent attention to what is expected under one or more alternatives (Klayman & Ha, 1987, 1989). A similar phenomenon is found in research on covariation assessment: People generally pay more attention to the distribution of outcomes when a hypothesized cause is present than when it is absent (e.g., Wasserman et al., 1990). The preference for extreme conditional probabilities noted by Slowiaczek et al. (1992) applies more to probabilities given the focal hypothesis than given the alternative. Pseudodiagnosticity also implies concern with probabilities given the hypothesis, with little concern for probabilities given alternatives (Mynatt et al., 1993). Conversely, a number of studies find significant facilitation of hypothesis development when alternatives are made explicit, as in the Dax/Med reframing of the 2-4-6 task (Tweney et al., 1980), or when people are asked either–or questions (Is she introverted or extroverted?) rather than being asked to judge the truth of one hypothesis (e.g., Hodgins & Zuckerman, 1993). Generation of explicit alternatives was also associated with success in Klayman and Ha's (1989) rule discovery tasks.

Merely having explicit alternatives available may not be sufficient to facilitate hypothesis development, however. For example, even when there is a well-defined set of several alternative hypotheses, people may think about them separately, responding to new data by changing their degree of belief in one hypothesis without any corresponding change in beliefs with regard to the others (Robinson & Hastie, 1985; Van Wallendael & Hastie, 1990). Generating one's own alternatives may not help much, either, if one does not accord them serious consideration. It seems that under many circumstances, people find it difficult to divide their focus among more than one hypothesis at a time. This is particularly so when people believe that there is a single best answer and they already have a viable hypothesis about what it is (Gnepp & Klayman, 1992; Mynatt et al., 1993; Tweney et al., 1980). The failure to give due consideration to alternatives may be part of a larger tendency for people to draw relatively few inferences in reasoning. Johnson-Laird and Byrne (1991), for example, base their theory of deductive inference on the idea that people's representations of problems are often incomplete and tend to include only information that is explicitly stated or that is otherwise made salient (see also Evans, 1989).

In addition to such cognitive propensities, researchers have noted the importance of motivational forces in shaping hypothesis development. The presumption here is that people are motivated to maintain self-esteem and positive regard by others. In this view, we face a motivational trade-off between being accurate and preferring to believe some things over others (see Kunda, 1990). Certainly, some beliefs are more pleasurable to hold than others. We might then expect preferred beliefs to be more often the focal hypothesis, and for people to require extra pushing to give them up. Indeed, psychic pain can be thought of as simply a potential cost of relinquishing a preferred hypothesis. If so, it might be considered normative, from an expected utility point of view, to require more evidence to give it up than a neutral Bayesian would. Aside from such preferences for particular beliefs, people may just find it painful to give up hypotheses in general. To do so requires an admission of error, which presumably hurts self-esteem and the positive regard of others. The cost of changing one's mind may also be raised by societal values favoring consistency and the courage of one's convictions, independent of accuracy. Such motivational factors could promote a number of the observed confirmatory tendencies, such as the tendency to regard disconfirming evidence as suspect and confirming evidence as valid, the tendency to give the benefit of the doubt to the prevailing hypothesis when interpreting ambiguous data, and the practice of asking questions biased in favor of answers that support the hypothesis and then treating the results as unbiased.

Confirmation biases are a diverse enough collection of phenomena to accommodate a diverse set of causal explanations, and each specific phenomenon may have multiple causes of its own. It is likely that each of the cognitive and motivational explanations mentioned here, as well as others, contributes to the way people develop hypotheses. Nonetheless, I do not feel that we have an entirely satisfactory picture of the causes of confirmation biases. Many of the explanations offered explain phenomena that do not constitute true confirmation biases, such as positive testing, feature-positive effects, or pseudodiagnostic thinking. Furthermore, none of the proposed general causes covers the range of observed phenomena. As important as cognitive limitations are, many hypothesis-testing tasks are not overly demanding of cognitive resources. Moreover, there is a missing link between saying that some kind of information requires extra milliseconds to understand and saying that people will not or cannot use that information. Is it really so hard to understand that, say, if you observe something you did not expect that it argues against your hypothesis? As important as motivation is, many tasks elicit minimal ego involvement, with subjects arbitrarily handed one of a set of possible alternatives. Simplified, impersonal tasks often do not elicit more optimal hypothesis development; sometimes quite the contrary.

A. AN INTEGRATIVE STORY CENTERED ON LEARNING

The inherent interest and complexity of the confirmation bias picture invites speculative interpretation, to which I will now contribute. What follows is a framework that might be useful in pulling different findings and localized explanations into a unified story about confirmation biases, with attention given to both motivational and cognitive components. The organizing theme of this story is learning, that is, the acquisition, shaping, and retention of cognitive processes for testing and revising hypotheses.

I begin with the assumption that people's hypothesis-testing strategies, like cognitive processes in general, are reasonably well adapted to their environment at large (see also Anderson, 1990, 1991). Evolution certainly plays a role in making this true, although, in my view, probably not at the level of providing us with genetically preprogrammed cognitive strategies or schemas. Rather, adaptation of processes to tasks comes about largely by means of learning, through instruction, observation, and feedback.

Learning is necessarily a function of motivation, cognition, and environment. Motivation is critical because behaviors are reinforced according to what the organism finds rewarding. Cognitive factors determine what the organism is capable of learning, how fast it can learn, what kinds of feedback promote learning, and how information from the environment is interpreted. The nature and quality of information available in the environment affects what can be learned and how difficult it is to separate signal from noise. Any and all of these factors can contribute to making learning slow, difficult, and imperfect. People are subject to multiple, and often conflicting, motivations. Cognitive processes are limited and effortful. The information we get from the environment is incomplete, untrustworthy, and often biased.

At the same time, the task people face in learning how to test, evaluate, and revise hypotheses is a very difficult one. Hypothesis development takes place in a wide variety of different environments, and processes well suited to one are not necessarily well suited to the next. Figuring out which strategies suit which environments requires multiple-cue learning of considerable complexity. Consider, for example, the process of positive testing. Klayman and Ha (1987, 1989), Friedrich (1993), and others identify a number of task variables that determine the payoffs of using positive testing. These variables include the base rate of occurrence of the target property, the proportion of all cases that fit the hypothesis, the relative costs of false positive and false negative errors, and the a priori probability of the focal hypothesis and of specific alternatives. Moreover, if one is going to use a positive test strategy, one had better take into account the base rate of occurrence for the feature being tested, possible acquiescence biases, feature-positive effects, and so on.

People are good learners, but they have their limits. There are too many potentially relevant environmental variables to expect people to learn to customize their strategies to every task. In a noisy environment, it is necessary to average across enough experiences (or natural selections, for that matter) to detect a signal. This precludes dividing the world too finely or considering too many variables. Plus, fine-grained adaptation would require people to notice the relevance of relevant variables and to separate their effects from the effects of others.

Other potholes in the road to adaptive behavior arise from the need to perceive correctly the values of important task variables. (How costly are false negatives vs. false positives here? How much effort/capacity will this take? How likely am I to mess this up?) Then, even if the appropriate variables are attended to and measured, different cues may point in conflicting directions. In that case, doing the right thing requires a sense of the relative importance of different determinants, an aspect of learning that is especially difficult for people (see Klayman, 1988a, 1988b).

The likely upshot of all this environmental complexity is that people learn to respond effectively to a few, important, salient task-to-strategy relations. This is compatible with Klayman and Brown's (1993) idea that cognitive processes may be well adapted but only modestly adaptable. An explanation of hypothesis development based on complex multiple-cue learning also fits research findings indicating that subjects perform better in specific domains in which they have considerable experience and when problems can be fitted to well-established schemas. In the case of familiar domains, people can gather enough experience to connect process–outcome relations to situational variables. Concentrated experience within a single domain reduces the number of competing variables and allows the learner to use less abstract variables (e.g., "when hiring for low-skill vs. high-skill positions" rather than "when the base-rate of occurrence for the target property is high vs. low"). More general schemas, such as those proposed by Cheng and Holyoak (1985) and Cosmides (1989), may also carry information about what to look for when. Such general schemas have a wide potential base of application, although there is then the problem of correctly perceiving the fit between situations and schemas. Direct instruction in abstract reasoning concepts may also help by identifying relevant task variables and providing training in applying appropriate procedures, rather than requiring people to learn such things by induction (see Nisbett, 1993).

B. But Why Confirmation Bias?

So far, this learning-based account for biased reasoning still leaves open the question of why the preponderance of errors should seem to line up in one direction, namely toward confirmation. The answer may involve learning–motivation interactions. If people generally find confirmation of their hypotheses to be rewarding, then they will tend to learn behaviors that produce more confirmation. It is plausible to hypothesize that it hurts to find out that one's favored beliefs are wrong, and it feels good to find out that one is right. Moreover, there are cognitive costs associated with having to generate new ideas, and possibly social disapproval for waffling. Just keeping an open mind can have psychic costs. Mental effort must be devoted to continued information gathering and consideration of alternatives, and actions contingent on settling the question may seem riskier or may need to be postponed.

This does not mean that people have hypothesis preservation as a goal, however. People are often motivated to test their theories and to learn the truth. But rewards and punishments for correct or incorrect judgments are often delayed or absent altogether. The results of one's judgment are prone to self-fulfillment (Einhorn & Hogarth, 1978). Social interaction can confound these feedback problems because of norms against giving other people bad news, and because the truth of some social judgments is negotiable (Swann, 1984). Indeed, when other people lack good information about the accuracy of one's judgments, they may take consistency as a sign of correctness (Prendergast & Stole, 1993). In summary, it is difficult for people to discern the connections between cognitive processes and eventual successes or failures of hypothesis development. The benefits of confirmation over doubt and revision are more immediate and local. Thus, processes that promote confirmation have a reinforcement advantage, even if people are in principle motivated to develop cognitive processes that promote accuracy in general and in the long run.

VII. Conclusions

Earlier, I drew a distinction between bias as inclination and bias as faulty judgment. The case for confirmation biases constituting at least an inclination seems solid. The case for their constituting systematically faulty judgment is necessarily harder to make, because it implies some standard of optimality. Bayes' equation is the most common norm here, but people have a lot to worry about that Bayes did not, such as cognitive effort, self-esteem, and social standing. It is important to try to account for the full range of an organism's goals and motivations when trying to understand its behaviors. On the other hand, some speculations along these lines flirt with tautology. If we start with the assumption that people simply would not make serious, systematic errors, it will almost always be possible to find a set of goals for which the observed behavior is optimal. Many studies in the confirmation bias tradition demonstrate behaviors that seem grossly off the mark, not only to theoreticians, but also to the people who engage in the behavior. A subject's reaction is more often "Oops" than it is "So what?" People generally have the intuition that their real-world reasoning and decision processes are also far from optimal. Is that intuition itself biased? Besides, if people can learn to do better (which it seems they can), this implies that they were not already performing optimally. Despite some intriguing interpretations by people like Cosmides (1989) and Friedrich (1993), I think the burden of proof still lies with those who maintain that people's hypothesis development processes are basically optimal.

Even if confirmation bias is real, there do not seem to be any straightforward answers to the question of what causes it. If confirmation biases arise from a direct motivation to stick to one's beliefs, why are biases still found in tasks in which people are primarily trying to be accurate or in which they have little personal stake in the hypothesis? If a trade-off between cognitive costs and benefits is driving hypothesis development, why do we see strong biases in simplified, easy-to-process tasks? Confirmation biases seem to emerge primarily in the connections between different cognitive and motivational processes. One interpretation is that cognitive limitations and imperfect heuristics serve as enabling conditions for systematic error in hypothesis development; motivational factors act as a force lining up the errors in a predominant direction, like a kind of magnetic field.

There is still a lot that we do not know about how this works, but there are several emerging themes that help tie together some of the bits and pieces.

1. People treat positive things and positive relations differently from negative; the former seem to have priority in a number of different ways.
2. People possess schemas that they can use, either directly or by analogy, to guide the development of hypotheses concerning particular types of relations.

3. The presence and salience of alternatives plays a critical role in promoting hypothesis revision.
4. Much of hypothesis development can be understood in terms of how the person constructs a mental representation of the problem, especially with regard to which elements are seen as relevant or not (e.g., Holland, Holyoak, Nisbett, & Thagard, 1986; Johnson-Laird, 1983; Johnson-Laird & Byrne, 1991; Klahr & Dunbar, 1988; Thagard, 1989).
5. Learning processes may provide important links between various cognitive and motivation processes, and may help explain why processes and performance vary so much from one situation to another.

In the final analysis, the one thing that can most confidently be said about confirmation bias is that it is not a unitary phenomenon, but rather an emergent property of the complex system of processes underlying hypothesis development. That complexity can be daunting. Consider, for example, that after scores of 2-4-6 studies over the past 35 years, we still do not have a really clear picture of what subjects are doing in that one little task. In some ways, however, the complexity and diversity of confirmation biases can be considered good news. The fact that confirmation biases are so dependent on context, information, and training implies that there are multiple routes to take when trying to engender better hypothesis development. These include domain-specific training and practice (e.g., Feltovitch et al., 1984), general training in principles of reasoning (e.g., Nisbett, 1993), and the engineering of environments to accommodate people's cognitive processes instead of vice versa (e.g., Klayman & Brown, 1993). Plus, as Dunbar's (1995) observations of research laboratories illustrate, social mechanisms can play an important role in ameliorating (as well as exacerbating) biases in hypothesis development.

I doubt that, in the end, there will prove to be any simple, unifying explanation for confirmation biases that has eluded researchers so far. This is because the more we look at hypothesis development, the more it becomes clear that the components are not separable and distinguishable. Cognition versus motivation, conscious versus preconscious, abstract versus concrete, testing versus evaluating versus revising: all are interconnected. Ironically, it may prove easier to develop a broad, systemic picture of confirmation biases and their role in hypothesis development than it is to nail down explanations for individual pieces like the 2-4-6 task. As the broader picture develops, we learn more about what to expect from people when, and what we can do to help.

ACKNOWLEDGMENTS

I thank Sema Barlas, Jackie Gnepp, Chip Heath, Steven J. Sherman, and the editors for their valuable assistance and advice. This work was supported in part by Grant SBR-949627 from the Decision, Risk, and Management Science program of the National Science Foundation.

REFERENCES

Agostinelli, G., Sherman, S. J., Fazio, R. H., & Hearst, E. S. (1986). Detecting and identifying change: Addition versus deletion. *Journal of Experimental Psychology: Human Perception and Performance, 12,* 445–454.

Anderson, J. R. (1990). *The adaptive character of thought.* Hillsdale, NJ: Erlbaum.

Anderson, J. R. (1991). Is human cognition adaptive? *Behavioral and Brain Sciences, 14,* 471–517.

Baron, J. (1985). *Rationality and intelligence.* Cambridge: Cambridge University Press.

Bem, D. J. (1972). Self-perception theory. In L. Berkowitz (Ed.), *Advances in experimental social psychology* (Vol. 6). New York: Academic Press.

Beyth-Marom, R., & Fischhoff, B. (1983). Diagnosticity and pseudodiagnosticity. *Journal of Personality and Social Psychology, 45,* 1185–1195.

Brunswik, E. (1956). *Perception and the representative design of psychological experiments.* Berkeley, CA: University of California Press.

Cheng, P. W., & Holyoak, K. J. (1985). Pragmatic reasoning schemas. *Cognitive Psychology, 17,* 391–416.

Cheng, P. W., Holyoak, K. J., Nisbett, R. E., & Oliver, L. (1986). Pragmatic versus syntactic approaches to training deductive reasoning. *Cognitive Psychology, 18,* 293–328.

Cosmides, L. (1989). The logic of social exchange: Has natural selection shaped how humans reason? Studies with the Wason selection task. *Cognition, 31,* 187–276.

Cosmides, L., & Touby, J. (1992). Cognitive adaptations for social exchange. In J. H. Barkow, L. Cosmides, & J. Touby (Eds.), *The adapted mind: Evolutionary psychology and the generation of culture.* New York: Oxford University Press.

Doherty, M. E., & Mynatt, C. R. (1990). Inattention to P(H) and P(D|-H): A converging operation. *Acta Psychologica, 75,* 1–11.

Doherty, M. E., Mynatt, C. R., Tweney, R. D., & Schiavo, M. D. (1979). Pseudodiagnosticity. *Acta Psychologica, 49,* 111–121.

Doherty, M. E., Schiavo, M. D., Tweney, R. D., & Mynatt, C. R. (1981). The influence of feedback and diagnostic data on pseudodiagnosticity. *Bulletin of the Psychonomics Society, 18,* 191–194.

Dunbar, K. (1995). How scientists really reason: Scientific reasoning in real-world laboratories. In R. J. Sternberg & J. Davidson (Eds.), *The nature of insight.* Cambridge, MA: MIT Press.

Einhorn, H. J., & Hogarth, R. M. (1978). Confidence in judgment: Persistence of the illusion of validity. *Psychological Review, 85,* 395–416.

Evans, J. St. B. T. (1982). *The psychology of deductive reasoning.* London: Routledge & Kegan Paul.

Evans, J. St. B. T. (1989). *Bias in human reasoning: Causes and consequences.* Howe, UK: Erlbaum.

Evans, J. St. B. T., Newstead, S. E., & Byrne, R. M. J. (1993). *Human reasoning: The psychology of deduction.* Howe, UK: Erlbaum.

Farris, H. H., & Revlin, R. (1989). Sensible reasoning in two tasks: Rule discovery and hypothesis evaluation. *Memory & Cognition, 17,* 221–232.

Fazio, R. H., Sherman, S. J., & Herr, P. M. (1982). The feature-positive effect in the self-perception process: Does not doing matter as much as doing? *Journal of Personality and Social Psychology, 42,* 404–411.

Feltovitch, P. J., Johnson, P. E., Moller, J. H., & Swanson, D. B. (1984). The role and development of medical knowledge in diagnostic expertise. In W. Clancey & E. H. Shortliffe (Eds.), *Readings in medical AI* (pp. 275–319). New York: Addison-Wesley.

Fischhoff, B., & Beyth-Marom, R. (1983). Hypothesis evaluation from a Bayesian perspective. *Psychological Review, 90,* 239–260.

Fratianne, A., & Cheng, P. W. (1993). *Assessing causal relations by dynamic hypothesis testing.* Unpublished manuscript. Department of Psychology, University of California, Los Angeles.

Friedrich, J. (1993). Primary error detection and minimization (PEDMIN) strategies in social cognition: A reinterpretation of confirmation bias phenomena. *Psychological Review, 100,* 298–319.

Funder, D. C. (1987). Errors and mistakes: Evaluating the accuracy of social judgment. *Psychological Bulletin, 101,* 75–90.

Gnepp, J., & Klayman, J. (1992). Recognition of uncertainty in emotional inferences: Reasoning about emotionally equivocal situations. *Developmental Psychology, 28,* 145–158.

Gorman, M. E. (1986). How the possibility of error affects falsification on a task that models scientific problem solving. *British Journal of Psychology, 77,* 85–96.

Gorman, M. E. (1989). Error, falsification, and scientific inference: An experimental investigation. *Quarterly Journal of Experimental Psychology, 41,* 385–412.

Griggs, R. A., & Cox, J. R. (1982). The elusive thematic-materials effect in Wason's selection task. *British Journal of Psychology, 73,* 407–420.

Hearst, E., & Wolff, W. T. (1989). Additional versus deletion as a signal. *Animal Learning & Behavior, 17,* 120–133.

Hoch, S. J. (1985). Counterfactual reasoning and accuracy in predicting personal events. *Journal of Experimental Psychology: Learning, Memory, and Cognition, 11,* 719–731.

Hoch, S. J., & Ha, Y.-W. (1986). Consumer learning: Advertising and the ambiguity of product experience. *Journal of Consumer Research, 13,* 221–233.

Hoch, S. J., & Tschirgi, J. E. (1983). Cue redundancy and extra logical inferences in a deductive reasoning task. *Memory & Cognition, 11,* 200–209.

Hoch, S. J., & Tschirgi, J. E. (1985). Logical knowledge and cue redundancy in deductive reasoning. *Memory & Cognition, 13,* 453–462.

Hodgins, H. S., & Zuckerman, M. (1993). Beyond selecting information: Biases in spontaneous questions and resultant conclusions. *Journal of Experimental Social Psychology, 29,* 387–407.

Hogarth, R. M. (1981). Beyond discrete biases: Functional and dysfunctional aspects of judgmental heuristics. *Psychological Bulletin, 90,* 197–217.

Hogarth, R. M., Gibbs, B. J., McKenzie, C. R. M., & Marquis, M. A. (1991). Learning from feedback: Exactingness and incentives. *Journal of Experimental Psychology: Learning, Memory, and Cognition, 17,* 734–752.

Holland, J. H., Holyoak, K. J., Nisbett, R. E., & Thagard, P. R. (1986). *Induction: Processes of inference, learning, and discovery.* Cambridge, MA: MIT Press.

Johnson-Laird, P. N. (1983). *Mental models.* Cambridge, MA: Harvard University Press.

Johnson-Laird, P. N., & Byrne, R. M. J. (1991). *Deduction.* Howe, UK: Erlbaum.

Kahneman, D., Knetsch, J. L., & Thaler, R. H. (1990). Experimental tests of the endowment effect and the Coase theorem. *Journal of Political Economy, 98,* 1325–1348.

Kahneman, D., & Tversky, A. (1972). Subjective probability: A judgment of representativeness. *Cognitive Psychology, 3,* 430–454.

Kao, S.-F., & Wasserman, E. A. (1993). Assessment of an information integration account of contingency judgment with examination of subjective cell importance and method of information presentation. *Journal of Experimental Psychology: Learning, Memory, and Cognition, 19,* 1363–1386.

Kern, L., & Doherty, M. E. (1982). Pseudodiagnosticity in an idealized medical problem-solving environment. *Journal of Medical Education, 57,* 110–114.

Klahr, D., & Dunbar, K. (1988). Dual space search during scientific reasoning. *Cognitive Science, 12,* 1–48.

Klayman, J. (1987). *An information theory analysis of the value of information in hypothesis testing.* Working Paper No. 171. Center for Decision Research, Graduate School of Business, University of Chicago.

Klayman, J. (1988a). On the how and why (not) of learning from outcomes. In B. Brehmer & C. R. B. Joyce (Eds.), *Human judgment: The social judgment theory view.* Amsterdam: North-Holland.

Klayman, J. (1988b). Cue discovery in probabilistic environments: Uncertainty and experimentation. *Journal of Experimental Psychology: Learning, Memory, and Cognition, 14,* 317–330.

Klayman, J. (1991). *Seeking and finding in hypothesis revision: Some interactions.* Paper presented at the meeting of the Society for Judgment and Decision Making, San Francisco, November, 1991.

Klayman, J., & Brown, K. (1993). Debias the environment instead of the judge: An alternative approach to reducing error in diagnostic (and other) judgment. *Cognition, 49,* 97–122.

Klayman, J., & Ha, Y.-W. (1987). Confirmation, disconfirmation, and information in hypothesis testing. *Psychological Review, 94,* 211–228.

Klayman, J., & Ha, Y.-W. (1989). Hypothesis testing in rule discovery: Strategy, structure, and content. *Journal of Experimental Psychology: Learning, Memory, and Cognition, 15,* 596–604.

Kleinmuntz, D. N. (1985). Cognitive heuristics and feedback in a dynamic decision environment. *Management Science, 31,* 680–702.

Koehler, J. J. (1993). The influence of prior beliefs on scientific judgments of evidence quality. *Organizational Behavior and Human Decision Processes, 56,* 28–55.

Koriat, A., Lichtenstein, S., & Fischhoff, B. (1980). Reasons for confidence. *Journal of Experimental Psychology: Human Learning and Memory, 6,* 107–118.

Kunda, Z. (1990). The case for motivated reasoning. *Psychological Bulletin, 108,* 480–498.

Kunda, Z., Fong, G. T., Sanitioso, R., & Reber, E. (1993). Directional questions direct self-conceptions. *Journal of Experimental Social Psychology, 29,* 63–86.

Lord, C., Ross, L., & Lepper, M. C. (1979). Biased assimilation and attitude polarization: The effects of prior theories on subsequently considered evidence. *Journal of Personality and Social Psychology, 37,* 2098–2109.

Mahoney, M. J. (1976). *Scientist as subject: The psychological imperative.* Cambridge, MA: Ballinger.

Mahoney, M. J., & DeMonbreun, B. G. (1977). Psychology of the scientist: An analysis of problem solving bias. *Cognitive Therapy and Research, 6,* 229–238.

McKenzie, C. R. M. (1994). The accuracy of intuitive judgment strategies: Covariation assessment and Bayesian inference. *Cognitive Psychology, 26,* 209–239.

Millward, R. B., & Wickens, T. D. (1974). Concept-identification models. In D. H. Krantz, R. C. Atkinson, R. D. Luce, & P. Suppes (Eds.), *Contemporary developments in mathematical psychology: Learning, memory, and thinking (Vol. 1,* pp. 45–100). San Francisco: W. H. Freeman.

Mynatt, C. R., Doherty, M. E., & Dragan, W. (1993). Information relevance, working memory, and the consideration of alternatives. *Quarterly Journal of Experimental Psychology, 46A,* 759–778.

Newman, J., Wolff, W. T., & Hearst, E. (1980). The feature-positive effect in adult human subjects. *Journal of Experimental Psychology: Human Learning and Memory, 6,* 630–650.

Nisbett, R. E. (Ed.) (1993). *Rules for Reasoning.* Hillsdale, NJ: Erlbaum.

Nisbett, R. E., Krantz, D. H., Jepson, C., & Kunda, Z. (1983). The use of statistics in everyday inductive reasoning. *Psychological Review, 90,* 339–363.

Payne, J. W., Bettman, J. R., & Johnson, E. J. (1993). *The adaptive decision maker.* Cambridge, UK: Cambridge University Press.

Prendergast, C., & Stole, L. (1993). *Escalation of commitment: An economic analysis of decision-making rules.* Unpublished manuscript. Graduate School of Business, University of Chicago.

Robinson, L. B., & Hastie, R. (1985). Revision of opinion when a hypothesis is eliminated. *Journal of Experimental Psychology: Human Perception and Performance, 11,* 443–456.

Simon, H. A. (1957). *Models of man.* New York: Wiley.

Skov, R. B., & Sherman, S. J. (1986). Information-gathering processes: Diagnosticity, hypothesis-confirmatory strategies, and perceived hypothesis confirmation. *Journal of Experimental Social Psychology, 22,* 93–121.

Slowiaczek, L. M., Klayman, J., Sherman, S. J., & Skov, R. B. (1992). Information selection and use in hypothesis testing: What is a good question, and what is a good answer? *Memory & Cognition, 20,* 392–405.

Smith, J. F., & Kida, T. (1991). Heuristics and biases: Expertise and task realism in auditing. *Psychological Bulletin, 109,* 472–489.

Snyder, M., & Cantor, N. (1979). Testing hypotheses about other people: The use of historical knowledge. *Journal of Experimental Social Psychology, 15,* 330–342.

Snyder, M., & Swann, W. B., Jr. (1978). Hypothesis-testing processes in social interaction. *Journal of Personality and Social Psychology, 36,* 1202–1212.

Spranca, M., Minsk, E., & Baron, J. (1991). Omission and commission in judgment and choice. *Journal of Experimental Social Psychology, 27,* 76–105.

Swann, W. B., Jr. (1984). Quest for accuracy in person perception: A matter of pragmatics. *Psychological Review, 91,* 457–477.

Thagard, P. (1989). Explanatory coherence. *Behavioral and Brain Sciences, 12,* 435–502.

Trope, Y., & Bassok, M. (1982). Confirmatory and diagnosing strategies in social information gathering. *Journal of Personality and Social Psychology, 43,* 22–24.

Trope, Y., & Bassok, M. (1983). Information gathering strategies in hypothesis-testing. *Journal of Experimental Social Psychology, 19,* 560–576.

Trope, Y., & Mackie, D. M. (1987). Sensitivity to alternatives in social hypothesis-testing. *Journal of Experimental Social Psychology, 23,* 445–459.

Tversky, A., & Kahneman, D. (1982). Judgments of and by representativeness. In D. Kahneman, P. Slovic, & A. Tversky (Eds.), *Judgment under uncertainty: Heuristics and biases* (pp. 84–98). Cambridge: Cambridge University Press.

Tweney, R. D., Doherty, M. E., Worner, W. J., Pliske, D. B., Mynatt, C. R., Gross, K. A., & Arkkelin, D. L. (1980). Strategies of rule discovery in an inference task. *Quarterly Journal of Experimental Psychology, 32,* 109–123.

Van Wallendael, L. R., & Guignard, Y. (1992). Diagnosticity, confidence, and the need for information. *Journal of Behavioral Decision Making, 5,* 25–37.

Van Wallendael, L. R., & Hastie, R. (1990). Tracing the footsteps of Sherlock Holmes: Cognitive representations of hypothesis testing. *Memory & Cognition, 18,* 240–250.

Wason, P. C. (1960). On the failure to eliminate hypotheses in a conceptual task. *Quarterly Journal of Experimental Psychology, 12,* 129–140.

Wason, P. C. (1966). Reasoning. In B. Foss (Eds.), *New horizons in psychology.* Harmondsworth, UK: Penguin.

Wasserman, E. A., Dormer, W. W., & Kao, S.-F. (1990). Contributions of specific cell information to judgments of interevent contingency. *Journal of Experimental Psychology: Learning, Memory, and Cognition, 16,* 509–521.

Wharton, C. M., Cheng, P. W., & Wickens, D. T. (1993). Hypothesis-testing strategies: Why two goals are better than one. *Quarterly Journal of Experimental Psychology, 46A,* 743–758.

Yates, J. F. (1990). *Judgment and decision making.* Englewood Cliffs, NJ: Prentice-Hall.

Zuckerman, M., Knee, C. R., Hodgins, H. S., & Miyake, K. (1995). Hypothesis confirmation: The joint effect of positive test strategy and acquiescence response set. *Journal of Personality and Social Psychology, 68,* 52–60.

INDEX

CONTENTS OF RECENT VOLUMES

ISBN 0-12-543332-8

90040

9 780125 433327